Forging American Communism

_____

Forging
American Communism

THE LIFE OF
WILLIAM Z. FOSTER

Edward P. Johanningsmeier

PRINCETON UNIVERSITY PRESS
PRINCETON, NEW JERSEY

Copyright © 1994 by Princeton University Press
Published by Princeton University Press, 41 William Street,
Princeton, New Jersey 08540
In the United Kingdom: Princeton University Press,
Chichester, West Sussex

Library of Congress Cataloging-in-Publication Data

Johanningsmeier, Edward P., 1956–
Forging American communism : the life of
William Z. Foster / Edward P. Johanningsmeier.
p. cm.
Includes bibliographical references and index.
1. Foster, William Z., 1881–1961. 2. Communists—
United States—Biography. I. Title.
HX84.F6J65 1994 324.273′75′092—dc20
[B] 93-27539 CIP

ISBN 0-691-03331-5 (acid-free paper)

This book has been composed in Adobe Sabon

For Lisa, with love

———————————

CONTENTS

CONTENTS

ILLUSTRATIONS

ACKNOWLEDGMENTS

WHATEVER ELSE may be said about him, it cannot be denied that William Foster was a wanderer, zigzagging across the geographic as well as political landscape. Thus I owe a particularly large number of debts in tracking him down, incurred in locales as diverse as Spokane and Moscow.

Beginning in Philadelphia, Walter Licht supervised the dissertation upon which this study is partially based. I am greatly indebted to him for his confidence in this project, his patience with detours, and his ready willingness to expand upon and complicate my thoughts about William Foster. I would not have been able to trail Foster beyond Philadelphia without generous support from the American Civilization Department at the University of Pennsylvania. At Penn, Drew Faust and Antoine Joseph provided crucial encouragement and helpful readings early on; Jan Radway and Michael Katz provided methodological inspiration. Rick Halpern offered not only his encyclopedic knowledge of the Chicago labor movement, but his optimism and interest as well.

I am greatly indebted to Joe and Jennifer Kolko for generously opening their memories and household to me, and for allowing me to work with their wonderful collection of documents and photographs. Thanks also to Harold and Zelda Foster, Arthur Zipser, Dorothy Healey, Harry Epstein, Gil and Helen North Green, Albert Glotzer, George Meyers, Sam Darcy, and Philip Foner for the patience and care with which they offered their recollections. Mary Carr, Charlton Brandt, Harvey Klehr, and Reiner Tosstorff shared their knowledge and research with me, and Deborah Vernon DiMicco and Moira Donovan provided authoritative translations of French and medical documents, respectively. I am grateful to Maurice Isserman, Nelson Lichtenstein, and Gavin Lewis for their readings of the manuscript in its later stages, and for their editorial suggestions. I owe a special debt to Lauren Osborne and Beth Gianfagna at Princeton University Press for their excellent guidance at even the very last stages. Any shortcomings or errors are, of course, the results of my own stubbornness.

My research was well supported and enlarged by expert archival assistance from Mary Anne Hill at the Woodruff Library, Emory University; Edward Weber at the Department of Special Collections at the University of Michigan; Archie Motley at the Chicago Historical Society; Peter Filardo and Dorothy Swanson at the Tamiment Library; Pat Proscino at the Balch Institute, and Elaine Miller at the Washington State Historical Society. I am especially grateful to Lee Pugh and the staff of the interlibrary loan department at the Van Pelt Library of the University of Pennsylvania for their relentless pursuit of difficult-to-locate documents. Thanks to Tim Wheeler and Ken BeSaw for their assistance with photographs from the archives of the *People's Weekly World*. I owe an especially large debt to the staff of the Center for Research and Preservation of Documents on Modern and Contemporary History in Moscow for their courtesy and professionalism. In particular, I wish to thank Galina Gorskaya, Eleanora Shaknazarovna, Andrei Doronin, and Maria Vedenyeva for their expert guidance and unfailing patience. The assistance of Jim Heinzen and David Shearer was absolutely vital to my research in Moscow. My friends Galina Khartulary and Valery Klokov ensured that my visits were both productive and enjoyable.

This book is dedicated to my wife, Lisa Vernon, upon whom I have long depended for her fearlessness and wisdom.

NOTE ON SOURCES

THIS STUDY has made use of a number of manuscript collections held by the former Central Archives of the Communist Party of the Soviet Union, now called the Center for Research and Preservation of Documents on Modern and Contemporary History (CRPDMCH). These include William Foster's personal papers (donated by his daughter to the Soviet Communist party), the archives of the Communist International, and those of the Red International of Labor Unions.

The Center's manuscript collections are catalogued according to the following order: *fund*, (e.g., Comintern or William Z. Foster); *opis* (a catalog listing subcategories within the fund, often but not always divided chronologically, i.e., "United States" or "1919–1923"); *delo* (individual file) and *listok* (document page reference within each *delo*). My citations generally correspond to this arrangement, for instance, f. 495 (Comintern archive), op. 261 (personal file of individuals), d. 15, l. 5.

ABBREVIATIONS

ACLU   American Civil Liberties Union Papers, Seeley Mudd Library, Princeton University.

BTS   William Z. Foster, *From Bryan to Stalin* (New York: International Publishers, 1937).

Comintern   Archive of the Communist International, CRPDMCH, Moscow, f. 495.

CPUSA   Communist Party of the United States Papers, CRPDMCH, Moscow, f. 515.

DS   David J. Saposs Papers, Historical Society of Wisconsin, Madison.

EB   Earl Browder Papers, microfilm edition.

FOIA   Freedom of Information Act Files, FBI, William Z. Foster.

JMK   Private Papers of Joseph Manley Kolko.

LH   *The Labor Herald* (Chicago) published by the Trade Union Educational League.

NM   *The New Majority* (Chicago).

PH   Powers Hapgood Papers, Lilly Library, Indiana University.

PWL   William Z. Foster, *Pages from a Worker's Life* (New York: International Publishers, 1939).

RILU   Archive of the Red International of Labor Unions or
       Profintern, CRPDMCH, Moscow; f. 534, op. 7,
       "United States."
TD   Theodore Draper Papers, Special Collections Department,
       Woodruff Library, Emory University.
VOL   *The Voice of Labor* (Chicago).
WZF   William Z. Foster Papers, CRPDMCH, Moscow, f. 615.

Forging American Communism

———————————

INTRODUCTION

AMONG twentieth-century American radicals, William Z. Foster will surely stand as one of the most implacable. His was an obstinate revolutionary temperament, unadorned by complex ideological convictions and only lightly constrained by legal or political convention. Driven by a deeply held hostility to many of the central assumptions of American politics and economic life, his career as a socialist, Wobbly, syndicalist, labor organizer, and Communist spanned five decades.

Foster's long and circuitous political journey began at the turn of the century in Philadelphia, where a compelling soap-box speaker inspired his first identification with the American socialist movement. However, his articulate public life as a radical began in the 1910s. During these early years as an itinerant labor agitator and journalist, he sought to adapt the complex dynamics of the "new unionism" to the development of a coherent revolutionary program for American labor. At the end of the decade, working as a "free-lance" radical within the American Federation of Labor, he was the architect of unprecedented organizing drives in the meat-packing and steel industries. During World War I and immediately afterward, he was considered by many to be one of America's most effective (and dangerous) labor organizers. Yet, despite his activities during these years, it was his subsequent career in the Communist party that would largely define his place in the history of the American labor movement.[1]

In the early 1920s, when Foster joined the American Communist movement, it was a tiny underground sect engaged in a debilitating factional quarrel over whether or not it should function openly as a "legal" party. Moreover, at the founding conventions of the Communist and Communist Labor parties in 1919, few in attendance had any knowledge of or experience in the trade union movement. By 1936, the Party could portray itself as an organization with substantial roots in American labor unions. As the Party's chief labor organizer during its early years, Foster played an important role in bringing about this transition in the Party's membership and orientation. Yet, in many respects his personality and outlook were not suited to the new politics of labor that emerged in the 1930s. Later, during the Cold War, he would preside over a period of sharp decline in the Party's influence among American radicals. At the end of his life, he was a deracinated figure, tragically out of touch with the native oppositional traditions that had nurtured his career.

Despite his prominence, historians have not been particularly attentive to the man whose activities and ideas contributed significantly to the character of American Communism. Foster was one of the few leadership figures to remain in the movement from the first years of its development through its decline in the 1950s; understandably, treatments of his personality and politics have focused on these years. Generally, he has been portrayed within this milieu as an adroit factional infighter and opportunist, a politician more in tune with the ideological requirements of the Comintern than with the needs of the American working class. Theodore Draper, in his two detailed studies of the early years of the party, *The Roots of American Communism* and *American Communism and Soviet Russia*, documented Foster's rapidly shifting positions on issues such as the labor party movement of the early 1920s, "American exceptionalism," and trade union organizing strategy. According to Draper, these changes illustrated Foster's "ability to change, or appear to change, his convictions as often as the party line demanded."[2] Draper's view of Foster corresponds to his thesis that the American Communist Party was chronically hindered by its fealty to policies and strategies set in the Soviet Union.

This study of Foster's life seeks to address a different set of issues. Most basically, it begins with the assumption that it is impossible to understand Foster's career in the Communist party in isolation from his earlier radicalism. When he joined the Communist movement in 1921, he was forty years old. A stubbornly independent figure, he was a fully formed personality with coherent ideas about the problems confronting American unionism. He commanded a respectful audience among influential progressives in the mainstream labor movement. In other words, he was hardly a cipher upon which a political movement, however disciplined, could easily inscribe its ethos and ideology. One measure of this was the fact that Foster was never trusted by the Comintern with a confidential overseas assignment, a rite of passage for most Communist leaders. When he acknowledged toward the end of his career that he had made "many political mistakes," his confession was meaningful beyond the ritual requirements of Communist self-criticism.[3] Foster was deeply attracted to Communism, but the movement was hardly a monolithic phenomenon; its appeal encompassed a wide variety of political personalities. Thus, this study has not devoted much effort to pushing Foster into any particular objective category of "Communist," or specifying a moment of conversion. Foster's education as a radical began many years before the founding of the Comintern. At the same time, in certain very significant instances, his ideas departed from Communist orthodoxy after 1921.

Once Foster's Communism is grounded in the history of modern American radicalism, the influence of the Comintern becomes less important in explaining his motivations. There is no doubt that Foster was a devout admirer of the Russian Revolution and respected the revolutionary authority and resources of the Comintern. But the more important question addressed by this study is: What was it in Foster's personality, politics, and experience that led him to devote his life to international Communism? He was, after all, an American, and his life cannot be fully understood without reference to this basic fact. Foster fought for years after he became a Communist to establish an "exceptionalist" perspective for American Communism. Before he joined the Communist party, Foster's experiences had convinced him that the revolution in the United States could be brought about by radicals working within the trade union movement. He held himself aloof from the American Socialist party and remained suspicious of Marxist doctrine. After he joined the Communist party, he retained much of his syndicalist outlook. His unfamiliarity with Marxist thought often left him ill-prepared for the numerous theoretical disputes that characterized party life at its upper echelons. He was a somewhat anomalous figure in the Party; in an organization that was dedicated to working-class revolutionary activity, he was one of the few members of the leadership who was of undeniably proletarian background. He was also the only leader who had any real experience leading "mass struggles" or large-scale strikes. Bertram Wolfe, who joined the Communist party at its inception, once suggested that Foster's belief that the unions were the most important focus of revolutionary activity in America was "the first expression" of American exceptionalism in the Communist party.[4]

While this study seeks to locate William Foster in a native tradition of labor radicalism, in several important respects his career represented a significant departure from an earlier socialist legacy. For instance, during the years that Foster was most active in the labor movement, Eugene Debs was perhaps the figure who best represented what twentieth-century socialists inherited from earlier American radicalisms. Foster and Debs, however, were strikingly different figures. While the two agreed briefly in the early 1920s on the best strategy that radicals might pursue in the mainstream labor movement, Foster was generally disdainful of Debs. This disdain, however, not only arose from conventional differences of strategy and politics, but was complexly rooted in each man's personality and experience. These differences, as well as Foster's critique of the Socialist leader, provide insight, I believe, into some of the fundamental disjunctures that American socialism confronted in the early twentieth century. Debs and Foster, ultimately, could not share a viable definition of "community" or "citizenship," and this had profound implications for one of Foster's central failures: his inability to develop a powerful and credible vision of an alternative American social order. Partly this was a failure of language; Foster never developed a radical lexicon that was anywhere near as evocative as was Debs's. This study, however, assumes that Foster's uniquely disabled voice was the expressive correlative of a particular historical experience, an experience that was, in the end, profoundly American.

This study pays particular attention to the history of Foster's rhetoric. He and his generation of radicals, after all, are often remembered for their distinctive political grammar. Foster was an eclectic thinker and improvisational activist whose rhetoric borrowed from American trade unionism, various currents in American and European syndicalism and anarchism, prevailing notions of gender, and to a certain extent, the ideologies of American corporate enterprise. He was not a learned or original theorist by any means, and it is tempting to dismiss much of Foster's writings as mere propaganda or factional posturing. There is a lack of veracity in his public speech that many found repellent, but there is another sense in which his language was profoundly honest. He did, after all, believe that he lived in a world of large economic imperatives and ubiquitous capitalist power; the terminology of Communism (as well as its "Aesopian" evasiveness) did, in this sense, fit with much of his experience. It was a world, he believed, in which dialogue was not particularly valuable. Nonetheless, ideas were important and useful to Foster, and the public presentation of his politics was closely related to his successes and failures as a radical.

Ironically enough, despite the reams of political writing that Foster produced, his personality was characterized by certain "voicelessness" or aphasia. Of course, his voice was often circumscribed by powerful forces outside his control, but he himself often denigrated the "talk" of politics in favor of decisive action and the power of organization. Related to this was his tendency to downplay the importance of workers' voice not only in politics, but in the management of their own labor. The economists Richard B. Freeman and James L. Medoff have proposed that one vital function of labor unions in our society is to provide workers with a "collective voice" in regard to the day-to-day conditions of their employment. Tragically, despite his lifelong devotion to labor unionism, Foster only rarely acknowledged the necessity for developing a truly democratic, participatory "voice" in the workplace. However, Foster's peculiar failure of voice and language, I have assumed, can be explained as much by an inquiry into the complex social history of his times as by an understanding of his unique personality.[5]

From the very beginning of his career in the Communist movement, Foster was among the leadership of the Party. Just as I believe that he was not merely a cipher for decisions about policy and orientation made at the international level, so do I believe that an examination of his career in the

Party can provide important insights into the nature of the Communist movement. Like any political party, the Communist party was organized around a set of hierarchical relationships. In this context, the rank-and-file membership did not act completely autonomously, even though it is now clear that the relationships between shop-floor and community-level organizers and the party hierarchy were characterized by a significant degree of independence.[6] Whatever the exact nature of Foster's political influence within the Party at different times, he was able to leave a large and distinctive imprint on its general orientation.

I argue that Foster's syndicalism was particularly influential in this regard. Earlier accounts have acknowledged the syndicalist background of the many of the Party's early leaders, but generally have not traced how these personal histories affected Communist policy after the founding of the Comintern.[7] I believe it is possible to detect significant continuities between Foster's earlier syndicalism, as formulated in the 1910s, and the texture of later policies adopted by the American Communists. In the 1920s, originally as a result of Lenin's injunction that American radicals should "get into" the trade union movement, the party hesitantly adopted much of what had come to be known as "Fosterism," the idea that the revolution in the United States would come about as a result of the activities of a "militant minority" in the trade union movement. This idea may seem anachronistic today, but Foster and his allies in the Party held to it years after the death of Lenin and through a number of changes in line. This orientation was by no means inevitable, neither was it always in accord with the views of powerful ideologists in the apparatus of the Comintern. Within the American Communist movement, opposition to Foster's policies was often bitter and intense. I do not believe that such opposition was merely opportunistic; rather, it reflected genuine differences of interpretation and background among American radicals, differences which, of course, predated the Bolshevik Revolution. Outside of the Communist movement, Foster's strategy met with determined resistance by both the leadership and much of the rank and file of the trade unions. Nevertheless, "Fosterism" proved to be a strong enough interpretation of American conditions to help the Party gain some of its most important successes in the labor movement, though it was not ultimately compelling enough to create a unified Communist movement in this country.

Earl Browder, who perhaps knew Foster better than any other of his contemporaries, once claimed despairingly that the wily Communist leader could "abandon his ideas with the greatest facility of any man I've ever met—and repudiate them publicly, without the slightest embarrassment. . . . So, if you're trying to develop a line of Foster's over the years, you may be able to do it but it'll be filled with the most God-awful contradictions."[8] Jay Lovestone, a bitter political opponent of Foster's, fastened on him the nickname "Zig-Zag." I have attempted in this study to explain in detail some of the more notable and astonishing zigzags in Foster's career, but in a larger sense it may be useful to the reader to think of this biography as comprising three large parts, each documenting the most basic transformations in his life and identity.

As a young man Foster was a drifter, a member of the large class of floating American workers at the turn of the century who are only intermittently visible as individuals to today's historians. The first three chapters of my account of his life follow his early wanderings as closely as possible, and document his developing political awareness. Like many others of his disposition and social class, Foster left no journals, and only a few early letters. Despite such impediments, I believe it is possible to offer a complex portrayal of Foster as an important historical actor. He wrote detailed autobiographies, and his actions and thoughts can be discerned as well in the correspondence, testimony and memories of his associates. Thus there is an abundance of sources for the historian to consider.

The middle (and largest) part of this study deals with Foster's career as a labor organizer and Communist. During World War I, his roles in the meat-packing organizing drive and the Great Steel Strike placed him at the center of momentous conflicts among giant corporations, Progressive politicians, and organized labor. His activities during these years show him to be a transitional figure, gaining national prominence at the end of a particularly violent half-century of labor unrest, but also before and during the emergence of the modern labor movement in the United States. Ever the modernist and organization man, he was nonetheless an idiosyncratic figure—either a new type of labor organizer, as some styled him, or a "lone wolf sort of operator," as Earl Browder described him. Both as a labor organizer and Communist, Foster personified the contradictions of the "borer from within." While professing loyalty to the organization, he in fact never quite fit—either in the American Federation of Labor or the American Communist movement.

The final four chapters of this study, encompassing the period following his breakdown in 1932 to his death in Moscow in 1961, address Foster's role in the most important transformations that the Communist party experienced in its recent history: the abandonment of sectarianism for the Popular Front during the Great Depression and World War II, and finally the reversal of this policy during the Cold War. Foster unquestionably played his most important role in the later shift toward sectarianism; without his powerful presence in the crucial period after 1945, it is quite possible that the American Communist party would have evolved into a different organization than it is today. However, both hardened and transmogrified, "Fosterism" became a logic of decline, isolation, and helplessness during the Cold War era. With his death in 1961, William Foster left a legacy of complex and often negative lessons for later generations of activists.

Chapter 1

BEGINNINGS

I cannot remember the time when I was not
imbued with that class hatred against employers
which is almost instinctive to workers.
—William Z. Foster, *Twilight of World Capitalism*

IN THE INTRODUCTION to his 1937 autobiography, *From Bryan to Stalin*, William Z. Foster explained that "I have tried to show those forces which impelled me, an American worker, to arrive at revolutionary conclusions, to become a Communist." Similarly, in the introduction to his collection of more personal sketches, *Pages from a Worker's Life*, Foster noted that the rationale for the book was to illustrate "the forces that made me arrive at my present political opinions." In his deterministic analysis of his own life, he left little room for a consideration of his family and the subjective experiences of his early childhood. Yet there is no doubt that the circumstances of Foster's early life, especially the poverty in which he grew up, decisively shaped his political identity. When asked by a Senate committee investigating the Great Steel Strike of 1919 to explain his political views, he began by asserting that "I am one who was raised in the slums."[1]

In Foster's portrayals of his childhood, only one personality emerges from the formidable welter of "forces" he describes to influence his life in a decisive manner: his father, James. Even so, his father as well as his mother remain shadowy figures, possessing neither complexity nor dimension in Foster's accounts. His reminiscences reveal no deep affection for either one, and he offers no elaboration at all when citing the fact that both died while he was still in his teens.

James was born in County Carlow, Ireland, and was twenty-seven years old when he arrived in the United States as a Fenian political refugee in 1868. A vigorous, combative, and intensely political man, he was a devoted member of a secret revolutionary brotherhood that had conspired to raise an armed revolt by Irish soldiers of the British garrison in Ireland. James told his son of a "traitor" who betrayed him and his comrades. At the time, British officials were acting decisively to purge the garrison of nationalist plotters; the Habeas Corpus Act was suspended and police were making wholesale arrests of suspected Fenian insurrectionists. Hundreds of others besides James fled to the United States to escape imprisonment.[2]

James's forced emigration brought him first to Boston, then to nearby Taunton by the late 1860s or early 1870s. It is quite possible that James was initially drawn to the town by family ties, but the only evidence for this is an occasional proximity of addresses recorded in the city directories. When he arrived in Taunton, the town already possessed a sizable population of first- and second-generation Irish immigrants, many of whom worked in the town's large textile factories. James, however, appears not to have been directly employed by the mills. His name first appeared in the Taunton city directories in 1874, with his occupation listed as "hostler"; this is consistent with William's description of his father's occupation as that of a livery stableman and carriage washer.[3]

James's wife, Elizabeth McLaughlin, was born in Carlisle, England, into a family of textile workers. It is unclear when or where James and Elizabeth met or were married, but James may have met his wife during his residency in Taunton. She was ten years younger than James, and unlike her husband was a devout Catholic. Neither James nor Elizabeth possessed any formal education. Of the two, Elizabeth may have had more experience as an industrial laborer; James, a stableman, was "of peasant stock." In the mid-nineteenth century, Elizabeth's family, which for generations had made their living producing textiles from the hand loom, witnessed first-hand the terrifying starvation conditions that had attended the transition from the hand to the power loom in the British textile industry. Although William recalled that Elizabeth's "political activities were nil," it is quite likely that his mother possessed at least an understanding of the traditions of labor unionism, which were well developed in the English textile industry by the 1850s, particularly so in Carlisle.[4]

It is difficult to speculate on the nature of James's and Elizabeth's relationship, but the family raised one child whose baptismal record shows another woman's name listed as the mother, with James as the father.[5] In addition, the elder Foster was a heavy drinker whose "special predilection" for fighting Irish policemen often landed him in jail. A restless man with few attachments, his most valued possession was a fine homespun overcoat that he had brought with him from Ireland.[6] In Taunton, James was unwilling or unable to establish a home of any permanence for his family. When William was born in 1881, the family's address was an apartment located on an interior alleyway near the center of town; however, James and Elizabeth made their home at nine different addresses during the years in which they lived in Taunton, between 1872 and 1887. During this period, according to various records, Elizabeth gave birth to nine children, including William E. Foster (the "Z" was added much later). Of these nine children, four survived into adulthood; three are recorded in Taunton municipal records as having died at age three or younger. Two of the children succumbed to common respiratory infections, croup and bronchitis, while two other children "disappeared" in the sense that they cannot be accounted for in either municipal records or census manuscripts.[7] They are not mentioned by name in either of William Foster's autobiographies. It is possible that they were given for adoption, yet, according to Foster's account in *From Bryan to Stalin*, most of the twenty-three children his mother bore died in infancy.[8]

Through these years of frequent moving, the family continued to have their children baptized at St. Mary's Catholic Church; the congregation may have provided a center of support and orientation for the immigrant family, as it did for many of the Irish that settled in Taunton in the 1860s and 1870s. The extent of the Fosters' involvement in church, community, and ethnic organizations in Taunton remains unclear, however. Such memberships, if they were indeed a part of the Fosters' life at this point, apparently did not enable them to overcome the problems that resulted in frequent childhood deaths in their family: poor health care, inadequate nutrition, and uncertain housing.

In the winter of 1887, James and Elizabeth moved their family to Philadelphia. While the reasons for the family's move remain obscure, the family's mobility itself is significant, for it is a theme that persists in William Foster's early life. Geographic mobility was an important part of an immigrant family's strategy for survival and advancement, yet many such families cannot be traced by historians or demographers studying the social life of a particular community. Not only did William's family relocate frequently, its members appear and disappear in municipal, census, and church records and are often never mentioned. However, despite the incomplete evidence available on the precise composition of the family, it is possible to locate William Foster in a particular Philadelphia community during the years 1887 to 1900, and to establish what kind of "forces" were at work there, as well as the kind of choices that may have been available to him.

It is easy to imagine that the family's relocation in Philadelphia was a jolting experience. Census records and city directories reveal no other Fosters or McLaughlins living in the vicinity of the neighborhood where they settled, suggesting that the family could not rely on the cushion of clan loyalties upon arriving in the city. While the Fosters had moved often within the medium-sized mill town of Taunton, Philadelphia was a different environment altogether. In the 1880s, the city was a booming industrial metropolis, second only to New York in the size of its manufacturing work force and the value of its product. Although Philadelphia was noted in the nineteenth century for the exceptional architecture of its public and commercial buildings, developers imposed an efficient yet stark uniformity on the residential neighborhoods of the city's working-class population. In the districts that housed the city's immigrant laborers, vast grids of row houses fronted rear alleyways where thousands of families could be found living in crowded and squalid backyard houses or shacks.[9] While visitors to Philadelphia were apt to remark on the cleanliness of the city or the beauty of the huge Fairmount Park, ugly court and alley slums, or "horizontal tenements," characterized districts like Southwark, Grays Ferry, Kensington, Port Richmond, and Moyamensing. For some, these areas symbolized the promise of Philadelphia's burgeoning industrial economy; one civic booster reminded observers that "wherever a great city is, extremes meet."[10]

William Foster wrote that one street on the block where his family lived in South Philadelphia, Kater Street between Sixteenth and Seventeenth in the old Moyamensing district, "was a noisome, narrow side street, made up of several stables, a woodyard, a carpet cleaning works, a few whore-houses and many ramshackle dwellings." He also described two alleyways on his block where there was no running water, and where "half-starved, diseased, hopeless" people lived by "casual labor, begging [and] petty thieving." An impoverished African American community centered only two blocks north of the Foster residence harbored a "dangerous criminal class," according to W. E. B. Dubois's 1896 study, *The Philadelphia Negro*. Here, according to DuBois, were gathered "shrewd and sleek politicians, gamblers and confidence men"; prostitution thrived as it did in many other parts of the city. Despite the proximity of Dubois's famous Seventh Ward to Foster's neighborhood, Irish gang members routinely attacked African Americans who ventured into their district.[11]

An 1895 Philadelphia atlas portrays a residential alleyway of small wooden dwellings in the center of the block where James Foster and his family lived, but the Fosters occupied a three-story brick row house, described as a tenement in its property deed, facing South Seventeenth Street. The atlas also gives an idea of the mixed economy of the area, and suggests that in this district in Philadelphia, work and community were closely intermingled. The neighborhood at that time contained several small woolen mills, a chemical works, and a smelting works, as well as lumberyards, liveries, and stables. While horse-drawn streetcars were available in Philadelphia at the time, they were generally too expensive to be utilized on a daily basis, and most manual workers lived within a mile or so of their place of employment.[12] It is therefore reasonable to assume that James Foster worked in one of the stables near his home. As for Elizabeth, it was unusual for the wife in a working-class family in Philadelphia to be regularly employed outside the home during this period. In a routine autobiographical questionnaire completed years later, William pointed out that his mother "did not work after marriage" and that his family was dependent on his father's income.[13]

The Fosters did not own the house in which they lived during their years in Philadelphia, although many Irish immigrants who had arrived in the city a generation earlier had been able to achieve home ownership. Few of the residents of Foster's neighborhood owned their own houses, but it was not unlikely that the owner of a tenement such as the Fosters occupied might have an Irish surname. Writing in 1893 of the apparent low proportion of "Paupers and Vicious Classes" in Philadelphia, the sociologist Lorin Blodget concluded optimistically that Philadelphia's experience showed that "it is not a necessity of the creation of great wealth, that there should follow great poverty to the creators of that wealth." Although Blodget attributed Philadelphia's apparent success to the "great numbers engaged at wages in productive industries," many observers at the time were alarmed by the existence of what seemed to be an idle, lawless, and degraded working class in areas like Moyamensing, where the Fosters lived. William Foster noted that in his neighborhood, many residents never worked, and lived only by their wits. His own family occupied an uncertain position in the industrial society that Philadelphians were creating, both as an ideology and as an existing milieu of limited opportunity, in the last decades of the nineteenth century.[14]

Although many Irish immigrants lived in Moyamensing in the 1880s and 1890s, it could not have been accurately described as an ethnic ghetto. Several streets near where the Fosters lived were almost entirely populated by Irish immigrants, but other blocks were more ethnically diverse. In this respect, the area was similar to many other districts in Philadelphia. In 1880, while roughly a third of the city's total population was of Irish stock, only one person in five of Irish background lived in the concentrated clusters of Irish ethnicity. Even in areas that included the highest concentrations of Irish, they composed only about half the total population. Moreover, in the 1860s the Irish in each residential cluster were largely heterogeneous with regard to occupation, unemployment rates, and extent of property holdings. As Philadelphia became more industrialized and transportation systems improved, increased social differences in the workplace began to influence choice of residence more than ethnicity; unskilled workers, in particular, became more isolated. Similarly, social class was steadily becoming more important as a factor in determining membership in Irish fraternal or community organizations in Philadelphia during this period.[15]

Foster remembered that the small area in the Moyamensing district that constituted his neighborhood was known as Skittereen. The street gang to which he belonged rigorously defined this district as extending from Sixteenth to Seventeenth Streets, between South Street on the north and Fitzwater Street three blocks to the south. An examination of the census manuscripts of 1880 and 1900 reveals that this neighborhood was changing quite rapidly during the period the Fosters lived there. In 1880, seven years before the Fosters arrived, the area included a large number of poor Irish-born workers, especially on the smaller side-streets. Kater Street, for instance, was home to mostly unskilled Irish laborers living in tiny two-story row houses, the majority reporting their occupation as "carter" or wagon driver. However, the area was still diverse in ethnicity and occupation. While far from predominant, skilled workers such as carpenters, coachmakers, machinists, metal smiths, printers, and jewelers, as well as businessmen and proprietors with boarding servants resided on the block in which the Fosters were to live and the streets facing it, along with teamsters, other unskilled laborers, and immigrants from Germany, England, Scotland, Italy, France, and Cuba. In this diverse neighborhood, however, there was a significant sign of economic uncertainty. A large number of the residents—on some streets, over half of the census respondents reporting an occupation—stated that they had been unemployed at some point in the previous year.[16]

By 1900, the year that William Foster finally departed, this small section of Philadelphia was home to a large proportion of African American workers, with some streets still showing a mixture of Irish and American-born white laborers. Many of the recently arrived African Americans listed birthplaces in the South, and simply described themselves as laborers. Those who gave an occupation were often domestics, waiters, bootblacks, janitors, and porters. On Kater Street, at the center of the block where the Fosters lived, of the approximately sixty-five individuals over age twenty who lived there in 1900, only five, comprising one family, had resided there in 1880. The relatively fluid ethnic composition of Foster's neighborhood is suggested by the fact that the three-story tenement in which the Foster family had resided from 1887 to the late 1890s was occupied in 1900 by three African American families, two of which were headed by laborers. Symbolically, a building across the street from the Foster residence that housed a workingmen's club in 1889 had been converted into a relief mission by 1901.[17]

James Foster did not bring his family into a stable ethnic community in Philadelphia, but few Irish who moved to the city in the nineteenth century possessed a coherent national identity in the first place: most loyalties were focused on the family, clan, town, or home county. Even fewer such immigrants were devoted to the political ideal of Irish nationalism, but for James Foster, the idea of a free and united Irish state was of tremendous importance.[18]

William Foster characterized his father as a "militant" nationalist who made his home into a gathering place for Irish patriots as well as Molly Maguires fleeing persecution in the mining regions west of Philadelphia. Irish nationalism was the "intellectual meat and drink" of William's early youth, and he later wrote that it was his father's politics that first impelled him to become a "rebel." Philadelphia was indeed a hotbed of Fenian activity, the center of Irish nationalist plotting in the United States in the 1880s. James undoubtedly had some contact with William Carroll, a prominent and militant leader of the émigré movement who held meetings at his home on South Sixteenth Street, only two blocks from the Foster residence at the time. Carroll was a leader of an extremist faction of the Clan-na-Gael, which advocated violent revolutionary methods to gain Irish independence.[19]

At the level of style at least, James's revolutionary politics are evocative of his son's later activities as a syndicalist and Communist. The Fenian organizations to which James belonged in the 1850s and 1860s were secret revolutionary brotherhoods, carefully ordered elite groups enveloped by complex initiation and other rituals. The movement itself was suffused with various kinds of special terminology as well as signs, passwords, and oaths. Promotion within the brotherhood brought higher responsibility and esoteric knowledge, and its initiates thought of themselves as members of a larger international movement. E. J. Hobsbawm has noted the resemblance between such ideals and the strong globalist perspective of later socialist movements. Moreover, the brotherhood itself did not normally operate as part of a broader movement that was identified with its policies, but rather permeated conservative institutions; thus the largest kind of revolutionary designs were combined with a defensive, secretive pragmatism. In their strategizing, the Fenians conceived of uprisings directed by small groups of devoted initiates who would draw the masses behind them in some unspecified way.[20] For William, the central metaphor would be that of radicals "boring from within" the American Federation of Labor. Despite his cursory treatment of his father in his autobiographies, there is no doubt that William formed an intense bond with his father: as a boy he determined to devote his whole life to fighting to free Ireland. It was from his father, undoubtedly, that William first absorbed the tantalizing idea that small groups of men (minus "traitors") could accomplish so much. Finally, William admired his father as a "rebel" and a fighter for his political ideals, but his own radicalism would be limited by the obvious maleness of this conception. In the traditional iconography of the American labor movement women have historically been excluded from roles as "fighters." In Foster's conception as well, the ideal organizer is always the militant working*man*.[21]

From 1892 to 1898, James Foster listed his occupation in the city directories as that of a seller of birds and dogs. William noted that his father attempted unsuccessfully to establish a small store while working as a stableman, but also points out that James, being an "ardent sportsman," made his home a "rallying point" for cockfighters and dogfighters, as well as runners, boxers, ball players, and "race-track men."[22] Writing in 1884, a Philadelphia historian observed that while before the Revolution cockfighting and dogfighting had been occasionally sponsored by "men of the highest respectability," these "barbarous amusements" were, by the 1820s, "shunned by all who laid a claim to social standing." The type of business that James conducted in his home typically drew the attention of middle-class reformers who investigated unsanitary conditions in immigrant neighborhoods.[23]

James undoubtedly began his business as a way to supplement his low wages; if his income as a hostler or stableman approximated that of an unskilled industrial worker of the time, he would have been unable to achieve the "minimum adequacy" household budget that has been calculated by Michael R. Haines for Philadelphia in 1880. In a world far removed from Philadelphia's "good society," whatever income James Foster may have been able to bring in from selling birds and dogs, or possibly sponsoring animal fights, could not be depended upon to provide for much economic security. During the depression of the mid-1890s, the "half-starved" family eked out a living from the neighborhood soup kitchen, presumably the one that was operated only right around the corner from the Foster residence at the time.[24]

Because of the family's difficult economic situation, it was important for James and Elizabeth's children to be employed outside the home. The wages of working children were the chief means of survival during this period for a family where the head of household's earnings were not large.[25] However, according to the best information available, when the Foster family first moved to Philadelphia in 1887, the eldest child, John, was only ten years old. Records from St. Teresa's Church in Philadelphia show that four children were born into the Foster family and baptized between 1889, when Elizabeth was thirty-eight years old, and 1893. By 1893, the first year of a major depression, there were a minimum of five children in the family aged sixteen or younger, and it is possible that the family included as many as five children under the age of ten. By the 1890s, earnings from the older children may have begun to make a difference for the family, but even then, for many months during the depression, James and his eldest son John were unemployed. William attended a nearby public school for four years until 1891, and also managed some income hawking newspapers before being forced at age ten to find regular employment. He wrote much later that during this period, "the task of being the family providers fell upon my sister and myself, both of us children hardly in our teens." His older sister, Sarah-Anna, listed her occupation as that of a domestic on her 1898 marriage license.[26]

Survival for a working-class family in South Philadelphia during the last half of the nineteenth century was predicated on a variety of "memberships." Belonging to a community group or fraternal organization, church, political party, street gang, or, most basically, a stable family, could ensure a measure of security within a larger milieu of uncertainty and poverty. It is difficult to judge the extent to which the Foster family participated in community-level fraternal or church organizations, but William remembered that several kinds of networks existed in his neighborhood. Besides his father's militant Irish nationalism, there were the life of the street gang, the loyalties of the Republican political machine, and the influence of the Catholic Church.

The family attended St. Teresa of Avila Church at Broad and Catharine streets, not far from where the Fosters lived in South Philadelphia. William recalled that his mother and Father Joseph V. O'Connor, a priest at St. Teresa's Church and a "friend" of his, unsuccessfully pressured him to attend a Jesuit college in order to be educated for priesthood.[27] As for his own Catholicism, Foster's memory is ambiguous. He claimed in one essay that his readings in natural science had taken him "far and away beyond the control of the Catholic Church" at an early age. Elsewhere, he admitted that he "took Catholicism earnestly" in his youth. Evidently, he maintained some ties to St. Teresa's Church until the late 1890s: Father O'Connor was a priest at St. Teresa's for only one year, from 1897 to 1898. Yet, Foster's few years of formal education were apparently in the public school system, despite the distrust of many Irish Catholics for the public schools and the fact that there was a large parish school at St. Teresa's. Despite his mother's entreaties, his father's activities were more appealing to him at the time, and it is noteworthy that he characterized his mother's Catholicism as a form of "control." Elizabeth, a pious Catholic of English background, may have frowned on her husband's militant Fenian politics, questionable business enterprises, and religious negligence. If William associated his identity as a fighter and "rebel" with his father's influence, the autobiographical fragments in which he describes his mother and her Catholicism are related in a contradistinctive way to his understanding of himself as a revolutionary modernist. In his later recollections, he associated his mother's religiosity with what he held to be some of the worst aspects of working-class tradition: such beliefs, he wrote, were mired in "unsubstantiated myths and legends," "blind" faith and irrational superstition. Foster's radicalism would always be informed by a kind of stark economism or "system thinking" that denigrated the complex ontology of faith, custom, and political symbolism in workers' lives.[28]

The most important fraternal organization in Foster's small neighborhood was the street gang. Such gangs had a long history in Philadelphia, and they were commonly seen by the city's upper-class citizens as dangerous manifestations of Irish criminality. Foster's gang was named the Bulldogs. The younger members participated in a baseball team, a fife-and-drum band, and a social club, while the older gang members had a "big social-political club" and a mummers' band known as "The Bright Star." However, Foster's memories of the Bulldogs were largely negative. There were conflicts within the gang between Protestants and Catholics; its members were animated by strong "religious, national and race prejudices." Many of the Bulldogs were criminals, while some were "drunks" and "degenerates," "the ripe fruit of the slums." The gang was an "efficient school for crime," and a "foundation of the corrupt Republican Party" as well.[29]

While there may have been a political dimension to the gang's activities, party loyalties probably did not allow for much self-determination for the neighborhood within the larger context of Philadelphia city politics. In Philadelphia, the Republican party organization in the last decades of the nineteenth century was dominated by Anglo-Saxon business interests and the Scotch-Irish bosses of the state party. As a result, the Irish Catholics in Philadelphia never came to dominate the urban political machine as did their counterparts in Boston and New York. Yet, despite the uncertain and fragmented status of the Bulldogs, Foster remembered that "there was much real proletarian spirit in our gang." As an example of this spirit of solidarity, he cited the gang's participation in the strike of the Amalgamated Association of Street Railway Employees in 1895.[30]

Foster's memory of the 1895 street railway strike is a central event in his portrayal of his own childhood. According to his autobiographies, he and his family were quite conscious of the struggles of American organized labor in the 1890s. James apparently knew Molly Maguires who had been involved in strikes in the Eastern Pennsylvania coalfields, and William remembered having paid close attention to the Homestead strike of 1892 and the Pullman strike of the American Railway Union in 1894.[31] Despite their apparent sympathy with striking workers, William does not mention that either he or his father belonged to a union during this period. The Knights of Labor, an organization that included manual laborers in its ranks, had organized some hostlers serving the early horse-driven streetcar lines, but in Philadelphia the union entered a period of deep decline after a series of lockouts and unsuccessful strikes in the late

1880s. Unionism was not a significant force in Moyamensing in the last decades of the nineteenth century, and in this sense as well the residents of Foster's neighborhood remained vulnerable and largely powerless.[32]

Nevertheless, William Foster was an active participant in the street railway strike. This strike was an unusually violent episode in the turbulent history of labor relations in the city in the 1880s and 1890s. Foster considered it his "introduction to the class struggle," even though the conflict was more complex than he portrayed it.[33] If the strike was a "class struggle," it was one in which the workers enjoyed widespread public support and sympathy. Many of the citizens of Philadelphia apparently felt that the demands of the trolley conductors for recognition of the right to belong to the Amalgamated, and for impartial arbitration of employee grievances, were legitimate. However, there was less support for the violence and disorder that the strike seemed to engender. It was recognized that the strikers themselves were not involved in the riots and widespread wrecking of streetcars that accompanied the strike. The *Philadelphia Inquirer* editorialized that "there can be no mistaking the fact that the sympathy of the people [was] heartily with the strikers—not with disorder and riots, for which the strikers were not responsible, but with the cause itself."[34]

Near Foster's neighborhood, there were several serious disturbances. At one point, "fully three-thousand people" gathered in the vicinity of Bainbridge and Fifteenth Streets. Only blocks from the grand new city hall then under construction, the mob wrecked four trolley cars before being dispersed by mounted policemen. Foster himself participated in an episode near his house where a street was barricaded and a streetcar destroyed. At a gathering near City Hall, he was clubbed by a mounted policeman.[35] The rioting that Foster participated in seemed to involve much more than the specific grievances of unionizing workers. The *Inquirer* noted that "it is the mob—the half grown youths, the idle population—that is to be blamed. The strikers themselves have little to do with the barricading of streets, the smashing of windows, the overturning of cars." The newspaper decried the "arrogance" of the Philadelphia Traction Company, and urged that the corporation recognize the legitimate demands of the strikers. The president of the Amalgamated noted that "the best people espoused our cause as right and just." Nevertheless, what was alarming about the strike, according to the *Inquirer,* was the associated civil disorder, caused in part by "men walking the streets out of employment and too lazy to work."[36]

Thus, in 1895, the excluded and powerless came briefly and violently into the consciousness of Philadelphia's citizens. Years later, when Foster's comrades spoke glibly about the "masses" and "mass movements," he must have unconsciously referred back to his memories of this brief but spectacular social conflagration in Philadelphia. To speak of "the masses," for him, was not to speak of political formulae and complex gradations of revolutionary consciousness. Instead, in this instance at least, the political energy of "the masses" was fueled by a volatile mixture of resentments, impulses, and rumors, as well as by quite rational identification with the grievances of the streetcar operators. For Foster as an adult, organization would always be the key to mastering the revolutionary potential of the modern working classes.

Foster remembered that the strike ended with a compromise, and that the conflict was for him his first practical lesson in the "harsh realities of the labor movement." His memory of the strike settlement was correct, for while the Philadelphia Traction Company did recognize the right of its employees to belong to a union, the agreement stated that the union itself "must not enter into the relations between employees and the company, and cannot be recognized in the business conducted between us."[37] As for the rioters, newspaper accounts of the disturbances and their aftermath emphasized that such men had not been legitimately associated with the strike itself, and indeed were not to be considered "citizens" of the city in the first place. In his autobiographies, Foster failed to draw such a distinction between the strikers and the rioters, even though rioting continued sporadically after the settlement of the strike. He consciously identified with both the strikers and the rioters who disrupted the life of the city for nearly two weeks.

Although Foster remembered the outcome of the strike in ambivalent terms, his direct involvement in the demonstrations did not fail to impress upon him the possibilities of solidarity and militant direct action by an otherwise excluded community of supporters for a grievance of labor. The streetcar strike represented a briefly successful exercise of collective power in a community that Foster portrayed as otherwise fragmented, normless, and politically impotent. Although his career as a radical would always be characterized by a certain uneasiness with street demonstrations and protests, for the young Foster, caught up in the crucible of violence and unrest occasioned by the streetcar strike, the ideal of trade unionism was dramatically fused with the impulse for power, community, and order. The 1895 strike caused him, he later reflected, to "become a trade unionist, in theory at least."[38]

If the street railwaymen's strike was a central public event in Foster's memory of his childhood, the circumstances of his first employment were important at a different level. Here, the private life of his family and childhood seems to have been overwhelmed by impersonal economic exigencies. His first job was as an assistant to Edward A. Kretchman, a craftsman whose shop was at Franklin and Noble streets, nearly two miles from the Foster residence in South Philadelphia. This was an unusually long distance; it is quite possible that William boarded with his employer at least periodically. Kretchman was a respected die-sinker and metal-worker, and he took his young helper with him on trips to New York, Boston and Washington to sell the souvenir medals that he produced. Foster probably gained much of his traveling confidence, later put to much use, from Kretchman. As well, his work in Kretchman's shop un-doubtedly underlined the vast difference between the stubbornly inde-pendent world of craft production, still much in evidence in industrializ-ing Philadelphia, and the world of uncertain wage labor in which his family was immersed.

Despite Foster's admiration for Kretchman and the craftsman's strong liking for him, at age thirteen he quit this job and began working in a series of industries, beginning in 1894 with the MacKellar, Smith and Jordan Type Foundry in Philadelphia.[39] Foster has written two different versions of his decision to quit Kretchman's shop; in *Pages from a Worker's Life,* he claims that he "felt no call to a life of art," and instead "wanted to become an industrial worker and was drawn as by a magnet to the shops."[40] Despite the implication that he decided quite eagerly at this young age to become an "industrial worker," in another account Foster portrays this decision in a different light. Here, he sees his decision in the context of the depression of the 1890s, and the fact that "I had to make more wages somehow" in order to help support his family, with his elder brother and father unemployed. Contrary to his account in *Pages from a Worker's Life,* Foster's introduction to the world of industrial labor was probably a wrenching one, fraught with physical hazard. Dur-ing his approximately three years in the type foundry, he became "satu-rated with lead." Foster himself describes his earliest work experiences in a bitter and angry tone. "Men could find no work but there were always places for child slaves," he wrote. He remembers that, "denied the oppor-tunity for an education and living in a poverty-stricken home, I early felt the iron of the class struggle sink into my heart. . . . I deeply resented the poverty in which I had to live." He reflected bitterly that it was "super-hog capitalist greed" that had been responsible for the joblessness that his father and brother had experienced in the 1890s.[41]

Perhaps as a result of the economic stresses of the 1890s, William's family had come apart by 1898. There is very little dependable informa-tion available about it during this period, but several facts seem most important. James disappears from Philadelphia city directories in 1898; Foster states that by 1901, both of his parents were dead. It was during this year that the family's three eldest children leave the city. Foster does not mention the specific reasons for his own departure, but it is clear that he believed that Philadelphia did not offer the opportunity to escape from the poverty and powerlessness in which his family had been immersed in Skittereen.[42]

Like many others who became industrial workers at a relatively young age, Foster had difficulty forming any lasting attachment to a particular job or employer. He worked at the MacKellar, Smith and Jordan type foundry until 1897, and then found employment as a furnace tender at the Harrison White Lead Works in South Philadelphia. This job lasted for approximately a year; he evidently moved to Wyomissing, near Reading, sometime in 1898. In Wyomissing, Foster lived with his recently married sister, Sarah-Anna, and her husband, George McVey; both men worked in a fertilizer plant. John, Foster's older brother, joined the United States Army in July, 1898, during the Spanish-American War, and was released in October of the same year. In the winter of 1900, at age nineteen, Foster left Wyomissing because he had begun to develop tuberculosis as a result of his work in the fertilizer business.[43] The hazards that Foster faced as a young worker are salient features of his recollections of his early life. Whatever other centrifugal forces may have caused his departure from Philadelphia and later Wyomissing, the very real physical threats that were posed in earning a livelihood as a young, unskilled worker seemed to shadow him wherever he went. Because he was without a trade and was unable to secure union membership, quitting was one of the few prerogatives he could exercise over the conditions of his employment.

One characteristic of William Foster's youth was that neither he nor his family were members of any geographically stable industrial working class. The area in which the Fosters lived in Philadelphia was one where skilled laborers were giving way to a group of individuals who struggled to eke out a living on the margins of a developing urban capitalism. Skittereen was isolated from the rest of South Philadelphia by virulent race, ethnic, and gang prejudices. In a city where participation in the manufacturing sector traditionally provided the most promise of economic security or advancement for new arrivals, James Foster's occupation as a carriage washer was decidedly preindustrial in nature.[44] William Foster's first work experience as a child was as a craftsman's helper, and his introduction to industrial labor may have been a bitter and unhappy experience, despite his later disclaimer. Foster's experiences as a worker varied quite dramatically. He was undoubtedly familiar with the life of industrial labor by the time he reached age nineteen, yet he had also been involved in a declining craft milieu. By the time he was twenty, he had become an itinerant laborer. At this point in his life, his location in the American working class was ill-defined, without clear ethnic, religious, or geographic dimensions.

Furthermore, living in the urban backwater of Skittereen, William Foster's family had experienced a kind of powerlessness that was similar to that which many African American families living in the city at the turn of the century understood. In Philadelphia, blacks had few opportunities to achieve economic security, and the vast majority of black males worked at the unskilled, manual jobs that many Irish once filled. At the same time, Irish immigrants were subject to a racism that could be as virulent as that which many blacks experienced. One historian, writing in 1901 of Philadelphia's impoverished Irish, noted that they had "revolting and vicious habits. Being of the lower order of mankind, they were repellent to those who were further advanced in the social scale."[45]

Foster felt that his involvement in the street railway strike "exerted a profound influence" on his identity. During this period, his identification with Irish nationalism "began to sink into a secondary position." He remembered that the Pullman and Homestead strikes of the 1890s had helped develop his "proletarian class instinct." In 1893, he had followed the progress of Coxey's Army; he frequented the army's recruiting office at Thirteenth and Filbert streets, reading bulletins on the progress of this early movement of unemployed workers. In 1896, at age fifteen, he attended political meetings of the Bryan campaign, and heard the Great Commoner speak once. The failures of Coxey's Army and the Populists were important events in Foster's memory of his youth. However, in 1900, during a return visit to his neighborhood in Philadelphia, he heard a speech given by a socialist that "marked a great turning point" in his life. The speaker's arguments and analysis seemed to provide a perfect distillation into political terms of Foster's experiences. The soapboxer distributed a leaflet inscribed with a cartoon that Foster never forgot: a large, powerful worker, "Labor," cowered under a whip wielded by a puny figure, "the Boss." The whip was "the Job." Although Foster had devoured books on the French Revolution that he acquired from the Philadelphia Free Library, by 1900 he had "never encountered a Socialist book or pamphlet" in his neighborhood. That same year, while living in Wyomissing, he walked six miles with his brother-in-law to "help" him vote for Eugene Debs for president. Foster wrote of his growing interest in socialism that "forces were at work which were rapidly developing my native proletarian instinct into genuine class consciousness."[46]

In 1946, Foster admonished a high-ranking member of the Communist party for her decision to have a second child. He told her that once her child was born, "you [will] have given a hostage to capitalism."[47] This startling declaration was probably meant to be practical advice to an important party cadre, yet it is a conclusion that seems consistent with Foster's account of his own childhood. His politicized and occasionally bitter descriptions of the conditions in which he lived as a child suggest that he remembered his life in Philadelphia as that of a "prisoner" in a class war in which family, ethnic, religious, and political influences had been rendered superfluous or irrelevant. Such a portrayal is to a certain extent a simplification of a more complex historical reality; the concept of a class war seems inappropriate as a way of understanding the dynamics of Foster's neighborhood in the 1880s and 1890s, or the street railway strike that was so central to Foster's memories of the period. Yet the fact remains that for him, his participation as a child in the public sphere of work and industry was far more significant than involvement in the more private worlds of ethnicity, family, and fraternity.

Still, while Foster's self-portraits commence with a seemingly determined childhood, his account unconsciously reveals a somewhat more complex and contradictory set of themes that would be manifested in different guises throughout his later career. A useful key to this thematic structure is Foster's portrayal of his family's fertility. Although his mother's fertility was indeed high for impoverished working-class women in Philadelphia, it is very likely that her prodigious childbearing was consistent with trends and attitudes within her original family milieu, the rapidly industrializing mill towns of northern England. In such towns, despite very high levels of infant mortality among workers, a spasmodic yet generally expanding demand for industrial labor provided a positive incentive for working-class families to attempt to establish and maintain large families. Surviving older children could become positive contributors to the family economy as early as the age of ten. In light of this, Elizabeth's childbearing may be understood as a rational reproductive strategy, not a symbol of her helplessness. However, in William's autobiographies she is a character without voice and animation, an essentially passive figure whose "political activities were nil" and whose life of "hardship and drudgery [was] made worse by her excessive childbearing."[48]

As his comments reveal, William Foster came to be a convinced Neo-Malthusian, believing that strict birth control would enhance the economic power of the working class. A radical syndicalist, he declared in 1912, "knows that children are a detriment to him in his daily struggles, and that by rearing them he is at once tying a millstone about his neck and furnishing a new supply of slaves to capitalism." It is noteworthy that he was thinking along these lines even late in his career, as a Communist. In his autobiographies, he portrays his family's fertility (and, indeed, working-class sexuality in general) in negative terms. Rather explicitly in other contexts, he located the problem of working-class poverty and powerlessness partly in the inability of the poor to control their reproductive lives; limitations on fertility could be a key to empowerment, he thought, by increasing the effectiveness of a "militant minority" of childless activists and by constricting the supply of labor. Foster limned James's and Elizabeth's fertility as disabling and irrational in the modernizing economy of Philadelphia in the 1880s and 1890s, and he himself fathered no natural children.[49]

What is striking is that Foster's attitude to some extent replicates that of modernizing bourgeois reformers who similarly invoked the ideals of discipline and restraint in their negative portrayals of working-class fami-

lies. William Foster himself would always be somewhat of a labor disci-
plinarian, and despite his strong admiration for his father's primitive
rebelliousness, a manifest characteristic of William's life was that he relentlessly sought the achievement of a thoroughly modern revolutionary
movement, which could be achieved primarily through organization, the
productive channeling and restraint of impulse and spontaneity. Here, his
portrayal of his family and childhood in Philadelphia merges with the
idea of an inherently disorderly working class whose lives were punctuated by periods of solidarity as well as dangerous collective emotion.

Foster's own understanding of his childhood is dominated by the central facts of his family's poverty, and his own experiences as a child
worker in Philadelphia's huge and diverse economy. By the time he was
nineteen, he had largely abandoned any ethnic, religious, or political milieu of which his family may have been a part. One historian has proposed that Foster's thinking was dominated by his rejection of the importance of the social dimensions of American life; all that is necessary to
know about American society "can be learned from the economic sector." While there was an ethnic and collective dimension to the small
community in which Foster lived in South Philadelphia, it proved to be
quite impermanent, and many of the neighborhood's residents undoubtedly experienced the kind of debilitating powerlessness that is the result
of extreme poverty.[50] While Foster the "system thinker" undoubtedly imposed his later structure of beliefs on his account of his own childhood,
his experience in Philadelphia appears to have been one in which the "system" loomed most large and destructive, the city's vast economy at once
inaccessible and fatally intrusive. James Foster's Irish nationalism, Elizabeth's Catholicism, or William's participation in the gang life of the Bulldogs may have provided a semblance of order for the family within the
rapidly changing neighborhood in which they lived. Yet, by his own account, William Foster had difficulty identifying with these allegiances.
Instead, he joined the Socialist party rather suddenly at age nineteen, and
departed from Philadelphia without a committed vocabulary of religious,
communal, or civic metaphors with which he might have framed his subsequent political experiences.

Foster's attachment during the period immediately after he left Philadelphia appears to have been with his sister, Sarah-Anna, and her husband,
George McVey. Between periods of wandering, he would return to this
family. He lived with them in Wyomissing, Pennsylvania, while working
in the fertilizer industry there. He remained with them only briefly, however, and in 1900 began a hobo existence as a transient worker that
would last for approximately a decade. From Wyomissing, he traveled to
Havana, but was unable to find employment there. Leaving Cuba for

Foster as a street railwayman, 1901, age twenty,
New York City. His first union.

Florida, he worked briefly with a railroad grading company and later at
a backwoods lumber camp near Tampa. After two weeks at the lumber
camp, Foster "beat it" to Jacksonville, where he found "a pretty good
job" at Armour and Company's large fertilizer plant there. Nevertheless,
he also quit this job and soon left for New York City, where he worked
as a streetcar motorman for several months and participated in a failed
effort to organize the workers into the AFL. After being fired from his job
for his attempts, Foster shipped to Galveston, Texas, where he worked
briefly at a railroad construction camp. From here, he hoboed by train to
Portland, Oregon, arriving sometime in the winter of 1901. He worked
for a short time in nearby lumber camps, on railroad construction crews,
and as a laborer on the thriving port city's docks.[51]

In Portland, Foster would become an active participant in local Socialist politics, thus beginning a career in radical and labor politics that
spanned nearly half a century. Yet, before his immersion in Socialist party
activities in Portland, Foster's "revolutionary development suffered a
rude interruption," as he put it. Beginning an interregnum as a sailor, he
signed on as an ordinary seaman aboard the *Pegasus*, a British bark engaged in the still-thriving Cape Horn trade to South Africa and Australia.[52] When the ship arrived at Newcastle, Australia, in November 1903,
Foster deserted, and using the alias "Tom Donahoe," signed on to the
Alliance, a British iron bark bound for Peru. There he joined the *County
of Cardigan*, a British iron sailing ship, bound around Cape Horn for
England. Evidently, the *County of Cardigan* had had difficulty retaining

its crew. In March 1904, the British Consul in Callao, Peru, wrote to the ship's captain recommending that he discharge "the mutinous members of [the] crew," and hire replacements as soon as possible. Foster and six other able seamen joined the ship and signed an agreement that guaranteed wages of £3 per month until arrival in England. Foster later wrote that he participated in a "refusal of duty" when the ship arrived in Talcahuana, Chile, although this incident is not recorded in the ship's articles.[53]

Sailors on British merchant ships often deserted. Of the 120 men who sailed on the *Pegasus* for any period of time during her around-the-world voyage in 1903–1904, for instance, 56 are recorded in the ship's crew agreement as having deserted in various ports, unable to collect their wages. Because most of their wages were paid only at the end of a ship's voyage, a captain possessed a large degree of economic, as well as statutory authority over his men during a voyage, which could be as long as three years. If life on board proved intolerable or difficult for a seaman, he could desert but was subject to penalties and a blacklist. Foster signed his correct name to the *County of Cardigan*'s articles when he boarded in Peru, but he later feared that he would be identified as a deserter from the *Pegasus*. The crew of the *County of Cardigan*, according to Foster, had all deserted British ships in recent years, and feared that because of wage penalties imposed on deserters, "when we hit a British port each of us would be confronted with an agent of our previous ship who would take away every shilling we had coming to us as wages on the *County of Cardigan*." Foster and several other crew members thus refused duty for a short time while the ship was in Chile, were imprisoned briefly, and finally rehired with the understanding that they would be paid in full when the ship reached port in England. Evidently, this "strike" was won, for the ship's articles record that Foster was paid in full when he was released from duty at North Shields, England, in December 1904.[54]

Before arriving in England, however, Foster received a letter from his sisters announcing the engagement of his younger sister Clara; the letter also mentioned an attempt by the McVeys to establish a homestead in Oregon. "I examined the map of your places thoroughly and from what you say in your letter I consider you have done a wise thing in taking up the land," Foster replied. However, he planned to join the Atlantic Coast Seamen's Union and intended to work on steamers serving American ports. He noted that conditions on American steamers were better than on English ships, and that "a quartermaster or steersman in any good line like the Fall River [Massachusetts] line receives about $40 a month all found." Nonetheless, life as a sailor struck Foster as hazardous; he mentioned an occasion when two crewmen from the *Pegasus* were washed overboard and drowned in a storm off Cape Horn. In addition, "you have no home, no friends, and are the prey of all kinds of land sharks and are liable to unsteady employment and other ill conditions too numerous to mention." He composed the following verse to illustrate his attitude towards being a sailor:

> A British ship comes sailing with the wind going free
> With all sails drawing a noble sight to see
> But again that old saying, it seems always true
> That distance its enchantment lends to the view
> Like a frightened bird as she goes rushing past
> With foam covered bows and spray flying past
> And while she goes pitching into the billows high
> Her masts are writing hunger all over the sky

Writing from Queenstown, South Africa, in November 1904, Foster told his sisters that "your letter has set me to thinking seriously again as I had just about adopted the sea as my means of livelihood." Although he joined the Atlantic Coast Seamen's Union upon arriving in the United States in 1904, Foster soon made his way across the continent to Oregon, in order to rejoin the McVeys.[55]

By the time he returned to Oregon, when he was twenty-three years old, William Foster had lived and worked in Taunton, Philadelphia, Wyomissing, New York City, Havana, Florida, Texas, Oregon, and at sea. Any description of Foster as an essentially detached, uninvolved, and peripheral figure during this period must fail, however. If he was unable or unwilling to attach himself to the social and economic life of Philadelphia or any other town at this point, his work in a variety of places and industries nevertheless engaged him in the large drama of the nation's economic development. For instance, as a young man, Foster gained his knowledge of railroads while working in construction camps and hoboing across the country. When he returned to Portland, he would work as a laborer in railroad yards near the city, and briefly as an engine fireman.[56] As an adult, Foster's chief means of mobility and economic survival would be his employment as a railroad worker. In this way, his "rootlessness" would deeply involve him in the work culture of the country, and provide him with a large perspective from which to view American life.

Foster's first involvement in radical politics in Portland, he believed, was the end result of a process that began during his childhood in Philadelphia. In his 1919 Senate testimony, given two years before he became a Communist, he invoked the stark economic conditions of his childhood as a sufficient explanation for the development of his beliefs. In his autobiographies, looking back on the "forces" that created his personality and politics, his memory focused on the bitter realities and limitations he faced while growing up in an atmosphere of powerlessness in Philadelphia slums in the 1880s and 1890s. For him, these "slums" did not encompass an idealized ghetto of ethnic or religious solidarity, nor a mythical arena from which upwardly mobile Americans emerged strengthened in character and personality. Any account of Foster's political life must begin, then, with the fact that his socialism was not informed by the memory of a stable and self-determining American community life, as was Eugene Debs's, for instance.[57] While Debs has been described as a socialist and citizen, Foster's "citizenship" was ambiguous, and was not centered on a particular American community. In Philadelphia, the residents of Skittereen demonstrated a measure of power and solidarity during the 1895 street railway strike by resorting to tactics that only placed them, according to many observers, outside the realm of citizenship. As a sailor, Foster lived and worked among a highly transient group of workers who exercised few rights other than the ambiguous freedom attendant upon the abandonment of their employment. Finally, it is significant that Foster, after leaving his neighborhood in Philadelphia in the late 1890s, did not visit it again for thirty years. When he did return, he found that the tenuous governance of the Bulldogs had vanished long ago; "even their tradition was unknown to the new crop of poverty-stricken slum dwellers" in Skittereen.[58]

Chapter 2

SOCIALIST AND SYNDICALIST

The revolutionary Working Class ignores
obnoxious "majority" made laws wherever it has
the power to do so.
—William Foster, 1910

The workers' movement has been a series of daily efforts
linked to the efforts of the previous day, not by any
rigorous continuity but uniquely by the attitude and
state of mind ruling the working class. The action of the
working class has not been, I say it again, ordered
by formulae or by any theoretical affirmations;
nor has it been a demonstration following a plan
foreseen in advance by us.
—V. Griffuelhes, *L'Action Syndicaliste*

WHEN WILLIAM FOSTER wrote that the drifting workers of the American West at the turn of the century "usually had no homes or families, and often no religion," and were "voteless and took little or no part in the political and social life of the cities," he was describing a way of life with which he was quite familiar by the time he had reached age twenty. He considered himself to have become an "industrial worker" after he quit his apprenticeship to Edward Kretchman in Philadelphia, but he also remembered this period of his life as a time of "floating": for more than a decade he would be "perpetually beating back and forth over the western railroads." Nonetheless, Foster's travels certainly did not resemble the desultory wanderings of a diffident personality. Despite his floating status, he seemed to possess a sure internal compass. In the rapidly developing Pacific Northwest, he quickly attached himself to communities of highly committed radicals and dissenters, and always sought to make sense of his experiences in larger intellectual and political terms.[1]

When he signed the crew agreement on board the *Pegasus* in Portland in 1903, he listed his address as "c/o George McVey, The Dalles, Oregon." It is not clear whether he lived with his sister and brother-in-law in Oregon before going to sea, but McVey was a Socialist, and seems to have been the only member of the family circle at the time who held such beliefs. He may have been the person who first introduced Foster to party life, but both men were also infected with the dream of establishing an independent stake for themselves in the West, far from the world of proletarian Philadelphia and Skittereen. When Foster arrived back in the United States in 1904, he made his way across the continent to Oregon, where he took up a 320-acre homestead in the foothills of the Cascade Mountains next to the claim that the McVeys had only recently established. He cleared timber on his land and planted potatoes during the summer months. In the winter he found temporary employment in lumber camps, on railroads, and once as a sheep herder, in order to support himself and earn enough capital to make improvements on the land. His hard physical labor on his claim earned him very little monetary return; and in 1907, as a depression swept through the West, he was forced to sell out.

However, in those three years Foster found another kind of sustenance and reward through his involvement in the Portland local of the Socialist party. He became a "party worker," hawked subscriptions to the enormously popular Socialist weekly, the *Appeal to Reason*, read Marxist classics and, significantly, "nearly all" of the pamphlets written by Daniel DeLeon.[2] Thus began his involvement in the radical labor movement of the American West. However varied his interests and political wanderings would be during this period, this unattached, circumspect, and self-contained young man always sought the company and special knowledge of militant brotherhood.

By 1904 the Socialist party was becoming a powerful force in national politics as well. At the height of its influence in the years before World War I the party would enroll over 150,000 dues-paying members, sponsor or endorse hundreds of periodicals and newspapers, elect nearly a thousand of its members to political office, and wield heavy influence in the American Federation of Labor as well as the radical Industrial Workers of the World. The appeal of the Socialist party would prove wide enough to encompass immigrant industrial workers in the eastern metropolis as well as hard-pressed farmers in the Southwest. The electrifying rhetoric of its most prominent spokesman, Eugene Debs, promised a humane alternative to the grinding cycles of helter-skelter industrialism, as well as a credible vision of resistance to the insolent dominance of large corporations over American politics and community life.

However, despite socialism's expanding influence and appeal, it was not a tolerant, ecumenical version of the movement that first attracted Foster to radical politics in the Pacific Northwest. The Portland Socialist party was dominated by Tom Sladden, a contentious left-winger who dreamed of a revolutionary movement shorn of bourgeois sympathizers. An ardent expositor of the ideal of proletarian purity and heroic mission, Sladden doubted whether a doctor, lawyer, preacher or even "a woman with radical ideas on the sex question," no matter how nonconformist, could be a true revolutionist. He had the cuspidors removed from the

Oregon party headquarters upon taking office as state chairman, on the grounds that such furniture was characteristic of the bourgeoisie, and that authentic proletarians had no use for such conveniences. He argued grimly that the effective working-class revolutionist was unencumbered by profession, trade, or property, and was contemptuous of education, religion, and patriotism. "Upon his shoulders rests the problem of freeing society."[3]

After selling his homestead, Foster worked briefly as a fireman on a Portland railroad, hoping eventually to join the Brotherhood of Locomotive Firemen and Engineers. The security of membership in this elite railroad brotherhood proved to be an elusive goal, however; he lost his job because of the lingering depression and was forced to look elsewhere for employment. He moved to Seattle, where he was able to join a building trades union and gain work as a construction worker and in local sawmills for two years, from 1907 to 1909. Once again he sought out the Socialist party local, which in Seattle was bitterly divided by seemingly interminable controversies between reformists and "revolutionaries." A central figure in the increasingly sectarian atmosphere in Seattle was Dr. Hermon Franklin Titus, a querulous left-wing socialist and editor of the *Seattle Socialist* who has been cited as the "father" of socialism in Washington state. He served as Foster's earliest mentor in the complex world of radical journalism and politics.[4]

Titus was a former Baptist minister from New York and Massachusetts who had quit the pulpit in the 1880s in order to attend Harvard Medical School. After graduating, he emigrated to Seattle, where he worked as a contract physician for James J. Hill's Great Northern Railway and as a social worker among the city's transient population of timber workers. He joined the Fabian Society and familiarized himself with the ideas of Lawrence Gronlund, whose book *The Cooperative Commonwealth*, published in 1884, was one of the earliest popular syntheses of Marxian ideas in the United States. Titus became a prominent figure in Seattle's municipal reform movement, and played an important role in composing a new charter for the city in 1900. He was a restless, energetic, and ambitious man whose Socialist politics were deeply influenced by the evangelical and scientific training of his youth and his experiences tending the injured and exploited workers of the developing West. At some unspecified point he concluded that "reform was impractical and revolution necessary." He began publishing the *Seattle Socialist* in 1900, which in turn gave impetus to the organization of the Socialist party in Washington. The purpose of the new organ was to "Organize the Slaves of Capital to Vote their Own Emancipation."[5]

Titus was a full-fledged scientific socialist. "The attitude of the Revolutionary Socialist is the scientific attitude, the modern scientific attitude in contrast with the ancient superstitious attitude," he wrote. There was no room for "dreams," "schemes," or "utopias." In addition, he proclaimed, "there are probably not ten thousand people in the United States who thoroughly understand the simple Principles of Revolutionary Socialism." The process of the education of the working class must begin with the "facts." The concept of a strictly inductive, evolutionary socialism as opposed to normative socialisms based on "dreams" recurs in Titus's writings. "To the scientific man, facts are everything, theories nothing," he explained. How can a socialist, or revolutionary, look to the future, given the necessity of focusing simply on the "facts"? A prominent feature of Titus's political writing was his belief in Darwinism and the inevitable evolution of society according to the laws of natural history. "Karl Marx," after all, "scientifically investigated the facts of human society and formulated its laws of development, as Charles Darwin did in the life history of animals other than man." Thus, "Marxism, like Darwinism, must be accepted and believed, if its facts are well established." Titus proposed that the revolutionary socialist, like the scientist, "never guesses at anything."[6]

Titus had a propensity for accusing Seattle's AFL-affiliated trade union leadership of corruption, and his obsession with doctrinal purity and exclusion of those not wholeheartedly committed to revolution alienated him even further from the union movement. Among unionists in Seattle, "Titusism" and the doctor's "college-bred" didacticism were considered highly disruptive; at one point, The Seattle Union Record, referring to Titus, averred that one "full-fledged 'scientific' socialist" could be more effective in destroying a labor union than a dozen strikes. Titus's inability to establish a working relationship with the AFL-affiliated unions effectively cut him off from the most powerful labor organizations in Washington at the time.[7] Finally in 1909 the zealous former skid-row physician and his supporters walked out of a Socialist party convention in Everett, claiming that a reformist right-wing element had unfairly seized control of the party. The National Executive Committee of the party promptly declared Titus's rival group illegal. By October, this tiny left-wing group, to which William Foster belonged, reconstituted itself into something called the United Wage Workers Party of Washington, and had changed the name of the Seattle Socialist to the Workingman's Paper.[8]

For less than a year, Foster remained among the small group of devoted radicals who followed Titus into the Wage Workers party. He later stated that his failure to return to the Socialist party "was perhaps the greatest political mistake" of his career. In retrospect, he judged the schismatic Titus to have been "a brilliant speaker, a forceful writer, an energetic agitator and one of the outstanding Marxists then in the United States" who nonetheless had a tendency to "incurable 'leftism'" and "bureaucratic arbitrariness." Despite these critiques, Foster as a young man was irresistibly drawn, like his mentor, to the vision of a revolutionary movement unadulterated by the corrupt yearnings of the bourgeoisie. Both dismissed the Socialist party as it was constituted in 1909 as "hopelessly" middle class. Titus's Wage Workers party was to be composed exclusively of proletarians, "as defined by *The Communist Manifesto*."[9]

Despite their vast difference in backgrounds, Titus and Foster shared certain characteristics that may best be described as stylistic. Both were uncomfortable in the world of genteel reformism and "regular" trade unionism. Instead, they were drawn to the milieu of the unassimilated working-class autodidact, purist and impertinent. Titus's disquisitions were heavy with a ponderous naturalism; both Foster and Titus held socialism to be as much a codified special knowledge as an irresistible historical movement. Both Titus and Foster accepted that while the working class possessed the immanent force of the revolution, most workers were simply not prepared to accept or comprehend revolutionary science because of their blind acceptance of capitalist propaganda in their churches, schools, and press. This was a common theme in socialist polemics of the era, but it was especially evident in Titus's disquisitions. Foster's distrust of the working class was a deeply felt and insoluble mixture of disdain and unrequited devotion more than it was an intellectual construct, but in 1910 he considered himself well tutored enough to conclude that the working class, being "raw and undeveloped," mindlessly accepted middle-class illusions and strove for outmoded "individualist ideals." Titus the socialist who "never guesses at anything" shared with his young protégé a sense of confidence and destiny, even though Foster's revolutionary certainty would be tempered by a certain patience and willingness to compromise that Titus usually lacked.[10]

Moreover, both Foster and Titus were heavily influenced by the ideas and writings of Daniel DeLeon. Foster described Titus's Wage Workers party as a "hybrid" between DeLeon's Socialist Labor party and the Industrial Workers of the World, and claimed that the "DeLeonist training" of many of its members, including himself, led them eventually to the IWW and syndicalism. When the Wage Workers party faltered, Foster and other followers of Titus considered joining the SLP.[11]

Daniel DeLeon, the brilliant and acerbic leader of the Socialist Labor party, was one of the earliest theoreticians of twentieth-century American syndicalism. He is often cited as an early "orthodox" American Marxist, but his writings show a notable willingness to innovate. Although he would not have described his own politics as "syndicalist," by the turn of the century he was increasingly enamored of and impressed by the powerful potential of militant industrial unions like the Western Federation of Miners and Eugene Debs's American Labor Union. DeLeon became one of the founders of the Industrial Workers of the World in 1905, an organization dedicated to building a radical alternative to the more conservative, craft-oriented policies of the American Federation of Labor. He wrote that same year in the Industrial Union Manifesto that "the political movement is absolutely the reflex of the economic organization," and that revolutionary industrial unionism should be conceived of as the "muscle" that would enforce a socialist political victory. Labor unions, rather than any particular political party, would play the primary role in bringing about the revolution. DeLeon began to define "political" action as an instrument for propaganda and recruitment rather than a means of winning office. When Foster concluded in 1910 that the "ballot" was "on the bum entirely," he was echoing DeLeon's theory of "industrialism," which included the idea that "the value of the 'ballot' as a constructive force is zero."[12]

In 1909, William Foster, after having left the Seattle Socialist party with Titus and his followers, was at a crucial juncture in his life. It is not clear at what point, exactly, he decided to make a career of labor politics, but it was evidently quite important to him to belong to a viable and coherent political movement. A variety of choices were available to him. He could attempt to rejoin the Seattle Socialist party, but this was apparently not an acceptable option for him because of what he felt was that organization's "hopelessly" middle-class orientation. Foster's involvement with Titus and the short-lived Wage Workers party brought him close to the ideas of Daniel DeLeon's SLP, but he later claimed to have been "repulsed" by DeLeon and his "crass sectarianism" and "dogmatic utopianism."[13] These, however, are adjectives that could just as easily have been applied to Hermon Titus, and Foster's judgment must be considered in juxtaposition to his own membership in Titus's schismatic and ephemeral party, which echoed many of DeLeon's theories. The Wage Workers party dissolved by 1910; Titus never again achieved anywhere near the prominence he had previously enjoyed in Washington state politics. True to his obsession with proletarianism, he seems finally to have become either an elevator operator or hotel doorman, and died in obscurity in New York City in 1931. Joseph Pass, an individual who was quite active in Washington radical politics, claimed to have visited Titus, then quite ill, at the doctor's Greenwich Village apartment in 1930. Pass recalled that Titus had asked about Foster, and "talked of him as a teacher of his pupil."[14]

Titus was still struggling to locate a constituency and focus for his new party when he sent William Foster to cover an explosion of workers' protests and social unrest in Spokane in the winter of 1909. Both men could not have helped but be fascinated by the potential of the Industrial Workers of the World, which was seeking to organize the workers in Spokane. The IWW had led a huge strike of immigrant steel workers in

McKees Rock, Pennsylvania, in July. The strike was especially significant because it showed that immigrant workers, previously largely neglected by the American Federation of Labor, could successfully organize against a corporation as huge and seemingly omnipotent as United States Steel. In November, workers belonging to the International Ladies Garment Workers' Union in New York City and Philadelphia called a giant industry-wide strike that dramatically illustrated the power of workers organized on an industrial basis to resist the demands of their employers. Foster, a member of his local AFL craft union in Seattle, the Building Laborers, and a former Socialist, began to achieve a name for himself in the labor movement at a time when workers' struggles at the point of production were the most visible manifestations of working-class militancy. Soon, he would wholeheartedly embrace the vision of working-class emancipation through militant trade union action, culminating in an apocalyptic general strike.[15]

It is noteworthy, however, that the workers that the IWW sought to organize in Spokane were not trade unionists in the conventional sense, and their struggle was conducted far from the "point of production." The Spokane free speech fight was one of the earliest efforts by the Wobblies to dramatize the issue of the lack of civil rights among the unorganized floating laborers of the West. At the time, Spokane was considered the hub of what was then called the Inland Empire, a commercial center for the region's lumber and mining industry. Hundreds of unemployed men would journey to Spokane in order to buy jobs from the local employment agencies or "sharks," which held a monopoly on transient jobs in the area. Such employment agencies worked in collusion with foremen to buy and sell temporary employment; agencies would occasionally sell nonexistent jobs to the vulnerable itinerant workers. Wobbly organizers were dispatched to cultivate and focus the discontent of these workers, and by November the jails were filling with IWW soapboxers and others who, in defiance of local restrictions on street speaking, were arrested while haranguing passersby against the employment agencies. One participant in the fight wrote that before the IWW arrived, there had been no semblance of organization among Spokane's floating workers. "They were a faceless, wandering mass of workers, moving from job to job, with no sense of direction or unity. The IWW proposed to change this state of affairs."[16]

When Foster departed for Spokane as Titus's chosen correspondent, it was decided that his name should be embellished with a "Z." A friend of Foster's, Harry Ault, later asserted that he had suggested the added initial as a way of adding distinction to the byline "William Foster." Titus himself explained that the "Z" was added so that Foster could be sure of receiving mail that otherwise might be delivered to another "William E."

in Spokane. In any event, Foster never referred to himself as William "Ze-bulon," and the "Z" was never intended by Foster to indicate a middle name. Elizabeth Gurley Flynn, a nineteen-year-old IWW organizer who had arrived in Spokane in November, met William Z. Foster during her trial on charges stemming from her participation in the free speech fight. She described Foster, then twenty-eight years old, as "tall, slender, blue-eyed and soft-spoken," a regular "skinny marink." Titus described him only as a "quiet, gentle-spoken man, of slight build."[17]

The desultory but determined struggles of the "faceless, wandering mass of workers" in Spokane were immediately compelling to the novice socialist reporter. Foster's dispatches to the *Workingman's Paper* in No-vember and December were sympathetic to the IWW and the free speech fight, but the feature of the protest that seemed to impress him most was the "excellent discipline" of the participating men and women. Soon after he arrived, he was arrested, as Titus put it, "for standing on a sidewalk in Spokane." Evidently, police had identified Foster as the correspondent for the *Workingman's Paper* and the IWW newspaper, *Solidarity*, with which Foster was sharing his reportage, and arrested him at a free speech gathering. Foster's first foray into radical journalism and street protest landed him an assignment on the rockpile. At one point he was put in solitary confinement, on a bread-and-water diet, accused of helping or-ganize IWW meetings and activities in the jail itself. A visitor remarked that Foster looked "pretty seedy. He made no complaint, but his hands were cut and in bad shape. His shoes were worn out and I know his feet are cold." He was finally released after spending forty-seven days in the city jail on a charge of disorderly conduct.[18] Shortly afterward, he and two other men were elected as an IWW executive committee to negotiate a settlement of the fight with the Spokane mayor and other officials. The final agreement ratified by the authorities and the ragged army of deter-mined Wobblies allows some insight into Foster's later critiques of the IWW and its tactics.[19]

The IWW executive committee that met with the mayor and his aides made four basic demands: that the meetings in their hall be conducted free from police harassment; that the *Industrial Worker* be allowed distri-bution on the street without interference; that all IWW prisoners in city and county jails be released; and finally, that the police would not inter-fere with street speaking. The final agreement fell short of these objec-tives. It provided that the IWW would be permitted to speak only in "un-restricted" areas like vacant lots, and offered a vague promise that the mayor would ask the city council to revise the street speaking ordinance. It was agreed that the police would not interfere with IWW meetings, and *The Industrial Worker* was to be allowed free distribution. Wobblies who were prisoners in the county jails were to be released only gradually, pending the return of IWW national organizer F. W. Heslewood from Coeur d'Alène, Idaho, where he had been resisting extradition for prosecution in Spokane on criminal conspiracy charges. The IWW agreed to drop all of its civil suits against city authorities. At a mass meeting held the evening following the agreement, this "Treaty of Spokane" was endorsed "pending the good faith of the authorities." However, one Spokane newspaper reported that "some of the rank and file of the IWW whose leaders agreed to a peace pact with the city authorities are disgusted with the turn of events." The Spokane *Press* concluded that the "treaty" with the IWW brought matters "to exactly the same conditions that existed before the fight was taken up." Police allowed use of the IWW hall and publication of its newspaper, but Wobblies "will not be permitted to speak on the streets."[20]

In his later writings on the outcome of the free speech fight, Foster emphasized that the Spokane demonstrations were a victory for the IWW and for the principle of "direct action." Yet, he also intimated that the committee to which he belonged had been negotiating from a position of weakness: "The I.W.W., having pretty much used up its resources of men and money," considered the concessions of the city authorities, "if not a complete victory, at least a satisfaction of their proposed arrangement." Yet, Foster was undoubtedly aware that the "treaty" was a somewhat ambiguous accomplishment. While judicial decisions by Washington State courts eventually declared the Spokane street speaking ordinances unconstitutional, the hated employment agencies continued to operate freely after the conclusion of the free speech fight. Indeed, in the next two years, the number of employment agencies operating in Spokane increased markedly. Moreover, the IWW proved unsuccessful at provoking the kind of labor solidarity that would have been necessary for fundamental change to take place. The AFL unions in Spokane gave little support to the fight, and Foster implied that the Spokane police chief had decided to move aggressively against the IWW only after it became clear that most craft unions in the city viewed the Wobblies with hostility. The IWW and the AFL remained fundamentally separate organizations in Spokane, with different constituencies and conflicting philosophies of organization and tactics.[21]

In 1909 the IWW had yet to prove itself. Its membership had declined drastically since its founding in 1905. From afar, Daniel DeLeon harshly criticized the IWW for its exclusive reliance on direct action (he implied that the Spokane fight had actually resolved into a "political" struggle anyway) and was finally expelled on the basis of the fact that he was not a "wage earner." The powerful Western Federation of Miners had withdrawn from the IWW by 1908, and by then Eugene Debs had let his membership quietly expire. Despite the fact that workers across the nation were showing signs of militancy and willingness to engage in strikes for industrial unionism and workers' control, editorialists were asking by 1910 "Is the IWW to Grow?"[22]

Foster wrote from Spokane that his experiences in the free speech fight were invaluable to him. "Through it I have learned a few of the possibilities of organization and direct action, and more especially of the marvelous effectiveness of the passive resistance strike, in addition to learning many new wrinkles about the law, police, etc." While he was in the Spokane jail, he noted approvingly that the Wobblies held regular meetings, set aside separate evenings for "business" and "propaganda," established 10:30 P.M. as lights out time, elected a secretary and propaganda committee, and had enacted "dozens of other rules and regulations." Yet, despite what he witnessed during the Spokane struggle, Foster would never be able to accept what he saw as the IWW's dependence on spontaneity and its inability to build lasting organizations in the towns where its strikes and free speech fights took place. In his later formulations of revolutionary tactics, he would embrace the idea that small groups of militants were best able to encourage strikes when they operated under a decentralized organizational form. However, he more often equated power not only with system and order, but organization with centralization. As a Communist, he would end up writing of "the paralyzing effects of the naive and infantile decentralization tendency" among the Wobblies in Spokane."[23]

An incident that occurred a continent away, in his former home city of Philadelphia, undoubtedly reinforced Foster's interest in the "possibilities of organization and direct action" and belief that "it is really possible to organize the working class." In May 1909, the city was once again shaken by a strike of street railwaymen against its giant streetcar monopoly. Then in February 1910, after a settlement had broken down and the renewed strike had turned violent, representatives of Philadelphia's central labor union ordered the first general strike in modern American history. Two Socialists were on the strike committee, and one observer noted that "socialist philosophy tinctured the whole movement." When the general strike took effect, thousands of nonunion workers left work in a huge show of solidarity with the street railwaymen. Eugene Debs addressed an overflowing crowd at the Labor Lyceum. Ultimately, the strike came apart when a conference between representatives of the company and the car men created the impression that a settlement would soon be made. Despite the disintegration of the strike, the disturbances in Philadelphia created a strong impression among labor radicals throughout the country. One noteworthy feature of the strike was that it was initiated and organized by AFL trade unions; socialists pondered the meaning of a general strike in which organizations that they had often derided for their voluntarism and conservatism, took such a prominent role. One writer concluded that "unionism and socialism clasped hands as never before. The incident taught, better than can tomes of theory, the wisdom of working in harmony with the trades unions to the very utmost."[24] In Spokane, the Philadelphia strike was front-page news at the time when Foster was engaged in negotiating the end to the free speech fight. He could not have helped but be impressed by the fact that while the IWW campaign in Spokane was coming to an inconclusive end, the AFL central council in Philadelphia was organizing a massive general strike.

In the meantime, Spokane was itself experiencing an episode of labor unrest that confirmed the power of local AFL-affiliated unions decisively to influence city politics. Simultaneously with the calling of the general strike in Philadelphia, within days of the settlement of the free speech fight, the Spokane Central Labor Council announced plans for a large demonstration. The labor unions demanded a higher wage rate for workers who were employed under city contracts and the hiring of three police matrons to be stationed in the city jail. Initially, it was proposed that the demonstration be held on a large lot near the town center, since speakers were still "being denied the right to hold meetings on the streets by virtue of the street speaking ordinance." However, the police chief finally granted a permit to "organized labor" to conduct a parade, the purpose of which would be to pressure the Spokane City Council, meeting the same day, to adopt the measures endorsed by the Central Labor Council.[25]

When the parade took place, forty-nine unions marched in a parade that was estimated at between two and five thousand strong. In the list of participating unions, however, the IWW was not included. Indeed, the size of the parade dwarfed any protest the IWW had been able to generate during the free speech fight. The procession culminated in a large protest meeting near the jail, and the city council chamber was subsequently disrupted by a "near riot" when council members threatened to ignore the demands of the unions. Responding with a haste untypical of such bodies, the city council reversed itself and acceded to the demands of the protesters at a meeting the following day. Significantly, the council finally voted unanimously to repeal the street-speaking ordinance under which the Wobblies had been arrested. The prevailing sentiment was that "now that the IWWs have been crushed . . . there is no need to make citizens hold meetings in the mire of barnyards and back doors, as was done at the protest meeting in the rear of city hall jail last night."[26]

Thus, during the weeks that he lingered in Spokane at the conclusion of the free speech fight, William Foster both read of the AFL's success in calling a general strike in Philadelphia, and witnessed a display of power by the local AFL central labor body that was far more persuasive in its effects on the city's government than anything the IWW had heretofore been able to manage. Writing in 1911, he called it a "veritable political uprising . . . equally hostile to the IWW and to the corrupt local government."[27] Despite his role in negotiating the end to the Spokane free speech fight, Foster retained his membership in the IWW for only a short period. Soon, he would be arguing vehemently that Wobblies could best serve the labor movement by joining local AFL unions and seeking to convert these bodies into revolutionary organizations.

Rather suddenly after the conclusion of the events in Spokane, Foster departed for Europe. Elizabeth Gurley Flynn suggested that Foster's organizational and negotiating abilities during the Spokane free speech fight had "attracted the attention" of IWW leader Vincent St. John, and that Foster left for Europe with "the Saint's blessing." It is likely that there was some informal agreement between St. John and Foster under which the latter would write articles about the European labor movement for the IWW press and represent the IWW at a conference of the International Trade Union Secretariat in Budapest in exchange for an initial grant of travel expenses. The trip represented a great opportunity for Foster to establish a name for himself in the world of radical politics and journalism, and because of his relentless curiosity and traveling confidence, he was able to take good advantage of St. John's assignment. As he neared his thirtieth birthday Foster was unconnected by close family ties and without dependable employment. He aimed to travel to France in order to "learn a little," as he put it, about direct action.[28]

This statement implies that Foster considered his "education" in Spokane incomplete, but American labor radicals had been entranced by the well-publicized activities of the French Confederation Générale du Travail (CGT) since the turn of the century. Itinerant agitators and radical journalists like Foster as well as many rank-and-file Wobblies read widely in European philosophy and followed events in the labor movements of other countries quite closely. It is striking that Foster claimed to have read Gibbon, Darwin and Spencer as a young man, yet these authors were familiar to many other socialists and Wobblies at the time as well.[29]

Foster's reporting from both France and Germany was in the same style as his writing for Titus's *Workingman's Paper*: dry and carefully detailed, with occasional lapses into bitter sarcasm. He began his reports in Gary, Indiana, where he stopped on his way across the continent to New York City from Spokane. The future organizer of a giant strike against the steel industry carefully examined one of the town's mills, fortified against attack from the outside by strikers. As he watched workers streaming into the plant by way of a bridge, he contemplated "how vain all these fortifications will be against an army of educated workers who thus have the privilege extended to them of capturing the works daily by way of the main gate." Writing from New York City, he indulged in a dark and deprecatory meditation upon his visit to an East Side ghetto, a slum not unlike that in which he had lived as a child: "In streets covered with stinking filth and litter, a densely-packed mass of squalling, brawling, fighting, crying, playing, hawking, bargaining human beings live their allotted span in this 'best of worlds.' The pitiable part of it all is that these poverty-stricken wretches take their miserable fate almost as a matter of course. Ignorance rules supreme among the denizens of the 'Ghetto.'" He described Coney Island as merely "the playground of New York's vast army of slaves."[30]

Foster's steamer landed at Cherbourg in August. Upon arriving in Paris, he was amazed by the prominence of the labor movement in the life of the city; "all over Paris on every wall are flaming syndicalist posters, calling on the proletariat to unite, giving notice of strikes, lockouts, etc." At first, his correspondence reflected his belief that organized labor in France was far more "advanced" than the American movement in nearly every respect. It seemed immediately evident to him that "the American labor movement is in its swaddling clothes." Moreover, the "slaves" in France struck him as "not so submissive as they are in the States." At one point, after witnessing a demonstration by French workers, he remarked that he was "filled with disgust when I thought of the tame and unfeared American labor movement that I am doomed to return to in all likelihood. If it were possible for me to learn French in a couple of years, good enough to speak it fluently, I would surely stay here and cast my lot with these red-blooded syndicalists."[31]

Foster was fortunate in the timing of his voyage to France, because he arrived in time to observe the French syndicalists in action during the "general" railroad strike of 1910. The strike was ultimately crushed when Aristide Briand, the French premier and former Socialist who had once authored a popular pamphlet on the uses of the general strike, ordered a general conscription of all railway workers. Faced with courts-martial as army deserters, the strikers finally capitulated; at one point the entire strike leadership was arrested for hindering the operation of the trains. The strike itself was widely considered to have been unsuccessful; it showed, in part, that the radical syndicalists within the CGT could not effectively extend local strikes into national ones. Only small numbers of workers, all from the building trades, obeyed a call by the CGT for sympathy strikes. The "betrayal" of the workers by Briand and the strong governmental measures taken to defeat the strike impressed upon Foster the lesson that "when the government deems it necessary it will proceed to any length, regardless of law."[32]

During his weeks in France, Foster befriended several internationally prominent organizers, and searched diligently for ideas that could be useful in the United States. He noted that in France, power within the organized labor movement lay overwhelmingly with the *syndicats* (trade unions), or the local federations of unions, the *bourses du travail*. French syndicalists within the CGT did not always perceive the question of craft as opposed to industrial organization as a primary issue. In the United States, the development of a highly centralized industrial economy seemed to require, according to radicals in the IWW, a centralized industrial union movement as way of balancing the growing power of large integrated business concerns. Radical syndicalists in France, while in favor of the idea of the *grève générale* (general strike) and industrial unionism, believed that the realities of French economic development, which remained localized well into the twentieth century, required radicals to make their demands felt through participation in the existing craft unions, rather than through the formation of separate industrial unions.[33]

Many French syndicalist leaders eschewed formal doctrine in favor of the ideal of working-class spontaneity. When the revolution came, victory would depend not so much on philosophical purity or precision as on the élan of the workers, their fighting spirit, expressed in class warfare at the point of production. Furthermore, as in any war, the ideal of class warfare entailed no compromises, no complex blurring of categories between contestants. Thus, the French syndicalists eschewed the idea of democracy and political action because these involved bargaining and collaboration with the bourgeoisie, and inevitable betrayal of the working class. The idea of the class war was most appealing to Foster, and no other American radical of his generation would elaborate the idea as thoroughly as he. It was a concept that satisfied deeply felt and complex urges in his personality, and promised a transcendence that reformist socialism was not able to offer.[34]

Foster was also struck by the fact that within the CGT, the syndicalist leadership was a militant minority that was able to dominate a trade union movement very similar, in its decentralized structure and cautious, craft-conscious membership, to the American Federation of Labor. The French movement, Foster noted approvingly, is "dominated by 'dangerous leaders,' who are attempting to force a rather reluctant and ignorant rank and file to adopt the most approved methods of class warfare." During his visit, however, Foster had still not concluded that American radicals should "bore from within" in the AFL; the American federation, he reaffirmed, seemed "incapable of evolution," and "time after time" reactionary cliques had "frustrated the attempts of progressive members of the rank and file to make the organizations more in accord with modern conditions."[35]

Rather, Foster seemed enamored of the overtly insurrectionist style of Gustave Hervé, a prominent figure on the left of the French labor movement. During the 1910 strike Hervé called for widespread sabotage and "individual terrorism." Foster reported assiduously on the posturing of Hervé's journal *La Guerre Sociale* and the arrest of its editors, and implied that sabotage of the rail system seemed to be the only effective method for forcing the employers to rehire strikers who had been fired. Foster had a chance to visit Hervé in prison, where the French radical urged Foster to "teach American workers to practice sabotage" and even advocate assassination "when necessary." While in France, Foster wrote that "government laws should be entitled to no more consideration than the rules of the factory, if they oppress the workers. It is the workers' privilege to break them in any manner they see fit, or are able to do." Moreover, the French workers understood that sabotage "stands for the most revolutionary sentiments the working class can have, i.e., utter contempt for capitalist life and property."[36]

Foster's dispatches were permeated with his belief in the great importance of what he was witnessing, a sense that the European working class and its leaders were making history. Determined to make the most of his European visit, he moved on from France to Germany. If he was attracted to the style of the French labor movement, the opposite was true of his impressions of German socialism. He was dismayed by the lack of a militant demonstration by workers on May Day in Berlin, and, after observing a mass funeral for a Socialist party leader, noted that "to one who has been taught to consider the German movement as the very acme of revolutionary endeavor, the demonstration was a disappointment." He expressed amazement at how well dressed were the German socialists attending the funeral, and noted bitterly that he had been excluded from participating in the funeral procession and ceremony because of the fact that he lacked the proper attire. This incident underlines the fact that Foster, the future chairman of the Communist party in the United States, nursed a profound distrust of Marxian socialism at this vital and formative stage of his career. Alienated as he was both by the fruitless polemics of Hermon Titus and by the respectable gradualism of the Social Democracy, his instincts drew him to the syndicalists of the IWW and the French movement.[37]

We can gain a revealing glimpse of Foster's personality through accounts of his participation in a conference of the International Secretariat of National Trade Union Centres in Budapest. He attended the conference, dominated by socialist and reformist European unionists, at the behest of St. John, who hoped that Foster would gain a measure of international recognition for the IWW. Foster angrily contested the credentials of James Duncan, the official AFL delegate, on the grounds of the AFL's association with the "class collaborationist" National Civic Federation. He was able to tie up the entire first full day of the conference with his protest against the seating of Duncan. He was finally supported only by Léon Jouhaux, secretary of the CGT, and George Yvetot, the other CGT delegate. During the discussion of the motion, Foster lost control of his temper. "His language was foul, vulgar and vehement. He even threatened assault, and subsided only to prevent [his] expulsion from the room," according to one delegate. Despite his generally stolid demeanor, Foster's temper could be quite explosive. Back in the United States the president of the American Federation of Labor, Samuel Gompers, in his report to the annual AFL convention in 1911, referred to Foster's "effrontery" and "the repudiation of the so-called Industrial Workers of the World" at the Budapest conference.[38]

Foster's difficulties at the conference were exacerbated by the fact that he was arrested for vagrancy the night after the first session. Having no money for lodging, Foster had attempted to sleep in a horse-drawn moving van on the outskirts of Budapest. His predicament came to the attention of the convention when a subscription paper was circulated, soliciting contributions to secure his release from jail. A Hungarian trade union official gained his release, and Jouhaux and Yvetot lent him ten dollars until St. John wired more money. St. John considered the episode embarrassing to the IWW, perhaps because it underlined its image as an organization of hoboes and "bums."[39]

While in Europe, Foster paid particularly close attention to denigrating the "patriotism" of the working class—whether manifested in participation in military parades and ceremonies, or in simple obedience to the laws of the state. He admired Hervé's Blanquist "antipatriotism," and upon observing a military ceremony in Berlin in which troops were being reviewed by the kaiser, he remarked that the soldiers' patriotism "shows what damned fools working men can make of themselves." Foster's disdain for the intelligence and patriotism of the majority of workers was unexceptional among American Wobblies, and French anarcho-syndicalist leaders were, as Albert Lindemann has put it, "unapologetic elitists who frequently expressed contempt for the mundane concerns of the average French worker."[40]

Foster possessed a fiercely seditious temperament, and his revulsion at patriotism and patriotic displays applied to the United States as well as to foreign countries. Although the rhetoric of citizenship surfaced occasionally in his writings, it inevitably seemed awkward and synthetic in his hands. For him, America was a set of conditions to be transcended. If earlier radicals had seen America as representing certain democratic ideals that might be utilized in the construction of a better society, Foster's radicalism was deeper and more unappeasable, for the very reason that he had not experienced, let alone believed in, the possibility of such a transformation. In an article in 1911, he ridiculed the fact that Eugene Debs delivered his lectures from a platform "smothered in American flags." When he asserted that "the best socialists are the best patriots," he was writing in an entirely negative, sarcastic sense.[41] He was on his way to becoming what chamber of commerce patriots of his time most feared: an unattached working-class agitator, the "familiar outsider" whose alienation could not be discerned in his ethnicity, race or physiognomy. Long before he became a syndicalist, or even a Communist, however, Foster was an "un-American" American.

Foster returned to the United States in time to attend the sixth convention of the IWW in Chicago in September 1911. At this convention, which was attended by only thirty-one delegates, he raised the possibility of dissolving the IWW, reconstituting the organization as a propaganda league, and "getting into the organized labor movement" for the purpose of "revolutionizing" existing unions. This audacious proposal was consistent with his experiences and observations in the United States as well as Europe, but soon he would be accused of promulgating a "foreign" idea within the IWW. At the convention, he was nominated by a faction of "decentralizers" as a candidate for the editorship of the Wobbly newspaper, *The Industrial Worker*. With an article published immediately after the convention, he began his campaign radically to reconstitute the organization that he had joined only two years earlier.

From mid-November to mid-December 1911, the editors of *The Industrial Worker* and *Solidarity* opened their columns to letters arguing for or against Foster's proposal to change the character of the IWW. His arguments, coming so soon after his return from Europe, were carefully thought-out and organized, suggesting that they had been formulated well before his arrival in the United States. Foster presented the idea that the AFL constituted the "organized" labor movement in the United States as an almost self-justifying argument in favor of radicals focusing their activities within it. Yet he was also supremely confident that a small cadre of disciplined activists could bend just about any organization to its ends. This syncretism would always lurk near the core of Foster's radicalism, and informed his tendency to understand revolutionary transformation in tactical, rather than historical terms.[42]

Foster's arguments contained a formidable critique of the IWW, especially in light of developments in the European labor movement and the apparently declining significance of the IWW in the United States. As he noted, European industrial union movements organized along the lines of the IWW remained pathetically isolated and ineffective. In the United States, membership in the IWW had stagnated in the years between 1905 and 1911, while by 1912 workers belonging to industrial unions within the AFL vastly outnumbered the membership of the IWW, and those unions seemed more vital than industrial unions outside the federation.[43]

Nonetheless, rank-and-file Wobblies rushed to defend their organization against Foster's rhetorical assault. One argument was that many Wobblies, belonging to what one correspondent characterized as the "floating element" of American workers, could not even get into the craft unions to "bore from within," because of high dues and the culture of craft exclusiveness that permeated the AFL. It was often pointed out that Wobblies would simply be expelled if they attempted to undermine the traditional structure of the AFL unions.[44]

Foster was not at all convinced that Wobblies were the victims of that much persecution. He knew that in such AFL unions as the Western Federation of Miners, the United Mine Workers, and the Shingle Weavers, Wobblies were tolerated and some even held official positions. In an unpublished article that was refused by *Solidarity*, Foster outlined his thinking about boring from within: "Let [the Wobblies] forsake the doctrine that in order to change the minds of the workers and educate them, it is necessary to destroy their present unions and to organize themselves into brand new ones—a mode of reasoning that the workers seem unwilling to accept. Let them adopt a policy of always standing squarely for the best interests of the unions of which they are members—*which are synonymous with those of the working class*—and, it will become next to impossible to expel even the most militant of them."

He went even further, though, meditating that craft unions would be fully justified in expelling Wobblies "by the present hostile attitude of the IWW towards them." This was an odd sentiment from one who only months earlier had been denied a seat at the conference of Social Democratic trade unionists in Budapest, having been characterized by the AFL as a "disrupter." Yet it reflects that despite his seething anger at self-satisfied and complacent union officials and gradualist Social Democrats, Foster understood the powerful appeal of "immediate" demands for the American working class, and still yearned for some measure of the stability and legitimacy afforded by the AFL. He signed his letter "Yours for an Effective Organization."[45]

When Foster's critics accused him of using the history of the labor movements of other countries as a template for American activists, he pointed to the successes of British syndicalists. In the summer of 1911, while Foster was in Germany, two huge strikes in Great Britain, by the dock workers and the railwaymen, riveted the attention of the European labor movement. Tom Mann, a hard-nosed English labor leader who had played an important role in developing these paralyzing nationwide transport strikes, had unabashedly borrowed from the ideas of the same French syndicalists whom Foster had found so inspiring. Thorough preparatory organization, solidarity actions, sympathetic strikes, and "Amalgamation Committees" designed to coordinate the actions of the disparate craft unions were tactics that the English syndicalists borrowed from the French. According to Foster, the experiences of the British syndicalists, as well as the unprecedented solidarity exhibited by British craft unions, suggested that the tactics of the French radicals could be applicable to labor movements operating in highly industrialized economies. He accused the Wobblies' leadership of unthinking "patriotism" in dismissing the ideas of European radicals. The debate raged in the pages of the IWW paper *Solidarity* for weeks, until finally the editors declared the discussion over.[46]

Foster, of course, failed in his efforts to convert the IWW from a revolutionary industrial union into a propaganda league. He blamed his lost bid for the editorship of the Spokane *Industrial Worker* on a rigged vote, and finally he had to decide whether to repent and remain in the IWW or choose another path to the revolution. At the Chicago IWW convention where he first publicized his ideas, Foster and several like-minded Wobblies decided to carry on a propaganda campaign within the IWW in order to "win it over to the policy of boring-from-within." At this point, he was designated national secretary of a proposed federation of small propaganda groups that would be created within various IWW locals. In January 1912, he duly established an organization called the Syndicalist Militant Minority League in Chicago.[47]

Foster worked hard in Chicago to win influential trade unionists to his views. One evening, he appeared before a "well-attended" meeting in which the audience included "several men prominent in the AF of L," as well as "some of the Old Guard of Industrial Unionism in America." Before this audience, Foster argued that contrary to IWW "dogma," the AFL "could evolve," and that "the militant worker should be within its ranks playing his active part in that evolution." He pointed to the UMW as an example of an AFL union that had become increasingly a "class organization no less than an industrial one" in recent years. The French railway strike and the industrial unrest in England showed the results of the activity of militants within existing unions, according to Foster. An observer at the meeting succinctly recorded his aims: "Make industrial unionism our program from within unions and further its propagation and application as circumstances dictate." The policy of Foster's proposed militant minority would be "abolition of contracts; closer affiliation, thereby extending the scope of organization, and so giving growth to industrial unionism in application; reduce high initiation fees, advocate General Strike, Sabotage, and when need be, dual organization. . . . fight political socialists within unions."[48]

On February 15, an article appeared in *The Agitator*, a small but influential anarchist newspaper published at Home Colony in Washington state, announcing that Foster would make a tour of the West Coast and discuss his ideas at IWW locals along his route. Foster's trip west to build up his Syndicalist Militant Minority League coincided with the successes of the IWW during the spectacular Lawrence textile strike. It was a stressful period for him, as the events in Lawrence had suddenly made his proposal to change the course of IWW tactics from within seem "quite barren." Moreover, his six thousand-mile trip by railroad from Chicago to the Pacific Northwest proved to be difficult and hazardous. His route took him through St. Louis to McCook, Nebraska, and from there to Akron, Colorado. He rode from Nebraska to Colorado on an open car full of bridge steel; during this ten-hour ride he nearly froze to death. However, he found a welcome haven at Home Colony.[49]

The colony was an unpretentious utopian community located on the banks of Joe's Bay, a scenic inlet off southern Puget Sound. The founding principles upon which the colony was based included, simply, the statement that each member should be allowed "the personal liberty to follow their own line of action no matter how much it may differ from the custom of the past or present, without censure or ostracism from their neighbor." Some Home Colony residents, free to pursue their personal panaceas, practiced free love, or "variety" as it was called. Other practices included vegetarianism, various kinds of spiritualism, and nudism. Portraits of Karl Marx, Ferdinand Lasalle, Peter Kropotkin, and Michael Bakunin graced the walls of the colony's schoolroom. Residents contributed to support various IWW free speech fights, the Russian revolution of 1905, and the defendants in the Haywood-Moyer murder trial. The anniversaries of the executions of the Haymarket protesters were ceremoniously observed, and patriotic holidays like the Fourth of July were mocked and ridiculed. Occasional visitors included Harry Ault, Hermon Titus, Emma Goldman, Alexander Berkman, Elizabeth Gurley Flynn, William D. Haywood, Ben Reitman, and Elbert Hubbard. Later, a former anarchist described Home as a haven for "crackpots, cultists and radical high-binders," an "old time get-away for reds, *real* ones: dynamiters, riot-provokers, slackers, anti-military propagandists, and all around 'unAmericans.'"[50]

When Foster appeared there in 1912, Home Colony's most notorious resident was perhaps Jay Fox, editor and publisher of *The Agitator*. Fox, born in 1870, grew up in Chicago's "back of the yards" district. Like Foster, he was the son of an Irish immigrant and had belonged to an Irish street gang in his youth. At age sixteen, while working at the Malleable

Jay Fox.

Iron Works in Chicago, he joined the Knights of Labor. He was shot and wounded by police during a demonstration by striking workers at the nearby McCormick Reaper Plant on May 3, 1886, and witnessed the tragedy at Haymarket Square the subsequent evening. A metalworker by trade, he became a charter member of Debs's American Railway Union in 1893 while working in the machine shops of the Illinois Central Railroad in Chicago. He was among those arrested during a roundup of anarchists after the assassination of William McKinley in 1901. In 1905 he attended the founding convention of the IWW but remained skeptical about the new organization's chances of success. A collaborator of Lucy Parsons, the widow of Haymarket martyr Albert Parsons, Fox was quite active in Chicago anarchist circles before he came to Home in 1908.[51]

Within a few years Fox had attracted a swirl of attention to tiny Home Colony, above all because of his probable background role in the dynamiting of the offices of the staunchly open-shop *Los Angeles Times* by individuals connected with the Los Angeles local of the Bridge and Structural Iron Union. Following the arrest of the brothers John J. and James McNamara for the notorious bombing, detectives for the William Burns agency, convinced that Fox had been either involved in the bombing or was helping to hide accomplices of the McNamaras, visited Home and placed him under surveillance. Burns was at least on the right trail, for an informant at Home was able to lead him to the McNamaras' accomplices, who were arrested and extradited to California. Later, in a self-promoting book about the affair, Burns titillated readers with descriptions of Fox's unmarried living arrangement with an unnamed anarchist woman and her children. That woman, Esther Abramowitz, would soon thereafter enter into a lifelong relationship with William Foster.[52]

Esther Abramowitz evidently first met Jay Fox in Chicago; they attended the 1905 convention of the IWW together. The radical journalist and author Hutchins Hapgood described Fox and Abramowitz in his 1907 book, *The Spirit of Labor*. He wrote that Fox "had more fibre and calmness and strength than the rank and file of the anarchists. He talks well, and reasons, not emotionally, but coolly; and in character he is balanced, tolerant and kind. He is a learned man . . . school-masterly in look, and talks in a slow, deliberate way." During her years in Chicago, Esther was apparently a "varietist" or "free lover."

> Esther is what Jay calls his "companion." She is a beautiful Jewess. . . .
> She is melancholy and affectionate and gentle and sensual, and has had an unhappy experience with men. She left her husband some years ago, "because we didn't develop together." And Jay and his wife separated for the same reason. Then these two met, and each discovered that the other had "high ideals."
>
> So they simply live together. They have a great respect for one another, and Jay is so tolerant that Esther's "longings" are completely satisfied, even when they lead her away from Jay for weeks at a time. But Jay's soul is fortified and tested: he is not emotionally vulnerable. . . .[53]

William Foster claimed that Esther Abramowitz became his wife in 1912; however, they were in fact married in Chicago in 1918. Foster's relationship with Esther began through their mutual acquaintance with Fox, who had once editorialized that "a consistent belief in natural selection, in justice, in liberty, will lead to free love." Esther had been born in the Russian province of Kovno; her family came to the United States when she was a young girl. Before she began living with William, she had three children as a result of earlier relationships: Rebecca, Sylvia, and David. Of these David and Sylvia eventually adopted the Foster name; Rebecca, much more distant from the family, died in 1922. As William relentlessly pursued his labor and syndicalist enterprises, Esther and her children remained largely in the background. Foster, according to the description of one of his contemporaries, resembled Fox, "though [Foster] was younger and more sociable. They were both about the same height, slim and lithe, and both imperturbable. Between them moved the dark and voluptuous Esther Fox, a figure of Oriental

Esther Abramowitz and her children, Sylvia and David, at Home Colony.

romance." Fox and William and Esther Foster would remain lifelong friends.[54]

Thus William Foster, with a seemingly insatiable appetite for political and geographical wandering, began moving in an anarchist milieu soon after his return from Europe. Here, the legacy of Haymarket, as interpreted and articulated by Jay Fox, was particularly resonant. Fox wrote that Home Colony was merely "a place where people out of harmony with capitalism could associate together and enjoy each [other]," but he was preoccupied intellectually with an attempt to update, in light of "modern" developments, the radical traditions to which he had been exposed as a young man. Fox's theories before 1911 were a curious amalgam of the old anarchist "Chicago idea" and Social Darwinism. The "Chicago idea" harked back to the conceptions of the anarchists Albert Parsons and August Spies—the idea that the trade union was an instrument of social revolution that, in its ideal form, "would be satisfied with nothing less than the elimination of capitalism." It advocated a "militant, a revolutionary unionism, which sought to get at the root of bureaucratism and compromise." At the same time, for these anarchists, the trade union was to be the "embryonic group of the future 'free society.'" Significantly, in the early 1910s, Foster and Fox would operate a syndicalist league out of the Chicago home of Lucy Parsons.[55]

Fox was confident that as modern society evolved, the unionist would come to understand that the ultimate aim of the union was to gain "the full value of labor expended" for workers. Unions were noncoercive in that they were based on the "scientific" principle of voluntary, evolutionary organization. "The anarchist sees in the growth of the trade union an evidence of the tendency towards the simple, natural, yet scientific state of society he is working for." As labor unions grow and strikes become more extended, "it only requires time and experience to develop the desire for a GENERAL STRIKE," he wrote. The aim of the anarchists, he averred, "is the abolition of capitalism and every vestige of authority; this is to be displaced by a society of free socialism in which the various trade unions own the means of production and distribution in common, and freely exchange with each other on the mutual basis of social equality, individual liberty and real justice."[56]

Fox was critical of the IWW, which he believed had centralized power in the organization's general executive board. For this anarchist, the AFL was appealing because of its voluntarist model of organization. In addition, while "the AFL is slow to move, like all large bodies," it was nonetheless "advancing towards industrialism." He noted that the IWW had failed "to reach the masses of union men with its propaganda." The French syndicalists, on the other hand, "did not organize unions except where no unions existed," and have shown that "the form of organization makes little difference if the membership has the revolutionary spirit." Syndicalism is "the evolutionary method, growing out of the ranks of labor, instead of the philosopher's brain." Foster seemed to share this outlook; the IWW made a "fetish" of the form of industrialism, he wrote, and the conservatism of German industrial unions showed conclusively that the idea of industrial unionism alone was an insufficient basis upon which to build a radical labor movement.[57]

Fox's brand of anarcho-syndicalism was evident in the series of articles that Foster wrote in the *Agitator* beginning in the spring of 1912, entitled "Revolutionary Tactics." Foster's writings for the *Agitator* showed that he had embraced an eclectic brand of anarchism and syndicalism, strongly influenced by the examples of the British, French, and American labor movements. The articles argue for the creation of a national propaganda league, modeled explicitly along the lines of the British syndicalist leagues created by Tom Mann. From the French and British labor movements Foster reiterated the lesson that syndicalists must "bore from within" in existing labor movements, although this policy had definite antecedents in the United States, most notably as part of the anarchist movement to which Jay Fox belonged. This anarchist tradition provided an analogue in the American labor movement for what Foster had observed in Europe, especially with regard to the issue of decentralization and voluntarism. Fox wrote, in support of Foster's proposals, that "the plan of organization and the spirit of the IWW is towards centralization. Syndicalism moves in the opposite direction." For Foster, at this stage of his career, centralization meant bureaucracy and conservatism; decentralization would enable the "autonomy of militant minorities." These *noyaux* would be in a position to form new unions if the present trade unions "proved incapable of evolutions." He noted approvingly that in France, railway workers, mindful of the "abuses and incompetence" of the railway union's strike committee, "launched a new railroader's union, claiming the national committee had outlawed itself." In the United States, he wrote, the creation of new unions, if carefully undertaken, "would doubtless go far towards breaking up the notorious job trust unions."[58]

It was clearly an exciting time for Foster. He had quite literally traveled around the world in search of his ideal of militant brotherhood. He knew that the labor movements of Europe and America were in upheaval and that the new philosophers of syndicalism were often in the forefront of events. It seemed as if anything might be possible for a clear-sighted militant minority, gifted at once with an understanding of the science of history and the will to move workers' organizations in a progressive direction.

Chapter 3

THE SYNDICALIST LEAGUES

The real "radicals" are in the labor movement; those
hanging on the outside began with the movement, too,
but then became too weak for it. . . . My experience
is that the radicals make a mistake in neglecting the
trades-union movement. If they are trades-unionists they
can have a hall to speak in undisturbed by police.
—Anonymous anarchist, 1907

THE HISTORY of the nomenclature of American radicalism includes certain terms that seem to have been wholly and immediately unassimilable, incapable from the moment of their introduction of achieving any widespread use other than in a negative or entirely derogatory sense. Such terms appear, in retrospect, to have required no huge mobilization of public opinion in order to guarantee their estrangement from public discourse. Yet, these "disabled" terms, categories, and labels, described particular social ideals or modes of action that were influential enough to elicit a response from certain elites, and were perceived by them as distinctly threatening in a very material sense. Somehow it is appropriate that William Z. Foster would be associated with several such terms throughout his career; these included "anarchism," "bolshevism," and the unfortunate "boring from within." During the years after he returned from Europe the concept with which he was most closely associated was "syndicalism," a word that loosely described aspects of an indigenous social movement, but which was at the same time widely disparaged as an un-American "ism."

From 1910 to 1914, "syndicalism" became a most important topic for American editors and journalists, a matter for extended debate and careful consideration. One writer nervously declaimed that syndicalism is "more dangerous than labor unionism because it is less stupid and less corrupt." A recurring theme in numerous articles in the mainstream press was that although syndicalism originated in Europe, its prospects in the United States must be taken quite seriously. A writer for the New York *American* proposed that European workers had learned the tenets of syndicalism from the managers of trusts and monopolies. European monopolists operated under the assumption that power only resided in the workplace and in control of the means of production, and had thus "turned law and politics into mere tools of deception and repression." Unless legal and political reforms were undertaken quickly, according to this correspondent, American workers might readily adopt the direct action tactics advocated by European labor leaders. Another writer emphasized that syndicalists were a radically new type of labor agitator, unattached to traditional forms of working-class ethics and custom. Quoting a letter from Jay Fox's *Agitator*, the reporter proposed that syndicalists "are out for plunder and respect nothing their enemies venerate. You may talk to them of country, of duty, of law and order, and they will shrug their shoulders at these words, which have no meaning to them." Most alarming was the prospect that modern society would simply be overwhelmed by the "unattached proletarian elements" it had bred.[1]

Most observers, of course, associated syndicalism with the Industrial Workers of the World, and the huge strikes of textile workers at Lawrence and Paterson in 1912–13. By the summer of 1913, however, the IWW appeared to many observers in the labor movement to be on the verge of disintegration. Wobbly leaders like Frank Donovan and Elizabeth Gurley Flynn decried the reliance of the IWW on spontaneity, and the accompanying lack of emphasis on building stable organizations.[2] However, the American Federation of Labor, which had criticized the IWW strikes in Lawrence and Patterson as "anarchistic," showed no more promise than the IWW in addressing the problem of how to organize unskilled, immigrant workers in the face of the massive opposition of employers. At the level of semantics, the IWW eschewed the syndicalist label, socialists debated the exact meaning of the word, and, by 1915, there were indications that "syndicalism" had been "defeated" in the arena of public discourse as well. By 1915, the debate and alarm over syndicalism had largely subsided in the American press.[3]

In the period before the outbreak of World War I, only one American organization was bold enough to identify itself specifically as "syndicalist," and that was William Foster's Syndicalist League of North America. As early as November 1910, in the first issue of *The Agitator*, Jay Fox had called for the establishment of "agitator groups" that would spread propaganda for industrial unionism among organized workers. After Foster and Fox met at Home Colony, they went to work to realize their common plans. "I was impressed by him as by few other labor agitators I have met," Fox wrote of Foster. "I was struck by his great determination to carry out [his plans]. He was devoid of that riotous egotism I had found so common in propagandists. I took to the chap right away and was ready to go along with the program."[4] Foster's relentless efforts in the next few years justified his friend's assessment. As Fox intimated, he was a restless but extremely dedicated personality, an individual endowed with extraordinary willpower. In this respect he personified a favorite syndicalist slogan: "Vouloir, c'est pouvoir."

During the Western tour that first brought him to Home Colony in the winter of 1912, Foster was able to convince several groups of disaffected Wobblies of the relevance of his ideas; these small nuclei eventually developed into the groups that would constitute the Syndicalist League of North America. One such group, convinced of the impossibility of changing the IWW from within, quit the revolutionary union and joined AFL locals. From the beginning, they saw themselves as part of an international movement. Writing from Nelson, British Columbia, in April, J. W. Johnstone reported to *The Syndicalist*, a British newspaper established by Tom Mann and his Industrial Syndicalist Education League, that "we have started a Syndicalist League here, and are making headway." Johnstone wrote that he had been a member of the IWW for five years, and had recently begun to realize that the aim of the IWW, "building up an entire new Labour movement," was impossible. The IWW claimed that the AFL couldn't be made "revolutionary," but, according to Johnstone, "there are a great many of us, members of the IWW, who not only deny it, but have arguments so strong that the IWW Press refuses to publish any of them."[5]

After his hobo propaganda tour in February of 1912, Foster returned to Chicago, but he did not establish a permanent residence there. He found a promising job as a railway car inspector, and joined the AFL local in his trade, but the following summer he spent three months as a canvasman with a wagon tent show that wandered throughout the Midwest. Foster's account of these experiences is revealing. He remembered that the show "went over big" in corn belt towns in the Midwest, and wondered how the small-town audiences could be so credulous when some of the actors were obviously drunk. The "natives," as he called them, could remember the smallest details about performances given by the same tent show three or four years earlier. The people in the small towns that the show visited were "starved for diversion."[6] Having lived most of his life in large urban environments, Foster had difficulty comprehending the lives that people in these rural communities led. As he traveled around the Midwest with a troupe of actors and charlatans, he wrote a pamphlet that revealed his understanding of the traditional narratives of American politics as illusion and farce. His was a radicalism that was profoundly antinostalgic. He had little use for or interest in the kind of theatre and traditional emotive symbolism that characterized the populist socialism that was then sweeping parts of the West and Midwest.

The forty-seven-page pamphlet, *Syndicalism*, bore the names of William Foster and Earl Ford. According to Foster, Ford's role in the production of the booklet was mostly to supply the funds to enable its publication. Despite the obscure origins of the booklet, it gained a certain amount of attention. The conclusion of an alarmed reviewer for the *Independent* was that the implications of this "lurid red pamphlet" could be ignored only at the nation's peril. Citizens must face the fact that there is "a faction in federated labor that is trying with an eager passion, which would be religious if it were not so demoniac, to capture all federated labor and all socialism to the methods of merciless violence, murder and ruin." A perusal of *Syndicalism* revealed that its authors advocated nothing less than a "reign of terror," and government by an "aristocracy of assassins." A somewhat less frightening assessment appeared in the *Journal of Political Economy*, and the pamphlet provoked serious analyses by William English Walling and Louis Fraina in separate articles in the *International Socialist Review*.[7]

Syndicalism is a detailed attempt to explain an idea about revolutionary tactics that many American radicals had themselves dismissed as essentially inapplicable to American conditions. The booklet reiterated many of the positions that Foster had articulated in his previous writings. The importance of the general strike, the uses of sabotage, the hopelessness of Socialist electoral politics, and the necessity of building a class-based revolutionary labor movement from within existing trade unions are all familiar elements of Foster's thinking as it had developed by 1912. Certain features of the pamphlet, however, are noteworthy because they show Foster's politics at their most radical. Relatively early in his analysis, he repudiated outright the notion that modern revolutionists must look to an American republican tradition for their vocabulary. The syndicalist, according to Foster, has "learned that the so-called legal and inalienable 'rights' of man are but pretenses with which to deceive workingmen." Capitalists can only understand "naked power," and this the syndicalist must accumulate through the careful choice of weapons, without consideration of traditional issues of what might be "fair," "just," or even "civilized." He must not allow legality, religion, patriotism, honor, or duty to "stand in the way of his adoption of effective tactics."[8]

Foster's polemic calls openly for industrial warfare, unmitigated by reciprocal obligations of any kind with "capitalists." "Every forward pace humanity has taken has been gained at the cost of untold suffering and loss of life, and the accomplishment of the revolution will probably be no exception," he observed. Moreover, the prospect of bloodshed during a general strike does not frighten the syndicalist, for he is "too much accustomed to risking himself in the murderous industries and on the hellish battlefields in the niggardly service of his masters, to set much value on his [own] life." Indeed, in the context of the most threatening situation for a syndicalist, scabbery, murder is justifiable. Despite his later denials that his rhetoric implied that it was appropriate to take the life of a strikebreaker, the sense of Foster's writing is unmistakable. In France, he noted, strikebreakers are becoming "pleasingly scarce and expensive," for they are "literally" hunted by militants "as they would wild animals." In such a situation, a scab "becomes so much vermin, to be ruthlessly exterminated." In the pages of *Syndicalism*, Foster's rage is only partly subsumed by his attempt to couch his polemic in the style of "scientific" certainty. For Foster, syndicalism was "the science of working-class direct action."[9]

Syndicalism showed that in the course of his geographical and intellectual wanderings, Foster had managed to immerse himself in the writings of Michael Bakunin, who was widely admired by American anarchists. His portrait was prominently displayed in the main hall at Home Colony, and his voice echoed in Foster's writings of this period. Thus Bakunin had written that the revolutionist "despises and hates present day social morality in all its forms. He regards everything that favors the triumph of the revolution. . . . All soft and enervating feelings of friendship, love, gratitude, even honor must be stifled in him by a cold passion for the revolutionary cause. . . . day and night he must have one aim—merciless destruction." In addition, "every forward step in history has been achieved only after it has been baptized in blood." The true militant was to "renounce all egoistic and vain interests of patriotism." For Bakunin, as for Foster, the proletariat lacked two things: organization and science.[10]

What is perhaps most striking about *Syndicalism* is Foster's conception of the postrevolutionary society. He thought that given the spread of industrial warfare in Europe and the United States, it was important to address such issues as soon as possible. While he discussed his ideas in this respect more fully in a later article for *The Toiler*, a newspaper published by a group of syndicalists in Kansas City, his understanding of the future society was apparently developed while traveling with the tent show in the summer of 1912. According to Foster's theory, after a violent general strike overthrew the established order, there would of course be no state mechanism, but the future society would be far from anarchic. Traditional syndicalist theories proposed that unions would assume control of their particular industries; Foster had no faith in this conception. He argued that the unions' "democratic character" rendered them incapable of exercising control over production. Instead, he proposed a government based on what he called "shop organizations." While these would include "every worker" in a particular industry, they would be governed by experts or foremen who would guide production and introduce new technologies according to "scientific" principles.

Here, Foster took the momentous step of extending the syndicalist disdain for democratic politics to the workplace. He would retain "monopolized" industries, which he conceived as the "autonomous" structures of the future shop organizations. He imagined that under these organizations production and distribution would be "automatic," merely a process of filling orders as efficiently as possible. In this sense, "chance and arbitrary industrial dictatorship" would be eliminated; the "whole industrial process," after all, is "becoming a matter of obeying facts and figures." Thus, industrial life would be hyperorganized and instantly calibrated according to supply and demand; plants would be opened or closed automatically in response to consumer wants. In the plants themselves, the workers of the shop organizations would choose their own superintendents and foremen "by examination," but Foster strongly implied that in the future society expertise would everywhere take precedence over majority preference. There would be no place for politics in "the adoption of far-reaching measures, such as the creation of new industries, reorganizing old ones, adoption of new industrial process, etc.," regardless of their social impact. For instance, the introduction of a cheaper, more efficient productive process in the steel industry would be settled simply by "figures" determining whether it would pay interest on the cost of its installation. There is no mention of traditional craft prerogatives or the problem of unemployment. Lurking in his conception is the idea that the mass of workers are simply interchangeable.[11]

Confident that in the future society they would have no interest "to bilk their fellow beings, as they now have," Foster would endow "thoroughly organized specialists" with the power to make social law. In the shop organizations, such specialists would be chosen "on the score of their fitness," rather than "on the score of their ability to secure the support of an ignorant majority, through their oratorical powers, good looks, influence, or what not, as is the ordinary democratic procedure." During a period when workers across the nation were striking against the introduction of Taylorism and scientific management techniques in industry, he betrayed little sense of the possible uses of "science" as ideology. As workers' knowledge of the process of production in industry was being continually constricted and fragmented, Foster proposed that workers could have authority only if they were "specialists."[12]

Foster claimed to have derived his theory of the "producing organizations" of the future society from J. A. ("Jack") Jones, Elizabeth Gurley Flynn's first husband, a drifting labor agitator and former Wobbly with a reputation as a dynamiter, whom he may have met in Chicago. With his mangled hands (supposedly the result of his bomb-making efforts), long hair, and wild clothing, Jones was a remarkable figure in Chicago radical circles.[13]

Whether from Jones or elsewhere, Foster's ideas certainly had antecedents in American radical and socialist thought, as well as in the writings of European anarchists like Bakunin and Peter Kropotkin. Bakunin wrote of postrevolutionary "free productive associations," organized on the basis of "special knowledge" and expertise, which would manage production according to statistics. Kropotkin wrote in his *God and the State* that "In the matter of boots, I defer to the authority of the bootmaker; concerning houses, canals or railroads, I consult the engineer." Kropotkin envisioned quasi-authoritarian "producers' associations" that would carefully measure individual performance and supervise the distribution of goods and services in the new society.[14] Such ideas had proved easily adaptable to more modern American conceptions. Foster's idea of an authoritarian, "automatic" producing organization is reminiscent of Edward Bellamy's industrial army, as outlined in the earliest versions of *Looking Backward*, for instance,[15] and similar themes surfaced in the philippics of Daniel DeLeon.

As a relentless modernizer concerned to update anarchist theory, Foster was clearly outside the tradition of criticism of the alienating effects of industrial process, standardization, and consumerism, to be found in the works of such writers as John Ruskin, William Morris, and even Kropotkin. During the period when Foster was writing, intellectuals of diverse political persuasions sought to adapt the form of "modern" industrial organization to their particular conceptions of utopia. After all, once abstracted from self-interest and profit, the social relationships within large-scale corporate enterprises "looked a great deal more promising than the traditional social divisions and organizations that then divided and dominated the United States," as one historian has put it. Also, Foster probably understood his proposals as an antiutopian counterposition to that of the IWW, wherein a mass-based "one big union" would somehow govern industries democratically.[16]

It is striking that *Syndicalism* is composed of violent revolutionary rhetoric, mixed with insights that are essentially managerial in nature. Foster portrayed his theory of syndicalism as essentially detached from considerations of politics or ideology. The problem of tactics is addressed by reference to the theory of the "militant minority." In every group, Foster noted "there are to be found a certain few individuals who exercise a great influence over the thoughts and actions of the rest of the mass of individuals composing the group. They are the directing forces of these groups—the sluggish mass simply following their lead." Foster held out the prospect that through sheer strength of personality, dedicated revolutionaries could succeed in driving history. For him it was a fundamental principle that workers themselves were blinded by their own "political, moral, religious, patriotic, craft and other illusions"; the "masses" consisted not of an active citizenry, but of malleable consumers of capitalist propaganda. At a time when workers were increasingly confronting a separation of conception from execution in the workplace, Foster was valorizing a similar kind of alienation in the realm of radical unionism. Not only do syndicalists possess superior acumen and "scientific" expertise, their understanding has been perfected through a kind of social Darwinism; syndicalism as a doctrine is "a product of natural selection."[17]

Thus, Foster's *Syndicalism* combined the rhetoric of nineteenth-century anarchism with elements of managerial ideology, all in the service of "workers' control." His vision of a reconstituted workers' community or "future society" in which order was the predominant value perhaps arose from his experiences in Philadelphia; Foster's distrust of the ability of workers to organize themselves remained a strong theme in his writing, even after the Spokane free speech fight. At the same time, years before the Russian Revolution, his writings foreshadowed Lenin's enthusiasm for the accomplishments of American scientific management. Writing in 1937, Foster proposed that there were certain parallels between his theory of the producing organizations and the nature of Soviet government. He wrote that in the Soviet Union, industries were directed by "economic bodies under the direction of the state . . . somewhat akin to our Producing Organizations, while the trade unions . . . play only an auxiliary role in production." However, in an ominous and revealing passage, Foster noted that his earlier theory had proven inapplicable to Soviet experience. According to his conception in *Syndicalism,* the entire economic organization of capitalist society, presumably including its managers and intelligentsia, would be carried over into the new society. In the Soviet Union, such an apparatus had to be "rebuilt" through the "creation of a new technical personnel." Significantly, Foster conceived of the "producers" in the new society not as individual, autonomous citizens, but rather as "organizations" in which there was little collective control.[18]

Ironically, Foster's pamphlet contained certain themes that expressed the dynamism and some of the contradictions of the developing "new unionism" of the 1910s. Largely based on renewed militancy within older AFL affiliates, the new unionism aimed at the recruitment of unorganized workers, the development of proto-industrial methods of craft-union amalgamation, and a general rejection of labor "Progressivism" and labor-management cooperation. *Syndicalism* attacked piecework and advocated slowdowns and sabotage despite Foster's apparent fascination with modern managerialism.[19] His ideal union was one that maintained local autonomy in order to eliminate the power of bureaucrats and officials and guarantee the power of the rank and file. Foster's interpretation was that craft autonomy would lead to working-class solidarity, not frustrate it; it was the officialdom, through their interference and opportunism, that perpetuated the lack of coordination between crafts. At the same time, the ideal union would be composed of all the workers, skilled and unskilled, in a particular industry.

While *Syndicalism* concluded with the assurance that the Syndicalist League of North America was a "possibilist organization with a practical program," the overall approach of the pamphlet must have seemed foreign to many of its readers. Foster accepted the necessity of violence and bloodshed in the course of revolutionary struggle, and bitterly denounced patriotism and democracy. His polemic was filled with references to the ideas of French, German, and English socialists and syndicalists. He advocated neo-Malthusianism, or strict birth control, since the syndicalist "knows that children are a detriment to him in his daily struggles." At the same time, Foster averred that a syndicalist accepted the anarchist position on marriage.[20] His vision of the postrevolutionary society contained intimations of Taylorism, a doctrine that undoubtedly held little appeal for most workingmen. What Foster was promising in *Syndicalism* was violent class war that would culminate in the establishment of a society in which traditional conceptions of family, law, work, and nation had little or no meaning.

Syndicalism was strongly flavored by the radical positivism and teleology that were characteristic of the writings of Hermon Titus and Jay Fox. These themes would resurface continually in Foster's own writings as a Communist, and they underlay the mechanistic quality of some of his later conceptions. However, the central problem of Foster's pamphlet revolved around the contradiction between the need for autonomy and spontaneity among workers making their demands felt through direct action, and the feeling that "democracy" had somehow become inappropriate as a way of securing revolutionary change. This contradiction is implied in the theory of the "militant minority"; in Foster's conception, unorganized workers can be readily provoked into large strikes by a small cadre of highly disciplined radicals. Yet, "great strikes break out spontaneously and, also . . . spontaneously produce the organization so essential to their success." Foster the anarcho-syndicalist affirmed that syndicalists must be "anti-authoritarians, their national labor unions being decentralized and their local unions possessed of complete autonomy." Foster the future Leninist proclaimed the necessity of a militant "vanguard" cadre that would inevitably lead workers' struggles. While he claimed that what was needed in the American labor movement was "not less autonomy, but more of it," workers must be organized into unions that included "all skilled and unskilled workers directly connected with a given craft or industry." Foster's tangled arguments about the nature of the worker, as well as his attempt to reconcile the voluntarism of the anarchists with the efficiencies of corporate forms of organization, were the most important features of his thinking as a syndicalist. His ideas reflected an acute tension between an older, craft-based radical impulse and the organizational ethos of the Progressive era.[21]

One salient feature of *Syndicalism* that was to prove so threatening and alarming, not only for several reviewers in 1912 but for a wider public during the 1919 steel strike as well, was the rhetoric of class war that served as the background for much of Foster's analysis. A tone of bitterness and anger was present in some of his writing for the IWW press while he was in Europe, but it is in *Syndicalism* that one can most readily sense Foster's rage. It is a rage against capitalists, "utopians" in the IWW, and the "horde of doctors, lawyers, preachers and other non-working class elements" that "infested" the Socialist party. The revolutionary must be prepared for violence, bloodshed, and destruction during the course of his struggles, and he must take "no cognizance" of "Society." Foster's vision is a kind of twentieth-century Hobbesianism in which social transactions consist of maximally organized, yet unmediated, violence against the working class in the form of the wages system. As a result, the syndicalist must be as

"unscrupulous" in his choice of weapons to fight his everyday battles as for his final struggle with capitalism. . . .

The only sentiment he knows is loyalty to the interests of the working class. He is in utter revolt against capitalism in all its phases. His lawless course often lands him in jail, but he is so fired by revolutionary enthusiasm that jails, or even death, have no terrors for him. He glories in martyrdom, consoling himself with the knowledge that he is a terror to his enemies, and that his movement, today sending chills along the spine of international capitalism, tomorrow will put an end to this monstrosity.

Syndicalism is nothing less than "daily warfare" against capitalism, since capitalism has "organized the whole fabric of society" in its attempts to maintain the working class in "slavery." No other American radical of his generation would embrace the metaphors of warfare as completely as did Foster. The central images of Foster's *Syndicalism* revolve around the idea of the destruction of subjectivity; workers are "slaves," without essential motives or inalienable rights, and capitalism itself is so highly organized and insidious that for the syndicalist, mere survival is a tenuous proposition. The capitalist class is not a remote or abstract entity, but rather the worker's "mortal enemy" which must be overthrown for him merely to "live."[22] Foster's vision of society and revolutionary struggle is a bleak one, in which a syndicalist must be utterly unattached to family, country, or society in order to survive.

By 1912, at age thirty-one, Foster's personality must be considered to have been more or less fully formed. By all accounts, he was a quiet man, but possessed of a quick temper and a willingness to engage in bitter argument with those who disagreed with him. He was uncomfortable speaking before large audiences, yet during one speech before a group of workers in the 1920s he leapt from the podium and physically assaulted a heckler. His lifestyle was ascetic in the extreme. Throughout his life he accumulated few personal possessions, and he sought, quite successfully, to live without concern for property or even personal financial security. At least in his later years, Foster never purchased clothes for himself, and habitually gave away whatever cash he possessed, much to the chagrin of his immediate family. Despite the fact that he claimed to have married Esther Abramowitz in 1912, he does not mention that she accompanied him on his numerous hobo trips or agitation tours in the 1910s. His contacts with his sisters, who settled into conventional lives on the West Coast, were "rare," and he never mentions the fate of his older brother. The man who came to play such a significant role in the American Communist party was essentially a loner. He was not a particularly gregarious man, and had few close personal friends outside of his immediate family circle.[23]

During the 1919 steel strike, a reporter for the *New York Tribune* described the alienation and anger that lay at the center of Foster's personality. "Soft-spoken though he is, it is not difficult to perceive a certain hard bitterness underneath. An almost academic vocabulary is occasionally made picturesque by a selection of hot expletives spoken coolly. It is then that you see the bitterness." In 1912, Foster's bitterness was plainly evident in the pages of *Syndicalism*. His personality was undoubtedly complex, and perhaps so evasive that the exact sources of his alienation will remain obscure. However, a number of vignettes from *Pages from a Worker's Life* help to put Foster's rage in context. The *New York Tribune* reporter who observed him closely in 1919 sensed that Foster's persona was partly attributable to the rough work and "unticketed" experiences of a railroad carman. Foster, he noted, was undoubtedly quite well acquainted with the world of "break beams and bumpers," and his appearance easily approximated that of an off-duty railway worker.[24] The reporter's observations provide a conceptual link between Foster's occupation as a railroad worker in the 1910s and his personality; this connection can be explored through reference to *Pages from a Worker's Life* as well. A variety of incidents in which Foster was a participant or witness serve to elaborate Foster's self-conception as a revolutionary syndicalist, and confirm certain themes contained in his pamphlet *Syndicalism*.

As an autobiography, *Pages from a Worker's Life* is a valuable account of Foster's life, yet many of the incidents that the book records are simply unverifiable; they often occur in isolation, without a social or organizational context of any permanence. The individuals, places, and work situations in Foster's stories are themselves presented as prosaic and ephemeral. As an author or observer Foster is socially decentered, even though the work milieu which he observed and recorded is itself part of a specific

Foster, ca. 1912, railroad worker and syndicalist.

historical reality. The "syndicalist" must be, as Foster noted in his pamphlet, "anti-Society."

Although Foster rejected much of American society, its structures of belongingness and hence its means of verifying experiences, his employment as a railway laborer engaged him quite deeply in the nation's work culture. From 1901 to 1919, he worked and lived in many different capacities on American railroads, the network of transportation that helped the nation define itself as a coherent commercial and political entity. For the men who were employed on the railroad, however, work among the cars, engines, and machinery could be dangerous and violent. Foster had ample opportunity to witness this kind of violence; during his years as a railroad worker, he found employment as a fireman, second cook on a grading crew, airbrake repairman, interchange car inspector, car carpenter, and brakeman, mostly in Chicago's switching district. Between periodic hobo trips to the West, and an interregnum as an organizer of timber workers in Washington state, Foster worked in Chicago railway yards from 1911, the year of his return from Europe, until 1917, when he became a full-time organizer for the American Federation of Labor. During this period, he witnessed workers being crushed, decapitated, and crippled as they worked among the heavy machinery in the car shops. Foster's descriptions of these accidents are simple and unemotional; in one incident, a worker's body was "crushed flat, almost cut in two, between the car sills and the wheel, and he died instantly without uttering a sound." In another case, as a result of a braking error, both trucks of one railroad car passed over a worker. "His head was cut off completely."[25]

The subject of these stories is the danger of railway work, and the greed of employers. Foster's accounts of his years after he returned from Europe and attempted to organize a syndicalist movement in the United States are permeated with a sense of utter insecurity. The recurring themes of Foster's descriptions of his experiences working on different railway lines and hoboing across the country are transience, invisibility, and the obliteration of lives in obscure and meaningless circumstances. These themes are especially evident in his accounts of his "unticketed" experiences on the railways. Far from romanticizing the hobo lifestyle, Foster emphasizes its utterly ephemeral and violent nature. As a brakeman and car inspector, Foster was familiar with trains and knew how to ride inside the trucks, or wheel structures under passenger cars. He described the dangers involved in cramming into the complex wheel mechanisms of the trains and riding inches above the tracks in high-speed passenger trains. It is a striking evocation of the possibilities of violence and personal destruction that are implied when a hobo attempts to adopt modern machinery and technology to his own purposes. Foster noted that one wrong calculation as he was riding the "trucks" could cause him to be "instantaneously cut to pieces, as hundreds of hoboes had been before me."[26] Foster's narrative reflects a kind of fatalism about the ubiquity of technological power in modern society melded with an intensely felt resistance to capitalist exploitation.

In other instances, the theme of obliteration recurs. Many hobos, miscalculating their leaps as they sought to board moving trains, had "been picked up along the right-of-way, a bloody, mangled mass," Foster recounted. In a small town in Idaho, he witnessed the aftermath of an incident in which a shifting load of lumber had crushed a hobo in a railway car; "his bones were crushed like pipe-stems and his flesh was smeared against the shattered car end. . . . they gathered up what they could of the shapeless mass and put it into a wheelbarrow." While riding on top of a car in Maryland, Foster saw a fellow tramp killed instantly when the train passed under a low wagon-road bridge. Once, while hanging precariously between two cars, Foster narrowly escaped being "thrown beneath the wheels and ground to pieces." Another time, he and several other hobos saw a hobo attempt to board a train only to be dragged under the wheels and cut to pieces: "it happened so suddenly that he never even screamed." A special fear of hobos, Foster remembered, was being locked in a car and left at an isolated siding to starve to death. "Many's the time trainmen and car inspectors have opened foul-smelling box-cars and discovered dead hoboes, starved to death."[27]

The literal truth of these stories is not so important as their thematic structure. At the heart of the syndicalist ideal lay the concept of the class war, but there is never any sense of the possibility of "return" in Foster's vignettes; no Edenic community or vitalizing participatory life exists at this point in his autobiography. The overwhelming sense is of incipient invisibility and obliteration. Indeed, those chapters of *Pages From a Worker's Life* that describe his life in the years after his return from Europe seem to affirm his implied self-description in *Syndicalism*. It is a convincing portrait of brutality, alienation, resistance, and survival.

After the production of *Syndicalism* in the summer of 1912, Foster returned to Chicago and found a job as a railway car inspector. He worked diligently to bring some semblance of organizational coherence to his embryonic syndicalist league.[28] By October, Fox had decided to leave Home Colony and devote his energies to the development of Foster's tiny syndicalist movement in Chicago. From Home, he wrote to Joseph Labadie that "This berg is becoming too small for the A[gitator]. It's outgrown the state. We want to take the center of the industrial stage. The syndicalists want me to go there and make the paper the central organ of the movement. And this movement is going to grow, Jo. It's better than our pure and simple anarchy at this stage."[29] Thus, Foster and Fox hoped to adapt their peculiar brand of anarcho-syndicalism to the task of organ-

izing a mass revolutionary movement in Chicago, a huge and diverse metropolis. Each man prided himself on his "realism"; Foster always took
care to present himself as an anti-utopian, and Fox had left Home Colony
and moved to Chicago so that syndicalism might "take the center of the
industrial stage." In line with these sentiments, both men sought to bring
about the revolution by helping to speed the evolution of "higher" forms
of working-class organization. In November 1912, the last issue of Fox's
The Agitator appeared. By January 1913, Fox had renamed his paper *The
Syndicalist*, though legal entanglements kept him in Washington until
early spring.[30]

Foster and Fox operated the Syndicalist League out of the rooming
house operated by Lucy Parsons at 1000 South Paulina Street, in a heavily
Slavic community in Chicago's Near West Side. The league attempted to
collect dues of five cents per month from its members and forbade, on
pain of dismissal, the use of official titles or funds in support of any political party.[31] On Sundays, the two men read together and carried on the
correspondence necessary to keep the league functioning. It was a sign of
the increasing influence of syndicalism among radicals that after Foster
and Fox arrived in Chicago, Parsons, the widow of the famous anarchist
and "Haymarket martyr" Albert Parsons, increasingly embraced syndicalism as the focus of her political activities. She added *Syndicalism* to her
literature list, contributed to *The Syndicalist*, and changed the title of her
standard speech from "Anarchism: Its Aims and Objects" to "Syndicalism: Its Aims and Objects."[32]

The new organ of Foster's league, *The Syndicalist*, advocated industrial sabotage. It carried a column entitled "Society Notes," in which its
author, J. A. Jones, provided readers with insights such as "A few drops
of sulphuric acid placed on top of a pile of woolen or cotton goods never
stops going down," or, "Engine cylinders are expensive articles. A
clogged lubricator means a cut cylinder. Dirt in the oil can mean a clogged
lubricator." Other "hints" were more ominous. One proposed that ar-
sonists might employ sausage skins strung on wire and filled with gaso-
line to accomplish their aims; another noted that "New York's gangsters
are using Maxim silencers to silence their opponents."[33] While Foster
later claimed that as a syndicalist, he had accepted the "revolutionary
economics, class struggle and historical materialism of Marx," the
"Worker's University," a list of books for sale through *The Syndicalist*,
did not contain a single work by Marx. Rather, books by Proudhon,
Emma Goldman, Tolstoy, Nietzsche, Kropotkin, and Pouget were recommended as those that would ideally fill the shelves of the informed syndicalist. In *Syndicalism*, Foster made a point of recommending Kropotkin's
The Conquest of Bread, the classic text of "communitarian" anarchists.[34]

The Syndicalist League of North America developed into a small but widely noticed propaganda society for radical trade unionists. Foster later recalled regretfully that because of his belief in decentralization, the national league was incapable of developing into a very unified organization. At the local level, groups were organized in Kansas City, St. Louis, San Diego, and Omaha that were affiliated in a vague way with the league. The various syndicalist groups that came into existence were highly autonomous, Foster wrote, and "collected what funds they saw fit, issued their own journals, and worked out their own policies." He estimated that the membership never exceeded two thousand, and was mostly concentrated in Chicago.[35]

In that city, Foster's league included a small group of militants, among whom were Jones, Joseph Manley, and Samuel Hammersmark. Manley, who would later marry Esther's daughter Sylvia, was a bridge and structural iron worker. He was born in Dublin, Ireland, and told the labor biographer Solon DeLeon in the 1920s that his father had been a physician and African explorer. He probably met Foster at Home Colony, where he was an infrequent visitor; the two men would work together closely in the Chicago Federation of Labor, the 1919 steel strike, and the Communist party. Hammersmark was an anarchist who was also listed as the publisher of *Why?*, a short-lived radical journal with Tacoma, Washington, as its address. He became actively involved in the Chicago Federation of Labor, but ended up managing the Communist party's bookstore in that city in his later years. Another anarchist who became involved with the Syndicalist league was Foster's future wife, Esther Abramowitz. Esther's relationship with the Chicago anarchists went back much further than Foster's. Besides having been Jay Fox's lover, she was associated with a milieu at the turn of the century that included Parsons, Emma Goldman, Alexander Berkman, and Anton Johannsen. By the 1920s, Johannsen had become the chairman of the Organization Committee of the Chicago Federation of Labor.[36] It was the Kansas City syndicalist group that developed into the strongest component of the national league, and its activities give a fairly clear picture of the league's ambitions with regard to the labor movement. It had "practical control" of the Cooks, Barbers, and Office Workers unions, and "virtually controlled" the Kansas City Central Labor Council according to Foster. Moreover, working under Max Dezettel, a former Wobbly, the group was instrumental in launching a strong Labor Forward Movement in the city. Employing aggressive, quasi-evangelical methods, Labor Forward activists organized a number of trades in the city, including shoe repairers, retail clerks, waitresses, laundry workers, bootblacks, telephone operators, and packinghouse workers. The movement attracted the attention of Gompers, and was officially cited for its efforts at the AFL national convention of 1914. The Kansas City radicals were able to publish a newspaper of their own, *The Toiler*. The editorials were in line with SLNA theory, and Foster contributed several articles during the paper's run from October 1913 to January 1915. "Toiler Boosters," including Foster, were selling between eighty and one hundred subscriptions per month by early 1914.[37]

A good indication of the league's general philosophy was the central illustration on the first page of the premier issue of *The Toiler*. It showed a group of workers, tools in hand, gazing upon a rising sun. Inscribed upon the sun were the initials "AFL." Beneath the illustration was the epigram: "The Hope of the Workers." However, none of the local syndicalist leagues subscribed to the spirit of narrow reformism and wage-consciousness typically associated with AFL-style unionism. "In America today," according to the organ of the St. Louis league, "we find the whole country in a turmoil of strikes and lockouts. These strikes, undoubtedly, are but the skirmishes preceding a series of great general strikes that will make every institution of capitalism creak and tremble to their very foundation."[38]

It was the activities of the Kansas City syndicalist league that first brought Foster into contact with a personality with whom he would have a very long, complex, and difficult relationship, which in certain respects would end up defining both men's political careers: Earl Browder, future general secretary of the American Communist party. Born in Wichita in 1891, Browder had joined the Socialist party at age sixteen, and left home for Kansas City in 1912. By 1914, as an accountant for a subsidiary of Standard Oil, he had become president of his office workers' union, and a delegate to the Kansas City central labor body.

In the early 1910s, as a young socialist in Kansas City, Browder read Friedrich Engel's book *Socialism, Utopian and Scientific*. He wondered whether the IWW constituted a form of "utopian" trade unionism as Engels defined the term. "If there [was] one thing I didn't want it was to be a utopian," he reflected much later. "I was trying to find some connection between the ideas about a better world and practical everyday life." In 1913, at a meeting in the city's labor temple, Foster came down from Chicago to speak before his union. At this first meeting, Browder came away impressed by Foster's practical program, and the fact that he had had "outside experience, even in Europe." Throughout the publishing history of *The Toiler*, Browder is listed as one of the most successful of the "Toiler Boosters," and in February 1914, the newspaper contained a reference to him as secretary of the "Kansas City Syndicalist League." While Browder had evidently been impressed by Foster, he did not meet him again until 1915.[39]

The rhetoric of industrial warfare echoed in many Midwestern railheads during one of the most bitter and prolonged strikes of the era, the revolt of the shopworkers on the Illinois Central–Harriman lines from 1911 to 1915. Working as a railway carman in Chicago at the time, Foster was closely acquainted with the logic and means of the strike, and the Syndicalist League participated in a campaign to defend L. M. Hawver, a leader of the revolt who had killed a railroad policeman in self-defense. In certain respects the strike represented a paradigm for Foster's conception of syndicalist revolutionary activity. It was sparked by an attempt by the officers of the Illinois Central to introduce time study and incentive pay into the railroad car shops, but another issue was the right of the railroad shop unions to federate and secure a joint contract. It began as a revolt by rank-and-file craft unionists, and precipitated the development of a "system federation" of allied craft unions that presented unified demands to the employers. Many striking shopworkers explicitly rejected the leadership of the recently elected Socialist officers of the International Association of Machinists. Nonetheless, the strike had implications that the management of the Illinois Central perceived to have been nothing less than revolutionary. C. H. Markham, president of the Harriman line, flatly declared that if the strike and the federation plan had been successful, workers' control of the entire railroad industry would have been the result.[40]

It is important to recognize that the shop crafts unions, including the railway carmen to which Foster belonged, possessed an outlook and membership that was fundamentally different from that of the elite railway brotherhoods whose heyday had been in the late nineteenth century. The brotherhoods of engineers, firemen, trainmen, and conductors maintained a fairly stable membership, and it was not unusual for them to be looked upon as assets by the railroad companies. Occasionally they named their lodges after prominent railway officials. The shop unions, however, had a far more transient membership since their work was not so steady as that of the men handling the trains. They tended to be nomads or "boomers," and often floated from "shop to shop and from road to road." As a result, they were commonly considered far more militant than the brotherhoods had been. The shop unions proved much more willing to experiment with new organizational forms as a way of ensuring closer cooperation among the crafts.[41]

The shopmen's strike lasted until 1915, when it was finally broken. As Foster noted, it turned into a rank-and-file struggle against both the railroad companies and the craft union officialdom. Among the reasons for the defeat of the strike, according to Foster, was the fact that the craft union leaders were mistrustful of federated action, which they saw as a step in the direction of industrial unionism; the officials of the engine, train, and yard service unions kept their men at work. In the eyes of IWW and Socialist writers at the time, this confirmed that the craft unions could never transcend their voluntarist form. However, in Foster's view, the strike was not a complete failure. After the strike, the major railroad companies "never forced another important strike over the right of federated action by the railroad companies," and even negotiated several agreements with federated unions during the strike itself. During World War I, as an organizer for the railway carmen in Chicago, Foster asserted that the strike had aided his union's negotiations with the railroad companies. Carl Person, one of the leaders of the violent 1911 strike, wrote that "there was no mistake made by going on strike, or the strike taking place, for out of this strike the federated movement blossomed into importance all over this country." The experiments with the federated form of organization that the AFL sanctioned in the early 1910s provided much of the conceptual framework for the wartime organizing campaigns that Foster led in packing and steel.[42]

In line with his previous views, Foster also stood on the radical side on the issue of sabotage, which was a central source of controversy among Socialists and labor unionists of the 1910s. No event illustrated this tension better than the events surrounding the bombing of the *Los Angeles Times* building in 1910 by individuals connected with the Los Angeles local of the Bridge and Structural Iron Union. Twenty workers in the building were killed by the blasts. James B. McNamara and his brother, J. A., the secretary treasurer of the union, were arrested and charged with the crime. Many in the labor movement were at first convinced of the McNamaras' innocence, yet the brothers were eventually tried and convicted on the basis of their own confessions. The incident doomed the candidacy of Job Harriman, a Socialist, for mayor of Los Angeles, and this helped convince many politicians in the Socialist party that they had to separate themselves from those radicals in the labor movement who advocated sabotage.[43]

In the angry debates that ensued, Foster was certainly among those who defended the McNamaras; his friend Jay Fox may have played a role in hiding fugitives in the case from the authorities. He wrote in the French syndicalist journal, *La Vie ouvrière* that there was no reason for revolutionaries in the labor movement to regret the use of violence against capitalists. Although there was no doubt that they participated in the bombing of the *Times*, according to Foster, the McNamaras were the kind of radical AFL unionists whom he admired, just "good militant workers." The use of dynamite during the struggle of the Structural Iron workers against the open shop in the Los Angeles area was entirely justified, he felt. In the meantime, "constructive" Socialists fulminated that sabotage was ultimately counterproductive. The tactic was merely a cathartic release for the slum proletarian's "blind class rage" according to one spokesman.[44]

While coming under attack from Socialists for their views on sabotage, Foster and other like-minded syndicalists promulgated a compelling argument about the tasks facing militants in the labor movement in the 1910s. In a decade when aggressive strike action was often based in the existing craft unions, the IWW played a comparatively small role. Indeed, as David Montgomery has pointed out, syndicalist tendencies among American workers during the period "may have reached far beyond the limited influence of the IWW." For the majority of American workers, the IWW simply proved unable to provide the kind of organizational continuity and protection that twentieth-century industrial labor seemed to demand. "It became increasingly apparent that the immigrant machine tenders wanted something more from their organization than oratory and strike leadership." Many AFL unions remained isolated and powerless as well, but there was evidence, as Foster claimed, that the craft organizations were capable of "evolution." When the famous English syndicalist Tom Mann visited the United States in 1913, he appeared before meetings organized by Foster and the Syndicalist league and asked of the IWW, "if one looks to find definite, tangible, effective organization, to what extent does it exist?"

Considered in the context of Foster's life, it is easy to see why many workers might seek the security and organizational coherence that the AFL ideally offered. While the paradigmatic business enterprises of the era were becoming ever more thoroughly rationalized and integrated, workers like William Foster struggled in an economic environment which to them seemed increasingly uncertain and chaotic.[45] As a young man, Foster's life was marked by a level of insecurity and transience that many historians have equated with the traditional membership of the IWW, yet he conscientiously sought, and attained, AFL membership wherever he went.

Foster's life in Chicago during the years that he was attempting to establish his league of trade union radicals can be reconstructed only through details gleaned from his own writings and testimony, some of which is contradictory and unclear in its exact chronology. It is not certain, for instance, whether or not Foster and Esther Abramowitz were living together before 1918. In testimony before an arbitration board in 1918, Foster stated that he had no children at the time he worked in Swift's car shops in 1915.[46] Esther, as previously noted, had three children in 1912. She and William were married only in 1918, perhaps then only so that Foster could avoid the draft. As an anarchist and "varietist," Esther may

have been unwilling to accept any formal living arrangement or relationship with Foster until then, and of course Foster himself thought that
family and children were a handicap in the class struggle.[47] In Lucy Parsons's rooming house he had the opportunity for frequent interaction
with the group of anarchists and labor activists to whom Parsons was an
important symbolic link with the past as well as an adviser and friend.
This may have provided at least a semblance of a community life for
Foster. However, he must have been struck by the difficult conditions
under which many families in this particular Chicago neighborhood
lived. A study completed in 1910 was highly critical of the crowding and
inadequate sanitary conditions in rooming houses in the area where Foster lived on the near South Side, bordering on South Paulina Street. The
housing of families in single rooms was most appalling, according to a
survey completed in 1910. "Only the very poor, or those who are less
than ordinarily competent, will consent to live in this manner, and for
such there seem peculiar advantages in renting by the week a furnished
room which will make possible the most transient and irresponsible kind
of family life," the author concluded.[48] Regardless of the exact circumstances of his own boarding arrangements, Foster once again found himself in a community where the lives of its members were considered
wretched and incomprehensible by middle-class observers.

Between occasional organizing ventures, Foster worked as a railway
car inspector at the nearby Chicago and Northwestern railway yards,
often for twelve hours a day, seven days a week. Despite the long hours
and danger of such work, he finally began to achieve a measure of economic stability and security. He earned between sixty-five and eighty dollars a month; this was a comfortable wage for a working man, and was
the highest standard rate paid to railway mechanics in Chicago at the
time. A car inspector was among the most skilled of railway workers,
often having years of experience building and repairing cars. Working
under little direct supervision, his responsibility was primarily to determine the condition of cars at interchanges, and make light repairs when
necessary. Since many railroads carried cars from other companies, the
inspector had to make a careful record of the defects of cars taken on in
a switching yard. In addition, he was expected to be thoroughly familiar
with many different sets of rules and Interstate Commerce Commission
regulations, all of which were often changed. As a result, a car inspector
had to possess a prodigious memory and concern for detail. As Foster
himself wrote, the inspector "had to be familiar with the innumerable
parts of hundreds of types of wooden freight cars in use upon scores of
railroads. Besides, he had to know the equipment all these cars were supposed to carry and he had to work so rapidly that he had to gauge at a
glance the condition of the cars."[49]

In many ways, Foster's occupation as a railway car inspector was suited to his temperament and abilities. An indefatigable organizer who could involve himself in the most complex details of his work, Foster was at his best when he combined his knowledge of bureaucratic minutiae and procedure with a certain inherent flexibility and adaptiveness. In his political life he often preferred to work alone, seeking personal leadership and direction of distinctive working-class organizations.

The Syndicalist League of North America, or at least its organizational center, broke up in early 1914. By November 1913, Fox had returned to Washington state. It is unclear whether or not Foster accompanied him, but Fox remembered that "after a year in Chicago promoting the new adventure in Syndicalism we decided to lay off for a while. . . . Later when things looked brighter we would stage a comeback." According to Foster, in early 1914 "the [SLNA] crumbled away into disconnected groups of militants working here and there in the trade union movement." *The Syndicalist* had lasted until September 1913, through only nine months of publication. By January 1915, the newspapers that had been associated with the Syndicalist League in San Diego, St. Louis, and Kansas City had expired.[50]

Also, while he was in Chicago, working as a car inspector, Foster developed severe difficulties with his vision. The job demanded excellent eyesight, and its requirement for continual, rapid, and accurate visual examination of the cars could result in severe eyestrain. In addition, as the national secretary of the SLNA, Foster "devoted every available waking moment to reading and to writing letters." As a result of his eyestrain, Foster's eyes "gave out" and he had to quit his job on the Chicago and Northwestern railroad. For some time, he wrote, he could not look upon any kind of motion. These difficulties apparently persisted for some three years until 1917, the year in which he finally stopped working as a railway carman and involved himself in the campaign to organize Chicago meatpacking workers.[51]

Much later, writing as a Communist, Foster reflected that the failure of the Syndicalist League was "primarily due to its incorrect syndicalist program." This program, he concluded, was fatally flawed because of its simplistic concentration on trade union struggles, abandonment of electoral activity, and dependence on worker spontaneity. Yet, he pointed out that these were symptoms of a broader malady: nearly all American radicals at the time were affected by what he called the "syndicalist confusion." He ignored the concrete, historical factors that led him to reject the Socialist party and the IWW in the 1910s. It is a strikingly self-negating, ahistorical position.[52]

While the Syndicalist League belonged to a specific historical context, the organization was also a profoundly personal creation. As such its limitations encompassed, to a large extent, the limitations of its founder. As an organization, the SLNA sought a national scope. It is difficult to imagine that Foster, often working extremely long hours as a railway car inspector, was capable of devoting enough time and energy to the task of establishing such a national organization. At the same time, Foster's personality and experiences influenced the substance of the SLNA's message in a way that may not have appealed to many of the AFL unionists whom he sought to recruit. Later, after he had long since publicly renounced syndicalism, Foster wrote that the SLNA's "leftist direct attacks upon the workers' nationalistic feelings and their religion also needlessly alienated the masses of workers afflicted with such illusions and made for sectarianism."[53] Problematic as such rhetoric may have seemed to many of the individuals who read *Syndicalism* or listened to his speeches, it was grounded firmly in Foster's own experiences as a worker and radical.

Foster's retreat from Chicago came at a crucially important juncture in his life. Faced with the failure of the Syndicalist League and unwilling or unable to commit himself to his trade as a car inspector, he cast about for a role in the organized labor movement. In his search, he once again benefited from his relationship with Jay Fox. In 1914 Fox was appointed vice president of the AFL-affiliated International Union of Shingle Weavers, Sawmill Workers and Woodsmen, headquartered in Seattle, by a close friend of his, J. G. Brown. At the time, the union of highly skilled shingle weavers was attempting to establish a semi-industrial form for itself by expanding its jurisdiction to loggers and sawmill workers; in the midst of this campaign, Foster was appointed to his first full-time job as a labor organizer. Soon he found himself working to bring about a statewide strike, which had been planned by the union for May 1 if employers did not grant the eight-hour day, overtime pay, a minimum wage, and safety features in the mills. However, the employers began dismissing union members wholesale, and because of a severe depression in the logging industry the timber workers themselves seemed to have little confidence that a strike could achieve their objectives. The union decided to pin its hopes on an eight-hour day referendum being sponsored by the Socialist party for the November elections. The referendum was defeated, and the union disintegrated. Even though the reasons for its defeat were complex, the lesson Foster drew from this campaign was simple: unions seeking to "evolve" into more powerful forms had to avoid Socialist politics at all costs.[54]

Foster had occasion to witness another setback for AFL-style industrial unionism in 1914. In that year, copper miners belonging to the powerful Western Federation of Miners Local No. 1 in Butte revolted against the administration of president Charles Moyer, and ended up demolishing the union's office with dynamite. Moyer had autocratically suppressed or defeated all attempts to challenge his authority, and the local itself was commonly assumed to have become a mere subsidiary of the Anaconda Copper Company. Dissidents sought to organize another union, and at the height of the rebellion, Samuel Gompers wired all international unions with affiliates in Butte to send representatives to assist Moyer in fighting what he believed was IWW influence. J. G. Brown sent Foster to Butte, and at a meeting of AFL officials in Helena at which Moyer was present, Foster advised that the WFM authorize a new election of officials in Butte. Moyer angrily rejected this proposal, but when Foster traveled to Butte to meet with leaders of the new union and attempt to convince them to rejoin the WFM, he was accused of being an agent of Moyer's. At the time, despite his status as AFL organizer, Foster wrote approvingly of the militants' grievances without endorsing their formation of a new union. In any event, Moyer's intransigence and the miners' rebellion resulted in a disastrous split from which the once-powerful WFM would never entirely recover.[55]

When his appointment as organizer for the Shingle Weavers expired in early 1915, Foster returned to Chicago. Unfortunately, he arrived in the midst of a severe industrial downturn. He was able to find work as an inspector in Swift's refrigerator car shops in the stockyards district, but at drastically reduced wages. He lived in a tiny flat, "a little box of a place," and felt that the longer he worked the less secure he became. He needed glasses and dental work.[56]

Yet Foster retained his dogged belief in the Syndicalist project. Thus, in January 1915, a few months after the outbreak of World War I, he organized a "syndicalist conference" in St. Louis, the purpose of which was to establish another league of trade union militants. The new group was called the International Trade Union Educational League, the nomenclature being exactly parallel to that of Tom Mann's organization in Great Britain, the International Syndicalist Educational League. An executive board was established, consisting of Foster as secretary, with Jack Johnstone, Joseph Manley, Jack Carney, and Jay Fox, all future Communists, among the other individuals on the governing body. Max Dezettel, who had been the editor of the old SLNA paper in Kansas City, *The Toiler*, was delegated the task of establishing a national organ for the ITUEL in Chicago, which was called *Chicago Labor News*. At first, the conference endorsed the program contained in Foster's SLNA pamphlet, *Syndicalism*. However, because the opinions of many of the old Syndicalist league members had "undergone radical changes," Foster was instructed to prepare a new statement of purpose. The new organization planned to sell a series of pamphlets to be authored by Fox, Tom Mann, and Pierre Monatte among others. The group was frank about its entrepreneurial appeal: "You pay us 8c a copy and then re-sell them for 10c." Members were instructed to "agitate for the six-hour day" and join the American Federation of Labor.[57]

In April 1915, Foster somehow secured an open-ended appointment as a general organizer for the AFL. During a period of economic recession in Chicago this appointment was undoubtedly welcome. However, it meant that during at least part of the period he was working to establish the ITUEL, supposedly part of a coalition of progressives in Chicago against what he later called the "Gompers national machine," he was on the AFL payroll.[58]

Foster wrote a treatise entitled *Trade Unionism: The Road to Freedom.* It was the "only formal statement of policy ever issued by the ITUEL." In this booklet, he apotheosized the function of American trade unions. Regardless of whether they were organized along craft or industrial lines, or whether or not there was any degree of class consciousness among their members, the trade unions were by their "very nature driven on to the revolutionary goal," according to Foster. American trade unionism, he wrote, "has transformed the workers, employed and unemployed, from a mob of human commodities and articles of commerce into a disciplined army of freemen fighting collectively against the common enemy for their rights." Foster looked explicitly to the example of the huge strikes in Great Britain in 1910–11 as the inspiration for his new organization. Here, the guiding principle was federation. Through an inevitable process of craft union amalgamation, organized labor would eventually gain absolute control of capitalist society. He noted that since the beginning of World War I, the British transport workers', miners', and railroaders' federations had "combined themselves into one gigantic offensive and defensive alliance," the so-called Triple Alliance. Because unions always made demands according to their strength, and inevitably increased these demands as their strength grew, organized labor would eventually overthrow the wages system. By making "immediate" and partial demands for their members, craft unions were "as insatiable as the veriest so-called revolutionary union."[59]

In his writings of this period, Foster tied together the themes of organization, power, and manhood. Among craft workers threatened by the divisive forces of technological change in the early twentieth century, a manly bearing on the job entailed maintaining a dignified pose toward the boss or foreman, and required that workers respect shop-floor traditions of mutual respect and solidarity. Foster clearly sought to evoke such traditions when he wrote that unorganized workers were neglecting their duties to their families: workers outside the union constituted a "miserable picture of incompetence and cowardice," and "the sufferings of their women and children awaken no echo of revolt in their dull hearts." On the other hand, "trade unionism binds together the hosts of individually helpless workers into one mighty organization." He exhorted: "Be a man! Join the Trade Union Movement and be a fighter in the glorious cause of liberty!" Although the current administration in the Chicago Federation of Labor owed a great deal of its power to the white-collar and mostly female teachers' union, Foster's appeal was aimed explicitly at "all workingmen."[60]

At some point in early 1916 Foster was elected as business agent, or organizer, for the Chicago District Council of the Railway Carmen. This vote was the result of a referendum by thirteen locals, and marked Foster's growing visibility within the Chicago Federation of Labor, the AFL's aggressive and self-confident central union affiliate in the city. Foster's election was remarkable, considering the fact that he had lived and worked in Chicago, with frequent absences, only since September 1911. From the beginnings of his participation in the more radical dimensions of the American labor movement, Foster had proved able to gain a measure of personal notoriety. This was partly the result of his ability to sell his pamphlets and "subs" to literate workingmen and unionists who were curious about the latest trends among radicals in the labor movement at home and abroad. In addition, Foster's reputation as a virulent critic of the wage system may have aided his rise—it was not unusual for AFL unionists to put such men in office as a show of their independence from the bosses.[61]

At the same time, in Chicago, Foster probably gained some access to the inner circles of that city's labor movement through his relationship with Fox, Parsons, and Esther Abramowitz. The connection between these anarchists and the Chicago Federation of Labor was illustrated by the early career of Anton Johannsen, whom Earl Browder later described as the brains behind the CFL in the 1920s. Johannsen was an itinerant labor activist who found his forte and voice as a leading troubleshooter and specialist organizer for the powerful San Francisco Building Trades Council in the years before World War I. In Chicago, he maintained a friendship with Jay Fox, and had once helped him find work in the city. Esther was a friend of Johannsen's wife, Maggie. Johannsen told Hutchins Hapgood that his relationship with the Chicago anarchists had helped him make a favorable impression in national AFL circles. "I began to meet the big fellows, men like John Mitchell and Sam Gompers, and I found that my acquaintance with radical ideas, slight as it then was, helped me with these men, no matter how conservative they were—and they always seem more conservative than they are in reality." Johannsen concluded that "there is no conception so close to trades-unionism as anarchism," but that a radical must not "advertise" his strong position in the unions. Despite his pragmatism, it was difficult for Johannsen to

Esther and William.

maintain a low profile; he "at least knew" of the McNamara bombing conspiracy before it had been carried out, and was indicted in 1912 by a federal grand jury for crossing state lines to aid the structural iron workers' bombing campaign.[62]

A few years earlier, in 1913, John Spargo had predicted that syndicalism would tend to "degenerate to the level of the most conservative labor unionism." In certain respects, this prediction was borne out by the ideology and activities of the ITUEL. The logic of Foster's position implied that, since unions were moving automatically toward revolution, there would be no point in fighting reactionary leaders, because these, too, would be caught up in the inevitable process. The ITUEL even laid "far less stress" than did the SLNA upon the importance of revolutionary consciousness among workers. Because unions were revolutionary by their very methodology and structure, there was no real reason to attempt to convert workers to a particular point of view. In 1937, Foster wrote that this theory was a "sag into right opportunism." At one point in his new pamphlet, he quoted Samuel Gompers on the beneficent effects of craft unionism.[63]

Foster gained the attention of the AFL president through their mutual interest in organizing a Labor Day parade in Chicago in 1916. Despite the great significance of May 1 for the Chicago labor movement and the preference of many radicals for observance of May Day, Gompers endorsed the official Labor Day, thinking it generated favorable publicity for the unions. He wrote to Foster acknowledging him as "an advocate and defender of true trade unionism," based on his reading of some of Foster's articles for the Timber Workers' journal. It is unclear whether Gompers remembered Foster's angry challenge to the AFL at the Budapest convention in 1911, but now he wrote that Foster "might render a valuable service to the toiling masses of our country to a [sic] clearer understanding of their duty as workers and trade unionists than prevails in the minds of many. Your past experiences and associations, together with your mental development should certainly prove an advantageous lesson to those who have not yet seen the true light of all that trade unionism portends."[64]

The ITUEL came into being in the middle of the industrial crisis of 1914–15, before the boom brought on by war orders and the American preparedness campaign. Although it was a period of rapidly rising living costs and "spreading discontent among workers," the AFL unions were stagnant, the IWW had declined, and the Socialist party was still suffering from its 1912 split. Thus the ITUEL, conceived as an organization that could unify the relatively secure base of militants within the AFL unions, must have seemed to Foster to have been a promising proposition. Earl Browder, speaking in March 1945 after years of acrimonious factional debates with Foster, asserted that in the 1910s, the function of Foster's small syndicalist group was to find a "few intelligent men and women here and there over the country who shared some common ideas about progress, and who had some sort of practical approach of how to bring it about and were not content with dreaming and ideals."[65] Foster had clearly traveled some ideological distance since 1910. Symbolically, when his old mentor, Hermon Titus, showed up at one CFL meeting attempting to convince workers to pledge to a general strike for the four-hour day on May 1, 1925, delegates complained impatiently that he was needlessly taking up their time.

For Foster, what was "practical" meant abandonment of active opposition to American participation in World War I. In the first months of the war he had inveighed bitterly against the conflict. In 1914 he submitted an article to the official AFL newspaper, the *American Federationist*, in which he excoriated the "patriotic attitude" of European Socialists, blaming them for failing to prevent the developing conflict. He predicted that the war would forever change the Socialist movement and predicted ominously that rank-and-file workers "will abandon the Socialist program of endless sentimental talk and will act." However, in 1916, at an ITUEL conference in Kansas City, Foster argued that the league should not take sides in the European conflict, and that American involvement was inevitable. Unionists should not have any illusions that they could prevent it. According to Foster, radicals within the unions should ignore the moral issue of the war and focus their main attention on preparing to "take advantage of war conditions to organize the workers and raise bigger and bigger demands." To cinch his argument, he recounted how he had received a letter from Pierre Monatte, in which the French syndicalist leader warned that radicals within the French labor movement had been severely weakened by its extreme antiwar attitude prior to August 1914. Foster won overwhelming support for his views from the conference. In 1919, before a Senate committee investigating the steel strike, he even admitted that he had sold Liberty Bonds at one point during the war. Although this would later be used by his opponents in the Communist party to impugn his revolutionary purity, militant trade unionists at the time evinced little willingness to expose themselves to patriotic recriminations by opposing the war.[66]

Max Dezettel, the editor of the league's organ, the *Labor News*, drifted away from the organization as he entered into alliances with corrupt unionists against John Fitzpatrick, the president of the CFL. Later Foster wrote darkly that he was finally killed in an accident in a "scab" taxicab. However, Foster claimed that the ITUEL had members in Chicago locals of the Painters, Railway Carmen, Carpenters, Machinists, Barbers, Retail Clerks, Tailors, Ladies Garment Workers, Metal Polishers, and Iron

Molders. The activities of the ITUEL generally revolved around attempts by Foster, J. W. Johnstone, and several other delegates to the CFL to gain the support of that organization for progressive causes. Foster himself worked to establish a Chicago railroad council; his models were the Chicago building council of craft unions, and the federated council of railroad crafts that had just conducted the long and violent Illinois Central–Harriman strike. On a theoretical plane, Foster's activities were consistent with Bakunin's conception of the role of the "militant minority": here the aim was to "foster the self-organization of the masses into autonomous bodies, federated from the bottom upward." Still, many workers were suspicious of the federation idea, thinking that it merely allowed the railroads to save the effort of negotiating with a number of different crafts, and that it created another layer of jobs for union officialdom. Nonetheless, in May of 1916 Foster was able to report to the CFL that his committee of federated Chicago and Northwestern craft unionists had won a large increase in wages. Following the conclusion of the Harriman strike, he reported, "every railroad now concedes the federation system of organization, the railroads falling in line and dealing with them as such."[67]

One nonwage issue that aroused the indignation and anger of labor movement activists in the late 1910s, was the imprisonment of the left-wing socialist Tom Mooney in July 1916 for the bombing of a San Francisco preparedness-day parade. Defense committees sprang up all over the nation. Most observers agreed that he was innocent of the crime; it was not until 1939 that a governor's pardon released him. For a generation of young radicals, the Mooney case was a "crisis of conscience." Many Socialists, and later Communists, could trace their active participation in the radical movement to their anger at the imprisonment of Mooney.[68]

Mooney had earlier belonged to the SNLA, and in 1913 Foster had aided Mooney in his unsuccessful agitation to turn his union, the Iron Molders, into a "militant industrial union." Now, Foster and the ITUEL were deeply involved in efforts to publicize the Mooney case and raise funds for his defense. John Fitzpatrick gave Foster the job of organizing a CFL mass meeting for the support of Mooney. An acquaintance of Foster's who had known him through Home Colony remembered that his efforts mobilized a large number of local anarchists and radicals. At the subsequent mass meeting, Foster spoke, as did William D. Haywood, Alexander Berkman, and the famous Sinn Fein rebel Jim Larkin. In March, another mass meeting was planned, this time organized by Foster's friend Jack Johnstone, and far more ambitious in scope, since it was to take place in the Chicago Coliseum. The meeting was a great success; John Fitzpatrick, president of the Chicago Federation, noted that the crowd, estimated to have been approximately seventeen thousand, was the largest for such an event in the federation's history.[69]

The ITUEL as an organization did not last beyond the spring of 1917, finally resolving itself into a small group of not more than one hundred radicals working within the Chicago Federation of Labor. Yet, by 1917 Foster and his small group of radicals had attained a certain amount of prominence and influence in the Chicago labor movement. Because of the willingness of John Fitzpatrick to encourage or at least acquiesce in his initiatives, a tremendous personal, political, and organizational opportunity arose that Foster proved adept at exploiting. A combination of social circumstances existed as well, which helped secure the acceptance and relevance of many of Foster's ideas. The complex development of the new unionism of the 1910s would eventually culminate in 1919 with the greatest wave of strikes in the nation's history.

American participation in World War I and increasing federal intervention in labor disputes were of overwhelming importance in establishing the context of labor relations in which Foster would operate after 1916. At the same time, the increasing centralization of large firms and corporations at the turn of the century created a crisis in labor management. As production became more and more complex, many businesses sought to establish rigid forms of hierarchical control that in turn inspired effective challenges by their workers. Increasingly, "as a naked and clearly visible system of power, hierarchical control revealed to the workers the oppressive nature of capitalist relations."[70] If government intervention and the ideological issues attendant on the war helped to obfuscate, to a certain extent, the nature of productive relations at the time, many workers were experiencing the exercise of capitalist power in its most transparent forms.

In certain basic respects, William Foster's temperament and outlook did not fit with the emerging complexity of the American economy in the immediate pre- and postwar periods. For him, the central feature of social relations, both as experience and theory, was the "daily warfare" of worker and capitalist on the battlefield of the wages system. This battle was direct and unmediated, of explicitly violent implications, with nothing less than personal survival depending upon the outcome. This is the Foster of *Syndicalism,* the uncompromising radical possessed of a deep and unrelenting rage against "Society." Yet, by 1917, when he was thirty-six years old, Foster had immersed himself in the activities of the progressive Chicago Federation of Labor; the trade union movement became, for him, the perfect expression of the possibility of working-class transcendence. His work in the Chicago Federation of Labor required a certain amount of circumspection and compromise, but it was a context in which his personal ambition could find expression. It may also have provided him a kind of security and community that had been otherwise lacking in his experience. Eventually, Foster's radicalism would reassert itself and cause him to sever his ties with the leaders of the Chicago Federation. In the interim, though, he set out to fulfill what he now held to be the primary duty of syndicalists in the class war: organize.

Chapter 4

LABOR ORGANIZING IN "THE JUNGLE"

IN THE YEARS after 1916 William Foster dedicated himself to a future of gradual trade union progress, which he thought would culminate in the abolition of the wages system. Although Foster's faith in the revolutionary potential of unionism was not borne out in his lifetime, it is difficult to exaggerate the extent to which employers in the last years of the 1910s perceived unions to be radically inimical to the very foundations of their enterprises. In the industries where Foster was working as an organizer in these years, meatpacking and steel, managers and owners were absolutely steadfast in their refusal to recognize the collective bargaining organizations that their workers were seeking to establish. Because employers were often unscrupulous and unyielding in their resistance to unionization, the basic issue in these organizing campaigns became, for Foster, the problem of power, and how workers, by themselves, might seize it. A few years before the beginning of the 1917 campaign to organize Chicago's packinghouse workers, he had been a member of a union delegation seeking to discuss a steamfitter's grievance with an Armour vice president. Upon being ushered into the executive's office, the workers were outraged to learn that he would only discuss the weather with them. According to Foster, the vice president finally shouted at the delegation that they should "go back to your trade union friends and tell them Organized Labor will never get anything from this company that it hasn't the power to take!"[1]

By 1917, Foster had involved himself in nearly every variety of American radicalism, from left-wing socialism to anarchism, but had finally found a niche for himself as a radical trade unionist in the Chicago Federation of Labor. His writings and activities there reveal that he had traveled some distance, intellectually, from the days of his involvement with the Industrial Workers of the World. At the beginning of the decade, he had embraced the syndicalist, antiformalistic idealism of French radicals like Griffuelhes, Pelloutier, and Monatte. At that time, what was most important for Foster was not the structure of a particular labor organization, but the extent of militancy of the workers. If there was a common theme in Foster's writings in the early years of the 1910s, it was the importance of organization, regardless of its form, and the need for revolutionary activity to begin where workers were already organized as a class.

Yet, as a syndicalist who flirted briefly with anarchism, he evinced a strong distrust and animus toward trade union bureaucrats, and believed that a strong centralized union organization would stifle the initiative of radical "militant minorities."

By 1916, Foster had embraced a kind of trade union teleology that enabled him to rationalize his work within the Chicago Federation of Labor. If trade unions are by their very morphology revolutionary or potentially revolutionary, then it is possible to work for purely trade union ends without compromising radical goals. Foster's syndicalism gradually emerged reformulated as a structuralism in which the rhetorical importance of revolution became secondary. The intellectual route from antiformalism to systematicity, however, was not as tortuous as one might expect. Foster, after all, was living in an age when the organizational imperative seemed to dominate social discourse. Early in his career, he exhibited an inclination to frame his radicalism in positivistic terms; the revolution would be brought about by recourse to "scientific" observations about society and its historical trends. Moreover, he continually portrayed his ideas as anti-"utopian," contrasting them with the tactics of the IWW and the socialism of Eugene Debs. Foster's search for a revolution that "worked" led him to posit a future society in which the great complexities of modern life might be rationally managed by technicians and experts. Finally, the Social Darwinism that crept into much of his rhetoric as a syndicalist allowed him to understand the development of "higher types" of unions as both inevitable and progressive.

Foster was growing increasingly enamored with the possibilities inherent in workers' urge for concrete forms of empowerment, and less certain of the transformative power of propaganda and "education." It is significant for a consideration of Foster's actions after 1919 that his two greatest successes in the 1910s came as a result of his abilities as an organizer, and his perception that workers must first seize and maintain organizational power before any vision of a society in which labor had a meaningful voice could be realized. In this sense, Foster's portrayal of his encounter with the Armour vice president signified an important break with his earlier syndicalism. It was perhaps the first time that he came face to face with the intransigence of corporate power and its mute functionalism. The lesson, in part, was that the crucial dialogue for workers would be between organizations, not between men and ideas.

Foster's hard pragmatism in this regard was best illustrated by his abandonment of any public or principled opposition to American involvement in the war. This was a timely adaptation, in line with both Fitzpatrick's attitude and the stance of other radicals at the time. It approximated the unofficial policy of the IWW, for instance, which was at the time minimizing its opposition to the war while attempting to establish organizational gains in the industries where it was strongest.[2]

However, the IWW, because it was widely perceived as a revolutionary movement, was mercilessly persecuted by federal and state governments after America's declaration of war in April 1917. By September, the Justice Department had launched coordinated search and seizure assaults against every major IWW local in the country. Shortly thereafter, a Chicago grand jury indicted 166 IWW members on charges that they had interfered with the war effort. In August 1918, William D. Haywood, nearly fifty years old, was sentenced to twenty years in Leavenworth prison. The incarceration of numerous other Wobblies, and later of Eugene Debs, showed how easily revolutionary movements in the United States could be disabled. It was clearly a time when prominent radicals were faced with a simple choice brutally formulated: to what extent did the survival of their organizational aims depend upon the renunciation of principle? Debs, on the one hand, spent years in prison as a result of his defense of the principle of free speech. William D. Haywood forfeited the bail raised by many of his friends when he decided to flee to the Soviet Union after his conviction in 1918. Moreover, the extent and depth of the IWW prosecutions showed that the federal government was quite willing to use its vast power to attack the entire organizational base of radicalism in America. Thus the dilemma between survival and principle was felt, perhaps more acutely, at levels far below the leadership of revolutionary organizations. It is difficult to imagine Foster, with his prejudice against the "talk" of politics, risking jail for the principle of free speech. Yet the fact that he was able during this period to fight effectively for goals he genuinely believed were revolutionary must be considered a significant achievement, even though his conception of trade union organizing was scoffed at by many radicals.[3]

By 1917 Foster had become convinced that the Chicago Federation of Labor could successfully organize the unskilled workers in the city's giant meatpacking industry. Later, he remembered beginning to contemplate this huge undertaking as he was walking to work one day in July 1917. He had proposed to Earl Browder's Workers' Educational League in Kansas City in 1915 that radical labor organizers should, during the world war, take advantage of labor shortages and escalating production in certain industries to raise greater and greater demands for labor. From Pierre Monatte, he had learned that vociferous denunciations of the Allied war effort had only served to isolate radicals from the labor movement in France. By 1917, Foster's prescience had been largely confirmed. No huge outcry against the persecution of the IWW and its leadership had developed among American workers by 1918. In meatpacking, the industry with which Foster was immediately concerned, production increased dramatically during the war years; American food, it was proposed in Chicago, would "win the war." As a result of the great demand for meat, and the manpower shortages caused by conscription, the huge numbers of unemployed who stood outside the packing concerns every morning seeking work began to diminish. Traditional sources of cheap labor were, of course, cut off as a result of the fighting in Europe.[4] Thus, the possibility of undertaking such a campaign may have seemed fairly realistic to Foster and John Fitzpatrick at the time.

Fitzpatrick, the man whom Foster had to convince of the realism of his project, was not an individual given to either quixotic daydreams or radical panaceas. Born in Ireland in 1874 and brought to America by his uncle eight years later, he began work at an early age on the killing floors at Swift and Company in the Chicago stockyards. He learned the trades of blacksmith and horseshoer, and became active in his local of the International Union of Journeyman Horseshoers, and, later, of the Blacksmiths, Drop Forgers and Helpers Union. A powerfully built man with a simple and direct manner, Fitzpatrick seemed to move easily into leadership positions in the Chicago labor movement. By 1902, he had been elected president of the Chicago Federation of Labor, an office that he ended up holding continuously, except for one term in 1908, from 1906 to 1946. Fitzpatrick participated in the 1894 strike of the American Railway Union, and thus had occasion to witness first-hand the overwhelming power of federal courts and injunctions in labor disputes, as well as the explicit boundaries of Samuel Gompers's voluntarist conception of American trade unionism. He was an ardent Irish nationalist, a friend of James Larkin. Until the 1920s, Fitzpatrick's Chicago Federation was known as a powerful center of progressive unionism, where radicals like Anton Johannsen and William Foster could be active organizationally while remaining otherwise circumspect. Fitzpatrick, like Foster, was committed at this time to the development of a more powerful unionism organized along "new lines." Both men considered industrial unionism an "evolutionary" principle.[5]

Despite Fitzpatrick's support for the meatpacking organizing campaign, it was not a foregone conclusion or inevitable by any means that unionism could succeed among Chicago's packinghouse workers. AFL unions had traditionally been unsupportive and suspicious of organizational campaigns that aimed at unionizing black workers. Despite the developing labor shortages, the packers aggressively recruited workers from new sources of unskilled labor, especially among women and southern blacks. Married immigrant women were employed in large numbers for the first time in the packinghouses during the war. Inflation and the decline of the boarding system helped to encourage women to enter the labor force in Chicago as a way of compensating for lost income. Concomitantly, the Great Migration of black workers from the South had translated into a doubling of Chicago's black population during the war years. In earlier strikes in the packing industry, especially in 1894 and 1904, the employers had aggressively recruited black strikebreakers; as a result, many unionists in Chicago considered blacks a "scab race."[6]

Moreover, the Chicago packing industry in 1917 represented a formidable array of consolidated business interests. Like many large industrial activities of the early twentieth century, meatpacking had become an oligopoly, with several large firms dominating all aspects of the business, each having expanded their concerns to include domination of the production, transportation, processing, and marketing of their product throughout the nation. At the same time, technological innovations on the shop floor continued to undercut traditional forms of workers' control over the process of production. As early as the 1890s, the perfection of the "disassembly line" and the increasing division of labor and decline of skill it entailed had begun to erode the power of the craft unions in the packing industry. During World War I, the most basic form of worker resistance, quitting, was a widespread phenomenon in the packinghouses, but this only made the task of establishing and maintaining coherent labor organizations more problematic. If, as Foster noted, the management of the packinghouse industry would only give to organized labor what organized labor had within its power to take, few observers at the time would have anticipated significant concessions on the part of the packers.[7]

For William Foster, the failure of the union impulse before 1917 was first a matter involving obsolete organizational forms, then a social difficulty attendant upon fragmentation and lack of unity within the community of workers. Later, he emphasized that from its inception, the idea behind the 1917 stockyards campaign had been that no group of workers was "unorganizable." The really important task, according to Foster, was creating an appropriate structure upon which to base the unionizing effort. It was essential, he wrote, for such a group to "organize itself rather than the packinghouse workers. Its problem was chiefly internal, not external." Because there was no such thing as an unorganizable group of workers, if a proper structure was established, "the actual bringing of the immense army of workers into the unions was bound to ensue." Foster's assumption was that if a small cadre of militant unionists, "an effective organizing force," could "organize itself" sufficiently, then workers would inevitably apprehend their own interests and join the union. Yet there was something coldly distant and manipulative about Foster's model. At first, he evinced little sympathy for the packinghouse workers themselves, and what he held to be their unwillingness or inability to organize themselves. At one point, he wrote of the "hopelessly and helplessly wretched, ignorant, starved-out and degenerate unorganized stockyards workers."[8] Foster's ideal was still that of a few stern and unyielding militants doing battle with exploitative capitalists over control of an essentially undependable workforce. However, it was certainly an intensively activist ideal: the burden for an entire social transformation rested on the abilities of a small group of activists.

Foster was quite aware of certain implacable social realities when he decided to initiate the stockyards organizing campaign, above all that of racism. The fact that Foster had witnessed routine, violent racism in the Philadelphia neighborhood where he grew up meant that he comprehended the difficult role that black laborers played in Chicago's stockyards in 1917 as well as the profound racial divisions that characterized the community. At the outset of the packinghouse organizing campaign, he seemed optimistic that blacks could be organized effectively, although by the 1920s his position in this regard would shift significantly. In 1917, his faith in unionism as the inevitable expression of workers' consciousness of their interests applied to blacks as well as whites and unskilled immigrant laborers. This faith in the power of organization allowed him to see in Chicago's packinghouse community the possibilities of solidarity and power rather than fragmentation and impotence.

Yet, as Foster noted, in 1917, African American meatpacking workers were very suspicious and distrustful of the unions. If Foster tended to minimize the importance of this legacy, it is certain that John Fitzpatrick thoroughly understood the problems that the organizing campaign faced in this regard. Apart from the memories among white stockyard workers of the strikes of 1894 and 1904, blacks in the packinghouse district had a variety of good reasons of their own for being resistant to unionization. Traditional craft union policies of exclusion or segregation proved to many blacks that the conditions to which they were exposed in the workplace and in the community could not be escaped merely through union membership. A significant number of recent migrants from the South in the packinghouse district undoubtedly had experience in unionism and collective protest as former timber and sawmill workers, dockworkers, and tenant farmers. However, many others from the rural South were unfamiliar with strikes and unions, or had perhaps migrated north in order to escape from localities where racist unions exercised job control. In Chicago, the packing concerns donated funds to African American community organizations and provided an immediate avenue of employment for recent black immigrants. Quite realistically, the "white man's union" was seen as an obstacle to economic survival.[9]

Despite the apparent difficulties that would impede any attempt to unionize the stockyards, Foster went to a meeting of the Chicago District

Council of his craft union, the Railway Carmen, and proposed an organizational campaign. After securing the endorsement of this body, Foster and a committee of the Carmen approached Local 87 of the Amalgamated Meat Cutters and Butcher Workmen and gained their approval for a resolution to be introduced at the regular meeting of the Chicago Federation of Labor. On July 15, 1917, Foster and R. T. McQuillen of the Railway Carmen (a member of the ITUEL Executive Board), with Dennis Lane and Joe O'Kane of the Butcher Workmen, proposed to the Chicago Federation that a conference be called, as soon as possible, "of representatives of all trade unions with jurisdiction over workers in the Union Stock Yards . . . for the purpose of launching and carrying on a united and vigorous campaign to bring within the protecting ranks of Organized Labor the vast army of exploited men, women and children in the meat packing industries of Chicago." After a brief speech by Foster calling for the cooperation of all trades in the meatpacking industry for the purpose of organizing the packinghouse workers, Dennis Lane of the Butcher Workmen stated that it "was about time the other trades took part in the work" of organization.[10]

The following week, the Stockyards Labor Council was formed. It consisted of representatives from a variety of trades with jurisdiction over the packinghouse workers, including the Butcher Workmen, Railway Carmen, Machinists, Electricians, Coopers, Carpenters, Office Workers, Steam Fitters, Engineers, and Firemen. The Stockyards Labor Council (SLC), however, was only proto-industrial in form. It was, as John Fitzpatrick noted, brought into existence primarily as a way of organizing the workers into the various craft unions. It did not, at first, have any power to propose wage scales or negotiate grievances; this authority remained in the hands of the international unions. Nonetheless, a great step toward unity had been taken. The SLC functioned under one executive board and one set of business agents and organizers. Although neither Foster nor Fitzpatrick could have gained support for a bona fide industrial union within the existing framework of the AFL, Foster wrote that "we infused our whole movement with the spirit of industrial unionism." According to Dennis Lane, the president of the Amalgamated, the SLC drafted a set of laws nonetheless which, if put into effect, would have overridden the authority of the affiliated international unions.[11]

Even without the enactment of such laws, the formation of the Stockyards Labor Council to direct an organizational campaign aimed at all workers in an industry as economically central as meatpacking was an unprecedented event. Foster compared the SLC with the system federations of railroad workers that had been established in the 1910s, but the tasks involved in organizing the packinghouse industry were on another order of magnitude. Moreover, the campaign was initiated only months after the United States had entered the war, at a time when the open shop was widely equated with Americanism. Employers and state militia had not hesitated to crush unionizing attempts by the IWW during the war in industries that were deemed just as vital to the war effort. Significantly, Foster again looked overseas for a concrete instance of the success of industrial unionism, for an example to illustrate the potential of a body like the SLC. In addition to the example afforded by the system federations of railway workers in the United States, he pointed to the recent successes of English transport workers, whose craft unions had been amalgamated into federations; he believed that "the power of the packing interests could be broken down in a similar way by the organization of all workers in the industry."[12]

Foster was elected secretary of the SLC, an important indication of the extent to which he had become a recognized and trusted figure in the Chicago Federation. He later remembered that at first, he, J. W. Johnstone and several former ITUEL members worked as volunteers to get the SLC started. Eventually, unnamed CFL officials prevailed upon the president of the Brotherhood of Railway Carmen to appoint Foster as a full-time organizer for a ninety-day period. According to Foster, the Amalgamated was suspicious of the SLC's endeavor from the beginning, and the CFL paid only the expenses of the first mass meeting. Eventually, an organizing corps was established that consisted of various officials and volunteers from the allied crafts, including members of the Chicago Women's Trade Union League. In August, Foster reported to a meeting of the Chicago Federation that the first session of the SLC had included delegates and representatives from nineteen separate craft unions. In September, some months after the formation of the SLC, the public phase of the organization campaign began in earnest. A mass meeting was held on Sunday, September 9, with only mixed results. It was reported that fourteen hundred individuals were present at this initial gathering; yet, when the call for joining the unions was announced, few responded. Workers were reluctant at first because of company informers in their midst, and, according to Foster, because of the "long years of AFL betrayal and incompetence" in the meatpacking industry.[13]

Nonetheless, the various business agents, delegates, and presidents of the unions affiliated with the SLC met every Monday night for four months, and gradually gains in membership were achieved. It is clear that before the SLC was organized, workers in the packing industry had become restless, mindful of the opportunities afforded by the wartime labor shortages. Several short strikes, initiated by the rank and file, occurred in 1916 and 1917; the companies responded by raising the common labor rate. By the end of 1917, this unionization impulse, together with the energetic work of the SLC activists, had resulted in some noteworthy successes. By early 1918, the extent of organization in the stockyards stood at 25 to 50 percent of the work force. Membership in the Butcher Workmen increased by twenty thousand from July 1917 to January 1918. Fitzpatrick noted with satisfaction as early as October that a number of unions had "added materially to their membership" as a result of the campaign.[14]

All involved in the packinghouse drive recognized that the single most important factor in determining its success or failure was the willingness of blacks to join the effort. J. W. Johnstone proposed in September to the CFL that some African-American packinghouse workers, despite the fact that they had no organization as yet, were voluntarily organizing meetings in response to the SLC's campaign. Yet, the resistance and suspicion among blacks remained strong. Of the approximately twenty unions affiliated with the SLC, most drew the color line quite sharply. No union was more notorious for excluding African Americans than Foster's Brotherhood of Railway Carmen, for instance. By September, rumors were spreading in Chicago that the packers were seeking a strike as a way of crushing the unionizing drive, and that the companies were recruiting a huge force of black strikebreakers from the South.[15]

The SLC secured Samuel Gompers's permission to enroll African Americans who were excluded from membership in the various allied craft unions into separate "federal" locals. At first, it was planned that black butcher workmen would be organized into the large Amalgamated locals of unskilled workers, but some African Americans protested their minority status in these unions. In response, an all-black local was established, but this device proved untenable because of accusations that the new union was a "Jim Crow" proposition. Realizing that this criticism would be fatal to the campaign, Foster and the SLC agreed that mass Butcher Workmen locals should be established on a neighborhood basis, with membership in both white and black community-based unions being theoretically interchangeable. At the time, Foster believed that African Americans should be organized into "existing unions." These workers, he noted, object to "Jim Crow" unionism and "insist, rightfully so, that if they are to come into the trade union movement they should come into it upon the basis of equality." However, in the end, the butcher workmen's unions into which blacks were organized were de facto segregated locals. The placement of African Americans belonging to the affiliated trades into "federal" unions was only a temporary expedient; when the AFL unions refused to permit blacks to transfer their membership to their respective craft locals, many dropped out of the federal organizations.[16]

Nonetheless, between July 1917 and January 1918, the Stockyards Labor Council had established a precarious unity among stockyard workers. Estimates of black membership in the SLC-created mass locals

Foster addressing a meeting of packinghouse workers, 1918.

varied, and immigrants joined the movement in uneven increments. Although Foster had envisioned an industrial-type union solidarity in the stockyards, tensions and differences existed that would ultimately help bring about the defeat of the unions. The complex structure of the SLC divided skilled packinghouse workers, who joined the Amalgamated locals, from unskilled laborers who were organized into the various community-based unions. Similarly, the neighborhood locals ended up as separate ethnic unions in practice, with women, Polish workers, and blacks in different organizations. To an overwhelming extent, the most dedicated unionists proved to be the Poles; they were the largest foreign-born group in the packinghouse labor force. Much of the SLC's success in organizing this group was attributable to the efforts of John Kikulski, a charismatic speaker who helped bring Polish workers into the unions in huge numbers. Foster reported that "a great deal of the credit for the success of the movement will be due to the energetic work of Kikulski and . . . if he had not turned out and taken the grip on the situation that he does, it is very questionable whether the campaign would have been successful."[17]

The stockyards campaign was the first time that Foster appeared as a speaker and leader before large audiences. While he was undoubtedly effective, and was able to hold the attention of his audiences, Foster was not a particularly charismatic figure. His appeal consisted in a straightforward delivery, made without artifice or embellishment, that progressed logically through each point that he established. Jeanette Pearl, a Chicago trade union activist, noted that Foster embodied a "new type of labor leadership."

> [He] does not possess the overpowering, gigantic force of a DeLeon, the emotional sweep of a Haywood, nor the great humanitarian ebullition of Debs. His power is centered on an elemental simplicity for interpretation, combined with a dynamic force for "putting it across." Foster rivets one's attention and the subject matter he presents is made so vivid, so plain and so elementally obvious, there is no need for intellectual straining and exertion. Listening to Foster, one does not feel as if in the presence of the mighty.

Pearl, writing in 1922, noted that "there is nothing overbearing in his personality," no "straining to dominate and capture control." Foster, she wrote, was a "technical expert" more than an orator or compelling intellectual. Foster himself understood his abilities in these terms. Later, he reflected that from the very beginning of his career in the labor movement he had seen himself as a "specialist" in "mass organizational work." Foster's power as a speaker was derived from his ability to frame his arguments for complex economic and organizational issues in lucid and astringent terms, coloring his rhetoric only incidently with irony or a smoldering, carefully controlled outrage. He was mostly concerned with establishing the simple logic and means of empowerment, and increasingly, because of his position as a trade unionist, he left the implications of his tactics for others to decide.[18]

Foster's self-conception mirrored that of the central personalities of the era in which he lived. It was the era of the ascendant social science specialist, especially personified by the sociologists and reformers (especially active in Chicago at the time) who found receptive audiences in expanding state and local bureaucracies as well as in the Roosevelt and Wilson administrations. At the same time, some turn-of-the century Progressives, notably Theodore Roosevelt, embraced a kind of warrior ethos that defined manhood at least in part as the quest for the kind of authenticity that only warfare could provide. Foster explicitly sought an identity as both a syndicalist "warrior" and a trade union specialist; his bureaucratic, reformist, and managerial impulses both melded and conflicted with those of the proletarian class warrior throughout his career.[19]

In spite of the disappointing immediate results of the September mass meeting, in the following months, as Foster wrote in 1918, "a living torrent poured into the unions." At a November 4 meeting of the Chicago Federation, Foster reported that the SLC had gone on record for "immediate action" in response to the organizing efforts of the previous months, and was pressing officials of the international to call a conference in Chicago. He noted that the "contagion for organization had sprung up all over the country," and that this meant that the campaign was now a "national proposition" that was effectively "out of the hands of the locals." He proposed that much of the responsibility for the success of the campaign now rested with the internationals, and that if these organizations would exert 5 percent of the energy that the Chicago campaign had exhibited, "every packing house in the country will be organized." According to Foster's autobiographical account of the campaign, he was, at this point, attempting to push the Amalgamated officials into a situation where they would eventually have to call a strike. Foster noted that the more militant SLC organizers were "proceeding on a militant strike policy," and that the workers themselves were "strike minded."[20]

As a result of growing pressure from the rank and file and Foster's group of SLC organizers, the Amalgamated convened a conference on November 11 in Omaha, where they formulated a set of demands, including union recognition, wage increases of a dollar a day, overtime pay, equal pay for women, and the eight-hour day. Subsequently, representatives of the international unions in packing met in Chicago and adopted a similar set of demands. This confident formalization of grievances, concomitantly with the growing organizational strength of the movement, helped build further momentum for the unionizing drive. At this point the Stockyards Labor Council was beginning to act like a union, pressuring the internationals to prepare and endorse a negotiating position. According to Fitzpatrick, the council had "outlined their propositions" to the international officers before the Omaha conference, even though the actual presenting of grievances was the responsibility of the international unions. A week after the formulation of demands by the Amalgamated and the internationals in Chicago, Foster told the Chicago Federation that the next move was up to the packers, and that if they "do not move in the right direction, we will have to insist on our rights." Foster noted, according to the minutes of the meeting, that "the 70,000 people working in the packing plants throughout the country for many years have had nothing to say about the conditions under which they shall work, but within the last three or four months they have been able to raise their hands and say they want something."[21]

Yet, the employers remained confident. Despite the successes of the unionizing campaign, they refused to meet with a delegation consisting of Lane, Fitzpatrick, and Foster that had been chosen to present the workers' demands. In one plant, sixty workers who were wearing union buttons were summarily discharged. Again, the Stockyards Labor Council took the initiative, deciding by unanimous vote to ask the international unions to take a strike vote. A conference of the international representatives was duly called, and a strike vote was authorized. On Thanksgiving Eve, the packinghouse workers voted overwhelmingly to give the union leadership the power to call a strike. Foster, Johnstone, and other SLC organizers were eager for a walkout, but Fitzpatrick and Lane were not. Faced with the strike dilemma, the Chicago labor leaders were apparently relieved by Samuel Gompers of the responsibility for making a final decision. According to Foster in 1918, "a telegram was sent to the officials of the A.F.L. [in Washington, D.C.] advising them" of the strike vote. In turn, the AFL immediately "notified the Department of Labor and a mediator, Fred L. Feick, appeared upon the scene." Writing in 1937, Foster recalled that "we were immediately infested with agents of the Federal Mediation Commission." Judging from the later actions of the SLC in resisting government mediation, it is indeed likely that Foster and Johnstone were adamantly opposed to the prospect of arbitration. Foster made his attitude toward mediation explicit in a contemporary account:[22] "In a number of recent Chicago strikes Government mediators have intervened, been defied and ridiculed by the employers and have had to pack their grips and depart, leaving the workers infinitely worse off than if the mediators had stayed out of the affair altogether. In such cases the workers naturally conclude that if the Government can do nothing with their autocratic employers it is useless for them to keep up the fight, and a lost strike results."

Foster's vision of the dangers of federal intervention came close to realization when Feick and his agents left Chicago, unable to bring about even a meeting between the packers and the labor representatives. Apparently, once it had been decided to attempt to secure government mediation, it was felt necessary by the unions involved to increase pressure still further through political channels. Foster himself, while distrustful of mediation, knew that a strike would have been difficult to win, given the opposition of the AFL and the leaders of the national officials of the dozen federated stockyard unions. Fitzpatrick later testified that Feick had told him after the breakdown of the first mediation effort that the packers were eager for a strike. Subsequently, representatives of the Amalgamated, the SLC, the Chicago Federation, and the various affiliated crafts traveled to Washington and ended up, through Gompers's offices, in a conference with Newton Baker, the secretary of war. As a result of this meeting, a binding arbitration agreement was signed that provided that there would be no strikes or lockouts during the period of the war, and no union recognition. Even so, the packers refused to participate meaningfully in the process, and again a committee of Chicago labor leaders went to Washington. Finally, under pressure from the Wilson administration, the packers agreed to involve themselves seriously in the arbitration process. Not the least threatening to the packers had been the prospect, widely discussed at the time, of government seizure of their plants.[23]

Thus, in the first months of 1918, the federal government emerged as the most important broker of power in Chicago's stockyards, an arena where the day-to-day relationship between the companies and their employees had generally been dictated by the brutal logic of the labor market. It is possible to see Fitzpatrick and Lane arrayed on one side of the labor equation in the developing conflict, each man acutely mindful of the history of the major strikes in Chicago in which packinghouse workers had been involved. On the other side of the equation, Foster, Johnstone and other militants sought to develop the threat of a strike, fully intending to bring about another open conflict if the packinghouse workers' grievances were not addressed. Each side, in 1918, was essential to any favorable outcome of the situation for labor. Fitzpatrick and Lane benefited from the activities of the radicals, employing the SLC's agitation and aggressive organization campaign as a way of building their organizations and pressing the packers into arbitration. Foster and Johnstone, former Wobblies, needed the cover of legitimacy afforded by their affiliation with the Chicago Federation of Labor in order realistically to pursue their own aims. Far from being atypical, this kind of syncretic arrangement was basic to much of what organized labor was able to achieve in the twentieth century. John L. Lewis, for instance, never hesitated to employ the threats of radicals as a way of pushing labor's demands at the highest levels of state and local government, and his skillful management of such threats became the basis for much of his influence outside of the labor movement.[24]

However mistrustful of government interference he may have been at first, Foster must have been pleased at the outcome of the first phase of the arbitration. The final decision by Samuel Alschuler, the arbitrator, awarded the workers the basic eight-hour day, overtime pay, and significant pay increases. A parade of witnesses at the public hearings had testified to the horrific working conditions in the stockyards. "It was as if the characters in *The Jungle,* quickened into life, had come to tell their story from the witness chair," Foster wrote. During the hearings, Foster played a significant role, helping to organize the workers' testimony and assisting with the portrayal of conditions in the yards. In 1919, during the height of the steel strike and amid accusations that Foster, the chief organizer, was a dangerous radical, Alschuler wrote that Foster's activities during the packinghouse hearings had seemed innocuous enough. During the arbitration, according to Alschuler, Foster "seemed to act as an adviser to the representatives of the employees, and was apparently relied on for the production of documents, figures and references as they were wanted in the hearing. After that award was made many questions arose, both as to interpretation and compliance, which necessitated many hearings of grievances, wherein Mr. Foster often represented the employees." Furthermore, Alschuler wrote, "In his representation of the employees in the various controversies before me in which he participated he impressed me as being particularly intelligent, honorable, moderate, tactful, and fair. His manner of presentation and his occasional apt literary references led me to inquire of others as to his early advantages, and I learned with some wonder that they were absolutely nil, and on the contrary all the very reverse of advantages."

Alschuler's statement shows how easily Foster was able, in the highly charged atmosphere of 1918–19, to restrain his more radical impulses and assume the persona of moderation. His career to this point might easily have served as an encyclopedia of American radicalisms, but by the time he was gaining a degree of prominence and success as a labor organizer, his radicalism had become even more imprecise and protean. Alschuler concluded that "if in his earlier wanderings he imbibed for a time fantastic, extreme or destructive social ideas, I am sure there was nothing developed in the many conferences and hearings in which he participated which would indicate that he still harbored them."[25]

It is possible to gain an understanding of the nature of Foster's abilities as a labor leader through an examination of his role in the conflict that erupted between workers and employers in the Union Stockyards and Transit Company—the corporation, formed by a combination of railroad and packing interests, that coordinated the arrival and distribution of cattle at the stockyards—shortly after the first Alschuler award. The managers of the company refused to sign the Alschuler agreement, so Foster, still secretary of the Stockyards Labor Council, and J. W. Johnstone, who was the improbable chairman (he was a member of a painters' local at the time) of the recently organized Livestock Handlers' Union, immediately took the fifteen hundred workers in the yards out on strike. Johnstone's organization was acting in this case as a de facto industrial union; the workers it represented included engineers, oilers, firemen, and electrical workers as well as steamfitters, tinsmiths, bricklayers, carpenters, cement workers, painters, roofers, and sewer workers. Instantly, as Foster later described it, the strike stopped the transfer of all cattle, sheep, and hogs into the stockyards, bringing the industry to a halt. Foster and Johnstone were threatened by Department of Justice officials, who claimed that the strike was harmful to the war effort.[26]

As a result of the strike, the U.S.Y. & T accepted the terms of the earlier Alschuler award, and agreed to submit the stock handlers' demands for a further wage increase and double time on Sundays and holidays to Alschuler for arbitration. William B. Wilson, the secretary of labor, had sent telegrams to the Union Stockyards Company and Foster, urging that the strike be suspended.[27] Significantly, the final agreement was negotiated between the U.S.Y. & T and the Stockyards Labor Council; the SLC was acting in this case as the bargaining agent for all of the affiliated crafts. In this whole situation, Foster and Johnstone showed that they would not hesitate to call a strike as a way of accomplishing their demands. At the level of the workplace and in the union, Foster was instinctively a radical, aggressively creating the impetus and organizational framework for strikes and job actions. Testifying at the arbitration hearings, he showed that he could master statistical minutiae and details concerning complex wage scales, as well as the history and conditions of the stock handlers' work. In the context of negotiation, Foster could argue the subtleties of contracts and work rules with the most legally sophisticated company lawyers. As a strike leader, he was capable of militant and decisive action in the defense of what he believed to be the workers' interests.

Yet, Foster remained circumspect about his aims. Near the conclusion of the arbitration hearings, he argued eloquently within the framework of traditional trade union rhetoric. Proposing that he felt personally that the concept of a "living wage" was a "disgraceful standard," he asserted that "we have just reached a point where we can demand a living wage, and we are going past that living wage standard and are going to ask for a share in the product of industry. They are already doing that in England, and we believe that we are entitled to it." However, he did not propose anything as drastic as expropriation. The time will soon come, he believed, when "we shall be recognized as partners in industry, and our standard of living will not be set to [*sic*] by competition nor by figuring out just how little we can barely live on, but it will be figured out on a basis of a partner in industry." He believed that this vision of asking for more of a share of the product of labor and "partnership" in industry would ultimately result in the destruction of the wages system. Yet in 1918 he was skillful enough to persuade his interlocutors, including Alschuler, that such demands merely encompassed the legitimate rights of labor.[28]

During the months leading up to the Alschuler decision, Foster had evidently been contemplating the initiation of an organizing campaign in the steel industry. After all, he reasoned, if the trust-dominated meatpacking industry had shown itself vulnerable to organization, then a similar campaign might be aimed at America's very largest monopolized business. Furthermore, he wrote, "I had no idea of settling down as a trade union official in the packing industry."[29] There is no doubt that Foster was an ambitious man, an individual who envisioned the possibility of leading mass national walkouts against powerful and integrated modern corporations. His avowedly internationalist perspective lent a sense of confidence to his initiation of the packinghouse and steel campaigns. Thus only a little more than a month after the first Alschuler award in the packinghouse industry, Foster proposed a resolution before a meeting of the Chicago Federation of Labor on April 7, 1918, that called upon the AFL to begin an organizing drive in the steel industry.[30]

By the summer of 1918, Foster's activities in initiating the steel campaign were taking up much of his time, and he began to turn responsibility for the Stockyards Labor Council over to J. W. Johnstone. The work of Johnstone and Foster in the stockyards campaign seemingly verified Foster's idea that mass organizational campaigns and strikes would gain vital momentum and coherence through the activities of a militant minority. Foster had gained his position as secretary of the SLC and AFL organizer as a result of his aggressive work in the Chicago Federation. The movement appeared to have little regard for established procedure or traditional conceptions of trade union "democracy." Dennis Lane, the secretary of the Amalgamated, noted that after the various packinghouse internationals had given up some of their jurisdictional rights to the Stockyards Labor Council, the "self-elected" leaders of the SLC went on to "make laws to suit themselves." He also observed that "when Foster left to take up his new duties as Secretary-Treasurer of the organization committee in the iron and steel industry . . . [he] turned the office of Secretary-Treasurer of the Stock Yards Labor Council over to 'friend Johnstone' without an election or even consulting the delegates of the council, and Johnstone has perpetuated himself in that office ever since."[31]

By 1916, Johnstone, Foster's former IWW and Syndicalist League associate, had insinuated himself into the CFL by way of the Mooney defense campaign. During the later phases of the packinghouse organizing effort, Dennis Lane reflected bitterly on Johnstone's tenuous relationship with the Chicago labor movement, and provided some insight into the tactics of the group of militants with which Foster was associated. "J. W. Johnstone blew into Chicago along with a small band of IWW's from the Northwest only a short time before the organization campaign was put on in the stock yards at Chicago. He claimed to be a member of the Painter's Union, but to this day I have never met a soul that has ever known Johnstone to do a day's work at this trade or any other trade where manual labor is required." Johnstone, according to Lane, "injected himself" into the stockyards campaign.[32]

The importance of federal intervention in the stockyard unionizing drive is illustrated by the fact that by November 1918, after the first Alschuler award, the Amalgamated had 62,857 members on its rolls, over twice the number that had been achieved as of January 1918, when the campaign was several months old. "The Alschuler award was but a dream for the workers, it meant so much to the average men and women," wrote Arthur Kampfert, a packinghouse worker who witnessed the 1917–19 organizing drive. According to Kampfert, the award "established a pattern for human decency, education and independence" for packinghouse workers. However, for Kampfert at least, it was the unions that best symbolized the aspirations of the workers. The lesson gained by the organization campaign and the subsequent improvements in the stockyards was that "you had to fight; live and die for the union." Yet, Kampfert was expressing an ambiguity that lay at the very heart of the organizing campaign. Where did the locus of power ultimately reside?[33]

The answer to this question would be determined in the postwar period, when the Alschuler administration expired. Foster, in midsummer, was optimistic about the future of unionism in the stockyards. He wrote to Frank Walsh, who had acted as the workers' attorney in the arbitration hearings, that "we are doing very well here in the Yards. The organizations maintain themselves very good, in spite of the croakers who said they would fall to pieces as soon as the excitement died out. I think the foundations of unionism have been solidly laid in the packing industry for a long time to come." At the same time, the Stockyards Labor Council was acting aggressively to extend organization into different branches of the meatpacking industry. One of the by-products of the industry was soap, and the Fairbanks Company, which made the "Gold Dust Twins" detergent, had a big plant in Chicago. In order to stave off the unionizing drive, the company fired several union activists and then attempted to establish a company union. Foster noted that an elaborate employee benefits plan was instituted that included pensions, organized sports, and improved sanitary conditions. Despite these improvements, Foster and Johnstone worked assiduously to get across the message that the workers' "only protection was in a trade union." Foster wrote to Walsh that while the company refused to meet with the SLC, "all the trades are standing together. I think we will soon bring the company to its senses." Once again, the SLC was acting as a union. It not only organized the Fairbanks workers, but presented demands and threatened to call a strike. Finally, the company was forced to negotiate a settlement with Johnstone.[34]

Despite Foster's optimism, as the war drew to a conclusion, it became increasingly evident in the packinghouses that the gains of the unions were not as solid as they appeared. The SLC and Fitzpatrick had been able to secure government intervention and mediation only under the condition that the union was not to be formally recognized as a bargaining agent for the workers, and that no preferential shop would be established. In the last months of 1918, Alschuler began to back away from the wage standards he had established during the war. On the basis of hearings held in December 1918 and January 1919, only small wage increases were granted to the unions. As the war ended, foremen in the packinghouses told workers that after the war, when the arbitration agreement expired, the packers would reestablish their ascendancy on the shop floor by dismissing those individuals who had been active in the union. Also mindful of the impending end of the wartime labor shortages, workers began to back away from the union, or, as Lane described it, "place themselves in a position where they might deny their affiliation with the union." In the declining months of the unionizing drive, according to Kampfert, rumors circulated in the plants that the "concessions granted were not through the efforts of the union, but that the government had ordered them granted."[35]

Furthermore, the unions were beset by factional maneuvering and jealousies. Lane became jealous of the SLC's power. It is noteworthy that by the summer of 1919, the Stockyards Labor Council was beginning to resemble what Foster had long warned against, a dual industrial union. By March 1919, the Stockyards Labor Council had thirty-eight "affiliated organizations" on its letterhead. These allied locals included steamfitters, laborers, office employees, stock handlers, steam engineers, structural iron workers, machinists, railway carmen, shipping clerks, and the Women's Trade Union League, in addition to locals more directly involved in the meat industry like stock handlers, hog and cattle butchers, boners, casing workers, butcher workmen, and laborers. The SLC fought with Lane's Butcher Workmen in June 1919 over the issue of whether to force a showdown with the companies on union recognition or extend the Alschuler agreement for a period of one year after the war had ended, as the packers proposed. The SLC favored a strike, but the internationals decided to pursue the more cautious policy, and the agreement was extended. The SLC leaders claimed that Lane and the officials of the internationals had signed the agreement without consulting them. Lane was determined not to allow the development of a bona fide industrial union within his jurisdiction.[36]

In a bid to reestablish his authority, in July Lane established a new council, District Council 9, as a way of countering the SLC's power in the stockyards. The locals into which the vast majority of the newly organized packinghouse workers had been enrolled by the SLC refused to join Lane's new council. The national office of the AFL stood behind its international president, Lane. Secretary-treasurer Frank Morrison of the AFL wrote to Fitzpatrick in September and demanded that Kikulski and John Riley, an effective African American organizer, cease their organizing efforts on behalf of the SLC. He asked pointedly if the SLC was indeed a branch of the Chicago Federation as it had been advertising. Lane fulminated that the jurisdiction of the SLC "was stretched to such an extent that their noses were stuck into the national affairs of our movement." Foster, of course, identified the organizational incoherence and factionalism that beset the unions in the summer of 1919 as the most important cause of the unions' eventual downfall. "The great weakness of our Chicago Stockyards Labor Council," he observed, was that "actual control of the international unions involved remained in the hands of reactionary A.F.L. officials." The introduction of a second council echoed the split in union forces that had helped bring about the failure of the 1904 strike.[37]

The split between the Amalgamated and the SLC occurred at a turbulent and vital juncture for Chicago's organized labor movement. Angered by postwar wage cuts, layoffs, and the increasing cost of living, workers throughout the city engaged in job actions and strikes. Foster's steel organizing campaign was just beginning in earnest in Gary and South Chicago. By July 1919, according to one estimate, approximately 250,000 workers in Chicago were on strike, threatening to strike, or locked out. A telegram sent on July 19 by the Chief of Staff of the U.S. Military Intelligence Division in Chicago to his superiors in Washington implied that the situation was revolutionary: "Estimated 150,000 men on strike in Chicago. Probably 200,000 or more by Wednesday morning. Russians, Poles, Lithuanians predominate. Russian radicals dominate. Situation critical." A military intelligence agent visited the IWW headquarters and heard it reported that J. A. Jones was developing various sabotage plans aimed at the meatpacking companies. Jones was a delegate to the CFL from the same Painters' Union local as Johnstone, Local No. 147. Foster noted that the ITUEL group in Chicago had made "it a special point to work with the 'educational' or sabotage committees of the locals involved" in Chicago strikes of the late 1910s. Most alarming to domestic intelligence agencies was the fact that in August and September, the American Communist and Communist Labor parties held their founding conventions in Chicago.[38]

Foster witnessed the final breakup of the stockyards organizing campaign from the perspective of his involvement in the steel unionizing drive. By the end of the summer of 1919, he must have been both saddened and alarmed by the failures of the Stockyard Labor Council, which he had played so large a role in establishing. The end of the council, after all, did not bode well for the AFL's efforts in steel, an industry where organizers had to face many of the same difficulties that packing had presented, only on a much larger scale. Other than the confusion created by the retrogressive maneuvers of Dennis Lane, what was most salient about the tragedy that unfolded in Chicago's packinghouse industry was that the problem of race helped to undermine the initiatives of the progressive unionists. While the history and etiology of the open racial conflicts that erupted in Chicago in the summer of 1919 are quite complex, the Labor Council's organizational efforts suffered as a result of the violence. Employers took advantage of racial, ethnic, and organizational divisions within the Labor Council and the Chicago Federation. Despite the best efforts of the council, racial attacks on unorganized blacks occurred in some districts. At the same time, Lane escalated his campaign to restrict the prerogatives of the SLC's organizers. By January 1920 the council was finally forced to resign from the Chicago Federation.[39]

During a subsequent investigation of the Chicago race riots, Foster acknowledged the idea that African Americans had been particularly susceptible to the blandishments of the employers. The only way that black workers could advance in the industry, according to one leaflet he cited, was to "stick in with the boss and then when there is a strike to step in and take the jobs that are left. . . ." Foster's choice of words seemed to reinforce the beliefs of conservative unionists: blacks were "constitutionally opposed to unions," he testified, "and all our forces could not break down that opposition." However, the reason for the reluctance of African Americans, he stated, was racism: "The colored man as a blood race has been oppressed for hundreds of years. The white man has enslaved him, and they don't feel confidence in the trade unions." Nonetheless, Foster remained optimistic, despite the conflicts that attended the unionizing efforts. He observed that "there is more real fraternal feeling among the black and white workers than in any other grade of society." As soon as blacks became "a factor in industry" they would come to understand the power of unionism, he thought.[40]

It is possible to see Foster's optimism as emerging from his role as a "new type" of labor organizer, one who perceived the problem of working-class unity in mostly technical terms, undeterred by the seemingly insoluble complexities and emotions of community life. At the inception of the stockyards campaign, he believed that trade unions, as purely functional entities, were the "road to freedom" for America's workers. The Stockyards Labor Council promoted the idea that the common economic interests of workers could overcome divisions of race, ethnicity, and craft; in this sense it was able temporarily to slip the bounds of AFL traditionalism. A remarkable spirit of solidarity was demonstrated by workers belonging to the SLC during the organizing effort and even at the height of Chicago's race riots in 1919. The council ended up being the primary vehicle through which thousands of workers experienced a degree of collective power for the first time.

Despite later accusations by his enemies in the Chicago Federation, Foster's "detachment" from the stockyards milieu of work and community was not as clear as it may seem. His own early life certainly predisposed him to comprehend the nature of working-class racism and the experience of cultural and economic adjustment to a large urban environment as well as any resident of Chicago's Packingtown. His anarchist "antipatriotism," so bitterly expressed only a few years earlier in his pamphlet *Syndicalism*, was distinguished from that of the IWW by his belief that radicals could act under the cover of AFL "legitimacy" in ways that might otherwise be construed as insurrectionary. This, too, was an insight consistent with the tradition of the anarchist "Chicago idea." According to Foster, the AFL had the "vital advantage" as a vehicle for radicals, because it spoke "the same language of the broad masses of workers."[41] Foster's faith in the ability of trade unions to represent the aspirations of all workers was severely tested during the campaign to organize the packinghouse industry. However, the idea of trade unionism in Foster's mind had become not unlike the idea of community, and he held to it tenaciously.

Even so, Foster's vision was tragically unfulfilled. In the end, the SLC was a structure that, despite the promise it held out to thousands of workers, proved unable to supplant the power of the packing concerns and the government, or compel or support working-class unity for very long. Part of the difficulty lay in Foster's own position as an innovative organizer in a time of transition for American unionism. Working in the SLC, he sought to harness the anger and emotions of an older-style unionism in the service of industrial unionism, a task that required that workers adopt a new language of solidarity in the face of bitter opposition by the employers. In his battles with the packing concerns, Foster exhibited something of the cool realism and peculiar reticence of his corporate adversaries, and, while articulate about the need for racial unity, he expected that organization itself would compel solidarity. Sympathetic observers understood and accepted Foster's pursuit of this activist vision.

Foster's rise to prominence in the Chicago Federation symbolized a departure from an older style of labor radicalism that drew on ideals based on the normative social relationships of small-town America. One particularly effective and vital such strain in American socialist and radical thought at the time intermingled themes of productive individualism and self-reliant personal integrity with attacks on the inhumanity of corporate methodology. Perhaps the most effective communicator of this vision was Eugene Debs, for whom the memory of the intimate social relationships of his childhood in Terre Haute, "where all were neighbors and friends," continued to animate his discourse well into the twentieth century.[42] In contrast, William Foster perceived Upton Sinclair's *The Jungle* as an accurate description of life in Chicago's Packingtown, and instinctively operated on the assumption that the city in which he lived and worked was governed by men who only understood the language of power. Foster's unusual ability to act on this basic insight would catapult him to a position of great influence in the labor movement. Soon, he would become America's most notorious labor organizer.

Chapter 5

THE GREAT STEEL STRIKE

Can it be possible that in this critical time in our
Nation's history such men as William Z. Foster are
spokesmen for the working classes of the country?
—Congressman John G. Cooper (1919)

ON AUGUST 28, 1919, William Z. Foster, in the company of Samuel
Gompers, John Fitzpatrick, and several other labor leaders, was ushered
into a palatial room in the White House for a meeting with President
Woodrow Wilson. The subject of the conference was the imminence of
economic warfare in the various towns and communities that were the
homes of America's vast steel industry, the vital heart of the nation's economic and military preponderance. When William Foster spoke during
this discussion, he did so as the person who was responsible for the day-
to-day functioning of the organization that represented one side in the
developing conflict. Despite his central role in the proceedings, those who
knew Foster must have wondered about the process that had brought him
to a conference with the president of the United States. As an anarcho-
syndicalist, he had written in 1912 that a revolutionary must be prepared
to accept martyrdom, consoling himself only with "the knowledge that he
is a terror to his enemies." Foster now arrived at the White House as a
representative of the most "legitimate" American labor organization, the
AFL.[1]

In a later age, it would be difficult to conceive that an individual with
Foster's background could gain access to such an important position in a
national labor organization. By 1961, the year of his death, radicals had
been effectively purged from such positions in the American labor movement; Foster himself was deeply implicated in the process that led to this
state of affairs. However, in the first months of 1919 he had a reputation
only as a particularly adept organizer for the Chicago Federation of
Labor. In April, a Pittsburgh newspaper had printed a story about Foster's syndicalist past, but no one had paid much attention. Thus, when
Woodrow Wilson met with Foster and other labor leaders that August,
the radical past of the secretary-treasurer of the steel organizing drive was
not yet an important public issue. According to Foster, as the discussion
with Wilson progressed, the president felt comfortable enough to speak in

colloquial English and slip into "roughneck talk" which, amazingly enough, did not "look a bit like pretense" to him. Wilson, however, was not able to give the labor leaders what they wanted, a conference to discuss their demands with Judge Elbert Gary, the "czar" of United States Steel. Despite the entreaties of Wilson's emissary, Bernard Baruch, Gary would not deign to meet with the steelworkers' committee. Within a month, upward of a quarter of a million workers were on strike.[2]

The steel strike that William Foster helped bring about in the last months of 1919 was a vitally important event in the history of American labor. Yet, while the strike itself was the largest single walkout that the nation had yet witnessed, its intensity and violence were typical of many other labor disturbances that year. Journalists and scholars typically described the unrest as "warfare." Before the end of the year, over four million workers, 22 percent of the nation's work force, had fought their employers in thousands of strikes and lockouts. Policemen and telephone workers in Boston, textile workers in Lawrence, the United Mine Workers under the leadership of John L. Lewis, and railroad shop workers in the Southwest, were some of the most significant participants in the huge strike wave. In certain respects, Foster was an incongruous figure in the maelstrom. Few would have guessed that he sought revolutionary change. Quiet and generally mild-mannered in demeanor, he struck some observers as more like a poet or university professor than a labor leader. Yet Foster had assiduously prepared himself for his role in 1919.[3]

When William Foster chose to focus his seemingly boundless energy on the development of an organizing campaign in the steel industry, he was attacking the most formidable bastion of the open shop in American business. As in meatpacking, the history of previous unionizing efforts was dismal and unencouraging. In 1892 the Amalgamated Association of Iron, Steel and Tin Workers of North America, then one of the most powerful unions within the AFL, was defeated during a bitter and violent strike at the Carnegie Steel Company's works in Homestead, Pennsylvania. The strike was deliberately provoked by Carnegie's managers, who had been confident that they could import strikebreakers, maintain production, and thus eliminate the Amalgamated from the huge Homestead Works. The success of the Carnegie company encouraged other steel manufacturers to step up their pressure against the Amalgamated. An ill-planned strike in 1901 further weakened the union. By 1909 U.S. Steel had summarily announced that all its plants would henceforward be operated on an open-shop basis. A fourteen-month strike ensued; its defeat effectively eliminated the Amalgamated as a collective bargaining agent in the steel industry.[4]

The defeat of unionism in steel in the first decade of the twentieth century was also linked to major changes that were taking place in the technology and organization of steel production. On the one hand, astonishing advances in mechanization reduced the importance of human labor and craft unions as factors of production. Increases in productivity resulted in increases in hours of labor since it was assumed that machines lessened the "hard labor" of steel production. However, workers did not see a corresponding rise in wages, and unionism was actively repressed in the plants in the traditional ways. On the other hand, management introduced company unions and a network of paternalistic benefits in order further to reinforce its hold over the workforce. A new generation of steelmasters after 1900 was generally less concerned than their predecessors had been with driving wages lower to cut costs, and the largest corporations valued "labor stability." The assumptions under which the new steel managers operated was made explicit by Elbert Gary in a speech in New York in 1911: "We have the advantage [of the workers] in education, in experience, in wealth, in many ways, and we must make it absolutely certain under all circumstances that we treat them right."[5]

William Foster's experience as a worker and radical unionist before 1918 did not encompass industries where the more sophisticated experiments in labor-management relations that surfaced in the Progressive Era were employed. As a result, his vision was in a sense limited and inappropriate to the new world of industrial labor that emerged after the First World War. As a young man, he had understood work as a direct and unmediated exploitation of labor by capital. In his job as a railroad car inspector in the 1910s he had witnessed the introduction of piece rates in the shop crafts and the destruction of the lives of workers who had little protection in the workplace. Before 1918, he had no experience with company unions, "welfare capitalism," or government mediation of labor disputes. "Slavery" was a recurring metaphor in his descriptions of workingmen's lives. "Industrial democracy," the shibboleth of labor relations in the early 1920s, would have been an incomprehensible term for him; even in Foster's vision of the postrevolutionary society such a conception was deeply problematic. He had abandoned his efforts to organize Chicago's meatpacking workers before the full implications of the mediation efforts of the federal government had been realized. As a syndicalist, Foster was most comfortable in the context of direct conflict between organized workers and their employers. During the 1918–19 organizing campaign in the steel industry, he was forced to confront a far more complex reality. Here, the battle would be fought as much on the ground of politics and ideology as of organization.

As in the packing industry, in steel the intervention of the federal government in labor relations during World War I presented an opportunity to unionists. Even before the United States entered the war, workers had engaged in violent strikes in Youngstown, Braddock, and Pittsburgh.

Taking advantage of the wartime labor shortages, the Amalgamated began to register some gains in membership, especially in the finishing plants where the more highly skilled workers were employed. However, despite the labor shortages, the larger plants were still mostly unorganized by the summer of 1918. The steel companies unilaterally raised the common wage rate during the war, and the factories were inundated with propaganda that equated unhindered steel production with patriotism, citizenship, and the fight for democracy abroad. Ultimately, however, the federal government began to restrict the prerogatives that the steel managers enjoyed with respect to their workers. The National War Labor Board, under the co-chairmanship of William Howard Taft and Felix Frankfurter, intervened in a labor dispute at the Bethlehem Steel Company in July 1918. Much to the dismay of men like Elbert Gary, who had enjoyed essentially untrammeled authority in the sphere of relations with his employees, the NWLB forced the companies to meet with committees of their employees and ultimately pressured them into the adoption of the eight-hour day.[6]

In this context of increasing federal intervention William Foster took the first steps to initiate the steel organizing campaign in 1918. In April, as the position of the Allies in Europe worsened and American troops were being rushed to the battlefront, Foster and sixteen other delegates from various unions introduced a resolution before the CFL that began with the declaration that "the organization of the vast armies of wage earners employed in the steel industries is vitally necessary to the further spread of democracy in America." Speaking for the resolution, Foster noted that while any attempt to organize the half-million workers in the steel industry could not be undertaken lightly, until the job was done, "organized labor would never be safe from any attacks that might be launched against it." Moreover, while he had been told repeatedly that the task was an impossible one, he, for one, refused to allow himself to be placed in any such frame of mind. Foster's proposal was given an important boost, though, when several days after this resolution was passed, Frank Morrison, secretary-treasurer of the AFL, sent John Fitzpatrick a letter that included an optimistic report from an organizer in Gary. Morrison asked "whether or not you believe the time is ripe to move on Gary for the purpose of organizing the steel workers." Gompers referred the CFL steel resolution to the May convention of the Amalgamated Association, which lent the proposal its endorsement.[7]

Next, Foster concentrated on his campaign to be elected as a delegate to the upcoming AFL convention in St. Paul. He perceived the proposed steel campaign as a personal initiative, and in addition, the job of AFL delegate was a prestigious one, providing an opportunity for an ambitious trade unionist to make contacts at the level of the national officialdom. Taking advantage of the prestige he had attained as Secretary of the Stockyards Labor Council, Foster was elected unanimously to the job of delegate.[8] The AFL convention in St. Paul convened in June of 1918, more than a year before the tragic Chicago race riots that marked the dissolution of the SLC. At the convention, Foster was undoubtedly struck by the irony of his position as delegate from the largest central labor body in the nation. Six years before, he had been a subject of ridicule when James Duncan recounted the role Foster had played as an IWW delegate to the International Secretariat in Budapest. In 1918, he arrived in St. Paul as an individual who was widely credited with being responsible for one of the largest and most successful organizing campaigns in AFL history. It is easy to imagine, however, that as Foster mingled among the crowds of delegates he was not entirely comfortable. He was not an individual who was given to back-slapping camaraderie or easy sociability. Moreover, his feelings about his new status may have been quite ambivalent; he had embraced a theory that saw trade unionism as inevitably progressive, but temperamentally he was still a radical, retaining a certain Wobbly disdain for the union officialdom upon whom he depended for the furtherance of his aims.

Foster's immediate task was to introduce a resolution calling for a steel organizing campaign. This being duly referred to the committee on organization, he turned his attention to convincing delegates from the steel industry unions to attend preliminary meetings. Later, Foster wrote that he felt that the campaign was being sabotaged by Gompers from the start. However, in a letter written during the St. Paul convention to Fitzpatrick, who had remained in Chicago, he noted that he had received a "very friendly greeting" from Gompers, and that the AFL president had "held up the whole proceedings to inquire a minute as to how we are progressing in the Stockyard[s]." After the resolution was passed, Foster convinced Gompers to call a meeting of delegates from the steel industry unions, but Gompers did not attend, and scheduled it during a lunch recess, "an almost fatally inopportune time." Undeterred, Foster took down names, scheduled a further meeting, and convinced Gompers to preside. At this conference the AFL president declared, according to Foster, that the AFL was prepared to "go down the line on the proposition." Yet during the meeting the wily Gompers made a deft but unmistakable reference to Foster's background, warning of the dangers of the movement being "turned over to any other than legitimate trade union ends." Morrison, who also attended, seemed enthusiastically in favor of the campaign, and assured the delegates that he would do his utmost to guarantee its success. Many of the delegates must have been skeptical at first that the AFL would be willing to risk its resources and prestige on a unionizing effort in an industry as powerful as steel. However, the example of the successful packinghouse drive was a significant factor in the minds of the union officials. Foster reported to a CFL meeting upon returning from the convention that much of the enthusiasm for the proposed steel drive came from the knowledge of what had been accomplished in packing. Thus, in St. Paul, it was agreed that within thirty days a conference of international presidents or their representatives would be held for the purpose of formally launching the campaign.[9]

As Foster pointed out in retrospect, it was quite important for this conference to convene as soon as possible, since the success of the organizing drive was dependent to a certain extent on the course of the war in Europe. Putting off the conference of international presidents, he wrote in 1920, "involved further waste of probably the most precious time for organizing work that Labor will ever have." In June of 1918, though, he was more sanguine. The response he received to his proposals in St. Paul, he wrote to John Fitzpatrick, "far exceeded my expectations. I honestly believe a big movement has been set on foot to organize the steel industry." To Fitzpatrick, whom he was attempting to persuade to become the national chairman of the organizing drive, he averred that "as Sam Gompers has said the stockyards movement has blazed the way and shown labor how to organize the basic industries. In this big movement everybody is looking to us in Chicago to take the lead." By this time, it was clear that Foster himself had taken a very large role in developing the campaign. At the very first conference of the steel organizing committee in St. Paul, he was elected temporary secretary; at the second his position was made permanent. Gompers lent his verbal support to the initial efforts, but Foster had to hustle to generate support among the officials of the internationals. Even Fitzpatrick's support seemed tenuous. Foster evidently had expected the CFL president to attend the St. Paul convention to help him "handle the heavyweights and get them interested," but he never showed up, despite repeated telegrams from Foster urging him to do so. Fitzpatrick was, at this point, immersed in efforts to organize a labor party in Chicago.[10]

At a conference in Chicago on August 1, the National Committee for Organizing Iron and Steel Workers was formally established. The committee consisted of representatives of fifteen national craft unions; as in the packinghouse campaign, it was agreed that while the organizing effort would be a joint one, each particular craft union would maintain jurisdiction over a particular segment of the workers. The Amalgamated had potentially the most to gain; it claimed jurisdiction over the majority of unskilled workers in the steelmaking and finishing plants. The National Committee was an entirely voluntarist entity; theoretically, it had no authority over its constituent unions. In utilizing a uniform initiation fee and application blank, the committee consciously imitated the AFL Railway Employees Department. Foster, the secretary-treasurer, was put in charge of the committee's organizing work with the caveat that his policies must be approved by the chairman. Yet, while Gompers was chairman in name, he participated very little in the committee's deliberations; Fitzpatrick had assumed the "temporary" chairmanship by the time the body met again in mid-August. Although he ended up playing a public role in the organizing campaign, Fitzpatrick, according to Foster, took no actual part in it for six months after it had begun.[11]

Although the steel organizing drive was quite traditional in its careful attention to craft union jurisdictions and autonomy, as Foster proudly remembered, this group of unions represented the "largest body of workers ever engaged in a joint movement in any country"—approximately one-half the membership of the entire American Federation of Labor. This fact showed quite clearly how important the campaign would be, for the defeat of the committee's initiatives would represent a setback for quite a large segment of the organized labor movement in America. Despite the huge stakes, certain decisions were made at the outset of the campaign that did not bode well for its success. Foster wrote to Frank Morrison that he planned a "lightning," simultaneous campaign on a national basis.

> As soon as the workers begin to respond by joining unions, we should knock on the doors of the Steel Trust and demand a national settlement. My experiences in the packing industry convince me that such an action on our part would tend to bring the workers into the union in great numbers. And very shortly the Steel Trust will be confronted with the alternative of giving us some consideration, facing a far-reaching strike, or submitting to government compulsion.

Unfortunately, at first Foster was able to extract only $100 from each international to finance the activities of the committee. The limited funds that were appropriated meant that the committee would instead have to focus on one district at first. In mid-September, he declared to Morrison that the committee's finances "were entirely inadequate to the tremendous task" that lay ahead, and an alternative method of fund raising was devised. By the end of 1918, only a little more than $6,000 had been raised for the purpose of organizing the entire steel industry. By then, precious time had been lost. Foster and others perceived that the success of the steel venture depended upon American participation in the war; by late September the Germans were retreating and an Allied victory seemed imminent.[12]

In August and September 1918, however, the success of unionization in the Chicago area, where the committee chose to focus its initial efforts, had little to do with such distant events. Here, social and economic conditions at the level of workplace and community had aggravated a whole range of grievances against the management of the giant steel mills. Gary, the city on the banks of Lake Michigan that had been conceived and built by the United States Steel Corporation, saw some of the unionists' first successes. When the city was founded in 1906, U.S. Steel had consciously sought to avoid the heavy-handed paternalism that had resulted in labor strife at nearby Pullman, Illinois. However, even though the corporation did not at first plan to involve itself overtly in local civic and business affairs, it and its subsidiary development corporation, the Gary Land Company, ended up collecting rents from the many immigrant and un-skilled workers who lived in the houses that were erected for them. Widely divergent building patterns and the desire of U.S. Steel to extract the maximum value from its housing in the form of high rents helped create dismal slum districts. The organization of work and community by the ascendant steel managers tended to reinforce divisions of skill and ethnicity among Gary's working class. In addition, World War I provided an ideological context wherein the distinction between Americans and immigrant "Hunkies" whose loyalty was suspect could be drawn more explicitly. An atmosphere of intolerance and chauvinism pervaded Gary before the unionizing efforts began to take hold.[13]

At the very outset of the steel organizing campaign in Gary, the city's newspapers and public officials portrayed organizers and unionists as in-dividuals whose "citizenship" was at best ambiguous. U.S. Steel's origi-nal vision of a thriving community of secure, homeowning families did not materialize in the first decades of the twentieth century, and Gary's elite had seemed nervous about the loyalty of its immigrant work force during World War I. In 1920, 60 percent of Gary's population consisted of immigrants or their children; blacks comprised another 10 percent. When the organizing campaign in Gary began to meet with success, an effort was made to equate the appeals of the unionists with un-American subversion. Yet, very few of the immigrant workers in Gary were Social-ists or radicals, and their grievances had mostly to do with wages, hours, and working conditions. As late as the 1920s, approximately 80 percent of Gary's steel workers were on twelve-hour shifts, seven days a week. Wages were often barely adequate to support a family. As in most steel towns, wages had risen uniformly during the war, but inflation had effec-tively negated gains in real income for most workers.[14]

In Gary, as well as at South Chicago, Joliet, and Indiana Harbor, or-ganizers reported in September that great progress was being made in signing up members, even though in Gary, U.S. Steel had discharged sev-eral workers who had affiliated with the campaign. Other than these dis-missals, U.S. Steel in Gary did not make a concerted effort to counter the first efforts of the unionizing campaign. Foster himself reported triumphantly to Morrison that "in this district the spirit of unionism is raging through the mills." In Gary, "many thousands, in every department of the steel mills, are lining up in the organizations." At the first organizing meeting on September 9 the crowd was so large it blocked all surrounding streets. By February 1919, an organizer was able to claim that the steel plants there were "at least 75% organized." David Saposs, a close follower of the strike, conjectured later that U.S. Steel itself did not actively oppose organization of its workers in Gary, knowing that it was sufficiently entrenched in Pittsburgh to prevent the unions from gaining an effective foothold. In any event, the successes of the first organizing efforts in Gary and in the Chicago area inspired the committee to create a "Chicago District," appoint a secretary, and move their efforts to Pittsburgh, the real heart of the steel industry. Despite their successes, Foster understood that the committee's accomplishments remained tenuous so long as they confined their efforts to Gary. He pleaded with Gompers for more money and organizers—the committee was "still sadly lacking in both," he wrote—in order to establish a truly national campaign.[15]

Foster described Pittsburgh and the constellation of steel communities surrounding it, where approximately 70 percent of the country's steel industry was concentrated, as an "amazing and bewildering network of gigantic steel mills, blast furnaces and fabricating shops." Theodore Dreiser, who worked as a reporter for the Pittsburgh *Dispatch* shortly after the Homestead strike, remembered that the city, "in spite of the wealth which it has created for certain individuals," is "almost always in trouble. If it is not a steel strike it is a [railroad] car famine, and if it is not a car famine it is a society scandal, which is almost as bad. . . . Poverty, filth, wretched laboring conditions on one hand, and, set over against this, great wealth and great display." While the technology and profitability of steelmaking undoubtedly improved since the 1892 strike, according to Dreiser the community still wore the visage of defeat. Many steelworkers in 1919 maintained vivid memories of the demoralizing failures unionism had suffered in previous decades.[16]

Perhaps no other American city provided as clear an illustration of the transformation that industrialism had wrought in working-class communities by 1919. During an 1877 strike against the Pennsylvania Railroad, striking trainmen in Pittsburgh generated wide support in the city for their grievances. Miners and ironworkers struck in sympathy with the railroad employees, and as in the violent Philadelphia street railway strike in which Foster participated as a young man in 1895, newspapers and local officials expressed an understanding of the complaints of workingmen against corporate "monopoly." However, by 1919, the development of the steel industry had entailed a new set of social relations in the city. One of Foster's central insights, derived from a decade of involvement in conflicts arising from the "new unionism," was that a strong impulse toward workers' control could arise within the context of active craft traditions. However, in Pittsburgh, the steelmasters had long since understood this truth, and had acted decisively to constrict the influence and power of skilled workingmen in their factories. The reorganization of work, in turn, resulted in drastic changes in the community.[17]

The relentless erosion of the culture of the craft worker in Pittsburgh and the arrival of thousands of immigrant laborers to man the new steel mills helped to undermine the kind of community-wide consensus that had characterized reaction to the 1877 labor unrest. The expansion of industrial capitalism in the city, according to one historian, took workers from different backgrounds and "molded them not into a unified working class but into a segmented mass with deep fissures running along occupational, neighborhood, racial, and cultural lines." In a milieu of increasing fragmentation, U.S. Steel came to exercise more and more influence in the social life of Pittsburgh. The corporation pursued a bifurcated strategy for maintaining its ascendancy. As it sought to achieve unmediated and direct authority in the workplace, the steel industry invested heavily in the social and cultural life of the city. Accordingly, its status in the wider community grew; by 1919, the workers had lost many of their allies in the steel towns. Yet, resistance to the imperatives of the companies remained, however altered in form and extensiveness. Strikes continued to upset the new equilibrium. The McKees Rock strike of 1909 was in some ways a prolegomenon to the 1919 strike, showing that "Hunkies" and immigrants could not be dismissed as unorganizable. Moreover, the city's laborers contended for political citizenship while evincing dissatisfaction with the industrial order in which they were immersed. Immigrant workers in 1912 voted heavily for Eugene Debs, and began to make their political influence felt in Pittsburgh. In certain respects, the fact that the new ethnic working class increasingly sought to participate as full citizens in the new Pittsburgh generated even more enmity and fearfulness among the city's elites. Thus, when Foster moved the offices of the steel committee to Pittsburgh, hoping to bring the city's unskilled immigrant steelworkers into the AFL, he was entering hostile territory. Floyd Dell wrote in the radical monthly *The Liberator* that "Pittsburgh does not represent ordinary capitalism, the capitalism that bickers and dickers with organized labor. Pittsburgh is capitalism militant—capitalism armed to the teeth and carrying a chip on its shoulder."[18]

As expected, in Pittsburgh and in the nearby mill towns along the Monongahela River, Foster's committee met with immediate opposition. Most notably, the mayors and city officials of the towns surrounding Pittsburgh refused to allow public meetings to convene. The inability of organizers to secure permits to speak, as well as the harassment, beatings, and arrests of the committee's representatives is a continually recurring theme in Foster's descriptions of the strike and the organizing drive. As a former Wobbly who had experience in free speech fights, Foster was familiar with the problems that radicals confronted in securing a platform for their views. To employers and civil authorities, however, the IWW had always represented a revolutionary organization, and had been treated as such. In 1918, Foster and his organizers represented the AFL, the putative "legitimate" voice of American workers. After all, Gompers had served for years on the National Civic Federation, and signs of AFL power were quite evident in Washington in 1919. William B. Wilson, the secretary of labor, was a former Mine Workers' official, and the administration had applied pressure on the meatpackers in 1918 in favor of the employees. Yet, following the Armistice, the balance of power in the steel industry began to return to the employers, as the War Labor Board's statutory authority expired. In December, Frank Walsh, the joint chairman of the WLB, described it as "a disappointing mirage to the working people of the country" in a letter to John Fitzpatrick. Walsh believed that "the employers, by some sort of agreement are holding things back."[19]

Foster was encountering resistance from other quarters as well. He wrote to Gompers pleading for a meeting of the AFL Executive Council in Pittsburgh to "reestablish right of assembly in western Pennsylvania." If such a conference failed to materialize, "the present campaign to organize the iron and steel workers will almost certainly fail, so great is the need." For the campaign to lose its hard-won gains would be "one of the worst defeats in the history of trade unionism in this country." Citing the fact that a total of only $6,000 had been raised in contributions by the internationals, and that besides the organizers delegated by the internationals only one AFL organizer was working full time on the campaign, Foster complained pointedly that "since its inception, the National Committee has lacked the backing necessary to the accomplishment of its great task in hand. It has been neglected and starved, with the present urgent results." If the committee had been able to pursue its plan for a national, simultaneous campaign, unionism "would now be entrenched in the steel industry beyond all hope of dislodgement." He made a personal appeal to Gompers: "I am convinced that there is but one man in the Labor Movement who is equal to our emergency, and that is yourself." Despite Foster's plea, Gompers refused to risk the prestige he had accumulated during the war by entering into a quarrel with Pennsylvania politicians; he probably believed that in any event he could have had little influence over the situation in the steel towns. He wrote a letter to the mayor of McKeesport, but the proposed conference never materialized.[20]

The committee also felt that Eugene Debs was resisting the movement they had created. In appearances in the vital Youngstown district, Debs

complained about the limitations of AFL-style unionism, severely criticizing the plan of organizing into separate crafts. Foster and two others went
to meet with Debs, bearing a letter signed by twenty-four organizers exco-
riating him for his "reckless" statements. There is no surviving record of
this first meeting between the two labor leaders, but Foster harbored a
deep-seated distrust of Debs. Writing in 1914, he had ridiculed Debs's
"well-known" failures as a union organizer and his "scientific socialist"
attitude toward the AFL. Now, the caustic letter from the National Committee carried Foster's unmistakable imprint: "What in fact, is this movement, with its broad-sweeping scope and solidarity, its low initiation fees
and urgent appeal to the common laborer, but the embodiment of many
ideas long advocated by yourself, stripped of their utopianism and rendered practical?" Debs, after being confronted with the letter, toned
down his attacks, but he could not be induced to lend his prestige to the
organizing campaign. When the strike finally erupted, he sent the committee a message of support from the Atlanta Penitentiary.[21]

As early as November 1918, the committee concluded that a fight for
free speech would be quite vital to the success of their efforts. It was
agreed that "drastic action must be taken to establish the right of assembly in Pittsburgh, or no hope of success could be expected in this campaign." In the Pittsburgh district, officials in Braddock, Homestead,
Rankin, and McKeesport refused to permit meetings and pressured the
owners of halls not to accommodate organizers. Moreover, according to
the committee, the Pittsburgh press was carrying out a "conspiracy of
silence" against the organizing campaign.[22] It was not until May that
organizers were able to convene their first street meetings in McKeesport
without interference. But in mid-June the Mayor issued a summary decree
prohibiting street meetings, and threatening any violators with arrest.
The National Committee decided to force the Mayor to throw organizers
and street-corner speakers in jail. Confronted with this opposition, and
the fact that the organizers were holding large meetings on the street, the
Mayor relented and allowed the use of a hall. In July, a speaking permit
was formally issued that provided that meetings be "subject to police
regulation" (approval of speakers in advance), and that "no speaker shall
talk in any other languages, except the English Language."[23]

Elsewhere in the Pittsburgh district, the story was the same. The campaign seemed to precipitate a clear delineation: the steel companies and
the civil authorities stood arrayed against the unionists and their supporters. At Homestead, J. G. Brown, for whom Foster had worked as a timberworkers' organizer in Seattle, was told point-blank by the burgess that
he would not be able to hold meetings there, nor advertise in the newspaper, nor pass out leaflets. Finally, "flying squadrons" of organizers went
into the steel towns around Pittsburgh, determined to hold meetings re-

gardless of the opposition of local magistrates. Speakers included Foster, "Mother" Mary Harris Jones, James Mauer of the Pennsylvania Federation of Labor, and Philip Murray, then President of United Mine Workers District 5. Foster himself was arrested in Duquesne, Homestead, and North Clairton.[24] The free speech tactic worked in most places, but there was a tremendous cost. Organizers, despite arrests and beatings, were able to hold large meetings throughout the Pittsburgh district, in McKeesport, Homestead, Donora, and Duquesne. However, when meetings were held, company officials and private detectives often stood outside the doors, intimidating workers and threatening them with the loss of their jobs. Walking through "pickets of bosses" to attend organizing meetings at towns like McKeesport, workers "joined the organization at the peril of their economic lives," Foster told the Interchurch World Commission. Around Pittsburgh, "the influence of the Steel Corporation is so great that it's almost like sticking your head into the lion's mouth to undertake a meeting like that."[25]

By early summer the organizing drive had exacerbated tensions in the mill towns to the point of explosion. Foster wrote to Frank Walsh of the War Labor Board that in Johnstown, the Cambria Steel Company was "using every stratagem to brand this a bolshevik, hence an illegal, movement." He and a local organizer were arrested in July for holding a meeting in defiance of the authorities.[26] Thousands of newly recruited union members in Johnstown and elsewhere sought immediate action; unauthorized strikes threatened to break out before the movement was strong enough to sustain a coordinated national walkout. In Gary, organizers were having difficulty holding their men on the job, according to one investigator, partly because the IWW was propagandizing heavily among the workers. In response to this pressure, Foster proposed in April that a "general conference" of union delegates be held in Pittsburgh. This tactic, which was used so successfully during the stockyards organizing drive, was a favorite of Foster's; he would employ it often during his career in the Communist party.[27]

In the spring of 1919, however, Foster proposed before the steel workers committee that a conference of rank-and-file delegates from newly organized steel locals would "speed up the work of organization." By formulating demands and grievances, such a conference would have the effect of giving the newly organized workers "something tangible to look forward to." At the same time, it would "pacify" restless workers who threatened to disrupt the national movement by going out in uncoordinated local strikes. Even so, everyone present knew that calling a conference was a potentially dangerous step; once a set of demands was publicized, the pressure would be on the union to present the grievances to the employers. A number of delegates from the participating internationals warned against such a conference. Several cautioned against "anything that would tend to make the movement go off half-cocked." It was feared that restless workers might "get . . . started into action that might catch us unprepared."[28]

Nevertheless, the committee voted in favor of a conference. When 583 rank-and-file delegates convened in Pittsburgh the following month, most came with the idea that they would be in a position to take "decisive action." The workers, however, were quickly disabused of this notion by the few international officers present who, in the words of David Saposs, "took it upon themselves to guard the powers of the Internationals." Michael Tighe, the president of the Amalgamated, "warned the conference of the danger of usurping powers not properly belonging to it." Quite pointedly, he read a letter to the gathering that he had written "along these lines" to Foster. Clearly, the conference would not be permitted to call a strike, or even recommend one. By the spring of 1919, the experience of Dennis Lane's Butcher Workmen with the Stockyards Labor Council was undoubtedly a factor in Tighe's thinking. However, the Pittsburgh conference did take several important steps that pressured the steel workers' committee and the internationals in new ways. First, demands were stated, but not yet formalized, in numerous resolutions. The eight-hour day with double time for overtime and holidays, minimum wage scales, and protection against arbitrary dismissal were among the grievances represented in these resolutions. In addition, proposals were submitted for a universal transfer card, as well as a broadened iron and steelworkers' department that would formalize the *ad hoc* structure of the National Committee. Both proposals were referred to the forthcoming convention of the AFL in Atlantic City. There, the ideas were shelved. Most important, though, were proposals for a universal transfer card and an iron- and steelworkers' department, both of which would begin to infringe upon or blur craft jurisdictions in the steel industry.[29]

In his later writings, Foster focused on the "sabotage" on the steel organizing campaign by AFL officials. It is true that the top leaders of the AFL trades involved only rarely participated in the deliberations of the National Committee. This, however, may have worked to Foster's advantage. Without high officials present, it was probably easier for him to push through votes and resolutions to pressure the internationals into action. Even so, few AFL officials of any importance spoke in Pennsylvania during the important free speech struggles. Gompers himself never delivered a speech in the organizing districts, preferring to remain in Washington much of the time. At a crucial juncture in the campaign, in the weeks before the Pittsburgh conference, the Amalgamated sought a separate understanding with U.S. Steel. This move openly threatened the existence of the larger movement, and probably served to underline its weakness to Elbert Gary. During the organizing campaign, representatives of the internationals on the National Committee complained that their presidents were reneging on promised financial aid, were not delegating enough organizers, and were themselves not showing enough interest. Although Foster in retrospect believed that there was a conscious effort by AFL officials to undermine the campaign, the internationals were also justifiably cautious about committing many resources to an effort that had failed so disastrously in the past.[30]

Moreover, in April, an important article had appeared in *The Nation* that probably alarmed high AFL officials. The author, George P. West, proposed that the progressive unionists in Chicago, under the leadership of John Fitzpatrick, were seeking to undermine the Gompers regime. Citing the steel and packing campaigns, West proposed that "today the most important industrial movements, or economic movements, as Mr. Gompers calls them, are entirely out of the hands of Mr. Gompers and his lieutenants." Instead, "they are in the hands of John Fitzpatrick and his associates of the Chicago Federation of Labor." Although Gompers had given his perfunctory support to the steel drive, it "is the most important enterprise undertaken by organized labor in the industrial field in a generation. Yet officials of the Federation not only did not initiate it, but they had to be dragooned into giving it aggressive support." West, apparently, had arrived at this perspective while loitering in the committee's Pittsburgh office, and through conversations with Foster. His article, according to Foster, "created consternation in our ranks." Gompers demanded a refutation. In response, Fitzpatrick wrote a reply to *The Nation*, in which he lauded Gompers and gave him credit for the success of the packinghouse drive and the initiative behind the steel campaign. Fitzpatrick's rejoinder to the West article was reprinted in the *Chicago Labor News*. However, the question of Fitzpatrick's and Foster's aims had been raised quite publicly.[31]

Thus, at the Pittsburgh conference, little could be done, given the limitations imposed upon it, than appeal for negotiations with the steel companies. Yet, most present, including Foster, anticipated that the steel industries would never consent to meet with the committee. After all, that would be tantamount to union recognition. Six weeks earlier, Gary had refused to meet with representatives of the Amalgamated who, acting on their own, had requested a separate conference. "As you know," Gary wrote, "we do not confer, negotiate with, or combat labor unions as such. We stand for the open shop." Thus Foster, by calling a conference of the discontented steel workers, had maneuvered the committee into a position where it had to begin considering a strike.[32]

Realizing that the Pittsburgh conference had accomplished very little in the way of addressing their demands, many recently organized steelworkers began to lose faith in the committee, and it became evident that "immediate action" had to be taken in order to maintain the allegiance of the rank and file. By July, Foster was pushing for the taking of a strike vote; he reported that "some action must be taken that will secure relief. All over the entire steel district the men are in a state of great unrest." He confronted the committee with a letter from Samuel Gompers that indicated that efforts to arrange a conference between Elbert Gary and the steel committee had been unsuccessful.[33] The committee, faced with Gary's refusal and the desire, continually reiterated by Foster, of the rank and file for immediate action, resolved to ask the internationals to take a strike vote. Fitzpatrick was in favor of pressing ahead, thinking that a strike vote would impel the government to intervene. However, two crucial unions, the Amalgamated and the UMW, voted against Foster's proposal. Despite this breach, the other affiliated unions voted to go ahead; the final vote was twelve to two in favor—not unanimous, as Foster later reported. A list of twelve demands was presented, which included the right of collective bargaining, reduction of hours, standardized wage scales, and abolition of company unions.[34]

As Foster had likely anticipated, the decision to go ahead with the strike vote, as well as the formalization of the steelworkers' demands, gave the organizing campaign an important boost. Again, he knew from his experience with the stockyards campaign that such an action would help bring workers into the unions. Two days after the decision of the National Committee, he met with Tighe and Davis of the Amalgamated. "They stated frankly that they would do the best they can to make the move a success and would go along with it all the way. They showed a very good spirit," Foster told John Fitzpatrick. By this time, the Amalgamated was not really in a position to resist. After the humiliating rebuff of their independent overture to Judge Gary, and given the overwhelming vote of the National Committee to canvass the workers on the question of striking, Tighe and Davis had to at least appear to go along with the national movement. A little over a week later, as workers surged into the unions in anticipation of the strike vote, the officers of the Amalgamated were even more enthusiastic. To Fitzpatrick, Foster reported that "the campaign is going along like a house afire now." In Monessen, six hundred workers signed up in the space of two days, and in McKeesport, the committee was in the process of distributing one thousand applications to the respective craft unions. Most importantly, according to Foster, the Amalgamated was "going along fine with the strike vote proposition." He had had a "long talk with Mike Tighe and he takes a very friendly attitude towards me." The Amalgamated had one important reason to support the idea of a strike vote: it promised to boost membership. Between August 1, 1918, and December 1920, the union would sign up seventy thousand members. Thus, Foster was encouraged in late July, as the unions were taking the vote. "I think there will be good cooperation all along the line in this big move," he told Fitzpatrick. "From all indications at this end of the line, I think we have the steel companies on the hip."[35]

The response to the strike vote was overwhelming; upward of 90 percent voted in favor of authorizing their internationals to call a strike. However, the committee itself did not have the authority to call a strike or set a date; this power still rested in the hands of the internationals. Again, Foster took the initiative. On September 4, he called a "special meeting" of the committee, where he outlined the increasingly vigorous steps the steel companies were taking to interfere with the organizing effort. He reported that it was necessary that "some measures" be considered "to protect our men and to defend their rights." In late August, Fitzpatrick, Foster, and Davis had called on Gary at his offices in New York; their overtures for a conference were summarily rejected. This is what led to the futile appeal to Woodrow Wilson in the White House on August 28.

Thus, at the "special" meeting of the committee, "the advisability of setting the strike date was discusse[d] pro and con at great length." It was finally decided to convene the committee in Washington, and invite the presidents of the internationals with the power to put out a strike call to attend. At this important conference, a thorough review of the situation was made. It could not have surprised many in attendance that Gary had continued to refuse to negotiate with the National Committee. Foster confronted those present with a series of telegrams and letters from steel organizers across the country stating that "unless the National Committee does something they would have to take the matter into their own hands." A typical telegram from Youngstown read: "We cannot be expected to meet enraged workers who will consider us traitors if strike is postponed." He argued that "conditions are as favorable for a determined stand in the steel industry as they are likely to be." Joseph Manley, an associate of Foster's from Home Colony, the SLNA, and the ITUEL, who was the representative of the Bridge and Structural Iron Workers on the committee, stated that he believed the "situation is such that defensive action is absolutely necessary." Foster proposed that "if no action is taken now our movement will rapidly go to pieces, thru spasmodic strikes. To stop the movement now is out of the question." He even voted against sending yet another telegram to Woodrow Wilson seeking intervention with Gary. However, he was in the minority, and the telegram was sent. Wilson's reply, received the next day, contained no assurances; the strike date was then set for September 22. According to Foster, Tighe was the one who finally proposed the date.[36]

Foster with Mary Harris ("Mother") Jones and steel organizers.

Even then, after the committee had put out the strike call, Gompers and Wilson requested that the walkout be postponed, pending a national industrial conference of representatives of labor, management, and the "public" that was planned for October 6. For some reason, Gompers had kept the committee uninformed about the possibility of postponing the strike, even though he had promised Bernard Baruch that he would bring influence to bear "to have all demands held over until that time." On September 17, five days before the scheduled strike, the committee met to consider Gompers's plea and the public pressure brought upon them by Wilson for postponement. Once again, Foster confronted the committee with telegrams from the steel centers urging that the strike go ahead. Fitzpatrick swung his influence in favor of action, writing bitterly to Gompers that "you may not be aware that seven of our organizers have been brutally murdered in cold blood during the past few days and the campaign of terrorism on the part of the steel companies is beyond description." Convinced that to hold out any longer would fatally damage the movement, the committee voted twelve to three to maintain the strike date. Later, Gompers would lay responsibility at Foster's feet for the timing of the strike. "This is the same Foster," he declared, "who in the face of definite information that the U.S. Steel Corporation was prepared for and wished a strike in 1919 and in the face of a request of the President of the

United States that the strike be at least postponed, insisted on that disastrous struggle."[37]

Foster himself received some pointed personal challenges. James Kline, the influential president of the Blacksmiths Union, argued that Gompers was wrong in urging a delay. "You will not be able to hold the men in the shops longer than the 22nd," he wrote. Workers "feel the humiliation of being ignored and when statements are made to Chambers of Commerce by the Capitalists to 'treat 'em rough,' and that they have the ammunition and foodstuffs enough inside the plants to last them a long while, they are red-blooded enough to go to a test." Besides, "delays are going to put members in the 'O.B.U.' [One Big Union or IWW]." From the other side in the developing war, Foster received a number of arrogant missives. One sheriff wrote to forbid meetings of "your Anti-American movement," warning that he "represents the majesty of the law, and is absolutely required to maintain peace at all hazards, and hence is given whatever powers are necessary to this end." An "Employer" wrote "strike—you fools and get your licking. The public is sick and tired of your arrogance. . . . Such undesirables as you should be deported with the rest of the IWW and the quicker it is done the better for the Country. You agitators are never satisfied unless you are breaking up homes and causing misery. The only thing that will settle you is powder and shot and you will get it, if you keep up your performance." It was simply not in Foster's character to decline such challenges.[38]

The type of movement that William Foster had helped build among the nation's steelworkers in 1919 is indicated by the fact that by the scheduled date of the strike many workers had already walked out. By September 20, the Friday before the strike date, five hundred immigrant workers had ceased work at the Pittsburgh Steel Company in Monessen. Also, mills in Martin's Ferry, Ohio, as well as the Laughlin Plant of the American Sheet and Tin Plate Company in Pittsburgh were closed by early walkouts of immigrant steelworkers. Only hours before the strike, constabularies rode their horses through an "unauthorized" meeting of "potential" strikers in North Clairton, clubbing onlookers and arresting strike leaders. In Allegheny County, a proclamation was issued that proscribed gatherings of three or more individuals in one place; in McKeesport, local unions were prohibited from holding even business meetings. Nationally, approximately a quarter-million steelworkers were on strike by the end of September. This represented nearly half of the industry's total work force. In western Pennsylvania, however, the strike was not as immediately successful as in other districts. Here, a fundamental divergence arose between native-born and immigrant workers; the latter proved much more willing to strike. As a result, local authorities found it easier to attack the strike movement in the area surrounding Pittsburgh as essentially "un-American." The local and national press followed suit. A correspondent for the *New York Tribune*, filing his front-page dispatch the day before the strike, reported from Pittsburgh that "foreign steel workers have been told by labor organizers that the general strike of the employees of the steel mills, which is to begin tomorrow, is the revolution. . . . There is no doubt that many of the Slav workers, with hazy but rosy visions of the Russian economic revolution in their minds, think that Monday will mark the beginning of the revolution in America."[39]

In other districts, the unity of the strikers was more pronounced, at least in the first weeks. Skilled and unskilled, native and immigrant workers stood together. In Gary, South Chicago, and Johnstown, for example, the mills were nearly empty on the first day of the strike. Even in numerous smaller steel towns, including some in the Pittsburgh district like Donora or Monessen, workers successfully ignored intimidation and stayed away from their jobs.[40] For Foster, of course, the dominant metaphor for the organization and conduct of the strike was warfare. His classic account of the strike, *The Great Steel Strike and Its Lessons*, is replete with references to wartime "tactics," and he often refers to the actions of authorities in the steel towns as if the conflict had been an armed battle.[41] To a significant degree, he was correct. Burgesses and police chiefs deputized numerous citizens in preparation for the strike, and often laid away storehouses of weapons to be used in the event of violence. An atmosphere of oppression descended over the towns of the Pittsburgh steel district. Heavily armed mounted constabularies patrolled streets in immigrant neighborhoods. As a syndicalist Foster had, years earlier, proposed that capitalism had "organized the whole fabric of society with a view to keeping the working class in slavery." The belief that strikes were capable of creating systemic and generalized crises for capitalism had provided much of the framework for Foster's conception of labor organizing in the 1910s. During the 1919 steel strike, he observed, western Pennsylvania was "controlled body and soul by the Steel Trust. The whole district has the psychology of a company-owned town. All authority centers in the steel industry. From there practically every institution takes its orders."[42] Foster's conception of society as system was seemingly vindicated by many of his experiences during the steel strike, but in many places, labor achieved a significant degree of power and unity when forced to confront capital on its own terrain.

There was a much larger sense of the stake for labor as well. Hundreds of local unions throughout the United States, from the Theatre Ushers in Brooklyn and Ice Cream Wagon Drivers in Washington, D.C., to the Garment Workers in New York City contributed over $400,000 to the strike effort.[43]

Breaking up a suspected strike meeting.

Foster addressing an open-air meeting, Braddock, Pennsylvania.

Like the McKees Rock strike of 1909, the 1919 strike was a movement in which unskilled, immigrant workers, heretofore considered unorganizable by the AFL, played a large role. Foster pointedly termed the opposition to the strike by civil authorities a "white terror." He noted that "the backbone of this strike are the foreign workers." Before the Interchurch World Commission, he repeated the standard AFL line on immigration: "Any criticism about the unions being un-American is all to be directed against the employer for bringing that class of men over here and putting them into his mill. We organize them after they get here—we don't bring them over here." Although the American-born worker "makes the best type of union man," he is "hard to organize," Foster continued. However, the immigrant worker, he asserted, "has that group idea very strongly developed," since in Europe he had come to learn that "if there is any possible chance for him to do anything he feels that it is as a group, not as an individual." During a strike, the immigrant "is a splendid fighter. He has the American beaten when it comes to a fight." Foster, characteristically, was optimistic about the possibility of organizational unity among the foreign-born and unskilled steelworkers; otherwise he would not have attempted the drive in the first place. Nevertheless, deep ethnic divisions marked the conduct of the strike. In Johnstown, for example, immigrant strikers held their own meetings in separate neighborhood enclaves, and picketed in national groupings at the mill gates. National Committee organizers sought to convince more skilled native workers that "hothead" demands of immigrant strikers for the establishment of industrial unionism and the immediate satisfaction of shop-floor grievances could be delayed, or at least settled within the context of traditional AFL-style bargaining.[44]

Foster seemed obsessed with the figure of Fannie Sellins, a highly effective United Mine Workers organizer and activist who was shot to death during a violent confrontation between unionists and vigilantes in August. The national office of the committee had grotesque photos of the dead Mrs. Sellins displayed prominently on its walls, and Foster mentioned her death whenever the opportunity arose. Despite Foster's attempts to make her into a martyr, Judge Gary argued that his company had no plants in Breckinridge where Sellins was killed, and the press made very little of her murder. Foster later wrote to Upton Sinclair that the fact that she had been killed at a non–U.S. Steel plant "was purely an accident, as any of the other steel companies would have been just about as glad to do the job." Those who were implicated in the shooting were not brought to trial until four years after the fact, and were finally acquitted by a jury that issued a statement implying that Sellins's death was justified because of her involvement in "bolshevik" activities.[45]

Foster's office in Pittsburgh was unprepossessing. Mary Harris ("Mother") Jones remembered that chairs were not allowed in the office during the steel strike since any gathering would then be construed as a "meeting" and hence subject to regulation by the authorities. Besides the photos of Fannie Sellins, many posters were on the walls; one was a wartime poster entitled "Americans All," showing men of many different nationalities fighting under the American flag. The office employed only a stenographer and a publicity director; Sylvia Manley, Foster's adopted daughter, worked as a secretary. Esther was a frequent visitor. There was no reception area outside the small office, so organizers, strikers, and reporters filed in and out in an unregulated flow. Mary Heaton Vorse, who had the opportunity to observe Foster during the strike, remembered him as an indefatigable worker who, despite the long hours he put in at the strike center, remained "composed, confident, unemphatic and imperishably unruffled." Journalists generally focused on Foster's executive ability and found that unlike the stereotypical radical of the time, he was "quiet mannered" and "soft-spoken." He had "an unusual memory and carries in his head what most men would keep in elaborate files," according to one reporter; "the general judgment of those who have been in close contact with him is that he is a leader of exceptional ability." *The New Republic* even noted that Foster "speaks elaborately of the details of the scientific management of strikes." At a time when it was often assumed that the "distorted" minds of radicals were readily discernible in their supposedly misshapen features, Foster's physiognomy seemed normal enough. "He has a good head, small ears, keen, clear eyes, the jaw and chin of a leader of men," one reporter observed. On the other hand, John Brophy, then a delegate from the UMW to the National Committee who saw Foster speak several times, recalled that while Foster lacked the grandiloquent style of a Fitzpatrick, Gompers, or John L. Lewis, he "talked a vigorous militant language, in the conventional terms of trade unionism."[46]

From the very beginning of the strike, Foster was portrayed as the brains and active force behind the organizing drive. One steel company official even referred to the strike as being led, not by the AFL, but by the "Foster organization." To some extent, individuals who had a stake in the failure of the strike sought to portray Foster as the plotting "genius" behind the movement in order to discredit it. However, much of the organizational impetus for the strike had in fact originated with Foster. Within the organization itself, there were unmistakable signs of Foster's influence. Two close associates of his, former SLNA members Joseph Manley and Samuel Hammersmark, showed up in the National Committee's minutes as playing significant roles in the organizing campaign.

Manley, Foster's son-in-law, surfaced as the committee's delegate from the Bridge and Structural Iron Workers in July 1919, at a crucial point in the organizing drive, and served with Foster and one other individual on the important committee in charge of organizing the strike vote. Hammersmark was a local organizer in the Youngstown district. J. G. Brown, a friend of Jay Fox's for whom Foster had worked as a timberworkers' organizer in Washington, was a member of the national organizing committee, and belonged to the "flying squadrons" that spoke in the steel towns despite the prohibitions of local authorities. One observer described Brown as Foster's "chief aide in the conduct of the strike." Later, he took over the steel committee after Foster resigned.[47]

An important question in the minds of observers of the strike in its first days was the extent to which Samuel Gompers supported the strike. Despite Foster's claim in *The Great Steel Strike and Its Lessons* that Gompers's last-minute request to delay the strike was "qualified," the meaning of the AFL president's entreaty had been unmistakable, and the National Committee's rejection of his request provided a powerful argument for those who sought to portray the movement as being in the hands of radicals.[48]

How did the AFL president perceive Foster's role? In his autobiography, Gompers remembered that he had listened to a speech by Foster at a CFL meeting before the war in which he stated that he "supported in full the fundamental principles, the ideas, the methods, philosophy, and policy of the American Federation of Labor." Gompers claimed to have been convinced by Foster's change of heart: "He was a man of ability, a man of good presence, gentle in expression, a commander of good English, and I encouraged him." As a result, Gompers was, initially at least, "really pleased with his selection as secretary of the organizing committee."[49] There is no question that without Gompers's acquiescence, at least, the officers of the internationals would not have participated in the campaign in the first place. However, as the committee's organizing efforts took shape throughout 1918–19, Gompers may have had some misgivings. The AFL assigned a high-ranking organizer the task of secretly monitoring the content of Foster's speeches.[50] It was during this period that the Stockyards Labor Council was engaging in open warfare with Dennis Lane's Butcher Workmen international in Chicago; the SLC had been organized by Foster and Fitzpatrick along much the same lines as the steelworkers' committee. Gompers, whom Foster later characterized as "nobody's fool," was undoubtedly aware of Foster's radical past in the early stages of the steelworkers organizing campaign. If Gompers himself did not remember Foster's disruptive attacks on the AFL at the Budapest conference of the international trade union secretariat in 1911, then James Duncan, an AFL vice president who had witnessed Foster's performance there, undoubtedly reminded him at some point early in the campaign. Foster offered to resign if his secretaryship proved harmful to the movement.[51]

However, Gompers went along with the organizing campaign. To some degree, he had little choice. As the steelworkers' campaign escalated, Gompers was hardly in a position openly to resist, especially given the fact that Foster repeatedly emphasized that he intended to employ only strict "trade union principles." Because he was in Europe during crucial periods, Gompers was not in an advantageous position to exercise close control over the development of the organizing drive. Moreover, the steel campaign, at least initially, promised to increase AFL membership quite dramatically. Yet, at the crucial point when it was necessary for Gompers to demonstrate some control over the steelworkers movement, too much momentum had already accrued. When the strike date arrived, the public pressure increased even further on Gompers to take a stand. In the first week of the walkout, the *New York Tribune* editorialized that "for the first time in its history, the American Federation of Labor turned over its vast power, its good will, its organization, to a wild revolutionary, an avowed advocate of violence and bloodshed." The question was: "What does Mr. Gompers say?" At the same time, it was not unusual for newspapers to interpret Foster's actions as an attempt to take over the leadership of the AFL from the aging Gompers. "If the strike is successful it is expected by labor leaders here that Foster, who has been the chief figure in it, would bulk large in the councils of the AFL, and might succeed in giving the policy of that organization a turn in a more radical and socialistic direction," the *New York Times* warned.[52] Gompers may have overestimated the degree of control he could exercise over both the strike and his "dangerous ward," as one newspaper described Foster. He was undoubtedly dismayed by the position he found himself in, and resentful of the roles played by Foster and Fitzpatrick.

Inevitably, Foster's authorship of *Syndicalism* became an important public issue. Congressmen and senators fulminated against the phrases it contained, editorialists expressed outrage, and AFL officials sought to portray Foster's pamphlet, written seven years earlier, as inconsistent with the aims of the strike. Several of the more violent and radical passages in the small book were quoted at length in many newspapers and magazines. The rhetoric of *Syndicalism* and the fact that Foster had written the tract were as much as many Americans ever knew about the strike.[53] Indeed, Foster's pronouncements seemed to lend credence to widely held suspicions that radicals and bolsheviks were conspiring to undermine American institutions. Foster's statement in *Syndicalism* that the radical trade unionist must be absolutely "unscrupulous" in his methods heightened the tension, and rendered his own disavowals problematic. The unfortunate phrase "boring from within" was resurrected, and, moreover, his methods seemed to fit perfectly not only with Foster's avowed aims in *Syndicalism,* but with his later pronouncements in *Trade Unionism: The Road to Freedom.* While he accused the steel companies of ordering massive reprints of *Syndicalism* for distribution in the steel towns and among the press, Foster himself passed out copies of *Trade Unionism* at strike headquarters in Pittsburgh.[54] Although the rhetoric in this pamphlet was much less violent and anarchist in tone, it essentially reaffirmed the message of *Syndicalism* that radicals should "bore from within" in the AFL in order to bring about the new society. If Foster tried to illustrate the evolution of his views by distributing *Trade Unionism,* he was only partly successful. "Foster's Latest Pamphlet Shows Views Unchanged," the *New York Tribune* headlined.[55] At the same time, because his intelligent and quiet demeanor seemed to contrast so starkly with his writings, Foster posed more of a threat, somehow, than other "agitators." "Critics of Foster believe that, owing to his manner of address and his appeal to thought, he is doubly a menace," one observer noted. Foster seemed to embody too many contradictions to fit comfortably into the mold of the archetypical American radical during the developing red scare.

Yet he was the leader of a movement that expressed the deep contradictions and schisms of American society at the end of the Progressive era. Although he was American-born, a highly skilled railway worker, and an adherent of the methods of the AFL, he had taken a large hand in organizing a movement that many Americans associated with the foreign-born, or those whose "citizenship" was considered ambiguous. At one point, he found it necessary publicly to affirm his citizenship "in face of doubts that he is an American." Speaking on the floor of the House of Representatives, Congressman John G. Cooper of the Mahoning district in Ohio proclaimed that Foster was a leader of the radical element within organized labor, which is "especially appealing to men of foreign birth who have little or no conception of American ideals and institutions." Furthermore, Foster himself, "by his own words, shows his unfitness as a labor leader and disqualifies himself as an American citizen enjoying the protection of the American flag."[56] One writer proposed that Foster was "a revolutionary of the Lenine type," while another observer noted that "this man Foster is a native-born citizen. He is a most dangerous leader and a dangerous domestic enemy."[57] Thus Foster seemed, as an individual, to symbolize the collapsing of previous social categories, and the reordering of traditional conceptions of radicalism and its origins. As his statements in *Syndicalism* suggested, Foster had little or no regard for the rhetoric of "democracy" or the traditional "rights" of workingmen and citizens. Yet as a new type of labor radical, one who putatively sought

Parade of strikers, unidentified steel mill. Note veterans.

only to build larger, more efficient, and more powerful labor organizations, he worked within the same conceptual terrain as the leadership of
the new managerial capitalism.

How did Foster himself understand the steel strike and its aims? In
certain respects, the contradictions implicit in the public construction of
his personality and motives corresponded closely to Foster's own politics,
and the theory of radical trade unionism that he developed throughout
the 1910s. By 1916, he had embraced a kind of instrumentalism that

looked to workers' empowerment through unionism as the most important end that radicals could pursue, given the "underdeveloped" state of
workers' consciousness at the time. Foster believed, as did many capitalists, in the radical implications of the new unionism. The problem, of
course, was how to convince revolutionaries and socialists that trade unionism was implicitly radical, while maintaining the vital advantage of
"legitimacy" that protected the movement from various forms of repression.

Foster's solution to this problem entailed a full-blown rationale for
deception, which he clearly explained in his more recently published writings—not just in the rhetoric about revolutionary "unscrupulousness" in
syndicalism, which company publicists and newspapermen delighted in
quoting, but also in his later polemic, *Trade Unionism: The Road to Freedom*, published in 1916. In *Trade Unionism*, Foster's belief in the necessity of deception is more understated, but the implication is clear. Because
trade unionism "strikes at the very heart of capitalism" and is a "radical"
solution, its advocates must dissemble and deceive:

> True, the Trade Union Movement itself doesn't generally propagate the
> idea that it aims at the overthrow of the wages system. But this is because it
> has not yet become conscious of its full mission. Consequently, too much
> weight should not be given such conservative slogans as "A fair day's pay for
> a fair day's work," and "The interests of Capital and Labor are identical."
> These expressions are not basic. In actual practice little or no attention is
> paid to them. They are for foreign consumption. Their purpose is to deceive
> and disarm the opposition. This form of deception, which is usually uncon-
> scious, is used by all aggressive social movements.

Foster's rationale for this tactic was bound up with Social Darwinism,
and his habitual dismissal of the social conventions of modern capitalism
as epiphenomenal. "Even the great ruling capitalist class finds [deception]
indispensable. Strong as it is this great class would be speedily squelched
did it not continually hide its nefarious schemes of exploitation under a
hypocritical mask of patriotism, morality, benevolence, and the like."
Shortly after the conclusion of the steel strike, Foster again reflected on
the necessity for subterfuge, using many of the same phrases as in *Trade
Unionism*. Why have radicals dismissed trade unions as "merely pallia-
tive bodies?" It is because, "like various other aggressive social movements," unions have to instinctively camouflage their aims, in order "to
pacify and disarm the opposition. This is the function of such expressions
as, "A fair day's pay for a fair day's work," "The interests of Capital and
Labor are identical," etc."[58] It was a common-sense approach, but it effectively limited Foster in the war of labor against capital to the gray

nether world of "deceptive" phraseology and hard organizational imperatives.

For Foster, the steel strike was part of an essentially radical enterprise, yet this did not entail the necessity of establishing or even advocating industrial unionism as a primary issue. Earlier in the decade, as a result of his visit to Germany, he had decided that industrial unionism did not, as a form of organization, necessarily indicate the existence of revolutionary consciousness among workers. In the United States, he believed, true industrial unionism was an unrealistic objective at the time. He had an important tactical reason to reject the idea of One Big Union during a period when the term was often associated either with the IWW or "foreigners." However, Foster later claimed that he had sought, through the strike, to "break down the old system of craft unionism and lay the basis" for the development of industrial unionism.[59] Foster was characterized by the Interchurch World Commission as having "combatted the natural tendency of sections of the rank and file toward industrial unionism." The commission took pains, in its reports on the strike and its outcome, to emphasize that the strike had been conducted according to accepted "trade-union methods." Foster, it was reported, "was constantly complaining of fighting the radicals, meaning those who wanted a general strike called." David Saposs was closest to the mark when he termed the organizational theory behind the steel strike as "opportunistic-industrial unionism."[60]

Saposs, a close acquaintance of Foster's who had occasion to discuss the strike with him, affirmed Foster's long-held animus against the "utopian" IWW, which, because of its impossibilist perspective, "narrows its function to propaganda purposes only." Neither was Foster in sympathy with "the one big union idea which would scramble together the workers of various crafts and industries. . . . This he regards as artificial and visionary." Fitzpatrick, at one point, was quoted as saying that "only idiots believe in the general strike." "Mother" Jones, at a Chicago Federation of Labor meeting, had a purely pragmatic, ecumenical message for strikers and radicals: "I want to say to you men and women: Stop quarreling about 'isms.' Put aside your sentimental rot, get into the trenches and demand a civilization where men can live." Eugene Debs, who was not ordinarily sympathetic to AFL–style unionism, wrote from his prison cell in Atlanta that "If I should get out of this prison today, I would be in Gary or Pittsburgh tomorrow." He now warned that the nation's workers might "lay down their work and be swept into a revolution with cyclonic fury" in sympathy with the steel strikers.[61] Foster knew, quite realistically, that the central issues for most steelworkers in the fall of 1919 were wages, hours, and working conditions. However, his belief in the necessity of the "evolution" of the labor movement did not prevent him from bringing up the issues of a steelworkers' department and universal membership transfer in AFL councils. If the extent of the walkout confirmed that a truly "general" strike was an untenable proposition at the time, Foster welcomed and encouraged indications of solidarity with the steelworkers. Shortly after the strike began, he expressed enthusiasm over the fact that in some districts railway trainmen and switchmen refused to participate in the hauling of steel to and from the plants that had been struck. At the same time, he was always careful to present his objectives in prosaic terms. When asked whether he favored the socialization of the steel industry, he replied that "I'm just an organizer. I'm not a steel man. I organized the packing industry, and then moved on. After I get through with this strike I'll take up something else."[62]

It is impossible to know whether Foster hoped statements such as these would reassure authorities. In any event, as the strike entered its first months, local police, civic groups, and elected officials treated the strikers as if they were dangerous revolutionaries. Gary and Chicago, where organizers had initially met with their most encouraging successes, were the focus of much anti-"bolshevik" activity. *Syndicalism* was widely circulated in Gary by U.S. Steel and the Loyal American League as evidence that extremists were in control of the strike. Foster, according to the league, believed in "the overthrow of American institutions . . . and the domination of all America by the labor tyranny known as syndicalism." Unfortunately, amid such hysteria, the real issues of the strike in Gary were obscured. Workers' demands for collective bargaining, an eight-hour day, six-day week, and increased wages became secondary concerns in the local press. The *Gary Daily Tribune* advocated the denial of free speech to radicals and the deportation of "disloyal" aliens, while the organ of the CFL, *The New Majority*, was banned during the strike.[63] State and then federal troops arrived in the city in response to the entreaties of General Leonard Wood. The "steel city" was quickly transformed into a garrison town. Machine-gun squads were established at strategic points, and infantry patrolled the streets. Martial law was declared, strike meetings were restricted, picketing was prohibited, and the military raided the homes of Gary's socialists and radicals. Despite the assiduous efforts of the Army Intelligence Division, investigators failed to turn up any concrete evidence that the strike in Gary was led by radical elements.[64]

Foster wrote soon after the strike that "ours are days when the organized employers, inspired by a horrible fear of the onward sweep of revolution in Europe and the irresistible advance of the labor movement in this country, are robbing the people over-night of their most precious rights,

Pennsylvania Constabulary.

the fruits of a thousand years of struggle." There is no doubt that in western Pennsylvania, especially in the Pittsburgh district, strikers were met with bitter resistance by state police, the American Legion, company guards, numerous armed and deputized "citizens'" groups, and various local burgesses and civic authorities. By October 14, James Mauer, president of the Pennsylvania Federation of Labor, had written a letter to Governor W. C. Sproul in which he was able to detail the evidence of repression in the steel towns. In communities like Homestead, Clairton, McKeesport, Braddock, New Castle, Monessen, and Butler, terrorism was routine, he noted. Men and women were arrested at their homes and beaten. Those who were arrested were often not informed of the charges against them. Strikers were fined exorbitantly for ill-defined misdemeanors and told to go back to work or risk further imprisonment. Mounted state policemen rode through the streets, arbitrarily searching, arresting, or clubbing "suspicious" individuals. Shots were fired at strikers' homes, and in Monessen citizens were detained by company guards in makeshift private "jails." In New Castle, most of the attorneys in the town were deputized, and refused to take up the cases of arrested strikers. Outdoor meetings of strikers were strictly prohibited in the towns along the Monongahela Valley; the earlier victories of the free speech campaign quickly evaporated. Sproul, when confronted by Foster with the denial of constitutional liberties in his state, remarked merely that "experience has shown that it is dangerous to permit the congregation of large numbers of people during times of stress and excitement."[65] Numerous full-page advertisements were taken out in newspapers claiming that the strike was a failure and urging workers to return to the plants. Mary Heaton Vorse attempted to generate a publicity campaign to counter the propaganda and accusations, but Foster, much to her dismay, couldn't "bear to spend a cent for anything but relief." In the meantime, in Pennsylvania, "civil liberties became a dead letter." The *Wall Street Journal* justified the repressive measures with the imprecation that "the leaders of the steel strike are apostles of violence with the destruction of any form of law as a first principle."[66]

Foster proved unable effectively to refute such charges. On October 3, he was called to testify before a Senate committee that had been hurriedly assembled to investigate the strike. If one were to specify a vital and most illuminating moment in Foster's life as a radical, this was surely it. His testimony embodied the contradictions, dangers, and tautologies that would pursue him in his later career as a Communist. He had always been, in a certain sense, an "invisible" man; now the protean labor organizer, radical, anarchist, "bolshevik"—each label had been applied with equal conviction—was called publicly to account.

Foster's performance must be considered in light of two basic facts. First, he was in a situation where a complete and convincing renunciation of his radical past would undoubtedly have helped to relieve the public pressure that was being brought against the strike and its leadership. Secondly, Foster had no compunction about not telling the truth to the committee; indeed, he was theoretically committed to the necessity of "camouflaging" labor's cause. Besides, ominous statements had been made recently by men in government. Representative Julius Kahn, chairman of the Military Affairs Committee of the House of Representatives, had proposed that in light of Foster's authorship of *Syndicalism*, the steel strike leader might be prosecuted for murder. As in the Haymarket affair in the previous century, the possibility was raised that a radical could be tried for a crime simply by appearing to advocate it. Here, the focus was on Foster's statement, in *Syndicalism*, that strikebreakers should be "exterminated." By 1919, Foster may have reasoned, quite realistically, that if society would not tolerate activities that it deemed radical, then society could not reasonably expect a radical to be forthright about his motives.[67]

Almost immediately, the issue of Foster's authorship of *Syndicalism* was raised. Although the booklet had the names of two authors on its cover, Foster assumed complete responsibility for these writings. He was asked, straightforwardly, if he believed in "the doctrine of revolution" that the pamphlet contained. He equivocated, noting that the small book had been written "eight or nine years ago; I do not know exactly when," and that "since then I have become possibly a little less impatient, a little less extreme, possibly, in my views, considerably so, in fact. . . . Today I am an advocate of the system of unionism as we find it in America and England." When asked again if he believed in the doctrine of *Syndicalism*, Foster replied, "How far [my ideas] have changed I am not going to make an issue in this campaign if I can help it." At one point he responded, when pressed, that he no longer entertained such views, and that he no longer called himself a syndicalist.[68]

Yet further on, he carefully stated that he did not believe in syndicalism only as it was expressed in the pamphlet. Samuel Gompers, sitting next to Foster at the hearings, "hissed" at him to make a categorical repudiation, but the circumspect former railwayman remained evasive. He expressed an undeniable truth when he stated that "if I was still a believer in that book and tried to use it and put it into practice I would not be in the position I am in."[69] Even so, the next day, the *New York Times* headlined that "He Dodges Direct Answers: Admits Belief in Employees' Control of Industry, Extermination of Scabs, and Race Suicide." Even in his post-strike evaluation, Foster equivocated on the issue of whether or not he remained a believer in the tenets of *Syndicalism*.[70] Foster's testimony stood as lesson in the difficulties that faced the radical seeking the cover of "legitimate" institutions. Occurring at the height of the postwar "red scare," the congressional hearings were a rehearsal for later inquisitions that Foster would endure as a Communist. The irony of his situation at the steel strike hearings was that, at the point of his very highest visibility in American life, as a radical with a political identity he came closest to disappearing. "I have no teachings or principles," he pleaded. "I apply the principles of the American Federation of Labor as best I understand them."[71] His statements that he had sold Liberty Bonds during the war and supported AFL unionism made him an easy target of criticism by the IWW and later, by factional opponents in the Communist party.

If the steel strike was a very public event, subject to the manipulations of politicians, newspaper editors, and publicity men, it was at the same time a "private war." At this level as well, the steel strikers were facing defeat in the last months of 1919. The prospect of some kind of federal mediation of the strike had disappeared once and for all in early October, when the President's Industrial Conference proved unable to force Judge Gary to enter into negotiations.[72] Gary's refusal to move toward union recognition during the conference appeared to confirm that the original decision not to postpone the strike had been an appropriate one. Encouraged by the inability of labor to exert effective pressure in the realm of purely public affairs, the steel companies stepped up their efforts to defeat the strike in the mill communities, where their power seemed equally formidable. Company-influenced newspapers claimed that the strike had been defeated. Workers feared for their future livelihoods as an extensive network of company spies and agents infiltrated the communities in order to identify strike leaders and unionists. Black strikebreakers were recruited from the South in increasing numbers. After the strike, Foster laid much of the blame for widespread use of blacks in the struck mills at the feet of the unions: "Many of them sharply draw the color line, thus feeding the flames of race hatred." In the future, the success of unionization required that unions "open their ranks to negroes, make an earnest effort to organize them, and then give them a square deal when they do join." However, at the height of the strike, he made an ill-considered assessment of the motives of the black work force, and in so doing revealed his growing pessimism on the possibility of unity. "The colored worker," he asserted, "is not very responsive to trade unionism. He seems to feel that the best way he can solve his problem is to break down the white working man. He acts as a scab at all times."[73]

Given the degree of official repression and opposition to the walkout, it is remarkable that workers stayed out as long as they did. However, many were able to survive on Liberty bonds that they purchased during the war, and many immigrants relied on their savings. In the National Committee office in Pittsburgh, Foster, when told over the phone of an organizer who had been arrested, replied sardonically: "Dig up your Liberty Bonds and buy a little liberty."[74] As the strike wore on, it became clear that the forcible interdiction of free speech and assembly extended even to the highest levels of the National Committee. On November 7, when Foster arrived in Johnstown to address a meeting of steelworkers, a group of plain-clothes policemen and prominent businessmen forcibly escorted him back to the train station, ordering him to leave town. The largest hall at the local Labor Temple had been jammed with strikers waiting to hear him speak. Organizers continued to be arrested in Johnstown despite this publicity.[75]

Faced with such opposition, the strike began to lose momentum. There was some strike relief, but as the walkout continued, families found it increasingly difficult to survive. In Monessen, one resident remembered, "they starved, let me put it very straight to you. The strike [failed] simply because the people didn't have any food and didn't have any money to pay their mortgages, what have you."[76] In November, production in the steel mills began to rise significantly. Skilled, native-born American workers returned steadily to their jobs; the Amalgamated made a crucial decision to allow certain of their members to honor previous contracts. By early December, the National Committee had sent a telegram to its organizers acknowledging that the strike was lost. Judge Gary, however, showed that he was willing to maintain the level of hyperbole that had prevailed throughout the strike; he proposed that the nation had been saved from "the closed shop, Soviets and the forcible [re]-distribution of property."[77]

In order to discredit the movement, employers, the national press, and local authorities had emphasized Foster's prominent role in organizing and carrying out the strike, implying that he was something of a self-appointed dictator. However, it is possible to see that Foster was a central figure in the movement without subscribing to the notion that he was merely hungry for power or a "master conspirator." Above all, Foster was an opportunist who was impatient with the niceties of union "democracy." Understanding that significant resentment existed in the mill towns toward the steelmasters, he had worked diligently to develop an organizational vehicle through which rank-and-file grievances could be addressed; in so doing he was able to exercise a significant degree of individual leadership. However, as the employers perhaps understood, Foster's leadership represented a challenge to traditional craft union ideals about the way in which strikes should be conducted. According to traditional formulae, the conduct of a strike was to be carefully circumscribed by elaborate procedures that combined membership approval with "control" by the international officers. At National Committee meetings where often only half of the affiliated international unions were represented, Foster developed aggressive policies and then presented the international leadership with a series of *faits accomplis*. William Hannon, the representative of the Machinists on the National Committee, commented revealingly on the conduct of the strike machinery:[78]

> The steel strike was handled differently from any strike that I have ever been connected with. In practically every other strike . . . the officers of the International organizations affected have handled the situation, acting as an executive committee to direct the strike. In this strike, the Secretary of the National Committee assumed the leadership, the International representatives having but little to say about its direction. Of course, when the National Committee met, the action taken was generally approved.

David Saposs, who witnessed several National Committee meetings, later recounted how "Foster was an exceedingly able man and at these national committee meetings [AFL leaders] were helpless. They couldn't take issue with Foster or with Fitzpatrick—they were tongue-tied." Moreover, at the level of a national organizing campaign, the old-style skills of the craft union leaders seemed irrelevant. "It was something that they didn't know anything about and they might have been good at negotiation, but it was so strange, so foreign to them that they felt helpless and they acquiesced with everything that Foster and Fitzpatrick suggested. They were glad to get the damn thing off their hands. They never had any faith in it anyhow."[79]

Foster himself became a leadership symbol to the strikers and organizers. In the last weeks of the strike, Heber Blankenhorn, an investigator for the Interchurch World Commission, recounted how Foster had faced a district organizers' meeting for five or six hours. "Men's nerves [were] rasped by three months of strike with all sorts of accusations of bad faith, betrayal, shortage of commissary, etc." Foster, despite his pleas that he had come only "to listen," was forced to speak the moment he arrived. "At the end of the session, criticism had quite disappeared, no personal criticism of him stood anywhere and there was a general feeling that everything had been explained and everything done that could be done." Foster took some pride that his skills also encompassed the ability of the "modern" trade unionist to channel radicalism among the rank and file into "constructive" channels. He told Blankenhorn that his role as the conflict ended was to argue against radicals who could "sweep an entire meeting off its feet and get wild applause for any sort of drastic proposal." In reality, according to Foster, the radicals "have no reason in their plans," or "really have no plans but only very destructive criticism." Even so, David Saposs, who interviewed numerous steelworkers as an investigator for the Interchurch World Commission, remembered that Foster was the figure to whom most steel strikers attached their personal loyalty.[80]

As the strike ended, Foster pushed for the continuation, rather than disbandment, of the National Committee. "The fight must be made a permanent one," he proposed. This in itself may have been interpreted as a rather ominous move by AFL officials, since the Amalgamated had withdrawn from the committee almost immediately upon the demise of the strike and had claimed that the committee had been infringing on its jurisdiction in the late stages of the conflict. D. J. Davis of the Amalgamated claimed later his union had withdrawn "because irresponsible men had been appointed [as organizers] by Secretary Foster, in charge of various cities."[81] Foster proposed that a large corps of organizers stay in the field, and that a steelworkers' bulletin in several languages be distributed regularly. Activist nuclei would be maintained in each steel community. "A vigorous campaign of education and reorganization will be immediately begun and will not cease until industrial justice in the steel industry has been achieved," Foster promised, quite optimistically.[82]

Nevertheless, he resigned as secretary of the steelworkers' committee in favor of his friend J. G. Brown effective February 1. He later claimed that he had resigned "entirely of my own volition," but admitted also that he desired that a "new phase of the work go ahead with a clean slate," presumably meaning that he wished that the committee not be further discredited by his presence.[83] However, it was rumored that Foster had had a direct hand in choosing Brown to continue as secretary, and that Foster and "other radical members" of the committee continued to decisively influence its deliberations.[84] Meanwhile, workers returned to work bitter, uncertain, and discouraged. In Monessen, strikers were required to personally apologize to the plant superintendent before reclaiming their old positions, and in Colorado workers submitted to mandatory physical examinations and signed statements vowing their cooperation with management and loyalty to their country. "A feeling of despondency runs through the ranks of the workers," Saposs reported after the strike. "Many vow that they will never join a union again." While some workers felt that they had "demonstrated their power quite effectively against these giant corporations," the predominant feeling seemed to be that "the steel corporations are invincible and that striking is useless." In the spring and summer of 1920, Roger Baldwin and the newly formed American Civil Liberties Union inquired with the National Committee about the possibility of beginning some kind of free speech campaign in Western Pennsylvania in support of a new organizing drive. Brown replied that the withdrawal of the Amalgamated had caused the collapse of the committee's organizing work, and that he was "winding up its affairs."[85]

Despite Foster's claim after the walkout that it had "raised the prestige of the trade union movement wonderfully with the steel workers," the strike was unmistakably defeated. The prospect of collective bargaining in the steel industry was as dim as it ever was, and the power of the companies in the mill towns remained undiminished and was, perhaps, even enhanced. The steel strike was, as Foster put it in more sober moments, a "tremendous defeat" for unionism and had a lasting effect on all American workers in the sense that it foretold the powerlessness of labor in the face of the open-shop movement of the 1920s. It was not until 1923 that the eight-hour day was finally established in the steel industry.[86] Moreover, the crushing of the unions in 1919 showed how easily a progressive labor cause could be crippled by accusations that its leadership was "red."[87] Thereafter, radicals would never be as comfortable in the "legitimate" American labor movement, and many, including Foster, searched for other avenues by which to pursue their aims. Foster himself would never openly lead another strike.

Despite its defeat, the steel strike and its complex lessons became part of the historical consciousness of an emerging generation of activists and organizations. Men like John Brophy and Philip Murray, who were central in the establishment of the CIO nearly two decades later, participated in the 1919 organizing campaign. Roger Baldwin, who helped to found the American Civil Liberties Union in 1920, walked picket lines in Chicago during the strike and offered Foster a position on the body's first national board.[88] The packing and steel campaigns provided the Communist party with its first substantial issue in the labor movement of the early 1920s, "amalgamation."

As for Foster, the steel strike marked the high point in his career as a labor radical. The historian Philip Taft termed the organizing campaign "one of the great organizing feats in American labor history." However, the movement's defeat was also an ominous affirmation of Foster's own problematic position in American society. Theodore Dreiser, in a 1941 tribute to Foster, wrote that the steel strike was "where, perhaps for the first time, America began to see itself clearly."[89] Dreiser did not explain what he meant by this remark, but the 1919 strike was remarkable at least in part because it acted to momentarily precipitate and clarify the deep divisions that had developed within American society in the first decades of the twentieth century. Most importantly, in respect to a consideration of Foster's life, it was an event that symbolized that the boundaries of American citizenship had become more tightly constricted and more explicitly delineated. During the years in which Foster was most active in the American labor movement, immediately before and after World War I, the exclusion and deportation of aliens, immigrants, and dissenters reached an unprecedented level. Anarchists, Wobblies and "bolsheviks" were the primary targets of chauvinist hysteria. Between 1912 and 1917, as one historian put it, the United States Congress "abandoned the conviction that radicalism could be a home-grown phenomenon."[90] In this atmosphere, Foster was deemed most "dangerous" because he was a radical and also most demonstrably an American.

During this period Foster also sought, as did thousands of others, to achieve economic citizenship through unionization. Such citizenship may have represented to some a vehicle by which workers could merely achieve a larger share of an expanding American capitalism. To others it meant gaining the means to resist the increasingly powerful and arbitrary control of managers and foremen in the workplace. For the leadership of one of the largest sectors of the economy, the organizing campaign and the empowerment that it promised was perceived as radical enough to deserve unyielding opposition and suppression. If the steelmasters justified their intransigence by invoking their own paternalistic and ultimately benign interest in their employees and their communities, the history of the decline and dissolution of American steel towns must stand as testimony to the fragility of their intentions. Yet this history is also a testimony to the limitations of Foster's vision. Needless to say, the establishment of powerful, integrated industrial unions in the 1930s did not prevent what took place in the steel industry in later decades. During Woodrow Wilson's second Industrial Conference, which met immediately in the aftermath of the steel strike, a group of labor leaders was asked by *The Survey* to propose solutions to the "labor problem." Among the replies were "Equal Citizenship," "Nationalization," and a "National Labor Board." Foster's solution, predictably enough, was "Organization." For him, unionization would remedy the central problem in the steel industry: "property rights are supreme and human rights negligible. The representatives of property have complete control." In the *Great Steel Strike and Its Lessons*, Foster concluded that "when our militants generally adopt English methods, and turn their whole-hearted attention to building up and developing the trade-union movement—that hour will be the dawn of a new day for American Labor."[91] Much of Foster's later career would show the immense difficulties involved in accomplishing this vision.

Chapter 6

LABOR ORGANIZER AND COMMUNIST

This is not the first time that I have been a guest of a city,
and as I looked around me I saw many others who had
been guests of the American government and of almost
all other governments in the world. But it certainly
was the first time that any of them were honored
guests. . . . You can tell my enemies to go to hell.
—Jack Johnstone, writing to John Fitzpatrick from
Petrograd during his first visit to Russia

In a 1924 article in which he described his role in the Chicago Federation of Labor during the meatpacking and steel campaigns, Foster reflected that his position had been that of "a free lance in the general trade union movement." To a certain degree, this was an accurate description. He did not belong to any explicitly revolutionary organization at the time that he gained his most notoriety as a radical, even though the leadership Chicago Federation of Labor was classified in some official circles as "revolutionary."[1] During the 1910s, he had woven ephemeral groupings of trade union radicals around his unique brand of anarcho-syndicalism, but these had dissolved by 1918–19, the years of the most militant strike activity in American history. These organizations drew their inspiration from broad and eclectic sources. In addition to referring to trends in the international labor movement, they seemed peculiarly suited to the aggressive activities of many radical unionists during the Progressive Era. They sought, in varying degrees, to combine elements of the radical syndicalism of the IWW with the pragmatism of the Socialist party's "boring from within" approach. Yet the SLNA and the ITUEL bore certain characteristics that marked them as uniquely personal organizations. Foster was advertised prominently as secretary-treasurer of each of the syndicalist leagues, and their founding manifestos were authored by him. He himself had refused, for various reasons that seemed to him purely realistic, to adapt his radicalism to membership in either the IWW or the Socialist party. In a sense, his greatest successes at the end of the decade were personal successes; no particular workers' organization ultimately enhanced its power or gained prestige as a result of the packinghouse and steel organizing drives.

In notes for a 1923 article entitled "What Lies Back of Foster," David Saposs meditated on the role of the "free-lance" radical within the labor movement. These "borers from within" had come to appreciate, through their experiences, that "aggression leads to isolation," and that an essentially pragmatic attitude was the soundest way to further their goals. Also, they sensed that American workers and labor leaders had grown "touchy" on "isms," and that "any idea that appears tainted with 'high browism' or foreign contact" impaired their usefulness to labor organizations if they were so labeled. Free-lancers thus keep "their [social] aspirations and ultimate ideals under cover." Foster, according to Saposs, embodied the difficulties and contradictions of the "detached" labor activist within the AFL. He did not publicly criticize AFL leaders or officers during the steel strike, and "resented criticism of his own course by the intellectuals and revolutionary radicals." While the free-lancer found it always necessary to subordinate his own goals while working behind the scenes, if the steel strike had been successful, Saposs conjectured, Foster would have been able to assert his independence of AFL officials and step out of his subordinate role. Then, he could have been more free to speak his mind. However, more often the free lance had to content himself with remaining a "regular" in order to remove suspicion from himself. Saposs was a friend of Foster's at the time, and understood his motives as well as anyone. "His is very largely the position of the stepchild or adopted citizen, he is there by sufferance," Saposs wrote.[2]

In the period immediately after the steel strike Foster's organizational affiliations changed, yet Saposs's insights into the nature of his career remained essentially accurate. In the previous decade, he had been seeking the status of "radical regular" in the AFL. In the early 1920s, he would become both a Communist and a free-lance radical working within the AFL; however, in each case he remained, for the time being, "in" but not "of" each organization. In each cycle he showed that he was willing to accommodate his views somewhat to his new affiliation, but the process was not entirely opportunistic. In the 1910s, his activities in the AFL were not inconsistent with his earlier theorizing about the way in which the wages system would eventually be abolished. In the early 1920s, he might have inflected his radicalism in a more conservative direction, as John Fitzpatrick eventually did, in order to maintain a significant role within the Chicago Federation of Labor. Instead, he became a part of the central leadership of the Communist party. However, despite a period of experimentation with united front labor politics in the 1920s, the *sine qua non* of Foster's radicalism remained his idea that the revolutionary movement in this country would develop out of the trade unions. Immediately after and during the steel strike, the newly founded American Communist parties did not come close to sharing this view, and the tactics and orientation of the Socialist party were based on an under-standing of political citizenship that Foster rejected. Thus Foster once again determined to create a league encompassing the militant minority within the AFL, while at the same time publicly promoting his particular brand of syndicalism, which some critics called "Fosterism."[3]

When he resigned as secretary of the National Committee for Organiz-ing Iron and Steel Workers in late 1919, Foster did so with the idea in mind of creating a new organization of trade union militants. This objec-tive was momentarily delayed; it would be nearly a year before he was able to pull together another syndicalist league. In the meantime, his ac-tivities seemed to lack coherent purpose. Certainly the events of 1918–19 had provided him with much to ponder. Later, he wrote that the defeat of the steel strike required a revision in his strategy. His hopes of using the steel strike as an entering wedge in a campaign to organize American mass-production industries were gone, as also was his "hope of over-throwing the Gompers machine by the mass organization of the unorgan-ized."[4]

Did Foster, as a result of the defeat of the packing and steel campaigns, begin to doubt that his strategy of revolutionizing the AFL from within could be successful? As would be true throughout his career, his "scien-tific" perspective on the inevitable development of unionism remained the basis of his faith when the workers and the unions failed to perform as anticipated. However, Foster was no grim determinist; he blamed the de-feats of the immediate postwar period in large part on the lack of a well-organized militant minority in the AFL, and his statements at the conclu-sion of the steel campaign indicate that he felt that the next phase of his activities in the labor movement must proceed as much along educational as organizational lines. Foster occasionally used the term "education" interchangeably with "sabotage," but his formation of yet another educa-tional league after the war can also be seen as consistent with his admira-tion of the ideas of Lester Frank Ward, a progressive theorist whose writ-ings Foster admired at the time.[5] His shifting focus in 1920 was in part reflected by the fact that immediately after the strike he concentrated his energies on writing his classic account of the conflict, *The Great Steel Strike and Its Lessons*. It was a relatively unusual undertaking for a labor organizer. He wrote to Roger Baldwin in February, 1920 that "for the past few weeks (or should I say for the past few years) I have been so damned busy that I hardly know which end of me is up. . . . I am so busy, as peculiarly busy in fact as a fish out of water—I, a roughneck, am writ-ing a book."[6]

Foster's nebulous status in 1920 is illustrated by his lack of direct in-volvement in the "outlaw" railroad strike of that year. As a result of wartime legislation, American railroads had remained under federal con-trol, and strikes were thus prohibited. However, the government repeatedly refused to grant wage increases in the industry in spite of the steadily increasing inflation, and after the government control was lifted in March 1920, wildcat strikes of switchmen, engineers, conductors, and firemen spread throughout the nation. Attorney General A. Mitchell Palmer publicly accused Foster of being behind the walkout, but Foster issued a blistering denial. He asserted that he knew none of the individuals who were advertised as strike leaders, and dismissed Palmer's accusations as an attempt to boost his campaign for president. Still, the strike suggested to Foster the need for organizational coherence among the militant railroad employees. He noted that it was likely that "there never was a big strike in this country more spontaneous and unplanned than the one in question." Indeed, in its monthly reports to the Department of Justice early in 1920, Military Intelligence reported that Foster "and his former associates are now in Chicago, where an active interest in railway circles is being manifested by them."[7] When he formed the Trade Union Educational League later in the year, much of its propaganda was aimed at discontented railroad shop workers.

Although he was not listed as an official delegate, the "red radical" of the recent steel strike attended the AFL convention in Montreal in June. The issue with which the convention was most concerned was the Plumb Plan for nationalizing the railroads. Since 1919, the International Association of Machinists and its Socialist president, William Johnston, had lobbied intensively in Congress for some form of continuance of federal administration after the war ended, even though during the red scare, nationalization was met with intense opposition. The *New York Times* editorialized that the Plumb Plan was "a venture into radical socialism— a very long step towards the principles of Lenin and Trotsky and of Soviet Government." Nonetheless, at the 1920 AFL convention, the IAM delegation was influential in securing approval of a resolution favoring government ownership. Foster was seated with the Railway Carmen delegation during the voting on the issue, and knew Martin Ryan, the union's influential president. Foster interpreted the convention's approval of the Plumb Plan as a defeat for Gompers, and may have felt that the AFL president's days were numbered, since even Matthew Woll, one of Gompers's most trusted associates, voted with the railroad unions. A Wobbly who was in Montreal at the time and who was acquainted with Foster carefully noted his demeanor. "Foster was in high favor around the convention hall. He was a conspicuous figure around the lobby and among the groups of delegates. I met him in the lobby after the roll call vote on the Plumb Plan resolution, and [he] said to me in great glee, 'You see what we're doing? We've put the skids under the old man.'"[8]

The support of Socialists like Johnston in pushing through the Plumb Plan resolution cannot have failed to impress Foster, for the only serious contenders as an alternative leadership to that of Gompers were the Socialists. As far back as 1912, writing for *La Vie ouvrière,* he had recognized the importance of this socialist opposition; despite his profound mistrust of their policies, he predicted that "the capture of the AFL by the socialists will mark a deep change in the workers' movement."[9] In addition, Johnston's IAM aggressively took up the issue of amalgamation in the immediate postwar period; this was a progressive program that was very close to Foster's own position on the problem of pushing the AFL toward industrial unionism. Thus, it is not surprising that in May of 1920, months after the formation of the Communist and Communist Labor parties, Foster was a prominent guest at the Socialist party's national convention in New York. In a well-received address, he envisioned a new strike in the steel industry that would be a signal for a general strike of all workers. "When the big strike comes, we want the steel workers, the mine workers, the railroad men and every trade in," he proposed. When he was introduced, the *New York Times* noted, Foster was greeted with "a tremendous demonstration of approval." Only the mention of the name of Eugene Debs, who was incarcerated at the federal penitentiary in Atlanta, gained a more enthusiastic reception by the delegates.[10]

Despite his prominence in labor and radical circles after the steel strike, Foster drifted in his "free-lance" role in 1920. He resigned his position as a Brotherhood of Railway Carmen organizer, and was unable to secure employment as a car inspector because he had been blacklisted in Chicago.[11] His position in the AFL was ambiguous, as illustrated by his status at the Montreal convention. As if to underline his uncertain situation, Foster became business manager for the *New Majority* in July. This would be perhaps the most incongruous position he would ever hold, for Foster was temperamentally unsuited for office work despite his tremendous organizing ability. His job required that he work to increase the paper's circulation and promote labor party initiatives among Chicago unionists. His tenure proved to be quite unsuccessful; the newspaper ran up huge deficits during the summer of 1920. During this period, *New Majority* noted, there was a notable "apathy" among unions affiliated with the CFL in generating subscriptions. The AFL national office pressured many locals of international unions to withdraw support from Fitzpatrick's labor party initiative. Interestingly enough, beginning in November, immediately after Foster's resignation and the defeat of the Farmer-Labor party ticket, the paper began to generate surpluses once again. Nonetheless, his resignation was abrupt, and the *New Majority* implied that this had created a "burden" for the editorial staff.[12]

The end of the steel strike marked the beginning of a kind of "united front" period for Foster, in which he found himself involved with causes and groups that were not strictly trade unionist in orientation. During the strike, he began an interesting relationship with the American Civil Liberties Union. In November 1919, he had invited the ACLU to investigate civil liberties in Pittsburgh. As the strike wore down, he proposed that ACLU speakers in Pennsylvania might "help get civil rights for the strikers" and generally "open up" the situation.[13] Although these proposals came to nothing with the collapse of the strike, Foster's relationship with the ACLU showed that he had begun to look outside purely working-class organizations for support of his initiatives and ideas. B. W. Huebsch, a member of the ACLU national board, published Foster's book on the steel strike. Beyond the ACLU, liberals seemed to receive Foster positively. In 1920, the publication of a sympathetic interpretation of the steel strike by the Interchurch World Commission, an interdenominational body of socially conscious Protestant clerics, drew widespread negative comment by a variety of groups that had been opposed to the unionizing drive, including the National Civic Federation. The commission itself, during its investigation of the strike, questioned Foster in a sympathetic manner and refused to resort to the kind of red-baiting that the Senate investigatory committee had indulged in. Articles in the *New Republic* were uniformly supportive of Foster and his activities. The difficulties encountered by unions in gaining favorable publicity and free speech seemed uppermost on Foster's mind when he assented to Roger Baldwin's request that he become a member of the national board of the ACLU. "Altho [sic] I make it an inflexible rule to belong only to strictly trade union organizations," he wrote, "I feel that I should make an exception in the case of your body. If there is anyone in this country who should realize the necessity of free speech and do all possible to achieve it, it is my humble self."[14]

Foster remained mostly aloof, though, as organized labor sought to redefine and reassert its citizenship in the first years of the decade. Despite his syndicalist background, he could not have helped being exposed in 1920 to the widespread sentiment among unionists that some type of political action by labor would be necesssary in the postwar environment. John Fitzpatrick had been a persistent opponent of Samuel Gompers's nonpartisan political stance, and had helped create the Labor party of Cook County in 1918. In April 1919, he polled a sizable fifty thousand votes in his candidacy for mayor. In November, as the steel strike waned, Fitzpatrick called a conference in Chicago that resulted in the formation of the American Labor party. During the summer of 1920, the new party merged with the Committee of Forty-Eight, a group of ex–Bull Moosers and Liberals led by Amos Pinchot; the result was the Farmer-Labor party. In 1920, Parley Parker Christensen ran for president and Max Hayes for vice president under the aegis of the new party; in November, they polled three hundred thousand votes. The labor party movement in 1920 had broad support, not only among Chicago unionists, but also among garment workers in New York City, the International Association of Machinists, the railroad brotherhoods, and mine workers. For Fitzpatrick, the widespread use of the injunction against strikes in Chicago and the successes of the British Labor party were powerful arguments impelling him toward involvement in labor politics.[15]

During the steel strike, Foster had refused to allow labor party exhortations to be published in the National Committee's official strike bulletin. Finally, John Fitzpatrick prevailed upon him to allow some publicity to enter the strike literature.[16] By 1920, however, there are indications that Foster the syndicalist was developing closer ties with the labor party movement. He was a delegate at the Farmer-Labor party convention in Chicago in 1920. Two of his closest associates, Samuel Hammersmark and J. W. Johnstone, had also established significant relationships in this direction. Hammersmark was the secretary treasurer of the Cook County Labor party in 1920. Though he resigned in May 1921, as late as 1922, his name appeared on a Cook County Farmer-Labor party primary election ballot. Johnstone was head of the party's organization committee in 1920.[17] Harry Ault, a friend of Foster's from his days in Seattle, was prominent at the FLP's founding convention in Chicago in 1919, and helped establish a ticket in Washington State during the 1920 elections. In a letter to Ault, Foster seemed positively disposed toward his efforts: "From the faint echoes of the strife reaching here it would seem that you fellows have a dandy chance to carry your state. If so it will be an epoch-making achievement. More power to you, say I." Working as business manager for the *New Majority*, Foster himself occupied a prominent position on the Farmer-Labor party's official organ. Later, he wrote that "during the course of the meat packing and steel campaigns my old Syndicalist anti-politics had started to collapse. So much so that by 1920 I had begun to be active in the Labor Party, then centering in Chicago."[18]

This, however, was somewhat of an overstatement. The alacrity with which Foster dropped his affiliation with the *New Majority*, and the fact that he was willing to embark upon a new venture almost immediately after the November elections suggests that he had been thinking along other lines for some time. Writing to Ault in October, he hinted at his plans: "After the election a few of us here are about to launch a project which I think will interest you very much." By mid-November, the Trade Union Educational League had come into being. Its headquarters during its first months of existence was in the Chicago Federation of Labor Building at 166 West Washington Street. While Foster had broadened his scope somewhat since the steel strike, the new league was essentially a reprise of the Syndicalist League of North America and the International Trade Union Educational League, albeit with minor adjustments. For instance, Foster now called much more explicitly for industrial unionism. In a letter to Upton Sinclair, he asserted that "it seems to me that it is time that the left wing of the great labor movement develop an industrial program. It had one fifteen years ago, but that led to the IWW and all these years of impotency. The time is ripe for another, and the new one, if it is to fare better than the last, must call for the development of the inevitable industrial unionism thru the old trade unions."[19] Foster was clearly excited about the prospects for starting up another syndicalist league, and it is easy to imagine that despite his uncertain affiliation (and income) during this period, he worked day and night to develop contacts and a credible program for his new venture.

One of the few published documents relating to the new league contains a classic statement of "Fosterism." The emphasis on the militant minority, the belief in the "evolutionary process to industrial unionism," the reference to trends in the international labor movement, and the almost overwhelming sense of personal leadership are reflected in this one-page leaflet, called quite simply "A Statement of the Aims of the Trade Union Educational League." Although it implores the reader to subscribe to *The Labor Herald*, there is no evidence that any issues of this newspaper ran until 1922. It concludes with a request that "all workers desirous of making a real effort to put the labor movement upon an industrial basis are requested to communicate with the undersigned [Foster]." In some respects, this statement of aims is even less radical than that of the previous ITUEL. While there is an overt emphasis on industrial unionism, it is unmistakable that progress in that direction would be gradual and "natural" rather than revolutionary. It is enough for Foster merely to point out that unions "are constantly broadening and extending their scope of action. This they are doing through a whole series of get-together devices, familiar to all experienced trade unionists, such as amalgamations, federations, departments, local councils, joint agreements, common organizing campaigns and strikes, extensions of jurisdictions to include women, negroes, the unskilled, etc. etc." There is no talk of the abolition of the wages system or a labor party. It was a program calculated to find approval among a wide spectrum of progressive unionists.[20]

True to the putative intent of his new league, Foster departed on a long speaking tour for the Amalgamated Clothing Workers in late November. His friend David Saposs, educational director of the ACW, organized the tour. The ACW had been able to donate the huge sum of one hundred thousand dollars to support relief for the steel strikers in 1919. In 1920, the fact that Foster was engaged by the union to embark upon a lecture tour during which he would supposedly promote the program of his new league illustrated his strong ties with progressive trade unionists. Indeed, a central focus of Foster's lectures, the need for the amalgamation of craft

unions, while consistent with his earlier statements, was essentially con-
gruent with the views of Sidney Hillman, the Socialist president of the
Amalgamated.[21]

In early 1921, Foster gave a lecture for an organization called the Chicago Workers' Institute that developed into an acrimonious debate with
his audience. He began his talk with an admonition: "Quarantine your
ideas by taking them away from the unions where the masses are, or
spread them by fighting the conservatives on the floor of the unions—that
is the choice you radicals have to make." This led to a hot dispute with
IWW partisans in the crowd, who violently objected to his arguments. He
accused radicals of having "violated the first principle of working class
solidarity. They have forsaken the real organizations of labor, based
upon common economic interests, and have formed outside organizations, based upon a revolutionary creed."[22]

It is impossible to know whether or not his audience that evening included Communists, but if so, Foster's message could not have helped but
antagonize them. The two American Communist parties that had been
founded in Chicago by dissident left-wing factions of the Socialist party
at the height of the steel organizing campaign were, at the time of Foster's
speech, entering into unity negotiations. However, the two parties would
not finally merge until May. At their inception, the Communist groups
resorted to underground, conspiratorial tactics, partly as a result of their
members' infatuation with the revolutionary élan of the Bolsheviks, and
partly because they were driven below the surface of American life by the
red scare and the Palmer raids. Although in early 1921 the issue separating the two parties was the difficult question of whether or not the movement should emerge from the underground and engage in "legal" tactics,
on the issue of unionism and the AFL, there was still a general consensus.
The Communist Labor party endorsed the "revolutionary industrial unionism" of the IWW, "whose long and valiant struggles in the class-war
have earned the respect and affection of all workers everywhere." The
Communist party merely noted that "the A.F.L. is reactionary and a bulwark of capitalism. It is actually an enemy to the workers."[23]

However, during the steel strike, both the IWW and the fledgling Communist parties had seemed uncertain about how they should react to the
unrest. On the one hand, they offered sharp critiques of Foster's syndicalist aims and methods. *The Communist* gave him a nickname that must
have seemed appropriate to those who scorned his "evolutionary" approach to industrial unionism: "E. Z. Foster." The organ reiterated that
the AFL, into which Foster sought to organize the workers, was in fact
"the arch enemy of the militant proletariat." As a result, both Communist
parties had no immediate program for the strike, and did not have a plan
for organizational work. All that was offered were two slogans: "Make

the strike general and seize the State power." Yet, all workers were urged to somehow support the steelworkers in an attempt to "crush the capitalists." Louis Fraina wrote of the 1919 strike wave in general that "these strikes . . . must cease being strikes and become revolutionary mass action against capitalism and the State. Every strike must be a small revolution, educating and disciplining the workers for the final revolutionary struggle."

Despite these criticisms, other radicals offered rhetorical support to Foster and his aims. The *Ohio Socialist*, a left-wing organ at the time, published a favorable assessment of the strike. Later, a writer for *The Toiler* pointed to Foster's unique position in the labor movement, and unwittingly foreshadowed the difficulties the organizer of the steel strike would face as a Communist in the 1920s. The publication of *The Great Steel Strike and Its Lessons* marked "the arrival of a new type of labor leader in the labor movement, corresponding more closely to the new conditions and temper of the masses; a type, at once canny and practical, intelligent and efficient, fearless but not revolutionary. As clearly as Foster is distinct from the Communists, he is as clearly distinct from the old trade union bureaucrats."[24]

Foster himself would have recognized certain elements of the founding desiderata of the Communist parties as quite close to his own views. After all, as it emerged in 1919, the Communist movement in America was the confluence of two general currents in American radicalism: left-wing socialism and IWW-style syndicalism. The Communist Labor party, for instance, proposed that "the most important means of capturing state power for the workers is the direct action of the masses, proceeding from the place where the workers are gathered together in shops and factories. The use of the political machinery of the capitalist state for this purpose is only secondary." Furthermore, "in America there is a highly-developed Labor Movement. This makes it impossible to accomplish the overthrow of capitalism except through the agency of the organized workers." In calling for "shop branches" and shop committees to conduct revolutionary propaganda, both parties were echoing the concept of the militant minority, which Foster had embraced since 1911. Likewise, the founding manifesto of the Communist Party implored its members to "participate in mass strikes, not only to achieve the immediate purpose of the strike, but to develop the revolutionary implications and action of the mass strike."[25] Despite these statements, Communists in the United States operated in a rarefied sphere far beyond the mainstream labor movement. Few American Communists possessed the experience of participating in a "mass strike," let alone developing its "revolutionary implications."[26]

How, then, is it possible to recognize Foster in late 1920 as an incipient Communist? While there was still a gulf separating "Fosterism" and

Communism, his outlook toward such issues as industrial unionism and political action seemed to be becoming more flexible. Moreover, David Saposs remembered that criticism of the steel strike by the Communist *New Masses* worried Foster more than any other criticism. While he had been disdainful of commentary on his tactics by "radicals" during the strike, by 1920 Foster was "drifting away" from the AFL. He thought "Communism was the wave of the future," according to Saposs.[27] As a close follower of trends in the international labor movement, he probably shared the official viewpoint of the Chicago Federation of Labor on the Russian Revolution. Since 1917, the CFL had gone on record as favoring the recognition of the Soviet government. In 1920, the body endorsed a resolution which in effect called for a general strike in Chicago if the Soviet Union were invaded. At the Farmer-Labor party convention that year, which Foster attended, Fitzpatrick expressed the hope that "the day was only near when the workers in the United States would be able to concentrate their efforts and do a job such as Russia has done." Samuel Gompers, long since convinced that the Soviet regime was essentially undemocratic and hostile to labor unionism, wrote defiantly to a CFL official that "it cannot be possible that a single delegate to the Chicago Federation of Labor is in possession of the real facts concerning Russia and the slavery of its workers maintained by militarism."[28]

Foster probably had some personal contact with the Communist movement as well. As he maintained his connections in the Chicago radical community, he could not have helped but cross paths with individual Communists at some point. Moreover, a significant proportion of the leadership of Foster's earlier leagues was moving in that direction by 1920. Interestingly enough, four members of the "executive board" of his ITUEL eventually became Communists: Jack Carney (one of the founders of the Communist Labor Party in 1919), J. W. Johnstone, Jay Fox, and Joseph Manley.[29] As for Johnstone, he had become a Communist sometime before Foster first sailed to the Soviet Union in early 1921. It was not unusual for Foster to be assailed as a Bolshevik or Communist even before he departed for Russia. Late in 1920, the chairman of the Americanization Committee of the Chicago Association of Commerce gained attention when he told a women's club that "I believe that Foster and the 15 percent who are urging bolshevism upon America with Russian gold, should be stood up against the wall and shot by a firing squad, and I would like to be one of them."[30]

While it is tempting to see Foster's trip to Europe in 1921 as the first step in a quasi-religious conversion process, it is more appropriate to recognize certain features of his thought, expressed years earlier, in the political philosophy of the Bolshevik revolution. The concept of the militant minority, which structured much of his activities in the 1910s, bears a striking resemblance to classical Leninist doctrine. Foster's moral skepti-

cism, his disdain for ideological expressions of "democracy" and nationalism, his opportunism, and even his vision of the future workers' society
are consistent with what came to be labelled "Bolshevism." It is no coinci-
dence that when he arrived in Moscow, he was in the company of many
of the leading figures in European syndicalism. Pierre Monatte, whom
Foster had befriended in Paris in 1911, Alfred Rosmer, Gaston Monmos-
seau, and Tom Mann were all syndicalist acquaintances of Foster's who
were in the process of entering the Communist movement at the time.
Many European syndicalists were entranced by the writings of Lenin,
whose *State and Revolution*, published in 1919, repudiated the idea of
gradualist political action and called for the immediate destruction of the
state in a revolutionary upheaval. Lenin's writings, at the time, were
called "Blanquism with *sauce tartare*." His proposal that the proletarian
state was only transitional ("in a community without class antagonisms,
the State is unnecessary and impossible") was appealing to anarcho-syn-
dicalists and radical unionists who had been accustomed to thinking of
Marxists as political reformists. However, the relationship between internationalist syndicalism and Communism would prove to be a difficult
one.[31]

For Foster, it was the publication of Lenin's *"Left-Wing" Communism: An Infantile Disorder* that accelerated his interest in Communism.
This pamphlet, which became available in the United States in 1921, was
an acrid polemic against the separatist assumptions of the new Western
Communist parties. The Bolshevik leader discussed an issue close to Foster's heart: the problem of revolutionary work within reformist trade unions. The pamphlet was written in the spring of 1920, when the possibility of revolution in Europe seemed increasingly remote and a number of
revolutionary uprisings had failed disastrously. Lenin referred sardonically to those Communists who, in light of recent developments, did not
understand the need to "compromise" and "maneuver" within reactionary trade unions by whatever means necessary. "We cannot but regard as
. . . ridiculous and childish nonsense the ponderous, very learned, and
frightfully revolutionary disquisitions . . . to the effect that Communists
cannot and should not work in reactionary trade unions," he wrote.
Communists "must imperatively *work wherever the masses are to be
found.*" In this pamphlet, Foster "found revolutionary dual unionism
condemned and the boring from within policy endorsed much more
clearly and forcefully than we had ever expressed it." It is safe to conclude
that what initially drew Foster to the Communist movement was not
Marxist philosophy, but rather a powerful exposition of a particular
tactic.[32]

However, despite what he later termed his "joy and amazement" at the
appearance of the pamphlet, there were aspects of *Left-Wing Communism* that were inconsistent with "Fosterism." Ever since his experiences

in Seattle with Hermon Titus and the Workingmen's party, Foster had rejected the concept of a leading role for a political party in the labor movement. In 1912, his advice to his fellow syndicalists had been simple: fight political Socialists in the unions. James P. Cannon, a Communist and the future founder of the Socialist Workers' party, evidently had some contact with Foster in 1920 or 1921 before the latter's trip to Moscow. At that point, Foster was still suspicious of the Communists' political orientation and close relationship with the IWW. Although the aftermath of the steel strike found him experimenting with a labor party idea, this was a venture whose leadership was drawn from labor unions. For Lenin, however, there was no doubt of the leading role of the party. He began his disquisition on trade unions in *Left-Wing Communism* by invoking this principle: "Actually, all the directing bodies of the vast majority of the unions, and primarily, of course, of the all-Russian general trade union centre or bureau . . . consist of Communists and carry out all the instructions of the Party."[33] Foster would spend much of the rest of his career grappling with the implications of this conception of the role of unions in the revolution.

Despite these problems, the powerful example of the Bolshevik revolution and the pronouncements of Lenin on the necessity of "boring from within" finally inspired Foster to visit Russia. The Bolshevik leaders already knew of Foster as a possible U.S. ally. Lenin himself had received a copy of Foster's *The Great Steel Strike and Its Lessons* from John Reed in the fall of 1920. Reed occasionally discussed American conditions with Lenin, and wrote to him that Foster "has original ideas, a number of which are very valuable. I know him personally." That Reed may have known Foster "personally" by late 1920 is suggestive of Foster's previous ties with the fledgling Communist movement in the United States. Reed may have met Foster at the 1919 convention of the American Federation of Labor, where the radical journalist interviewed a number of officials.[34]

The formal invitation to visit Moscow came from Foster's old acquaintance, Earl Browder. Browder's political wanderings found him in New York in 1920, a member of the United Communist party. It was his acquaintance with American radical trade unionists, including Foster, that would provide him with his first substantial responsibility as a Communist. Browder was assigned the task of recruiting an American delegation to the forthcoming first congress of the Red International of Labor Unions (RILU) or Profintern in Moscow, and he promptly went to Chicago and looked up Foster. He found Foster to be a "sort of 'lone wolf' sort of operator"; moreover, "E.Z." Foster was still suspicious of Marxist politics in early 1921, according to Browder. Browder understood that Foster was "in cold relations with the official leadership of labor," and Foster later admitted that at the time of his first contacts with the Communists his newly organized TUEL "faced a most unpromising struggle for existence." After reading *Left-Wing Communism*, he sensed that there might be a place for him and his struggling league in the Communist movement. The role of traveling radical delegate was of course a familiar one for him. The internationalist ideal retained a powerful appeal to Foster, as it did for many other American and European syndicalists. In advance of the Bolsheviks, syndicalists had taken steps toward the creation of a revolutionary international of labor unions as early as 1913.[35]

Foster joined the international Communist movement during a period of retreat and reassessment for both. In the period immediately after the revolution in Russia, the Bolsheviks had no real use for an international trade union policy; given the perceived imminence of revolution in western Europe, what was most important was the organization of workers into Soviets or workers' councils under the leadership of Communist parties. By September 1919, however, such tactics seemed increasingly irrelevant. After the war, instead of joining Soviets, masses of European workers had flooded into the reformist trade unions. In order to counter the prestige of the reformist International Federation of Trade Unions or "yellow" international, the Bolsheviks moved to create a "red" trade union center, and European and American syndicalist organizations, including the IWW, were invited to join, even though the new international was founded with the intent of reasserting the predominance of politics within the trade unions.[36]

At the first formal Profintern congress, convened in July 1921, a large delegation of syndicalists argued stubbornly against the idea that the Communist union movement should be ultimately and organically connected to the Communist political apparatus. However, Albert Rosmer and Tom Mann, two of Foster's old syndicalist acquaintances, were among those who argued for closer cooperation between the trade unions and the Communist parties. Solomon Lozovsky, the head of the Profintern, assailed the syndicalist aloofness from politics, maintaining that politics was nothing other than "the active opposition of one class to another." He argued indignantly that to speak of the separation of economic and political action was nonsensical. Foster, never punctilious about theory, either agreed or acquiesced. His experiences of 1918–19 had driven home the idea that industrial struggles were to some extent political in nature. More important, he was more often thinking in terms of centralization and discipline, as his frequent mixing of strike and military terminology illustrated. According to the Bolsheviks, the revolution could not succeed without "the strictest discipline, without complete centralization." In other words, the Russians and their allies replied to the syndicalist invocations of spontaneity and decentralization with the argument that the class war must be fought with thoroughly "modern" organizational methods—a difficult argument for syndicalists like Foster to resist. The writer André Tridon had written as early as 1912 that "syndicalists are modern if anything. . . . The past is dead and the future is unknown. The immediate needs of the present hour are to them the sole object of interest."[37]

Ironically, while Foster was undoubtedly sympathetic with the Bolsheviks on these points, he may have calculated at first that he could have his TUEL and the advantages and prestige of international affiliation without sacrificing a great deal of independence. Reflecting the intense controversies at the congress, its final "Program of Action" contained several compromises. The four points of the resolution affirmed main tenets of the revolutionary syndicalists: the importance of direct action, industrial unionism, workers' control, and organization of factory committees. Differences of interpretation between Communists and syndicalists on each point were left unresolved. It was publicly acknowledged that the links between the RILU and the parties of the Communist International would be of "an organic and technical character," but that neither organization would be subordinate to the other. Recognizing the importance of gradually winning the allegiance of the organized sectors of the working class in the West, the Comintern early on tended to allow a degree of independence for the Profintern, which E. H. Carr has termed "by far the most powerful and important" of the Comintern's auxilliary organizations. During the 1920s, the Profintern developed into "more than a mere subsidiary organ." However, in an unpublished Profintern protocol, it was determined that "On all bureaux established by the [Profintern], the Communist party of the same country shall have adequate representation with decisive vote. Where disagreement arises between the party and the bureau, the position of the party shall prevail, pending appeal to and decision by the [Central Executive Committee of the Comintern]." Browder and William D. Haywood signed a document at the congress which stated that "in case of disagreement between the American Bureau of the RILU and the Communist party, the party decision prevails until final decision in Moscow." Foster's own "instructions" from the RILU upon being appointed "special representative" of the RILU in the United States carried the same requirement and stipulated that "your work in the United States will be to follow STRICTLY the principles and general policies laid down by the Congress of the RILU." To keep an eye on things, Browder, in acting as Foster's assistant, would also function as "information agent for the Executive Bureau of the RILU in Moscow."[38]

With regard to the matter closest to Foster's heart, the Profintern was quite specific: "The question of creating revolutionary cells and groups inside the American Federation of Labor and the independent unions is of vital importance. There is no other way by which one could gain the working mass in America, than to lead a systematic struggle within the unions." As for the IWW, its members "should join their respective trade unions and spread their propaganda among them." Despite this ukase, desultory opposition to the boring-from-within idea continued at the second Profintern Congress in 1922. It would not be until 1923 that the TUEL was officially recognized as the sole American section of the Profintern.[39]

While in Moscow, Foster must have been impressed with the figure of William D. Haywood, the Wobbly leader who had been the personification of western labor radicalism in the prewar era. A refugee from the American justice system, Haywood had arrived in Moscow at a time when the Russians favored the IWW perspective in the United States. At the third Comintern congress, which overlapped the Profintern gathering, Haywood's line on the IWW was ridiculed. In *Left-Wing Communism*, Lenin had specifically associated IWW tactics with "infantile" labor politics. In an interview, Haywood bitterly attacked Foster's position without referring to him by name. "There are some fellows around here who say that there are 159,000 good reds in the AFL. Anybody who says that is a damned fool," the expatriate Wobbly declared. At the end of the Profintern conference, Haywood wrote to Lenin trying to convince him that the IWW was not an "illegal" or "underground" organization. Yet, when the American delegation to the Comintern Congress submitted a "Budget for American Work," $100,000 of the roughly $350,000 total budget was proposed to be allocated for legal defense of Communist leaders of the IWW or to make good on the bonds of individuals like Haywood who had fled their appointments in court. In contrast, only $10,000 was to be allocated to organizing among mine and railroad workers.[40]

Still, Foster's views on the IWW, which he had held for nearly a decade, were now endorsed by the only successful revolutionary party in the world. Suddenly the TUEL, which had gotten off to an extremely shaky start, was endowed with tremendous significance. Profintern congresses were truly impressive events. At such gatherings Foster was in the company of radical unionists from all over the world, and he might observe Lenin or Trotsky in action or attend a reception, for instance, for veterans of the Paris Commune. Nonetheless, Foster remained in the background while he was in Moscow. Alfred Rosmer, who knew Foster as a result of the latter's sojourn in France in 1911, observed that his visit to Moscow was "notable for its discretion." Browder, on the other hand, played a more visible role. He was secretary of the American delegation, and represented the TUEL in discussions. He worked hard to promote Foster and the TUEL, writing to Trotsky in reference to the strike movement of 1919 in which Foster had played so large a role that "the events of 1919 provided the American workers with more fundamental Communist education by one hundred times than was accomplished by the Communist parties. Specifically, these events showed that it is within the realm of possibility for the Communists of America to take over the direction of the American labor movement" with an organization like the TUEL, in a short amount of time. Browder attempted unsuccessfully to set up a meeting between Foster and Lenin, writing somewhat overoptimistically to Lenin that Foster is "the leader of the Left Wing of the American Federation of Labor." Although Foster had a chance to hear Lenin speak a number of times, he spent much time composing dispatches for the Federated Press and the *Voice of Labor*, a recently founded Chicago newspaper edited by Jack Carney. He seemed to be responding to Gompers's challenge that Chicago unionists did not know the "real facts" about Russia. Along with dispatches extolling the political virtues of the revolution, he composed detailed reports on the state of Russian agriculture and the currency system.[41]

In the Soviet Union, Foster found that "the new Russian government is really a workers' republic." Noting that all adults over eighteen could vote, but that capitalists were disfranchised, he compared the situation to the United States, where capitalists "set up all sorts of residence, sex and other ridiculous voting qualifications that deprive millions of toilers of any say in the government." He quite simplistically portrayed the soviets as democratic workers' councils, chosen directly by workers in their place of employment. Otherwise, there were "no general elections as Americans understand the term." Although he observed that the delegates to the soviets could be recalled at any time, he did not elaborate the process by which this would come about. Moreover, Foster wrote admiringly, there is no "ridiculous" separation of powers in the Soviet Union: "Once the workers' government has spoken that settles the matter."[42]

Foster, of course, was most interested in Soviet trade unions, and his ability to convince his audience that they functioned in the workers' interests was vital in light of Gompers's frequent attacks on the "undemocratic" nature of the Russian labor movement. In some respects, his reports on this issue reflect his earlier meditations on the role of unions in a post-revolutionary society. In *Syndicalism* and elsewhere, he had proposed that the "fighting" functions of unions would disappear, and that government would be carried on efficiently by a technical intelligentsia. In 1921, he bowed to Lenin in noting that the trade unions in the Soviet Union were "the very foundation of the whole soviet structure." Yet, he observed, the unions had played very little part in the actual revolution. After all, "at the outbreak of the February Revolution in 1917 there were in all Russia only three unions." Here, Foster was confronted with a direct challenge to his previous thinking. Trade unions had played a marginal role at best in establishing the only revolutionary government in the world.[43] Continuing, he became entangled in yet another inconsistency. The Russian unions, he observed, were purely industrial in nature. Previously, he had believed that industrial unionism could come about in the United States only through a process of steady evolution. In the Soviet Union, Foster reflected, in a clumsy stab at the IWW, "the industrial unionism prevailing . . . is not due to the sudden realization of a beautiful scheme. . . . On the contrary, it is the result of the every day experiences of the movement, the culmination of a constant structural evolution to meet the needs of the workers." Yet, in a country that was far less industrially developed than the United States, the "evolution" of industrial unionism could not have lasted very long—especially if, only four years earlier, there had been only three unions in all of Russia.[44]

Moreover, the Russian unions were indisputably different bodies than those in America, as Foster recognized. Affirming his earlier prognostications on the "future society," he proposed that after the October Revolution, the unions had merely been transformed from "organs of combat to organs for carrying on production." During the revolution, the militant minority, or in this case, the "shop committees," had carried on most of the struggles in the industrial sector. However, these were "mostly independent of the unions." For Foster, "workers' control" was a means to power, but was largely inapplicable to the management of industry in a socialist society. After the revolution, these fighting bodies had to give up their control of industry "into the hands of the various boards and committees of the supreme economic council." The shop committees merely recognized that "special ability" was necessary for the complex task of managing production, and that "this ability must not be hedged about with red tape or ignorant meddlers." Because of this, the workers on the shop floors no longer insisted upon "mechanical representation" in the bodies that govern industry. Instead, they "aid" in the selection of such groups, but then "give them power to go ahead in purely technical matters." Under the crisis conditions in the new society, where the task was rebuilding industry, strikes were "nothing less than so much scabbing on the revolution."[45]

However, in 1921, as Foster probably knew, trade unions and their leaders represented a powerful and relatively independent bloc within the Soviet Communist party itself. There was significant worker resistance to Party domination of the unions, as well as opposition to the introduction of individual management by experts (as opposed to the system of committee or collective management). Moreover, until 1928, there would be constant factional struggles within the Bolshevik leadership over the nature and role of trade unions in the new Soviet state. Powerful figures like Lozovsky and Mikhail Tomsky, chairman of the All-Union Trade Union Council, argued that unions should be relatively independent of the party and retain a role as protectors of workers' interests. Others, including Trotsky and Bukharin, advocated the militarization or complete "statification" of the unions in order to facilitate the rebuilding of the shattered Russian industrial base. As the emergency measures of War Communism were revised after 1920 and opposition to party domination of the unions persisted, Lenin himself steered a middle course, recognizing unions as vital linking mechanisms between the state and the masses, but acknowledging both that unions themselves should retain a powerful voice in the management of their members' labor and even proposing that workers would require union protection against the Soviet state. In 1921 Foster endorsed the concept of strong Party control of the unions, individual management "for efficiency's sake," and compulsory labor as a temporary measure until the old habits of capitalism are "eliminated from the workers' minds by proletarian education." After all, "the people are still afflicted with the ignorance, selfishness, and short-sightedness of the old dog-eat-dog competitive system. Discipline is still necessary. Only a minority are intellectually prepared for the new society. And it falls as naturally to this intelligent minority to set up the essential discipline in Russian industry as it does to the corresponding minority in American trade unions to create the discipline absolutely necessary to make the masses function in those bodies."[46]

Foster's doubts about the ability of workers to understand the imperatives of industrial development in the postrevolutionary society led him even further from traditional syndicalist ideals. If, as he had asserted in 1912, unions could not effectively manage economic relations in a new social order, then it was necessary to establish another form of control. In Russia, he found that "not only have the unions been unable to operate industry by themselves, but the whole syndicalist conception of a purely industrial social mechanism has proved unworkable." Because of the conditions faced by the Bolsheviks, "the workers have been compelled, in spite of themselves, to create a political state with all its organs of repression in order to achieve communism." The political state, in the Soviet Union, was administered by the Communist party, which, he observed, "is more than a political party in the accepted sense of the term. It is really a scientific system of social control: an organization which makes every institution function in the spirit of the revolution." In all his meditations on the Russian Revolution, Foster was as much concerned with production, efficiency, and order as with social justice. He did not attempt to specify the point at which these elements were potentially divergent.[47]

If Foster's admiration of the Russian Revolution could be anticipated in his earlier syndicalism, other qualities of Bolshevik governance appealed to him at yet another level. A central assumption of Foster's thought had always been the ubiquity of the capitalist wage relation in

American society. In *Syndicalism,* he had proposed that capitalism had organized all dimensions of society in its own image. The only "space" or independent social sphere that might be established was within the trade union movement. However, by 1922, his faith in the transformative power of labor unions, as well as his belief in the inevitable evolution of unions into higher forms of organization, had been dramatically called into question. Within this historical context of defeat, he was led to posit an alternative teleology, as well as a more explicit (because it had seemingly been actualized by the Soviet Communists) vision of the "new society." It is not surprising that his understanding of capitalism as a "total" form of social organization caused him to project as its alternative a totalizing, uncategorical revolutionary ideology. He quoted Zinoviev approvingly: the Communist party "is an organization dealing with all sides of all questions, without any exception." Foster wrote admiringly that the party, "if it is omnipresent, it is also omnipotent. Although it is entirely unofficial in character, it has the deciding voice in all social questions."[48]

While certain aspects of Soviet society appealed to Foster and seemingly confirmed aspects of his earlier speculations, there is no doubt that a careful observer would have entertained doubts about the survival of the revolution in the summer of 1921. Traveling near Leningrad, Foster saw that "the countryside was devastated, many bridges were lying in rivers, the people were poverty stricken." In Moscow, the whole population seemed to be "living on the edge of starvation, everybody looked thin and wasted." Significant political dissent existed as well; "it was the period of the Kronstadt revolt and many peasant uprisings" and "numerous threatening strikes" in Moscow. Foster's dry and empirical dispatches as well as the abundant evidence of the fragility of the revolution suggests that he was first attracted to Communism because of the power and discipline of the Party, not because of any messianic faith in the future of the socialist ideal in Russia.[49]

In the midst of this, Foster witnessed a spectacular ritual affirmation of his revolutionary ideal. "Once in a while one has an experience that can never be forgotten so long as life lasts," he wrote. In June, he was present at a mass demonstration held in Red Square in honor of the Third Congress of the Communist International. In the huge cobblestone square, he watched a parade of the Red Army, after which Leon Trotsky in plain military uniform reviewed the troops. It seemed to be a completely different scene from years earlier, when as a young man he had observed Kaiser Wilhelm review his troops on the eve of World War I. The Soviet officers were "conspicuous by their lack of the usual military swagger and bluster." Foster was overwhelmed by this display of the power of the Red Army. The symbolism here was democratic and international, with heterogeneous groups of civilians, students, factory groups, and trade unionists marching with crack military regiments. Yet the Communist party groups particularly impressed Foster. The party, he noted, "is the brain and backbone of the Russian revolution," its elite shock troops. In uncharacteristically exaggerated prose, Foster proposed that "no capitalist country possesses armed forces which, man for man, could meet them successfully in battle." Significantly, the party groups marched at the very head of the parade. "In Russia the Communists are first in war and everything else." He watched them march by "with more interest than I have ever bestowed on any other body of human beings in my life." Foster reflected that "it seemed as though I saw the soul of the revolution." Witnessing this military display was clearly the emotional high point of Foster's first visit to the new Soviet Union.[50]

Before he left the Soviet Union, Foster went on a day trip with five other international delegates to what Foster described as a "workers' rest home" approximately twenty miles from Moscow. Accompanied by Solomon Lozovsky, the party drove to a confiscated Russian estate where they were warmly greeted. The other guests were supposedly workers who had been chosen by their unions to enjoy the privilege of a vacation at the retreat. Foster's personality was ascetic, almost to an extreme. Yet it is striking that beginning in 1921, he was always afforded the trappings of prominence and a degree of physical comfort in the Soviet Union that he never enjoyed in the United States. This would be true, quite literally, to the day of his death. In 1921, the group was shown around their hostel, which "was furnished with the still-barbaric splendor characteristic of Russian mansions, with gilt and gold everywhere." After a hearty dinner Foster and the others played Russian games. The next day there was fishing, as well as boating, swimming, and hikes throughout the estate. In the evening, a concert was given in the huge ballroom, followed by a singing of the "Internationale." Foster had witnessed a demonstration of the fruits of the revolution, seemingly available to everyone according to merit.[51]

It is interesting to imagine how Foster conceptualized the new order in the Soviet Union. Prominent Communists seemed to have access to privileged treatment. During the parade that he witnessed, the army seemed to him well fed, despite the scarcity of food. Foster understood that there was a certain inequality in the distribution of goods, despite the egalitarian impulses behind the revolution. There is no evidence, however, that participation in the privileges accorded Communist party membership in the Soviet Union prompted contradictory feelings in Foster, who had always written bitterly about inequality in the United States, and who dedicated his life to the idea of working-class empowerment. The sacrifices and hard work of the few extraordinary militants in the Soviet Union justified their special status. On the other hand, there is no doubt that

Foster harbored the revolutionary's ambivalent feelings about the inert masses. Occasionally, his assumptions about the deep inadequacy of the workers could be expressed quite brutally. In an advertisement for the pamphlet he wrote on his experiences in Russia, Foster wrote honestly about the role of the "militant minority":[52]

> I am not astonished or discouraged that the workers are making a poor job of establishing the new society in Russia—I have had too much practical experience with the masses to expect anything else. Have I not organized as many as three or four thousand packinghouse or steel workers in a single union and then searched in vain among them for even one skilled or adaptable enough to keep the simple financial accounts of the organization or conduct its meetings? What, then, could I expect from the even less experienced Russian workers with the enormous tasks of the Russian revolution suddenly thrust upon them? Nothing more than the shrieking incompetence and indifference of the masses that I found—with a few live wires doing all the real work.

However, after his return to the United States, Foster wrote that "by their heroic and wonderful achievements in the past the Russian workers breed confidence for the future."[53]

In his later autobiographical accounts, written after years of participation in Party factional fights, Foster's descriptions of his visit to the Soviet Union are characterized by an inflated literary style that seems to border on cynicism. In 1921, "in the midst of . . . chaos and ruin, triumphant over its world of enemies," he wrote, "stood the brave Russian working class, led by the indomitable Communist Party with the great Lenin at its head." He had realized at the time that he "must stand shoulder to shoulder with the embattled Russian workers, win, lose, or draw." He had been, in 1921, "deeply certain that the Russian workers had found the way to Socialism and eventual Communism." As for his own views, "in Leninism I found the answer to every major revolutionary problem."[54] While traces of this kind of rhetoric are evident in his writings in 1921, by 1937 examples would abound in his prodigious output of books, pamphlets, and articles. Foster's public presentation of his politics was characterized by a peculiar doubleness, rendering his political "self" problematic. His gradual adoption of the inflated style of the Communists symbolizes as much as anything the devaluation of the rhetorical means to his political self-definition. In 1921, joining a vigorous debate in American labor circles about the nature of the new Soviet regime, Foster's propaganda often seemed cold and ersatz.

Foster's journey into the world of Communist politics was also a journey into a lexical environment that was different from the one in which he had been immersed during his years in the Chicago labor movement. Although he came to understand himself as a Communist "theoretician" only much later in his life, after 1921 he gradually, and perfunctorily, began to adopt the terminology of orthodox Marxism. It was not an altogether unfamiliar language to him; after all, he had begun his career in radical politics as a member of Hermon Titus's Socialist local in Seattle. However, while working within the Chicago labor movement, where "isms" were often greeted with skepticism, he had largely eschewed the phraseology of Marxian radicalism. He believed that he and a small coterie of militants could advance the revolution without embracing the language of "ultimate" demands. To a large extent he would continue to believe this, as his early years in the Communist movement would illustrate.

It is impossible to understand Foster's attitude toward the language of American radicalism without reference to his organizational ethos, and the historical context in which this ethos emerged. In his earlier career, Foster's thinking had been characterized by a curious combination of elements of American Progressivism, with its emphasis on organization and integration, and the nineteenth-century anarchism of the "Chicago Idea." Increasingly, however, he embraced the undemocratic implications of the organizational ethos, and rejected the assumptions of the anarchists, which he considered retrogressive and threatening to his conception of the way a revolution would be brought about. What Foster admired about the Russian Revolution was the discipline (and power) of the Communist party, and its ability to inspire the submission of individual will to a larger, ultimately progressive imperative. Despite the fact that elements of his syndicalism would remain with him during his career as a Communist, Foster conceived of his entrance into the Communist movement as a kind of conversion, an act that was radically discontinuous from his earlier politics and which set him free, so to speak, from his own history. According to *From Bryan to Stalin*, in 1921 he accepted his new identity as a Communist "without difficulty, though I had been a syndicalist for a dozen years."[55]

Foster's admiration of the revolution and his willingness to become a Communist are consistent with the central assumptions of the "borer from within," that the primary responsibility of those seeking fulfillment of a particular goal is to seek first a viable organizational base. "The Russian Communist Party was the highest type of organization ever produced by mankind," he concluded.[56] Once inside, the true voice of the "borer from within" can be found only with difficulty because it has been confined by the requirements of the organization. This never really troubled Foster, for unlike American socialists like Eugene Debs, he would always be more concerned with the structure of the revolution than with its moral authenticity. In addition, his belief that it is natural for a progressive movement to "camouflage" its aims with "phrases" confirms his devaluation of the language of revolution. This devaluation was part and parcel of Foster's whole analysis. "The Socialist party in this country collapsed because it was built upon talk, instead of upon the solid foundation of the trade union movement," he wrote shortly after becoming a Communist.[57]

In Foster's world, power and "talk" were oppositional categories, not related to each other in any stable way. The influence of the Communist party derived from its organizational strength, which in turn originated with the skill and energy of the cohesive, elite militants of the Leninist vanguard. On the other hand, according to him, the Socialist party had "degenerated into a movement of the poor and discontented of all classes." In Foster's mind, the Socialist party was associated not only with an expansive definition of citizenship and the politics of inclusion but also with "talk" and powerlessness. Communism was fundamentally exclusive, and associated with organization and the conquest of real power. It is striking that this series of oppositions contains intimations of gender: like many of his contemporaries, Foster associated organization (and executive ability) with manhood and Socialist politics with traits like "utopianism" and impracticality. In the class war the rhetoric of citizenship was futile and empty; the socialists, Foster averred, had given up the "vitalizing" doctrine of the class struggle.[58] These themes can be traced backward as well as forward in Foster's autobiographies. In a more basic and elemental sense, this aspect of his politics was consistent with his portrayals of his childhood: he was opposing the Catholicism of his mother, which he had rejected at an early age as ineffectual and superstitious, with the militant, insurrectionary Fenianism of his father.

Foster returned to the United States at the end of the summer of 1921. During the journey home, he had much to ponder. In the aftermath of the steelworkers' organizing campaign, he had brought together another syndicalist league, but the direction this organization would take seemed uncertain. Was the Trade Union Educational League to become only a clearinghouse for the ideas of progressive unionists, or a center for the dissemination of a more radical program? Foster's aversion to "talk" meant that he would not be entirely comfortable with either orientation. However, if the league was to be an organizing vehicle, how could momentum for unionizing drives be built in the context of the defeats of 1918–19? As Foster considered these questions, he was entering into an uncertain relationship with the American Communist movement. There is no evidence, however, that he was particularly wary of his new allies; indeed, he seemed to embrace the Communists and the Russian Revolution wholeheartedly. His accounts of his visit to the Soviet Union, written before he became a Communist, exude a sense of vindication. He secretly joined the American Communist party soon after he returned from Moscow. David Saposs remembered that when he, his wife, and Esther met Foster at the train station in Chicago upon his return from the Soviet Union, he seemed like a "new man."[59] Thus, once again Foster returned to the United States inspired, convinced that practical trade union militants in America could learn important lessons from the experiences of European revolutionaries.

Chapter 7

THE "FREE LANCE" AND THE COMMUNIST PARTY

The fate of the Communist party depends upon the
control of the masses, through the capture of the trade
unions, without which revolution is impossible.
—William Foster, 1923

ALTHOUGH William Foster secretly became a Communist shortly following his return from Moscow in September 1921, he would remain somewhat of a "free lance." For nearly a year and half, he publicly denied that he belonged to the Party. This denial represented more than simple prevarication or wariness about possible prosecution; the defining characteristic of his career in the 1920s would be his discomfort with his new allies, his uncertain fit within the early Communist movement. In his first years as a Communist, the Trade Union Educational League would be the primary focus of his activities. The dichotomy was not a rigid one, but during this period the two organizations developed along different lines. The early Communist movement, based primarily in New York, sought unabashedly to impose the model of the Russian Revolution on its activities in the United States. In this milieu, Foster was often viewed as a trade unionist without deeply held Communist convictions. On the other hand, despite his admiration of the Russians, once Foster returned to the United States in 1921, he sought to create a radical movement for industrial unionism that would be peculiarly adapted to American conditions. He expected that his TUEL, centered in Chicago, could function relatively unhindered within the Communist party apparatus as its trade union section.

It is striking that very little of the practical program that was called "Fosterism" in the war years changed after he became a Communist. In March 1921, shortly before his trip to Moscow, Foster defined the issue that would be the Communist party's central focus in the labor movement in the early 1920s: amalgamation. For him, amalgamation was as much a result of natural "evolution" in the unions as it was a strategy developed by devoted militants seeking to reorganize the existing trade union bureaucracy. Its advocates "have no plan or theory, but [work] pretty much as immediate circumstances dictate," he noted. Events after the war showed that the railroad unions in particular were ready for the next phase in this evolution. "Amalgamation of the sixteen railroad craft unions into one industrial union—that's the railroader's next step," Foster proposed.[1]

In Foster's conception, amalgamation meant full-scale industrial unionism. A decade earlier he had denied that the labor movement must move toward centralization in lockstep with the gigantism of large corporations, and had decried the "utopianism" of IWW-style industrial unionism. Now, following a series of demoralizing defeats, the earlier federation idea seemed outmoded. Whereas industrial unionism had been as much a state of consciousness as an organizational form in Foster's understanding of revolutionary tactics, now the idea of solidarity became more purely instrumental. The duty remained, however, for a few radical specialists to work within the existing unions to achieve their aims. While trade unions were revolutionary "at heart and in their daily actions," their structure was to be elaborated with networks of minority organizations, shop steward and shop committee movements, amalgamation committees and educational leagues. Beyond the workplace, labor politics should be subordinated to the initiative of that fraction of American workers who were organized: "The trade unions are the only possible basis for a successful Labor Party." However, Foster still had no coherent idea about the role of politics in establishing his planned fusion of the unions. He would prove unable effectively to manage his new relationship with the Communists during his first years in the party, and while he understood the strength of labor's impulse to political action in these years, he viewed the labor party initiatives of both Communists and progressives with a mixture of resignation, suspicion, and contempt.[2]

Nonetheless, by early 1922 Foster had come to believe that with the support of the Communists, the TUEL could develop a radical and realistic movement for industrial unionism in the United States. He achieved some noteworthy successes. For a brief period, amalgamation occupied the center of debates over the future of the labor movement in the United States, and the TUEL and a small but active group of non-Communist militants openly challenged the defensive posture assumed by much of the mainstream leadership of the American Federation of Labor following the setbacks of the war years. Yet, Foster's uncompromising aversion to any form of "class collaboration" set him apart from many progressive unionists during this period, and his deep ambivalence about the role of politics in the labor movement would sharply limit the scope of the small movement for industrial unionism begun by him and his dedicated group of union radicals.

While Foster calculated that the future of the TUEL lay with the Communists, his antipathy toward the Socialist party gradually sharpened.

During the steel strike he had worked closely with Socialists like James Maurer, president of the Pennsylvania Federation of Labor, and after the war he was still held in high regard by figures like Kate Richards O'Hare and Eugene Debs. His growing involvement with the Communists obviously rendered such relationships more problematic, despite the fact that he joined the Communist party at a time when it was being pressured by Moscow to act more like the Socialist party from which it had split in 1919. Foster's affiliation with the Communists after his return from Russia coincided with the Comintern's turn toward a united front perspective and its campaign to convince the American Communists to assume a more realistic attitude toward the trade unions. In the last months of 1921 the Communists organized the Workers' party as a "legal extension" of their underground party even though many Communists still quite adamantly refused to participate in "open struggles." Despite these changes, a defining characteristic of this stage of Foster's career would be the retention of his disdain for the Socialist party and the democratic ideals it represented. When a delegation of Communists approached Eugene Debs seeking his support shortly after his release from the Atlanta Penitentiary in the spring of 1922, he promised a meeting with Foster, but had other things to say as well. "The Communists are finally waking up to the fact that they should work in the unions. But perhaps they do this with the wrong motives—not to build up a vigorous labor movement, but simply to use the unions as channels of Communist propaganda," he told the delegates. "Some groups propose to take orders from men in Moscow who know absolutely nothing about American conditions. I know more about American psychology and conditions than all the leaders in Russia know in five years, and I will not accept my orders from a maniac like Zinoviev." Debs went on to ask, "since when, I want to know, has socialism become synonymous with Communism? I am not a Communist and I don't want to be one, and I do not believe in MINORITY RULE."[3]

Partly as a result of his association with the Communists, Foster the dangerous wartime labor leader achieved an intensely controversial public identity in the first years of the decade. The *New York Times* termed him "America's most prominent exponent of Soviet Russia's regime." This, of course, would have implications for his activities in the labor movement, where Foster preferred to portray himself as only a "radical regular," and where, in the early 1920s, discretion would become ever more highly valued. At the University of Wisconsin, the influential labor economist John R. Commons stirred up criticism when he invited Foster to address a mass meeting at the University Armory. Commons remembered that in a classroom meeting, Foster gave "the most scholarly account I have heard of the evolution of Communist doctrine from Marx to DeLeon to Lenin." At Columbia University the faculty refused to allow

Foster to speak on campus, shunting him to an off-campus location where he was attacked by egg-throwing protesters. Charlie Chaplin incurred the curiosity and wrath of red hunters when he held a reception for Foster at his home in Hollywood.[4]

In his first years as a Communist, Foster remained a flexible tactician who was untroubled by the nuances of Marxist theory. His earliest pronouncements added up to an inchoate version of American exceptionalism, the idea that unique conditions in the United States required fundamentally different tactics than those pursued by other Marxist parties. While still in Moscow, he wrote that America was the exception to the idea, still "prevailing in Marxist circles," that nations with the greatest industrial development also have highly developed labor movements. Furthermore, his experiences led him to believe that ethnic diversity and a high degree of prosperity did not explain America's particularly weak labor movement. Rather, it was purely because of the intellectual "backwardness" of American militants that the unions were peculiarly attenuated in the United States; the strategizing of labor radicals was too often infected with the impractical, utopian ideal of dual unionism. This kind of analysis did not go unchallenged. Later, responding to another airing of this idea, one Comintern authority, Z. Leder, accused Foster of confusing the American labor movement with the American labor bureaucracy, and pronounced that "Foster does not perceive the obliquity of his politico-historical outlook." Leder implied that the central assumptions of the militant minority were fundamentally flawed; "We must not forget that human beings and organizations alike, are merely the instruments of history," he intoned. Despite the fact that the review carried the imprimatur of high-level official sanction, Foster wrote an impertinent private rebuttal to its author and complained bitterly about its publication to Solomon Lozovsky, the head of the Profintern.[5]

Lozovsky, whom Foster had met during his first trip to Moscow, proved to be an important political ally in the Russian party apparatus. A short man with a large black beard and a nervous manner, Lozovsky remained director of the Profintern from its founding until its dissolution in 1937. A Bolshevik exile who had returned to Russia in 1917, he was nonetheless expelled from the party the following year because of his views on trade unions: he was an early and vociferous advocate of union independence from state control. Nonetheless, by 1920 he had surfaced once again as secretary of the All-Russian Union of Railway Workers and shortly thereafter as head of the Profintern. During his long subsequent career, he was known as an agile politician and "survivor"; after his service as head of the Profintern he was elevated to deputy foreign minister, a post he held from 1939 to 1946. In his later years, the American party held him in high esteem: in an unusual gesture, it presented him with an

American automobile as a gift. A popular figure with Western journalists, Lozovsky managed to evade every Stalinist purge but the last. He was arrested in 1949 for "plotting against Stalin" and was executed in 1952 for conspiring to "tear the Crimea away from the USSR" and create a Jewish state as a bulwark of American imperialism on Soviet territory. He was rehabilitated in 1956. Nikita Khrushchev remembered Lozovsky as an intensely committed and indefatigable antifascist, and recalled his demise with particular regret.[6]

During Foster's visit to Moscow Lozovsky had promised financial support for the TUEL, and soon after arriving back in the United States Browder wrote a letter reminding him of the agreement. "The plans made with Borden [Foster] are being carried out. . . . We don't need a great deal but we must have our journal," he importuned in a letter intercepted by the Bureau of Investigation. In early 1922, Browder telegramed that notwithstanding the sale of ten thousand copies of Foster's pamphlet *The Russian Revolution*, the league still needed ten thousand dollars to start up the *Labor Herald*. He promised Lozovsky that "Foster will lead National Movement. Starting throughout country March to organize Left Wing under name of TUEL. Connections estimated in 500 towns; Foster comes out publicly for RILU."[7]

However, when the *Labor Herald* finally appeared in March, it would have been difficult to identify it as a Communist journal. Its opening statement of principles did not mention anything about a labor party, dictatorship of the proletariat, or support for the Soviet Union, even though the Russian Revolution was cited as proof of the validity of the concept of the "militant minority." All this was in line with Foster's belief that all "aggressive" social movements had to "camouflage" their aims, yet he immodestly declared that "the launching of the Trade Union Educational League marks a turning point in American labor history."[8]

Before the first issue of the *Labor Herald* appeared, Foster mailed out preliminary circular letters that carefully outlined the rules, objectives, and methods of his organization. He imagined a movement that would be national in scope and focus, in which all of its adherents acted in synchrony under the guidance of an elite cadre of militants. The campaign to organize the TUEL "will be carried out somewhat along the principles of a military drive," he wrote. His first mailings went to one thousand "specially selected live-wire workers." Membership was limited to members of the trade unions in good standing, but the organization was divided into sections according to industry rather than craft. An "army" of radicals would exercise influence in the labor movement through "rigid application of modern organizational methods." These methods "are the very heart of the league's program," he wrote. The first objectives were not centered around any particular grievance of labor against their employers. The initial step of the local leagues would be a campaign to amalgamate the sixteen railroad craft unions, with the aim of influencing an upcoming convention of the AFL railway employees department.

In Foster's rhetoric and strategizing, there was a predictable blending of modern business and revolutionary methodology: mass mailings, marketing, sales, and bureaucratic efficiencies were all adopted to insurrectionary purpose. All League members would be required to subscribe to the *Labor Herald*: "anyone who does not realize the necessity of a powerful official organ can be of no service to the League." Moreover, an enterprising militant "can make considerable money" selling subscriptions. The circular letters carefully outlined the order of business for the first meetings of the local groups, with precise guidelines for election of officials. In presenting his aims to local unionists and workers, Foster drew upon the familiar dichotomies. At one meeting in New York, he made it clear that his organization had no place for "utopian dreamers." He had come to New York to "talk business," and there would be "no oratory," just plain "man to man" talk about the task of revolutionizing the labor movement.[9]

As he began the campaign for industrial unionism among the railroad unions, Foster's new organization quickly gained the attention of the National Civic Federation, which in turn sought to involve the United States Department of Justice in suppression of his activities. As the first issue of the *Labor Herald* was circulated, the Civic Federation sent copies of Foster's "correspondence and material" to the presidents of the railroad companies. Moreover, the federation asked J. Edgar Hoover to "get inside" the TUEL and supply the names of "key" men. The "leading labor men" of the NCF could then see to it that the TUEL leaders were expelled from their unions, it was explained. The Justice Department was assured by the NCF that this process would remain "absolutely discreet." William J. Burns, the director of the Bureau of Investigation, wrote that this was "a wonderful idea and we will be delighted to help out."[10] Subsequently, Burns had his agents follow Foster and take careful notes on his speeches and meetings. The erstwhile private investigator assured one concerned citizen that the bureau was "keeping in touch with all of [Foster's] movements." Robert H. Lovett, then assistant attorney general, wrote to a concerned vice president of the Pennsylvania Railroad that the Bureau of Investigation considered "Foster's organization as one of the most dangerous in this country today."[11]

The small group of radical unionists who worked with Foster and the TUEL operated in an extremely difficult economic environment in late 1921. That year saw a major depression, during which the unemployment rate hovered near 20 percent. Employers, unnerved by the huge increase in union membership that had occurred during the war years, took advantage of the high rate of joblessness and aggressively pursued the "American Plan" to introduce "freedom of choice" and the open shop in union strongholds. Unemployment and insecurity would shadow workers in large sectors of the economy throughout the decade; some well-informed observers estimated that it was as high as 13–15 percent in 1929 on the eve of the stock-market crash. In this context, the TUEL early on focused its efforts on "education" of embattled unionists rather than organization of the vast majority of unorganized workers. From its inception the TUEL offered little to unemployed workers.[12]

As the economy lurched into recovery after 1922, TUEL cadre would face other strategic challenges. The decade witnessed a significant overall rise in real wages and decline in working hours for most industrial workers, but also an exponential increase in the intensity of most jobs and a suffocating constriction of traditional forms of shop-floor independence as managers resorted to a variety of techniques to boost productivity. Time-and-motion experts and machine-paced production lines were now ubiquitous features of many workers' worlds. Perhaps most symbolic of the industrial ethos of the 1920s were the successes of Henry Ford in thoroughly mechanizing and subdividing the work process while providing his workers with an unprecedented standard wage. To workers confronted with the tribunes of modernity on the shop floor, the TUEL offered the prospect of a stronger, more militant unionism and an end to "class collaboration." More penetrating criticism of the newest forms of industrial production was generally absent from the propaganda of the league. Despite the fact that the paradigmatic Ford regime was exhausting and dehumanizing for many assembly-line workers, Foster was an admirer of Ford's techniques. He was delighted that Fordism was being widely imitated by Communist industrial managers in the Soviet Union in the 1920s; he predicted that this would enable the Soviets to catch up with the United States in consumption and industrial production within a decade.[13]

In contrast to the war years, the leadership of organized labor was in a coldly pragmatic and minimalist mood, weakened by a number of major defeats. Samuel Gompers, in particular, actively sought to repress the initiatives of radicals within the AFL, and his regime generally acquiesced to the introduction of new techniques of managerial control on the shop floor. Yet, spreading rank-and-file discontent with conservative unionism and the activities of the TUEL would test Gompers's approach severely. Most importantly from Foster's perspective, progressives and socialists in the unions, despite their experimentation with "new forms of struggle" such as labor banks and productivity agreements, would also act decisively to assert discipline in their unions in the face of challenges to their leadership by the rank and file and the Communists.[14]

The TUEL made its debut at the AFL railway employees department convention in April 1922, where a vocal minority of industrial unionists conducted a campaign for increased cooperation among the railroad shop crafts. Approximately forty amalgamation resolutions were submitted by various system federations and local unions; debate was long and intense. At a TUEL caucus during the convention, Foster and William Ross Knudsen, who would later mount a challenge for leadership of the International Association of Machinists, pushed the amalgamation idea. In response, conservative unionists pointed to the Knights of Labor, Debs's American Railway Union, and the IWW as past examples of the futility of industrial unionism. The failure of the Pullman Strike and the American Railway Union should remind railroad workers that " 'one big union' leads to dictatorship, chaos and quick dissolution," the editors of the *Railway Carmens' Journal* pointed out. Nonetheless, in the months following the convention, Foster and the TUEL conducted amalgamation campaigns at the conventions of four railway brotherhoods, the Locomotive Firemen and Enginemen, the Conductors, the Trainmen, and the Clerks. Progressives like Warren S. Stone, the chief of the Brotherhood of Locomotive Engineers, invoked the traditional interpretation of "amalgamation," calling merely for "closer cooperation" short of industrial unionism.[15]

The efforts of the league were given a boost by the Chicago Federation of Labor. In March, the federation approved a resolution favoring industrial unionism and requesting that the AFL immediately call conferences of its international unions for the purpose of arranging to "amalgamate all unions in the respective industries into single organizations, each of which shall cover an industry." Jack Johnstone, who was at the time chair of the organization committee of the CFL, introduced the resolution and Foster was the principal speaker in its support at the initial meeting, although several unionists rose to attack him as a Wobbly and "disrupter." Soon after this victory, Samuel Gompers hurried to Chicago. At a hastily convened meeting of local officials he denounced Foster as one who "wants to become the Lenin of America." He pronounced that he had never known such a "self-appointed autocrat." In this highly charged meeting, Fitzpatrick strongly defended the amalgamation measure. Foster, who had been absent from the meeting but had hurried over when he heard what was going on, faced cheers as well as angry shouts to sit down when he sought to defend himself. He challenged Gompers to a debate, and invited him to appoint an auditor to examine the TUEL's bookkeeping. The AFL president challenged Foster's motives, but he apparently retained a degree of admiration for his adversary. He was later quoted as asking "Is it not a pity that so much ability should be subverted to disrupt our labor movement?"[16]

Despite such publicity, amalgamation was not an issue raised by the rank and file during the nationwide walkout of approximately four hundred thousand railway shopmen that began in July 1922. In 1921, in response to company requests, the Railway Labor Board had approved deep reductions in wages for most workers while acquiescing to the widespread practice of "contracting out" of work to nonunion employers. Conditions in Foster's craft became particularly difficult as a result; in Chicago, nearly 50 percent of the carmen's work in the city had disappeared because of the practice of outside contracting.[17] Gompers and Secretary of Commerce Herbert Hoover, through the offices of the National Civic Federation, worked to prevent the strike, and both were instrumental in settling it. However, Foster and the TUEL worked to inflame the strike beyond the reach of injunctions and high level labor-management détente. In Omaha, league activists encouraged the city's Central Labor Council to endorse a call for a general strike to break the federal injunction against picketing and leafleting. A Bureau of Investigation agent reported to J. Edgar Hoover from the city that Foster was "gaining [a] foothold among all the radical labor unions in this part of the country"; an informer claimed that Foster had formulated "extensive plans" for sabotaging the railroads. Foster went on a speaking tour during the strike, followed by federal agents. In Kansas City, he implored the strikers to amalgamate their unions and, according to the BOI agent present, ended by proclaiming that "Labor and Capital have no interest in common and that labor will not come into its own until Capital is crushed and destroyed." His speech held his crowd of two hundred for two hours, and he was interrupted by prolonged cheering. The agent in charge in the city wrote to Hoover that "it is my opinion that the less this bolshevik is allowed to talk during the present railroad and coal strikes, the better it will be for the country." When Foster showed up in Denver to speak before a local chapter of the TUEL about the strike, he was summarily arrested by Colorado Rangers and driven to Wyoming, where he was left on the side of a road near the state's eastern border, minus his suitcase and belongings. Nonetheless, the TUEL "flooded" strike centers with propaganda and its members appeared on picket lines to distribute pamphlets and handbills.[18]

As the strike began to gather momentum, Attorney General Harry M. Daugherty gained approval for an injunction against the strikers so sweeping that even Hoover and Secretary of State Charles Evans Hughes agreed that it was a transgression of the workers' fundamental rights. It provided that strikers could not "loiter" near any railroad station or office, and could not "congregate" near yards, shops, depots, or terminals. Furthermore, they were enjoined from picketing or actively discouraging the use of strikebreakers through "letters, circulars, telegrams, telephones, or word of mouth [!], or through interviews in the papers." The railroads hired thousands of workers to replace the strikers, and surrounded stations and freight yards with armed guards. The strike had largely disintegrated by September, a resounding defeat for the strikers. In order to save jobs, the AFL Shop Crafts Council agreed to negotiate separate settlements with different systems. Out of this settlement grew the famous "B & O Plan," a Taylorist-inspired scheme for labor-management cooperation in which union committees participated in implementation of cost-cutting measures on the shop floor. Foster saw the defeat of the shopmen's strike and the development of the B & O Plan as the beginning of a momentous "new orientation" in the labor movement. What enraged Foster most about the settlement was its endorsement by a number of progressive unionists in the metal trades. To him, this represented an intolerable retreat in the class war.[19]

In the aftermath of the defeated strike, workers themselves were far from resigned to the "new orientation" in their unions. While many blamed scabs and the Daugherty injunction for the debacle, others proposed that the larger lesson of the strike was that the railroad workers must "use the ballot." Letters to the *Carmen's Journal* echoed the theme that "clearly our form of organization is not what it ought to be." An Ohio worker wrote that in his lodge "they are all filled with the amalgamation idea." Another proposed that "there is on the part of the rank and file of the Brotherhoods a desire for consolidation," and that the AFL conception of "loose confederations" was clearly outmoded. While it is impossible to judge the extent of rank-and-file sentiment for amalgamation from such letters, clearly the TUEL had latched onto a very "live" issue. At a subsequent TUEL conference over four hundred delegates from every railroad craft and every district attended, despite warnings by union officials to stay away.[20]

In the railway shop unions, the TUEL focused its activities on the International Association of Machinists. Over 80,000 machinists participated in the 1922 strike; at its conclusion, IAM membership stood at 97,000 after a high of 330,000 in 1920. During the period after the shopmen's strike to 1927, sixty-two railroads established their own company unions of shopmen. In this atmosphere, the TUEL proposed its own candidate for the union presidency. William Ross Knudsen, who was on the California executive committee of the Socialist Labor party and had led large strikes of machinists in Akron in 1919 and in Cincinnati in 1920, ran on a platform of industrial unionism, an end to compromises with employers, affiliation with the Red International, and "preparation of the machinists, through their union, for establishment of a Workers' Republic, in which workers shall run the industries." L. M. Hawver, a leader of the 1920 outlaw strike, ran as vice president with Knudsen. The ticket lost by a three-to-one margin, but in December the TUEL gathered a national conference of metal trades unionists that approved a plan for a new union, the first step being the merging of the executive boards of the twenty-four trades. Within a month, the IAM initiated an expulsion campaign aimed at TUEL members.[21]

Another vital focus of TUEL activities in the early 1920s was in the nation's largest union, the United Mine Workers, already an industrial, amalgamated union. Here, Foster and the TUEL were integral elements in the growing opposition to the union's flamboyant president, John L. Lewis. Lewis's critics were particularly aroused by his acceptance of government demands in settling the 1919 strike, but a whole variety of labyrinthine and often violent local controversies undermined Lewis's regime during this period as well. The Harding and Coolidge administrations were less willing to compromise with Lewis than the Wilsonians had been. In April 1922, Lewis called six hundred thousand miners out on strike, but was only able to accomplish an agreement with the operators to maintain wages at their 1920 level. Lewis and his allies saw this as a substantial victory given the extensive wage cuts that almost every sector of American labor was experiencing at the time. However, during this period Lewis backed away from his proposals for nationalization and a "triple alliance" of miners with railroaders and longshoremen as a way of protecting the UMW's gains. His critics redoubled their attacks.[22]

One of Lewis's most bitter opponents was the mercurial former president of District 14, Alexander Howat, who had encouraged wildcat strikes of local unions, despite a contract that District 14 had negotiated with the operators in 1920 and a ban on strikes by the Kansas state legislature. Lewis in turn suspended the district charter, thereby removing the popular leader from office. At every Mine Workers' convention in the early 1920s, the issue of Howat and his appeals for reinstatement was used by oppositionists as powerful weapons in their attacks on Lewis and his increasingly dictatorial machine. In the midst of these fights, Howat moved closer to Foster and the TUEL. Of the TUEL, Howat noted, "I am for it. Foster is doing great work. The TUEL has got hold of a big idea. The best fighters in the trade unions are naturally radical and progressive. When they learn to organize and act in one body in the unions, a new day will dawn for American labor."[23]

Foster's entrance into UMW politics began in earnest in early 1923 when the league proposed that left-wing miners in Ohio and Pennsylvania establish "a new international organization of progressive miners within the union, which would gradually absorb it and eliminate its international and district officials." Thus, in February 1923 a conference of the Progressive International Committee of the UMW gathered in Pittsburgh; at a conference in April, three thousand miners listened to Howat speak in support of the Progressive Miners' platform, which called for nationalization of the mines, reinstatement of the expelled Kansas officials, a six-hour day, national agreements, and "affiliation with the militant trade unionists of other countries." The new organization attracted not only rebellious miners, but free-lance TUEL militants like Frederick Merrick, a prewar Socialist who had helped lead a large strike against Westinghouse Electric near Pittsburgh in 1916. At a subsequent June conference the flavor was more revolutionary and the attendance far smaller. At the time, Foster was under pressure from Communist party leaders who believed that the issues the insurgent miners were putting forward were not "political" enough. Even so, within a month an expulsion campaign was begun, targeting those who had attended the conference. Joe Manley, Foster's son-in-law, was badly beaten by Lewis henchmen during a Scranton UMW meeting. The *New York Times* summed up Lewis's strategy when it headlined: "Coal Miners Demand a 20 Percent Rise; Eject Communists."[24]

Aside from mining, the most important of the early TUEL efforts was in the needle trades. In the International Ladies Garment Union in New York City, the expression of radicalism in the immediate postwar period was the shop delegate movement, which aimed to establish rank-and-file control through the creation of an assembly of delegates from each shop that would govern the union. At several conferences in late 1922 and 1923 the TUEL was able to both absorb and strengthen this movement. By 1923 the league, with its demands for Profintern affiliation and active support of Russia, had gained a majority on the executive board of Local 22, gained a foothold in Locals 1 and 9, and had established its presence in ILGWU locals in Chicago, Boston, and Philadelphia. In the Amalgamated Clothing Workers the TUEL established a strong influence as well, but generally deferred to the administration of Sidney Hillman, who was strongly pro-Soviet before 1923. During this period Foster endorsed the Hillman regime's proposals for wage reductions and "production standards," to the disappointment of other left-wingers who bitterly opposed these concessions to management.[25]

For workers in a variety of American unions after 1921, the TUEL had become an important voice for industrial unionism. By October 1922, the amalgamation movement had gained the endorsements of hundreds of labor groups across the nation, including sixteen state federations, fourteen national unions, dozens of central labor bodies, and thousands of miscellaneous locals. By December, Foster could with reasonable accuracy report to his mentor in Moscow, Lozovsky, that the league was "a powerful and respected factor in the whole trade union movement." However, he was choosing his words quite carefully when he claimed that policies "based entirely on the program of the RILU are attracting the widest attention and support," and that amalgamation is "considered a leading communist policy." For twenty-five thousand dollars a year, he suggested, there could be a "powerful left movement within the trade unions of America within a short time." Although the amount of the Profintern's subsidy for the TUEL remains unknown, support from the Soviet party clearly helped the league produce highly polished propaganda and disseminate it to a wide audience.[26]

Despite local successes, the TUEL continually emphasized its national scope and the need for a high level of national coordination. At one point, Foster even suggested that the league "was not to be allowed to develop local movements." He was pragmatic enough to tailor the league's rhetoric to conditions in particular industries. Yet, his activities and rhetoric continued to reflect his deep-seated urge to substitute organization for politics and community. It was only through a genuinely national orientation that workers could achieve "system, order, program and power," according to one *Labor Herald* editorial. In order to get away from the "localist psychology," national conferences became the focus of the movement. In addition to conferences of militants in the mining and needle trades and railroad industries, "national" meetings were held by the TUEL in the shoe, textile, and printing trades.[27]

Yet, the league still bore the marks of a personal organization. Only rarely was the Communist party mentioned in its literature. Foster was by far the most prolific contributor to the *Labor Herald*, and many other articles appeared under one of his pseudonyms, "John Dorsey." The prominence of Foster's imprint is partly a reflection of the fact that "Fosterism" had few other champions in America before the publication of Lenin's *Left Wing Communism*. Few American Communists at the time could write authoritatively about the trade union movement, and even fewer had experience outside their particular craft, if they did happen to belong to a union. Because of its personal nature, "Fosterism" remained as much a style as a methodology. This was consistent with Foster's syndicalist temperament and the militant minority's ideal of personalist élan. By the 1920s, however, Foster represented what might be called "corporate syndicalism." Whereas earlier syndicalists had placed much of their faith in the alchemy of working-class spontaneity, Foster intimated that the "masses" could be organizationally and psychologically manipulated by a militant minority employing the most modern techniques. "You must know every curve in the psychology of the masses," he told one gathering of TUEL recruits. "It is amazing how tame and stupid the workers rest under the control of the Gompers machine," he wrote to Lozovsky. Observers continued to characterize Foster in terms of his astonishing "executive" abilities. One in-depth journalistic profile noted that Foster's ability to convince people that he is sincere, his "organizing power," and his nonideological emphasis on the material rewards of a more efficient unionism "have made him the outstanding radical labor leader in America." If not for his background and "secondary personality" as a "fighter," he "might have become a successful business or professional man." This writer implied that it was Foster's salesman-like ability to change his language and personality to fit a given situation that made him so effective.[28]

Despite its endorsement by the CFL and numerous trades locals across the nation, amalgamation was not a central rank-and-file demand during strikes in the major industries that the TUEL had penetrated by the early 1920s. The issue arose primarily as a demand among activists in conventions prior to the central strikes of the period, and was proposed as a remedy for the structural weaknesses of the unions after such strikes had been concluded or defeated. It was, in short, a demand that could be taken up only internally, and was by nature an issue that was capable of causing intense controversy within the unions themselves. As debates escalated, Foster came under sharp personal attack. Officials portrayed amalgamation as a cover for a power-grab by the Communists. An editorial in the AFL *American Federationist* accused Foster of the "hallucination" of "imagined greatness," and concluded that the TUEL was composed of "recruits from the physical and mental fringes of society, along the line which divides crudely between the fit and the halt." As in the steel strike, conservatives sought to discredit the movement by explaining it as a conspiracy that Foster had masterminded. The fact that the amalgamation campaign did bear the marks of Foster's personal leadership reinforced this view. J. B. S. Hardman, for instance, termed Foster "the organizing genius of the amalgamation drive. He gave the movement direction, oneness of purpose, and a detailed, uniform organization. All the argumentative literature came from [his] pen. He provided the charts and diagrams showing how amalgamation would work."[29]

Foster's relationship with the fledgling Communist movement in the United States was clarified somewhat when he appeared before a secret convention of Communists on an isolated farm near Bridgman, Michigan, about an hour's train ride from Chicago, in August 1922. Following his return from Russia nearly a year earlier, the Communists had written an urgent memo to the Comintern reminding it of a secret agreement whereby representatives and organizations of the RILU were to remain subordinate to their respective Communist parties. However, for nearly a year Foster and his associates had built the TUEL with little guidance from the leadership of Communists other than Foster himself. In this he had the support of Lozovsky, who had lectured the American Communists in 1922 that the TUEL must retain a relatively independent role. Its program could not have the "precise character" of Comintern and Profintern resolutions, he argued. Even the political leadership of the Communist Party must maintain its distance, for "influence in the working-class movement is secured neither by resolutions nor by certain successful decisions of the Central Executive Committee, but by the work done by Communists in their respective labor organizations. We must, therefore, speak less or, if you will, not at all about control of the activities of the league, for such talk leads only to mechanical control, or rather an attempt at mechanical interference in work which by its very nature the party can neither carry on nor accomplish."

Certainly this was a doctrine that fitted nicely with Foster's orientation at the time, but Lozovsky's views surfaced with regard to American party activities as late as the 1940s when he told one American cadre that "in trade union tactics it is not the job of a labor leader to cooperate with the more radical political leaders but it is the job of the radical political leaders to cooperate with the labor leaders."[30]

The main purpose of the convention at Bridgman was to work with an undercover Comintern plenipotentiary to bring to an end the disputes within the Party over the issue of underground work. It was Foster's appearance, however, that was the highlight of the meeting. By now Foster was one of America's most famous radicals, and many delegates were apprehensive that he had been followed by Department of Justice agents. Introduced to top Communists for the first time at a nighttime meeting, with lanterns and torches illuminating the scene, Foster lectured the assembled would-be Bolsheviks that "the fate of the Communist party depends upon the control of the masses, through the capture of the trade unions, without which revolution is impossible." Of course, this meant a corresponding central role for Foster in the revolution, and once again Foster's conceptions led him into the realm of American exceptionalism. Lenin himself had endorsed the concept of "boring-from-within," but the idea that the trade unions were the most important focus of Communist activity was a quite controversial proposition in 1922. Only a little over half of the Bridgman delegates, representing the leadership of the party, were even union members, for instance. In the wider membership, only 5 percent were actively involved in trade union work. In a party of five to six thousand members, only five hundred at most could be called "American comrades." Many had come to the party out of the IWW or the prewar left wing of the Socialist party.[31]

The Communists at the convention recognized that the TUEL had played, in its first year of existence, a relatively independent role. One of the resolutions approved by the gathering held that contact must be "established between the executive committees of the party and the executive committees of the [TUEL]." Earl Browder told the convention that there had yet to be an "actual functioning connection between the Workers'

[Communist] Party and the TUEL." Because so little of the "effective manpower" of the Party was involved in the league, the Party might not be able to control its development, he asserted. He urged that the Party involve itself "right down in the ground . . . in every local group" of the movement. Browder, who was the designated liaison between the Party, headquartered in New York, and the TUEL, based in Chicago, remembered that in the early years of the TUEL, "the party learned of the TUEL program only from TUEL officers. . . . The Central Committee [of the party] assumed direction of the trade union work only after 1924." One Communist at the time complained privately to Lozovsky that "the Workers' Party is supposed to control the [TUEL]," but "the league controls the industrial policy of the Workers' Party."[32]

Perhaps the most important and revealing aspect of Foster's speech before the assembled Communists was his explicit definition of the distance between the TUEL and the Socialists; Foster the revolutionary technician criticized Debs the revolutionary moralist. He proposed that one reason the Socialist party had declined in influence was because "it fell into the hands of Debs, and Debs has been a man who never really grasped the significance of mass organizations." Then, in remarks that illustrate the fundamental divergence between the two men's outlooks, Foster noted that under Debs, the Socialist party "seemed to go along with the idea that [it] should be an organization of citizens in general, and did not realize that the foundation had to be the workers, and not only the workers but the organized workers."[33]

Unfortunately for the Communists at Bridgman, the Department of Justice was able to locate the convention before it concluded. Foster recognized an undercover agent at one gathering and alerted the delegates, the most important of whom were able to flee before the authorities arrived in full force. When the convention was raided, federal agents seized a huge cache of documents which had been hastily buried in a barrel in the woods. Foster returned to Chicago to face other ominous developments. A huge train wreck in Gary had aroused suspicions among police that the TUEL had somehow sabotaged the train in support of the railroad strike. At midnight the evening of the wreck, Chicago police broke into the TUEL offices in Chicago and ransacked Foster's files and desk. News of this raid could not have reassured TUEL activists who had had direct contact with Foster in the recent past. The Illinois district attorney's office turned a list of *Labor Herald* subscribers over to Burns; a subscription to the paper constituted TUEL membership, since the league was not a dues-paying organization. Also turned over as a result of the raid was a complete list of Foster's correspondence. Burns, of course, had previously agreed to provide the National Civic Federation with the names of TUEL members in order to effect their expulsion from the unions to which they belonged. Foster himself was arrested in Chicago for violation of a Michigan criminal syndicalism statute as a result of his participation in the Bridgman fiasco.[34]

Although he was freed on bond pending his trial in Michigan, Foster could not have helped but look upon his prosecution as a serious threat. Just past his forty-second birthday, he faced a five- to ten-year sentence in state prison if convicted. He wrote to Roger Baldwin that "at last the powers that be believe they see their long-awaited chance to get me." Baldwin replied that "you are singled out because you have an effective means of putting the idea [of industrial unionism] into operation; the other advocates have not." Foster was being prosecuted under one of a score of criminal syndicalism statutes that had been passed in various states during and after the war. Typical laws, like the one in Michigan, held it illegal to advocate violence or sabotage as a means of political or, pointedly, industrial reform. Some states were quite specific. The law in effect in Idaho included in its definition of "sabotage" such activities as loitering on the job, improperly done work, waste, publication of trade secrets, and slowing down work or production. Understandably, organized labor perceived these laws as real threats; as early as 1919 the Michigan Federation of Labor had called for the repeal of the statute under which Foster was arrested.[35]

Foster's trial in the Bridgman case was one of the American Communist party's earliest and most successful attempts to establish a united front among Communist, labor, and progressive groups. The American Civil Liberties Union offered its services to Foster and the other defendants; a "Labor Defense Council" secured the services of Frank Walsh, a noted labor attorney, to defend Foster. At the request of the ACLU, the council kept its rhetoric focused on the issue of free speech and free assembly, portraying the Bridgman arrests as part of a drive against "organized labor." The LDC's (and Foster's) connections with the Chicago labor movement were shown by the prominent roles played by Robert Buck, editor of *The New Majority*, Anton Johannsen, and Lillian Herstein in fund-raising for the defense effort.[36]

The trial itself symbolized that Foster's career stood at a crossroads. In some ways, it was a community affair, with jurors free to mingle with their fellow citizens from the small town of Bridgman during recesses. Foster offered a benign interpretation of the "dictatorship of the proletariat" to the jury, but admitted that he sought to overthrow the government of the United States and the establishment of a workers' republic. He frankly admitted that he had visited Moscow and that the Communist party supported the work of the TUEL in the United States. However, he denied that he belonged to the Communist party, or that the TUEL had any "organic connection" to the party. One reporter described Foster as a "quiet, mild-mannered man" who spoke thoughtfully and deliberately under cross examination. At times, Foster's voice was so low that the court stenographer had difficulty distinguishing his words. He seemed to the reporter "almost like a poet and dreamer." Foster's "pensive attitude, his amiable manner and his soft answers to the questions of the Prosecutor made it hard for one to realize that this was the man whom many people regard as the most dangerous Red agitator in the country."[37]

The self-portrayal that Foster offered was that of a "free lance," an independent radical who was nonetheless sympathetic with the Bolsheviks and the Russian Revolution. He recited his background as an itinerant American worker who, during the course of his geographical and political wanderings, had renounced the IWW and chosen instead to work within the established labor movement. He listed the unions to which he had belonged throughout his career, as if to emphasize his roots in the indigenous working class. When the prosecutor asked him if he would advocate revolution by insurrection and civil war, the courtroom hushed and Foster paused dramatically before stating in a calm and matter-of-fact manner that he could not say whether he would or not. As the jury was out, he, Frank Walsh and Esther sat quietly awaiting the verdict. The deliberations lasted nearly five days before it was announced that the jury was deadlocked. The presiding judge dismissed the case pending a new trial. Although Foster would remain under heavy bail until 1933, when the case was finally dismissed, it was an outcome that had a profound meaning. A jury of small-town Americans who had been in contact with their friends and acquaintances throughout the trial split evenly over the issue of Foster's purported "syndicalism." Those who voted for acquittal included a "prosperous grocer" and several farmers, as well as a self-described suffragist whose husband was the superintendent of a nonunion factory in nearby St. Joseph. Following the trial, one regretful commentator implied that such women were temperamentally unsuited to the difficult business of rooting out deceptive Communists: "She was evidently more or less emotional. . . . Her sympathies were successfully aroused." She was simply "unable to grasp that Foster was heading a great conspiracy against civilization and Christianity."[38]

Foster's "Colorado Kidnapping" during the railroad strike had become a national issue during this period as well, with a similarly favorable outcome. Thanks to the legal and publicity machine of the ACLU, the issue became prominent in the Colorado gubernatorial campaign of 1922. A pro-labor governor was elected, and dozens of officials of the Colorado Rangers were forced to resign.[39]

Thus, by early 1923, Foster had secured two important public-relations victories in addition to the successes that the TUEL was experiencing in its amalgamation campaign. While Foster's largest debt in the

Bridgman prosecution was owed to the Communists and their Labor Defense Council, in the past Communists had been easily convicted in similar prosecutions, and the Communist leader Charles Ruthenberg was
convicted later on the same charges that had been brought against Foster
arising from the Bridgman arrests. Thus, the outcome of the Bridgman
trial was in some sense a personal vindication. However, soon after the
trial it was revealed that Foster was indeed a Communist, although he
himself did not bother to make a public announcement to that effect.
Instead, it was left to the Communists themselves to declare that Foster
was "a Communist," a statement Foster merely let stand. Thus Foster
came to his public identity as a Communist with reluctance, but this was
nonetheless a momentous step, for it would end his career as a "free
lance."[40]

For the time being, though, all the elements in William Foster's political universe were in precarious alignment. Despite signs of trouble, the
TUEL had attained a significant voice in the American labor movement.
The outcome of the Bridgman trial suggested that he had found a place in
American public life, however uncomfortable and insecure, for his particular brand of revolutionary politics. He might function openly as an outspoken radical in favor of the Russian Revolution and the American
Communist movement, as well as an advocate of progressive labor reform. This achievement arose from the deep contradictions inherent in
Foster's personality and experiences. Possessed of a complex awareness
of American life that was the result of having lived and worked in nearly
every imaginable working-class milieu, he had shown that he was capable
of pragmatic leadership of large numbers of American citizens. His voice
had been heard by a president of the United States as well as by impoverished steel workers. Although he possessed a profound and abiding sense
of alienation from American society, among progressive intellectuals he
was widely praised as merely a good manager who sought to bring modern methods of organization to bear on the problems of the labor movement.

In the spring of 1923, Foster and the TUEL even gained the potent
endorsement of Eugene Debs. The Socialist leader pointedly singled out
Foster in his statement, without mentioning the Communist party: "The
Trade Union Educational League, under the direction of William Z. Foster, is in my opinion the one rightly directed movement for the industrial
unification of the American workers. I thoroughly believe in its plan and
in its methods and I feel very confident of its steady progress and the
ultimate achievement of its ends."[41]

It was a typically generous albeit somewhat risky endorsement, especially considering reports publicizing the disparaging comments about
Debs made by Foster at the Bridgman convention and Foster's obviously

close relationship with the Communists. Debs and the Socialists may even have entertained thoughts of enticing Foster away from the Communists at a time when Foster still publicly denied that he belonged the Party. Moreover, Foster had just been ignominiously rebuked in a Comintern organ for his theory of American exceptionalism. With Debs's endorsement and the support of a number of influential allies among progressives in the labor movement, Foster might have chosen in the period following the Bridgman trial to move the TUEL away from the Communists. However, by early 1923, Socialist unionists had clearly allied themselves on the wrong side of war between labor and capital, according to Foster. Although in the prewar years the Socialist party had represented an active opposition bloc within the AFL bureaucracy, now the party was daily "becoming closer and closer affiliated with Gompers," he observed in May. Writing privately, he accorded little significance to Debs's endorsement: "Debs is still a member of the Socialist party, which for the most part bitterly hates the TUEL. . . . The chances of winning him entirely to our cause seem to grow worse than better." Although Foster went along with Debs's continued attempts at a rapprochement by blaming the capitalist press for distorting his Bridgman comments, the gulf between the two men's outlooks was simply too wide. In contrast to Debs's endorsement, William D. Haywood wrote an angry critique of Foster and the TUEL, which circulated at the highest levels of the Comintern. Writing in Moscow on Foster's views of the "bankruptcy" of the AFL, Haywood asked, "What material advantage would it be to amalgamate units that are intellectually blind? Is not some education necessary before amalgamation for industrial unionism can be brought about?" Haywood was clearly incensed and embarrassed by Foster's continued attacks, in pamphlets financed by the Communist party, on his beloved IWW. On Foster's boring-from-within strategy, he asked, "What becomes of the revolutionary slogan 'To the Masses! To the Masses!' Where are the unorganized? What about the colored race?" Haywood's observations had merit, but he offered no real solution to the problems facing labor radicals in the postwar era other than to assert the continuing relevance of the shrunken IWW and inveigh against the signing of contracts as the "death warrant of labor." Nonetheless, the essentials of Haywood's cirtique were summoned against the TUEL by Foster's factional opponents in the party leadership through the 1920s.[42]

Soon, however, the terrain upon which Foster operated in the period following the Bridgman trial began to shift rapidly. Although his immersion in the Communist movement by no means signaled the end of his career as a labor organizer, the formalization of his ties with the Party would restrict his flexibility in this sphere significantly. Additionally, it meant that he would become more deeply involved in the intense factional controversies that had characterized the Communist movement from its inception. These controversies centered mostly on the problems of the Party's role in labor politics, and once again he became swept up in the labor party activities of the Chicago Federation of Labor. It was a movement with which Foster undoubtedly had some sympathy, but ultimately, the Farmer-Labor party would prove unable to function as a point of connection between the Communist party and the Chicago Federation. Its failure showed that the kind of relationships that Foster hoped to build between the Party and the mainstream labor movement were quite fragile.

As for the TUEL, in an era when unions were under seemingly unceasing assault from employers, labor leaders continued to preach solidarity and portray the league as dangerously disruptive. And there is no question that it was, in the sense that it sought to dislodge the established union leadership and "incorporate" older, parochial craft interests. However, despite the increasingly uncertain position of the TUEL in the labor movement, the league continued to provide a functioning organizational framework for a cadre of energetic and articulate Communist unionists, above all in Chicago. In January 1923, despite his pending trial for the Bridgman fiasco, Foster was elected secretary of the Chicago Federation's powerful organization committee, with Anton Johannsen, an old acquaintance, as chairman—this in spite of the fact that Foster wrote quite openly in the Communist press of the necessity for American revolutionaries to seize control of the trade unions.[43]

Of the Communists in the CFL, J. W. Johnstone was, next to Foster, the most important figure. He had worked closely with Foster ever since founding the first local branch of the Syndicalist League of North America in Vancouver in 1911. His experience as chairman of the Stockyards Labor Council after 1918 qualified him as one of the few Communists who had actually led and organized American workers. Earl Browder, despite his tendency to exaggerate his role as an independent figure in the Chicago party, had been a stranger to the city before his meeting with Foster in 1921. He was perceived as little more than Foster's "messenger boy," acting as the liaison between Foster and party headquarters in New York. Samuel Hammersmark was another TUEL figure associated with Foster at the time; he was a hard-working and well-liked individual with close ties in the Chicago anarchist community. Arne Swabeck and Charles Krumbein were Communist delegates to the CFL who would later play important roles in the party as labor organizers. In 1923, they were examples of a new type of Communist cadre, individuals who came to the party through the TUEL and the labor movement, rather than vice versa. Joe Manley, Foster's son-in-law, also began to play a significant role in the CFL-CP axis in the early 1920s.[44]

After his Bridgman trial in April and his public acknowledgment that he was a Communist, Foster's relationship with the Chicago Federation and its leaders became progressively more difficult. First, Foster's speeches at the Bridgman convention about converting the unions to the cause of Communism were now public knowledge, and some Chicago unionists openly cited his comments about Debs in an attempt to discredit him. Moreover, throughout the previous year, especially after the CFL had endorsed amalgamation, the national leadership of the AFL had increased its pressure on Fitzpatrick. Gompers and Fitzpatrick had been at odds for decades over the issue of a political party for labor. Now, in light of the amalgamation resolution and calls for recognition of the Soviet Union, Gompers's accusation that Foster and the Communists were exercising an inordinate amount of influence in the CFL could not be easily sidestepped. Perhaps most damaging was Gompers's notification in late April that the AFL would henceforth cease paying a subsidy that amounted to one-half of the expenses of the CFL, which included rent on its offices and Fitzpatrick's salary. In a letter to Fitzpatrick announcing this decision, Gompers noted that the AFL only paid the expenses of organizers who came under its "own direction." After these funds were withdrawn, the CFL began to run a monthly deficit. Gompers was clearly attempting to rein in Fitzpatrick on the labor party issue and the presence of radicals in the CFL. Obviously, in this atmosphere, it became necessary for Foster to act much more cautiously in his relationship with the CFL.[45]

In the postwar period, a trade union radical like Foster with strong syndicalist tendencies faced a dilemma. Many progressive unionists had become convinced of the necessity for some kind of political action by labor. In order to maintain his ties to this sector of the labor movement, it had been necessary for Foster to support or at least acquiesce in these initiatives. As his friend Jay Fox put it in describing his own conversion to political action, "only fanatics fight against facts." In the 1920 elections, he had gone along with Fitzpatrick's Chicago Labor party, but immediately after the election he turned his attention to more familiar pursuits and organized the TUEL. In 1922, while Foster and his new league agitated among railroad workers for industrial unionism, TUEL propaganda contained an ill-defined call for political action, always presented as a secondary issue. That year, a group calling itself the Conference for Progressive Political Action emerged as a tangible result of the wide demand among railroad unionists for political organization. At its first formal gathering in Chicago in February 1922, Warren S. Stone of the Brotherhood of Locomotive Engineers, William Johnston of the Machinists, and William Green of the UMW were in attendance. The Chicago Labor party, under the leadership of Fitzpatrick, was also represented. Foster attended as well, and he was impressed by the breadth of trade union support for the CPPA initiatives: "I found fourteen or fifteen of the railroad organizations there; I found the United Mine Workers of America represented there; I found the Amalgamated Clothing Workers, the International Typographical Union, several other big international unions and fifteen or twenty state federations of labor represented there." Although Foster understood the appeal of the CPPA to beleaguered unionists, at the second convention of the organization in December he and Ruthenberg, as representatives of the Workers' party, were ignominiously refused credentials in a move that was supported by powerful progressives like Johnston, a prewar militant and supporter of Soviet Russia in 1920 who now denounced the Workers' party as "un-American." While this must have reinforced Foster's convictions about the timidity of the Socialists, in 1922 the CPPA, acting not as a political party but within Gompers's paradigm of nonpartisan labor lobbying, was able to exert a strong influence in local and national elections, defeating a number of antilabor candidates. One hundred seventy CPPA-endorsed candidates won seats in the House of Representatives. "Never before had the American working class asserted itself so decisively at the polls."[46]

By 1923, the Chicago Farmer-Labor party organization, headed by Fitzpatrick, had constituted itself as the left wing of the larger mass movement symbolized by the CPPA. Fitzpatrick had even supported an attempt by the Workers' party to gain credentials at the second CPPA convention in December 1922. He and his Chicago cohorts boldly resigned from the CPPA in early 1923 because the latter organization had not moved to create an independent labor party; this was the issue upon which Gompers refused to budge. But Foster was certainly closely involved in the relationship between the Communists and the Chicago Federation's political ventures in 1923. Only he possessed a real following within both the CFL and the Communist party, and only those Communists familiar to the CFL leadership were welcome in the Farmer-Labor political enterprise. Foster, as a friend of Fitzpatrick and Nockels, was the focus of the first contacts between the FLP and the Communists.[47]

Yet, the position Foster had established was increasingly difficult to maintain in early 1923, as Fitzpatrick sought support for his Farmer-Labor party among progressives in the labor movement. First, within the Communist party, rumors circulated that the Party had begun to come too much under the influence of the Chicago "reformists," that is, the Party's union delegates to the Chicago Federation. Simultaneously, Fitzpatrick began to distance himself from the Communists. In April, the month in which Foster's membership in the Communist party was revealed, Fitzpatrick pointedly declined to address a May Day meeting sponsored by the Workers' party in Grand Rapids. "The vast majority of American workers, both native and foreign born, resent what they regard as imported programs and they subscribe to the home-grown variety," wrote Fitzpatrick, who so often in the past had endorsed the actions of European labor movements. In April the AFL Executive Council sent out a notice to the Seattle Central Labor Council declaring that "unions affiliated with the AFL cannot have dealings with the Soviet Government of Russia and remain in the Federation." The AFL demanded that the council repudiate a resolution calling for the recognition of Soviet Russia and resumption of trade relations.[48]

Nonetheless, the Communists decided to aggressively pursue their entrée into Fitzpatrick's organization. Foster himself was not particularly enthusiastic about the proposition, even though, as had been true in 1920, many of his long-time associates were more involved than he. As the Chicago FLP prepared for an important convention in July, Foster "took very little part directly in events," according to Arne Swabeck, a Communist CFL delegate at the time. When the Communists sought agreements with Fitzpatrick, they did so with Foster's blessing, but he still preferred to avoid outright political activity.[49]

At this crucial point, a European Communist with only months of experience in the American party began to play a crucial role. Joseph Pogany, who was in the United States secretly under the pseudonym John Pepper, was a refugee from the failed Hungarian revolution who had made his first appearance before the American party at the Bridgman convention as a delegate from the Comintern. Pepper was a charismatic, self-aggrandizing international revolutionary who mesmerized the Americans with his amazing political prognostications, his arcane "theses," and his aura of secretive Comintern *savoir faire*. His influence was particularly strong among the Communists in New York, but he was taken by Foster as well. Like Foster, Pepper harbored a visceral dislike of "opportunistic" trade union leaders, who, it was generally agreed in Communist circles, had played a large role in the "betrayal" of the Hungarian revolution only two years earlier. During the Bridgman trial, Pepper wrote a flattering article entitled "William Z. Foster—Revolutionary Leader" for the Communist newspaper, *The Worker*. In it, he described Foster as "the American face of Communism." For the first time, he wrote, "there appears before the American workers a man who is at once blood of the blood, flesh of the flesh, of the working masses: a worker himself: a leader of the masses, a trade unionist, a revolutionist, a Marxian and Communist." Given Foster's still uncertain status in the Communist party, this encomium from an international figure may have been seen as a welcome gesture. "Those of us who [did] not enjoy an international reputation were disposed to accept as correct Communist tactics everything to which Pepper said *yes* and *Amen*," Foster later related. However, at a time when Foster still denied belonging to the Communist party, it was Pepper's statement (which Foster himself could hardly deny) that finally, irrevocably, brought his political affiliation into the open.[50]

In the months before the Chicago convention, Pepper pushed relentlessly for a strong Communist role in the FLP. Simultaneously, the Socialist party decided against sending delegates; Foster later admitted that this robbed the upcoming convention of its "respectability" among progressive unionists. Foster himself still hesitated, aware of Fitzpatrick's sensitive position. He still moved quite uncertainly in inner party circles. Browder noted that he was "still very clumsy and awkward in everything relating to the Party." Foster was reluctant even to attend meetings of the Party Central Executive Committee, and sought to maintain contact with the Party through a small liaison committee, which was presumably headed by Browder. Yet, Communist functionaries based in New York, including Pepper and head of the Party's CEC Charles Ruthenberg pressured Foster to play a larger role as a party leader and resisted his inclination to restrict his function to a narrow trade union sphere. Thus unwilling to challenge the authority of Pepper, and under pressure to play a more prominent political role in the Party, Foster drifted.[51]

The Chicago convention proved to be a debacle for the Communists. Foster's strong influence in the CFL was apparent. His old friend J. G. Brown was secretary of the FLP and was able to pack the convention with Communist delegates from fictitious fraternal and labor organizations. Joe Manley was secretary of the conference's organizing committee.[52] Fitzpatrick finally proposed only to convene a "unity conference" instead of a formal party convention. In a humiliating defeat, he was forced to walk out of the convention when the Communists and other delegates formally endorsed the immediate creation of a "Federated Farmer Labor Party." From all accounts, before the convention Foster had argued against a split with Fitzpatrick. He saw the Labor party issue as "strictly a rank-and-file proposition," strongly opposed by the higher officials of the AFL, but thought it was "impossible for the Workers' party by itself to lead the rank-and-file revolt to establish the Labor Party." Nonetheless, he admitted that he was "dazzled" by the discipline the party exhibited at the convention itself. He seemed to have little idea of the depth of Fitzpatrick's bitterness, and suspected that he would come around eventually because some of his closest friends were in favor of the immediate creation of the labor party. Foster just "tried to bull it through and make the best of it," Browder recalled.[53]

Thus, writing immediately after the convention, Foster called the formation of the FF-LP "a landmark in the history of the working class." The Fitzpatrick delegates, he now declared with Bolshevik certainty, had "had no constructive policy, but quibbled, hemmed and hawed about, hesitant and undecided." One of Fitzpatrick's friends quoted Foster at the convention as saying "the center has no guts, no program, and while I am sorry, they don't count." To Lozovsky, Foster enthused that "the formation of the new Party weakens Gompers's control just that much more. When his bureaucracy collapses, as I believe it will before another two or three years have passed, we can look forward to profound changes in the labor movement of this country." Fitzpatrick, though, accused the Communists of "killing" the Farmer-Labor party, and with it "the possibility of uniting the forces of independent political action in America." He observed that "as a practical proposition . . . the minute the Workers' party is identified with this movement, then that will be the battering ram that is going to be used against every group."[54]

Within weeks of the convention, Foster reported to the Comintern that "we are going up against a stiffer opposition all along the line. The old guard everywhere seems to be alive now more than ever." Cannon observed that the miners' and needle unions were waging "open war" on the TUEL. "You know the old sickness of the American party, the tendency to get unduly excited, to overestimate the radical development and plunge into premature actions which bring disastrous defeats and paralyzing reactions in our own party," he wrote to a friend. When the gravity of Fitzpatrick's warning finally became clear, Foster moved quickly to attempt to repair the damage. He told Cannon that the trade unionists in the party were suffering from the "hangover" that was the result of the split, "but the others in New York are still living in a fool's paradise. Something has to be done to change this course." In party councils, Foster protested that the labor party policy was making him appear as a traitor to Fitzpatrick and his friends in the CFL. Privately he now complained to Lozovsky that many unionists were "frightened off" by the prospect of the whole FF-LP enterprise "being formed in Moscow." One CEC member recalled that, at the time, "it seemed so unworthy of a Communist leader to base his conclusions on opinions and desires of friends who were not even Communists." Pepper pressed for the Chicago Communists to agitate for the stillborn Federated Farmer-Labor Party in their unions, haranguing these "opportunists" for their "betrayal" and "criminal cowardice" when they showed signs of demurral. He accused Foster of having a stronger attachment to the CFL than the party, and bragged that the FF-LP was "the first real mass party of American workers and farmers." Cannon seemed to have little faith that the Party could solve its problems on its own. He implored a friend in Moscow to "write to me soon and let me know if Radek, etc. are paying very close attention to the activities of the American party and what they think of them. I hope they are not thinking we do not need any more advice from them."[55]

In the following months, the issue of the proper role of the stillborn FF-LP became the vortex of a bitter controversy that was to have broad implications for the future of the Communist movement in the United States. The origins of the dispute can be traced, ultimately, to the recurring American debate between syndicalists and "political" socialists. For Foster this was a familiar debate, except that this time he was operating in the unfamiliar milieu of the Communist party. It would be unrealistic to suppose, however, that the Party itself could remain separate and immune from differences of opinion that had afflicted American radicals for several generations. Beginning in 1921, a new generation of Communists had entered the Party. Unlike the left-wing and language-federation Socialists who had dominated the early years of the movement, this new cadre was predominately syndicalist in background and orientation. Foster was the exemplary figure in this new membership cohort, but individuals like Browder, Johnstone, and James P. Cannon would also play central roles in arguing for a strong trade unionist emphasis to party policy. Cannon, a colorful and charismatic figure who would emerge as a founder of the American Trotskyist movement in 1927, was not a Foster follower in the sense that Browder was, but he formed a factional alliance with Foster in late 1923 as a result of the FLP imbroglio. Alexander Bittelman, an accomplished Russian-speaking ideologist and a convinced member of the Foster faction, remembered that "in the period that followed the organization of our party in 1919, it was through the left wing in the trade unions, headed by Foster, that the Communist movement began to derive its main strength and influence." The assumptions behind Foster's approach were that "Communists with trade union contacts and experiences ought to constitute the core of the party's leadership." This leadership, though, remained unrepresentative of the Communist party's membership as a whole. Foster himself admitted in Comintern circles that the TUEL was "exceedingly few in numbers," and that the Party, upon which the TUEL was dependent for most of its strength, consisted of 90 percent foreign-born workers who "have little effect on the trade union movement because of the language barrier."[56]

In the midst of the difficulties attending the new Labor Party enterprise, Lozovsky pressured Foster to give the league a more Communist flavor. Following his first trip to Moscow, Foster had parried suggestions by Lozovsky that he establish a united front with the IWW and other "independent" unions, organize agricultural workers, establish a "Red Federation" of labor unions to rival the AFL, and run a Communist candidate against Gompers for the AFL presidency. In response to one missive that he had not acted quickly enough on a Profintern resolution to establish a united front "Council of Action" with the IWW and other independent unions, Foster protested to Lozovsky that while he did his best to implement such policies, "you must bear in mind how far away America is from Russia." Now, in the midst of intense pressure on the league,

Lozovsky wanted more attention to international events in the *Labor Herald*. Foster replied that as it was, nearly one-quarter of the space of the paper was devoted to foreign news, and that he often had to deal with complaints that it paid too much attention to the European situation. "If we are to remain a fighting institution, we must deal with the living problems in this country, which means that we must have a certain amount of space in our paper to do it," he wrote. Furthermore, "In the United States one of the most difficult phases of our work is to give publicity to the Red International. You will recall, of course, that our labor movement is not even affiliated with [the reformist international of labor unions]. There is practically no feeling of internationalism in the American working class. The workers share pretty much the same sentiment of the people at large, which is to keep out of foreign affairs." Nonetheless, Foster vowed to put Profintern resolutions into action as soon as he received them, and to continue to advocate "international affiliation."[57]

As Foster belatedly took a stand within the Workers' party on the importance of its ties in the organized labor movement, it became increasingly difficult to maintain those ties. At a crucial meeting of the Illinois Federation of Labor following the split, Fitzpatrick disowned a labor party resolution merely because, as the CFL organ put it, "Foster and his friends supported the amended resolution." In every instance, the issues upon which the Chicago Federation had previously taken a positive stand, including industrial unionism, recognition of Russia, and support for rebellious miners in the UMW, were tabled or voted down. Fitzpatrick collapsed under Gompers's pressure on each of these issues; John H. Walker, the president of the Illinois Federation and another putative progressive unionist, engaged in unabashed red-baiting of Foster at the convention. He had been threatened with loss of financial support for the federation if the organization persisted in its support of labor party activities.[58]

The meeting of the Illinois Federation of Labor was of tremendous significance, not only for its retrogressive stands on several resolutions supported by the TUEL, but because it represented a final repudiation of Foster by the leadership of the CFL. The character of this repudiation, in turn, revealed much about the increasing conservatism of an important sector of the labor movement in 1923. First, Foster had clearly overstepped his boundaries in his recurring attacks on the official leadership of the AFL. Oscar Nelson, vice president of the Chicago Federation and that organization's leading conservative voice, seemed particularly incensed by Foster's attacks on "pie counter" jobs held by AFL bureaucrats. Yet, the resolutions that the TUEL and Foster endorsed still commanded significant backing by the rank and file. The amalgamation resolution, for instance, was cosponsored by representatives of eighteen local unions. Many of these delegates openly resented the red-baiting of the officials, who had claimed, in essence, that the resolution should be rejected simply because Foster and the TUEL had promoted it. "I have found out that anything that is brought into this convention that is for the benefit of the rank and file is called an IWW movement, a red movement, or something," noted one exasperated delegate. Other delegates objected that the instructions of their constituents on the amalgamation issue had not been influenced by Foster and the TUEL; two of the unionists in favor of the industrial unionism resolution spoke for entire district councils representing thousands of members. On the first day of debate, the amalgamation resolution gathered momentum as numerous United Mine Workers delegates from southern Illinois, many denying their affiliation with the TUEL or the Communist party, rose to speak in its favor. However, at this point, as Foster rose to defend the amalgamation resolution for the first time, John Walker, presiding over the convention, abruptly closed debate and adjourned the delegates before Foster could begin his address. The conservatives seemed determined to demonstrate that they, too, could manipulate a convention.[59]

When the delegates reassembled the same afternoon, Matthew Woll, vice president of the AFL, took the floor before debate on the amalgamation resolution was allowed to resume. It is not surprising that Woll surfaced at an important state federation gathering in which numerous TUEL-supported resolutions were to be decided upon. Woll was a high-ranking AFL "fixer," an experienced veteran of such contentious meetings, and a master of the rhetoric of AFL unionism.

In his speech Woll placed the league in a collectivist tradition in the labor movement that he blithely traced backwards a century to the Chartist movement in England. In the United States, he proposed, the TUEL had its antecedents in the American Labor Union, the Knights of Labor, and the IWW. Each of these, he suggested, had been disastrous experiments, and to embrace the idea of industrial unionism would prove destructive to the progress of the labor movement. The AFL vice president concluded that Foster, whom he repeatedly characterized as "Mr. Imposter," sought only "the limelight, so that there may roll into his coffers more dollars and cents to continue the nefarious work that he is doing." The TUEL was an "insidious and . . . subtle and dangerous" movement that threatened to "destroy" the AFL, he proposed. Foster, in his defense, sardonically noted that "I do not have to break up the labor movement, the labor movement is pretty badly broken up as it is."[60]

For Foster, from a personal standpoint, the full significance of the Illinois Federation convention became clear as the outraged officialdom groped for a way to portray him in the most unfavorable light. Woll's characterization of him as "Mr. Imposter" was close to the mark, for

Foster's career in the Chicago Federation had been built by "camouflaging" his ultimate aims. Victor Olander, who had observed Foster for many years, hammered at this theme. He recalled how the labor radical had, in CFL meetings in the 1910s, apparently repudiated his syndicalist past. He remembered how Foster had at that time "frequently [been] on his feet, attacking and ridiculing the socialist delegates present in the Chicago Federation of Labor, always in a laughing, pleasant, mild-mannered sort of way." What emerged in the descriptions by Olander, Woll, and the others was, ultimately, a devastating if disingenuous portrayal of one of Foster's characteristic disabilities: his inability to establish a consistent normative vocabulary by which he might describe his radicalism. Olander was accurate when he sensed that Foster's peculiar aphasia before the committee investigating the steel strike symbolized his career in the labor movement. When the issue of Foster's radicalism was taken up, Gompers had "hissed" at Foster to "talk," but that finally "word went out over the country that this man would not say anything."[61]

Yet, surely no one could question Foster's "ability to step into a debate," Olander asserted, pointing to Foster's performances over the past several days. He cautioned that he "never minimize[d] Brother Foster's intelligence, I think he is one of the shrewdest psychologists in the labor movement in this country." The theme of Foster's attachment resurfaced continually. His sincerity had already been impugned; however, it remained for his essential "dishonesty" to be placed in context. The idea of community was invoked, as it would be continually during Foster's career, in order to establish his status as an outsider who could not be trusted. Nelson, in the course of an attack on the resolution endorsing the labor party, sought to contrast his motives with those of Foster: "I grew up in Chicago, I worked in Chicago—I haven't moved around from Seattle and other points, depositing my card." Local unionists often looked with suspicion on strangers who used their cards to avail themselves of the liberal benefits and advantages that were afforded by the unions for "travelers," often refusing such benefits to workers who had belonged to the union only a short time. In addition, Nelson asserted, Foster "came into" the packinghouse organizing campaign and had used it in order to promote himself. Foster attempted to parry these attacks, in his purely literalist, logical manner. "It seems I have been accused of moving about," he replied. "It seems I have lived in the West for a while. That seems to be quite a disgrace." In reply to accusations that he "came into" the stockyards campaign, Foster struggled to repudiate the logic of localism: "I have lived twelve years in the city of Chicago, I don't think all the respectable Americans live in Chicago; in fact, I know of about 107,000,000 who do not live there."

Thus, according to the emerging grammar of labor conservatism, Foster operated in a strange, deracinated world of psychological manipulation, self-promotion, publicity, and insidious bureaucratic centralization. According to nineteenth-century republicanist evocations of the nature of subversion, the political "confidence man" used deceit and cunning to undermine citizens' independence of mind, especially in urban environments where, increasingly, the presence of large numbers of strangers challenged traditional criteria of trustworthiness. Now the images of Foster the confidence man and radical charlatan were merged with portrayals of the Communist leader as an unscrupulous utilizer of "modern," essentially corporate forms of persuasion and self-promotion. Elsewhere, Woll jumbled patriotic and anticorporate images when he asserted that the only thing new about Foster's program was "his method of commercializing old and imperialistic and autocratic ideas." While it is impossible to gauge the effect that Foster's rebuttals had on the assembled delegates, the rhetoric of community with which he and his program were attacked was framed in a vocabulary that Foster was ill-suited by temperament, inclination, or experience to utilize in his own defense.[62]

At the American Federation of Labor national convention in early October, there was a further unraveling of the TUEL position. Resolutions favoring recognition of Russia, industrial unionism, and independent political action were defeated. Although such actions were not unexpected at AFL conventions, an important precedent was affirmed whereby a Communist could be expelled merely because of his political opinions. This, of course, would have repercussions at other levels. William F. Dunne, outspoken Communist editor of the *Butte Bulletin*, was unseated and his credentials revoked. Philip Murray, then a United Mine Workers vice president, introduced the measure to expel Dunne. Matthew Woll proclaimed that anyone "who has direct connection with the Communist party and is playing for the Soviet and Moscow government has no right in this convention as a trade unionist."[63]

Publicly, Dunne was defiant toward the "bureaucrats" who engineered his expulsion. Privately, he was defiant toward the Party's own Central Executive Committee. Dunne was a hard-nosed, hard-drinking Western unionist; a joke circulated in the Comintern that he was one of the few American party members who, if given a gun, wouldn't shoot himself with it. Following his expulsion, he wrote to Browder about the whole Labor party debacle: "We have alienated a lot of support to which we were entitled, and are now completely isolated. I do not know what steps are now being taken to remedy this condition, but I want to tell you that this being run out of the trade union movement after fourteen years of activity, makes one stop and consider if our tactics have been correct. . . . I have no wish to become a party hack. My field is the labor movement."

Blaming the New York party faction for its "demagogy," Dunne bitterly complained that "our most valuable comrades have been sacrificed in a futile attempt to carry out a policy that was doomed to failure from

the start, but which satisfied the egos of men to whom the labor movement is a closed book." Noting that it wasn't just officers of the internationals who had voted to expel him, he noted that "when I see real militants lining up with the machine, I know that we have blundered somewhere."[64]

Although Foster and his allies were wont to portray the problems of
the TUEL in terms of the internal factional situation in the Workers'
party, other forces were at work as well. From the beginning of its existence, Foster had claimed that the TUEL was not a dual union, but it was
apparent even before the Chicago split that the league was building an
alternative structure within the unions it targeted. Foster explained to
Lozovsky that the TUEL itself could not assume a "mass character" for
fear of being branded a dual union, but that the National Committees
organized by the league in the different unions were another matter. By
the summer of 1923 such committees existed in the mining, needle, textile, and shoe and leather industries, and the railroad crafts. The national
conferences held by these committees, while formally renouncing dualism, nonetheless had the explicit aim of replacing the existing union leadership and completely reorganizing the individual unions. The National
Committees were "ostensibly independent of the league but in reality part
of it," he explained. And, one of the stated policies of the league at the
time was "to support the foundation of new unions where the present
ones are impractical." The organization of national conferences by the
TUEL industrial committees represented a potential threat to the real
power base in the AFL: the internationals. State and local federations,
such as those in Chicago and Illinois, were comparatively powerless.[65]

In the ILGWU in New York, where the league had managed to establish its most influential presence, the accusation of dualism dogged the
Communists and provided the central rationale for an effective expulsion
campaign aimed at TUEL members. Meyer Perlstein, vice president of the
union, pointed out that the local league was deciding shop-floor rules and
piece rates, and calling work stoppages. Thus, "the League does the same
work which the unions are doing, and the League is really an economic
organization guided by the Communist party of America and the Third
International." It is "a pure and simple opposition union pledged to replace [the ILGWU] gradually and to take it in and make it a department
of the TUEL." Morris Sigman, the president of the union, and Perlstein,
both Socialists, pointed out that the league prohibited its members from
belonging to the Socialist party, and eventually drew Eugene Debs into
the controversy. Debs attempted unsuccessfully to negotiate a detente,
but refused to interfere in the expulsion campaign, much to Foster's chagrin. "The same thing will happen again, and more repeatedly, I fear, in
the future," Debs warned Foster privately. When Debs parted company

with Foster over the expulsion campaign in the ILGWU, he was splitting over the issues of dualism and "disruption," not Communist domination of the Federated Farmer-Labor party in Chicago. Debs's unwillingness to defend the TUEL was a decisive blow to the Communists.[66]

In the last months of 1923, the Communists thought they had one more chance to redeem themselves. Despite the well-organized quashing of TUEL-supported initiatives at labor conventions throughout the country, Foster and the Communist-dominated Federated Farmer Labor party extracted an invitation to a conference of the powerful Farmer-Laborite coalition in Minnesota. In 1922, the Minnesota Farmer-Labor party, dominated by farmers' Non-Partisan Leagues, was able to establish a strong enough electoral coalition to elect a United States senator, two of the state's ten congressmen, and a majority of the state legislature. In 1923, Magnus Johnson, the Farmer-Labor candidate, captured the governorship. William Mahoney, an influential figure in the Minnesota movement, was one labor leader who had publicly supported Foster during the Bridgman trial. He remained an outspoken critic of the AFL's red-baiting campaign, and publicly defended Foster for his stand on industrial unionism and the recognition of the Soviet Union. Mahoney thought Foster was being made a "martyr" for his advocacy of such progressive measures. Foster and the "industrialist" faction of the Workers' party sought to steer a careful course of support for the Minnesota FLP, as a way of resurrecting a semblance of the earlier united front with progressive unionists.[67]

Foster was ambivalent about the Minnesota movement: he privately sneered that it was made up primarily of farmers rather than industrial workers, and he understood that its upcoming convention intended to endorse Robert LaFollette for president. LaFollette, who would run under the CPPA banner in 1924, represented precisely the kind of middle-class reformer that Foster had always abhorred. Even so, Foster was against any policy that might provoke a split with Mahoney and thus endanger the tenuous efforts of the Communists to rehabilitate themselves with the left wing of the labor movement. In the meantime, the self-described "politicals" of the Party's Central Executive Committee in New York still promoted the Communist-led FF-LP as the potential vanguard of a mass movement of American workers. While Foster liked to think of the FF-LP as potentially the political equivalent of the TUEL, Pepper theorized that LaFollette was an American Kerensky and that the Federated party had revolutionary significance. Pepper's faction, which included Charles Ruthenberg, Jay Lovestone, and Robert Minor, complained that mere "industrialists" had taken over the party, and openly accused Foster of being a syndicalist without coherent Communist principles.[68]

Foster with Charles Ruthenberg, St. Paul, Minnesota, 1924.

Despite these difficulties, Foster was a compelling enough figure among the American Communists to be elected chairman of the Workers' party at its third convention in January 1924. Despite the fact that this was one of the few such elections to occur without overt Comintern involvement, Foster was soon on his way to Moscow, the occasion being a meeting of the Executive Committee of the Communist International (ECCI) to be held in April and May. There, Foster hoped to settle once and for all the difficult problem of the Federated Farmer-Labor party and its stance toward the larger movement for political action in the American labor movement.[69] Pepper, for his part, now sought to connect the American dispute to the political struggles in Moscow that had erupted in January 1924 following Lenin's death. The Comintern had offered no guidance in the vital events of 1923, but now the general attitude in Moscow toward third-party alliances was hostile.

In Moscow, Foster derided Pepper's infatuation with the FF-LP, proposing that the idea that it could become a mass party of American workers was "simple idiocy" and "laughable in practice." Foster had argued that the FF-LP had to go along with the LaFollette movement despite its political limitations, giving up any attempt to organize as a separate labor party. However, while Foster and Pepper were in Moscow, the Comintern ordered a split with the Minnesota FLP and a repudiation of LaFollette. Foster proclaimed that "if you do that, then the Communist party of America will be hurled backwards upon its path, it will be isolated from the masses and its work will be very much hindered and not only for a few months . . . but for a long time."[70]

However, Foster finally acquiesced to the Comintern's new policy; he had little real choice. Appearing in his first debates in Moscow forums as a Communist, and defensive about allegations that he was a barely reformed syndicalist, he was under tremendous pressure to accept the need to put distance between the American party and the LaFollette movement. In a rather desperate political ploy he even went a step further, proposing that if the Communists split with the pro-LaFollette forces in Minnesota, they should dispense with the FF-LP and run their own candidates for office in the 1924 election.[71]

Despite his fast backpedaling on Farmer-Labor politics, the issue upon which Foster staked the most in Moscow was a demand to have John Pepper "recalled." He declared that Pepper was engaging in a "reckless struggle for power" and that "he is gambling with the life and health of the Party; in his search for 'issues' he takes the slightest differences of opinion among the entire group, which ordinarily could be adjusted without any real difficulty, and makes them into life and death struggles." He evidently felt quite strongly about the situation; to demand the exile of an adept politician with Comintern ties like Pepper was a risky proposition. Yet, the Comintern granted Foster's request, much to the consternation of Pepper's allies.[72]

Why did Foster move so quickly to abandon his previous approach? He was not temperamentally inclined to resist when confronted in Moscow with the requirements of Communist discipline for the first time. At the same time, while understanding the pragmatic value of an alliance with a pro-LaFollette coalition, he was contemptuous of the Wisconsin senator and his program of ameliorative reforms. While his actions of 1920 and 1923 showed that Foster had been willing to go along with a "class" labor party movement such as Fitzpatrick's, based on left-oriented trade unions, there was very little in his experience to suggest that he could be very comfortable campaigning for a liberal like LaFollette.

The price of Pepper's removal was a repudiation of the farmer-labor united front, which, while valuable, had already suffered defeats at the hands of Fitzpatrick, LaFollette, and Gompers. These setbacks had occurred months before the Comintern finally pushed the labor party united front over the precipice. Indeed, there were even some gains for Foster, who, wounded by defeats at Illinois, Chicago, and finally at the AFL convention in Portland, extinguished the difficult FF-LP enterprise for the time being while engineering the removal of Pepper and continued endorsement of his leadership by the Comintern. Foster shed no tears over the demise of the FF-LP. He wrote to Lozovsky that the party "had no masses behind it," and that for the Communists to belong to it "was tantamount to having a united front with ourselves. There was nothing to do but step out from it and put up our own candidates."[73]

Foster's critics, though unrealistic about the prospects of the FF-LP, were basically right about his syndicalist outlook. The labor party movement had always been of secondary importance in Foster's calculations; it was primarily a means to an end. The TUEL continued to be the centerpiece of his overall strategy; he had written that "except for condemning the fatal Gompers political policy and advocating the general proposition of independent working class political action, the league leaves political questions to the several parties. Its work is primarily in the industrial field." For Foster, the Farmer-Labor movement had primarily been a "powerful weapon with which to oust Gompers from control of the unions," not an end in itself. On the eve of the Chicago split, Foster had privately predicted that the "Gompers bureaucracy" would collapse within two or three years. The FF-LP, he had envisioned at its inception, would be useful only "in a propaganda way." Even after the implications of the split with Fitzpatrick became clear, the Ruthenberg group, with no significant ties to the indigenous labor movement, sought desperately to maintain the metaphysical Federated Farmer-Labor party. Without it, they had no program and no base of activities, and might easily be reduced to the status of headquarters functionaries. Later, Foster aptly termed this party a "legend."[74]

As the FF-LP and the Communists' labor party front went crashing down, the Communists ran Foster and Benjamin Gitlow for president and vice president, respectively, on a straight Workers' party ticket. Foster's mind was not, in fact, on presidential politics; he planned to use the campaign to "build our industrial connections" and begin to reestablish the TUEL. However, the campaign showed how far to the left Foster had moved as a result of the events of 1923–24. Foster prided himself on his adaptability and canniness, but after 1923 he showed that he was also prone to periods of stubborn dogmatism. His politics cycled between careful opportunism and a kind of sullen, cathartic orthodoxy in which sins are purged by the repetition of fealty to first principles.[75]

His attacks on LaFollette assumed a particularly vehement and resentful edge. After years of compromise and maneuver on the margins of the labor party movement, Foster the radical syndicalist reemerged, his voice more certain than ever. The task of the Workers' party, he fulminated, was to "destroy the LaFollette illusion." Neither the Wisconsin senator nor his program, he proposed, "touch the vital question of power—who is to rule. He throws a mask over the brutal and obvious fact that the present system is a dictatorship of the capitalist class." He admitted, though, that a significant sector of the Communist party had been inclined to support LaFollette. Indeed, when the party announced that it was to run presidential candidates of its own, "it was difficult for the membership to readjust itself to the new situation. Something of a crisis developed. It was evident everywhere." Nonetheless, Foster seemed reconciled to his new role as presidential candidate and touring propagandist, noting afterward that the campaign had been a "historical event."[76]

During the campaign, Eugene Debs came out with an endorsement of LaFollette, and Foster was outraged. To him, Debs's "capitulation" only confirmed the tendency of socialists to "desert" the working class. Foster excoriated Debs for endorsing a candidate who was not only not a socialist, but was avowedly antisocialist. Debs responded by attacking Foster's connection with the Comintern: "Having no Vatican in Moscow to guide me I must follow the light I have," he insisted. Debs questioned whether the Socialist party could afford to "disappear from the scene" by severing itself from the LaFollette movement. Both Foster and Debs were acting in response to their experiences; Foster's contempt for LaFollette was not a dishonest reaction, and Debs instinctively sought to participate in the wider movement. However, the depth of the antagonism between Debs and Foster was a tragic illustration of the extent of the split in the socialist movement in 1924.[77]

During the campaign, the Communist standard bearer admitted forthrightly that the policies of the American party were formulated in consultation with the Comintern; the Communists were "extremely proud" of their affiliation with the Bolshevik revolution. While he acknowledged that he did not expect to be elected, "some day a Communist will lead the government that rules over America, [but] when that time comes the position will not be called president, it will be the chairman of the All-American Soviet."[78] Increasingly, Foster's rhetoric departed from the vernacular and slipped into the style of the Third International. Spurned by and spurning his former allies in the Chicago Federation of Labor, he began to embrace a new political grammar, one based on the requirements of a new set of solidarities and commitments.

Immediately after the election Foster moved quickly to dismantle the remnants of the Party's electoral apparatus, the moribund Federated Farmer-Labor party. The election results, he noted rather too hopefully, "completely eliminated" the prospect of a mass farmer-labor party distinct from the Workers' party. He concluded that there was no reason to expect that the labor party slogan "can be profitably resumed in the near future, if at all." The chief task of the Communists in the immediate future, he proposed, was the development of "the only weapon at its command . . . militant mass struggle." This meant a return to promulgating the basic program of the TUEL, amalgamation of the craft unions into powerful industry-wide entities. In response to recent defeats, however, he proposed that this transformation would begin on the shop floor, at the level of the rank and file, through the "widespread organization of shop committees."[79]

Still, despite his rhetoric during the campaign, Foster was privately quite bitter about the whole episode. "As I stated in Moscow, the Workers' party is now isolated from the Labor party movement. We will have to begin all over again," he wrote to Lozovsky during the campaign. When the Party took a stand against LaFollette, it "cut off many of the most valuable sympathizing elements we had in the unions." The American Communists were now "almost completely isolated in the labor movement. As I foretold and argued in Moscow, the whole works has gone over to LaFollette. Both Debs and Gompers have lined up with him. We will have much trouble sinking our hooks into the labor movement again." Publicly Foster glorified the Comintern. Privately, he complained bitterly to Lozovsky that the Comintern's decision to break the third party alliance was responsible for the acute crisis in the Communists' "industrial connections." During this period, according to the radical journalist Max Eastman, Foster related in a conversation in Moscow that "there's a lot of things happen here that I don't like, but we've got to take it, for the present. [The Russians] have the prestige, and you can't build a revolutionary movement without them."[80]

Two months before the election, at which LaFollette gained nearly five million votes, Foster despaired that the circulation of the *Labor Herald* had fallen to the point where it no longer made sense to maintain it as a separate organ. Yet at this vital point, when Foster was confronted most painfully with the difficulties of functioning openly as a Communist, he chose to stick with the Communists. When Lozovsky objected that ending the newspaper would mean the liquidation of the league, Foster responded that its circulation was a mere five thousand, and that merging the newspaper with other Communist periodicals would bring the league closer to the party membership, most of whom were foreign-born and had little understanding of working in the trade unions. He admitted that "we must readjust our movement to the sharp isolation which it is now suffering."[81] Foster seemed eager to get out of the business of journalism and back to organizing.

Foster's complaint that the Comintern decision had forced a disastrous split on American Communists had merit, but he was overstating his case. The attacks on the TUEL antedated the split in Minnesota, and had to do as much with Foster's own miscalculations as with interference from Moscow. League activists faced expulsions as a result of Communist policy made in the United States prior to the decisions handed down by the

Comintern in the spring of 1924. Since the conclusion of the Bridgman trial, and the public acknowledgment that he was a Communist, Foster could not evade responsibility or accountability for Communist policy, wherever it originated.

As he had perhaps calculated, Foster himself emerged from the whole Farmer-Labor controversy of 1924 in a stronger political position within the Communist party. As chairman, his program was still centered on building up a movement within the AFL for industrial unionism and the overthrow of the "Gompers regime." By 1924 Foster was able to eliminate both Pepper and the Federated Farmer-Labor party, or so he believed; even after the election, he admitted privately that the Ruthenberg group would "still stick to the old program of banging for a labor party anyhow." He recognized that his ability to silence the factional debates within the Party was limited; he wrote dryly to a Party ally that the situation was still "very difficult and complicated. It will provide another intricate problem for the Comintern to decide, no doubt."[82]

By the conclusion of the 1924 national elections, Foster had reluctantly abandoned his ties with the leadership of the organized labor movement in Chicago and had embraced his role as Chairman of the American Communist party. This was a momentous step, but it did not mean that he had transcended the contradictions of his earlier syndicalism. Nor did it mean that he had become a prisoner of a totalitarian ethos, wherein personality and volition are surrendered in the interest of discipline. While he was undoubtedly attracted to the discipline and revolutionary style of the Communist party, he retained certain core beliefs that he had developed in the prewar period. The idea that a militant minority could fundamentally alter the course of the American labor movement by "boring from within," creating new forms of organization and focusing their rhetoric on workers' economic struggles, remained the *sine qua non* of "Fosterism." He fought relentlessly, if not always successfully, to establish this as the main basis of Communist activities in the United States. As a result of adroit factional maneuvering and party infighting, by 1925 he had seemingly achieved the organizational power within the Communist party necessary to carry out this objective, even though it was by no means inevitable that the shape of party activities in the early 1920s would assume the form he envisioned. In the years after 1924, however, the Foster "tendency" in the Communist party would begin to unravel at both ends. Foster himself would see his leadership of the Party successfully challenged, while at the level of union and shop, TUEL minorities would find their activities more restricted than ever.

Chapter 8

"PHRASES LEARNED IN EUROPE"

ON MARCH 2, 1924, approximately thirty men and women gathered in a small rented hall in Los Angeles for an evening meeting of the Trade Union Educational League. The guest speaker was to be Ella Reeve Bloor, then sixty-seven years old, a lecturer and fund-raiser for the Workers' party. The individuals who sat in the audience were all members of local trade unions; they were precisely the kind of unionized militants that the TUEL sought to attract to its organization. This night, however, Mrs. Bloor's speech was interrupted when members of the Los Angeles Police Department "Wobbly" squad and a U.S. Department of Justice agent burst into the room and placed everyone under arrest. When taken to the police station, where they were charged with violating the state criminal syndicalism statute, the suspected revolutionaries protested that they had been meeting under the auspices of a "legitimate" organization. Each declared their craft union affiliations to the authorities. This was precisely what the law-enforcement agents had in mind when they undertook the raid in the first place. The U.S. Department of Labor's local "Commissioner of Conciliation" in Los Angeles had been acting as an intermediary for the Department of Justice and conservative AFL officials who desired "concrete evidence" of union members who were also sympathetic to the TUEL. Once this evidence was obtained, the AFL leaders had intimated, steps would be taken at once to expel them from their locals by order of the internationals. The Department of Labor official wrote in a "strictly confidential" memo to his superior in Washington, D.C. that the raid was the "culmination of a plan to furnish certain conservative [AFL] leaders with the 'dope.'" Within weeks, as a result of the raid, a "general house-cleaning" took place in the local labor movement, during which the Central Labor Council took steps to have TUEL members expelled from their unions. Members of the Carpenters' Union were the first victims of this purge.[1]

The *Los Angeles Times* claimed that the raid uncovered "a gigantic plot to undermine the American Federation of Labor and convert it into a Communist organization for the purpose of overthrowing the United States government." Understandably, at subsequent TUEL meetings in the city (which were infiltrated by Department of Justice agents) somewhat more immediate aims were discussed. At one such gathering, a speaker who quite naturally claimed that he was neither a member of the

Communist party nor of the TUEL, noted that he had been fighting for amalgamation and industrial unionism for thirty years. He cited the Seattle general strike as an example of what militant craft unionists, acting in concert, could accomplish, but blamed treasonous union officers for sabotaging its success. Another speaker attributed the backwardness of the labor movement in the United States to the fact that radicals had historically withdrawn from their craft unions to form "some dual union." The themes considered at these meetings were essentially distillations of "Fosterism"; as if to underline the Communist leader's role in the enterprise, one TUEL official, after a meeting, proudly showed an undercover agent a copy of a letter he had received from Foster that lauded the progress of the Los Angeles radicals. The letter urged the local militants, in the words of the agent, to "watch the officers of the unions and pick them to pieces until they got their own men into these positions."[2]

One can easily imagine how Foster, with the syllogistic mind of the organizer, created the intellectual framework under which the TUEL and the Los Angeles radicals operated. Boring from within plus the requirement of establishing industrial unionism meant the creation, by the unions, of some kind of transitional structure that might bring this about. Since conservative officials could not be depended upon to create such a structure by themselves, it was necessary to replace these officials. Industrial unionism became, therefore, primarily a matter of radicals and progressives gaining office in the old unions. The united front alliances of 1923 were thus assembled primarily at conventions, state and city central body meetings, and district conferences. Here, it was believed, it would be possible to initiate the overthrow of the "Gompers bureaucracy." This was a dangerous ground upon which to operate. The simple converse of Foster's conception of the "militant minority" was that radical activity in the unions could be defeated or at least checked by an equally determined and militant conservative faction. This, of course, is what happened in Los Angeles and elsewhere after the early successes of the TUEL prodded the AFL hierarchy into action. Although he continued to cite the maneuvering of conservatives as a cause of the TUEL's setbacks, Foster understood the implications of these events and sought to readjust the party's course after the 1924 elections. However, continuing attacks by AFL officials and bitter factionalism within the Workers' party itself would contribute to the defeat of this reorientation.

While TUEL activities varied from union to union, its work in the International Association of Machinists illustrated the difficulties faced by the league in the early 1920s. There, the league had been associated since 1922 with an insurgent movement gathering around William Ross Knudsen, a popular figure whom the Communists had backed in an unsuccessful 1922 electoral challenge to William H. Johnston. As the international initiated expulsion procedures against groups of local unionists belonging to the TUEL in 1924, Foster was forced to explore ways of attaching the league to a more moderate opposition to Johnston, this time gathered around J. F. Anderson. In the prewar period, Foster might have moved easily within the kind of progressive milieu that Anderson and his allies personified. However, in the post-war period, Foster moved inexorably leftward, while unionists like Anderson retrenched. Anderson was skeptical about amalgamation. In 1923 he noted that "there are plenty of examples of trades banded together in amalgamated units having the same hard struggle to advance the interests of their members as so-called industrial unions." As an example, he cited the United Mine Workers, an industrial union that had "almost complete control over their industry. Still they are obliged to strike, and their strikes are not always successful." Faced with an overwhelming preponderance of government and employer opposition, Anderson had supported the settlement of the 1922 shopmen's strike. For Foster, the individual union agreements arising out of this strike marked an important turning point in the history of the labor movement, symbolizing the beginning of the decline of unionism into "class collaborationism" during the 1920s.[3]

In 1927, Foster wrote that "after the close of the 1922 railroad shopmen's strike the trade union bureaucracy plunged into an orientation towards an elaborated and intensified class collaboration." By 1925, the themes of the class war had resurfaced with a vengeance in his rhetoric; he attacked any cooperation between trade union leaders and business as "fascist." For him, nothing represented this tendency more clearly than the "B & O plan" which was widely implemented in railway shops after the 1922 strike. Such plans theoretically recognized the role of independent unions in improving productivity in the railway industry; under the agreements, workers' committees would work with shop managers in developing proposals for increased efficiency. In return, the union received a kind of de facto legitimacy, while the companies pledged not to engage in the hated practice of subcontracting work out of the shops. In the IAM, the earliest and most vehement opposition to the B & O plan came from TUEL activists. Many progressives favored the new collaborative labor-relations system.[4]

In early November 1924 the National Committee of the TUEL met to formulate strategy for the coming months in the IAM. Foster had delegated to Andrew Overgaard the task of creating an analysis and plan. Overgaard's report and subsequent events in the IAM reveal much about the methods and tactics of the earliest Communist unionists. It is interesting to note that at this relatively late stage, after the Chicago split and the political debacles of 1924, Overgaard was able to identify a significant group of individuals in the IAM who were allies of the TUEL but not CP members. The general opposition movement itself, he observed, was split between "progressives" like Anderson and pro-TUEL "left-wingers." The program of the left wing, it was proposed, should include: industrial unionism; organization of the unorganized; a labor party; opposition to the B & O plan; struggle against racial discrimination and support for a campaign to organize black workers; working against the expulsion of TUEL members; recognition of Soviet Russia; and "international trade union unity." One month later, Foster and William Dunne were delegated to approach the progressives to demand representation of the left wing on the opposition slate in the upcoming elections. They conditioned the support of the TUEL on the endorsement of a fight against the B & O plan, a campaign to reinstate expelled members, and a "militant" campaign for industrial unionism. Also included in the conditions were support of a "class" labor party, and opposition to LaFollette. Significantly, the latter two were "not to be splitting point[s]."[5]

Anderson at first rejected the TUEL overture, so the league ran its own candidates in the union's "primary" elections. These candidates were able to demonstrate that a significant amount of support existed for the TUEL platform. Yet, after these nominating elections, the league withdrew its candidates and gave its qualified support to Anderson. In the general election that followed, Anderson did not make any public statement as to his position on these issues, but three other candidates on his slates backed a program that was identical to the TUEL demands, minus the LaFollette proviso. In the election, held in March 1925, Anderson lost by only fifty votes.[6]

Soon after the election, Anderson accused Johnston of fraud in the ballot counting and was subsequently suspended from membership. However, by early 1926, Anderson's membership had been restored, and the Anderson and Johnston factions in the union had reached an understanding that isolated the Communists. Both sides agreed to support a compromise president for the international, Arthur O. Wharton, who was elected in 1927 without opposition. In an introductory circular, the new president wrote: "If we are wise, we will be less visionary and more practical by concentrating our efforts in the direction of securing immediate and material benefits." For the next ten years, Communist influence in the union was minimal. Following an ardent campaign in their behalf, TUEL members who had been suspended by Johnston were reinstated only under the condition that they renounce the league. Under the regime of Johnston, who was a Socialist, the powers of the international president had grown significantly. In 1925 he essentially outlawed Communism by ukase, as one historian has put it. Moreover, the logic employed in the expulsion campaign was broad enough so that any IAM member who endorsed progressive measures was subject to the sanctions of the international. This was made explicit in a *Machinists Monthly Journal* article published at the height of the factional struggle in the union: "Each Communist, whether he belongs officially to the TUEL or not, is bound by party discipline to act in all union matters, not as the interests of the organization would dictate, but in accordance with the orders of the secret Communist central committee. It is clear, therefore, that any one who openly supports in any manner Communist activity aids thereby our bitterest enemy in fighting our Union, and must therefore be regarded as an enemy of the Union."[7]

Foster, in response to the expulsion campaign, proposed that union members who were known Communists fight for readmission, while party members who were not so identified sign the statements that required them to deny membership. However, the policy of the Machinists' officialdom essentially precluded any public criticism of the union on the issues with which the TUEL had been associated.[8]

While the Machinists' expulsion policy was forcing the TUEL deeper underground in the union, any evaluation of the disintegration of league efforts in the IAM must include a consideration of Foster's own role, above all, his unwillingness to compromise on the B & O plan. Foster's experiences as a railroad worker were rooted in the 1910s, the decade of the interminable Illinois Central shopmen's strike and open class warfare on the roads. The "class collaboration" the B & O plan represented was anathema to him. Yet, on no issue in the 1920s was the ambivalence at the core of "Fosterism" so evident. While he sought to establish united fronts in the unions during the 1920s, his unalterable opposition to the B & O plan created significant dissent among progressive unionists, many of whom favored the plan as a way to save their weakened unions. Foster openly derided these progressives as "cooperationists" following a policy of defeat and "surrender."[9] No Comintern initiative motivated his stand on this issue, but his steadfast opposition to the B & O plan illustrated the difficulties confronting any league effort to construct a larger united front of progressives during this period.

As expulsions demoralized the league and progressive candidates for union office were routinely defeated, Foster began to formulate "the next task." In September 1924, after an unblinking assessment of the league's progress, he wrote that "the situation is extremely critical. The trade union movement is in the death grip of an officialdom almost totally unprogressive. The union leaders stand helpless before militant capitalism." The league had to find some way to arouse the rank and file in a campaign against the reigning bureaucrats. In an explicit rebuke of past policies and the earlier basis of the amalgamation campaign, he suggested that "the era of passing resolutions, to have them thrown into the waste basket by sneering and stupid officials, is past." By early 1925, Foster had come to the view that amalgamation "is essentially a movement from the bottom," rather than a matter of convention fights over resolutions. The fight for industrial unionism, he asserted, must be "brought closer to the workers' lives." Shop committees needed to be organized, with radicals fighting for the everyday interests of workers and eschewing abstract slogans. Industrial unionism, he asserted, would only take place when official representatives of national and international unions "assemble in conference, with all their own friends, or by dint of strong rank-and-file pressure, and formally fuse together the organizations concerned." The development of "rank-and-file conferences"—a tactic learned from the Harriman strike, the packinghouse campaign, and the steel strike—would be the primary focus.[10]

Foster's attempt to reorient the league's activities never gained much momentum, however. The reasons for this are apparent at a number of different levels. First, from Moscow, Foster heard that Grigory Zinoviev, the head of the Comintern, was opposed to his ideas. The details of Zinoviev's critique are unclear; yet, once again Foster had retreated into the arena of "mere" trade unionism, refusing to confront the conservative bureaucracy in the arena of resolutions, "talk," and politics. Foster, pessimistic about the outcome of election struggles in the miners and machinist unions, replied that TUEL cadre "need a fighting policy. To simply tell them to go on endlessly passing resolutions . . . is futile." Moreover, "to expect to defeat the bureaucrats in elections or conventions is just about out of the question." Nonetheless, despite his reservations, Foster and the TUEL continued to press convention and election fights in a variety of unions, often with disastrous, even violent results. The appearance of Foster and other Communist organizers at conventions continued to provide conservatives with excellent opportunities for red-baiting progressive opponents of all persuasions.[11]

The limitations of the new campaign for industrial unionism can also be seen in the personality of its main leader. Although he formally conceived the task of the union militant as one of "education," Foster was an organizer by temperament and instinct. Respected by other Communists for his "executive and organizing skill, his craftiness, his patience and driving energy," as a speaker and writer, he was at his best when outlining the logic of collective action and empowerment. He simply lacked the ability of the great propagandist to inspire a vision of an alternative normative community in his audiences. In the end, purely organizational activity would provide the means to putting across the radical program. "American workers are ripe for radical ideas," he explained, but they can only be convinced by radicals if they see them working on day-to-day details in the unions, going to jail during strikes, and making significant sacrifices in their interest. "The workers follow the man who organizes them," he told one group of Communist unionists.[12]

However, this approach remained limited and perhaps fatally incomplete. What, in Foster's vision, did industrial unionism promise beyond "conferences" and perhaps a newer, more powerful form of organization? He was reluctant to employ the term "industrial unionism" because of its association with the "utopian" IWW, preferring instead to use a term that had explicitly business and corporate connotations: "amalgamation." In the midst of bitter opposition to TUEL initiatives, Foster was often forced to yield the domain of "talk" to the conservatives. As a matter of realism he was unenthusiastic about contests on these grounds, but beyond this, he retained an ungenerous view of workers' potential for political imagination. The ideals of equality, community, self-empowerment, and freedom—ideals that had given resonance to the idea of industrial unionism for generations of American socialists and unionists—are largely absent from Foster's rhetoric because he considered them outmoded and irrelevant. Moreover, he could not and would not say to workers, as did Eugene Debs in a famous speech on industrial unionism, that "my strength is drawn from you, and without you I am nothing." He could not claim that workers themselves were the "vanguard" of the social revolution and that in the future society "the working class will stand forth the sovereigns of this earth." He would not say to workers that "there is nothing that you cannot do for yourselves," or that in a future society of "brotherhood and equality" workers "must make themselves the masters of the tools with which they work." Whereas for Debs industrial unionism meant a future in which workers would cease to be mere "cogs" or "hands" in the machinery of capitalist society, Foster envisioned no fundamental change in that machinery other than a transfer of ownership.[13]

It is ironic that while Foster came to the Communist movement at least in part because of its organizational coherence and discipline, the American Communist party found itself rent by disabling factional warfare by the mid-1920s. He had believed that the TUEL could essentially assume all the most important roles of a Communist party in the United States, but this proved to be a stunning miscalculation.

To be sure, he had a number of important factors operating in favor of his perspective. First, the TUEL often acted relatively independently of the party apparatus, and it showed far more potential to develop into something larger than itself than did the Communist labor party adventures of the early 1920s. At the Bridgman convention of the party in 1922, it had been proposed that "control" of the TUEL would be exercised through

Party fractions (i.e., cells) in the league. Until 1924, this meant merely that Foster's administration of its activities was uncontested. For almost the entire year of 1923, until September, the National Executive Committee of the TUEL met separately from the party and consisted almost solely of Johnstone, Browder, and Foster, with Samuel Hammersmark occasionally participating in meetings.[14] At the same time, as chairman of the Workers' party, Foster had by 1925 survived several different challenges to his authority.

In the last months of 1924, however, Ruthenberg and Lovestone revived their bitter fight against Foster's leadership. They derided him as "Zig-Zag" for his ability to shift positions quickly on political questions. Benjamin Gitlow, a Ruthenberg factionalist, offered his recollection of Foster in these days:[15]

> He would spend his free hours hanging around Communist club rooms and meeting halls, gossiping about small matters with the rank and file. He liked, at these times, to tell stories of his hobo past, of his experiences with the hoods and goons he had known in his trade union days. Or he would entertain the boys with loud, ribald humor, cleverly flavored from the rich stock of slang he had acquired in his youth. It was as though he were telling those around him that he had only contempt for the savants [at party headquarters in New York].

The controversy revolved mainly around the issue of the Labor party. Pepper, at the Comintern's fifth plenum in March 1925, continued to argue the so-called "minority" view that the American proletariat was poised to surge into a "mass" labor party similar to that which existed in Great Britain. The "Fosterites" were berated for their belief that the American masses had little desire for political independence from the two-party system. He accused the majority of spreading the word that the minority was merely a group of "uprooted intellectuals." The truculent Hungarian, whose experiences in the United States had consisted of two years of life in the party underground, fulminated at one plenum that "the standpoint of the Foster group is the standpoint of the elements who hopelessly repeat a few phrases which they learned in Europe, but who do not understand the entire process of development, the entire history of the American labor movement with all its specific characteristics and definite complexities." At one point Pepper called Foster a "scoundrel" and demanded his expulsion from the party for sending false reports to the Comintern.[16]

In an explicit rebuke to Foster's perspective, in the spring of 1925 the Comintern decided that the decision to abandon the Labor party idea was "incorrect." He and his allies were forced to acquiesce to vaguely-worded "Labor party" resolutions, but one prominent American observer termed

Foster an example of "a pilot accepting orders and at the same time showing unmistakable signs that he firstly does not consider the order a good one [and] that he considers essential parts of the order as unacceptable." Foster wrote defiantly to Zinoviev protesting the wording of a *Pravda* article on the plenum, demanding a correction and complaining that "we have worked under many disadvantages in Moscow and have been obliged to suffer many discriminations of which the foregoing is an example." Although he promised to begin labor party work "throughout the United States," he noted that sentiment for such a party "is at a very low ebb." The Comintern attempted to assuage Foster by endorsing the idea that "the first and most important task" of the American party was capturing the leadership of the conservative unions. Foster's acceptance of the Comintern's authority continued to be based not only on his personal admiration of the Russian leadership and the Bolshevik revolution, but on the idea that "Fosterism" was ultimately consistent with the aims of the international movement. However, the factional hostility in the party, aggravated by the Comintern's unwillingness to provide an unambiguous endorsement of Foster's leadership, was so intense that he complained that it was seriously hampering the "constructive work" of the party. "The minority absolutely refuses to obey discipline," he reported to Moscow. "They say in so many words that they will not obey anyone except the Comintern," he pleaded rather naively.[17] At the district level, moreover, as one former Communist recalled, "factional loyalties turned all party meetings into screaming, conniving sessions that often ended in fist fights." Such conflict so threatened the American Party that in 1925 the Comintern proposed the establishment of a "parity commission" and the appointment of an "impartial chairman" for that year's party convention. Soon, a veteran Bolshevik, Sergei Ivanovich Gusev, arrived in the United States, smuggled in secretly from Mexico, to help adjudicate the dispute. A figure of high standing in Soviet Russian party, Gusev was a convinced ally of Stalin and an embittered foe of Trotsky.

When the Workers' party fourth convention opened in August, Foster was elected chairman over Benjamin Gitlow by a vote of 40 to 21. His authority was based not only on the cadre of radical trade unionists who joined the party after 1922, but on the language federations; most powerful among these was the Finnish Federation, which alone encompassed one-third of the party's membership at the time. Ruthenberg groused that this new Fosterite majority "had not passed through the experiences" of the years of the party's founding, and, indeed, had "held aloof" from the Communist movement in its formative period. However, Foster's majority remained tenuous indeed, for on the final day of the convention, Gusev dramatically produced a cablegram from Moscow that declared that "it has finally become clear that the Ruthenberg Group is more loyal to the decisions of the Communist International and stands closer to its views." The precise origins of this cablegram remain obscure, but clearly, mistrust of Foster remained high in Moscow. For Foster, it was a devastating decision. He informed Gusev that he would not accept the conditions outlined in the cable and stormed out of the meeting.[18]

Foster and his allies attempted to rally their factional supporters in meetings in Chicago and New York, developing what Gusev termed a "rebellion" against the Comintern decision. However, Foster was deserted by his close factional allies, including James Cannon, who argued that Foster's actions were "disloyal." Cannon argued for "a complete break with the whole tradition of diplomatizing with the CI. . . . We must develop the understanding that the party and the CI are one inseparable whole." Foster was similarly obsequious in his public tributes to the revolutionary authority of the Comintern, but the fact remained that he had absented himself from a Central Executive Committee meeting immediately after the reading of the cablegram. Moreover, he continued to hold out for a right of "appeal" of the Comintern's decision, insisting that the Soviets had acted upon incorrect information. Cannon and Jay Lovestone, a spokesman for the "minority," argued that the Comintern was simply incapable of making mistakes. According to Gusev, Foster's actions had raised the issue of "the relation of the party to the Communist International." The insulted Bolshevik accused Foster and his allies of "double accounting," paying lip service to Moscow while "following a political policy against the Comintern."[19]

To Lozovsky, Foster was incredulous. More than a month after the arrival of the fatal cablegram, the former chairman of the party still had no idea what the Comintern's motives were. "The whole decision is so mysterious," he wrote. "We have not received a single word in connection with it, except the original cablegram." Nonetheless, "we believe that a great mistake has been made, one that will cost our party very much. On all sides there is bitterness at our integrity being so ruthlessly attacked." Furthermore, "We will probably have to send another delegation to Moscow. This means further confusion and delay in the reorganization of our trade union work. I cannot imagine how such a decision was ever made by the Comintern. What effect did they think it was going to have upon our party, to deal a loyal group like ours such a heavy blow? How can they expect effective work from us after placing us under such a heavy and needless handicap?"[20]

In 1923, upon Foster's ascension to the chairmanship, no wholesale removals of factional opponents had been initiated. However, in 1925, Lovestone, Ruthenberg, and their allies toured the country to install an entirely new leadership at the district level. How would Ruthenberg's approach work? The main objective of the party, he wrote, must be to "draw the workers into a struggle against the capitalist government." The party's policy was to see to it that "labor" candidates were on the ballot in every state and congressional district where the party maintained an organization. The Communists would support farmer-labor parties "where they existed," but otherwise it would be the duty of Communists to place Workers' party candidates in the field. In the new "politicized" party, trade union cadres would be faced with the necessity of supporting Communist office seekers in local elections. Ruthenberg, now "general secretary" of the party, took steps to bring the TUEL more strictly under the control of the Central Executive Committee, and campaigned to eliminate the league altogether by replacing it with party factions. For months Foster's name was absent from the Workers' party letterhead. Under Ruthenberg's administration, the party's organ, the *Workers' Monthly*, was dominated by articles on international and Soviet politics as well as philippics by Lenin, Zinoviev, and Stalin with titles such as "Lessons of the Moscow Uprising." For curious American workers, Stalin contributed "Lenin—the Mountain Eagle." Jay Lovestone's ability to organize the wooing of Gusev showed his promise as a Communist politician. He wrote to Bukharin thanking the Comintern for the "excellent services" rendered by Gusev. "I, for one, want to state emphatically that I owe very much to him in the way of my political development, my understanding of and desire to give over all my services to the development of a Bolshevik Party in the United States."[21]

Within weeks of Gusev's intervention, Foster was on his way to Moscow to argue his "appeal." Zinoviev was evasive when asked in a private interview to explain the cablegram. He had clearly put up with his share of impertinence from Foster; now he stated dryly that Gusev's reports to him had indicated that the Foster group had used "doubtful methods" to secure a majority at the convention. Nevertheless, he agreed that the Ruthenberg group had gone too far in persecuting the Fosterites, promised to send a cable to that effect, and concluded that his visitors should "be cheerful." Meanwhile, Lozovsky pressed a defense of the hapless TUEL; he remained a "bitter pro-Foster factionalist." Theoretically, the requirements of Communist organizational discipline held that the leadership of the party must have a majority in all the subsidiary committees. In February 1926, in a highly unusual decision, a Comintern "American Commission" awarded Foster's faction a majority on the all-important Trade Union Committee. According to Foster, Nikolai Bukharin, the new head of the Comintern at the time, even proposed a formal split of the American party, with the "politicals" and "trade unionists" each commanding separate organizations. Following his humiliation at the American party convention, Foster was clearly thinking along these lines: in one Comintern debate he even stated that "we must realize that the TUEL has to be a separate organization and proceed in that sense." Instead, he won approval for a plan of reorganization and revitalization of the TUEL. The league was to appear as a separate organization, "high politics" was to be kept out of its work ("substance and mass strength shall be given preference over ideological clarity"), a new journal was to be launched, and the party was to acknowledge its trade union work as its most important area of activity. Foster proposed that the TUEL program "must be simplified and concentrated around burning everyday issues in the class struggle." A high-ranking Ruthenberg factionalist, John Ballam, secretly predicted such a settlement, claiming that the Comintern feared a Foster split, "especially after his show of strength at the membership meetings" following the Workers' party convention.[22]

Yet, by early 1926 both the party and the TUEL were in deep decline. Ruthenberg fired TUEL cadres from their positions, and many trade unionists were expelled as a result of the new leader's purge of the Fosterites. Other union cadres who had been recruited to the party through the TUEL "almost completely absented themselves and stopped paying dues," Browder recalled. Three of Foster's oldest and closest associates, Joe Manley, Samuel Hammersmark, and Jay Fox ceased to play important roles in the party during this period. Years later, in a condescending and revealing assessment of his view of Foster's associates, James Cannon reflected that "like most of those whose ideas and methods of work had been shaped in the narrow school of trade unionism," a figure like Hammersmark was "lost in the complexities of party politics." Foster wrote at the time that under Ruthenberg the "whole TUEL conception has been liquidated by the conception of mere [Communist] fractions." In early 1926, Ballam predicted that pending Cannon's cooperation, "we can put a bit and bridle on Foster and either break him in to be safe—to gee and whoa under the bolshevik group—or boil him down for glycerine."[23]

If Foster had any illusions about the TUEL's organizational independence, they were dispelled shortly after his return from Moscow. In order to be closer to its main base of support, the Party leadership decided to move the entire apparatus of the Party, including the *Daily Worker*, from Chicago to New York. Foster loudly objected, explaining to Lozovsky that Chicago, as a steel and railroad center, was "more closely related to the basic industries" of the nation and that the city possessed a rich revolutionary tradition. He complained that the New York Communists had a "local outlook" and that this had "grievously hindered our work on previous occasions." The comrades there "rarely look beyond the Bronx River," he proposed. Locating the TUEL in New York would label it "as a Party organization." Nonetheless, Foster was powerless to prevent the move.[24]

As far as Foster himself was concerned, sympathetic observers lamented his continued involvement with the Communist movement. The *New Republic*, which had been intrigued by Foster's brand of progressive

unionism, now declared that "his futility is a curious example of the se-
duction of a naturally fertile mind by a sterile absolutist philosophy."[25]
This assessment of the evolution of Foster's thought, however, was mis-
leading. In the 1910s, Foster's outlook, with its political relativism, faith
in executive systematicity, and contempt for the "resistance of tradition"
and the obstructionism of "labor bosses of narrow vision," as the *New
Republic* put it, shared certain characteristics with the managerial liberalism that permeated American political discourse at the time. However,
his brand of trade union radicalism had always retained a "hard" concept
of class at its core. David Saposs, a closer observer, understood that while
"Fosterism" was in some respects quite similar to progressive unionism,
Foster himself had always been a "revolutionary radical at heart."[26]

While it is a mistake to see Foster as a misplaced progressive unionist
who was "seduced" by Communism, "Fosterism" did suffer as a result of
its originator's involvement with the American Communist movement.
By early 1926, an astute unionist (and former Communist) like J. B. S.
Hardman could comment that "the Workers' party leadership, irresponsible and incompetent, sank its teeth deeply into the TUEL. It reduced the
movement to party size, imbued it with an ungenerous, narrow and clique
esprit that characterizes the Workers' party."[27] How did Foster allow this
to occur? The central difficulty lay in an ambiguity at the heart of his own
radicalism. While he was acutely conscious of the need to build mass
movements, he could also state, before a gathering of Communists, that
the Bolsheviks had demonstrated that revolutionary movements could no
longer be judged solely by their size. Like a number of other prominent
syndicalists of his generation, Foster found the Communist movement
quite consistent with the idea of the "militant minority." The nature of
the syndicalist project, as well as his attraction to the style of Communist
radicalism and the power that the Bolshevik revolution represented, help
to explain his willingness to attach the TUEL to the destiny of the Workers' party.

While factionalism within the Communist movement undoubtedly contributed to the decline of the TUEL, larger forces were at work that undermined the movement Foster hoped to build for industrial unionism in the
early and mid-1920s. The TUEL, because of the disastrous wartime defeats for unionism in mass-production industry, had by necessity focused
in the early years of its existence on unions that had managed to maintain
a strong tradition of workers' control into the 1920s. However, by the
middle years of the decade, it had become clear that these traditions had
been seriously attenuated in a number of trades, as they had in steel and
packing in a previous era. While TUEL efforts in a number of trades met
with some notable successes in the immediate postwar years, league mili-

tants were portrayed as disruptive influences whose activities and propaganda invited further employer attacks and weakened union solidarity. While league demands promised increased unity in the long run, the immediate effect of TUEL agitation was consistent with the portrayals of the union leadership in many cases.

As for mass-production industry, where the majority of American workers remained unorganized in the 1920s, the TUEL did very little actual organizing in the early years of the decade. This was true even where unions already existed. While the TUEL relentlessly pushed the slogan "organize the unorganized," league militants, operating under the constant threat of expulsion, could attain neither the positions nor the political backing from the union leadership that Foster felt was necessary for effective organizing drives. Faced with this difficulty, Foster had begun to reformulate his tactics, seeking to refocus the movement for industrial unionism "from below." However, by the time this adjustment was being contemplated, TUEL cadres found themselves under attack by factional opponents within the Workers' party. By 1926, with unionism in retreat on all fronts and with Foster's position in the Communist party severely weakened, "Fosterism" had seemingly reached a dead end. Even Joe Manley told Lozovsky that the league could not prosper unless it changed its approach to organizing mass-production industry. Significantly, the largest Communist-led strike of the decade broke out in Passaic, New Jersey, in early 1926 while Foster was in Moscow arguing his "appeal," and was sustained by workers for whom the AFL was a ghostly presence at best. The Communists had established a few shop nuclei and mill committees in Passaic by 1925; in September a wage cut of 10 percent at the Botany Mills in the city incited an angry strike. The walkout finally fell under the tireless leadership of Albert Weisbord, a recent Harvard graduate who was working and organizing in the Paterson silk mills when he was shifted to the strike scene. The Passaic strike gave the new Ruthenberg leadership the opportunity to test its belief that a more straightforwardly Communist program could be successful in the arena of trade union politics and organizing.[28]

At Passaic, authorities arrested nearly a thousand strikers, and picketers were dispersed with firehoses, tear gas, and vicious beatings. Weisbord organized workers into a "United Front Committee," issuing dues stamps and membership cards. However, the employers refused to meet with the Communists, and the United Textile Workers refused to have any dealings with the committee until the Communists withdrew and Weisbord resigned. With the mills operating with about a third of their former work force, Foster and the Communist leadership ordered the strike turned over to the UTW. The AFL, however, proved unwilling to pursue the situation aggressively, finally gaining little for the strikers. Foster believed that he had made the correct decision; "all these maneuvers are unsatisfactory and quite dangerous. But they had to be undertaken in view of the extremely critical situation of the strike," he reported to Lozovsky. Lozovsky, however, was doubtful, despite the fact that the Comintern had issued an injunction against the formation of "parallel trade unions . . . in any form" during the strike itself. "I still think that your tactics during the strike in Passaic were wrong," he wrote months later. "Your sacrifice of Weisbord in fulfillment of the demands of the employers and the Trade Union bureaucrats was the beginning of the end." His friend suffered from "a fear of setting up and directing a union."[29]

Foster and his factional opponents argued endlessly over the "lessons" of Passaic. It is difficult to sustain the idea that the strike might have been won under the auspices of the Communist-led United Front Committee, which Foster stigmatized as an incipient dual union. On the other hand, the AFL demonstrated its own inability and unwillingness to protect the workers, thus casting doubt on Foster's orientation. The UTW expelled the Communists from its Passaic local within months of the end of the strike.[30]

In the garment trades, the TUEL built steadily on the presence it had established in the early 1920s. Despite a vigorous expulsion campaign begun early in 1923, the TUEL was able to gain control of the executive boards of the three largest locals of the ILGWU in New York by the end of 1924. Communist influence was not limited to New York; in Boston, Chicago, and Philadelphia the league was able to maintain a strong position as well. In June 1925, Morris Sigman, the ILGWU president and a former Wobbly, brought charges against the three TUEL-dominated New York locals. After a brief trial, the locals were suspended. In response, Foster proposed the organization of a Joint Action Committee, which proceeded to behave in many ways like a dual union. The JAC collected dues and negotiated grievances with employers, while simultaneously making the reinstatement of the expelled locals and democracy in the union the central issues. Because of the enormous popularity of the JAC among the rank and file, the Sigman administration was forced to readmit the expelled locals and negotiate a settlement with the left wing. Foster supervised the negotiations for the Workers' party.[31]

In the needle trades, the top TUEL fractions dealt directly with Foster; in early 1923, nearly a year before the formation of the JAC, he and the needle trades cadres worked out a policy whereby "unions of the expelled" were to be formed if expulsions took on a "mass character." In the meantime, the issues that the TUEL group were to emphasize would be issues "of shop, of trade, and union." During this period, Communists in the needle trades looked to Foster as the only trade unionist in the top ranks of the party; he was "cautious by nature and not given to revolutionary phrases," according to one organizer.[32]

Nonetheless, Foster allowed factional considerations to affect Communist strategy in the needle trades in 1926, a vital year for the New York garment industry. A commission established by Governor Alfred E. Smith recommended a sweeping reorganization of the industry that ignored union demands for a forty-hour week and would have allowed employers periodically to dismiss up to 10 percent of their employees. In July the Communist-dominated Joint Board succumbed to strong rank-and-file demand for a general strike against the reorganization. However, the unions almost immediately found themselves on the defensive; when an opportunity for a reasonable settlement arose, neither Foster nor Ruthenberg and Lovestone, fearing accusations of "opportunism," could bring themselves to order concessions. The effectiveness of the strike steadily eroded, and the walkout was finally settled on even poorer terms. Communist leadership in the union was discredited, and conservatives, with the aid of the employers, reestablished their influence in a severely weakened union.[33]

William Foster was an extraordinarily ambitious man, but this is hardly an unusual trait among highly committed radicals. As a Communist, after all, he sought nothing less than the overthrow of an entire social order. At the level of personality, ambition becomes interesting as a motive and explanation when it begins to override principle, when it offers an explanation for actions that are inconsistent with previous commitments. Yet, it is difficult to evaluate Foster's ambition in this way. What "principle" can he be said to have held most closely? As a radical, he represented not so much a body of coherent ideas as he did part of a diffuse, eclectic, and adaptive American syndicalist tradition. Here, the end of working-class power was primary; the achievement of this end was more important than principle (understood as arid and futile socialist "doctrine") to begin with. Within such a framework, personal ambition becomes even more difficult to disentangle from a multiplicity of purely pragmatic motives. For Foster, even the end of working-class power was complicated by an ambiguous commitment to the idea of workers' control and democracy in the future society. This suggests that his ambition was ultimately authoritarian in character, that he desired little more than personal power and the achievement of a subjective and ultimately obscure agenda.

This was the interpretation of several of those who worked most closely with him. For James Cannon, for instance, the Communist leader was "a fame fetishist who adapted himself to Stalinist power" in the same way that he had adapted himself to the needs of Fitzpatrick and even those of Gompers, "with the calculation that in doing so he could serve his own ends and his own career." Earl Browder proposed that the entire history of the Communist party from the early 1920s to the 1930s could be written in terms of Foster's desire to seize its leadership. Browder, like others, emphasized Foster's "unprincipledness": Foster, he claimed, could abandon ideas with the greatest facility of any individual he had ever encountered in radical politics. Although these are the recollections of ex-Communists whom Foster had defeated in bitter factional fights, both Cannon's and Browder's assessments contain a large measure of truth.[34]

There are several flaws in this interpretation of Foster's personality and influence, however. First, in his case, personal ambition did not reveal itself publicly, in his everyday style and posture. A quiet, extremely ascetic man, his personality was revealed to observers and acquaintances more through encounters on back staircases, in cluttered offices, and in organizing meetings than on the podium, parade, or election tour. Above all Foster was an organizer, an occupation that offers little to the self-aggrandizing personality. The organizer by temperament is inclined to the preparatory and background work; the aspiring celebrity leaves such details to others. To some extent, this character trait would prevent Foster from exercising decisive leadership: his pursuit of power was always assiduous and patient rather than bold and decisive. One writer had noted this quality about him during the steel organizing drive of 1919: "I have watched him. He moves slower than his twenty-four unions. He moves actually behind his twenty-four unions, not in front of them. He waits for authority. He follows it inch by inch, day by day." This description could well apply to Foster's career in the Communist party.[35]

Throughout his career, Foster rarely hesitated to defend a political stance when he was in the minority. He was entirely comfortable in the role of oppositionist, perhaps because this role left him the most room for maneuver. There were definite limits to his willingness to dissent, however; no one ever questioned his skill at adapting, that he was a political survivor. In every political controversy in the American Party, Foster proved able and ultimately willing to subordinate his own ambitions to "party discipline"; this was revealed in 1925, and would be evident again in the last years of the decade. Instead of departing when confronted with a rebuke to his personal leadership, he remained in the Party. This was not true of other central figures who ended up outside the Communist movement, including Jay Lovestone, James P. Cannon, and finally Earl Browder himself. Like Foster, none of these figures had a particular reputation for "principledness" while they were Communists. Lovestone and Cannon, after leaving the Party, achieved personal leadership of splinter movements. Foster always seemed willing to defer the question of personal leadership.

The wellsprings of Foster's radicalism were indeed deeply subjective, but they cannot be traced, ultimately, to personal ambition. When all other aspects of his complex personality and convictions are stripped away, what remained was a tenacious fighter, driven by very deeply held grievances against a social system he dedicated his life to destroying. When he exclaimed to a gathering of comrades at his seventy-fifth birthday party that "I have hated capitalism all my life with every breath in my body!" it is difficult to imagine that anyone present doubted him. Related to these intense feelings was his instinct always to distill rather than elaborate the Marxian idea of history as class struggle in his writings and speeches. What was important was the commitment and the struggle; the revolution would be brought about by dedicated combatants and a general staff of organizers, not intellectuals or theorists. Only much later in his career would he come to believe that the class war could be fought effectively on the grounds of theory, yet even then theory served rather more as an adjunct to his rage than as a realm for creative speculation.[36]

Foster's eponymous syndicalist formula of the 1910s was a profoundly optimistic one. Influenced by a diffuse reform ethos that had permeated much of American society during the Progressive era, he invested an almost positivist faith in unionism as an organizational form, a set of structures that would inevitably evolve into higher forms. However, postwar American reformers and radicals were in general far less sanguine about the possibilities of this kind of change, and, on a more concrete level, Foster's experiences in the meatpacking and steel organizing campaigns seemed to leave him at least momentarily less certain of his earlier conceptions. As a Communist, Foster continued to believe that trade unions were the vital enabling institutions of the class struggle. However, what if the unions themselves failed to "evolve" into more radical and class-conscious forms, but instead changed in an entirely unanticipated way? What about company unions, which as Foster himself recognized, often assumed many of the functions of the independent unions in the 1920s? Radicals should either join them and attempt to transform them into fighting organizations or "aim at their complete destruction," he wrote.[37] Foster's conception of the role of trade unions in American society originally came into focus when he imagined them as autonomous agents in an otherwise brutal environment where the "whole social fabric" was organized by capitalism. He had clung to this vision tenaciously, even when, in the 1910s, he witnessed first hand the difficulties of trade union "evolution" at Butte and with the Timberworkers' Union. However, in the 1920s, unionism in America declined so rapidly and so decisively that Foster found himself on uncertain ground, groping for balance and stance in a world where earlier categories had become blurred.

In the 1920s a profound paradox caught radicals like Foster in a grinding contradiction. The optimism of the time seemed far more conservative in its implications: Americans lived in a time of supposed general prosperity, while businessmen and capitalists seemed quite confident that any problems and contradictions that arose could be readily absorbed within the structures of their firms. Yet, significant levels of poverty and unemployment persisted throughout the decade. These social facts remained a kind of ominous shadow to the general prosperity and optimism. Radicals like Foster were left to fight in this "shadow" world, to contend with the disjunction between the widespread conviction of general prosperity and persisting reminders of the fragility of the new order. In 1927, J. B. McNamara wrote to Foster from prison that "your letter was full of gloom which is a very good sign. Conditions will have to get worse before they get better."[38]

Foster surely knew that for many workers, times were not very good. The kind of workers whom the Communists led during the Passaic strike would be most receptive to Communist leadership in the future, he proposed, without specifying exactly how those workers could be effectively mobilized. As long as there is a body of workers with as "intense" a spirit as those in Passaic showed, "there is no room for pessimism" in the Party, he thought. Foster, by 1927, was predicting a severe economic downturn which would deflate the pretensions of the efficiency engineers and render company unions and union-management cooperation plans meaningless; the Party had to prepare itself for mass discontent. Moreover, the agenda of "Fosterism" remained. Despite the fact that the Party had become more "trade unionized," "our party is still very much of an ultra-leftist party; very much of a propaganda party," he complained in the party press. The Party could become "Americanized," he suggested, primarily by focusing its activities on the concrete economic demands of the workers. Furthermore, "the Communists must shed delusions of grandeur if they would be successful in unionizing and organizing the unorganized." They must "learn their industries, know the workers and create an effective apparatus which will mean something in a given situation." As it was, the Party "is so weak numerically as to be most seriously embarrassed in its work," he wrote in a confidential assessment. Yet, if unionism was in decline and Communist organizers continued to face expulsion, how could the Party mobilize workers around wage and workplace issues?[39]

Predictably enough, although Foster reacted strongly to all forms of unionism that practiced any kind of collaboration in the production process with capitalist management in the United States, he did not apply the same standards to the Soviet Union. Despite the fact that hundreds of American and European workers who emigrated to the Soviet Union in the 1920s had returned by the end of the decade with tales of exploita-

Foster with editors of *Gudok*, the railroad workers' union newspaper, in the Soviet Union.

William and Esther in the Soviet Union, 1926.

tion, shop-floor authoritarianism, and difficult living conditions, Foster continued to offer celebratory accounts of life and work in the Communist state. Following one visit there in 1924, he remarked that while production was "under control of the Supreme Economic Council, an organ of the Soviet government," trade unions take part in management of industry by having "representatives in all the regulating and planning bodies.... They organize productive conferences between the workers and management, at which proposals for improving production practices and methods are made." He wrote pridefully of Soviet labor unions that "of the industrial disputes that have developed," "nearly all" were settled without strikes.[40]

At a time when ever larger numbers of workers were experiencing the deadening effects of mass production, assembly-line manufacturing, and the pernicious complexities and competition of "managed" piecework, Foster failed to offer a critique of "scientific" supervision and technical control in the workplace. He had never worked on an assembly line, and had never been exposed to a situation where his job was threatened by technological change. Foster had no objection to the widespread use of piecework systems in the Soviet Union, holding that such systems "accelerate the tempo of socialist construction" and increase productivity. Differential wage scales and "socialist competition" were justified as "part of the elaborate system of incentives in effect for Soviet workers." In the Soviet Union, he proposed, every kind of education and promotion was available to workers; "the advance to the better paid, more skilled and more responsible positions rests freely with every worker himself." Thus, Foster's portrayal of the Soviet work environment was never significantly different from the way capitalists in the 1920s were portraying their own ideal workplaces. While his critique of capitalist production included a critique of how an individual worker experiences his job, this critique always focused on problems like physical danger, overwork, and low wages, and only rarely on issues of authority and alienation.[41]

Foster's position in the Party became somewhat more secure in the period following the sudden death of Charles Ruthenberg in March 1926. However, Ruthenberg's death did not end the factional infighting. Jay Lovestone, a close associate of Ruthenberg's, fought successfully for control of the Party in the period following his mentor's death. He privately vowed to Ruthenberg shortly before his death that he was "determined to uproot Fosterism no matter how long it takes and no matter what price we pay." However, Lovestone had not achieved the eminence in the party that Ruthenberg had and was thus somewhat less of a threat to Foster. After achieving the mantle of leadership, he downgraded the labor party idea, reached a superficial detente with Foster over the importance of trade union work in the Party, and accepted Foster's abhorrence of dual union-ism. Even so, he was an agile factionalist whom one former associate described as "a fascinating and devious person for whom maneuvering was the chief joy of life." His favorite tactic was to send Foster cronies like Jack Johnstone off to "have a good time" in Moscow on Party assign-ments.[42]

Lovestone's family were Lithuanian immigrants; he attended the Col-lege of the City of New York and worked as a statistician, social worker, and drugstore manager before his immersion in socialist politics. Unlike Foster, Lovestone had "grown up" in the Communist movement, joining the Party at age twenty-one. In 1927, he was seventeen years younger than Foster, who referred to him as a "City College boy." Lovestone and his allies hammered at the theme of Foster's "limited" trade unionist per-spective, and even went so far as to raise, in one Moscow plenum, the question of whether or not Foster's syndicalist proclivities qualified him as a Marxist. In this particular instance, Alexander Bittelman, the chief ideologist of the Foster faction, rose to defend his mentor with a long-winded and apparently successful rebuttal, replete with arcane references from all corners of the Marxist canon. Foster, still the Party's most prom-inent public personality, simply did not possess the extensive knowledge of Marxist theory necessary to successfully execute such a defense.[43]

Instead, Foster flailed at Lovestone with the crude logic of proletarian-ism. In one memo circulated in Comintern councils, it was pointed out that of the eight highest figures in Lovestone's faction, only one belonged to a union. None of the nine district organizers were union members. One individual, Robert Minor, was tersely dismissed as an "ex-capitalist jour-nalist; cartoonist"; another, Louis Engdahl, simply as a "university grad-uate." The leadership of the Party, in other words, was promoting "com-rades with no mass contact or experience." In one bitter attack in Moscow, Foster alleged that the Lovestone leadership was composed of former "students, teachers, artists, philanthropic society and commercial investigators, insurance agents, etc." He complained that the *Daily Worker* had been taken over by "Greenwich Villagers." In Foster's eyes, the upper stratum of the Lovestone regime "is composed mainly of a spe-cial type of intellectual developed by the New York City College." On the other hand, one participant in the controversies of the 1920s described the style of the Foster group as "the blue flannel workshirt, the leather jacket, the tilted cap, the slouch of the tough guy and the glorification of slang."[44]

The factional wrangling between Lovestone and Foster after 1926 took place during a period of treacherous political infighting in the Rus-sian party. By early 1927 Stalin had engineered Trotsky's downfall over the issue of "socialism in one country." Bukharin, then an ally of Stalin's, emerged as head of the Comintern, and Lovestone managed to position himself favorably in all Comintern political matters. He accepted, at least superficially, Bukharin's perspective that Communists could establish a mass following among the working class in the West primarily by gaining leadership of the trade unions. He was able to gain the first interview with Stalin ever granted to American party members, and his personal friendship with Bukharin seemed to ensure favorable reviews for his policies in the Comintern apparatus. Lovestone and his closest associate, Bertram Wolfe, associated themselves with an essentially conservative perspective on the potential of the Left in the United States, holding that capitalism in America was still on an upward swing. As a result of his adroit political positioning, by 1927 Lovestone had engineered what one Communist observer termed a "palace revolution" in which he and the group formerly associated with Ruthenberg gained control of the Central Executive Committee of the Party.[45]

Despite the fact that he was set against Lovestone's control of the Party, Foster's primary concern continued to be in the trade union field during this period, above all with the Party's most important labor initiative of the last years of the 1920s, the Save the Union movement in the mining industry. The origins of this movement can be traced to the drastic weakening of the United Mine Workers in the middle years of the decade. After 1924, John L. Lewis had cited his ability to contain the "ultraradical" opposition to his leadership as a bargaining lever in his negotiations with employers, but increasingly the operators simply ignored UMW agreements. This led to the formation of the Save the Union movement in early 1926 as a bloc of progressives dedicated to overthrowing Lewis's regime, to which the Communists, forced underground in the union by expulsions, furtively attached themselves. The movement's form and activities were consistent with the broad principles of the TUEL, yet its dynamics would, in turn, establish the context for a shift in trade union policy by early 1928.[46]

In its earliest stages, the Save the Union movement closely resembled earlier TUEL efforts to remove the entrenched leadership in the Miners' and Machinists' unions; its efforts focused on developing an electoral coalition that could attract enough votes at union conventions to unseat the established bureaucracy. However, in its later stages, the Save the Union movement ended up behaving almost like a dual union. By early 1928 it was sponsoring organizing drives, strikes, and relief efforts in the western Pennsylvania bituminous fields where the UMW had largely ceased to function effectively. From the very beginning, Foster played a dominant role in the machinations of the Save the Union movement, even though his activities were largely confined to behind-the-scenes organizing. One

Communist organizer who was active in the coalfields remembered that "he was directing, he was in charge of it." Working in the background with Communist activists and affiliated progressives, Foster would end up taking on his largest role in an organizing campaign and strike since 1919.[47]

The central public figures in the Save the Union movement were dissident Mine Workers officials who had already established credible voices for themselves as critics of the Lewis regime. John Brophy was the Socialist president of District 2 of the UMW in western Pennsylvania who had been an outspoken opponent of Lewis's since the early 1920s. A soft-spoken, bespectacled man who nonetheless had a reputation as a "fighting" union man, he had worked with Foster during the steel strike but had pointedly refused to associate with the Communists' Farmer-Labor party adventures of 1923–24. Another individual who would play an important role was Powers Hapgood, Brophy's assistant in District 2. Hapgood was a Harvard graduate who had made a reputation for himself as a gifted organizer. He secretly joined the Party in 1926, explaining privately that the Communists "are certainly the most sincere, hard-working and intelligent group in the labor movement."[48]

Foster's strategy in mining as it developed in 1926 was two-phased, and was consistent with his philosophy of building a left-wing union movement from the bottom up. His program was calculated either to destroy the Lewis regime and replace it with progressives, or "to stimulate it into sufficient activity to save the union from actual destruction," he wrote. Although the Communists supported Brophy in a bid for the union presidency in 1926 Foster had little faith in the outcome, predicting that Lewis would easily steal the election. In certain respects, Foster resembled Lewis. Both men's formative experiences had been in the hard school of the labor movement of the 1910s, and each had led major strikes in vital industries during the wartime upheaval. Both Lewis and Foster were opportunists who thoroughly understood the mechanics of union power. Lewis, like Foster, was fond of using military metaphors to describe the nature of authority in a union, and each man understood himself as a labor "executive" as well as a fighter for the rank and file.[49]

Despite an agreement with the progressives to stay in the background, the Communists publicly supported Brophy's platform, which called for a six-hour day and five-day week, nationalization of the coal mines, establishment of a labor party, and union democratization. No political demands were made, even for "recognition of Russia." As Foster predicted, the Lewis machine proved invulnerable to the first efforts of the new coalition of radicals and reformers; once again the infinitely resourceful Mine Workers' president was able to bring enough influence to bear to defeat the opposition slate. Brophy himself was convinced that the election had been stolen from him, but he remained powerless to do anything but issue fruitless appeals for an investigation. At the subsequent UMW national convention, Lewis defiantly raised his own salary by 50 percent and eliminated a phrase in the union constitution to the effect that miners were entitled to the "full social value of their product." Lewis and his minions relentlessly red-baited his opponents, and Hapgood was brutally beaten in his hotel room by Lewis sympathizers. Lewis's control over a severely vitiated union seemed as strong as ever.[50]

Foster saw the purpose of the election fight as primarily to "mobilize" the left wing in the union. The key opportunity for the Communists and insurgents would come in April, with the formal expiration of the so-called Jacksonville Agreement, a wage pact negotiated by Lewis in 1924 with the employers. Many northern coal operators, faced with the rapid expansion of nonunion competition in southern fields and a worldwide crisis of overproduction of coal, were determined to repudiate the agreement and the union. Understanding that miners were angered by unilateral wage cuts imposed by the employers and that the union hardly existed in many districts in Pennsylvania, Foster perceived an opportunity to transcend the convention-based fights of the past by organizing from the ground up and perhaps creating enough momentum to eventually supplant the existing bureaucracy. In preparation for a strike, his program was to develop district and subdistrict organization committees, united front Save the Union committees, and mine delegate conferences in the unorganized districts. "The basis of the fight against Lewis is an energetic struggle against the employers," based purely on immediate demands, he wrote to Lozovsky. He was operating on familiar ground. Brophy later reflected that Foster had retained many contacts in the towns of western Pennsylvania because of the 1919 strike "and the prestige he established then."[51]

As Foster was in the middle of preparations for the April strike, Lozovsky suddenly offered his own interpretation of events. He was worried about the Americans' trade union strategy, especially in light of the difficulties at Passaic. He had some suggestions of his own. He pointed out the seeming futility of running candidates against Lewis, whom everyone expected to steal thousands of votes in the first place. If the progressives and the Communists did indeed command a majority in the union, why remain within the UMW? He pointedly asked why Foster remained dedicated to reforming the UMW from the inside, and proposed that "THE QUESTION OF SETTING UP AN INDEPENDENT ORGANIZATION MUST BE RAISED." Otherwise, the league would never escape the "vicious circle" of UMW corruption, he contended. "You will have to remain in the power of Lewis to the end of time." Given the difficulties that had attended the "boring from within" tactic throughout the 1920s,

Lozovsky's criticisms were obvious. Yet, Foster remained of the opinion that unions in which Communists had an open leadership role could not function in the United States.[52]

The mine strike and lockout that erupted in April 1927 as a result of Lewis's failure to gain a renewal of the Jacksonville Agreement were a disaster for the UMW. However, the Communists and allied progressives of the Save the Union movement played an important role in keeping the strike alive; Foster pushed for the development of a separate relief program for support of the striking miners from the very beginning. By October 1927 the Pennsylvania-Ohio Relief Committee was in place; the historian of the strike in Pennsylvania estimated that by early 1928 the organization had taken over the distribution of relief from the UMW in more than thirty mining towns in the western part of the state. The Communists especially emphasized the organization of African American miners, and the bringing of unorganized miners into the strike.[53]

As the strike ground on through late December 1927, Foster, Hapgood, and Brophy met together to discuss long-term strategy. Of Foster, Hapgood wrote that "I don't know anyone who can analyze tendencies more graphically and impersonally than he." The central problem was that of taking the giant step toward forming a new union. In the field, organizers reported growing rank-and-file sentiment for a new union. Foster preferred a more gradual approach, proposing instead an "open conference" of progressives and Communists in the union. Although this would expose them to expulsion and "terrorism of all sorts," there "is nothing else open to us," he wrote privately. However, Foster was skeptical that the progressives would attend; this would mean that the Communists might have to organize such a conference themselves.[54]

In the meantime, Foster was hearing again that Lozovsky thought he was "too afraid of dual unionism." In Moscow, it was the beginning of a period of incessant leftward pressure, coinciding with Stalin's analysis that Western capitalism was about to enter an era of accelerating crisis. Soon, what would be called for was a "Third Period" in Communist tactics, in which Western parties were to disdain alliances with reformists and seize aggressive leadership of working-class movements. To Lozovsky's warning about the need for a new miners' union, however, Foster wrote an acrid reply: "You have quite a wrong slant on our policy here," he told him. "I found this to be quite the case generally in the Profintern when I was there last." Despite Foster's stubbornness, the Save the Union movement was in a very difficult position, given widespread rank-and-file demands for a new union and relentless pressure from Lewis. Foster proposed to Lozovsky that although the policy was to defeat Lewis from the inside, "have we drawn back at the prospect of eventual establishment of a new union? We have not." He reminded Lozovsky that "nearly three years ago I told you that it might be necessary to grab this union by an open struggle with Lewis." Foster saw the upcoming conference as possibly leading to an open split with the UMW. While the Communists and Progressives have opposed such a split, "we cannot shrink from it." He noted, however, that Brophy, "a wavering type," was "disinclined to take the leadership" of a separate movement, and reminded Lozovsky that "I fear you have only a faint idea how weak we are in the miners union." The Communists could count their English-speaking leaders on both hands, he pointed out. Nonetheless, he concluded that "it is either a militant policy now or else stand aside and watch the union go to pieces without a fight, and, perhaps surrender the leadership of the left-wing to either the IWW or some other secessionist movement."[55]

In January 1928, Foster called together a preliminary conference of the Save the Union Committee. It was held in semisecrecy; 125 delegates attended, 25 of whom were party members. Brophy attended and was elected chair; Howat, who was hoping Lewis would reinstate him, was hesitant to involve himself in an open fight despite a long conference with Foster. Lozovsky, from afar, let it be known once again that he thought the Save the Union slogan was self-defeating. Foster now confessed that while the "question of establishing new unions is going to be enormously stressed in our policy from now on," with regard to discarding the Save the Union line, "I think you are in error." Despite its parlous condition, he was convinced that the destruction of the miners would "enormously stimulate the open shop movement in every industry." As the date for the founding convention of the Save the Union Committee approached, Lozovsky cabled for Foster to attend the Profintern's fourth congress in Moscow. Foster pointedly refused the invitation, but a secret resolution of the congress demanded that the left wing in the UMW "must prepare to become the basis of a new union."[56]

On April 1, eleven hundred delegates met at Pittsburgh's Labor Lyceum to publicly inaugurate the Save the Union Committee. The vast majority were "genuine coal miners, not party members," according to Hapgood. Exhausted but determined, it was a "queerly silent crowd, roared to anger only against Lewis," according to one reporter. Five blacks were elected to the national executive committee; one black miner from Indiana announced that the convention marked the first time in twenty-eight years he had been allowed to express himself at a union function. The delegates set a strike for the middle of the month, aiming at the strategic Pittsburgh Coal, Bethlehem, and Carnegie Steel pits in western Pennsylvania. If it succeeded, it would shore up the UMW strike, now exactly a year old, in the vital bituminous districts, and establish enormous prestige for the union reformists.[57]

Reporting to Lozovsky on the Save the Union convention Foster showed he was determined to continue on his earlier path. He attempted to appease his patron by declaring that the committee would eventually declare the official positions of the Lewis machine vacant and elect new officers. Yet, more than a month after official Comintern resolutions and Lozovsky's explicit rebukes, he still refused to declare a dual union. Nonetheless, he now recognized that he had no alternative but to eventually organize unorganized miners into a separate union "should they strike." This union, he finessed, would be "under the leadership of the UMW left wing, but not affiliated with the UMW."

Shortly after the convention both Howat and Brophy drew away from the Save the Union Committee. Hapgood had been expelled from the union in 1927 and was having trouble finding employment as a miner; Lewis ordered Brophy's Nanty-Glo Pennsylvania local to expel him as a dual unionist in May. Brophy wrote to Hapgood that Foster had "definitely taken the road of dualism. . . . I am of the opinion that there is no solid group of support for a new union in the mining industry at this time." Brophy believed that while the UMW was "sadly weakened . . . it can still carry on." However, with both himself and Hapgood out of the union, he did not specify how the "boring from within" tactic could continue to be effective. Bitterly, Foster concluded that "the progressive leaders more or less collapse in the real fight."[58]

The Communists set up picket lines in key locations in the Pittsburgh area, still organized under the Save the Union Committee. Despite opposition from the UMW, the operators and the constabulary, hundreds of miners, many of them blacks, walked out in areas the UMW had long since deserted. Foster himself spent five months on the road doing organizing work in late 1927 and early 1928, but was forced to admit privately by the end of May that the strike was weakening rapidly and that "both the strike and the union are gradually disintegrating."[59] In the meantime, Foster faced rebellion from his closest associates in the Communist party over his refusal to change over to the new dual union line quickly enough. Browder wrote an article attacking the Save the Union slogan as "not a left-wing slogan." An internal party document, citing Save the Union Committee propaganda that was being distributed in the coal fields, claimed that Foster was "flaunting the authority of the Comintern and Profintern to their faces." At the same time, the three most important Communist organizers in the Save the Union Committee stated that they agreed with the idea that a new union must be formed eventually, but asserted that both Lozovsky and Foster were moving too quickly. To Lozovsky, Foster complained that "such bitter criticism as you make of our work cannot be explained away except on the basis that you were not informed of what is really taking place in America." Lozovsky's attacks in the Party press had opened Foster to accusations within the party that "our policy has been wrong all these years"; it is "simply impossible to work effectively in the face of such a situation," he fumed.[60]

Nonetheless, by July, the mine strike was over, and Foster was publicly reconciled to a new union. The National Miners' Union, created in September 1928, was the first of a number of new unions formed as a result of the shift in policy. Hundreds of UMW locals across the nation elected nearly seven hundred delegates to attend the union's founding convention in Pittsburgh. When they arrived, the hapless miners faced hostile police as well as a battalion of UMW thugs outside the convention site armed with bricks, bottles, clubs, truncheons, and taped chains. More than one hundred delegates were arrested; Lewis henchmen displaying UMW badges aided the police. Delegates were beaten in their hotel rooms. As a result of street fighting outside the Labor Lyceum, where the first meetings were held, the convention was forced to move to a workers' hall on an isolated hillside in East Pittsburgh. Brophy and Hapgood made brief appearances at the meeting, but the former Save the Union leaders were unpopular both with the UMW thugs and with the NMU delegates, and chose not to remain. It was clearly not a very auspicious start for the new union, but NMU organizers were soon quite busy. As sporadic and spontaneous "overnight" strikes swept the coal fields in the face of worsening unemployment and drastic wage reductions, Communist organizers focused on establishing a reputation for the NMU as a "fighting organization," in the words of one activist. The Communists found a receptive audience among many miners in the Pittsburgh district, many of whom were working for $1.50 per day, compared to the $7.00 they had received when the Jacksonville Agreement was in force. Foster admitted, though, that most NMU locals were only "shadow" or underground affairs.[61]

How did Foster understand the new line, and was he reconciled to it? There is no question that he publicly raised his voice against Lozovsky's policy at first, but by June, as the strike faded and as Lewis's apparatchiks expelled the progressives as dual unionists, his public stance had shifted significantly. Despite his concessions, at the sixth Comintern congress in Moscow at the end of the summer, Foster was confronted with an open rebellion by his factional allies for not moving quickly enough to embrace the new line, and was forced to give up leadership of his faction for nearly a year to Alexander Bittelman. There was little that he could do to erase the fact that he had openly snubbed Lozovsky, heretofore his only dependable ally in Moscow and now a figure of increasing importance in the Comintern apparatus. By 1927, Lozovsky had shrewdly cast his lot with Stalin, who in his drive for mastery of economic policy was about to launch a crushing offensive against stubbornly independent "right" trade unionists in the Soviet party. Foster's only solace in this humiliating turn of affairs was the privilege of an interview with Stalin in which, according to Foster, the Soviet leader seemed to predict the eventual demise of the Lovestone leadership. Foster related to his top factional allies how Stalin told him that "no good could come out of the Lovestone group, they simply liked to play with policies and mass work." While this meeting did not result in an open endorsement of his leadership, it undoubtedly encouraged Foster to bide his time until Lovestone's fate had been decided. Lovestone had an interview as well. He related how Stalin praised the party's work in the miners' union and seemed to endorse both Lozovsky's line and the idea of continued work in the existing trade unions. Stalin told him that the Comintern must soon make a decision that would prevent the further crystallization of separate groupings in the American party. When Lovestone suggested that Foster had "complete control of the TUEL apparatus," Stalin replied that "this is impossible. The CEC must have representatives everywhere." Stalin, according to Lovestone, praised Foster's "good trade union connections" and noted that while "he is connected with the worker, he is detached from general political questions." Then, "Stalin asked me whether Foster ever read any books. I told him yes, some, but that he does not study Marxist-Leninist literature." Stalin asked, "Why does Foster shriek so much?" and cautioned Lovestone not to "press him too hard." According to Stalin, the strength of Lovestone's group was that "we know very well how to put general political questions and react accordingly, but we must avoid being disconnected from the masses." In his account of the meeting, Lovestone betrayed no awareness of the impending split between Stalin and Bukharin.[62]

What is most notable about Foster's actions during the summer of 1928 was his ambivalence. As an astute organizer who was sensitive to different inputs and opinions from the rank and file and his own people in the field, he had difficulty moving beyond the task of developing coalitions into the realm of genuine leadership. Far from being a decisive or bold innovator in the arena of tactics, Foster was a cautious experimenter who usually moved slowly and defensively in pursuit of his aims. One close observer noted that he "was not respected for his . . . foresight. [He] was usually unsure of his own stand until the last minute with the result that he could not be depended on to exercise independent leadership." As Communist policy in mining floundered, Lozovsky's proposals at least provided a coherent set of objectives. Foster did not seem committed enough to any particular line of action to resist Lozovsky's imperatives for very long. His ambiguity and hesitation in adapting to the new line were conspicuous to many in the party. He tried to steer a middle course between those who thought the dual-union idea was doomed, and those, including several of his closest factional allies, who thought he was betraying their interests by not embracing the new line with enough fervor.[63]

Foster was never able to command a particularly cohesive faction in the sense that few of the trade union–oriented cadre in the party who tended to support his general perspective seemed to regard him with much personal loyalty. Earl Browder gradually built up resentment at the persistent portrayals of him within the party as no more than Foster's loyal "office boy." By 1929, having just returned to the United States from a mission to China for the Comintern, he felt the need to declare his independence. With regard to the change in line in Moscow, Browder was particularly obsequious, quickly and easily outmaneuvering Foster in the race to comply with the Third Period perspective on the unions. James Cannon had readily deserted Foster in 1925 when the Comintern reorganized the party leadership. Thereafter, he had gradually drifted back into the Foster faction in the party. In 1928, however, he castigated Foster for his stubbornness with regard to the new line, then departed the party altogether after the Comintern sixth congress. At one meeting of a caucus where he was being upbraided for his lack of enthusiasm about the new trade union perspective, Foster even attempted to physically intimidate his old crony, Jack Johnstone. Alexander Bittelman remembered that Foster was a "very hard taskmaster" who was "not above using threats and methods of intimidation with comrades who worked with him." Foster only rarely socialized with his factional allies, usually preferring to stay aloof.[64]

As early as 1927, Foster had pointed out to Lozovsky that under his direction, the TUEL's policy had been to support "independent" unions in the rubber, auto, boot and shoe, lumber, and marine transport industries, as well as in the needle trades. Would increasingly hard-pressed workers move into new unions or could the old unions revitalize themselves? Citing the "growing industrial depression" in 1928, Foster had preferred a wait-and-see approach.[65] However, in compliance with the new perspective, the Communists forged ahead with new unions in a number of different industries. Foster seemed relatively uninvolved in this process. For instance, Communist organizers were on hand when cotton mill workers in New Bedford, Massachusetts, struck against a wage cut and speedup in April 1928. Immigrant workers who had been ignored by the local AFL Textile Council were organized into a Textile Mills Committee, a tactic reminiscent of the Passaic strike. The strike lasted twenty-three weeks, but was fatally undermined when the AFL council settled on a 5 percent wage cut in July. Foster acknowledged that the New Bedford strike dramatically illustrated the need for new unions, but when the National Textile Workers Union was organized in September, he wrote distantly to Lozovsky that "our people" were making "quite a mistake in forcing the formation" of a new union. The proper steps, he suggested, were the formation of broad left-wing national committees, then left-wing conferences to organize the unorganized, then the setting up of local unions and shop committees, and finally the "eventual" calling of a convention to establish a new union.[66]

Predictably, the new Communist unions and the organizing campaigns they led were often brutally suppressed: the paradigm was in the Piedmont town of Gastonia, North Carolina, where a NTWU strike foundered in part because of vicious opposition and open red-baiting by employers and local officials. The intense resistance to the new unions seemingly confirmed Foster's perspective on the immense difficulties involved in openly Communist-led unions gaining permanent successes in the United States.[67]

How could the Communists organize the unorganized? Finally, Foster acquiesced to a new trade union "center," to be called the Trade Union Unity League, which would be a "coordinating" body for the new unions as well as workers who continued to belong to the AFL. He was still up to his old tricks. "Does the formation of the new unions and their concentration into a national center imply that the TUEL will give up its work in the old unions, that the new center will claim to be the whole labor movement and will ignore the existing mass trade unions? Does it call for an exodus of the left wingers from AFL unions?" he asked in one article in the party's labor press. "By no means. On the contrary, the TUEL . . . will redouble its work in the old unions." This rhetoric was still consistent with Comintern pronouncements, which, taken on the whole, conceded a continued usefulness for Foster's point of view. Lozovsky, for instance, warned in the party press against the "left sectarian" tendency of "not knowing how to work—often not wishing to work—in the reformist unions for the realization of the united front from below."[68] In the wrangling over the parameters of the new trade union center in 1929, Foster criticized the "high political phraseology" of the proposed call and declared that the TUUL would be "only a forerunner" to a new union federation, and was thus only of "a provisional character." Unions should only be established only after "serious headway is made in organizing the masses" around a program of immediate demands, he wrote in an internal party memo.[69]

Ironically, despite his reservations about the new line, Foster was presented with unprecedented political opportunities as a result of the shift to the left in Comintern policies. Lovestone, like Foster earlier, made several missteps in conforming to the new turn. Above all, although Bukharin now represented the "right danger" in the Soviet party, he had nonetheless hewed to Bukharin's line, predicting an upward trend for American capitalism and even resisting Lozovsky's call for new unions long after Foster had deserted the fight. Working with the benefit of Bittelman's ideological guidance, Foster quickly positioned himself on the left, now accusing Lovestone of representing the "right danger" in the American Party. He cynically attacked Lovestone for fomenting opposition to the new unions. His reward seemed imminent. In March 1929, when the American Party met in New York for its sixth convention, the Comintern representatives who were present declared that Lovestone's leadership was unacceptable. They had arrived in New York with a mandate that Foster was to be made new general secretary of the Party. However, Lovestone refused to relinquish his hold, and rushed to Moscow to make his appeal. Foster followed close behind.[70]

When a specially organized "American Commission" met in Moscow in April, Lovestone pressed his case. Arguing for days before the commission over the prospects of American capitalism in the immediate future, the proceedings of which were deemed important enough to include Joseph Stalin and a number of leading figures in the Russian party, Lovestone and his allies accused Foster of unprincipled factionalism and portrayed themselves as the true representatives of the majority of the American Party. The debate revolved around the question of which faction harbored the most dangerous right-wing tendencies. Lovestone's arguments, though dramatic and courageous, proved unsuccessful. Stalin's attitude toward the American Party leader became steadily less favorable as the days wore on; when it was all over, Lovestone and many of his followers had been unceremoniously deposed.

The proceedings proved of momentous consequence for Foster, as well. Stalin excoriated him for having consorted with "hidden Trotskyists" like Cannon in his grouping for so long, and indeed Foster's faction had attracted more than its share of activists who became Trotskyist dissidents. Stalin accused Foster of misrepresenting the confidential interview they had had months before. "What did Foster speak to me about? He complained of the unprincipled character of Comrade Lovestone's group. What was my answer? I admitted that Comrade Lovestone's group is guilty of these [transgressions] but immediately added that Comrade Foster's group is equally guilty of them. From this Comrade Foster comes to the strange conclusion that I sympathize with the minority group."

Stalin, who often addressed Foster directly in these sessions, termed him a speculator in the outcome of the affairs of the Comintern, a maneuverer and opportunist, as if the label could not be applied with equal justice to any other figure in the American leadership. According to the general secretary, appearing before the Commission in his trademark leather boots and tan tunic, Foster as well as Lovestone was guilty of "rotten diplomacy." It was "disgraceful" that Foster and Bittelman had at one point declared themselves "Stalinists" to demonstrate their loyalty to the Comintern. Because of these transgressions, Stalin finally rejected a motion to award leadership of the Party to Foster. Thus, once again William Foster had nearly grasped the leadership of the American Party, and once again it proved elusive.[71]

What were Foster's feelings at this point? It will probably never be possible to know with any certainty. One of the most glaring features of Foster's later career in the Communist party would be his public identification with and encomiums to Stalin's leadership. This was de rigeur for Communist leaders of all kinds, but in Foster's case this identification was particularly ironic. In the first decade of his involvement with the Communist movement, Stalin's regime had consistently thwarted Foster's attempts to establish clearcut leadership. In 1929 the American Communists reproduced Stalin's speeches with their denigrating references to Foster in pamphlet form, and the Soviets themselves went so far as to publish a "first edition" of one hundred thousand copies in Moscow. From afar, Leon Trotsky marveled at the spectacle of Foster's humiliation, speculating that the purpose of the pamphlets was "to show Foster that the boss is not joking."[72] Did Foster accept these ignominious defeats without resentment? It is difficult to imagine that he did, but his belief in the concept of Communist discipline and his assessment that there would be opportunities for the Party in the labor movement in the near future undoubtedly tempered whatever resentments he harbored.

In October 1929, a Comintern agent known as "G. Williams" arrived in the United States to assist with the reorganization of the Party in the wake of Lovestone's expulsion. A new, temporary leadership was installed, consisting of Max Bedacht, Robert Minor, and William Weinstone in addition to Foster, with Bedacht as acting secretary. During this period when the question of party leadership was seemingly up in the air, Foster's political stock was at a low ebb. Having barely survived a rebellion among members of his own faction, he was still not respected among a number of Party leaders because of his lack of Communist "theory or foresight," as Max Bedacht later put it. Increasingly aloof and distant, Foster endured an odd kind of personal and political isolation. He was a suspect figure who had been conspicuously deemed unworthy of leadership by Stalin himself. Yet, it was Foster who put forward the idea of Earl Browder as the new general secretary during this period, perhaps hoping to easily manipulate his former assistant. Browder, who was quickly elevated to more responsible posts after 1929, seemed to come out of nowhere when ascending within the Party. This achievement came at least partly as a result of Foster's sponsorship or at least acquiescence. How-

ever, Browder would quickly develop into a more or less independent
figure within the Party, openly defying Foster's attempts to influence
him.[73]

Whatever the mechanics of the inner-party situation, events in the
United States would once again provide the most critical challenges, and
opportunities, for American Communists. The implications of the stock-
market crash of October 1929 were not immediately clear to many in the
Party's leadership, but the developing economic crisis would soon draw
the Party from the shadows of marginality with which it had been surrounded in the 1920s. As for William Foster, his first eight years in the
Communist movement were undeniably difficult. Yet, despite accusations
that he lacked "Communist foresight," his instincts in a number of vital
areas were unerring. His caution about the strength of the labor party
impulse among American workers, his analysis of the fragility of company union and labor-management cooperation schemes, his belief in the
imminence of economic crisis, and his skeptical approach to Communist
dual unionism were largely vindicated in the coming decade. By 1929, he
had survived three periods of pointed controversy with Comintern authorities, emerging each time with concessions to his point of view. And,
despite the setbacks the TUEL suffered in the 1920s, Foster could still
point to the continuing work of Communist minorities who had "col-
onized" a whole variety of unions and industries: building and metal
trades, rubber, textiles, needle trades, autos, mining, electrical, railways,
and shoes and leather, to name only the most important. While these
unionists were often isolated, without significant influence and working
under the continual threat of expulsion, the Communists had been able to
establish a far wider scope for their activities in the unions than had
existed when Foster joined the party in 1921.

Chapter 9

THE RELUCTANT AGITATOR

[Agitation] is different from organizing work, which is
methodical, slow and quiet. Agitation is done in the
open . . . with the intelligent and full use of individual
mass emotions stirred up by deeds and words, capable of
creating strong passions of hatred,
sympathy, love and anger.
—Carlo Tresca

Like most good generals, Foster could command an
army—even a ragged and hungry army—
but he cannot improvise one.
—George Soule

THE DECADE of the Great Depression was filled with ironies for William
Foster. In certain respects, his was a radicalism of preparation and waiting; finally, "the masses got into action" as he later put it. On the other
hand, for Foster the vengeful fighter, the decade was punctuated by political uncertainty and physical sickness. The period of the "heyday" of
American Communism would belong in large measure to his former aide,
Earl Browder, an efficient organization man who had little experience
leading American workers. During a time of unprecedented national influence and acceptance for the Party, Foster's political and personal iden-
tities drifted in and out of focus. As a public figure he achieved a curious
kind of apotheosis. In 1930, he was general secretary of the TUUL and a
member of a three-person "secretariat" of the Party leadership.[1] He remained the personification of the Party's working-class constituency. He
published autobiographies that were worshipfully reviewed in the Party
press. Especially in the later years of the decade, he turned out a blizzard
of articles for the *Daily Worker* and the Party's theoretical organ, *The
Communist*, none of which were met by the kind of open factional rebuttals that his writings had often occasioned in the 1920s. Curiously
enough for a man whose career as a labor organizer had been informed
by a scorn for "talk," Foster would end his career as by far the Party's
most prolific writer.[2]

Following his debate with Lozovsky over the new trade union orientation, Foster would never again openly challenge an initiative from

Moscow as he had in the 1920s. Stalin's direct and personal repudiation in 1929, of course, underlined the insecurity of his situation in the Party. Moreover, the demise of the TUEL and his difficult relations with former factional allies like Bittelman and Johnstone meant that he could no longer rely on an independent base of support within the movement itself. On the labor front, Foster was still the Party's trade union authority, but his feelings about the TUUL and the new revolutionary unions were ambiguous at best. Thus, with the economy in sharp decline after 1929, Foster's position in the Party was unclear. In 1930, at age forty-nine, he seemed perilously close to becoming a figurehead.

The government of the United States clearly did not intend to take significant action to relieve the plight of the millions of Americans who had been thrown out of work after the crash of 1929. By the spring of 1930, Herbert Hoover was still convinced that the best way to solve the economic crisis was to balance the federal budget. The voices of conservative financiers and industrialists had an increasingly hollow ring: Bernard Baruch proclaimed that "no government agency . . . can cure this situation." Henry Ford asserted that the downturn was a "wholesome thing in general. If we could only realize it, these are the best times we ever had."[3] Such invocations only partly concealed the unease felt by the powerful at the scope of the crisis. It would become increasingly obvious that the old verities, always ritually intoned when the economy turned downward, might no longer hold.

For the Communists, the Depression portended a general crisis in world capitalism: Foster wrote delightedly that "the American crisis has deeply shaken and further undermined [the] capitalist world economy . . . laying the basis for still greater class struggles and revolutionary movements"[4]—although, typically, he also called for "careful analysis," and cautioned against what he called "putschist tactics." A Comintern directive implored Communist parties around the world to alter the "methods and pace of their work by concentrating their chief attention on the problems of the preparation and carrying out of mass *revolutionary actions of the proletariat*—strikes, demonstrations, etc." The American Party was clearly on the offensive; the demands of the international movement as well as the plight of the economy seemed to require immediate action. A Comintern resolution set March 6 as the date to hold demonstrations for "International Unemployment Day."[5] Thus the stage was set for the first major protest demonstration of the Depression years, the first eruption of social violence in a decade of unrest. William Foster, still the Communist party's best-known public figure, played a central role in the explosion on March 6 in New York City.

The demonstration was carefully planned. In preparation, "team leaders" were chosen and instructed in self-defense as well as propaganda. Leaflets read: "Work or Wages! . . . Unemployment insurance financed by taxes on profits and inheritances and administered by the workers. . . . Immediate relief for the unemployed by grants from government funds! . . . The seven-hour day; five-day week! No overtime!" The evening before the demonstration, Foster appeared as the principal speaker at a Charles Ruthenberg "memorial" meeting. A witness remembered him as "a tall, slender, handsome Irishman" with "physical vitality and great platform poise." He exuded the confidence borne of a lifetime of such speeches, but his style, as always, was restrained. He didn't work to arouse the emotions of the crowd; he seemed less an agitator than a skilled raconteur, often embellishing his narrative with working-class idiom. Foster's hand gestures were telling. Instead of gesticulating, imploring, or waving, one of his hands characteristically moved in a controlled chopping motion as he spoke, keeping cadence and registering emphasis. He delighted the crowd with a story about European aristocrats, suddenly impoverished, working as busboys and peddlers in Paris. He ridiculed the commissioner of police, Grover Whalen, a former salesman at the John Wanamaker's department store. At the conclusion of the speech, the crowd roared with approval.[6]

Undoubtedly, a number of government agents were in attendance at the meeting on the night of March 5. The next day, the city's security officials were clearly on edge, prepared for a major disturbance. All public buildings and churches, as well as the houses of high city officials and "prominent citizens" were watched by special police guards. Security was bolstered for Governor Franklin D. Roosevelt, who was in the city that day for a conference. The mayor canceled his appointments; a force of 250 policemen had surrounded City Hall and special squadrons of patrolmen on armored motorcycles were assembled, some armed with tear gas and submachine guns. Police manned the rooftops of the buildings surrounding Union Square, where the demonstrators gathered around noon. The Communists planned a rally at Union Square, then a march down Broadway to City Hall. The crowd, estimated by the *New York Times* to be about thirty-five thousand strong, packed the square, overflowing into the adjoining streets.[7]

As speakers agitated the crowd from five separate platforms, Police Commissioner Grover Whalen met with Foster and informed him that the march would not be allowed because no permit had been secured. Whalen was a brusque, egotistical politician who was prepared for a confrontation. A few minutes later, Foster appeared at the central platform, and proclaimed: "Whalen and the city officials have handed Broadway and other streets over to every monarchist and militarist exploiter of Europe and Asia to parade on, but now when the workers and the unemployed workers of New York demand the use of the streets Whalen's answer is that they cannot have them. Will you take that for an answer?" The crowd answered "No!" Foster motioned dramatically toward Broadway and City Hall.[8]

As the crowd began to move, the police rushed the demonstrators. The collision resulted in fifteen minutes of ferocious street fighting; hundreds of police and detectives lashed out with nightsticks, blackjacks, and their bare hands. Mounted policemen rode through the crowd, and firehoses sprayed the demonstrators. The conclusion of the battle left over a hundred civilians and four policemen injured. Foster found himself in a mass of surging demonstrators when he descended from the platform. Having worked his way down a side-street, he met with several other demonstration leaders at a prearranged location and then walked to City Hall to present a list of demands. Upon arriving at City Hall Plaza, Foster and the others were promptly arrested. The charge, initially, was felonious assault. No evidence surfaced that he ever struck anyone, but he was held without bail for seven days because of his arrest record; the judge cited his detention during the free speech fight in Spokane nearly two decades earlier. In the meantime, Whalen announced that his men had infiltrated the New York Communist party, had gained membership lists, and were informing employers of "reds" in their midst. He proclaimed his intention of having "communist children" expelled from city schools.[9]

We have no way of knowing what Foster's feelings were at the time; his description of the demonstration and his role in it in *Pages from a Worker's Life* is quite detached, almost as if he had observed the melée from a distance. Civil confrontations were never his forte as a radical, and at his age it is doubtful that he relished the opportunity for martyrdom that a jail sentence represented. Yet, it was a heady few weeks for the Party. Spectacular unemployment demonstrations had been held in large cities throughout the nation on March 6. The *Daily Worker* proclaimed that "a great movement is underway."[10]

Two days after being released on bail, Foster and a "workers' committee" appeared at a meeting of the Board of Estimate of the City of New York "to present the demands of the unemployed." Following a failed attempt to eject the committee from the hearing room, Foster confronted Mayor Walker not only with a set of meliorist demands, but the proclamation that "only by the abolition of the capitalist system and the building of a Soviet Government can the problem of unemployment be solved." An alderman asked if the Communists advocated the violent overthrow of the government. Foster replied that "as far as the use of violence is concerned, you folks at the head of the government of New

Foster under arrest with Robert Minor, following March 6,
1930, unemployed demonstration in New York City.

York City are very proficient at that." When pressed about whether he
would advise the workers to use violence, he noted ominously that "no
revolution has ever been accomplished without violence," and that he
would not object to the use of violence "on the part of the working class."
The following week, he and the "workers' committee" journeyed to
Washington, hoping to appear before a Senate committee investigating
unemployment. Their petition to testify was refused.[11]

At the end of March, the TUUL called a "national unemployment conference" to plan for a mass demonstration in Chicago in July. In its first
months, the developing unemployed movement, since it was organized
under the auspices of the TUUL, was entirely in Foster's hands. Yet, despite his position as secretary of the TUUL and the drama of his recent
arrest, he did not lend his presence to the conference. He was only mentioned (and his name dutifully applauded) when elected to something
called "the presidium." There is no evidence that such an office existed.
The keynote speech was given by John Schmies, who was formally national assistant secretary of the TUUL. Within a month the unemployed
councils were floundering. One leader lamented the lack of "stable lead-

ership," and noted that "the flesh and blood of the movement before
March 6th" have "gone to some other field of activity." The July 4 convention was a disappointment, and was barely covered in the Party press.
The fledgling unemployed movement had momentarily succeeded in ex-
posing the complex emotions of many ordinary people as they experienced the economic crisis. Yet, William Foster proved unable or unwilling
to contribute to the momentum necessary to sustain the movement.[12]

Foster was finally tried on misdemeanor charges of unlawful assembly
and "creating a disturbance." The charge of felonious assault would be
left pending until August. At his sentencing hearing he made a speech in
which he called for the downfall of the government and reiterated that
unemployment could only be solved by revolution. Found guilty by a
panel of three judges, he was sentenced to an indefinite term (the maximum being three years) and promptly sent to the prison on Hart's Island
in the East River. Breathlessly, the Communist press proclaimed that "already the jobless and militant workers are picking up the challenge
thrown down to them [by the verdict]." Plans were announced for a huge
"political mass strike" on May Day. The demonstrations that material-
ized were disappointing; this in turn provoked a round of self-criticism
within the Party. The emphasis in future, according to subsequent Party
resolutions, would be on thorough preparation and organizational work.
At a time when leadership of the Party was in flux, Foster lent his weight
to a more cautious approach. Soon he was calling for the Party to concentrate more on the "immediate interests" of the workers and "actual struggle" rather than "broad political slogans."[13]

Foster's humiliating job during his first weeks in prison was to work
alone in the basement of the warden's office as a custodian. Since he was
sentenced to an indefinite term of up to three years, it was important that
legal steps be immediately taken to reduce his sentence. Despite the revolutionary rhetoric of the Third Period, the Communists turned to the liberals of the ACLU for aid in arguing before the New York parole board,
which was responsible for determining sentences. In August, Foster's
term was finally set at six months, and earlier charges of felonious assault
were dropped. He was finally released on October 21. Despite his relatively short sentence, his prison term underlined his curious estrangement
from Party affairs. He was evidently permitted to write articles for the
Party press during his confinement, but obviously his connection to the
Party leadership was limited. Previous to his imprisonment, it had become evident that he was unwilling to provide leadership for the unemployment movement that he had helped initiate. During his term, he
missed the important seventh national convention of the Party, where the
leadership was reshuffled. The convention marked the beginning of the
ascendancy of Earl Browder in the Party apparatus. Finally, the TUUL,

Foster's bailiwick, seemed moribund; it did not bother to hold a national convention in 1930. Jack Johnstone observed in an inner-party meeting that "we ourselves have not yet convinced ourselves that the TUUL is a real trade union organization." A former Lovestoneite, Jack Stachel, was appointed to run the TUUL in Foster's absence. Foster had little regard for Stachel, a close ally of Browder's, but he would end up becoming the Party's organizational director.[14]

Despite his hesitance about the unemployed movement, the Third Period and the crisis of the Depression inspired some of Foster's most fervid hyperbole to date. In general, his rhetoric became more laden with Communist verbiage, his statements weighted by quotations from Marx, Engels, Lenin, and Stalin. As his independent organizational base within the Party weakened, his voice became more and more indistinguishable from that of the Party ideologists. Nothing illustrated this more perfectly than his testimony before the House of Representatives in December. In early March, Matthew Woll and the American Federation of Labor had charged that Foster had received funds from the Comintern to sponsor the unemployment demonstrations in the United States. The day after this accusation was made, Woll called for a congressional inquiry into the sources of Communist propaganda in the United States. The day following, Hamilton Fish of New York introduced a call in the House for an investigation along the lines that Woll had proposed.[15] The hearings were the precursors of the un-American Activities hearings of the 1950s.

Foster was the star witness. Edmund Wilson, who was covering the hearings for the *New Republic*, wrote an extended and perceptive commentary on the confrontation between Foster and Fish. He noted the contrast between the Communist leader's mien and his rhetoric, and offered a meditation on Foster's peculiar "speechlessness." The Communist leader looked "worried and harassed, his dropped hands with curled-up fingers make constrained ineffective gestures, his voice sinks to a whisper of pathos as if he were sighing to himself his hopelessness of ever being able to communicate with his opponents." Nonetheless, as the questioning began, it became clear that Foster would not shrink from employing the most ferocious-sounding propaganda before the assembled committee. What are the Party's relations with the Socialist party? "Socialism seeks to maintain capitalism; not to establish socialism. . . . The socialist is a fascist," Foster replied. What is the Communist view of the economic crisis? "The only possible guard for the future security of the working class is the dictatorship of the proletariat and the establishment of a Soviet Government." On religion: "Our party considers religion to be the opium of the people, as Karl Marx has stated, and we carry on propaganda for the liquidation of these prejudices amongst the workers." On the American worker: "The American workers realize that this world capitalism is already dead and giving way to the newer and higher social order, which is socialism." At one point, Fish asked if "the workers in this country look upon the Soviet Union as their country," to which Foster responded: "The more advanced workers do."[16] Clearly, Foster had traveled a long way since 1923, when he was able to portray Communism in a benign, populist light to a jury in Bridgman, Michigan.

Foster's Communist rhetoric struck Wilson as rather perfunctory, yet it seemed to allow him to confront his questioners effectively. Wilson noted that "never once in the course of the three hours' grueling does his courage or his presence of mind fail him. Though he may falter for a moment before answering, he always picks himself up and meets the question; and as soon as he meets the question, he is the dominating figure in the room." As for the propaganda,

> All this is merely the platform of radical oratory to which Foster is obliged to lift himself in order to reach a vantage point from which he can face the policemen, the fat congressmen, the marble Capitol, the eagle and shield of the Republic, the high imposing gilt and white ceiling, the wilderness of documents on the big table. . . . Once safe on the plane of his faith, he can meet his opponents with a logic, an Irish readiness and a New England conviction which contrast in a startling way with the unsureness and incompetence of the committee."[17]

The period following the Fish Committee hearings found Foster finally turning his attention to labor organizing and the TUUL. From the beginning, Foster had his own ideas about how the new trade union "center" should function, seizing especially on Third Period calls for "united fronts from below" to establish his own synthesis. In 1929, with Lovestone out of the picture, he had created the program for the first TUUL convention without first submitting it to Lozovsky for approval. All were welcome in the new league: new unions in textile, needle trades, and mining; "industrial leagues" that were to be "transitional" structures; fraternal groups; "left-wing" and shop groups; and TUEL remnants. However, at the convention there was a palpable undercurrent of pessimism, what Foster called in the weeks before the stock market crash an "underestimation of the radicalization of the workers." And, he reported to Lozovsky, the convention was still "too much of a party gathering of forces." By early 1930, acknowledging that the TUUL was "not growing but rather tending to vedge," he was proposing to Lozovsky a new TUUL constitution that would lay more emphasis on the organization of shop committees, "trade councils," and "local general groups," a euphemism for the old TUEL concept. By October, the Comintern was calling for increased concentration on immediate demands and the avoidance of "abstract politicizing" in the TUUL. Foster was intermittently optimistic about new TUUL unions in the auto, marine, packinghouse, and metal industries, but in early 1931 the TUUL national board decided to begin reestablishing its minorities in the old unions, building its agenda not around affiliation with the revolutionary unions, but around a program of simple economic demands. By December Foster had created a department within the TUUL to coordinate work in the AFL.[18]

The first years of the decade should have been extremely promising time for the TUUL, as factory orders continued to fall off and manufacturers imposed deep wage cuts. The AFL seemed helpless. Despite the weakness of the unions, noteworthy strikes broke out in a variety of industries across the nation. Jack Stachel admitted that most striking workers were unorganized and that neither the AFL nor the overextended TUUL was offering substantial leadership. In January 1931, the TUUL was able to step into a leadership role as ten thousand textile workers at the American Woolen Company in Lawrence, Massachusetts, went on strike to protest a wage cut. However, official repression was so efficient that within a week, the entire strike committee was arrested and placed under a deportation threat. The strike dissipated without the accomplishment of any concrete gains.[19]

The Party continued to bemoan the failures of the TUUL. Stachel admitted that there were not enough organizers to go around, that for the league, "organizing" often consisted of TUUL organizers arriving after the fact on the scene of a spontaneous strike. Usually they were met with the query: "Where were you before the strike?" Stachel, however, could come up with no alternative program or general method. The problem of preparatory organization in the textile industry had been especially compounded by the fact that, standing aloof from the AFL and the unions, league organizers had not previously established themselves in the struggle for "concrete demands," wages and hours. Partly as a result, the work of the organizers tended toward the "educational." As for the necessity of organizing revolutionary unions, Stachel observed that since early 1929, nearly two years previous, the TUUL had "fully accepted" the necessity of the decisions of the Red International, "but did not master them, did not study and apply them." He admitted that the international line had been pretty much ignored: "In Party resolutions we always endorsed the line of the Comintern and the RILU but in the practical every-day work we continued along the same old lines that had become outworn and obsolete."[20]

Foster weighed in with an opinion that managed to connect the issue of trade union democracy with the failures of the TUUL and by implication the entire Third Period line. He observed, typically, that "we cannot maintain our mass contacts with mere talk, however eloquent or revolutionary it may be." In the revolutionary unions, he asserted, it was too often the Party, and not the rank and file, that actually decided the program around which workers were to be organized. Such an attitude was a "serious error" which "assumes incorrectly that Communists have a sort of airtight monopoly on working class knowledge and wisdom." Then, in a striking critique of the general outlook of the Third Period, Foster proposed a modification in the way that demands were formulated by Party organizers. He used as an example of an ideal method the working out of a set of demands for steel workers in Youngstown. The first set of demands was established "by our top functionaries in their offices with little or no consultation with the workers." They included:

1. Seven-hour day, five-day week.
2. Abolition of the speed-up system.
3. Full social, racial, and political equality for Negroes.
4. Social insurance.
5. 25 percent wage increase.
6. Equal pay for equal work for young workers.
7. Recognition of the Metal Workers Industrial League.

An amended set of demands was finally adopted after consultation with a group of workers in the hot mill department:

1. Four six-hour turns, five-day week.
2. Against the tonnage and bonus system.
3. Half day's wages when called to work and sent home due to no work.
4. No less than $35 a week for the following jobs: meshers, cranemen, openers, doublers.
5. Equal pay for equal work for Negroes.
6. No doubling up.
7. No "voluntary contributions" weekly by the workers for the "unemployed and sick" who have been discarded by the company.
8. 10 percent of profits to go to fund for unemployed and sick relief.

The latter set of demands, according to Foster, was "a more realistic line" that the workers could fight for. It was notably less aggressive on the issue of the rights of African Americans, and contained no mention of the need for the recognition of the Communists' revolutionary union, the Metal Workers' Industrial League. It is surprising that his article did not provoke a rebuttal or "discussion." Only a few years earlier, the kind of departure that he was recommending would have precipitated a flurry of factional letters or articles.[21]

Foster was presented with an opportunity to test his interpretation of the Third Period line in the mines of western Pennsylvania in the spring and summer of 1931. Here, the National Miners Union had been in the field for months agitating against unilateral wage cuts by the operators. In May, one thousand workers struck the Carnegie mines in western Pennsylvania and by the end of June forty thousand workers were out in Pennsylvania, eastern Ohio, and West Virginia, a territory where the Communists and their organizers had much experience and many contacts as a result of their activities in the 1920s. Foster himself went into the mine districts to exhort, organize, and provide guidance. One organizer remembered that Foster, "more than any other, made this very difficult situation look very promising. He woke up at 5 a.m. every morning, spoke to the workers, cheered the picket lines, etc., etc." Another remembered Foster's abrasive organizing style in Party meetings during the strike: "he would tear down everybody. He was very much on the attack." Foster would go around a room and ask individual organizers what they had done. "He questioned each one so closely that [some] were destroyed. . . . They were so shaken by his questioning. But he did maintain discipline, and that's how he got all his mines out on strike." In dealing with organizers, Foster's personality was not easygoing. His assessments of a particular strike situation or of an organizer's accomplishments were often brutally frank and unsentimental; in meetings he could slip into an overwrought, easily provoked and contentious mode that some found intimidating. Later, he admitted privately that he was a "hard taskmaster," and not "the easiest guy to work around." He reflected that "I was always something of a driver in my work, inclined to explode once in a while."[22]

According to Third Period ideology the Party was to take open leadership of strikes, but in the strike districts in the Pittsburgh area the National Miners Union was only a background presence at first; instead, Communist organizers worked through a kind of ad hoc united front of grievance and strike committees. It was the first strike, Foster declared in a speech in Pittsburgh, "where a rank and file committee of miners has ever conducted their own strike." Foster was sensitive to charges that the Communists were slow in establishing their political presence, but admonished in one meeting of organizers that the Party should not take hold of such movements so closely "as to stifle them." The unions, he pointed out in inner-party councils, "have to be given a certain latitude." For Foster, the key to this strike was the establishment of a united front strike committee, a "thoroughly practical form of organization" in the absence of any tangible preexisting Party apparatus in the coal fields. At a conference in Pittsburgh in July a set of practical demands was drawn up, and a Unity Committee of Action established consisting of NMU members, sympathizing UMW locals and minorities, councils of unemployed and unorganized workers. Strike committees were elected by miners "regardless of union affiliation." Perhaps most important in keeping the strike alive was the aggressive and largely successful organization of African Americans into the NMU. In the realm of ideology, Stachel admitted in one meeting that the Communists "stopped talking about the 6-hour day and a workers' government and came down to brass tacks." Party organizers, involved in their first mine strikes in two-and-a-half years, often neglected to provide striking miners with NMU application cards.[23]

For Foster, the repression accompanying the strike was undoubtedly familiar, but demoralizing nonetheless. Miners' families were evicted from company-owned houses; credit at company stores was cut off; strikebreakers saturated the district; company thugs terrorized picketers; Department of Labor agents deported foreign-born activists. In June, Foster addressed a crowd of five thousand miners in the tiny town of Wildwood; the next day a demonstration and march resulted in the shooting of nine strikers, one fatally, by constabularies. The United Mine Workers recruited strikebreakers, and in August negotiated separate wage cuts with operators. Finally, a Comintern representative in the United States recommended that the strike be abandoned. By then the whole enterprise was faltering; nonetheless, Foster stubbornly resisted. An intense argument at Party headquarters in New York occurred when Browder subsequently summoned Foster to harangue him for "mistakes" made in the coal fields. What was the character of these mistakes? Browder had urged a more leading role for the NMU in the strike district; at one meeting in June, for instance, he had found himself under sharp attack from William Dunne, still an important field organizer and a Foster ally on procedural questions, for wanting to abandon the united front strike committee. A Comintern postmortem defined the issue: it concluded that while Communists must demonstrate that they can be successful strike leaders, the main object of the strike should be "the *revolutionization of the striking workers* [sic]," not the simple winning of "material results" (emphasis in original). Foster was finally forced to admit defeat, but the experience, according to a friend, left him "badly shaken." This was the last strike in which he would take a direct personal role as an organizer.[24]

During the strike itself, Foster complained bitterly to the national office that not enough organizers were being delegated to the coal fields. He later echoed this accusation in *From Bryan to Stalin*, implying that the strike was betrayed by the national office of the Party. Considering that this account was written in 1937, at the height of Browder's influence in the Party, this is a remarkable accusation, even in its carefully hedged terms.[25] During the strike, he wrote obediently that the strike was a "complete justification of the Comintern and the RILU line, and, of course, of the general line of our Party and the TUUL, for the building of revolutionary unions in the United States." However, Sam Darcy later remembered that the strike finally convinced Foster of the futility of the dual unions.[26]

Ironically, the 1931 strike marked the beginnings of a successful campaign by Lewis to reestablish the authority of the UMW, which was barely functioning the year before. The giant mining companies of western Pennsylvania were much more inclined to sign contracts with Lewis and the UMW than with the Communists, who had established a larger following by the summer of 1931. Lewis used the threat of radical influence in the coalfields to press his interests at the highest levels of government. He was unsuccessfully lobbying the Hoover administration and Congress for collective bargaining recognition and government-supervised price and production controls in the coal industry in 1931, but his ideas would find a much more favorable reception in the Roosevelt administration. John Brophy, who became the organizational director for Lewis's Congress of Industrial Organizations in 1936, remembered that following the passage of the National Recovery Act in 1933, it was not even necessary to organize the miners in Pennsylvania, "just have a good supply of application blanks." In 1931 the NMU strike helped keep the tradition of union militancy alive in the coalfields, and demonstrated anew the potential and vitality of biracial unionism.[27]

Foster continued to analyze the failures of the TUUL in terms of its lack of work in the AFL unions and the seeming inability of Communist organizers to create united front movements on the shop floor around programs of immediate demands. As for the new unions, Foster gradually stepped up his criticisms. In one meeting of top organizers, he gave a stern lecture:

> Comrade Schmies called attention to a certain tendency in the unions to lay down certain conditions—a worker must agree to carry out the full program of the TUUL and various other demands. This is all wrong, comrades. This is a sectarian tendency which we must not permit to develop in our unions. Who shall belong to our unions? Who shall belong to our minority organizations? Workers who agree to fight for even the smallest of our partial demands, these are the workers. We aim in our unions, particularly our unions, to have 100% organization in a given shop, that is where we are driving at—not to have the organization for some little elite of revolutionary workers. . . . no setting up of a revolutionary catechism as a basis for membership in the revolutionary unions.[28]

Despite his problematic position in the Communist party, the early 1930s found Foster reemerging as a public figure of national importance. As had been true during and immediately after the steel strike, he was the focus

of attention by newspapermen, business leaders, and domestic law-enforcement agencies. Earl Browder was not yet the central public person-
age of the Party; it was Foster who represented the face of the Communist
leadership most prominently. Typical of the attention he received in this
regard was his alleged role in inciting the March 7 riot and "massacre" at
Henry Ford's River Rouge plant in Dearborn, in which police and Ford
security agents opened fire on protesters with machine guns, killing four
marchers and wounding dozens more. Foster was blamed by the Detroit
press for the bloodshed because he had given an inflammatory speech to
the march organizers the day before the confrontation. Local police believed that he had played a principal role in inciting the riot. Headlines in
Detroit read "Foster's Smile Masks Heart of Dynamite," and "Communist Riot Provoker Sways Army of 250,000 with Gall-Laden Talks." A
warrant was put out for the arrest of Foster and four others on charges of
criminal syndicalism. Although the charges were eventually dropped,
Foster's parole board in New York revised his sentence, requiring him to
spend the rest of his parole in New York City.[29]

Foster was finally freed from his confinement in New York in May
when he was nominated by the Communist party to run for president.
Apparently, the parole board was concerned not to provide an issue for
the Party in the campaign. We cannot be sure that Foster was particularly
pleased—he did not relish his presidential campaigning. He complained
about "incessant traveling, perpetual speech-making, bad food, miserable hotels, boresome newspaper interviews, being talked half to death or
kept from badly needed sleep by comrades who felt it to be the function
of a Presidential candidate to adjust every local grievance, by after-meet-
ing home gatherings, 'banquets' and untimely talk fests." Despite the unprecedented opportunities offered by his platform and the unrest simmer-
ing in many communities, it was clear that Foster found his role as public
figure and political campaigner a stressful one.[30]

At the inception of the campaign, Foster produced a remarkable book,
entitled *Toward Soviet America*. Intended as a political platform, it is a
comprehensive statement of the aims of the American Communist party.
Foster mentioned to Lozovsky that he resented having to take time out of
his other activities to write it, "but I was commissioned to write it and
have managed to squeeze it in." Later, when the revolutionary exigencies
of the Third Period had been dispensed with, much of its contents would
be repudiated by the Party as irrelevant; contributing to the book's
ephemeral nature is the possibility that it was co-written by a Party publi-
cist. However, there is no question that Foster signed his name to it, and,
as usual, dedicated it to Esther. In the course of his travels in the first years
of the Depression he had encountered insistent questioning from American workers about life in the Soviet Union. The previous year, the Soviet

Union had advertised in New York for six thousand skilled workers and more than one hundred thousand Americans applied. Now Foster had a chance to explain how a Soviet America would function. The rhetoric of the book is consistent with that of Foster's 1920s factional documents, of his Fish Committee testimony, and in general, of his occasional departures into the realm of theorizing. It is heavy with line and jargon, statistics and apocalyptic predictions. The book's overall tone seems inconsistent with the essential pragmatism of Foster's ruminations on trade union organizing.[31]

Toward Soviet America is often ferocious-sounding, a tract in which discussions of the grim imperatives of the revolution alternate with curiously detached, dreamlike imaginings of what the future Soviet America will be like. It is these prophetic passages that are the most dramatic in the book. Arthur Koestler wrote of his experiences as a Communist that "the revolutionary's Utopia, which in appearance represents a complete break with the past, is always modeled on some image of the lost Paradise, of a legendary Golden Age." Yet what is remarkable about Foster's utopian projections is precisely their lack of a discernible "past," the absence of any historical compass. He never seriously attempts to tie his prognostications to the ideas of earlier American radicalisms.[32]

Except for the productive apparatus, the institutions of capitalism would be abolished in Soviet America. But as is typical of Foster's thoughts in general on the matter, nearly all aspects of social life under capitalism will need to be reorganized as well. Science? "A slave to the class interests of the bourgeoisie." Religion? "A monstrous system of dupery." Political parties? They "will be liquidated." Also to be "liquidated" are "all other organizations that are political props of bourgeois rule, including chambers of commerce, employers' associations, rotary clubs, American Legion, YMCA and such fraternal orders as the Masons, Odd Fellows, Elks, Knights of Columbus, etc." What of the family, and the role of women? The "American woman" is "either a gilded butterfly bourgeois parasite or she is an oppressed slave." In the American Soviet government, "woman" will be freed, "economically, politically and socially." She will be "free in her sex life," divorce to be "had for the asking." In the Soviet Union, "great factory kitchens are being set up to prepare hot, well-balanced meals for home consumption by the millions; communal kitchens in apartment houses are organized widespread."[33]

As for "bourgeois" culture, its aims are to make workers into "slave-like robots" who mindlessly accept whatever their employers decide to grant them; "unthinking soldiers who will enthusiastically get themselves killed off in defense of their masters' rulership," or "superstitious dolts" who are satisfied with a promise of heaven as a substitute for a decent earthly life. Thus, all of bourgeois culture will need to be reconstituted. In

Soviet America, "the press, the motion picture, the radio, the theater, will be taken over by the government." They will be "cleansed" of sex, crime, and sensationalism and "developed into institutions of real education." As for health, "the people will be taught to live correctly" through instruction in diet and physical culture. A common thread in Foster's critique of capitalism is its supposedly planless, anarchic nature. Yet, in his account, all the social institutions of capitalism turn out to be relentlessly and thoroughly organized in the interests of the ruling classes.[34]

In the future socialist world there will be no war, superstition, disease, ignorance, crime, unemployment, or poverty. However, what will remain of capitalism is its utilitarianism. In the first place, all who do not engage in "useful" occupations will be "liquidated." These include "wholesalers, jobbers . . . the entire crew of 'middlemen,' real estate sharks, stock brokers, prohibition agents, bootleggers, advertising specialists, traveling salesmen, lawyers, whole rafts of government bureaucrats, police, clericals" and others. All these are "socially useless elements." Scientists will serve socialism, and the "city intelligentsia" will be tolerated "insofar as these elements break with the old order and support the new."[35]

What Foster is attempting here is a modern analogy to an earlier producerist ethic, except that in Foster's hands the analogy is oddly deformed; the distortion stands out most meaningfully when he substitutes the trope "useful" for "productive" in determining the basic cleavage between workers and their potential enemies. An earlier strain in American labor radicalism had been relatively expansive in its definition of useful citizenship: "producers" might include small businessmen, for instance. Moreover, the focus of the earlier producer ethos was the notion of self-sustaining independence—providing for self and family within a complex community of interdependence and mutuality. For Foster, the idea of "use" dispenses with the idea of mutuality and community, and carries with it the ominous overtone of dependence on a larger entity, the socialist state, which, predictably enough, organizes all production. "The industrial system as a whole will be headed by a body analogous to the Supreme Economic Council of the USSR," he intones. This council is made up of a series of "united industries," "trusts," and "combines."[36] In earlier American socialist rhetoric it was the large corporation that represented the destruction of community and independence; for Foster a distant Soviet "trust" is the basis of social cohesion.

Foster's meditations on the future workplace are consistent with his writings on the subject in the 1910s. In the United States, he proposed, "the problem of the American working class in achieving socialism may be summed up . . . as the present American industrial technique plus Soviets." Soviet industry means "system, cooperation, efficiency." While he suggested that in socialist society trade unions "play a fundamental role," the precise role of workers' organizations is unclear. Although unions under socialism protect "the immediate needs of the workers," Foster is unable to posit any inalienable value for work in a society where the overriding concern is system, cooperation, and efficiency—which, of course, continued to be the bywords of capitalist efficiency engineers in the United States. There is no need for dissent. Since production is centrally managed, unions are reduced to primarily educational institutions: "schools for socialism." The idea of incorporation, as he first articulated and developed it in the 1910s, remained at the core of Foster's political and social outlook. It explains the ease with which he recomposed his utopian vision in the 1930s to conform with the totalitarian ethos of Stalinism.[37]

The crowds that Foster and his running mate James Ford were able to gather during the presidential campaign appeared large to observers. The campaign proved at least moderately successful in the domain of the salons as well. One important constituency that the Communist party courted in 1932 consisted of a number of writers and intellectuals who organized the League of Professional Groups for Foster and Ford during the summer of 1932. This organization grew out of an earlier group, the National Committee for the Defense of Political Prisoners, that had coalesced during the industrial warfare in Harlan County, Kentucky. A manifesto was written and signed by figures such as Granville Hicks, Sidney Hook, Edmund Wilson, John Dos Passos, Sherwood Anderson, Lincoln Steffens, Matthew Josephson, Theodore Dreiser, and Langston Hughes. Wilson voted for Foster in 1932, and Theodore Dreiser, who met Foster in Harlan County, once stated that he admired Foster "more than any man alive." The writers' manifesto stated that "as responsible intellectual workers we have aligned ourselves with the frankly revolutionary Communist party—the party of the workers." It reiterated the central themes of a standard campaign speech of Foster's: the lack of significant differences between Hoover and Roosevelt; the necessity for thorough "social reorganization" as a response to the economic collapse; the economic miracle of the Soviet Union, where there was no unemployment. The writers somewhat incongruously concluded that "The Communist party stands for a socialism of deeds, not words."[38]

One night at the end of May, Foster made an appearance as guest of honor at a campaign gathering at Edmund Wilson's apartment in Greenwich Village. For Foster, it was probably an uncomfortable occasion. Earlier, he had proclaimed that the crisis of the Depression meant that "the hotsy-totsy days for the intellectuals are over." He had predicted that most would become fascists or social fascists during the crisis; only a few, especially those with a "proletarian background," would become "real Communists."[39] *Toward Soviet America*, which had been published days before the meeting in Greenwich Village, was openly condescending toward what it termed the "trend among the petty bourgeois intellectuals towards Communism," which it attributed to the fact that the Depression had drastically curtailed their standards of living. "Even the intellectuals are being compelled to think," Foster wrote.[40]

Nonetheless, Matthew Josephson remembered that Foster "made a fine impression" that night, a "working-class type dressed in unfashionable though well-brushed clothes." He impressed those gathered with his "cool and logical" mannerisms; however, he was not, Josephson thought, "the man to magnetize crowds." As for the role of intellectuals in the radical movement, they were, Foster predictably observed, too much prone to talk and lengthy debate. Josephson quoted him as saying that the Communists, on the other hand, "having made their decision, cut out talk and go into action." He suggested that bourgeois recruits to the Party must adjust to this way of doing things. Later, thinking of writing an article on the Party for the *New Yorker*, Josephson visited its headquarters and met with Browder and Foster; of the two, Foster struck Josephson as having more of a common touch than Browder. The men gazed out the window at the newly constructed Empire State Building, which was nearly empty for lack of tenants. "Why we could take charge of the Empire State all right and fill it up to the top," Foster said.[41]

The presidential campaign was a grueling one. When his speaking schedule commenced, in early June, Foster was scheduled to travel thirty thousand miles and make 105 speeches. Shortly after the campaign began, he began experiencing "heart symptoms" that he never described in detail, but which caused him to eagerly "check off each meeting" as he completed it. To add to the stress, campaign meetings were held in an atmosphere of official harassment, and, of course, no little danger to Foster himself. He was arrested in Los Angeles at the end of June as he attempted to address an outdoor rally. The arrest provoked skirmishes between Foster's sympathizers and about a hundred police officers who had been assigned to prevent him from speaking. The police chief later explained that "I arrested Foster to keep peace in the city." Foster was arrested in August as well when he attempted to speak in Lawrence, Massachusetts.[42]

Two weeks following his arrest in Lawrence, Foster was complaining to his physician of recurrent attacks of pain in his left side while giving speeches. He collapsed in Moline, Illinois, on September 8, immobilized by severe angina pectoris. The *Daily Worker* did not report his illness until five days later, but finally acknowledged that he had suffered a "complete nervous breakdown" as well as a near-fatal heart attack. Foster later described himself as a "nervous wreck" and "helpless as a child" as a result of the collapse. Subsequently, on the advice of a physician, Communist party news was kept away from him as much as possible; for the better part of a year he did not even read the *Daily Worker*. He spent months in bed after the breakdown, and was only able to address a concluding election rally at Madison Square Garden from a telephone hookup at his home. In the summer of 1933, he journeyed to the Soviet Union for treatment, writing to a comrade that "what ails me now is the tail end of a bad nerve shattering—and believe me it was real hell. The heart symptoms have quite disappeared. What I need now is quiet, rest." However, Foster's recuperation in the Soviet Union of which he had written so glowingly began as a nightmare. In his ninth visit to the country since 1921 he was shuffled among three separate sanitaria, including Kislovodsk in the North Caucasus, a famous health resort with mineral springs and a physio-therapeutical institute. Nonetheless, Foster was unhappy being "sent" to Kislovodsk, preferring to be near the sea. At Sochi, a Black Sea resort, his condition deteriorated. A desperate letter to Lozovsky from Sochi reveals Foster, thirteen months after his breakdown, struggling to recover control of his mental health. He found his lodgings intolerably noisy, and he had to negotiate a large number of stairs in order to return to his apartment from walks. Feeling trapped in his apartment, he had "nothing to do" and suffered from insomnia. "I am absolutely isolated, but I cannot stand routine interactions—I cannot talk to anyone over one or two minutes, especially about politics. . . . I cannot play cards, read, write for any duration. . . . I don't know how to fill my days." He confided to Lozovsky that "the result of this unending loneliness is my constant nervous tension, and it is very difficult for me. This tension is increased by news of the struggle in the states. I am so helpless." He despaired, "I previously could work sixteen hour days even on Sundays, and under any conditions. But now I am being destroyed by details and features I didn't notice before." Sylvia traveled to the Soviet Union to take charge of her father's treatment, and apparently concluding that his health would not improve there, finally arranged for him to return to the United States in January 1934. Even at this point his condition was such that he was unable to return to work at his office. According to Sam Darcy, one of the few people in the Party who was close to Foster at the time, his physician warned him that if he was to survive he had to get away from New York City and Party headquarters. Thus, he went to San Francisco to live at the home of a relative; Darcy, who also lived in San Francisco at the time, remembered that Foster was in "shocking physical condition" during this period. His head shook constantly, his hands trembled, and he could walk only with great difficulty. It would be nearly three years before he could make a ten-minute speech. As late as June 1935 he was still being treated at Soviet sanitaria.[43]

Unfortunately, very little information is available about the critical interregnum in Foster's life between his collapse and his return to active Party life in late 1935. Because of his (and the Party's) reticence on the matter, it is only possible to speculate about the nature of the stresses that impelled him toward a physical and psychological breakdown. Clearly, the mine strike of 1931 was a severe test, and he admitted that at the end of the fight he thought he was "almost finished." A variety of other influences can be cited: the general problems associated with the TUUL and the failure of the organization to thrive during the economic crisis; the tension between his increasing visibility as Party spokesman and propagandist and his declining influence within the Party itself; and finally his evident unhappiness in the role of presidential candidate, as well as the stresses associated with the campaign itself. Foster, of course, viewed himself as a man of action. Despite the opportunities provided by the early years of the Depression, he had increasingly found himself operating in the realm of "talk."[44]

A subtle but marked shift had occurred in Foster's personality during the years leading to his breakdown. While observers in his pre-Communist career noted his easygoing, affable, even leisurely "executive" persona, as a Communist the more intensely driven aspects of his personality seemed to come to the fore more often. In his later years especially he was a fastidious man who was highly concerned with controlling and organizing the details of his own life; an acquaintance noted that during his illness he became more attentive than ever to such details: "Every minute of his day was organized to prevent the 'leakage' of time. So many hours for sleep, up early in the morning (6:00 A.M.) to scan the morning newspapers, then to write a thousand words. . . ." He neither drank nor smoked, and was inclined toward vegetarianism. One observer, Joseph Freeman, remembered that he "was ascetic by a standard which determined all his actions." Another recalled his "purposeful self-discipline" as his personal hallmark. On this level, Foster's personality was always different from that of gregarious, self-indulgent, and expansively sociable American labor leaders like Samuel Gompers and Eugene Debs. However, after his breakdown in 1932, Foster seemed to withdraw further from the contacts with the party rank and file he had maintained in the 1920s. He was "not the kind of guy you could go out to lunch with," one prominent organizer recalled. "He brought his own lunch and ate in his office while he worked. When Bill was through with his work for the day, he grabbed his briefcase and went home." Once, Foster had been characterized as "scientific" in his management of the details of strikes; now his discipline turned inward, finding an outlet in the management of his everyday life.[45]

It is difficult to gauge the effect that Foster's absence had on the Party and its direction. By 1932, it is safe to conclude, he had no firm political identity and no cohesive group of supporters within the Party. For the general membership, he was an important symbol of an older laborist perspective—a figure who advocated a kind of militant realism with respect to work within the mainstream labor movement. Yet, he also bore the stigma of the interminable factionalism of the 1920s. His illness coincided with Earl Browder's consolidation of influence in the inner councils of the Party, but Browder himself was coming to understand the need for a change of direction in labor policy by 1933. Foster would begin to compose a coherent political identity for himself only following his recovery and the emergence of the Popular Front perspective after 1935. Nonetheless, during the early years of the Roosevelt administration, when membership in the AFL surged dramatically, the Party was without the services of an experienced and respected activist with numerous contacts in the labor movement.

During his long recuperation, Foster began work on his autobiographies, *From Bryan to Stalin* and *Pages from a Worker's Life*. His physicians informed him following his collapse that his condition was serious enough to be life-threatening, and he was undoubtedly concerned to record and explain his political outlook and considerable life experience. If his brush with mortality in the 1930s occasioned a certain amount of introspection, neither of his autobiographies reveal it; the narrative is far more often political than personal. In his first book, *From Bryan to Stalin*, Foster presents himself as merely an actor in a much larger historical teleology, the rise and decline of American capitalism in the twentieth century. This autobiography reads like an exercise in self-conversion, a determined reassembling and reordering of a vast fund of experiences to conform with ritually reiterated doctrine. The second, *Pages from a Worker's Life*, published in 1939, purports to be a series of "more personal" reflections and memories, as he put it, but is largely devoid of self-analysis.[46]

Foster did not directly explain his reasons for writing a second autobiography, but simultaneously with the publication of *Pages from a Worker's Life*, he wrote a revealing article in *Political Affairs* in which he called for greater attention in the Party to the "human element in mass agitation." The task of Communists, he asserted, was to "put more of the stuff of real life into our agitation." Workers "see and feel the evils of capitalism primarily in terms of personal privations and miseries in their homes and workplaces," he wrote. Communists tended to pay too much attention to "mass trends, statistical quantities, social analyses and general political programs." In the Party, there was an "erroneous tendency artificially to separate political theory from 'human interest,' and grossly to belittle the latter." Communist agitators should study and reflect upon the "humanness" contained in the "moving speeches of Debs and Haywood," or the revelations of muckrakers like Lincoln Steffens and Upton Sinclair. The article reveals Foster's strong yearning for access to a more humane political rhetoric, and suggests that he hoped *Pages from a*

Worker's Life would reveal some of the "humanity" that is largely absent in *From Bryan to Stalin*.[47]

Yet, his attempt to humanize the class struggle in his second autobiography was only partly successful. Upon reading *Pages from a Worker's Life*, Elizabeth Gurley Flynn concluded that "there is no ego here; no cultivated 'complex'; no soul-searching to 'find himself'; no personal glory, amorous conquests nor 'success' recipes." As Flynn reflected, Foster's new autobiography revealed few prosaic human emotions such as ambition, love, pride, or play. Instead, Foster's self remained submerged in his class: "He 'lives and moves and has his being' as a worker; conscious of his class and its struggles, its needs and what its final aims must be. He has no personal life nor ambition outside of theirs. . . . Capitalism offers no attractions, no distractions, no interests to him."[48]

Foster's apparent lack of a personal "self" in his autobiographies cannot be understood simply as the hallmark of an authoritarian personality without a stable identity outside of his political organization. While Foster's autobiographies disguise, dislocate, and efface the "self," there is also a peculiar sense of dual consciousness, manifested in part by his construction of two different autobiographies, each with different purposes and structure. In one, the self and politics, person and theory, become nearly indistinguishable. The other aims at achieving a more "human" voice but ultimately falls short, revealing few details of personality distinct from that of the "working class." One purports to illustrate the "forces" that made him a Communist; it portrays Foster the theorist and historian. The other seeks a broader identification and acceptance, a more inclusive audience: it reflects Foster as agitator, attempting to employ the "human element." In publishing the two autobiographies with their different rationales, he undercuts and implicitly critiques the basis for each "self."

Foster's opposition of "theory" and the "human element," revealed symbolically by his dual autobiographies, can be elaborated further. In his *Political Affairs* article, he favorably relates the "human element" to the old-style emotionalism of Debs and Haywood, but also cautions against "sob-sister slobbering over the woes of the people," and his disdain for the sentimentalist appeals of earlier radicals like Debs was well known. He cites a vivid and compelling portrait of poverty and working-class sickness offered by one witness during testimony before a Congressional hearing on national health insurance as an example of "putting the breath of life into the dry discussion of the people's health." He noted that this testimony was given by a woman, a member of a trade union auxiliary. In the Communist party itself, women were not expected to contribute in the realm of theory, and they remained underrepresented in leadership positions proportional to their membership. Foster approved of the woman's testimony, but on the other hand, "sob-sister slobbering over the woes of the people" is definitely not consistent with the role of the "professional" revolutionary and scientific historian. When Elizabeth Gurley Flynn (the only woman on the National Board of the Party) published her autobiography in 1955, Foster saw fit to write a review of the book which somewhat condescendingly purported to place her experiences in "theoretical," historical perspective.[49] Foster's publication of *Pages from a Worker's Life* represented a carefully measured retreat from "theory" and a recognition of the need to utilize the "human element" in mass agitation. Harried as he was by official repression and incapacitated by illness, at this point in his career his excursion into the realm of agitator could proceed only so far. At the same time, even though Foster tried to demonstrate that the "human element" in mass agitation need not be inconsistent with hard-headed political theorizing, the dichotomy retained a gendered as well as professional meaning for him, and he remained a reluctant agitator.

Chapter 10

THE DEMOCRATIC FRONT

I haven't had an opportunity of close contact with the
other ruling elements of the American Communist
party—except, to be sure, Foster. The latter always
seemed to me made of more trustworthy material than
Lovestone and Pepper. In Foster's criticisms of the
official leadership of the Party there was always much
that was true and acute. But as far as I understand him,
Foster is an empiricist. He does not want to, or is not
able to, carry his thinking through to the end, and make
upon the foundation of his criticisms the necessary
generalization. For that reason it has never been clear to
me in what direction Foster's criticism is pushing him: to
the left or to the right of the official Centrism.
—Leon Trotsky

FOSTER's return to active involvement in the American party occurred in
the midst of momentous changes in the international Communist movement. The rise of fascism in Germany and elsewhere in Europe made it
imperative that Communists seek alliances with bourgeois politicians as
well as the formerly despised Socialists. In the summer of 1935, representatives of Communist parties from around the globe met in Moscow at
the Comintern's Seventh Congress, and were formally urged to abandon
Third Period tactics and slogans. The definition of what exactly constituted a "fascist" in the eyes of the Communists became far more restric-
tive and precise, and it now became necessary for the Communists to
stand on the side of traditional political liberties and democratic traditions. Despite the onslaught they faced, for thousands of activists in the
international movement the change in perspective offered a sense of renewed purpose. Following more than a decade of political and intellectual loneliness Communists began to achieve genuine leadership of working-class political movements, and would finally emerge as the dominant
force on the left.

By 1934 William Foster had endured a series of political reverses in the
Communist party and finally a shattering nervous breakdown, but as he
struggled back to health he remained committed to the Party and its in-
tensive and demanding culture of political comradeship. As revealed in

his private correspondence with Lozovsky and others, Foster retained a dogged and tenacious political optimism, based on a seemingly infinite willingness to compromise and maneuver. After 1934, there was ample reason for continued faith. As the Communists had predicted in the truculent philippics of the Third Period, the Western democracies seemed helpless to stem the growth of fascism in Italy, Germany, and Spain; only the Communists and Stalin seemed willing and able to forcefully resist. In the United States, the Communist party positioned itself favorably to play a large role in the powerful movement for industrial unionism that began to gather force after 1935. In this context, ex-Communists like Jay Lovestone and James Cannon and the splinter movements they led remained at the margins. The Socialist party, always condemned by Foster as irrelevant, now found itself decisively eclipsed in influence by the Communists.

In the United States, even before the Seventh Congress convened, many American Communists had been uncomfortable with the Third Period zeitgeist, and had moved in the direction of alliances with reformists before the line formally changed. The most notable instances of this kind of instinctive Popular Frontism came in the arena of labor organizing, which continued to be the Party's most important concern. While the impact of the TUUL revolutionary unions should not be minimized, in a number of industries organizers were searching for a more pragmatic approach years before the Seventh Congress. As early as 1931, Joseph Zack, an important Party organizer, acknowledged that "although we speak very much about strikes assuming a political character in the third period, in practice when we enter into a strike situation we look upon it pretty much in the old trade-unionist fashion. Our party transforms itself into a strike Party and the politics we leave pretty much to everybody else."[1]

During the early years of the Depression, AFL membership rose dramatically, and Communists were quite cognizant of that organization's successes. Moreover, Comintern and official Party resolutions from the very beginning had contained an element of ambiguity about the desirability of abandoning work within the AFL.[2] While his illness effectively removed him from the scene during this critical period, Foster's conspicuous hesitation about the new revolutionary unions and his continual emphasis on the importance of "boring from within" the established unions helped to create an atmosphere in which organizers could justify their involvement with the AFL as conditions permitted.[3] As early as February 1931, Foster told Lozovsky that the Party was "gradually re-beginning" work in the AFL unions, "in a number of practical situations." By April 1934, when the TUUL was finally abandoned, 30 percent of the Party's trade union members worked in Communist "factions" within the AFL.[4]

The TUUL unions were in difficult straits by late 1934, as Jack Stachel, still the organizational secretary of the league, readily admitted. In a pessimistic report issued in November, he reviewed the shortcomings of sev-

Foster with *left*, Elizabeth Gurley Flynn and *right*, Rose Wortis, 1937.

eral of the more important revolutionary unions, including those in the mining, textile, marine, auto and steel industries. He suggested that the auto and steel unions dissolve and join the AFL. One month later, the Comintern formally endorsed the move by the TUUL unions into the AFL. A final convention was held in March 1935 for which Foster, still apparently in ill health, provided a written address. He condemned the TUUL for its members' tendency to abandon the old unions, even though in virtually the same breath he asserted that the change in line that created the organization was "fundamentally correct." TUUL militants had gained valuable experience in mass-production industry. He maintained that a place still existed for a committee of independent unions, but added that "as for myself, I shall devote my chief attention to the work within the AFL."[5]

Foster, still quite weakened, began to reassert his voice in the Party just as the broad movement for industrial unionism in the United States was gaining momentum. Realizing that the AFL would never provide the kind of leadership necessary to undertake such campaigns, in October and November 1935 John L. Lewis and other AFL leaders, including David Dubinsky of the ILGWU and Sidney Hillman of the ACW, began to set up the Committee for Industrial Organization. By early 1936 the CIO had independently launched successful organizing campaigns in a number of core industries. From the beginning, Lewis and his associates called on experienced Communist organizers to assist in the drive for industrial unionism. For many, to be an American Communist during the Popular Front years meant not only membership in an international alliance against fascism, but belonging to a burgeoning and powerful movement in working-class communities for empowerment in the workplace. As Foster had predicted, Communist organizers would finally gain the respect of American workers more for their unstinting devotion to their unions than their adherence to Marxian ideology. One successful CIO organizer remembered that workers "didn't give a damn if you was actually a member of the Communist party, it was what you were doing in there. If you were contributing to the cause, good." However, at the same time, the leadership of the new CIO understood from the beginning that their movement was also a political movement, inextricably a part of a broader New Deal electoral coalition centering around Franklin D. Roosevelt.[6]

Foster publicly endorsed the new CIO as soon as it achieved organizational coherence. In his first published statement on the matter, he declared that as a result of the formation of the CIO, the "key problem" for the labor movement had now become organizing the unorganized into the AFL on the basis of industrial unionism. Despite years of enmity, the Communists would now support Lewis with "every energy" available to them. However, Foster still distrusted Lewis, his old nemesis, and worried that the CIO was holding back on its key steel organizing campaign in deference to Roosevelt's reelection campaign. "Lewis and the CIO leaders have based their movement too much upon Roosevelt, they don't want to embarrass Roosevelt," he worried in a top-level meeting. As for Lewis, "we must always remember that this man, up to a couple of years ago, was in the extreme right wing of the bureaucracy of the AFL and while we give him support, nevertheless we must be on guard that he doesn't revert back to his old practices." Foster continued to emphasize the importance of unity with the AFL, believing that the CIO risked a rank-and-file backlash by "splitting" too precipitously. To some extent, this mirrored the general approach of Lewis and his allies as well. Despite the suspension of the CIO unions from the AFL in August and October 1936, the new organization continued to insist on maintaining its ties to the AFL. For instance, it would not be until November 1938 that the CIO would formalize its break with the AFL, and even then, David Dubinsky decided to keep his union in the old federation. Foster emphasized that the CIO was "in no sense" a dual union, and at its inception at least, this was true. All unions represented by the CIO had been affiliated with the

AFL. Nonetheless, the CIO was essentially acting as a separate body by 1936, and Lewis had resigned from the AFL executive council. Despite his belief that a split was unfortunate, Foster blamed "bourbons" in the AFL for the rift, and reiterated Communist support for the CIO in the face of AFL demands that the new organization dissolve.[7]

Perhaps the most ironic aspect of Foster's career in the 1930s is that for the most part, both his physical and political powers were diminished at a time when his dream of a powerful movement for industrial unionism arising from within the AFL was reaching fruition. While his literary output began to increase steadily after 1935, it is difficult to ascertain the extent of his organizing activities in the trade union field. Browder and Foster would develop sharp differences over a variety of policy questions during the Popular Front period, and as a result, Foster's influence suffered in his former bailiwick. Browder put Roy Hudson, an ex-seaman, in charge of trade union work. As might be expected, Hudson and Browder both recalled that Foster gave union organizers in the Party "little guidance," and that despite meetings with organizers, they "didn't pay much attention to him." Hudson later admitted that he was not able to "bring about the collaboration between Foster and myself that I would like." Nonetheless, Foster wrote detailed manuals on organizing techniques and met fairly often with steel organizers to map out strategy; one prominent cadre reflected in a high-level meeting in 1939 that at Bethlehem Steel, "in every plant the whole program of [Foster] and his pamphlet is being put into effect. . . ."[8]

Others, working farther from the centers of Party leadership, recalled Foster's influence. Stella Nowicki and Herbert March, organizers in the meatpacking industry during this period, remembered that he and Jack Johnstone would provide important advice on tactics, as well as the names of individuals who could assist their efforts. Nowicki recalled that a pamphlet that Foster wrote during this period on steel organizing, *What Means a Strike in Steel?* was an organizer's "bible." March, a prominent and effective organizer for the CIO United Packinghouse Workers, remembered that he "learned how to organize" from Foster and Johnstone. One former Communist with wide organizing experience recalled that despite Browder's position as party chairman, Foster remained the "authoritative public spokesman" for issues pertaining to the labor movement during the 1930s. His influence extended to the level of personal contacts as well:

> The biggest overall memory of the way the rest of the Party felt about Foster in the 30s and 40s, 30s particularly . . . comrade after comrade would tell the same story, and that was that Foster was one of the few Communist leaders who, when he came to town, would sit with a group of people, com-

rades, workers, and would spend hours drawing out every detail of the work process of where they worked, every detail of the labor movement, every detail of the trends going on in that particular factory or union. He wasn't given to making big lectures to them, he would listen; and that was what impressed every comrade I knew in the labor movement. . . . I remember this quality which impressed me so, this sensitivity to workers' moods and trends, and his persistence in getting every detail.[9]

Foster published a number of organizing manuals during the 1930s, each of which drew on his experiences in earlier campaigns for industrial unionism.[10] In one remarkable instance, a red-baiting pamphlet entitled *Join the CIO and Help Build a Soviet America* was circulated that carefully detailed parallels between CIO organizing methods and Foster's own previously published advice. The parallels are indeed striking; everything from his advice on how to cultivate fraternal organizations and women's groups to the use of bands and radio is covered.[11]

Foster's role in the Party's successes during the CIO period must be considered in broad, general terms because of the lack of information about his Party activities. That the Party had developed a large cadre of aggressive and competent trade union organizers by the 1930s was testimony to the importance of his groundbreaking work with the TUEL and his relentless emphasis on the importance of workplace issues during the 1920s. In spite of the bitter attacks of Charles Ruthenberg and Jay Lovestone, Foster had helped preserve and strengthen the Party's trade union orientation. The stress on the importance of maintaining a relatively independent sphere of trade union activism, a distrust of electoral politics, an essentially syndicalist emphasis on workers' immediate demands, and above all the idea that the revolutionary activity of a "militant minority" of radicals in the trade union movement would prove most effective for Communists in the United States, were important aspects of "Fosterism" that survived the 1920s. As one organizer put it at the time, "experience bears out the fact that it is the union which is the mass bridge to the Party, politically and organizationally, and that the building of the union is the best mass approach to the building of the Party." In a larger sense, Foster's prediction was right: participation in the union movement in the 1930s brought American Communists closer to the reigns of real power than they ever had been.[12]

Yet, discontinuities existed as well. While "Fosterism" can be readily detected in the Party's trade union orientation in 1935, in particular industries and unions where this orientation was most strongly manifested in the early 1920s (for instance, in mining, the building trades, and railroad shop unions) Communists had very little influence by the 1930s. If Foster promoted the concept of semiautonomous Communist trade union organizing vehicles in the 1920s and 1930s, by 1935 nothing resembling the earlier TUEL or TUUL was in operation.

However, throughout the 1930s, Foster continued to cling to his belief that unionism was the most potent revolutionary force available to American radicals. True, late in 1935 he wrote an article for the theoretical journal, *The Communist*, in which he traced the history of syndicalism in the United States, noted that he himself had played a large role in creating the "syndicalist confusion" among American workers, and criticized syndicalist "theory" from the traditional Communist viewpoint, that syndicalism underestimates both the role of the state and that of the Party itself. Yet he left open the question of how power is to be attained, and in *Toward Soviet America*, his only contemporary meditation on the problem, he predicted that workers would "carry out a militant policy . . . in defense of their daily interests and finally, following the example of the Russian workers, they will abolish capitalism and establish Socialism." Despite his published disavowals, the syndicalist label continued to dog him. Browder, for instance, continually referred to him as an anarcho-syndicalist and "eclectic," both harsh adjectives in the Communist lexicon. Browder's inclination was to focus on developing the Party's political and electoral relationships within the New Deal coalition; gains in the CIO were important primarily as means to the development of this kind of political influence.[13]

Browder's accusation that Foster was an "eclectic" reflected his oft-repeated assertion that Foster's criticism of his leadership of the Party during the 1930s lacked consistency. At one level, Browder's assessment is accurate: Foster's conflict with Browder had a dimension that was as much personal as ideological in nature. Both men, undoubtedly, were intimately acquainted with each other's shortcomings; they had worked intermittently with each other in a political context since 1913. Of active Party cadres, only J. W. Johnstone had a longer association with Foster. Foster was known for his overbearing attitude toward subordinates, and Browder had undoubtedly been subject to all sorts of manipulations in his role as Foster's "office boy" in the early 1920s. Yet, by the 1930s, Browder had come to cherish his identity as an important figure in the international Communist movement. Later in the decade he would come to think of himself as the leader of a strong, independent national movement, like Maurice Thorez in France or Palmiro Togliatti in Italy. A Browder cult began to take hold: Popular Front iconography would juxtapose his picture with those of Jefferson and Lincoln; and Georgi Dimitroff, the Bulgarian Communist who served as the secretary of the Comintern in the 1930s, once termed Browder the greatest living Marxist in the English-speaking world. All this must have grated on Foster. The organizer of the Great Steel Strike found himself deferring to a man who had no

actual experience leading "mass movements" of American workers.
Browder's most important credentials, at least at the beginning of the
Popular Front period, seemed to be his strong relationship with the Comintern. Browder, for his part, understood this. Within the Party leadership, Foster continued to command respect, "a prejudice in his favor as
an old-time militant [of] the long tradition."[14]

Foster's "old-time" militancy inevitably conditioned his response to organized labor's growing involvement with electoral politics and the Democratic party after 1935. He remained sensitive to a number of different
political impulses in the ranks of organized labor, and the attitude of
American workers toward the New Deal in the months leading up to the
1936 elections required careful analysis. Support for candidates of electoral protest, both to the right and left of Roosevelt, had surged dramatically. Throughout 1935, both Foster and Browder had supported the idea
of a national farmer-labor party as a way of winning workers away from
FDR, who, they believed, had not yet proven himself as "a barrier to the
growth of reaction and fascism" in the context of the growing strength of
the Long and Coughlin movements. In top Comintern conclaves in 1935,
Foster emphasized a growing fascist danger as well as an increasing disil-
lusionment with capitalism among American workers, and argued that
for the first time in American history there was a potential mass base for
an independent labor party growing out of the labor unions. At the same
time, Foster criticized the early CIO for its seemingly unconditional support of FDR and its lack of support for independent parties. However, the
Comintern finally weighed in with an opinion that the Party must find a
way to support Roosevelt, and Foster complied by endorsing a policy of
Communist support of Roosevelt to avoid a split with the CIO; Browder
was more hesitant, believing that such a move would cost Roosevelt more
votes than he would gain. Finally, convinced that active support of a third
party would drain votes from FDR and possibly help elect Alf Landon,
the Party decided to run its own candidates, Browder and Ford, while at
the same time directing most of its criticism at Landon. This was a policy
Foster was comfortable with; he wrote privately to Darcy in August that
"I think our line is quite correct in the situation." Nonetheless, a continuing theme in his writings was that the CIO should be more independent
politically of FDR.[15]

Following Roosevelt's decisive victory in 1936, Foster began to develop and elaborate his objections to the Party's role in the new CIO–
New Deal coalition, while Browder came to embrace the New Deal alliance more wholeheartedly. Foster would continue to envision the possibility of a farmer-labor movement as a possible electoral alternative to
Roosevelt. In the emerging debate with Browder he raised themes that he

would consistently emphasize throughout the Popular Front years: his distrust of Roosevelt (a distrust which would come to be shared, among others, by John L. Lewis) and his belief that the Party was in danger of losing its identity by tying its fortunes too closely to the fate of the New Deal. He would continue to be reserved about electoral "coalitions" with the Democratic party: the point of the FLP, as Alexander Bittelman put it at the time, was "to win the masses from the capitalist parties."

In late 1937, the Party inaugurated the tactic of the Democratic Front, in which the Communists envisioned themselves as part of a united front of all forces "opposed to the fascists." The rhetoric accompanying the new orientation left out explicit references to the necessity of building socialism; Browder defined the Democratic Front as demanding "the minimum of those measures necessary under capitalism to preserve and extend democracy, all those things which have been the heart of the American tradition in the past, ever since the revolutionary foundation of the United States." He suggested that an independent farmer-labor party could only develop out of the Democratic party itself. Browder came to see the Democratic Front as the most vital component of Communist strategy, and he worked assiduously to develop high-level contacts with the Roosevelt administration. Foster, on the other hand, while not minimizing the importance of such contacts, continued to emphasize that the reforms of the New Deal had been primarily the result of pressure from below. One Browder ally in the top leadership remembered Foster's approach as: "Yes we have influence on the administration and policy, but it's to be gotten mainly by how you mobilize the masses. That's the key thing." Foster would "always say [labor] was the fulcrum for moving things."[16] His was a lonely dissenting voice during this period, and he continued to advocate what he called a "People's Front" strategy. The difference between the two strategies was significant.

In an article that gained a great deal of attention in Party circles, Foster laid out his reservations about the new line. The article reiterated his unease with the Party's attitude toward the New Deal, and reflected his essentially syndicalist perspective on the problem of Communist politics during the 1930s. In Europe, especially in France and Spain, he asserted, Communist parties had established strong People's Fronts in which they were "real vanguard parties." In the United States, the Party had made gains in membership, but much of these gains were proving to be ephemeral. Because the American Party had given over the role of winning "day-to-day struggles" to other forces (the CIO-Democratic coalition) it lacked the prestige of the French and Spanish parties, thus making recruitment and assimilation of members more difficult. Foster reaffirmed his belief that Communists could achieve leadership, which he defined as "appearing before the workers as their practical daily political leader," without sectarian, revolutionary sloganeering. "Workers cannot be expected to join a Party which they do not see definitely in action as a Party, nor do they want to affiliate themselves to a semi-underground organization," he asserted. As for the New Deal, he supported the idea of endorsing progressive candidates on Democratic tickets, but also warned of the necessity of cultivating independence from the established parties by supporting farmer-labor tickets wherever possible.[17]

Thus, the question was far more complex than a mere question of whether the Party should act as if it believed that American workers were ready to accept it as their leader in the field of "immediate demands." According to the Democratic Front theory of Browder and his supporters, American workers were simply less "advanced" than those of, for instance, France or Spain. Therefore, according to this reasoning, the Party was better off immersing itself in the broad coalition of forces gathering around the New Deal. Foster did not accept this logic. He had no illusions that the American working class as a whole was about to surge into a revolutionary Communist party, as his careful analyses of the broad appeal of the Long and Coughlin movements in the United States revealed. He simply believed that the Communists could maintain their identity as a party somewhere to the left of Roosevelt and at the same time attract the support of a significant number of workers. He continued to point to the successes of the TUEL, with its laborist orientation, in the early 1920s as an example of the Party achieving leadership in the arena of immediate demands. Foster judged the defeat of this orientation from a syndicalist perspective—the result of incorrect tactics, the introduction of divisive political concerns into the movement, and the sabotage of its efforts by a militant minority of conservative officials. The problem with his critique of the Democratic Front was that he never specified the point at which the Communists' tactics after 1936 would differ from earlier united fronts. His objections remained somewhat subjective, based more on style and contingency than doctrine or theory.[18]

Foster was uneasy about the CIO's growing estrangement from the AFL. While disdainful of the conservative leadership of the AFL president, William Green, he warned against making "a fetish of the form of industrial unionism." Here, he was picking up a theme from his pre-Communist, anti-IWW days. It simply cannot be said, he noted, "that the leadership of industrial unions is always progressive and that of craft unions always conservative." He asserted that the AFL could still "evolve," that industrial unionism could emerge within a craft union context. And in fact, by 1938, the AFL was surging in strength, having surpassed the CIO organizations in membership. In traditional AFL unions like the Teamsters, activists were indeed realizing that it was possible to convert local unions into mass-based, "industrial" organizations. Foster pointed out

that issues other than industrial unionism were potentially more important: democracy in the unions and support for independent labor parties,
for instance. Although he did accept the abolition of Communist shop
fractions and committees in the trade unions as a way of facilitating the
Party's relationship with the rank and file and allowing more independence for union cadres, he continually reiterated that the Party "cannot
become merely a tail to the C.I.O." While his thoughts on the Democratic
Front revealed a willingness to transpose international developments to
American conditions, his warnings about the CIO were grounded solidly
in his understanding of American labor history. He recalled the fate of the
progressive movement within the AFL in the early 1920s: the return of
prosperity, a decline in the militancy of workers, and the submission of
the progressives to the Gompers regime in the AFL had set the stage for
the mass expulsion of radicals, and for collaborative labor-management
agreements on productivity issues like the speedup. The parallels between
this set of developments and what happened to the Communists after
1947 in the CIO are striking.[19]

How did Foster's reservations about the CIO translate into practice? In
1937, a controversy erupted during a sit-down strike of UAW-Chrysler
workers in Detroit. Lewis reached a preliminary agreement with Chrysler
according to which the strike would be suspended while negotiations
began between the union and management. Despite tours of the plants by
Lewis and the UAW president, Homer Martin, many workers refused to
accept the agreement. Martin became convinced that Communists were
encouraging this revolt in order to undermine his leadership, and threatened to expel Communists wholesale from the union. William Weinstone, secretary of the Party in Michigan, backed the strikers, to the dismay of the Party leadership, which was loath to disrupt its relationship
with Martin and Lewis. Browder accused Weinstone of endangering the
Party's gains in Michigan, but Foster backed Weinstone, at least initially.
In another instance as well, Weinstone supported unauthorized strikers
only to have his decision questioned by Browder and his allies in the top
Party leadership, including Jack Stachel. Weinstone was finally demoted
and transferred. Foster endorsed this decision, but not without an argument with Browder in Moscow during which he reiterated his criticisms
of the Party-CIO relationship and the Democratic Front in general. Browder remembered that this was the "first, complete sharp and open opposition of Foster and I before the Comintern." Foster was "challenging my
whole leadership." As was true with all his Moscow trips during this
period, Foster returned chastened for his "sectarian" stance. In general,
however, while Foster complained of "tailing" to Lewis in the CIO, the
influence of the Party in the new industrial union federation was extensive; part of the price of their influence was the low profile they had been

cultivating for several years. This was a price Foster had shown himself willing to pay often enough in the past, in his relationships with progressive unionists in Chicago and elsewhere.[20]

Foster was uncomfortable with the Popular Front on other levels as well. As both a political figure and a symbol of the Party's supposed working-class provenance, Foster had always challenged the status and motives of nonproletarian Communists. However, it was increasingly clear that he had not been able to bring about the changes in the Party that he had envisioned when he joined the movement in 1921, convinced that it was only through influence in the trade unions that Communists could become a revolutionary force in America. In 1937, only one-third of the Party's membership belonged to trade unions, and by 1939, despite the Party's successes in the CIO, the proportion was precisely one-half. This did not represent an appreciable increase in percentage of union members since 1929, when the proportion was 48 percent. Moreover, only 50 percent of Party members were industrial workers. The Party had more members in the individual categories of office workers or professionals than in the steel, automobile, mining, marine, and textile industries combined.[21]

The 1930s saw a large and influential, if temporary, influx of artists and "cultural workers" into the Party and its auxiliaries. Within the Party, Foster was an adamant defender of the idea of "art as weapon," and continually emphasized that the cultural production of Party members should be understood in political terms. Even in the context of the class struggle, the contribution of artists and writers was questionable. He once wrote to V. F. Calverton, commenting on several of his essays, that "I think you run a danger of drifting off into work that is of too purely a literary character. It seems to me that this game is not worth the candle. There are so many much more important things to be done. A great need of our movement is a revolutionary intellectual who can analyze the broad developing social situation and help us map out policies with regard to them [sic]. . . . And I think this is a thousand times more important than literary work of however revolutionary a character."[22]

The Popular Front years saw the emergence of a unique cultural and political style that emphasized the Party's connections with American democratic and radical traditions. In parades and political pageantry, Communists sought to evoke the historical symbolism of American patriotic traditions; portraits of Lincoln and Washington were mingled with banners festooned with the hammer and sickle. In its everyday rhetoric, the Party often posited something called "Americanism" and then unhesitatingly sought to attach itself to this necessarily ill-defined concept. Communism, Browder proclaimed, was "twentieth-century Americanism." Often, the emphasis on the Party's indigenous roots took the form of simply asserting that Communists were Americans who liked to play baseball, spend time with their families, and exchange recipes. While previously the Communist self-image had revolved around the Leninist ideal of the professional revolutionary giving the whole of his life to the Party, now the emphasis was on developing strong nonpolitical ties to the "outside" community. Symbolic of the new orientation was that fact that it was not unusual for many young Communists to "Americanize" their names during this period. For instance, Saul Regenstreif became Johnny Gates, and Joseph Cohen became Joe Clark.

Such a change was not necessary for William Foster, but his particular self-conception as a professional revolutionary would prevent him from embracing attempts by the Party to search out a constituency larger than itself and the union movement. It is difficult, for instance, to conceive of Foster imagining an effective patriotic symbolism that might appeal to a wide American audience. For him, revolutionary transformation would come about efficiently and silently, beyond or behind the world of pageantry, emblems, allegories, or motifs.[23]

Likewise, even though Foster would remain the Party's preeminent symbol of its working-class Americanism, the rhetoric of Americanism proved oddly disjointed in his usage. In 1949, in the course of denying the charge that he and other Communists were essentially "foreign agents," he declared: "I, as other Communists, love the American people and their glorious revolutionary democratic traditions, their splendid scientific and industrial achievements. And I love, too, our beautiful land, in every corner of which I have lived and worked." Yet, he proposed, "building the Communist party in the United States, the citadel of world capitalism, is no easy job."[24] Here the alternating voices of detachment and belongingness ("their" glorious traditions and "our" beautiful land) are revealing. While Foster's invocations of his authentic American roots seem bogus and artificial, there is nonetheless a certain honesty in his inability to formulate a glib equation of Communism and "Americanism." Foster's attempts to evoke the Communist populism of the period revealed in an entirely unintended way that his radicalism was based on a powerful and genuine alienation from the central assumptions of American politics.

Foster was aware of Depression-era panaceas that advocated technocratic solutions to the nation's economic ills. The so-called technocracy movement of Howard Scott, as well as various other Veblenesque panaceas, gained his attention, not least because such movements often cited the Soviet Union as an ideal of technical and industrial unity. Obviously, such ideals had appealed to Foster, as they had to a number of American syndicalists—Scott himself had once been associated with the IWW. By the 1930s, however, he attacked "technocratic" ideas as "fascist," and indeed they were a key element of fascist ideology. However, Foster's critique rested only on a dubious supposition: that in the Soviet Union of the Five-Year Plans, technocratic organization was "democratic" because "social ownership inevitably involves social control."[25]

Foster traveled fairly frequently to the Soviet Union in the 1930s, and was undoubtedly aware of the murderous nature of Joseph Stalin's regime. He never hesitated publicly to endorse Stalin's actions, even long after the severely repressive nature of his rule was common knowledge in the West. He ardently supported the various show trials and executions of Stalin's political opponents. While it is true that his enthusiasms were widely shared in the progressive community at the time, his rhetoric was particularly worshipful at a time when he was in a uniquely knowledgeable position. Under Stalin, the Soviet system had become "the most profoundly democratic of all states," he wrote. Soviet citizens were "the masters of their social fate," and Stalin's constitution was "the most democratic in all the world." Moreover, "among the supremest [sic] achievements of this Socialist democracy were precisely the political liquidation of the reactionary Kulaks and the purging of the traitorous generals and politicians." How did Foster define the most important elements of Socialist "democracy?" While he included the right to vote and religious liberty ("the Soviet System provides for complete religious freedom") in his list of important "rights," others included the right to work, the right to labor's product, the right to organize, the right to education, and the rights to health, "rest and recreation," and "security." This is what "democracy" meant to Foster.[26]

Despite his clear statements on the issue, there is evidence that Foster's attitude toward Stalin's Soviet Union was more problematic than it appeared. Individuals who were close observers of Foster's career doubted his "conversion" to Stalinism. James Cannon, for instance, was convinced that Foster sought to adapt himself to Stalin's power in the Soviet Communist party just as he had with John Fitzpatrick and even Samuel Gompers in the American Federation of Labor during his days of "boring from within." Not surprisingly, Cannon's assessment mirrored that of Leon Trotsky. Trotsky thought that Foster tried "to conceal himself with the defensive coloration of Stalinism in order by this contraband route to move toward the leadership of the American party." Both were on firm ground in pointing to Foster's realism in matters of organizational power and how it is attained. Cannon believed that Foster came to Stalinism "with tongue in cheek." Indeed, there is a certain contrived quality to Foster's extravagant praise of both Stalin and Soviet society during this period. Statements such as "Stalin has the deep Marxian theoretical insight that enables him to see far more clearly than any of his contemporaries the correct path for the revolution" seem too worshipful when they appear under Foster's name. Was he seeking to attain his own ends by playing on Stalin's well-known susceptibility to flattery?[27]

Unfortunately, the truth about this central issue of Foster's personality and politics cannot be resolved with any certainty. However, he must be held accountable for his public stance; his accommodation to Stalin's regime undoubtedly heightened the dictator's prestige in the United States and within the American Communist movement itself. At a more basic level, his starkly instrumental politics as well as his statements on issues such as the inevitability of violence in the achievement of the revolution and the place of democracy in workers' organizations are not inconsistent with Stalinist politics. Part of his admiration of Stalin's Soviet Union stemmed from his belief that it was, as he put it, "a disciplined democracy." But if Foster continued to express admiration for the Soviets, deep reservations about Foster circulated in the Comintern *apparat*. "J. Peters," a shadowy Hungarian who supervised the American party's underground operations in the 1930s concluded in a report for Foster's private biographical file that "Foster never had any distinct outlook and generally speaking is very poor in Marxism." Moreover, "some comrades say that Foster joined the Communist party mainly for the Trade Union Educational League. . . . If we credit this analysis of Foster's activities we could come to the conclusion that he is rather a syndicalist than a Communist." He pointedly referred to Foster's "vigorous patriotism" during World War I and his sale of Liberty Bonds in "workers' districts" and added that "many workers blamed Foster for the failure of the Steel Strike." Peters concluded that "Foster is able to work long and hard and generally speaking he could be used well, but only under the condition of proper ideological and organizational leadership. Because of his instability and eclectic outlook he is unlikely to be able to lead the party. As a fellow he is good, straightforward and modest."[28]

Closer to home, Foster settled into his role as Browder's loyal opposition. There is no reason to believe that his opposition to Browder's polices was particularly devious. Indeed, during the years of the Popular Front, his dissent from Browder's policies helped isolate him politically in the American party, and as far as can be ascertained, no Comintern clique lent support to his perspectives. In short, he had little to gain from raising his voice against Browder, and he received little or no encouragement from other prominent cadres. The extent of his dissent from Browder's Democratic Front policies was not generally known to the Party membership.[29]

At a meeting of the Party's National Committee in 1939, Browder consented to a formal discussion of some of Foster's objections. Everyone present was familiar with Foster's particular policy differences with Browder; the meeting turned into a discussion of what Foster's role in the

Party was to be. Foster himself claimed that Browder was working to discredit him and limit his influence and activities, and that he was working at only half capacity. He implied that his underuse was a symptom of a general problem with the Party, that the Party's "organizational work" was not at the level of its "political work." After all, he noted, "ever since I had anything to do with the labor movement and revolutionary movement, I always had a natural inclination toward mass organization work, I mean particularly direct and immediate practical organizational work." He noted that Browder had openly accused him in Moscow of "wavering from the main line of the Party," portraying him as a sectarian influence.

In response, Browder's allies on the committee asserted that Foster and his writings had indeed been influential on a variety of issues, including the steel and auto drives in the CIO; one volunteered that Foster was developing a "persecution complex." Robert Minor, a founding member of the Party, suggested that Foster's mental powers had diminished since his illness. Eugene Dennis, a close aide of Browder's and rising influence in the Party, raised obliquely but unmistakably the question of Foster's possible expulsion. If there was not "a certain change" in Foster's attitude, he threatened, this would create large "problems" for the Party. One after another, the members of the National Committee disparaged Foster's motives, abilities, and political focus. It was a heady time for Browder and the Communist leadership. The party stood at its peak of membership and influence; "few liberal organizations were without a significant Communist presence" by 1939. Perhaps Browder believed that an open airing of Foster's grievances would allow him to discredit his adversary once and for all. However, international events would soon give Foster his opening, placing Browder and the whole Popular Front perspective on the defensive.[30]

The signing of the Nazi-Soviet nonaggression treaty in 1939 presented the American Communist party with a crisis of unparalleled dimensions. Suddenly the fighting in Europe was an "imperialist war"; shortly, Browder received a cable from Moscow instructing that the Americans "must cease to trail in wake of FDR, adopt independent position on all fundamental questions." One central facet of the Party's reputation among fellow travelers and liberals in the United States was its stand against Nazi aggression in Europe; with the pact of August, the antifascist stands of many Popular Front organizations were rendered meaningless. The ideology of the Popular Front had celebrated the Communists' defense of democracy in Europe and the United States; within a month or so of the pact it was common practice for journalists, politicians, and former political allies to lump Communists and Nazis together in one category: "communazis." Throughout the twenty-two months of the Nazi-Soviet Pact's effectiveness, the loyalty of American Communists to their country was openly challenged, and in the first years of World War II the Party once again had to bear the weight of official repression.

Clearly, Browder's carefully nurtured and complex relationship with the New Deal coalition and Roosevelt was in danger. Foster, who had been pressing for a more militant posture toward FDR for years, found this atmosphere congenial. The New Deal, he concluded in a lengthy article in *The Communist*, had provided some relief for those workers hardest hit by the Depression. However, such key pieces of legislation as the National Recovery Act and the Wagner Act had as yet failed to fulfill their promise to labor: five years after the creation of the CIO unionization in mass-production industries was still in a precarious state. For Foster, the New Deal had "remained under middle class domination, a bourgeois liberal at its head." Reiterating his basic objection to Browder's perspective, he proposed that what gains workers made up to that point were not the result of a diminution of class conflict, but were rather forced on the administration by mass pressure from below. Moreover, as the war in Europe escalated, workers should not allow the administration to "hog tie them under a paralyzing 'national unity.' " It is important to note that the Party's altered stand on the war was not as costly to its standing in the labor movement as it was in its relations with fellow travelers and New Deal politicians. Isolationist sentiment was still strong among the CIO rank and file, and the Party's new attitude toward FDR was shared by John L. Lewis, who continued to provide Communist organizers with important openings in the CIO and protected them against expulsion moves during this period.[31]

Browder was indicted by Roosevelt's Department of Justice for passport fraud in October 1939, and three-quarters of his time was taken up preparing for trial. Practical leadership was out of his hands. In March 1940, the hapless general secretary was finally sent to the federal penitentiary at Atlanta. Leading the obligatory chorus of outraged Communists, Foster noted solemnly that by Browder's imprisonment, "the Communist party, the working class, and the authentic progressive forces of the country have suffered a profound blow." Despite his incarceration, he stated, Browder "remains the heroic leader of the people." That same month Foster proclaimed that the Party's alliance with the New Deal was a failure. Robert Minor, a mercurial personality without particular prestige in the Party, was chosen by Browder to act as general secretary in his place. Thus, the Party entered a period in which Foster was restored to a more prominent leadership position. The remaining figures, Gil Green (head of the Young Communist League) and Dennis, were not yet solidly established. Bittelman tended to favor Foster's perspective.[32]

The period of the Nazi-Soviet Pact witnessed an outbreak of Communist-influenced strikes in several key defense industries. As early as 1931 Foster admitted in a top-level meeting that the Profintern placed particular importance on organizing workers in war industries, and the large involvement of Communist organizers in the 1941 strikes was consistent with the Party's perspective on international events. At the same time, as Maurice Isserman has pointed out, with Browder in jail, "an ideological mood resembling syndicalism took root in the party." Communist-led or -influenced strikes occurred at Allis-Chalmers in Milwaukee, which was producing turbines and engines for Navy destroyers, and at Vultee Aircraft in Southern California. Finally, when workers at North American Aviation in the Los Angeles suburb of Inglewood, California, came out, federal troops were called in to quell the strike, which was denounced by CIO and UAW leadership as well as Roosevelt. Foster wrote triumphantly that Roosevelt's use of troops at Inglewood was not an isolated act of impatience, "but a considered phase of a developing anti-labor strategy." The administration had shown itself to be "an enemy of the workers"; FDR's "whole line [is] dictated by Wall Street." Foster and the more aggressive labor wing of the Party may have relished the opportunity to attack Roosevelt and take advantage of growing worker unrest, but the strikes of early 1941 came perilously close to alienating key leaders of the CIO like Sidney Hillman, who were drawing ever closer to Roosevelt. The Communist role in the defense strikes inspired a round of antilabor red-baiting in Congress and the national media.[33]

The Communists' involvement in the defense strikes of early 1941 provided both impetus and controversy to a massive strike wave that rolled across the nation that year. In general, workers were in an aggressive mood, emboldened by large-scale government spending on defense contracts as well as by a widespread feeling that unionization was the only way that concrete gains in wages and standards of living could be achieved. In November 1940, the CIO had announced an ambitious organizing drive aimed at solidifying its heretofore uncertain status in America's central industries. The following months saw union contracts achieved at such companies as Allis-Chalmers, Weyerhauser, and International Harvester. Most important, in the spring of 1941 CIO organizers finally met success in their struggles against bitterly antiunion bastions such as the so-called "little steel" companies (especially the Bethlehem and Republic companies), and finally achieved the capitulation of the Ford Motor Company.[34]

For most Communists, however, the tide of worker militancy of 1941 was overshadowed in importance by Hitler's invasion of the Soviet Union beginning June 22, 1941. With breathtaking speed, Foster and the Communist leadership reoriented their attitude toward Roosevelt as well as labor unrest in industries vital to defense production. The defense of the Soviet Union suddenly became the primary responsibility of Communists everywhere, and unstinted production for the Allied war effort in Europe was imperative. In November, with German troops in sight of Moscow, Foster declared that strikes then being conducted by teamsters, miners, and by telephone and aircraft workers were unwise. They were danger-ous not only to the war effort, but to organized labor: they could be used as an excuse by reactionaries to draft antistrike, antiunion legislation. This, of course, had not been an issue only months earlier. He blamed the strikes on unpatriotic bosses who could not put national interests above their desire for profits. Within weeks, America was formally at war with Germany and Japan. Despite the fact that many patriotic Communists could now feel that defense of the United States and the Soviet Union were commensurate goals, American involvement in World War II would cre-ate vast challenges for the Party and its leadership.[35]

The war had a deep effect on the American labor movement, and these changes in turn had important ramifications for the Party. In general, the war years witnessed a growth in the bureaucratization of the CIO; labor relations more than ever became a matter of negotiation between union leaders and corporate and governmental officials. To some extent, the changing structure of labor relations after 1941 was foreshadowed by trends that were already in evidence during the New Deal and even ear-lier, during World War I. The war crisis mandated the creation of agen-cies whose primary goal was to manage production efficiently, and nego-tiate grievances before they resulted in strikes or unrest at the level of the shop floor. Foster, of course, was intimately acquainted with the require-ments and challenges of wartime labor-management relations. In World War II as well as World War I organized labor adhered to a no-strike policy; labor and production boards played an intrusive, if not dominant role in industrial relations in 1942 as well as in 1919. Foster had been able to utilize the government's wartime production bureaucracy to good advantage during the organizing campaigns of 1918–19, even though the gains thus achieved had proved to be ephemeral. In early 1942, declaring that "we are now in a war for our national existence," he endorsed a War Production Board and the proposals of CIO president Philip Murray for a powerful Industrial Council made up of representatives of labor, indus-try, and government. Only then, he proposed, could the necessary indus-trial efficiency be achieved. With the survival of the Soviet Union at stake, he did not hesitate to endorse the no-strike pledge made by both the AFL and CIO shortly after Pearl Harbor. Nonetheless, he did not rule out the use of strikes after "all other means of settlement have been exhausted." He also emphasized that the no-strike pledge was a temporary wartime expedient, and that "the unions should protect their legal right to strike. The unions must not surrender their primary right to settle wages, hours and working conditions in direct negotiations with the employers."[36]

To a large extent, the changing character of Foster's writings during the war must be ascribed to his forthrightly stated belief in the necessity of defending the Soviet Union and defeating Nazi Germany. During this period, his writings were never inconsistent with the requirements of Soviet foreign policy. However, he was also a keen observer of trends in the American labor movement; at no time did he embrace a perspective on the day-to-day problems of the labor movement that was not, at one time or another, also shared by prominent and effective labor leaders like John L. Lewis, Sidney Hillman, or Philip Murray. While there is no doubt that Foster's line shifted dramatically during this period, it never prevented the Communists from finding important and powerful allies in the mainstream of the labor movement. Nonetheless, by 1943 there were ominous forebodings of the price that the Communists would have to pay for their wartime stands.

In a widely circulated 1943 pamphlet entitled *Production for Victory*, Browder had proposed tying wage increases to increased productivity. For Browder, the incentive wage was a way to get around wage ceilings that had been imposed during the war. However, for many workers, especially in the auto industry, where the War Production Board approved a plan whereby the pay of all workers in a plant was to rise in proportion to increases in productivity, the incentive wage plan symbolized the hated speedup and piecework plans of an earlier era. Implementation of the plan nurtured the same kind of resentments and conflicts that earlier piecework plans had created. Walter Reuther, the ambitious vice-president of the UAW who led worker resistance to the plan, used an effective slogan to batter Communists and their allies in the union: "Down with Earl Browder's piecework." Foster attacked Reuther as a demagogue and reiterated his qualified support for both the no-strike policy and the incentive wage: "under present conditions of strong unions in the basic industries the incentive wage cannot harm labor conditions; for adequate measures can readily be provided by the unions to prevent the incentive wage from being used for speed-up and anti-union purposes." He tied his support of the incentive wage to the condition that local unions where it was established first gain the approval of their membership. Foster's stand was in line with WPB and NWLB guidelines, but he later admitted that the Communists enforced the no-strike pledge too rigidly "where shop grievance stoppages were concerned."[37]

Foster's positions on the no-strike pledge and the incentive pay plan reflect a desultory yet consistent evolution in his views during the years of the New Deal and World War II. The brand of radical syndicalism that

Foster brought to the Communist movement had been nurtured in an environment that was altogether different from the one that labor activists faced by 1942. Despite its shortcomings, the labor legislation of the New Deal created a new and often more favorable context for organizers. The New Deal and the vast expansion of government's role during World War II brought changes that were on a different order of magnitude than those wrought during World War I. Foster was obviously quite conscious of the increased importance of government in the arena of labor relations, and his writings often included the caveat that the gains workers achieved during the New Deal and the war were precarious and could be undone by hostile legislation or inattention to political organizing by labor.

At the same time, Foster was undoubtedly aware of the gains made by unions in the new atmosphere. In the Communist-led United Electrical Workers, for instance, James Matles and Julius Empsak were able to gain impressive concessions from management during the war through joint management-labor production committees. The union grew from 154,000 to 600,000 members during the war despite strict observance of the no-strike pledge. Moreover, in this union, the CP shift on incentive pay was not especially harmful; the union was able to negotiate contract clauses that minimized the more exploitative features of the incentive pay system. There was far less opposition to the concept in the UEW than in the UAW.[38]

More generally, Foster was evolving from his earlier syndicalism toward a growing sense of the importance of political action. "All economic questions are now taking on a political character. More and more wages and hours are being settled by government mediation and arbitration boards," he concluded in 1941. In such an arena, it was as important to maintain relations with the CIO leadership and hence a political lever with the Roosevelt administration as it was to keep in touch with the needs of the rank and file. As for the old syndicalist credo of keeping politics out of the union, Foster noted in 1939 that "the unions are concerned with wages, hours and working conditions. These questions have all become political issues."[39]

Thus, by the end of World War II, Foster's syndicalism, the core of beliefs and assumptions that had nurtured his radicalism since the 1910s, seemed to require yet another compromise. Jay Fox, years earlier, had proposed that a syndicalist never fights against "facts." Yet, the changes of the Roosevelt years were so profound and decisive that they in effect set Foster loose from his own history. His syndicalism would survive, but in a transmogrified form, devoid of the suppleness that memory provides strategy.

Chapter 11

"BROWDERISM"

The strangest result . . . of the Duclos article is to bring
forward Comrade Foster as the foremost Marxist.
Whatever his qualities in other respects, it is well known
to all who have had extended collaboration with
Comrade Foster that he has never understood Marxism,
that this is not his strong side. Comrade Foster is an
eclectic, subject to all sorts of theoretical influences;
and in addition he suffers from fear of responsibility;
he is by character irresolute and wavering on principle.
—Earl Browder

THE PERIOD encompassing the Communist party's support of the war
might have been a relatively unchallenging one for the Party. For many
Communists it was a time of unstinting patriotism; the crisis in Europe
required not professional revolutionaries but men and women willing to
devote themselves to the relatively uncomplex task of national defense.
The revival of the Popular Front after 1941 meant that the Party could
return to a politics of collaboration rather than confrontation; a soothing
measure of acceptance and legitimacy was the result. The progressive policies of the Roosevelt administration and the president's support for organized labor and the CIO made the Communists' tasks even easier.
However, there is no doubt that the Party's leadership worried about the
shape of policy and politics in the postwar world. After all, the majority
of the Party's leaders in 1943 had entered the movement in the 1920s; the
years following the end of the First World War had been comparatively
dark ones for both the Communist party and the labor movement.

Thus, the Party's theorists searched for a formula that would allow it
to avoid a repetition of the defeats of an earlier era. For Earl Browder, the
Popular Front was perceived not as a temporary exigency or a "maneuver," but a more or less permanent state of affairs. In a remarkable pamphlet entitled *Victory and After*, published shortly after his release from
Atlanta Penitentiary in 1942, he predicted that peace and cooperation
between the capitalist powers and the Soviet Union would continue after
the war. Here, he was beginning to tread on uncertain ground, moving
beyond the tactic of wartime alliance toward a theory about the emerging

Foster with Earl Browder, 1945.

character of world politics. Browder, who once confessed to Philip Jaffe that "When I was in Moscow I was like a child," seemed to be gaining ever more confidence as an "independent" theorist; the ideas about the postwar world found in *Victory and After* had no counterpart in Soviet pronouncements at the time. But in the spring of 1943, reacting to pressure and criticism from the Allies and intent on maximizing Western support for the struggle against the Nazis, Stalin formally dissolved the Comintern. While the Soviets would find ways to maintain their liaisons with other Communist parties notwithstanding the demise of the Comintern apparatus, American contacts with Moscow throughout the war were minimal, compared to earlier periods. Partly as a result, the perception arose among important American Communists, Browder included, that they would be freer to make their own decisions, and henceforth less encumbered by the aura of conspiracy that was part of their historical inheritance.[1]

However, as the Allies began to plan for victory in Europe the question of the Communist role in the postwar political environment became more urgent. For American Communists, an entire set of policies became associated with the outcome of the meeting in Teheran between Stalin, Roosevelt, and Churchill in December 1943—above all, the declaration in their joint communiqué that the Soviet Union, the United States, and Britain would "work together in the war and the peace that will follow," a peace that will be "enduring."[2]

For Browder, the Teheran communiqué represented nothing less than the basis for an entire theory about the nature of class relations in the postwar period. The agreement, he thought, was not merely a diplomatic instrument, a temporary accommodation of interests: "it means what it says, and it does not mean something else." It was, he stated, "history's greatest turning point," the "only hope for civilization in our time." To begin with, he proposed, the pact signified that the capitalist world powers had finally accepted the idea that the Soviet Union was a legitimate member of the "family of nations," that it was "in this world to stay"; and on the other hand, the Soviet Union would not seek to extend socialism into Western Europe. The postwar period would see the emergence of a consensus on democratic values and institutions, and in the United States it would be imperative for Communists to help foster "national unity" around such a progressive agenda. Toward that end, he announced in a speech given in Bridgeport, Connecticut, he would even be willing to shake hands with J. P. Morgan if that would promote the cause of peace and unity. After all, he proposed, "class divisions or political groupings" in the postwar world will "have no significance now except as they reflect one side or the other" of the issue of whether to support the "spirit of Teheran."[3]

In the weeks that followed, Browder erected an ambitious albeit precarious political scaffolding around the Teheran rapprochement. His boldest statement of his aims came during a speech at an enlarged meeting of the Party's National Committee in early January of 1944. The centerpiece of his program was the idea, symbolized by the Teheran agreement, that "capitalism and socialism have begun to find the way to peaceful coexistence and collaboration in the same world." In the United States, socialism could no longer be raised as an issue, because "It is my considered judgment that the American people are so ill-prepared subjectively for any deep-going change in the direction of socialism that post-war plans with such an aim would not unite the nation but would further divide it. And they would divide and weaken precisely the democratic and progressive camp, while they would unite and strengthen the most reactionary forces. In their practical effect they would help the anti-Teheran forces come to power in the United States."[4] Instead, American politics and labor were marked by liberal consensus, and American Communists should not actively oppose the slogan of "free enterprise," the new rallying cry of anti–New Deal conservatives.[5]

In one meeting, Browder abruptly proposed the dissolution of the Communist party "as a Party," and the substitution of a "Communist Political Association." The change, he concluded, would best reflect what the Party had in fact become: one of many "democratic and progressive groupings which operate . . . through the two-party system." The new Communist organization could expect to be "in a long-term alliance with forces much larger than itself."[6] None of the National Committee members present objected to Browder's proposals. Yet, at an annual Lenin memorial meeting convened in Madison Square Garden shortly after the meeting, Browder's proposals were met with only polite applause, and a number of cadres walked out of the arena after the midpoint of his speech, when he reasserted that socialism would cease to be a public aim of the Communists. Nonetheless, Browder moved confidently ahead with his new program. His theories represented an attempt to grapple with the political implications of the Popular Front for peacetime, but more was involved. In the first place, Browder was convinced of his own personal importance, not only to the Party, but to the progressive coalition surrounding Roosevelt. He was enamored with the new role of the Party in American life, its apparent acceptance and importance on the left wing of the mainstream of American politics. Thus, his personal ambitions melded with the needs and desires of a whole generation of Communists who had come into the Party during its "heyday." Both were dissatisfied with the old conspiratorial, sectarian style of Communist politics, and yearned for a measure of acceptance and legitimacy.[7]

William Foster offered his version of the postwar period at the same time Browder did, but with far less theoretical elaboration. In December 1943, the same month that Browder gave his Bridgeport speech, he revealed his fears of a far more dangerous postwar period in which a resurgent right wing could revive a "rampant American imperialism." The embodiment of the reactionary forces, according to Foster, was the Republican Party, which, if it was victorious in the presidential elections of 1944, could be depended upon to undermine the accomplishments of the New Deal. Moreover, a Republican administration, he wrote, "would encourage reaction all over the world" and "sow seeds for World War III." Republican rhetoric about the need for a return to "free enterprise" masked the desire of monopolists to reassert their power after the war. Communists, he asserted, should counter the free enterprise slogan by supporting the Roosevelt program for a new economic bill of rights: guaranteed jobs, social security, and national health insurance. The growing power of monopoly capital, "the poison source of fascism all over the world," would have to be "drastically curbed and eventually broken." This was in sharp contrast to Browder's feeling that decisive elements of monopoly capital could be won over to FDR's progressive program; it would later be cited by Browder as "the beginning of my head-on collision" with Foster's policies in the postwar period. Foster's perspective in early 1944 was shaped by the apparent fragility of the gains labor had made during the war, and also, undoubtedly, by the dark projections of a number of influential economists, sociologists, and political leaders who feared the domestic consequences of demobilization, foreseeing the possibility of dangerous social conflict.

On the right, by 1944 there was a growing and insistent clamor in influential business and corporate circles for a rollback of the "socialist" New Deal. This was illustrated most explicitly by a rightward shift in Congress and the swift passage of the Smith-Connally War Labor Disputes Act in June 1943, which gave the government increased authority to limit union activities. For many in the labor movement, the Smith-Connally Act represented an ominous attack on the structure of labor relations that had been built around the Wagner Act. At the level of the shop floor, militant employer opposition to federal labor legislation and unionizing drives had emerged with renewed force by early 1944. Thus, there was ample evidence to support Foster's projection of an uncertain and possibly hostile environment for labor during the reconversion period.[8]

We know of William Foster's reaction to Browder's startling initiatives primarily through the testimony of his friend, Sam Darcy. At the plenum where the momentous changes were proposed, Darcy took him aside and asked him if he agreed with the new line. Foster, according to Darcy, was in ill health and was "shaking as a leaf." He replied that he was against Browder's position, but could not take a public stand because he had been warned that any "factional" behavior might result in his expulsion. The two met for lunch, where Darcy pressed Foster to join him in presenting a dissenting report. Foster would not budge, but was visibly upset. Since Darcy had to leave the plenum early, the two were not able to consult further. However, the following week Darcy went to New York where he worked for hours with Foster at his tiny apartment on Nelson Avenue in the Bronx, formulating an opposition position. Foster decided to draft a dissenting letter to other members of the Party leadership, but he was clearly under a great deal of stress and was extremely concerned to avoid the appearance of organizing a faction. His behavior, from Darcy's account, suggests that he was plagued by intense doubts and uncertainty about the course he was about to take. Given the uncertain state of his health, as well as the fact that he was presenting a dissent without apparent sanction from Moscow, Foster's stand was a courageous one.

The Communist movement, obviously, offered no pensions for aging apostates.[9]

His letter was circulated only among the top leadership sometime between January 7 and January 20. It cannot be considered a factional document, since he could depend on no faction to support him. Nor was it a grab for power, since there is no evidence his appeal was aimed at the one audience that could possibly endow his critique with a larger significance, the Soviet Communist party. Foster, who had been sternly rebuked in an earlier time by Stalin for his factional behavior, was aware that his career was once again in danger. In demanding that the National Committee meet in special session to consider his critique of a policy that had already been approved, he was clearly violating the central tenet of "democratic centralism." Yet, what is perhaps most striking about Foster's letter are its theoretical pretensions. The objections that he laid out to the "Teheran thesis" are premised on what he called "some of the most basic principles of Marxism-Leninism." Browder's report, he indignantly proclaimed, projected the dissolution of class warfare in a "smoothly working national unity. The self-aggrandizing and imperialistic ambitions of the American ruling class would be tamed for the most part, and peace would descend on the family of nations. Differences of ideology would largely disappear."[10]

Foster's long letter to the National Committee is a remarkable document because it represents not only a competent critique of Browder's Teheran thesis, but an important shift in his own outlook. His career in the American radical and Communist movements had always been informed by a fundamentally improvisational outlook; here, he is engaged more than ever in the uncharacteristic role of prognosticator. In the past, the task of working out *post hoc* theoretical justifications for his policies had been left to others, notably Alexander Bittelman. His letter of March 1944 was entirely self-authored, according to Darcy. Yet, he remained self-conscious about his theoretical shortcomings. He admitted in one meeting that his "principal weakness" had always been a "lack of theoretical growth," that he had always conceived of himself as an organizational and trade union "specialist," and had thus been unable to "gain a broad comprehensive view of all the tasks of the Party."[11]

Despite its reliance on theoretical arguments, Foster's letter represented an instinctive reversion to the older categories of the class war. His thinking on almost all matters remained sensitive to what was happening in the labor movement and on the shop floor. By 1944 powerful rank-and-file opposition to the no-strike policy had emerged in a number of industries. Foster noted that some delegates to the plenum had interpreted Browder's report as implying a no-strike policy in the postwar period, given Browder's perspective of continued cooperation. While Foster remained adamant about the no-strike pledge during the war, he was clearly not committed to the idea of extending the agreement to peacetime. The idea of continuing the no-strike pledge "is nonsense," he wrote. "It would disarm the trade unions in the face of their enemies. The Teheran Conference did not abolish the class struggle in the United States."[12]

In February, Browder convened a special meeting of the National Committee to consider Foster's letter, which had plenty of time to circulate among the leadership. Darcy and Foster began the meeting by reiterating their positions. Foster was especially blunt and plain spoken. He made a speech of ten thousand words, an impressive achievement for a man of sixty-four years in precarious health. Browder, he asserted, was making a "serious mistake." He was placing too much faith on the influence of the few progressive "big capitalists" associated with Roosevelt. The bulk of capitalists are, simply, reactionaries, he proclaimed, and "we cannot cooperate with them." While Teheran opened the road for an enduring peace and social progress after the war, the Party had to be prepared for opposition to the Teheran perspective and a rejection of the idea of "national unity" by the main sector of American finance capital. Browder's report "completely left out the role American imperialism has been playing and will play in the sense of sabotaging the Teheran agreement." In the United States, there would be no "spontaneous industrial boom" following the war; "Capitalists have not become such saints that they will start doubling the wages of the workers" as a way of stimulating the internal markets and averting an economic slowdown. In this atmosphere, "it would be hard to conceive of anything more harmful to the workers than a no-strike policy in peace times in the U.S." Foster cited the postwar labor-management collaboration following World War I as a "surrender to the bourgeois." On the political front, the "forces of reaction" could be depended upon to exert every effort to attempt to defeat Roosevelt; therefore, it was of absolutely vital importance for the Communists to participate in the election struggle. "Our job is to join other forces to support Roosevelt for a fourth term."[13]

Foster's dramatic presentation was met by unanimous condemnation. For years, Browder had been cultivating the impression not only that Foster was out of touch and irrelevant, but that he represented an older, sectarian phase of the Party's history. Now, the reaction to Foster's report played on these conceptions. Gil Green accused Foster of "giving aid to the enemy" by exacerbating divisions in the Party. Eugene Dennis, perhaps the most unctuous of Browder's defenders, asserted that Foster's consistent criticism of Browder through the Democratic Front and war years showed that he "does not accept nor understand that Comrade Browder is the foremost, the outstanding leader of our Party. And also that Comrade Browder is a great leader of the international labor and Communist movements." According to Dennis, Foster was an instinctual troublemaker who "has become, consciously or unconsciously, the victim of factional considerations and a factional approach." Furthermore, if Foster continued to raise objections, he "may destroy his own prestige and usefulness in and to the Party."[14]

"Blackie" Meyers, a trade union "influential" associated with the National Maritime Union, noted that Foster "has a lot of prestige in our industry," and that "I am still a little shaken—this sounds strange, saying shaken—from reading that statement of Foster whom I have admired for years, since I was a kid. . . ." The statement, according to Meyers, was a "terrific mistake, and it is my hope that he tears the damn thing up; it does not belong in the Party." Others were more condescending, seeking to denigrate Foster's mental abilities. Dennis proposed that Foster brought up the issues he did because he was "confused." Browder sought to administer the coup de grace: "I think Comrade Foster is terribly confused, tragically confused; I think he has lost his way. The world has become too complex for him. But that in no way minimizes the damage he can do by clinging to his confusion." Despite the overwhelming opposition to Foster's ideas, there was a heavy air of defensiveness at the meeting. There was a consciousness of the "danger" of Foster's criticisms, and palpable concern about his intentions, best reflected in an apprehensive final question, posed by Gil Green: "does this mean you will bring your position to the Party?" Foster replied in the negative.[15]

Soon after the meeting, Foster requested that Browder cable a summary of his objections to Dimitroff. Foster probably did not expect a favorable judgment from Dimitroff, who was the foremost ideologist of the Popular Front and a consistent defender of Browder's perspectives. In the past, the powerful Soviet official had accused him of representing "certain sectarian remnants" in the Party. Nonetheless, the cable was sent, and Dimitroff in turn cabled Foster advising him to withdraw his opposition to Browder. So sure was Browder of his position that he had sent the entire text of Foster's January letter to Dimitroff.[16]

Foster toed the line. During the height of the controversy, when he was pressing his views most vigorously in the leadership circles of the Party, he stated in a speech carried on nationwide radio by CBS that the Teheran agreement ensured an "orderly, peaceful world after the victory," that it marked "the most decisive turning point in all modern history," and that Communists would no longer contest the ideal of free enterprise in their political activities. In July, he parroted: "As Browder has said, [the] hysterical shouting [for free enterprise] cannot be countered by demands for socialism or even for government ownership of key industries. . . ." He gave a keynote speech at the opening convention of the Communist Political Association. Foster's disciplined duplicity earned him the distrust of Party members who, like him, were dissatisfied with the Teheran perspective at the time. "So, in the secret files of the National Office, a letter of *disagreement*; but, for the party's membership and the toiling masses, a speech of *agreement* with the Party line," one long-time ally in the faction fights of the 1920s, Harrison George, bitterly reflected. Foster's posturing signified that he did not trust the membership, according to this cadre. On the other hand, Browder again made it clear to Foster by back channels that there would be "serious results" if he opposed the formation of the CPA. While Foster backed down, at least in public, Sam Darcy refused to recant. By summer, he had been expelled for opposing the dissolution of the Party; Foster chaired the hearing.[17] Once again, William Foster willingly submerged his convictions and feelings in the interests of Party discipline. It was obviously a period of great stress for him. Subjected to private humiliation by the leadership of the Party, he publicly retreated from his earlier invocation of his most cherished beliefs. He oscillated between abject belief and nervous uncertainty, dogma and compromise.

Nonetheless, the issues Foster had raised in his anguished dissent became increasingly salient in the last months of the war. At one level, the Communists were making significant gains as a result of their new orientation. The Communist Political Association played an important role in the activities of CIO Political Action Committee, which, despite the red-baiting of Dewey and the Republicans, contributed to Roosevelt's reelection in 1944. CIO political action committees had perhaps more of an impact at the local level, where they prevented the reelection of a number of virulently anti-Communist Congressmen, including Martin Dies of Texas. Thus, Browder's thinking was seemingly vindicated: the Communists by late 1944 had solidified and extended their influence in the left wing of the Democratic party. However, it was in the turbulent arena of union politics that Browder's Teheran perspective would meet its greatest challenges. It was here that Foster's assertion that the Teheran agreement and the end of the war would not result in an end to class conflict echoed most loudly.[18]

As the end of the war loomed closer, worker militancy surged dramatically. Increasingly unwilling to abide by the no-strike pledge, resentful at the continuation of the speedup, and concerned about unemployment and economic contraction after the war, workers in a variety of industries went on strike. This strike wave, however, illuminated more profoundly than ever the consequences of labor's marriage to the apparatus of wartime production. Often, union leadership was held responsible by government agencies for the enforcement of the no-strike pledge. Violation of contracts and agreements had implications for the survival of vital union prerogatives such as maintenance of membership protection, which were granted or revoked by government boards. A surge of unauthorized strikes in 1944 threatened the political standing of union leaders who had been increasingly drawn into a web of bureaucratic relations with government officials. This was especially true in the auto industry. In the UAW, the flagship union of the CIO, rank-and-file militants summoned a powerful challenge to the no-strike pledge in 1944. While the union's policy was allowed to stand as a result of a mail ballot, more members ended up going on strike during the war than voted to renew the pledge. In the UAW, the powerful Communist presence firmly aligned itself with the no-strike pledge. This policy was an integral aspect of Browder's Teheran perspective, but it created confusion. The idea of postwar class cooperation alienated many organizers, and helped to put what one organizer called a "stigma" on the left-center alliance the Communists had carefully cultivated in the auto industry.[19]

Thus, the no-strike pledge became far more than an issue of patriotism in 1944. What made the issue so explosive for the Communists was not only the wave of wildcat strikes, but the question, made suddenly legitimate by the Teheran "perspective," of how best to maintain industrial peace in the postwar world. The most salient factor in the thinking of CIO leaders in 1944 was the prospect of widespread layoffs, a sharp economic contraction, and a corresponding decline in union strength following the war. CIO leaders determined that their organizations could not benefit from a trial of strength with large corporations, flushed with profits, after the war. Thus, in March 1945 the CIO drafted a "Labor-Management Charter" with William Green of the AFL and Eric Johnston, president of the U.S. Chamber of Commerce. The document endorsed a postwar détente in which labor would offer to defend "a system of private competitive capitalism" and "the inherent right and responsibility of management to direct the operations of an enterprise" in return for management support of the Wagner Act and a liberal wage and employment policy. In general, Browder's perspective fitted nicely with that of CIO president Philip Murray. However, Communists and their allies went even further than Murray in supporting national service legislation that the CIO adamantly opposed, and openly projecting an extension of the no-strike pledge after the war.[20]

By 1945, Browder's endorsement of the central concepts of the Labor-Management Charter was consistent with his belief that in the end, the Communists could "enlist capital in the regulation of capital, overcoming its worst abuses." In general, Browder's vision was one of a depoliticized workplace, a milieu devoid of inevitable class conflict. There would be no "technical problems of production" during the reconversion period, he exulted, since "management and labor working with government, have demonstrated that they have the ability to solve any and all technical problems."[21]

Foster betrayed far less enthusiasm for such panaceas, even though Browder's "too uncritical acceptance" of the Labor-Management Charter was far down on the list of grievances he held against him. While he had endorsed increased production during wartime, and suggested that union work rules would have to be modified, he made it clear that unions should "secure guarantees that the alterations made shall be continued only for the duration of the war." Moreover, workers and unions should "insist uncompromisingly upon the maintenance of collective bargaining during the war," as well as the right to organize and to establish the open shop. He offered an endorsement of the Labor-Management Charter, but with the jarring proviso that the unions "must be on guard against the injurious class collaborationism of Social Democracy, which chained labor to the chariot wheel of reactionary capitalist interests." In general, Foster was positively disposed to labor-management councils, which he saw as "an important democratic development of the war years," and which, he thought, should be extended into the postwar period. Here, he was echoing CIO leaders like Walter Reuther who saw the committees as the beginnings of "industrial democracy," the opening wedge in a struggle for workers' control in the postwar period. Foster's postwar perspective would be far closer to that of Walter Reuther and his militant constituency in the UAW than to that of the more compromising forces of the CIO "center." His endorsement of postwar employer-worker cooperation was heavily conditional: it must, he proposed, be predicated on workers' rights to adequate representation in industry and government; it must not "degenerate into the speed-up practices of the 1920s, which almost cut the heart out of the labor movement," and it depended upon a "systematic and rapid increase in the real wages of the workers." These kinds of qualifications were almost entirely absent from Browder's rhetoric at the time.[22]

Foster's published and unpublished writings during the period of the Teheran thesis are in general more conditional and complex than Browder's writings were at the time. Yet, it cannot be said that Foster's outlook can be simply summed up as advocating a return to the "old verities": his recognition of the new role of politics represented a significant departure, a stance that he would never have entertained until the late 1930s, and then only hesitatingly. Nonetheless, Foster's syndicalism began to reassert itself by 1945, albeit in a new and more complex atmosphere, where questions of production had increasingly become affairs of the state. In a draft of an article that Browder did not approve for publication, he wrote that "the very heart of . . . efforts for national unity will lie in the relations between the workers and the employers." Despite his acceptance of the need for political action, Foster would continue to hold to this conception most tenaciously. In addition, he harbored doubts that state intervention would be a permanent feature of American economic life.[23]

It is impossible to know if Foster was certain that his critique of Browder's Teheran thesis would finally achieve vindication. A noteworthy characteristic of his career had always been the noncommittal nature of his political pronouncements; despite brief periods of orthodoxy and theoretical posturing, he was always willing to be disproven by forces larger than he. Thus, for nearly a year after his dramatic confrontation with Earl Browder, he blended easily into the changing political scenery. Signals from the Soviet Union suggested that the Teheran perspective was an appropriate one: in a speech in late 1944, Stalin declared that "the alliance between the USSR, Great Britain and the United States is founded not on casual, short-lived considerations but on vital and lasting interests."[24] Throughout 1944, Foster's prophecy of escalating world tensions and an aggressive, "greedy" American imperialism abroad found little confirmation in world events. At home, despite increasing labor unrest, Roosevelt's reelection seemed to preempt the likelihood of any "triumph of reactionaries" in the immediate postwar years.

In the first months of 1945, however, difficulties emerged in U.S.–Soviet relations that did not bode well for American Communists. Roosevelt's sudden death in April created uncertainty; no one seemed to be able to predict the character of Truman's leadership. At the same time, Averill Harriman and other prominent figures in the Democratic leadership began to advocate a far stricter interpretation of the recently concluded agreements at Yalta. Harriman, who had been urging a tougher line with the Soviet Union since late 1944, now warned Truman that America faced a "barbarian invasion of Europe" by the Communists unless firm measures were taken immediately. Truman met with Soviet foreign minister Vyacheslav Molotov weeks after Roosevelt's death to warn him bluntly to "carry out your agreements" regarding free elections in Eastern Europe. In the midst of this new atmosphere of uncertainty, in what could accurately be called the first months of the Cold War, the appearance of an article sharply critical of Browder in the French Communist journal *Cahiers du Communisme* was an event of decisive importance for American Communists.

The article was by Jacques Duclos, a leader of the powerful French Communist party. The article itself was considered to be an important indication of Soviet attitudes, since it quoted liberally from Foster's January 1944 letter to the National Committee, which, it was supposed, had been circulated only among the leadership of the American and Soviet parties. American policymakers pored over Duclos's article as carefully as did American Communists. It constituted, according to some observers, an important indication of Moscow's confrontational intentions in Europe after the war.[25]

While framed as an explanation to French Communists of the recent changes in the American party, Duclos's article represented a stern rebuke to Browder's leadership. Browder had, according to Duclos, drawn "erroneous conclusions in no wise flowing from a Marxist analysis of the postwar situation," and "despite declarations regarding recognition of the principles of Marxism, one is witnessing a notorious revision of Marxism on the part of Browder and his supporters, a revision which is expressed in the concept of a long-term class peace in the United States, of the possibility of the suppression of the class struggle in the postwar period and of the establishment of harmony between capital and labor." He accused the American Communists of "deforming in a radical way the meaning of the Teheran declaration and . . . sowing dangerous opportunist illusions which will exercise a negative influence on the American labor movement if they are not met with the necessary reply."[26]

In certain respects, the Duclos article is an ambiguous document. It does not constitute a point-by-point refutation of specific policies of the American Communists; indeed, the orientations of the French and American parties were remarkably similar at the time. The French Communists, though obviously confronted with a different situation than the Americans, were members of a united front coalition government after 1945. They, like the Americans, deliberately minimized their socialist goals and envisioned a period of uninterrupted production and class peace after the war.[27] Perhaps the gravamen of the article was its clear rebuke of Browder's projection that postwar Europe would be reconstituted on a "bourgeois democratic" basis. Stalin probably considered the article a means of exerting diplomatic pressure on the Truman Administration. At the same time, the scolding tone of the document and its unmistakable rejection of Browder's Teheran thesis meant that it was intended to stir the American Communists to drastic changes.

Duclos quoted extensively and approvingly from Foster's letter of January 1944, and portrayed him in unmistakable terms as the embattled defender of the Marxist-Leninist tradition in the United States. Thus, when the Party's leadership convened to discuss the article, Foster suddenly found himself at an obvious and distinct advantage over his rival of many years. What is striking and characteristic, however, is his initial hesitance in seizing the offensive against Browder in the first emergency meetings of the national committee after the arrival of the letter, despite having received Duclos's unambiguous endorsement.[28]

Nonetheless, at meetings of the National Board in May and June, one Communist after another reversed position in abject displays of repentance for their earlier "revisionist" stands. As one Communist leader reflected, cadres who had once called Browder a genius, "a great Marxist," and "our beloved leader," were within days relegating him to the category of "betrayer of the working class." Those who had only months earlier contemplated Foster's expulsion would soon be moving to beatify him. Browder, though, steadfastly refused to repudiate his earlier stands. For long periods he retreated to his office at the Party's headquarters, refusing to see visitors. His aloof and unapproachable demeanor did little at this time to endear him to his former followers. It was not until the middle of June, after continued long discussions of the errors of "Browderism," that Foster felt that he was on strong enough ground to attack Browder in unambiguous terms, criticizing his "bureaucratic" and "undemocratic" methods, and the "system of supercentralization" that he alone had supposedly created to manage the Party. He admitted, like most others, that sharp criticism of Browder was "no pleasant task." However, Browder's "revisionism must be ruthlessly exposed and combatted," he asserted, because it "plays into the hands of the worst enemies of the workers and the people—the finance capitalists, who are the generators of imperialist aggression, fascism and war." In a sardonic aside, he proposed that Browder's policies had created a whole category of Communists who were "worrying more about cajoling the enlightened capitalists than organizing the workers."[29]

The climactic episode in the whole affair came at the Communist Political Association's emergency convention in late July. There, Browder was removed as president of the association, and a new leadership was elected, consisting of Foster, Eugene Dennis, and John Williamson. The convention reconstituted itself as the Communist party. At the convention, Foster still betrayed some uncertainty about his course of action. In his hotel room prior to his keynote speech, preparing to deliver the final indictment of "Browderism," he wondered aloud to his aides whether or not his actions would create a new factional situation in the Party such as had existed in the 1920s. However, when he was called upon to give Browder's political reputation the *coup de grace*, his language belied little uncertainty. His indictment rested at least partly on a familiar concept, central to "Fosterism." Browder's central personal failing, he suggested at the meeting, was a "reverence for the spoken word."[30]

Earl Browder was expelled from the Communist party by a unanimous vote of the National Committee in February 1946. His removal did not result in an exodus of personal followers, as had been the case following the earlier expulsions of Jay Lovestone and the Trotskyists around James Cannon. He did not seek formally to organize an opposition, but instead lurked rather ominously on the fringes of the Party for years. He circulated a political newsletter aimed at Party members, hoping in the meantime that a change in the world situation might result in his rehabilitation. Surprisingly, in May 1946 he was granted a visa by the Soviet Embassy. He traveled to Moscow, where he was welcomed and entertained by high-ranking Soviet officials, including Lozovsky and Molotov. He was given a position as distributor of Soviet scientific books in the United States, a post that he held until mid-1949. His final estrangement from the Party came only in 1952. Foster himself was refused Soviet visas on several occasions in the postwar period; this undoubtedly raised questions in the American Party about his standing in Moscow. Indeed, confidential assessments of Foster in the Soviet Union remained negative. One review concluded that "despite his accomplishments in the Communist movement, he made serious mistakes in his party work," referring to his "factional struggle" in the 1920s, his consort with Trotskyists in his grouping, and his disagreement with the Comintern over new unions in 1928. In a report on Foster and Eugene Dennis, Gerhart Eisler, a German Communist who was a Comintern representative in the United States in the 1930s, concluded that both men, while "honest and devoted," were "not fit to lead masses" because they "often talk inconsistently and interpret American problems as foreigners." Surely the fact that Browder was allowed the pretensions of "government in exile" status grated on Foster. Browder's expulsion had not been dictated or even suggested from abroad; thus, doubts would continue to linger about the correctness of this course of action.[31]

No one could contest, however, that the American Party had entered a new phase after 1945. Suddenly, William Foster was endowed with unprecedented authority, and this would have far-reaching and profound implications during the Party's next two decades. His triumph was largely a personal one. Despite his position as national chairman, he had developed no large factional following previous to Browder's downfall. No group of followers and confidants existed whom he could place in key positions. Thus, few leaders of the uppermost echelons were replaced or purged; the National Committee continued to be composed primarily of individuals who had formerly been identified with Browder's discredited regime. This occasioned some anxiety among cadres who thought Foster was not going far enough in forcing a catharsis. Sam Darcy, for instance, from his perspective outside the Party, worried privately that Browder's "palace guard" remained influential despite the exit of their leader, and that Foster, now sixty-four years old, had not acted decisively enough to ensure a true Marxist-Leninist character for the leadership should he pass from the scene. Yet, because each of the former Browderites was tainted to some extent, their positions were precarious. Ironically, Foster emerged as the only leader with some claim to undeviating principle and Marxist-Leninist clairvoyance. It is important, therefore, to outline Foster's world view as it developed in 1945, when he finally stood on the brink of more or less undisputed leadership of the American Communist Party.[32]

Perhaps the most salient feature of Foster's thinking during this period was a near obsession with the bankruptcy of Browder's former policies, or, more accurately, what came to be known as "Browderism." Foster was not a dogmatist by instinct; his hesitance and uncertainty when called upon to exercise leadership in the initial campaign against Browder betrayed this fact. However, following his ascension to the chairmanship of the Party he launched a campaign of ideological "purification," a campaign that would be carried on with varying intensity for years. According to Foster, Browderism represented above all a shrinking from the class struggle, an abandonment of the idea of capitalism as a system of human exploitation, the end of the concept of the Party as a Leninist vanguard, and a rejection of the Leninist theory of imperialism as the final stage of capitalism. Browder had attempted nothing less than the "fastening of a right-wing bourgeois liberalism upon our Party," he thundered. For the campaign against Browderism, Foster donned the garb of high priest of Marxism-Leninism, but it was an ill-fitting garment. He simply lacked the knowledge of Marxist theory necessary to carry such a pretension successfully; it was as if the vehemence of his rhetoric alone could compensate for deeper uncertainties.[33]

Nonetheless, as penance for the sins of the Browder era, Foster proposed a frightening campaign for ideological conformity. "As never before," he averred, "we must train our Party in the fundamentals of Marxism-Leninism. To this end we must check over the curricula, teaching personnel and textbooks of all our schools. We must reexamine all our recent literature. We must prepare new propaganda and agitation material in harmony with our line. We must especially be alert to eliminate, not only Browder's wrong theories, but also all those opportunist ways of thinking and working that have developed. . . ." Moreover, a new leadership at all levels was required, complete with background checks of members' "qualifications," including their "social background, their Marxist-Leninist training, their previous Party record, their degree of participation in the present error, their connections with trade unions and mass organizations, [and] their present attitude toward Browder's revisionism. . . ." This call for an inquiry into the backgrounds of Party leaders was ironic, considering that Foster's history as a Wobbly, AFL organizer, and seller of War Bonds was far from pure, and had continually been dredged up by opponents of his in an earlier era. Strangely enough, at the same time that he made this strident call for conformity, he complained that one of the great weaknesses of Browder's leadership was that he stifled discussion and created a bureaucratic atmosphere in the Party.[34]

He seemed to be aiming for more than authority in its purely functional sense; he seemed to believe it was necessary to create an aura of unassailable moral authority around his leadership.

The campaign against Browderism showed Foster at his most extremist, but there is little evidence that he was imposing this mood on the Party membership. "Browderism" was excoriated at all levels. As noted, Browder's departure did not inspire a large exodus from the Party; in the immediate postwar period, membership remained relatively stable at around fifty thousand.[35] The remarkable persistence of "Browderism" as a derogatory political category suggests that the appeal of the campaign went beyond the pages of the Party's journalism. In certain respects, the crusade against Browder's "deviations" had all the appeal of a fundamentalist religious revival; one writer later characterized the political "correction" of the period as a type of "hysteria."[36]

Significantly, for Foster as well as others in the leadership, one of the main problems with Browderism was that it was insufficiently theoretical. Morris Childs, a member of the National Committee, implied as much when offering his analysis of the now-disgraced policies: "It is my opinion that all of us were influenced by our capitalist environment and ideology, that we did not develop our general tactical policy on the basis of general theory, but rather developed it empirically." Why was theory suddenly divorced from experience? Related to the feelings Childs expressed was a pervasive sense in the Party literature that Browderism had not provided a coherent set of norms by which the Party could identify itself in opposition to its surroundings. Hence the search for theory became, at one level at least, a search for principle. In his brilliant account of this crisis period in the Party's history, former *Daily Worker* editor Joseph Starobin reflected that the character of the Party's policies in the 1930s had seemed to weaken the sense of "revolutionary community" among Communists. Trade union leaders had been given more political flexibility and independence; shop and union fractions were abolished, and Communists, "participating in the wider world of public life . . . became subjects to all its temptations." For Starobin, in the 1930s the "revolutionary community tended to become a pseudo-community." A large part of what Foster promised and others were seeking, in the campaign against "Browderism," was a revitalization of original premises. Foster himself offered a symbolic connection with an idealized past and tradition; his return to leadership was invariably presented in the Party press as the "return of a veteran." Outside the party as well, Foster's ascension to leadership was taken to represent a reassertion of revolutionary purpose by the American Party at a time when Soviet-American relations were deteriorating. The Duclos article provided a perfect context for the revival of the House Committee on Un-American Activities in 1945. One member declared that the committee wanted to know "whether the Communists are still planning to destroy or overthrow the American system of Government."[37]

What was the nature of Foster's fundamentalist program? After 1945 he based much of it on the idea that Marxism-Leninism was a science. This was somewhat unexpected from a man whose career in the labor movement had been built, at least in its earliest and most successful stages, on his ability to dissociate himself from unpopular "isms." However, by 1945 his career had seemingly come full circle: his writings were eerily reminiscent of the tortuous reflections of Hermon Titus, the scientific socialist. In the years following the excruciating uncertainties and humiliations of the Popular Front years, Foster sought desperately to re-create his faith on the grounds of a fragile positivism.

After 1945, Foster continually asserted that a scientifically oriented Communist party was one that should struggle to develop new theoretical perspectives. In one letter circulated among the Party membership, he complained that "the greatest of all weaknesses of our Party [is] its lack of systematic theoretical work. The decay of world capitalism and the rise of world socialism are generating a whole series of new, major theoretical questions."[38] Yet, the campaign against "Browderism" would remain a potent weapon for stifling theoretical innovation or discussion. And discussion itself, despite assurances to the contrary, was valuable only to a point. After all, what Browder himself had been aiming at, according to Foster, "was to transform our Party more and more into an organization merely for talk." Near the end of one disquisition on the need for improved theoretical work, he proposed the establishment of a commission which would "carefully evaluate all our Marxist-Leninist theoretical writings, *before they are printed*" (his emphasis). Part of the problem was that Foster seemed unwilling or unable to explain what exactly was "scientific" about Marxism-Leninism. Paradoxically, as Starobin and others have pointed out, Communist theorists during this period often balked at the conventionally understood obligation of a scientist, which is to formulate hypotheses that are falsifiable, that may be proven or disproven by experience.[39]

In an earlier time, when he was at his most effective, Foster had brought a restless, experimental intelligence to the problem of building a revolutionary movement in the United States. "Fosterism" had been an eclectic, empirical, opportunistic, and highly personal mode of activism, more a style than a coherent body of doctrine. Theory and "science" had been an important element of "Fosterism," but only in an experimental sense as one aspect of an overall strategy, to be discarded or adjusted as particular situations demanded. By 1945, these characteristics of Foster's earlier syndicalism remained, albeit in a distorted form. He undoubtedly was aware that his theoretical shortcomings clouded his reputation in Moscow, but now he used the need for "theory" as a powerful weapon for the retention of power, for essentially conservative ends. And, Foster and the party leadership remained the final arbiters of "theoretical" discussions.

During a period when many Communists worried about the integrity of the political community to which they had devoted their lives, Foster's theoretical cogitations generally resolved into discussions of who should be included and excluded, of where the lines in the class war were properly drawn. Were bourgeois politicians, "progressive" capitalists, socialists, feminists, intellectuals, scientists, "professionals" to be considered potential allies or enemies? Leninism taught the need for alliances, but with whom? Significantly, Foster called for increased "theoretical" work at a time when he began to reembrace the idea of the Leninist "militant minority" most vehemently; thus the call for better theory was merged with the idea of revolutionary professionalism. The neglect of theory has resulted in a "weakening of the vanguard role of our Party," he wrote. The overwhelming concern for "theory" in Foster's writings was intimately connected to several of the central themes in his oeuvre. Communists of his generation had always prided themselves on their "professional" demeanor: Foster liked to think of himself as a "specialist," and James Cannon once reflected that being a revolutionary was the "highest and most honorable of all professions." For Foster, of course, the central problem of the earlier Debsian Socialism was also "wishy-washy" inclusiveness, and, he pointed out, "a great weakness of Debs was his theoretical inadequacy."[40] Lurking in this political grammar were echoes of his earlier neo-Malthusianism. By the 1950s, Foster had concluded that it was the task of the professional revolutionary to develop a dependable code of inclusion or exclusion (the proper end of theory), while a more dangerous and disabling influence (Browderism or an ecumenical socialism) would expand the community of revolutionaries beyond the bounds of coherence and effectiveness.

Other aspects of Foster's earlier syndicalism proved adaptable to the world of postwar Communist politics as well. Most salient was the idea of imminent revolutionary change. In 1948, at age sixty-seven, he told a group of Communist maritime workers that "we'll see Socialism before we die."[41] A main problem of Browderism had been that it had proposed an elongated perspective on the transition to socialism. Foster took his time in formulating an alternative conception, but for the time being, however, the idea of imminent economic collapse and war seemed to suffice. The United States, he never tired of asserting, was in its most degenerate, dangerous, imperialistic phase. "The world capitalist system is sick, very sick, as the two world wars and the great economic crisis, all within one generation, eloquently testify," he wrote in mid-1945. War with the Soviet Union, if not inevitable, was a continual threat, according to Foster. Undoubtedly, his convictions in this regard were bolstered by Duclos's endorsement of his critique of Browder's Teheran thesis and by the unfolding events of the Cold War. Yet Foster's apocalyptic rhetoric went beyond the expectations or requirements of the international movement. His writing and thinking in regard to the danger of war, economic collapse, and the aggressiveness of American imperialism anticipated rather than followed Stalin's earliest postwar pronouncements on these subjects.[42]

Just as he had understood the conflict between worker and capitalist on the shop floor as something resembling warfare, Foster had difficulty accepting the idea of peaceful coexistence between socialism and capitalism on the world stage. At the height of the discussions in the National Committee regarding Browder's projections for the postwar period, Elizabeth Gurley Flynn reflected on the reasons for her reticence in speaking out against the Teheran thesis, and made direct reference to Foster's syndicalist temperament: "I feel that I have applied this fear of being 'leftist' and being a 'Wobbly' to my estimation of Comrade Foster's position. I said, 'Well, Bill's an old Wobbly too and he has the same kind of deviations I could easily have." Foster's ideas helped move the Party further and further to the left after the war. For him, the coming crises seemed more than ever to require a "battle-ready" Communist movement, a militant minority shorn of "opportunist delusions."[43]

What of the central tenet of Foster's syndicalism, the idea that the trade unions could be the most effective instrument of revolutionary change in the United States? In general, the events of World War II and the postwar period offered the greatest challenges yet to his prewar conceptions. He undoubtedly recognized, as did many unionists at the time, that what might be achieved in collective bargaining could be undone by unfavorable legislation. However, while admitting that wages, hours, unemployment insurance, and strikes "have all grown into national political questions," he noted that organized labor was still "much weaker and far more vulnerable" in the "political field." As an example of these vulnerabilities, he cited the changing policies of Truman and the Democratic Party, which grew increasingly hostile toward labor after 1945. During these years the Communists would search unsuccessfully for an approach that would allow unions to exercise power in the political arena without succumbing to the sins of "tailing" and "Browderism." At a basic level, Foster remained mistrustful of the two-party system; the necessity of a developing a third-party movement would be a continual refrain. Ironically, the effect of his policies would be to return the Party to a stance similar to that of earlier AFL voluntarism, which posited a rough equivalence between the two parties. The CIO did not accept this formulation, however, and would develop closer and closer ties to the Democratic party throughout the postwar period.[44]

Chapter 12

UNIONISM, POLITICS, AND THE COLD WAR

IN SPITE OF his vision of a labor movement forced by political developments to defend its accomplishments in an arena where it was weakest
and most vulnerable, Foster clung stubbornly to his optimism about the
potential of the industrial union movement. American workers, he suggested hopefully in 1945, had largely lost faith in free enterprise, even
though they had not yet drawn the "correct socialist conclusions." Workers believed in what he called "New Dealism," which, while based on the
"illusions" of Keynesianism, nonetheless represented an advance in political consciousness.[1]

One reason for optimism, according to Foster in 1945, was that American workers were much less receptive to red-baiting tactics in the unions,
and were more positively disposed toward the Soviet Union.[2] Indeed,
there is no doubt that tens of thousands of rank-and-file unionists in a
number of CIO unions had consented to Communist leadership during
the previous two decades. Communist activists enjoyed a high reputation
as able and aggressive organizers. As a result, Communists or close Communist sympathizers controlled twelve of the CIO's thirty-five affiliates
by 1946. These included such influential unions as the United Electrical
Workers (UE), which represented nearly half a million members, as well
as the West Coast International Longshoremen's and Warehousemen's
Union (ILWU), and the National Maritime Union (NMU). Other powerful affiliates with close Communist ties or conspicuous Communist leadership were the Mine, Mill and Smelter Workers, the Packinghouse
Workers, and the New York–based Transport Workers Union. At the
national level, the Party had for years carefully cultivated an alliance with
the forces of the "center," personified by CIO president Philip Murray. In
the national office, the publicity director, Len DeCaux, was a Communist, and the union's chief counsel, Lee Pressman, consulted closely with
the Party. However, the Party's presence, despite Foster's optimism, remained controversial. Prominent Communist "influentials" in the unions
were conscious of their unique and somewhat precarious position, and
were used to carrying out union affairs with a degree of independence
from the Party. In this sense, many had adopted the familiar syndicalist
stance: the union took precedence over, and occasionally substituted for,
the Party.[3]

Beginning in 1946, this delicate relationship between the Party and its labor organizers would be severely tested, as an ominous anti-Communist temper began to stir in a number of unions. The origins of anti-Communist sentiment can, in part, be traced to the Party's wartime polices. To begin with, Communist support for the no-strike pledge and the speedup helped undercut the credibility of the Party among a rank and file that was increasingly restless under wartime controls. While endorsement of these policies was not especially costly to the Party during the war itself, its stand would be used effectively against the Communists by powerful union factionalists in the postwar period. This was especially true in the UAW, where Walter Reuther won the presidency in 1946 at least partly as a result of his ability to portray the Communists as vacillating on a number of wartime labor grievances.

Anti-Communist caucuses in a number of CIO unions gained an ideological advantage as a result of profound shifts in American and Soviet foreign policies. Mistrust of the Soviet Union and suspicion of the motives of American Communists resurfaced after the war. So strong had these sentiments become by 1946 that at the CIO convention in November, leading Communists were forced to acquiesce in the adoption of a resolution stating that "we resent and reject efforts of the Communist Party or other political parties and their adherents to interfere in the affairs of the CIO. This convention serves notice that we will not tolerate such interference." This resolution was the outcome of careful negotiation between Murray and the Communists. It was finally supported by important Communist figures: Michael Gold of the Fur Workers, and Mike Quill, the president of the Transport Workers. Communists, when called upon to explain their support of the resolution, justified it on the grounds that it was designed to preserve unity, and that it could be broadly interpreted, in classic syndicalist terms, as a repudiation of all political parties. Nonetheless, its logic signified that Communist union leaders occupied a special sphere. Foster, according to Quill, was directly responsible for the Party's decision to endorse the resolution. To Quill, it represented a "repudiation of the principle of Communist leadership in the Unions."[4]

The surfacing of anti-Communist sentiment in the unions roughly coincided with the outbreak of a number of strikes in the largest American industries. Beginning in 1945 and intensifying rapidly following the surrender of Japan, workers in the auto, steel, electrical, and meatpacking industries came out in the largest strike wave in American history up to that point. Fed up with wage controls and production demands, workers in mass-production industries emerged from the war in a militant mood. Foster wrote enthusiastically that the strike movement was of "a new kind," conducted on a "higher level" than ever before. Unions were at an unprecedented level of strength and membership. He noted a general absence of traditional repressive activities like red-baiting and the importation of strikebreakers. The inclusion of African Americans and women in the union movement created a new level of solidarity, he suggested. Moreover, he noted, workers were far more politically conscious than they had been after World War I. Though putatively acting on a higher plane of anticapitalist consciousness than previous strike campaigns, the strikers won few important victories. While workers were on the offensive, organized labor was clearly on the defensive.[5]

However, what was perhaps most significant about the strike wave was Truman's response, which was generally favorable to the employers. The new president employed his wartime powers to seize a number of industries, including coal, oil, meatpacking, and railroads, and threatened to draft striking railroad workers. Truman's actions threw the CIO leadership into turmoil. Philip Murray and Walter Reuther at one time or another in the immediate postwar period actively promoted the idea of a third-party movement. Foster remained hesitant and cautious about these initiatives. As early as September 1945, he bitterly denounced Truman as a militant imperialist, a term he used again in November in a public appearance before the House Committee on Un-American Activities, recently resurrected by Mississippi Democrat John E. Rankin. These were bold statements, considering that even the Russians had not yet employed such harsh terminology in reference to the new administration. In early 1946 he made a vague call for "an eventual broad progressive third-party movement" as a way to put labor on the offensive politically.[6] Yet Foster shrank from the implications of his pronouncements. His call for a third-party movement was accompanied by the usual caveat, that it must be "led by the workers, by the trade unions." He foresaw the "eventual" third-party "movement" as the result of a broad antiwar, antimonopoly coalition among workers, poorer farmers, African Americans, and "progressive" sectors of the middle classes.[7]

The third-party idea would remain in the background for nearly a year, but would resurface as the Cold War escalated. A widening rift in the Democratic party between supporters of Truman and a group generally sympathetic to the views of former Vice-President Henry Wallace seemed to endanger the New Deal consensus. Wallace, by late 1946, had emerged as a strong critic of Truman's foreign policy, and in several speeches essentially endorsed the idea of a Soviet sphere of influence in Europe. He resigned as Truman's secretary of commerce in the autumn of 1946. His aims were not entirely clear, but shortly thereafter a set of political action committees was created by an organization called the Progressive Citizens of America. This organization would provide the primary core of support for Wallace's third-party candidacy for the presidency in 1948. The Communist party cultivated a strong influence in this movement from the beginning.[8]

The question of how extensively to support and promote Wallace's developing candidacy would turn out to be of decisive importance for the Communist party. Foster, predictably, adopted a wait-and-see attitude, and shrank from leadership on the issue, at least at first. He traveled to Europe in the first weeks of 1947, ostensibly to attend the conferences of the Communist parties of Great Britain and the British Empire countries. In March, he journeyed to a number of Eastern European capitals: Prague, Sofia, Belgrade, and Warsaw. His visit to Europe involved more than mere tourism, however; in part, he was seeking a degree of "clarity" from European Communists on issues like the imminence of war and the third-party movement. Foster's activities and writings while he was in Europe were followed carefully by the staffs of local embassies, who in turn relayed transcripts of his writings and interviews directly to the Secretary of State George C. Marshall. Although Foster was pointedly criticized by some Communists, including Jacques Duclos, for his emphasis on the war danger, his rhetoric escalated dramatically while he was abroad. He painted a picture of American capitalism on the brink of fascism, with the new Congress poised to legislate a number of harshly anti-labor measures. "Wall Street is preparing its war of conquest," he told an Italian journalist in March. To a Polish interlocutor he proclaimed that "the chief aim of Anglo-American diplomacy in Eastern Europe is to re-build a ring of hostile reactionary states along the western frontiers of the USSR."[9]

Foster's sojourn in Europe coincided with a dramatic intensification of the developing Cold War. In March came the Truman Doctrine as well as an executive order requiring loyalty oaths of all government employees. The same month saw the introduction into Congress of the Taft-Hartley Act, a measure that would undermine many of the legal prerogatives that the unions had won during the New Deal. In May and June Secretary of State Marshall hardened his attitude toward Stalin, finally concluding that no bargain could be reached with the Russian dictator on the status of the countries of Eastern Europe. The Marshall Plan was announced in June.

Truman decided to veto the Taft-Hartley Act, but a majority of congressional Democrats had joined with Republicans in voting for passage of the bill. In June Truman's veto was quickly overridden. A key feature of the act was that it required affidavits from union officers certifying that they were not members of the Communist party. At first, leaders like John L. Lewis and Philip Murray refused to sign the oaths, but some, like the new president of the UAW, Walter Reuther, did not hesitate to utilize the oaths as a way of exploiting the spreading anti-Communist hysteria.

Foster, in the meantime, continued to equivocate on the issue of the third party. He evinced no fear of splitting the Democratic vote, for he had come to believe that Truman, if nominated, "would not only be valueless to the people, but would also have no chance whatever" of being elected. Indeed, at the time, Truman's popularity was at an extremely low ebb. Foster seemed convinced that conditions in 1948 were more favorable to a third-party candidate than they had been in 1924. In general, he wrote, workers recognized that capitalism had been "fundamentally weakened," sensed an imminent crisis, and understood that only political action could protect them from "the ravages of mass unemployment." In an astonishing leap of faith, he proposed that while the workers' mood "cannot yet be called mass class consciousness, they are nevertheless moving in this direction. They are ripe for a new mass party." However, in the same article, he exhibited an indecisiveness typical of this period in his career. He concluded at one point that "there must be a progressive Presidential candidate in the field in 1948, without fail, if not on the Democratic ticket, then surely on an independent ticket." In the same article, however, he stated that whether or not a new party would be strong enough to put up an independent presidential candidate and a slate of congressional and local candidates in 1948 "remains to be seen."[10]

To further complicate matters, in the summer and autumn of 1947 a rapprochement developed between the Truman administration and the CIO leadership. Despite his harshly antilabor rhetoric and actions in the earlier strike wave, Truman's veto of the Taft-Hartley bill was widely praised. Hard-pressed to retrieve the labor constituency, the president publicly endorsed repeal of what the CIO referred to as the "slave labor law." Truman's commitment to repeal of Taft-Hartley and restoration of the New Deal labor equation was not a deep one, as would become clear following his astonishing victory in 1948. Nonetheless, in 1947 Murray and his advisers eagerly pursued the opening Truman had offered them. The CIO's one-sided understanding with the Democratic administration would have profound, far-reaching consequences for the labor movement. Its immediate effects were to commit the CIO to Truman's anti-Communist foreign policy, and to rejection of the movement developing around Henry Wallace.[11]

In September 1947, FBI agents recorded a conversation in Foster's hotel room during a trip to California in which he betrayed far more skepticism about the idea of the third party than he was exhibiting in public at the time. The details of the conversation are quite striking, because they reveal Foster's forthrightly syndicalist perspective on the problem of the Wallace candidacy. He suggested that in many ways, the third party was no better than the Democratic Party. "Before we were tagging along with the Democrats, and now with Wallace," he complained. The third party could not be a success, he stated, unless the CIO could be convinced to support it wholeheartedly, but of course he held out little promise of that eventuality. He pointed out that "the Communist Party must not make the mistake it made twenty years ago regarding the Third Party movement . . . or history will repeat itself and the Communist Party will be no further ahead twenty years from now." He implied that the Party should concentrate on far more simple, prosaic objectives: "Send wages higher—get the money."[12]

Nonetheless, in December, the Party's top union leaders were summoned to a meeting in New York in which they were informed that Wallace would soon announce his candidacy on a third-party ticket. They were urged to help line up support in their organizations for Wallace's candidacy. By all accounts, the announcement was greeted with consternation and resentment, and Foster was conspicuously absent from the meeting. There is evidence that at the time two other high-ranking Communists, Eugene Dennis and Robert Thompson, were more aggressive than Foster in pushing for the third-party stand in the unions. Dennis was the Party's general secretary, in charge of electoral policy, and was known to be well tuned to political developments in Moscow as well. A somewhat mysterious figure who had spent years abroad in the service of the Comintern, Dennis was considered, according to Joseph Starobin, "the most authoritative party spokesman" after Foster somewhat incongruously nominated him to be general secretary in 1945. According to Foster himself, Dennis "led" in the decision to form a third party around Wallace. Thompson was the new chairman of the New York state party. He was a decorated veteran, a relative newcomer to Party politics, and was perceived as somewhat of a protégé of Foster's. While Foster undoubtedly had a significant amount of input into the formulation of the policy, it is interesting that as late as September he was complaining about the Party's "tailing" Wallace as if the enterprise was in some way beyond his control. One highly placed party official recalled that despite Foster's influence, he and his supporters were "often decisively defeated on issues" in the late 1940s.[13]

The Party's decision to support Wallace was fraught with danger. As the red scare gathered momentum, an endorsement of Wallace tarred a union official as a Communist sympathizer. Why, especially given Foster's awareness of the shortcomings of the Wallace campaign, did the Party attach itself so closely to the third party?

To begin with, Truman's support in the labor movement seemed precarious as the 1948 elections approached. Wallace, on the other hand, drew astonishingly large crowds on several precampaign speaking tours. This may have helped the Party's leadership convince themselves that Wallace, who would receive approximately one million votes in the general election, was a viable candidate. Even Foster was impressed by the crowds that Wallace was able to gather on a West Coast tour, and was surprised by the strength of pro-Wallace sentiment among steelworkers and miners in western Pennsylvania. However, it is difficult to imagine that Foster, remembering the problems attending the labor party enterprises of the 1920s, believed Wallace could draw a significant amount of national electoral support.[14]

Foster undoubtedly allowed international considerations to affect his stance on the third-party issue. In October 1947, *Pravda* announced the formation of a nine-member conference of European parties, the Communist Information Bureau (Cominform), whose purpose was to mobilize and coordinate the European resistance to American imperialism. The resulting manifestos and resolutions generally reflected a far more militant line than had previous resolutions of the kind, advocating especially the formation of aggressive united fronts "from below" in European countries. It was symptomatic of the new mood that the Yugoslav party openly criticized the Italian and French parties for having not seized power in 1944. American Communists interpreted the establishment of the Cominform as confirmation of their general outlook on the war danger and the menace of U.S. imperialism. In this respect at least, Foster's views seemed vindicated, a fact to which he later pointed with pride. However, the emphasis on the "united front from below" cut the ground away from his insistence that the leadership of a substantial section of the labor movement was essential to the formation of a viable third party; and this leadership was not, in fact, forthcoming. The only major left-led union formally to endorse Wallace was the Mine, Mill and Smelter Workers. The largest union in which the Communist influence was predominant, the United Electrical Workers, left the question of whom to support up to its individual locals. In general, pro-Wallace unionists justified their stance in traditional voluntarist terms: CIO resolutions could not be binding on individual unions.[15]

Yet, the Communist party's policies and pronouncements remained tied to international events and the demands of superpower foreign policy. The support of the Marshall Plan by the major labor federations, Foster wrote in 1948, represented a violation of "the most fundamental interests of the masses."[16] In an atmosphere of escalating anti-Soviet sentiment, the public stance of the Party on the Truman Doctrine and the Marshall Plan would prove extremely damaging. It is quite possible that Foster underestimated the impact of the Party's pro-Wallace rhetoric. As a newcomer to the Party in the 1920s, after all, he had scorned the idea that workers cared much about foreign policy issues.

Finally, Foster's role and motivations must be judged by how he anticipated the outcome of the Wallace debacle. He undoubtedly had misgivings about the Party's direction, but one undeniable result of Communist strategy in the 1948 elections was to rend the Party's ties to the CIO–Democratic party alliance, a goal that was consistent with Foster's skepticism and ambivalence about the role of labor in electoral politics. In his only major pronouncement on the Wallace issue in the months leading up to the election, he proclaimed that "a vote for either Truman or Dewey means a vote for eventual fascism and war." At the same time, the Wallace candidacy was also deeply flawed, from Foster's perspective: unlike the Progressive party candidate, "we Marxist-Leninists" do not "believe that the badly crippled world capitalist system can be saved and transformed into 'progressive capitalism,'" he wrote. Holding out little prospect for Wallace's election, he asserted that the main task of the third party would ultimately be to "[shatter] the deadly two-party system which for generations has politically paralyzed the working class."[17]

These statements reveal that Foster, while fearing a repetition of the events of 1924, had nonetheless neither offered nor developed a significantly new perspective on the problems of labor politics since then. In 1948, as well as 1924, the sectarian logic and aloofness of the Communists and Foster's own ambivalence culminated in a disastrous split. The Wallace candidacy, and Truman's surprising victory, helped set the stage for the swift elimination of Communist influence in the CIO after the election. This series of events had a far-reaching effect on both the Communist party and the American labor movement. After years of carefully building up an alliance with the "center" forces of the CIO, by 1949 the Communists suddenly found themselves estranged from the mainstream of the industrial union movement. In the CIO, the splitting away and expulsion of powerful Communist-led unions would drastically alter the face of the labor movement. The presence of Communists in the CIO had lent a militant and aggressive cast to American unionism during the 1930s; by 1949 the relatively young federation of industrial unions was well on its way toward acceptance of the precisely formalized labor-relations strategies of American corporate enterprise.

Certainly, William Foster was at the very center of these momentous developments in the American labor movement. Yet, he remained an enigmatic figure, his stands on different issues drifting in and out of focus or lurching wildly from left to right. It was undoubtedly a period of extreme stress, with the Party increasingly under attack on a number of fronts. Despite his demands for ideological unity and coherence, Foster seemed unable to provide consistent leadership. As he groped for political perspective in the midst of the developing crisis, his health began to deteriorate. In August 1948, already suffering from chronic hypertension and arteriosclerosis, he suffered a mild stroke. The stroke did not apparently affect his mental acuity, but resulted in a significant limitation of his physical activities. Suffering from numbness in his right side and extreme fatigue, Foster spent the next two months largely confined to bed in his Bronx apartment.[18]

Foster's private life in the period after World War II can be described only in outline. He and Esther lived in a one-bedroom apartment at 1040 Nelson Avenue in the Bronx, not far from Yankee Stadium. The apartment was very sparsely furnished and in a constant state of disrepair. Foster's closest family circle consisted of his two adopted children, Sylvia and David, and their spouses. The most frequent visitors were Sylvia and her second husband, Emmanuel Kolko, who would arrive once or twice a week to help Esther, who was suffering from severe arthritis, with household chores. Emmanuel was a stubborn family critic of the Soviet regime who had a brother, Abush, killed in Stalin's purges. Emmanuel would later accompany Foster to the Soviet Union and serve as his personal translator. Joseph Manley Kolko, Sylvia and Emmanuel's grandson, was also a frequent visitor; Foster dedicated his 1949 book *The Twilight of World Capitalism* to Joe with the words "To My Great Grandson Joseph Manley Kolko, Who Will Live in a Communist United States."[19]

Very little is known about William and Esther's relationship during these years, although their apartment was essentially divided at the time: Esther's domain was in the kitchen, where she slept, and living room. The bedroom was Foster's "workshop" and study. Although she was a Party member, Esther never participated in political discussions, and remained in the background. Sylvia and Emmanuel were aloof from the Party, and were absolutely adamant about keeping young Joseph out of Communist affairs, despite William's interest in schooling him in the Soviet Union. David was a devoted "union man" in his trade of printer and subscribed to the *Daily Worker*, but it is uncertain if he was a member of the Party.[20]

William Foster remained a very private person. Political acquaintances were welcome at his apartment, but only rarely stayed for dinner. Before his health problems limited his mobility, he would relax by going, alone, to Yankee games or the movies. Despite his almost puritanical deprecation of much of American art and culture, he was an avid film buff who often discussed movies in great detail with his colleagues. In the summer the family would stay for a few weeks at a cottage at the Mohegan Colony in Peekskill, with FBI agents lurking in nearby woods and bushes. For vacations, Foster would visit a relative in California, or his old comrade Jay Fox, who still resided at the Home Colony on Puget Sound. Foster's life-style was ascetic. His diet was very simple and most of his clothes were second-hand or gifts. He was adamant about not owning property: even the family automobile was in Sylvia's name. It was his habit to give money away during his occasional walks; thus, the family, never affluent,

Foster with his great-grandson, Joe Kolko, ca. 1948.

made a point of keeping money out of his hands. With his private time, Foster followed a rigorous routine. When he was healthy, he would usually rise at about five in the morning, and write for three hours before breakfast. After breakfast, there was a short walk to the corner newsstand, and then another four or five hours of writing.[21]

Foster's activities came under increasing surveillance by the FBI after 1945. His elevation to the chairmanship of the Party had qualified him for unblinking attention by the bureau, and he was on J. Edgar Hoover's list of subversives who were to be arrested in the event of a national security emergency. Subsequent trials revealed that the FBI had been able to infiltrate numerous informants into the highest ranks of the Party. By 1947, this infiltration had apparently extended to Foster's close associates; one informant gained access to his personal effects while he was traveling, for instance, and photographed documents in his possession and forwarded them to the FBI. By the late 1950s, Foster had become so security-conscious that confidential discussions in his own apartment were written out on notes that were burned immediately afterward and flushed down the toilet.[22]

In the last months of 1947, the FBI determined that Foster was carrying on a romantic liaison with an unnamed woman in Buffalo, New York. The bureau's conclusion was based on agents' interception and subsequent copying of Foster's amorous correspondence, as well as surveillance of Foster's meetings with the woman in Buffalo. A memo addressed to Hoover concluded that "while the Communist Party (from its point of view) was scurrying to protect its very existence, its National Chairman, William Z. Foster, took time out to prepare this type of letters and carry out an apparent personal escapade." This information, it was suggested, "may make it possible for us to put Foster some day in a very embarrassing position." However, whatever its parameters or intensity, the affair seems to have been broken off by early 1948.[23]

The Party seemed ill-prepared for the wave of legal prosecutions directed against it beginning in 1947. The most difficult challenge was presented by the Truman administration's decision to proceed with indictments against the twelve members of the National Board, including Foster, for violation of the Alien Registration law of 1940, known as the Smith Act. The act prohibited the teaching and advocacy of the overthrow of the Government by force and violence. The original indictments were returned by a federal grand jury in New York in July of 1948, on the eve of the Progressive party's convention in Philadelphia. Foster's case was severed from those of the others for medical reasons; according to two court-appointed physicians, the rigors of a prolonged trial would jeopardize his health. The trials of the rest of the Communist leadership began in New York in January 1949 and would last until October 1950, the longest criminal trial in United States history up to that time. The indictments alleged that in dissolving the Communist Political Association and reconstituting the Communist party, the leaders had entered into a conspiracy to advocate the overthrow of the government. The initial trial ended in conviction; the Party's leaders were free on bail until mid-1951, when the Supreme Court upheld the verdicts.[24]

Foster played an extremely important role in the Party's defense against the Smith Act indictments. Despite his severance from the trial, he continued to write prolifically and confer with Party leaders. This outraged J. Edgar Hoover, who continually directed his agents to follow Foster closely and accumulate evidence that he remained a threat to national security. Following the initial convictions Hoover would repeatedly importune New York District Attorney Irving Saypol, the mastermind of the espionage case against Julius and Ethel Rosenberg and "the nation's number one legal hunter of top Communists," to reopen Foster's case.[25]

Foster sought to transform the Smith Act trials into a political victory for the Party. He authored exhaustive analyses of Communist political doctrine that were circulated among the defendants. Convinced that the accused could not receive a fair hearing in a nation poised on the brink of war, he stubbornly maintained that the trials should turn on a defense of doctrine, and that the defense of the indicted leaders should deemphasize traditional First Amendment arguments. Foster's reference point was the prosecutions of the World War I era, when the First Amendment was essentially a dead letter for radicals. However, in the 1950s his policies effectively precluded support from the civil-libertarian Left. And, as it turned out, Foster would vacillate so much on the details of Party policy that it would be nearly impossible to determine what constituted Communist doctrine in the first place.

A key document in this regard was a deposition in which he argued that the Communist Party believed in a peaceful path to socialism. In a widely circulated pamphlet issued as a guide to Party policy during the trial, he acknowledged that the Party was "revolutionary," and that violence has accompanied all revolutions. However, he noted that in the meantime "we do have a program and that program is to elect a democratic coalition government which will have the potentiality of moving in the direction of socialism. I mean legally elected under the existing legislative or election machinery." Astonishingly enough, this was written following the Wallace debacle. Nonetheless, Foster cited the cases of Russia in 1917, as well as Czechoslovakia and Poland, as countries where "a group of [socialist] parties established a coalition government" as a prelude to Communism. Foster's ill-concealed admiration of the coup d'état as a revolutionary tactic did not prevent him from concluding that the peaceful transition theory was "the most important theoretical advance ever made by the CPUSA on its own initiative."[26]

However, there were problems with his theories, as Foster himself soon acknowledged. His writings during the trials represented somewhat of a retreat from his previous perspective on the imminence of fascism and war, but by 1950 his earlier prognostications were again coming to the fore. His convictions on the subject of the peaceful transition to socialism had been "at least very questionable" in the first place, one Party leader remembered.[27] Moreover, European Communists were increasingly minimizing the possibility of a peaceful transition to socialism. Thus, in an astonishing 1950 article, Foster backpedaled furiously. "In view of the drive of American imperialism toward fascism and war ... it is by no means certain" that workers would be able to democratically elect a socialist people's front government, he now asserted. "If the reactionaries should succeed in breaking down the democratic system and establishing fascism," the result would be "open, violent struggle." Of course, "one would be naive to speak of a peaceful election under such circumstances of sharp political struggle," he noted. By unhesitatingly aligning his writings with the outlook of the international movement, Foster risked the fate of the defendants in the trials, whose convictions were then under appeal.[28]

The Smith Act prosecutions coincided with a wide-ranging attack on the Communist presence in the CIO. Following the 1948 elections, Philip Murray and other CIO leaders embarked on a program of virulent denunciation of pro-Soviet labor leaders, accompanied by elaborate "hearings" that sought to prove that accused unionists were in thrall to the foreign policy needs of the Soviet Union. From 1948 to 1950, the CIO formally expelled eleven unions that were identified most closely with pro-Soviet policies. Subsequent CIO membership raids on the expelled unions were accompanied by near-hysterical red-baiting, vicious physical attacks on suspected Communists, and cynical alliances with McCarthyite politicians. A whole variety of circumstances helped to feed the red scare in the unions. It was the period of the Berlin blockade, the Communist takeovers in China, Czechoslovakia, and Poland, and later on the Korean War and an increasingly paranoid concern with internal security. In the CIO, Murray, a Catholic, aimed his anti-Communist rhetoric at powerful blocs of Catholics and unionists of Eastern European descent. In addition, for the CIO, it was an era of bureaucratic as well as ideological retrenchment. Communists, with their particular skills in local mobilization, were suddenly less useful. Party organizers had often depended on local solidarities and cohesive work groups to build the unions in the first place; after the war this social base for militant unionism was disappearing as worker mobility reached unprecedented levels. In addition, the developing social contract between labor and corporate management allowed for relatively steady wage increases and a new level of prosperity for workers in basic industries. Industrial unionism had finally achieved a measure of acceptance and legitimacy. However, as a result of the purges, CIO membership declined from a peak of 5.2 million during the war to only 3.7 million by 1950. The AFL, by comparison, could claim 8.5 members.[29]

At this crucial juncture, Foster's activities were increasingly limited. His health was poor; he spent more and more time confined to his apartment under care of a physician for his heart condition and was less able to offer functional leadership in the Party. Nonetheless, he continued to confer with Party leaders, and he certainly sought to offer ideological guidance. This phase of his career finds him turning out a veritable avalanche of articles, pamphlets, and books.[30]

A number of his treatises sought to comprehend the onslaught against the Communists in the labor movement. Foster cited historical precedents for the events of 1948–50. After all, he pointed out, the 1920s had also been a period of economic boom that had seen an increase in labor-management cooperation, a widespread belief that strikes would soon be unnecessary under a "new" capitalism, a climate of political conservatism and nationalism, and widespread expulsion of Communists from the unions.[31] This analysis seemed to be offering a cyclical interpretation of trends in the labor movement, but by 1953 Foster was once again hinting at darker uncertainties: the decline in the acceptance of Marxism in the United States had been long-term and continuous, he admitted. Even in the 1920s numerous union leaders had retained socialist sentiments and outlooks. Now, Marxism was rarely found among the organized working class. Why? He offered a half-hearted catechism of "exceptionalist" explanations: a ruthless and opportunistic antisocialist trade union bureaucracy; the uneven development principle (periods of ideological retrogression); imperialism and the resulting better living conditions of the masses; the "growth of bourgeois illusions," which he characterized as "Keynesian-Rooseveltian," in the labor movement. Whereas for a brief period he had previously admitted that the acceptance of "New Dealism" was a sign of progress in working-class consciousness, now he proclaimed Keynesianism "the most serious challenge ever faced by Marxism in this country." Despite his routine invocations of the increased prosperity of the American working class, he recognized that periods of working-class militancy and aggressive union building often came during periods of industrial boom.[32]

How was it possible to explain the decline in anticapitalist consciousness, and what hope could be held out for the labor movement in the future? Predictably, Foster placed great faith in the organizational strides made by the union movement. Organization of the unorganized, industrial unionism, and increasing racial tolerance were all the results, at least partly, of the successes of the Communist party, he wrote. He continued to hold out the distant possibility of a "strong and independent political organization." In the 1952 elections, faced with Adlai Stevenson, who favored the Taft-Hartley Act and endorsed the Smith Act prosecutions, and Eisenhower, he called for workers to endorse the candidates of the moribund Progressive party. Foster could only cite as a precondition for eventual electoral success his supposition that the CIO was finally organizationally strong enough to launch a third-party effort. In 1953, after years of red-baiting and expulsions, he could still conclude that the trade unions "are the force that must be depended upon, as against the destructive policies of the big capitalists, to keep the nation out of war, to protect and develop its democratic liberties, and to keep workers in jobs."[33]

What class consciousness there was, he wrote in 1955, was generally related to something he called "fighting spirit," or "the question of mass spontaneity." He cited the Flint sit-down strike as an example of "the spark that touched off the big series of strikes and organizing campaigns that built the CIO in the late 1930s." The trade union movement, he concluded, "like the working class in general, makes its main progress, not by slow evolutionary steps, but by militant leaps forward." This was bordering on a mystical conception of the origins of working-class militancy, but in nearly the same breath he asserted that "trade unions are born, advance, and decline according to ascertainable principles or laws." However, other than to assert that such development is generally uneven and that unions are subject to periods of retrogression and lessened class struggle, Foster left the historical etiology of trade union progress obscure.[34]

Shortly after the first convictions of the national leaders of the Party, the government initiated another wave of legal prosecutions aimed at destroying its cohesiveness at the local level. Dozens of leaders at the so-called "secondary" level were imprisoned, often after cursory trials conducted in an atmosphere of hysteria. At the time, it was not unusual for Party meetings and local headquarters to be attacked by angry mobs. It was becoming clear that the Party was honeycombed with informers, and the Party itself steadily became rife with suspicion and paranoia. The crisis seemed to demand an ever greater degree of conformity, discipline, and ideological purity from the Party's members. Thus, "trials" of deviating members were held that mirrored the grotesqueries of the government prosecutions. This internal witch-hunt would be recalled most vividly and angrily in a few short years, following Khrushchev's revelations of the horrors of Stalinism. Perhaps the most bizarre example of the Party's purification program was the campaign against "white chauvinism." Long-time Communists suddenly came under intense scrutiny for evidence that they held the slightest residual prejudice against African Americans. The campaign, which lasted roughly from 1949 to 1953, seemed in part an exercise in self-hatred; increasingly isolated and bewildered, Party members turned viciously on one another using the "white chauvinism" accusation as a club. It is noteworthy that Foster did not lend his voice to the special issue of *Political Affairs*, the Party's theoretical journal, that formally inaugurated the white chauvinism campaign, and that his authorship of a belated article condemning its "mistakes" and the fact that a number of comrades were "unjustly disciplined and even expelled" effectively brought an end to the hysteria. Nonetheless, it was clearly a time of chaos and horror for many Communists.[35]

Soon, Foster acquiesced to a plan to send much of the Party's remaining leadership underground. Although he later stated in a top-level meeting that he had been opposed to this maneuver and was "not present when this sectarian decision was made," he admitted that his belief that war between the Soviet Union and the United States was highly likely and that the Party could anticipate a long period of fascist-like repression meant that he bore responsibility for "one phase" of the policy. The tactic was indeed debated intensively in the Party's National Committee, but ultimately the "five minutes to midnight" perspective (the phrase was Eugene Dennis's) prevailed. Following the logic of imminent war and repression, the main element of the Party's leadership soon became "unavailable"; shortly after the Supreme Court's decision in June 1951 to uphold the convictions of the Smith Act defendants, a number of top leaders disappeared into an elaborate underground apparatus.

Undoubtedly, the persecution of the IWW during World War I weighed heavily on the minds of the Party leadership. Then, the decisions of numerous Wobblies to serve their sentences had helped to cripple the movement. Also, the American Communists may have convinced themselves that they could duplicate the feats of the Italian and Japanese Parties, which had endured vicious repression during the war and yet emerged with unprecedented power. This argument was typical of many others during this period. The glaring disjunction between the successes of the international movement and repression and decline at home intensified the search for paradigms from abroad; this in turn inevitably contributed to the surrealistic cast of Party propaganda. Foster, though, later vehemently condemned the underground phase in high-level meetings: "A well-developed security apparatus was, of course, indispensable," but such measures as closing bookstores, dissolving various fronts, and moving out of party headquarters were "carrying matters too far." He castigated the policy for having produced a "severe and unnecessary weakening" of the Party.[36]

Whatever his doubts about the Party's retreat from its routine political responsibilities, Foster's writings during this period are suffused with a sense of morbidity and angry detachment, almost as if he was a character shaped in another world. The election of Eisenhower in 1952 evoked from him stern warnings of intensified preparations for war. American society continued to sink into depravity. "The capitalist economic system is socially insane," he ranted, and this was illustrated most graphically by "the growing mental confusion of the people." In one Zhdanovist outburst, Foster proclaimed that in contrast to the conditions in socialist societies, American culture "is submerged by the ocean of filthy comic books, crime stories, and reactionary obscurantism. Unfortunately, this capitalist ideological trash has profound effects on the workers." While workers were increasingly confused and misguided, so too were the capitalists. The Smith Act verdicts, he concluded, were "the product of a capitalist system that is bewildered and doomed." The ruling class is "confused . . . as to its perspective," he suggested. Despite the apparent confusion at all levels of society, Foster continued to portray capitalism as a dangerous, aggressive system bent on world domination. Of course, concern about the imminence of war with the Soviet Union, paranoia about "internal security," anxiety about the potential of fascism in the United States, and obsession with symptoms of moral breakdown and alienation were characteristic of the writings of a wide range of non-Communist observers during this period. Thus Foster's diatribes cannot be dismissed as political fabulism; rather, they represent a curiously distorted mirror image of the Cold War zeitgeist.[37]

Foster remained an ambiguous, elusive figure. His writings of this period seem untethered in some basic way; they cycle wildly between calls for compromise and alliance and demands for revolutionary chastity. Taken individually, what force his articles possessed often dissipated in a morass of contradictions, endless nuances, and politically defensive qualifications. Yet, Foster's leadership was clearly associated with the conformist atmosphere in the Party, and at the local level it was often sufficient to end discussions with "that is the opinion of Comrade Foster." The Party came closest to imitating forms of Stalinist repression during his regime. Its authority structure was preserved in its basic outlines during the years of McCarthyism and the underground, and Foster himself was perceived as part of the surviving vital "center" of the Party leadership during these years. Articles for *Political Affairs*, for instance, were submitted to him for his sacerdotal consideration and approval. Thus, he remained a powerful influence during these years. Functioning during this period as a leader of an underground, internationalist, and tightly restricted revolutionary movement, Foster was working within his earliest paradigm of radical politics. An important characteristic of the Fenian organizations to which his father belonged was their rigorous attention to "security rituals."[38]

Foster casually referred to the continuing purges in the Soviet Union as "cleansing their leading forces of Zionist agents of American imperialism," and continued to write an occasional worshipful assessment of Stalin and his influence in the world Communist movement. However, he was conspicuously absent from the lineup of Party leaders who contributed encomiums for a special issue of *Political Affairs* celebrating Stalin's seventieth birthday, and abstained for a month from offering a eulogy following the Soviet leader's death in 1953. Since he was national chairman of the Party and thus obligated to act as its official spokesman, his inaction in these cases can be interpreted as a signal, however faint, that his opinion of Stalin had some significant reservations.[39]

As the Party searched for a way out of its crisis, Foster authored a number of ambitious books: *Outline Political History of the Americas* (1951), *History of the Communist Party of the United States* (1952), *The Negro People in American History* (1954), and *History of the Three Internationals* (1955). Together, these tomes amounted to some twenty-five hundred pages of densely composed orthodoxy. Foster credited a number of researchers and others in the preface to each book and later professed the works were the product of a collective authorship, but they nonetheless represent a significant individual accomplishment for a man who was essentially an autodidact. The fact that he composed these giant works while he was in precarious health and often bedridden is testimony to Foster's extraordinary willpower. Despite his age, he clearly possessed a powerful determination, as well as a comprehensive and disciplined, if not especially creative, intelligence. These had served him well in the American radical and Communist movements, and would continue to serve him in the fights that lay ahead.[40]

A kind of "cult of personality" grew up around Foster during this period. Clearly, his own ambitions and ego were being given full expression. The party press portrayed his books as triumphs of Foster's own immense Marxist-Leninist learning, and several were made required reading for Americans held in North Korean prisoner-of-war camps. *Outline History of the Americas*, according to Robert Thompson writing in *Political Affairs*, was the "product of one of the great scientific minds of the world Communist movement," and was "a really major event in the life of our Party and class." Moreover, according to Thompson, the book represented an "advanced" Marxism-Leninism; Foster was the foremost advocate in America of the "Stalinist concept of creative Marxism." One Party historian concluded, upon publication of *History of the Three Internationals*, that "Comrade Foster has mastered the law of social development." The Party issued special study guides for his *History of the Communist Party of the United States*. However, Foster's books did not gain a large readership among Party rank and file, a sign perhaps of growing skepticism about his leadership.[41]

Still, for many Party members, Foster's basic ideas and assumptions seemed to offer ready explanations for the repression that the Party endured during the darkest years of the Cold War, and his "old-time" militancy gained a devoted and powerful following within the Communist movement itself. The metaphor of social relations as warfare and the dismissal of popular politics as essentially epiphenomenal; the faith in the radical subjectivity and élan of a militant minority concomitant with an ultimately obscurantist historical analysis; and, finally, the assumption of persecution and the dismissal of workers' conservatism as merely a particularly pernicious kind of confusion: each of these found renewed usefulness for Foster and his followers during the Cold War. His syndicalism had always contained an element of personalist fiat and militant *vouloir* at its core. Now the central assumptions of this activist philosophy proved useful in the service of an essentially authoritarian political ethos.

Chapter 13

FINAL STRUGGLES

I was of my present general political opinions seventeen
years before the USSR was established, and no doubt
would have held the same opinions if history had not yet
given birth to that first Socialist country.
—William Foster, 1948

O Proteus conscience, never to be tied!
—John Dryden

DURING the Cold War, American Communists paid a terrible price for
their ideological connection to the Soviet Union; perceptions of and official policy toward American Communists were irrevocably tied to the
public's understanding of the role of the Soviet Union in world politics.
However, for a brief period in the first months of the Eisenhower administration, this connection between policy and perception appeared to dissolve momentarily. The Korean armistice was signed, the United States
Senate approved a censure of McCarthy, and the Supreme Court agreed
to reconsider appeals brought to it from a number of Smith Act convictions. Eisenhower inveighed against McCarthyite "thought control" and
proposed significant decreases in military spending. By 1955, it could be
said that the Cold War was in a period of remission. The previous month,
five members of the Party's National Committee who had been imprisoned under the Smith Act were released. That year, the unfortunate in-
habitants of the Communist underground apparatus began to surface,
and the Party resumed some of its normal operations.

However, the situation was still a dangerous one. In August 1954, Eisenhower had signed the Communist Control Act, or Public Law 637, "An
Act to Outlaw the Communist Party." The bill set fourteen broad indices
of membership and stripped the party of "all rights, privileges, and immu-
nities attendant upon legal bodies." Important Party leaders continued to
be vulnerable; Claude Lightfoot, the secretary of the Illinois Party, as well
as Junius Scales, the secretary of the North and South Carolina CP, were
arrested, convicted, and sentenced to prison terms for "knowing membership" in the Party. In March 1956, the New York District Attorney
moved to bring Foster himself to trial—the government's seventh attempt
to imprison him since 1948.[1] It would not be until 1957 that the Supreme

Foster with *left*, Paul Robeson and *right*, Benjamin Davis.

Court finally reversed its earlier rulings in the Smith Act cases and the legal edifice underlying the various prosecutions against the Party began to weaken.[2]

Despite the fact that his regime in the Party had drawn a large part of its ideological sustenance from the twin concepts of a war danger and a fascist threat, Foster seemed prepared to adjust his line somewhat when international tensions began to abate after 1954. In general, his writings took on a less sectarian cast. Although he continued to warn of the increasing danger of fascism in the United States, he cautioned against overestimating as well as underestimating the danger; the former could produce harmful "leftist moods," he wrote. The Party must work within the Democratic party, he admitted, not because that party could become a genuinely progressive organization, "but because the great masses of workers are there." He hailed the 1955 conference of the Big Four at Geneva as a "real victory for the cause of world peace," representing "at least a pause in the Cold War and perhaps its end." He warned again of the "left danger" in the Party, which "see[s] nothing new in the situation after Geneva." By January 1956 he was predicting "a more or less prolonged period of peaceful coexistence." However, he offered no programmatic changes.[3]

As the Party emerged slowly and cautiously from the shadows of McCarthyism, there was little consensus about the shape of the future. Many

Foster with *left to right*, Benjamin Davis, Eugene Dennis, and Robert Thompson.

foresaw continued repression, and in fact anti-Communism would remain a potent force in American politics at both the national and local levels for years. The Party continued to exist in an uncertain state of semilegality; in a movement that was frankly revolutionary, many expected this. However, a significant number of Communists were increasingly dismayed about the Party's powerlessness and obvious isolation from the mainstream of American politics and society. It was obvious that the Party had failed in ways that could not be explained merely by the facts of oppression and unfavorable "objective" circumstances. The failures of the period seemed to require a more searching reexamination. Without a positive strategy, leadership authority was at a low ebb. Moreover, the underground phase, by essentially dissolving the Party at its most dynamic levels, had undermined what one leader called the sense of "structured collectivity" that Communists had depended on to sustain themselves through periods of hardship and sacrifice. The Party, it seemed, needed to recompose itself at a variety of levels.[4]

As had been true in 1945, signals from overseas would once again provide impetus for a major reassessment. For some time it had been clear to a number of sensitive observers in the Party that the Soviets had been intermittently uneasy about certain aspects of Foster's leadership, particularly his emphasis on the war danger. The fact that Browder's name kept emerging, informally, in the ethereal atmosphere of international "discus-

sions" made this especially clear. As late as June 1955, at a United Nations gathering, Molotov had cryptically suggested to the foreign editor
of the *Daily Worker*, Joseph Starobin, that if the Party was not succeed-
ing in its present course, then it should try "another way." At the same
time, aware of dissatisfaction brewing among American Communists as
well as ferment in the Soviet party under Khrushchev, Eugene Dennis
began to call more openly for a "new look" at the old policies.[5]

It was the dramatic revelations at the Twentieth Congress of the Soviet
Party, however, that created a crucial opening for a number of articulate
critics. On February 14, Khrushchev delivered a report to the congress
that had explosive implications. In reference to Stalin's regime, it criticized the "cult of the individual," and called for a return to the Leninist
principle of "collective leadership." It was clear that the report represented the beginnings of an important change in perspective.[6]

Coincidentally, the news of Khrushchev's speech arrived at the time of
the year when the Party press was accustomed to celebrate Foster's birthday. This time, however, on Foster's seventy-fifth birthday, the editors of
the *Daily Worker* and *Political Affairs* were unusually conscientious in
printing every conceivable kind of tribute. A special issue of *Political Affairs* containing numerous testimonies to Foster's leadership also included the text of Khrushchev's initial report, which warned of the "cult
of the individual . . . alien to the spirit of Marxism-Leninism, a cult which
tends to make a particular leader a hero and miracle worker." About the
same time, the *Daily Worker* devoted a tremendous amount of space to
numerous routine birthday greetings to Foster from every foreign party.
All, of course, were couched in adulatory tones, but their number was far
out of proportion to those usually published on such occasions. The
paper even published a weird "Poem for William Z. Foster," fourteen
stanzas in length, which concluded:

> We who are yet to be born salute you
> Men and women of the new America
> (The tanks have been tamed to flowing steel, the atom pushes the levers)
> We who have followed the path that you have pointed,
> Out of the valley and up into the mountains
> Past the winding crags to the skyline of the dawn,
> We greet you, comrade,
> Today you are with us.[7]

In one issue, the editorial staff of the *Daily Worker*, as if to make their
point perfectly clear, juxtaposed yet more birthday greetings and tributes
with a letter from Ring Lardner, Jr., one of the "Hollywood Ten," which
raised the issue of an American "cult of personality": "I wonder if some
of the rather maudlin testaments to William Z. Foster on his recent birth-

day are really the most mature and effective way of acknowledging the respect due America's outstanding working-class leader." Following the letter was an editorial note: "Ring Lardner's letter raises a number of interesting and important questions of vital concern to the American Left. We are happy to have his views and by the same token invite our readers to submit theirs for publication." Soon thereafter, the *Daily Worker* transformed its letters columns into an open forum for discussion of the Party's predicament.[8]

Reports of Khrushchev's secret speech outlining the atrocities of Stalin's regime did not reach American Communists until late March, and the full text was not made available until June 5, when it was printed in the *New York Times*. In the meantime, however, Foster readily joined the controversy, obviously aware that the reputation of his regime was at stake. He was not going to repeat the mistakes of Earl Browder by isolating himself and refusing to debate. Nor, as would quickly become quite clear, was he prepared to quietly retire or accept a ceremonial post. The coming battle would be an arduous and divisive one, but Foster's defense of an essentially conservative course for the Party was perhaps his most impressive political performance. Ironically, his *tour de force* would come at the expense of an even more drastic diminution of the Party's influence on the American Left.

Publicly, Foster cautiously distanced himself from Stalin. The former Soviet leader had made "serious errors in his failure to develop a collective leadership," he ventured, but this was as far as he was prepared to go in mid-March, when the main burden of Khrushchev's critique had yet to become public. The American Party, Foster asserted, should not forget that under Stalin's leadership the USSR made "stupendous progress in nearly every direction in the building of socialism." Moreover, it was dangerous to criticize Stalin too harshly, for this opened the entire socialist enterprise to the hostile critiques of bourgeois politicians and journalists. According to Foster, final judgment on Stalin's regime was best left to the current Soviet leadership, for they were most thoroughly acquainted with him and his shortcomings. Thus, Foster mingled a call for a "thorough revaluation" of the Stalin legacy with the old shibboleths: defense of the Soviet Union and the need to maintain party unity.[9]

Within weeks, however, Foster's criticisms of Stalin had become much more vehement. Communists must condemn the "atmosphere of omniscience and extreme adulation with which he surrounded himself," he wrote. The list of Stalin's errors steadily became "more disturbing." He had

reduced collective leadership and Socialist democracy to a minimum, undercut the vigor and initiative of the Communist Party, put too much stress on the need for security measures inside the USSR, abolished self-criticism and cultivated an enervating adulation, exercised harmful controls over science, art and literature, made serious errors in the conduct of the war, needlessly antagonized Yugoslavia, committed mistakes on the "agrarian question," used brutality in combating dissident forces, prevented women from rising to high posts in the Party and the Government, misused Party cadres, etc.

Stalin's many mistakes and errors, according to Foster, were "appalling" and the character of many of his policies "reactionary." His errors and distortions "obviously did much harm to the USSR." These criticisms, seemingly quite severe, were still in line with the conclusions of Khrushchev's secret speech. Once again, however, the predictable equivocation was included: Stalin "consistently followed a correct general political line and . . . he has performed great services in the rapidly advancing Russian and World Revolution." By this measure, of course, there were few "errors" that could not be ultimately justified by the advance of the revolution.[10] Yet, Foster's history of equivocation would serve him well in the subsequent debates; the crisis in the Party seemed to require a villain and scapegoat, and his vacillation in the past on a number of issues would make it difficult to pin him down.

In late April, the national committee of the Party held its first meeting since 1951. There, Eugene Dennis presented his summation of the Party's situation and the reforms that needed to be undertaken. Although they were from quite different backgrounds, there was a certain resemblance between Dennis and Foster that Foster may have found uncomfortable. Dennis was primarily an apparatus-man and Foster's roots were in the indigenous labor movement, but both men could be reluctant and uncertain when confronted with a new situation that required decisive leadership. The current situation required Dennis to present not only a new general outlook, but a coherent set of alternatives. Ultimately, this proved to be beyond his capabilities, but his initial report was an inspiring document that provided a rallying point for the dissenters. In his summary, later issued as a booklet and entitled *The Communists Take a New Look*, Dennis asserted that the errors of the period after 1945 had been "left sectarian." The Party had been mistaken in portraying the nation as being on the brink of war, fascism, and depression. This mistaken perspective had led to disastrous results in the labor movement. Additionally, the sectarianism in the Party had been the result of "the mechanical and doctrinaire fashion" in which the Party had adopted as its own "the experiences of other parties." He called for a "creative" interpretation of Marxism based on American conditions, increased democracy, and discussion in the Party, and an abandonment of the concept of the Party as vanguard, the idea that "all those who really want socialism will have to come to us." Finally, he called for the formation of diverse democratic front coalitions and alliances. Foster, his appearances at the meetings occasionally curtailed because of his heart condition, was furious about the report, and was the only member of the National Committee to vote against it.[11]

In the meantime, the discussion of the Party's past errors continued in its press, most notably in the pages of the *Daily Worker*. The majority of the letter writers took what might be termed a moderate reformist view. Like Foster, they admitted past mistakes but refused to conclude that the crimes of Stalinism necessitated a rejection of the Party's fundamental principles. A clear majority believed that increased democracy and less bureaucracy could be achieved within a Marxist-Leninist Party. One expressed a typical sentiment: "While I agree with some of the generalities set forth (who doesn't), I don't see that there is any need to plunge ourselves into a long, tedious and demobilizing period of purging ourselves of 'Stalinism.'"[12]

Yet, the forum brought important and profound questions to the fore. The central problem, according to one correspondent, was how Marxism, which should be a guide to action, had become a dogma. "How does a science become a dogma? Science draws its theories from the facts; dogma selects (or invents) its facts to fit theories." A number of the rank-and-file editorialists, however, directly attacked Foster's leadership. He had acquiesced in the creation of a personality cult, one concluded. Others criticized Foster's statement that the Russians were best qualified to judge Stalin. Why couldn't American Marxists criticize the Soviet Union? Didn't a lack of serious criticism play into the hands of the reactionaries? In July, Foster wrote a letter to the Party's Administrative Committee complaining about the debate in the *Daily Worker*. The character of the discussion, he wrote, was "shocking." He cited "flagrant misinterpretation of policies, open advocacy of a return to Browderism, sniping at the Soviet Union, crass anti-leadership tendencies, and even proposals for the liquidation of the Communist Party." He concluded that "this is not Party democracy but political stupidity. It is high time that our Party take this situation in hand, and while welcoming constructive discussion and criticism, put a sharp stop to the anti-Party attacks now going on in our press." The Party secretariat, he proposed, should be empowered to "supervise" the Party discussion and "weed out from it such anti-Party material as has hitherto been cluttering it up."[13]

However, while privately seeking to limit the terms of the debate, in his writings Foster sought to both absorb and deflect the criticisms. Marxism-Leninism, he reiterated, could provide "no blueprint of the Revolution." The transition to socialism "was bound to take on different features in different countries in accordance with varying national conditions." He cited his Smith Act theorizing in support of his defense that he had supported the idea of a peaceful transition to socialism. He referred approvingly to the Popular Front strategies of the Italian and French parties, as well as Dennis's conceptions on the need for a "constitutional and democratic" road to a "peoples' democracy." The Communist party was the vanguard political party of the workers, he affirmed, but "under the pressure of the rapidly changing world situation, Marxism-Leninism must grow and evolve in a theoretical, strategical and tactical sense." The American Party, he rightly noted, had modified the perspective of imminent war following the Geneva Conference. He admitted that "in the period which is now developing," left sectarianism was becoming the main danger in the Communist parties. On all of these issues, the insurgents in the Party had proposed very little that was fundamentally new.[14]

The style of Foster's leadership was on trial as much as its ideology. Foster remained a difficult personality; the last years of his political career seemed to exacerbate his querulous manner. In general, he was a careful and patient listener, but was in turn extremely blunt and forthright in criticizing those with whom he disagreed, so that those who argued with him rarely came away with a sense that he respected their views. In Party meetings he was a lucid speaker who did not hesitate to employ a large and colorful vocabulary of expletives to make his point. Despite his health, he remained mentally sharp and alert. Occasionally he found it necessary to lie down on a couch during debates, shielding his eyes from the light. However, he would soon be back on his feet, arguing vehemently. He was undoubtedly somewhat of an intimidating figure, an individual with far more experience in American radical movements than any of his opponents. As one participant in the debates remembered, he was an individual who inspired respect, not affection.[15]

In the months following the path-breaking National Committee meetings, Foster found himself again isolated in the Party's national leadership, as he had been in the 1930s and early 1940s. The vindication of 1945 had perhaps contributed to Foster's sense of self-righteousness; undoubtedly memories of his personal triumph over Browder's "liquidationism" helped to harden his resolve during the summer of 1956.

In September 1956, after months of debate, the National Committee finally adopted a draft resolution as a discussion document for the coming national convention, which would convene in February of the following year. The resolution reiterated and confirmed the criticisms that Dennis and others had formulated earlier, and represented a clear repudiation of many of the Party's postwar policies. In particular, it called vaguely for a "mass party of Socialism." It was unclear whether or not this would be a substitute for the Communist party—some were already proposing that the Party transform itself into a "political association"—or a coalition to which the Communists would attach themselves in the future. Foster had initially voted, in the interests of Party unity, to endorse the draft resolution, but with qualifications to be published later. From all indications, he remained furiously opposed to the new formula, and finally he voted against it.[16]

The precise character of Foster's objections became clear in a remarkable dissent published in the October *Political Affairs*. It was a straightforward, formidable attack on the opposition. First, in the inevitable self-criticism, he admitted that a number of disastrous turns for the Party had occurred under his guidance. These, however, he still explained as an understandable reaction to repression: the fundamental cause of the Party's losses in membership and influence during the Cold War years was the anti-Communist hysteria whipped up by the government. Yet, the isolation of the Party had not been inevitable, he admitted. There had been serious mistakes: the support given the Progressive party in 1948 which alienated many in the labor movement and which also served as one of the excuses for expelling the left-led unions from the CIO; the failure of the Party convincingly to portray the possibility of a peaceful transition to socialism during the Smith Act trials; and, finally, the "approach taken to security measures to protect the Party." The trials and expulsions of members suspected of unreliability were the "worst error of the whole Cold War period," he asserted. The purges and resultant loss of membership had generally pushed the Party "too far to the Left." However, Foster pointed out that all of these policies had been approved by the National Board; the decisions were made before the Party leaders were imprisoned. The National Board at the time had included John Gates and Dennis, leaders who, he slyly suggested, were not left-sectarian by instinct. Gates himself scarcely needed to be reminded of his own past. Only a few years earlier he had published a pamphlet entitled *On Guard against Browderism, Titoism, Trotskyism* that had warned of the continuing "dangerous tendencies of liquidationism" in the Party and the "enemy ideologies of Browderism and Titoism."[17]

Privately, Foster readily admitted the "mistakes" of the postwar period, but he would never plead a full *mea culpa*. It was "not an easy proposition" to pin the problems of the Party during the Cold War on him, he later reflected in private remarks, because, he claimed, Eugene Dennis had been primarily responsible for instigating the Progressive party debacle and the disastrous adventures of the underground period. At the same time, Foster attempted to address fundamental questions that were on the minds of the reformers. While publicly stating that the American party must pursue a course of political independence consistent with "international proletarian solidarity," in one leadership meeting he stated bluntly that the problem of the Stalin cult really amounted to "an uncritical support of the USSR." The policy of following the Soviet party "has done grave injury to the Party in all its fields of work," he averred. Moreover, "the error runs back many years, and it affected not only our party but also every other Communist party in the world." Even considering the context, this was a startling statement for a leader of Foster's stature to make. Yet, the customary equivocation followed: in correcting the error, "we must do so skillfully, without committing excesses in the opposite direction."[18]

The heart of Foster's position was a defense of the fundamental idea of the Party as a Marxist-Leninist vanguard, "the vanguard political party of the proletariat and of the peoples in general," as he put it elsewhere. What particularly angered him was the fact that the National Committee, in its draft resolution, had rejected a proposal for a simple endorsement of Marxism-Leninism as the theoretical base for the American Party, in favor of an endorsement of Marxism-Leninism as it was "interpreted" by the Party. This, according to Foster, "would imply the end of Marxism-Leninism as embodying the principles of Scientific Socialism." The idea of a "broad, amorphous" party was particularly unsettling. The reformers who think such a party can exist in the United States and function effectively "are living in a dream world," he asserted in one talk. Elsewhere, while admitting that Marxism-Leninism was necessarily an "evolving" doctrine, he asserted that the resolution would tend to "destroy the international character of Marxism-Leninism and reduce it to the status of a Russian Socialist philosophy, subject to a maze of national 'interpretations' before adoption." The Communist Party of the United States "cannot be some vague 'Marxist' party, without a real theoretical basis," he concluded. "The Communist Party must be based upon Marxism-Leninism, but upon a newly invigorated Leninism, cleansed from Stalinist bureaucratic hangovers and fully adapted and applied to the American situation." Foster the syndicalist had always been more attracted to Lenin than Marx; in one leadership meeting this preference came through quite clearly. "Leninism is the Marxism of the imperialism epoch," he explained. "Outside of Leninism there is no Marxism." As to the cult of personality, he of course denied that it had been present during the period of his leadership, but pointedly reminded his critics that it had undeniably flourished during the Browder years, the period to which the reformers often implicitly referred as inspiration for their proposals.[19]

Foster's intransigence in the midst of the controversy was bolstered by several important signals from the Soviet Union. First came a review of Foster's recently published *The Negro People in American History* in *Pravda* that lauded Foster's thirty-five-year career "as a noted figure in the international Communist and workers' movement." The reviewer added that he had been steadfastly "devoted to the struggle for the purity and unity of the Communist party of the USA against opportunists and diversionists . . . in the spirit of firm loyalty to the teachings of Marxism-Leninism." At the same time, Khrushchev began stepping up his criticism of Tito, a sign that must have caused unease among the emerging "national" Communists in the United States.[20]

In general, much of the impetus for the proposed renovation of the Party had come from cadres whose defining political experiences had come in the 1930s. The center of the reformers' strength lay in the New York State Party, which comprised over half of the Party's national membership. The New York Party adopted the most vehement official call for reform; its report even called for a reconsideration of Browder's expulsion. However, in the period before the national convention, Foster could count on several important constituencies of his own. He had support in many Midwestern state parties among Communists who had perhaps felt the force of community repression during the McCarthy period most intensely. He liked to claim that his was the "workers' " perspective, and to some extent this was true. His leadership continued to elicit support among veteran needle trades workers in New York city, for instance, and perhaps his most vociferous supporters came from the Party's waterfront section. These individuals, veterans of the Party's heyday in the maritime union in the 1930s, were now increasingly bitter and isolated after a period of splits and expulsions in the National Maritime Union. One participant in the 1956 controversy termed them a "semi-anarchist group." However, Foster also elicited firm support from many of the Party's professionals and others classified as MAL (members at large).[21]

By late 1956, the reformers' position seemed to be weakening considerably. A number of factors were responsible. First, no one seemed willing to step forward to take firm leadership of the opposing forces. Dennis began to equivocate on a number of issues, and Gates's unfortunate proposal for a new "political association" rendered him vulnerable to accusations of "Browderism" and "liquidationism." No one of stature to replace Foster seemed to be available. Perhaps most important, the reformers were unable to agree on the exact implications of their arguments. The slogan "mass party of socialism" was a banality, subject to infinite interpretations. The Communist party, despite its Cold War ordeals, remained by far the largest party on the left. Was it to dissolve, or merge with other groups that were even more marginal than it was? Bereft of organizational meaning, slogans endorsing a "national road" to socialism, increased Party democracy, and an end to sectarianism were identical with what Foster himself had formally endorsed at various times in the past several years.[22]

Events in Poland and Hungary finally dissolved what unity of purpose the reformers possessed. In Poland, the workers' uprising in Poznań caused some to question the validity of the "people's democracy" that had been established under Władisław Gomułka. In Hungary, the brutal Soviet repression of the Nagy regime in 1956 was portrayed by Foster and his supporters as necessary to save the country from a counterrevolutionary uprising. This, surprisingly, was an assessment that would be shared by a significant number of the reformers in the Party. The Party was bitterly rent by the discussions surrounding the Hungarian invasion. A sense of demoralization gripped a number of Party members, a feeling that the tremendous task of theoretical and programmatic reappraisal simply could not be successfully completed as the Party was presently constituted. A wave of resignations further diminished the Party's membership.[23]

During the crisis of 1956 Foster had spoken vigorously and effectively in defense of his conception of Marxism-Leninism, but it would be a mistake to dismiss his performance as simply the stubborn obstructionism of an aging zealot. He, like other Communists during the period, struggled to assimilate the revelations of the Soviet twentieth congress. In one unpublished meditation, he wrote that the Soviets had yet to offer a satisfactory explanation of how the Stalin cult had developed in a socialist country; while Russian Marxists would undoubtedly come forth with an authoritative interpretation, "Khrushchev and other Soviet leaders have not been very helpful in this key respect." Elsewhere he asserted that "we must not confine ourselves merely to repetitious blaming it all upon the cult of the individual." However, in both his public and private pronouncements he settled on the entirely conventional idea that the Russian Communists had been guilty of "revolutionary excess" in defense of a Soviet Union encircled by hostile capitalist forces. "Other than this," he weakly concluded in one meeting, "we have no rational, not to mention Marxist, explanation" for the "barbarities" of Stalinism. Yet Foster was undoubtedly aware of the tautology: a Communist party in a socialist society could not convincingly ascribe the character of its governance to capitalism.[24]

At the end of the year, Foster received and inexplicably saved a letter from an anonymous writer, "one who has followed your career very carefully and with no little interest." It began with a brutal assessment of the recent developments: "Your life's work is now all shot to hell, isn't it?" The writer pointed to Foster's lonely position in the Party: "Dennis is a weakling and doesn't amount to a damn," and "Gates and others would like to see you die." The purpose of the letter, however, was not simple harassment. Reminding Foster of the Catholicism of his childhood, the writer continued:

It makes a man think, doesn't it? As a matter of fact, it is difficult for myself to know what course a man should pursue. You are a thinking man as I and many others well know. . . . Surely your mind must go back to your boyhood days when you believed in God and immortality of the soul. As we both know, these are profound concepts which have engaged the minds of the most brilliant men for centuries. They cannot be brushed aside lightly by thinking people. Has it occurred to you Bill as it has occurred to me, that dialectical and historical materialism might indeed be scientifically and philosophically invalid and that after all, the theists are the most cogent in their reasoning? It is a perplexing topic. Can plus come from minus?

In 1954, Foster had received a missive from a Catholic cleric which he publicly and ostentatiously rebuked with the statement that "as a Marxist, I find that the dialectical materialist viewpoint fully satisfies me in meeting the everyday problems of life." Now a writer proposed to him that "Christ certainly has fared far better than the leaders of history. They are gone. We are still confronted with Christ." Considering Foster's rhetoric and persona at the time, it is remarkable that he bothered to save this letter. Its significance for him can only be conjectured, in light of his actions much later.[25]

In February 1957, Foster attended what would be his last national convention of the Communist party. He was able to appear in person to officially open the convention, but was too weak to give his keynote address. Instead, his speech was read to the convention. In it, he reaffirmed his stubborn refusal to yield to the reformers on a number of issues. He spoke of "dangerous revisionist tendencies" and "prosperity illusions" among the workers, and warned against "sniping at the Soviet Union." He resurrected the familiar incantations of the campaign against "Browderism." The Party, he wrote, "must realize that world capitalism is sinking into general crisis in the face of the rising socialist world," and was in danger of underestimating the war danger and the aggressive role of American imperialism. He cited the Party's criticism of the Hungarian Communist party during the uprising as an example of a proper willingness to judge the affairs of other Parties, and spoke of the ultimately "harmonious" national and international interests of the masses. The Party "must cooperate freely with all other Communist parties," he wrote. The idea of a "so-called new mass party of socialism" was a chimera, he asserted; "for such a body there is no prospect in the political situation, neither now nor in the foreseeable future." While the Party must seek a broader membership base, he suggested "reducing our excessive numbers of full-timers" and cultivating "a strong core of professional revolutionaries." During one meeting in the preconvention discussion, he told one high-ranking organizer that he was not worried by the diminishing membership of the Party: "Even if we go down to 50 members, if we lose everybody but 50, and those 50 are true . . . Bolsheviks, we'll be back, it doesn't matter." By this time, Foster's conception of the "militant minority" had become nearly a parody.[26]

It particularly angered Foster that the "revisionists" openly rejected the logic of "boring-from-within" in the labor movement. "It is childish nonsense," one internally circulated draft resolution declared, to pretend that the modern trade union movement with its millions in membership can be "captured" or "dictated to." Instead, it would be the workers themselves who would eventually come to revolutionary conclusions as a result of their own experiences in the workplace. Foster of course rejected this logic, preferring to see the minds of the workers as profoundly malleable, citing the influence of "churches, army, radio, television." In 1958 he decried the fact that the Party had issued no official resolution on union work in three years, and finally invoked his distillation of the Party's history: "The Party itself was built upon the basis of active cooperation with the progressive forces in the trade union movement."[27]

Foster's perspective was vindicated at the convention on a number of key questions. The political resolution that was adopted rejected the idea of "liquidating" the party as a first step toward the creation of a "broader party of socialism at some future time." It reaffirmed the primacy of Marxism-Leninism and the Party's vanguard role. These had been the rallying points for the reformers, and their defeat was decisive. Yet, Foster's victory was not a personal one. The failed "left-sectarian" policies that had been associated with his leadership were repudiated. While he was reelected to the national committee, he failed to gain the votes of more than 100 of the 281 delegates who cast votes.[28]

It is difficult to imagine, however, that he was particularly discouraged or disheartened by the outcome of the convention. On the surface, at least, Foster seemed satisfied with the outcome of the Party crisis. Beyond the supposition that he had been aware of the nature of the Soviet regime for years, his reaction suggests that his Communism had never been held as a kind of quasi-religious faith, a body of beliefs sustained by infallible doctrine. Yet, there remained at the center of his politics one core belief that he defended with clerical certainty. This was the idea that a militant minority, a gifted priesthood of revolutionists, could somehow design the downfall of a corrupt and inefficient capitalist order.

Aside from this concept, with all its implications, the emotions and motives that drove him in the last years of his life clearly ran quite deep. While for him political resolutions were an ephemeral currency, his final speeches and writings cannot be said to be wholly mendacious. They reveal an extravagant anger, most of all, against "revisionists" whose qualifications and complexities would complicate the revolutionary enterprise. Foster was an individual who, as one of his associates termed it, "liked his class struggle simple and clear."[29]

Foster's last years were a testament to his astonishing determination. A crippling stroke in October 1957 affected his ability to speak and hold a pen, and he would remain mostly bedridden for the rest of his days. Nonetheless, he soon trained himself to compose notes, albeit in very shaky handwriting, and he dictated the substance of his articles to a typist. By 1959, he was back to a regular schedule of writing: in that year alone he produced eight articles for *Political Affairs*.[30]

In the meantime, the Party continued its decline in membership and influence; by the summer of 1957, it could claim only approximately three thousand members. In early 1958, the *Daily Worker*, whose management had been a continual target of Foster's wrath, was forced to close as antirevisionists choked off the newspaper's funding. Shortly thereafter, its editor, John Gates, resigned from the Party. Foster's victory over the fount of reformist "talk" was complete.[31]

Foster seemed anxious to build an enduring political architecture for the Party, and establish his credentials as a prominent Marxist theoretician. However, his writings contained little promise for a new approach. His hopes seemed to rely less on convincing analysis than on the continual invocation of the ultimate superiority of "world socialism" to a corrupt and decaying "world capitalism." For the American Party, Foster offered a prescription for isolation. In 1959, he criticized the draft resolution for the upcoming seventeenth convention of the Party, calling for a strengthening of its "international work" and a more explicit repudiation of the insidious revisionism of past years. The right danger to the Party, he held, continued to be the main danger. His perspectives found increasing support from abroad; articles in the Soviet press now explicitly condemned Gates and his allies by name as dangerous revisionists. The American Party dutifully echoed this critique, while offering little support for Foster's perspectives on the labor party and other issues.[32]

William Foster refused, however, to fit into neat political categories. This fact was underlined in the spring of 1959, when he sent a five thousand-word personal letter to Mao Zedong in which he extravagantly praised the accomplishments of the Chinese revolution and offered an extensive discussion of the political situation in the United States. The letter had not been approved by the Party's secretariat, and it caused no small amount of unease when the *New York Times* published it and Mao's warm response: "Allow me, on behalf of the Communist Party of China and the Chinese people, to extend hearty greetings to you, glorious fighter and leader of the American working class." In his letter, Foster suggested that he would like to visit the Peoples' Republic and be treated there for his medical problems. This raised the distinct possibility that the

National Chairman of the American Communist party might spend the last days of his life in Communist China. The Party was forced to reproduce the exchange between Foster and Mao in *Political Affairs*.[33]

Foster was certainly a close follower of the Chinese revolution, and an avid reader of Mao's writings as they became available. His *History of the Three Internationals*, which carried an extended discussion of the Chinese revolution and Mao, was published in 1955 during a period of debate over who would inherit the mantle of foremost Communist theoretician from the recently deceased Stalin. Foster termed Mao "a brilliant theoretician," a "creative Marxist genius" whose writings constitute "major contributions to the general body of Marxist theory." After 1955, Foster apparently remained unembarrassed by the refusal of the Chinese Communists to endorse Khrushchev's condemnation of Stalin. Certain Maoist themes were prominent in Foster's writings of this period; his continued emphasis on the dangerous and aggressive motives of American imperialism and the imminence of war were most noteworthy in this regard. Foster admired Mao's writings on military strategy and tactics, especially "the situation of a guerilla army gradually growing into a mass military force and carrying on the struggle in the face of a vastly stronger enemy." In any event, Foster would live only through the first months of the open Sino-Soviet split; hc was thus spared the necessity of taking an explicit political stand in the dispute. In 1963 the Chinese, by then bitter critics of the American Communists, would suggest that the Party "carry on and enrich the revolutionary tradition of Comrade Foster."[34]

During the years in which he had finally attained more or less undisputed leadership of the Communist party, Foster's politics were difficult to classify. His differences with the international movement on the issues of the war danger and the coming of fascism in the United States were ones of degree and timing, but significant nonetheless. His views on the nature of the Chinese revolution revealed that he was not as inclined to accept Soviet orthodoxy as were many of his comrades. During these years his politics essentially embraced one of the central tenets of Trotskyism, that world peace could not be accomplished without the overthrow of American capitalism.[35]

If there was any one area in which American Communists could have benefited from original theorizing, it was in questions of labor and electoral politics, and the relationship of the Party to state power. The unique and deeply rooted character of the two-party system in the United States required, on its face, an innovative approach to Communist tactics. The vehement repudiation of Browder's heresies rendered original thinking in this regard especially problematic after 1945, however. The political hostilities of the Cold War, as Foster never ceased to point out, had undercut many of the assumptions of "Browderism." Foster's writings, still suffused with themes from his earlier syndicalist years, offered very little prospect that the Communists could find a way to involve themselves in the hegemonic political culture. This was to be expected, since Foster for the most part eschewed contests over the symbolism and meanings of political culture.

At the level of political tactics, he was content to call for working within the two-party system toward the eventual establishment of a labor party. He declared privately that it was a "waste of time" to try to build unity among the various socialist sects. The political isolation of the Communist party in the 1920s and as recently as 1948, he concluded, was the direct result of its attempts to build up independent mass parties "instead of working with the masses" in the Democratic or even Republican parties. In this respect, Foster hewed rightward—in his eyes even the slogan "United Party of Socialism" was "sectarian," for instance.[36] While a labor party would come into existence at "the appropriate time," in the meantime it could not be forgotten that the trade union movement would be the backbone of any future progressive political coalition. In essence, he was foreseeing a situation in which the unions would take over or supplant one of the major parties. Trade unionism, as a purely organizational, instrumental phenomenon, was always prior to politics. This is how Foster could state, in a 1956 article entitled "The Road to Socialism," that the recent merger of the AFL and CIO was "a long stride towards independent working-class political action." Foster's laborist perspective and above all his belief in the historical progression of the union movement absolved him from offering a cogent explanation for the rejection by American workers of socialist politics.[37]

Foster's declining years were clearly challenging and difficult ones for him and his family. Although the Communist party itself had received significant subsidies from the Soviet Union since its founding, such payments were not enough to provide a particularly comfortable standard of living for even the highest officials of the Party. William and Esther continued to live in their one-bedroom flat in the Bronx, always badly in need of painting. His highest annual salary as a Party official was about thirty-five hundred dollars in the years immediately after the war; this was roughly equivalent to the average salary of a coal miner during the same period. Foster's life was not made easier by the United States government. In 1955 the Social Security Administration determined that a number of Communist party employees and their spouses were ineligible to receive retirement benefits because their service to the Communist party was in effect service to a foreign government. The government attempted to recover about a thousand dollars that had already been paid to Foster, but the policy of the Social Security Administration was finally overturned.[38]

At some point early in 1959 Foster and his personal physician, Dr. Harry Epstein, decided that he needed to travel to either the Soviet Union or China in order to receive proper medical care. Foster claimed that he simply could not afford treatment and rehabilitation in the United States. However, he was still under indictment for the Smith Act prosecutions, free on five thousand dollars bail pending his recovery from his illness. His attorney's repeated attempts to have the indictments dismissed so that he could travel out of the country were unsuccessful. In October 1960 the Supreme Court refused to hear his plea to be released from the terms of his parole, which limited him to the New York area, but ordered the government to make a determination whether his health would ever allow him to stand trial. While a physician finally determined that he was unfit for trial (he had suffered yet another stroke in July), the government delayed issuing him a passport, demanding that he appear in person in order to apply and make a sworn statement. Finally, he was delivered to the office in an ambulance. By January he was on his way to the Soviet Union.[39] In a parting letter to Gus Hall, the newly anointed general secretary of the Party, he wrote that "our Party is part of a great world wide Communist movement. Time has shown that it is indestructible, and is part of a movement which will eventually dominate the world. It is in this sense that we should fight to preserve and improve it. We must actually love our Party."[40]

Esther did not accompany him on his initial voyage, although he had for some time been seeking information from the Soviets about the possibility of treatment of her severe arthritis. Only his physician and his son-in-law Emmanuel—whose presence as a translator Foster insisted on because he distrusted the Soviet translators—made the initial trip with Foster. Once in the Soviet Union, however, he was upset for long periods about Esther's absence and worried about the state of the family he had left behind, especially whether they had enough money to live on. Esther, Sylvia, and Joe arrived in the summer.[41]

In March, the Soviets celebrated Foster's eightieth birthday. There were articles discussing his career in every major newspaper, and he was hailed as one of the world's "greatest Marxist theoreticians." Khrushchev himself visited Foster's bedside, only to be met with sharp criticism of the Soviet regime's growing hostility toward China. In his brief remarks, Foster offered praise for the Chinese revolution; the room, according to Emmanuel, fell very quiet. The Soviets, in turn, despite their celebration of his theoretical accomplishments, implied that Foster's syndicalism had limited his understanding of "dialectical" questions.[42]

Given his extremely frail condition, Foster must have known that he stood a very good chance of dying in the Soviet Union. His decision to

Foster's eightieth birthday, with *left to right*, Boris Ponomarev, translator, Mikhail Suslov, Nikita Khrushchev, and Frol Kozlov.

spend his last days there can be understood in purely pragmatic, as well as political terms: he believed that he could not afford the price of decent medical attention in the United States. Although in his last weeks he showed some signs of regaining partial use of his limbs, at a sanitarium outside of Moscow on September 1, he finally succumbed. A state funeral was held in Red Square at the Lenin Mausoleum; although Khrushchev was part of an honor guard at an earlier viewing, he was absent from this meeting. The two leading pallbearers for Foster's ashes at the Red Square service were Leonid Brezhnev and Mikhail Suslov, conservatives who would later engineer Khrushchev's downfall. Despite a solemn ceremony before the Kremlin Wall, where American Communists John Reed, William D. Haywood, and Charles Ruthenberg were interred, Esther finally accompanied his ashes back to the United States. At a memorial meeting at Carnegie Hall, raucous protesters paraded before the building carrying signs that declared: "We Hate Reds" and "One Less Red Pest."[43] His ashes were finally deposited in Waldheim Cemetery in Chicago, near the graves of the Haymarket martyrs. He was indeed, as his epitaph expressed, a "tireless fighter" for his dream of a socialist future.

Pallbearers at Lenin Mausoleum. *Foreground, left to right*: N. G. Ignatov, Leonid Brezhnev, Mikhail Suslov, Elizabeth Gurley Flynn (behind Suslov).

Memorial service, Red Square, September 6, 1961. *Left to right*: Mikhail Suslov, Elizabeth Gurley Flynn, Leonid Brezhnev, N. G. Ignatov, Dolores Ibarruri, N. M. Shvernik, V. V. Grishin, P. N. Pospelov, unidentified.

EPILOGUE

IN HIS later career Foster was often disparaged as an inflexible dogmatist. However, his final years were ones of deep uncertainty, which he was only partly successful in masking with a brittle scientism and hard determination. His often inconsistent meditations on the central problems of Communist politics during the Cold War betray something of an angry lashing out at phenomena that defy deeper analysis or betray understanding. Despite his relentless and obsessive efforts to locate a ground of certainty in Marxist theory, it was finally his voiceless rage that formed the inviolable core of his identity. Foster the "fighter" was in some senses an atavism, a throwback to the class-war syndicalism of the turn of the century and, even earlier, to the radicalism that his father had nurtured and which had been the "meat and drink" of his childhood years. All who knew him understood that his fighting temperament sustained him in his later years as well. This was reflected in his epitaph.

According to his family, Foster asked for the presence of a Catholic priest in the hours before his death. His request was somehow appropriate, representing a final and indissoluble ambiguity in his life and personality. In an earlier meditation on religion, he had somewhat defensively professed his comfort with the idea of oblivious death: his soul, he observed, betrayed no existence before his birth, why should he expect otherwise following his demise? Did his final plea represent a renunciation of this stark, logical materialism, or did it merely reflect a momentary confusion of faiths in a personality given by nature to abject belief and devotion to "canon law"? Here it is necessary to return to Foster's own uncertainty, reflected in the peculiar hesitation that lurked in many of his most important political acts. In the final analysis, he lacked the power of true belief that sustained many of the most effective activists in the Communist movement: "the power to hold convictions and to act on them," as one apostate characterized it. In this respect Foster the "fighter" was also a skeptical "professional revolutionary" and technician who harbored a certain cynicism about political ideals of all kinds, perhaps including those he himself professed. He understood and in some ways personified Zinoviev's dictum that "discipline begins where conviction ends." Ironically, this is why it is possible to trust his rage, because his anger always survived the test of his skepticism.[1]

While Foster held many convictions in his career, it was their very multifariousness and the ease with which he embraced, abandoned, or renounced them that defined his career for most observers. Some have compared Communist politics to religion, but Foster was an individual who finally refused to be constrained by a coherent set of beliefs. He was first attracted to Communism not because of the messianic faith that Bolshevism promised for some activists, but because its power and efficiency appeared to at least match that of the modern corporations that seemed to rule his world. Quite simply, he believed that Soviet power could be enlisted in the fight for social justice in America. At its most effective, his outlook was adaptive, experimental, and innovative; at its worst it could be crudely bureaucratic and aridly unhistorical. However, his aggressive modernism was not an alien, "un-American" mentality—its seeds were first planted into his consciousness in turn-of-the-century Philadelphia, where his family's powerlessness gave birth to his peculiar cynicism about working-class culture, tradition, and faith. It is impossible, though, to dismiss his alienation as based simply on narrow experience or a sullen, wounded memory. His wide and complex experiences as a worker and trade union organizer both contributed to his visceral hate of capitalist society and led him to embrace vital aspects of the worldview and methodology of his opponents. Part of the irony and tragedy of his life is that he never understood himself as an American in this way, fully a product of the society he so despised.

According to Max Eastman, Foster once explained privately to him that he and other American Communists did not like much of what they had to sign their names to in Moscow, but found it necessary to "go along" with Soviet pronouncements because, as the only successful revolutionary state in the world, the support of the Soviets was vital to the success of the American movement.[2] This is an entirely credible assessment of Foster's motivations, one that was at one time apparently shared, for instance, by both Trotsky and Stalin. It is especially suggestive to recall Foster's confidence in light of the collapse of Communism in the former Soviet Union. Undoubtedly, he came to place much of his revolutionary hope on the bureaucratic and military accomplishments of Communist state apparatuses, achievements that proved quite fragile. Yet, his radicalism was based on much more than opportunism or simple admiration of Soviet achievements. Because he was truly an American radical, we can be sure that the alienation and activism his life represents will survive the demise of Communist parties in other lands.

NOTES

INTRODUCTION

1. The only complete biographical study of Foster is Arthur Zipser's *Workingclass Giant: The Life of William Z. Foster* (New York: International Publishers, 1981). Zipser, a former aide of Foster's, puts forward a largely uncritical interpretation of Foster and his role in the Communist party.

Because Foster was such a prominent figure in the party, it is inevitable that histories of American Communism contain detailed discussions of his activities. Most thorough and insightful are the analyses of Theodore Draper, in his *The Roots of American Communism* (New York: Viking, 1957) and *American Communism and Soviet Russia* (New York: Viking, 1960). The only one-volume history of the party is Irving Howe and Lewis Coser, *The American Communist Party: A Critical History* (Boston: Beacon Press, 1957). Other discussions are contained in Harvey Klehr, *The Heyday of American Communism* (New York: Basic Books, 1984); Maurice Isserman, *Which Side Were You On?* (Middletown, Conn.: Wesleyan University Press, 1982); and idem, *If I Had a Hammer: The Decline of the Old Left and the Rise of the New* (New York: Basic Books, 1988). Also relevant is Bert Cochran, *Labor and Communism: The Conflict That Shaped American Unions* (Princeton, N.J.: Princeton University Press, 1977). Penetrating accounts by former acquaintances of Foster's are in Joseph Starobin, *American Communism in Crisis, 1943–1957* (Berkeley: University of California Press, 1972), and James P. Cannon, *The First Ten Years of American Communism* (New York: Pathfinder, 1962).

On Foster's activities in the labor movement before he became a Communist, very little of a systematic nature has been written. The most complete is Philip S. Foner, *History of the Labor Movement in the United States*, vol. 4, *The IWW 1905–1917* (New York: International Publishers, 1965). On Foster's participation in the meatpacking and steel organizing campaigns, the most thorough treatments are in James R. Barrett, *Work and Community in the Jungle: Chicago's Packinghouse Workers, 1894–1922* (Urbana: University of Illinois Press, 1987), and David Brody, *Labor in Crisis: The Steel Strike of 1919* (Urbana: University of Illinois Press, 1987). On the "new unionism" of the pre–World War I era, the definitive essay is David Montgomery, "The 'New Unionism' and the Transformation of Workers' Consciousness in America," *Journal of Social History* (Summer 1974).

2. Theodore Draper, *American Communism and Soviet Russia* (New York: Viking, 1960), p. 126.

3. William Foster, *Twilight of World Capitalism* (New York: International Publishers, 1949), p. 162.

4. Theodore Draper interview with Bertram Wolfe, Sept. 25, 1953, TD, Box 18, Folder 20.

5. Richard B. Freeman and James L. Medoff, *What Do Unions Do?* (New York: Basic Books, 1984), pp. 7–11, 14–16, 18–20.

6. Several of the numerous historical discussions and memoirs in this vein include: Kenneth Kann, *Joe Rapoport: The Life of a Jewish Radical* (Philadelphia: Temple University Press, 1981); Roger Keeran, *The Communist Party and the Auto Workers' Union* (Bloomington, Ind.: Indiana University Press, 1980); Paul Lyons, *Philadelphia Communists, 1936–1956* (Philadelphia: Temple University Press, 1982); Mark Naison, *Communism in Harlem during the Depression* (Urbana: University of Illinois Press, 1983); Steve Nelson, James R. Barrett, and Rob Ruck, *Steve Nelson: American Radical* (Pittsburgh: University of Pittsburgh Press, 1981); Nell Irvin Painter, *The Narrative of Hosea Hudson: His Life as a Negro Communist in the South* (Cambridge, Mass.: Harvard University Press, 1979); Al Richmond, *A Long View from the Left: Memoirs of an American Revolutionary* (Boston: Houghton Mifflin, 1973); Fraser M. Ottanelli, *The Communist Party of the United States: From the Depression to World War II* (New Brunswick, N.J.: Rutgers University Press, 1991). Recent studies in labor history containing accounts of Communist activity in unions include Bruce Nelson, *Workers on the Waterfront: Seamen, Longshoremen, and Unionism in the 1930s* (Urbana: University of Illinois Press, 1988); Joshua Freeman, *In Transit: The Transport Workers in New York City, 1933–1966* (New York: Oxford University Press, 1989); and Robin D. G. Kelley, *Hammer and Hoe: Alabama Communists during the Great Depression* (Chapel Hill: University of North Carolina Press, 1991).

7. On the relationship between Foster's syndicalist outlook and his career as a Communist, see James O'Neil, *American Communism* (New York: E. P. Dutton, 1947), p. 31, and James Weinstein, *Ambiguous Legacy: The Left in American Politics* (New York: New Viewpoints, 1977), pp. 49–54. Theodore Draper, in *Roots of American Communism* and *American Communism and Soviet Russia*, discusses prewar syndicalism in some detail but declines to investigate its influence on the later history of the party.

8. Earl Browder interview with Theodore Draper, pp. 36–37, TD, Box 1, Folder 8.

CHAPTER 1
BEGINNINGS

1. *BTS*, p. 9; *PWL*, "Foreword"; U.S. Senate, Committee on Labor and Education, *Investigation of Strike in the Steel Industry.* 66th Cong., 1st sess., 1919, p. 388.

2. James and Elizabeth's birth dates are from U.S. Bureau of the Census, *Tenth Census of the United States for 1880*, Taunton, Mass. E.D. 121; *BTS*, p. 11; John Devoy, *Recollections of an Irish Rebel* (New York: Charles Young, 1929), p. 130.

3. *BTS*, pp. 11–12. According to Taunton municipal birth records, James and Elizabeth lived in Taunton as early as 1872. James's first recorded address was in a section known as Whittenton, a mill village of company-owned houses and tenements north of town: *Taunton City Directory* (Boston: Sampson, Murdock and Co., 1874); D. Hamilton Hurd, *History of Bristol County, Mass.* (Philadel-

phia: J. W. Lewis, 1883), p. 823; *Atlas of Taunton City* (Boston: George Walker and Co., 1881).

4. *BTS*, pp. 11–12. Joseph North, in *William Z. Foster: An Appreciation* (New York: International Publishers, 1955), p. 7, states that James Foster "brought his wife, Elizabeth" from Ireland. However, in his autobiographies, Foster does not mention that James and Elizabeth emigrated together. E. P. Thompson, *The Making of the English Working Class* (New York: Viking, 1963), pp. 542, 706, on trade unionism in Carlisle.

5. St. Mary's Church, Taunton, baptismal record for Anne (Sarah-Anna) Foster, shows Anna Kelly as the mother with Elizabeth Foster's name crossed out.

6. "William Z. Foster," memoir by Samuel Darcy in author's possession. William remembered that his father was "a rough and tumble scrapper of local renown and his special predilection was to fight Irish policemen" (*BTS*, p. 12). See also Arthur Zipser, interview with the author, April 1980, and Zipser, *Workingclass Giant: The Life of William Z. Foster* (New York: International Publishers, 1981), p. 10.

7. William Foster's birth record cites only "Rear, Weir Street" as his family address. The 1880 *Taunton City Directory*, however, locates the family's address at "Rear, 50 Weir St." Various other addresses of the family during this period are cited in Taunton city directories; St. Mary's Church (Taunton) baptismal records; Taunton municipal birth and death records; 1880 Census. Anna, Mabel, Clara, and John are the only adult siblings that Foster mentions in his autobiographies. *BTS*, pp. 12 and 22. Taunton city birth records show William's original middle name as "Edward."

8. *BTS*, p. 12. According to various birth and baptismal records (which by no means should be considered all-inclusive), Elizabeth gave birth to thirteen children during the period beginning in 1872, when she was twenty-one years old, and 1893, the date of the last baptismal record available (see notes 7 and 26 for sources).

How typical was Elizabeth's experience with childbirth? We know that during the years Elizabeth resided in Taunton, at least three, and possibly five of the nine children she bore died in infancy. Samuel H. Preston and Michael R. Haines, in *Fatal Years: Child Mortality in Late Nineteenth-Century America* (Princeton, N.J.: Princeton University Press, 1991), pp. 91–92, provide an estimated proportion of children dying before age five (1900) of .19 for a representative US sample; .21 for Philadelphia parents; .23 for parents where the husband is a laborer; .21 where both parents are foreign-born. Gretchen A. Condran, Henry Williams and Rose Cheney, "The Decline in Mortality in Philadelphia from 1870–1930: The Role of Municipal Services," in *Pennsylvania Magazine of History and Biography*, April 1984, p. 155 found a general probability of death (age 0–1) of between 175 and 152 per thousand births for women in Philadelphia between 1870 and 1890. For poor and immigrant women infant mortality could be much higher than group samples indicate. "The poorer the woman was, the likelier she was to have more children, to be exposed to debilitating infectious diseases, to need to contribute her strenuous daily labor to provide food and shelter for her family, to live in ill-ventilated housing, to have access to fewer fresh foods, especially milk products and clean water, and to encounter more general daily hardships." Judith Walzer Leavitt, *Brought to Bed: Childbearing in America, 1750–1950* (New York: Oxford University Press, 1986), p. 72.

9. Bruce Laurie and Mark Schmitz, "Manufacture and Productivity: The Making of an Industrial Base, Philadelphia, 1850–1880," in *Philadelphia: Work, Space, Family and Group Experience in the Nineteenth Century*, ed. Theodore Hershberg (Philadelphia: University of Pennsylvania Press, 1981), p. 44; Sam Bass Warner, *The Private City: Philadelphia in Three Periods of its Growth* (Philadelphia: University of Pennsylvania Press, 1968), pp. 50, 52.

10. Edward Strahan, ed., *A Century After: Picturesque Glimpses of Philadelphia and Pennsylvania* (Philadelphia: Allen Lane, Scott and Lauderbach, 1875), p. 184.

11. *PWL*, p. 15; W. E. B. Dubois, *The Philadelphia Negro* (Millwood, N.Y.: Kraus-Thomson, 1973), p. 61.

12. The Fosters' address in Philadelphia, 619 South 17th Street, is from *Gopsill's Philadelphia City Directory* (Philadelphia: James Gopsill's Sons, 1887–1898) and "Consent to the Marriage of a Child or Ward" for Sarah-Anna Foster, January 21, 1898, Philadelphia City Archives, marriage records, 99919; *Baist's Property Atlas of the City and County of Philadelphia* (Philadelphia: C.W. Baist, 1895); Theodore Hershberg, Dale Light, Jr., Harold Cox and Richard Greenfield, "The 'Journey to Work': An Empirical Investigation of Work, Residence and Transportation, Philadelphia 1850 and 1880" in Hershberg, *Philadelphia*, pp. 128–75.

13. Claudia Goldin, "Family Strategies and the family Economy in the Late Nineteenth Century: The Role of Secondary Workers," in Hershberg, *Philadelphia*; Foster autobiographical statement, 12/26/32, Comintern, f. 495, op. 261, d. 15.

14. Ownership of Foster's home was verified in Philadelphia Department of Deeds, Philadelphia City Hall, #5-S-6–83. U.S. Bureau of the Census, *Tenth Census of the United States, 1880*, Philadelphia, Pa., E.D. 645–47. Dale B. Light Jr., "The Role of Irish-American Organisations in Assimilation and Community Formation," in *The Irish in America: Emigration, Assimilation and Impact*, ed. P.J. Drudy, Irish Studies, no. 4 (New York: Cambridge University Press, 1985), p. 119. Lorin Blodget, *The Social Condition of the Industrial Classes of Philadelphia* (Philadelphia: Philadelphia Social Science Association, 1883), p. 18; *PWL*, p. 17.

15. Light, "Irish-American Organizations," p. 127; U.S. Census, *Tenth Census 1880*, Philadelphia, Pa., E.D. 645–47. Theodore Hershberg, Alan N. Burstein, Eugene P. Ericksen, Stephanie Greenberg, and William L. Yancey, "A Tale of Three Cities: Blacks and Immigrants in Philadelphia, 1850–1880, 1930 and 1970," *Annals of the American Academy of Political and Social Science* 441 (1979): 64, 69.

16. Moyamensing is the traditional name of the large area in South Philadelphia where the smaller neighborhood that Foster called Skittereen was located. In using the term "Skittereen," I am referring to the geographical boundaries defined by the local street gang. *PWL*, p. 15. U.S. Bureau of the Census, *Tenth Census, 1880*, Philadelphia, Pa., E.D. 645–47.

17. U.S. Bureau of the Census, *Twelfth Census, 1900*, Philadelphia, Pa., E.D. 753–54; *Atlas of the City of Philadelphia, Vol. 8*, 26th and 30th Wards (Philadelphia: Geo. W. Bromley and Co. 1889); *Atlas of the City and County of Philadelphia* (Philadelphia: Geo. W. and Walter S. Bromley, 1901).

18. Light, "Role of Irish-American Organisations," p. 113.

19. Dennis Clark, *The Irish in Philadelphia: Ten Generations of Urban Experience* (Philadelphia: Temple University Press, 1973), pp. 132–35; Dennis Clark, *Erin's Heirs* (Lexington, Ky.: University of Kentucky Press, 1991), pp. 29, 147, 149; *BTS*, p. 14; Foster, "How I Became a Rebel," *Labor Herald*, July 1922, pp. 24–25.

20. E. J. Hobsbawm, *Primitive Rebels: Studies in Archaic Forms of Social Movement in the 19th and 20th Centuries* (New York: Norton, 1959), pp. 164–66.

21. Elizabeth Faue, *Community of Suffering and Struggle: Women, Men and the Labor Movement in Minneapolis, 1915–1945* (Chapel Hill: University of North Carolina Press, 1991), esp. pp. 73–74.

22. *Gopsill's Philadelphia City Directory*, 1892–1898; *BTS*, p. 12; *Boyd's Co-Partnership and Residence Directory of Philadelphia City* (Philadelphia: C. E. Howe and Co., 1896).

23. J. Thomas Scharf and Thompson Westcott, *History of Philadelphia, 1609–1884*, 3 vols. (Philadelphia: L. H. Everts, 1884), 2:941; *Housing Conditions in Philadelphia: An Investigation Made by Emily W. Dinwiddie* (Philadelphia, 1904), p. 23.

24. Michael R. Haines, "Poverty, Economic Stress, and the Family in a Late Nineteenth-Century City: Whites in Philadelphia, 1880," in Hershberg, *Philadelphia*, pp. 246–47, 255; William Z. Foster, "Unemployment," *World Magazine*, Sept. 28, 1974; Minutes, Nov. 27, 1894, Western Soup Society, Western Community House And Soup Society Papers, Urban Archives and Records Center, Temple University.

25. Haines, "Poverty, Economic Stress and the Family," p. 257.

26. Information about Foster's family from 1880 Census; Taunton birth and death records; *BTS*, p. 12; St. Teresa of Avila baptism record, St. Rita's Rectory, Philadelphia; Foster, "Unemployment"; *PWL*, p. 15; Marriage Certificate of Sarah-Anna Foster.

Foster attended public school before compulsory schooling laws came into effect in Philadelphia in 1895. On Irish immigrant attitudes toward public schools, see Clark, *Irish in Philadelphia*, p. 100. Foster's brief comments on his experiences in school are in *BTS*, p. 13; *The Worker*, Sept. 25, 1949, p. 1.

27. Warner, *The Private City*, p. 185. St. Teresa's Church no longer exists, but in the 1880s and 1890s it was a center of worship for many impoverished Irish immigrants in South Philadelphia; Joseph L. Kirlin, *Catholicity in Philadelphia: From the Earliest Missionaries Down to the Present Time* (Philadelphia: John Joseph McVey, 1909).

28. C. W. Baist, *Baist's Property Atlas of the City and County of Philadelphia* (1895); *BTS*, pp. 13, 14; Foster, *Twilight of World Capitalism* (New York: International Publishers, 1949), p. 159; "Priests of St. Teresa's Church," document at

St. Rita's Rectory, Philadelphia. Foster has been most convincingly portrayed as a "system thinker" in Aileen S. Kraditor, *The Radical Persuasion: 1890–1917* (Baton Rouge: Louisiana State University Press, 1981).

29. *PWL*, pp. 16–18. Foster writes quite negatively of a Bulldogs' social club that "was a gambling layout and a Sunday 'speakeasy,' a hang-out for bums, crooks, pimps, gamblers, racetrack touts, political henchmen and idle workers." (ibid., p. 17) This description has a suggestive similarity to his description of his father's activities in another context: "he made our home a rallying point for ball players, runners, boxers, race-track men, cock-fighters, dog-fighters, etc." (*BTS*, p. 12)

30. Dennis Clark, "The Philadelphia Irish: Persistent Presence," in *The Peoples of Philadelphia: A History of Ethnic Groups and Lower-Class Life, 1790–1940* ed. Allen F. Davis and Mark H. Haller (Philadelphia, Temple University Press, 1973), pp. 141–42. *BTS*, p. 11. *PWL*, p. 18.

31. *BTS*, pp. 11, 20, 22.

32. Nathaniel Burt and Wallace E. Davies, "The Iron Age, 1876–1905," in *Philadelphia: A 300-Year History*, ed. Russell F. Weigley (New York: Norton, 1982), p. 495; Warner, *Private City*, p. 184; Judith L. Goldberg, "Strikes, Organizing and Change: The Knights of Labor in Philadelphia, 1869–1890," (Ph.D. diss., New York University, 1985), pp. 111–12, 115, 205, 208, 269.

33. *PWL*, p. 143.

34. *Philadelphia Inquirer*, Dec. 25, 1895.

35. Ibid., Dec. 24, 1895; *PWL*, p. 143.

36. *BTS*, p. 15; *Philadelphia Inquirer*, Dec. 18, 1895, Dec. 24, 1895, Dec. 25, 1895.

37. *Philadelphia Public Ledger*, Dec. 24, 1895.

38. *BTS*, p. 15.

39. *PWL*, p. 19. Kretchman's address is in *Gopsill's Philadelphia City Directory*, 1893. Hershberg, Cox, Light, Greenfield, "The Journey to Work" in Hershberg, *Philadelphia*, pp. 134–35, for the average journey to work.

40. *PWL*, p. 20.

41. *BTS*, pp. 13–14; Foster, "Unemployment."

42. In *BTS*, p. 12, Foster states that his father died at age sixty. According to census records (Taunton, 1880), this would have been in 1901. Elizabeth, according to Foster, died in 1901 at the age of fifty-three; according to the 1880 Census, her date of death, if Foster's estimation of her age at the time of death is correct, would have been in 1903. No record of either James's or Elizabeth's deaths can be found in Philadelphia municipal records; neither is enumerated in the 1900 Census for Philadelphia. The last known address for Elizabeth is 1041 Dorrance Street in South Philadelphia; she was named as John Foster's guardian on his enlistment papers (National Archives) dated July 1898. James disappears from Philadelphia city directories in 1898. The year 1898 appears to have been an important one for the family, in which the three oldest children (and possibly James) depart. Sarah-Anna is married in this year, and William goes to Wyomissing, near Reading, to live with his sister, Sarah-Anna, and his brother-in-law, George McVey. John Foster enlists in July and is mustered out of the army in

Philadelphia in October 1898, but cannot be located in either the city directories or the 1900 Census. Foster goes to sea in 1901; he stated that "my parents were both dead and my two elder sisters were married." (*BTS*, p. 24) This is apparently partly incorrect, for of the three surviving sisters that he names in *From Bryan to Stalin*, Anna (or Sarah-Anna), Mabel, and Clara, Mabel and Clara were both younger. See Taunton City birth records, 1884, for Mabel; St. Teresa's Church baptism records, 1893, for Clara.

43. This account is pieced together from Foster's somewhat inconsistent narrative in *BTS*, pp. 13, 20, 23; *PWL*, pp. 21–22. Also, United States Bureau of the Census, Census for 1900, Wyomissing, Pa., E.D. 14. On the transience of young industrial workers during this period, see David Montgomery, *The Fall of the House of Labor: The Workplace, the State, and American Labor Activism, 1865–1925* (New York: Cambridge University Press, 1987), pp. 133–35.

44. Theodore Hershberg, "A Tale of Two Cities," p. 65.

45. Burt and Davies, "The Iron Age," p. 492; Clark, *The Irish in Philadelphia*, p. 38.

46. *BTS*, pp. 20–23; North, *William Z. Foster*, p. 12.

47. Dorothy Healey, interview with the author, Sept. 16, 1986.

48. David Levine, "Punctuated Equilibrium: The Modernization of the Proletarian Family in the Age of Ascendant Capitalism," *International Labor and Working-Class History* 33 (1991): 10–13; *BTS*, p. 12.

49. William Z. Foster and Earl Ford, *Syndicalism* (Chicago, 1912), p. 17; for Foster's attitudes on working-class sexuality as well as his parents' fertility, see *PWL*, pp. 17, 260; Foster, "Prisoners," *World Magazine*, May 3, 1975; *BTS*, pp. 12–13.

50. Aileen S. Kraditor, *The Radical Persuasion, 1890–1917* (Baton Rouge: Louisiana State University Press, 1981), p. 59.

51. This account is from *BTS*, pp. 24–25; *PWL*, pp. 21–23, 27. On Foster's experiences in Jacksonville, see ibid., pp. 126–27, and *The Worker*, May 5, 1923, p. 2.

52. "Agreement and Account of Crew, Foreign-Going Ship," *Pegasus*, March 6, 1902–Aug. 19, 1904; "Agreement and Account of Crew, Foreign-Going Ship," *Alliance*, June 6, 1902–Aug. 20, 1904; "Agreement and Account of Crew, Foreign-Going Ship," *County of Cardigan*, June 11, 1903–Dec. 5, 1904; Maritime History Archive, Memorial University of Newfoundland, St. Johns, O.N. 91144, 91239, 78749. *BTS*, p. 24; *PWL*, pp. 52–104.

53. Maritime records; *PWL*, pp. 85–89.

54. Maritime Records; "Account of Wages," William Foster, Dec. 4, 1904, *County of Cardigan*, JMK. See also Foster's claim that "I arrived in Oregon in early November, 1904, just in time to vote for Debs for President," in *BTS*, p. 26.

55. William Z. Foster to "Brothers and Sisters," Nov. 18, 1904, JMK (no punctuation in original); *BTS*, p. 25; *PWL*, pp. 131–33.

56. *Daily Worker*, Oct. 8, 1924, p. 4; William Z. Foster, *More Pages from a Worker's Life*, ed. Arthur Zipser (New York: American Institute for Marxist Studies, 1979), pp. 37–38, "Railroad Rules and Railroad Practice.

57. This aspect of Debs's politics is most convincingly portrayed in Nick Salvatore, *Eugene Debs: Citizen and Socialist* (Urbana: University of Illinois Press, 1983).

58. *PWL*, p. 18.

CHAPTER 2

SOCIALIST AND SYNDICALIST

1. *PWL*, pp. 20, 107–8; *BTS*, p. 27.

2. "Agreement and Account of Crew, Foreign-Going Ship," *Pegasus*; *BTS*, pp. 23–28; *PWL*, p. 30–38; *Daily Worker*, Oct. 8, 1924, p. 4.

3. David A. Shannon, *The Socialist Party of America* (Chicago: Quadrangle Books, 1955), p. 40; Tom Sladden, "The Revolutionist," *International Socialist Review*, December 1908, pp. 425–26, 430; *PWL*, p. 32.

4. *BTS*, pp. 27–28, 31.

5. Paul B. Bushue, "Dr. Hermon F. Titus and Socialism in Washington State, 1900–1909" (M.A. thesis, University of Washington, 1967); Carlos A. Schwantes, *Radical Heritage: Labor, Socialism and Reform in Washington and British Columbia, 1885–1917* (Seattle: University of Washington Press, 1979), pp. 95–96; Harvey O'Connor, *Revolution in Seattle* (Seattle: West Bank Books, 1964; repr. 1981), p. 12.

6. Titus, "Revolutionary Socialism and Reform Socialism," *The Socialist* (Toledo), Sept. 15, 1906.

7. Bushue, "Hermon Titus," pp. 26, 94, 31; Barbara Winslow, "The Decline of Socialism in Washington, 1910–1925" (M.A. thesis, University of Washington, 1967), p. 143; Schwantes, *Radical Heritage*, p. 139.

8. Ira Kipnis, *The American Socialist Movement*, (New York: Columbia University Press, 1952), p. 373; *Workingman's Paper*, Oct. 30, 1909, p. 1; *BTS*, pp. 31–33.

9. *BTS*, pp. 38, 51; Schwantes, *Radical Heritage*, p. 174; O'Connor, *Revolution in Seattle*, p. 15; William Z. Foster and Hermon F. Titus, *Insurgency, or, The Economic Power of the Middle Class* (Seattle: Trustee Printing Co., 1910), p. 10.

10. Titus, "Revolutionary Socialism," *The Socialist* (Seattle), Oct. 12, 1907; Titus and Foster, *Insurgency*, p. 10.

11. *BTS*, pp. 38–39, 33.

12. L. Glen Seretan, *Daniel DeLeon: The Odyssey of an American Marxist* (Cambridge: Harvard University Press, 1979), pp. 173–75, 178, 205; Titus and Foster, *Insurgency*, p. 14; Don K. McKee, "The Influence of Syndicalism upon Daniel DeLeon," *The Historian* 20 (1958): 275–89.

13. *BTS*, p. 36.

14. Ibid., p. 38; Bushue, "Hermon Titus," p. 37.

15. *BTS*, p. 47.

16. My account of the free speech fight is taken primarily from Philip S. Foner, *History of the Labor Movement in the United States*, vol. 4, *The IWW 1905–1917* (New York: International Publishers, 1965), pp. 177–85, and Melvyn Dubofsky, *We Shall Be All* (Chicago: Quadrangle, 1969), pp. 175–84. Foster himself offered a detailed analysis of the free speech fight in two articles written for the French syndicalist journal *La Vie ouvrière* (Paris), Jan. 20, and Feb. 5,

1911; Richard Brazier, "Looking Backward to the Spokane Free Speech Fight" [1966?] Unpublished manuscript, I.W.W. Collection, Reuther Library, Wayne State University, box 146, folder 13.

17. O'Connor, *Revolution in Seattle*, p. 16; Foster and Titus, *Insurgency*, p. 3. See William Z. Foster, "Theodore Draper's *Roots of American Communism*," *Political Affairs*, May 1957, p. 39, for Foster's denial that he ever used "Zebulon." See "Our Own Lenin" by Alva Johnston, *New Yorker* June 28, 1930, p. 19, for the assertion, for which there is no evidence, that at some point "it became strategic to identify himself with the old New England stock, and he developed the 'Z' into 'Zebulon.' " Titus's version of the "Z" is supported by the fact that there was indeed another William E. Foster, a railroad worker, living in Spokane at the time of the free speech fight; see *Spokane City Directory* (Spokane: R. L. Polk and Co.), 1909, 1910. Elizabeth Gurley Flynn, *I Speak My Own Piece: Autobiography of a Rebel Girl* (New York: Masses and Mainstream, 1955), p. 100; *Workingman's Paper*, Jan. 22, 1910, p. 1.

18. Ibid., Nov. 20, 1909, p. 1; Dec. 18, 1909, p. 1; "Foster in Jail," Jan. 15, 1910; Feb. 12, 1910, pp. 1, 2.

19. *Solidarity*, Feb. 19, 1910, p. 3; March 19, 1910, p. 1; *Spokesman-Review* (Spokane), March 4, 1910, p. 11.

20. *Solidarity*, March 19, 1910, p. 1; *Spokesman-Review* March 6, 1910, p. 2; *Press* (Spokane), March 4, 1910 p. 2; Glen J. Broyles, "The Spokane Free Speech Fight, 1909–1910: A Study in I.W.W. Tactics," *Labor History* 31(1967): 249–50.

21. *Vie ouvrière*, Feb. 5, 1911, p. 177; *Solidarity*, March 19, 1910, p. 2; *International Socialist Review*, March 1910, p. 828; Jonathan Dembo, *Unions and Politics in Washington State: 1885–1935*, pp. 73–74; Broyles, "The Spokane Free Speech Fight," p. 251; Elizabeth Gurley Flynn, "Memories of the I.W.W.," address of Elizabeth Gurley Flynn to students at Northern Illinois University, Nov. 8, 1962 (New York: American Institute for Marxist Studies, 1977), p. 4; Schwantes, *Radical Heritage*, pp. 138–39; *PWL*, p. 144; on the attitude of local AFL unions toward the IWW and the free speech fight, see *Evening Chronicle*, (Spokane) Feb. 1, 1910, p. 16; *Spokesman-Review*, March 2, 1910, p. 7; Foster, *Vie ouvrière*, Feb. 5, 1911, pp. 170, 177.

22. Dubofsky, *We Shall Be All*, pp. 220–21; *BTS*, p. 54. *Daily People*, Nov. 10, 1909, p. 1

23. *Workingman's Paper*, Feb. 12, 1910, p. 1; ibid., Jan. 22, 1910, p. 1; William Z. Foster, *More Pages from a Workers' Life*, ed. Arthur Zipser (New York: American Institute for Marxist Studies, 1979), pp. 40–41.

24. Frederick W. Speirs, *The Street Railway System of Philadelphia* (Baltimore: Johns Hopkins University Press, 1897), p. 114; *International Socialist Review*, April 1910, pp. 865–75; Selig Perlman and Philip Taft, *History of Labor in the United States, 1896–1932*, vol. 4, *Labor Movements* (New York: Macmillan, 1935), pp. 343–48. *Press*, March 6, 1910, p. 1; *International Socialist Review*, May 1910, p. 980.

25. *Press*, March 6, 7, 1910, p. 2.

26. *Press*, March 8, 1910, p. 1, March 9, p. 2; *Spokesman-Review*, March 8, 1910, p. 7, March 9, pp. 1, 3, March 10, p. 1.

27. *Vie ouvrière*, Feb. 5, 1911, pp. 177–78.

28. Gurley Flynn, *I Speak My Own Piece*, p. 160; St. John signed Foster's letter of introduction to the International Trade Union Secretariat credentials committee: *WZF*, d. 1, l. 4, Titus and Foster, *Insurgency*, p. 8.

29. Larry Peterson, "The Intellectual World of the IWW: An American Worker's Library in the First Half of the Twentieth Century," *History Workshop Journal* 22(1986): 153–72; *BTS*, p. 22.

30. *Industrial Worker*, Sept. 10, 1910, p. 3; Sept. 3, 1910, p. 3.

31. Ibid., Sept. 17, 1910, p. 2; *Solidarity*, Dec. 31, 1910, p. 3.

32. This account is taken from Harvey Goldberg, *The Life of Jean Jaurès* (Madison: University of Wisconsin Press, 1968), pp. 410–13; Peter N. Stearns, *Revolutionary Syndicalism and French Labor: A Cause without Rebels* (New Brunswick, N.J.: Rutgers University Press, 1971), pp. 30, 41; Harvey Mitchell and Peter N. Stearns, *The European Labor Movement, the Working Classes and the Origins of Social Democracy, 1890–1914* (Itasca, Ill: F. E. Peacock, 1971), p. 73; *Industrial Worker*, Nov. 24, 1910, p. 4.

33. Joseph Conlin, *Bread and Roses Too: Studies of the Wobblies* (Westport, Conn.: Greenwood Press, 1969), pp. 6, 10, 18; Louis Levine, "The Development of Syndicalism in America," *Political Science Quarterly* 28 (1913): 476–77; Larry Peterson, "The One Big Union in International Perspective," in *Work, Community and Power: The Experience of Labor in Europe and America, 1900–1925*, ed. James E. Cronin and Carmen Sirianni (Philadelphia: Temple University Press, 1983), pp. 56–57; *Solidarity*, March 26, 1911, pp. 1, 9.

34. Stearns, *Revolutionary Syndicalism*, p. 11; Louis Levine, *Syndicalism in France* (New York: Columbia University Studies in Social Science, 1911), p. 200; F. F. Ridley, "Syndicalism, Strikes and Revolutionary Action in France," *Social Protest, Violence and Terror in Nineteenth and Twentieth Century Europe*, ed. Wolfgang J. Mommsen and Gerhard Hirschfeld (New York: St. Martin's Press, 1982), pp. 230–34. See also Theodore Zeldin, *France, 1848–1945*, vol. 1, *Ambition, Love and Politics* (Oxford: Clarendon Press, 1973) pp. 229, 233; F. F. Ridley, *Revolutionary Syndicalism in France: The Direct Action of Its Time* (Cambridge: Cambridge University Press, 1970), pp. 177–78, 182–86.

35. Levine, *French Syndicalism*, p. 193; *Solidarity*, Nov. 5, 1910, p. 1, Nov. 19, 1910, p. 3, March 25, 1911, p. 1; *Industrial Worker*, Dec. 1, 1910, p. 4.

36. On Foster and Hervé, see Foster, "Ultra Leftism," *World Magazine*, March 8, 1975. In his testimony before the Senate committee investigating the steel strike, Foster admitted that he had met Hervé in La Santé prison, but tried to distance himself from prewar syndicalism by noting that Hervé had turned out to be, in 1919, "one of the biggest men in France." See U.S. Senate Committee on Labor and Education, *Investigation of Strike in the Steel Industry*, 66th Cong., 1st sess. 1919, p. 396. For a description of Hervé, see Paul Mazgai, *The Action Française and Revolutionary Syndicalism* (Chapel Hill: University of North Carolina Press, 1979), pp. 87–89, 214–15; *Solidarity*, Jan. 28, 1911, p. 3, Dec. 31, 1910, p. 4; *Industrial Worker*, Dec. 1, 1910, p. 4, Dec. 29, 1910, pp. 1, 2.

37. *Solidarity*, June 3, 1911, p. 2, June 10, 1911, p. 2; *PWL*, pp. 288, 290; *BTS*, pp. 49–50.

38. Foster was in effect contesting a rule that each country could be represented by only one labor organization. *PWL*, p. 291–93; *Solidarity*, Sept. 16,

1911, pp. 1, 4; Lewis Lorwin, *Labor and Internationalism* (New York: Macmillan, 1929), pp. 128–29; Lewis Lorwin, *The International Labor Movement* (New York: Harper, 1953), p. 40; William E. Bohn, "International Notes," *International Socialist Review*, October 1911, p. 245; American Federation of Labor, *Report of Proceedings*, 1911, pp. 29–30, 146–49, 153.

39. Ibid., pp. 29–30, 146–49, 153; Foster, *More Pages from a Worker's Life*, pp. 20–21; Conlin, *Bread and Roses Too*, p. 11.

40. *Industrial Worker*, July 13, 1911, p. 4; Albert S. Lindeman, *A History of European Socialism* (New Haven, Conn.: Yale University Press, 1983), pp. 172; Ridley, *Revolutionary Syndicalism*, p. 183.

41. *Industrial Worker*, July 13, 1911, p. 4.

42. *BTS*, pp. 55–56; *Solidarity*, Oct. 7, 1911, p. 1; *Industrial Worker*, Nov. 2, 1911, p. 3.

43. James Green, *The World of the Worker: Labor in Twentieth-Century America* (New York: Hill and Wang, 1980), p. 78. Philip S. Foner's *History of the Labor Movement in the U.S.*, 4:418–27, contains a more detailed discussion of Foster's debate with the IWW leadership.

44. For examples of these arguments, see *Industrial Worker*, Nov. 16, 1911, p. 3, and *Solidarity*, Nov. 18, 1911, pp. 2, 3.

45. WZF, d. 5, draft article "Refused Solidarity."

46. Geoff Brown, introduction to *The Syndicalist, 1912–1914: Reproduced in Facsimile* (London: Spokesman Books, 1975); Bob Holton, *British Syndicalism, 1900–1914: Myths and Realities* (London: Pluto Press, 1976), pp. 73–111, 144; Tom Mann, *Tom Mann's Memoirs* (London: Labour Publishing, 1923), pp. 251, 254; Michael S. DeLucia, "The Remaking of French Syndicalism, 1911–1918: The Growth of Reformist Philosophy," (Ph.D. diss., Brown University, 1971), p. 54; *Industrial Worker*, Nov. 2, 1911, p. 3; *BTS*, pp. 57, 58; *The Agitator*, Feb. 15, 1912, p. 2.

47. Foner, *History of the Labor Movement in the United States*, *BTS*, p. 58.

48. This account of the meeting in Chicago is from an account by Frank Pease in *The Agitator*, Feb. 15, 1912, p. 2.

49. Ibid., *BTS*, p. 57.

50. Schwantes, *Radical Heritage*, pp. 88–89; Bushue, "Hermon F. Titus," p. 21; Terry Pettis, "Sixty-Four Years a Union Man" (portrait of Jay Fox), *Our World*, Feb. 16, 1912; Charles P. LeWarne, *Utopias on Puget Sound, 1885–1915* (Seattle: University of Washington Press, 1975), pp. 171, 188–89; FOIA, Jay Fox file, 61-3-60-95, containing letter by Frank Pease.

51. *The Agitator*, Nov. 15, 1910, p. 1; Fox evidently met Esther during a sojourn in New York City: biographical information on Fox is from Jay Fox autobiographical MS., Jay Fox Papers, Gonzaga University, Spokane, Wash., and Mary M. Carr, "Jay Fox: Anarchist of Home," unpublished MS., pp. 2–5; LeWarne, *Utopias on Puget Sound*, pp. 208–9, 203–4; FOIA, Jay Fox file, 61-3-60-95; Fox is listed as a delegate in *Proceedings of the First Convention of the I.W.W.* (New York: New York Labor News, 1905), p. 612.

52. Mary Carr, "Jay Fox: Anarchist of Home," pp. 9–10; LeWarne, *Utopias on Puget Sound*, pp. 203, 206; William J. Burns, *The Masked War: the Story of a Peril that Threatened the United States by the Man who Uncovered the Dyna-*

mite Conspirators and Sent them to Jail (New York: George H. Doran, 1913), p. 82.

53. Hutchins Hapgood, *The Spirit of Labor* (New York: Duffield, 1907), pp. 286, 290–91, 383; for another account by Hapgood of Jay Fox's and Esther's lives in Chicago, see Hapgood, *An Anarchist Woman* (New York: Duffield, 1909), pp. 173–74; on Hapgood, see Leslie Fishbein, *Rebels in Bohemia* (Chapel Hill: University of North Carolina Press, 1982), pp. 177, 180, 197–98; Michael D. Marcaccio, *The Hapgoods: Three Earnest Brothers* (Charlottesville, Va.: University of Virginia Press, 1977), pp. 70–72, 141–46. *The Free Speech Case of Jay Fox* (New York: Free Speech League, 1912); LeWarne, *Utopias*, pp. 212–19; Mary Carr, "Jay Fox," pp. 11–12.

54. William Foster and Esther ["Ruff"], marriage certificate, JMK; Joseph Manley Kolko interview; Harold and Zelda Foster, interviews with the author, March 9, 1987, January 20, 1993; *The Agitator*, Feb. 15, 1911, p. 2; Lucy Robins Lang, *Tommorrow Is Beautiful*, p. 49; Mary Carr, "Jay Fox," pp. 4–7. Rebecca died of influenza in 1922. David was the son of Morris Martin Rasnick, who worked originally in the garment district in New York City as a presser, and met Esther in Chicago before becoming a dentist. In 1911 he had a dental practice in Seattle and advertised in *The Agitator* (for instance, Apr. 1, 1911). Rasnick remained on good terms with William Foster. In later years, he would advertise in the *Daily Worker* as well (for instance, Oct. 20, 1925).

55. Jay Fox autobiographical MS.; Paul Avrich, *The Haymarket Tragedy* (Princeton, N.J.: Princeton University Press, 1984), pp. 72–73. On the "Chicago Idea," see also John R. Commons, et. al., *History of Labour in the United States*, vol. 2, (New York: Macmillan, 1918; repr. 1946), pp. 290–300.

56. Jay Fox, *Trade Unionism and Anarchism: A Letter to a Brother Unionist* (Chicago: Social Science Press, 1908), pp. 5, 8, 9, 12–13, 15.

57. *The Agitator*, Nov. 1, 1912, p. 1; June 15, 1912, p. 1; July 1, 1912, p. 2. *Solidarity*, Sept. 30, 1911, p. 2; Oct. 14, 1911, p. 2.

58. *The Agitator*, June 15, 1912. Foster's series of articles ran April 15, May 1, May 15, June 1, June 15, and July 1.

CHAPTER 3
THE SYNDICALIST LEAGUES

1. *Current Literature*, June 1912, p. 685; May 1912, p. 555. From 1910 to 1914, there were sixty-one citations under "syndicalism" in the *Reader's Guide to Periodical Literature*. In comparison, only fifteen articles had the American Federation of labor as their subject during the same period.

2. Melvyn Dubofsky, *We Shall Be All* (Chicago: Quadrangle, 1969), pp. 227–87.

3. From 1915 to 1918 there were only four articles with syndicalism as their subject in the *Reader's Guide*.

4. *The Agitator*, Nov. 15, 1910, p. 2; Terry Pettus, "Sixty-Four Years a Union Man," *Our World*, Feb. 16, 1951; Mary M. Carr, "Jay Fox: Anarchist at Home," (unpublished MS.), p. 11.

5. BTS, p. 58; PWL, p. 128; *The Syndicalist* (London), July 1912, p. 6.

6. *PWL*, pp. 42–43.

7. Arthur Zipser, *Workingclass Giant: The Life of William Z. Foster* (New York: International Publishers, 1981), p. 38; *Independent*, Oct. 17, 1912, p. 94; *Journal of Political Economy* 21 (1913): 94; William E. Walling, "Industrialism vs. Syndicalism," *International Socialist Review* March 1913, p. 666; Louis Fraina, "Syndicalism and Industrial Unionism," ibid., July 1913, p. 25; *BTS*, p. 58.

8. William Z. Foster and Earl Ford, *Syndicalism* (Chicago: William Z. Foster, 1912), pp. 9, 18.

9. Ibid., pp. 13, 14; Typescript "Syndicalist League of North America Constitution," WZF, d. 86.

10. Michael Bakunin, *Catechism of a Revolutionary*, quoted Paul Avrich, preface to *Bakunin on Anarchy*, ed. Sam Dolgoff (New York: Knopf, 1972), p. xxiii; Bakunin, *Revolution and Revolutionary Violence*, in *The Political Philosophy of Bakunin: Scientific Anarchism*, ed. C. P. Maximoff (New York: Free Press, 1953), p. 372; Bakunin, *What the Workers Lack*, ibid., p. 316; *BTS*, p. 63.

11. Foster and Ford, *Syndicalism*, pp. 5–8; Foster typescript, "Is Government Necessary to the Operation of Industry?" WZF, d. 86. See also, for very similar conceptions of the "future society" by Foster: William Z. Foster and J. A. Jones, "The Future Society," *The Toiler*, (March 1914), pp. 7–8. In *Trade Unionism: The Road to Freedom* (Chicago: International Trade Union Educational League, 1915), p. 23, Foster allows that "each group of workers would have full power to carry on production in their own sphere," yet "scientific principles alone would regulate their activities. Foremen would be selected on the basis of efficiency, not by popular vote. New industrial processes would be adopted only after experts had approved their merit."

12. Foster and Ford, *Syndicalism*, pp. 7–8; on Taylorism and workers' response: David Montgomery, *Workers' Control in America* (New York: Cambridge University Press, 1979) and *The Fall of the House of Labor* (New York: Cambridge University Press, 1987), pp. 214–56; Richard Edwards, *Contested Terrain: The Transformation of the Workplace in the Twentieth Century* (New York: Basic Books, 1979), pp. 97–104; Harry Braverman, *Labor and Monopoly Capital* (New York: Monthly Review Press, 1974); on Taylorism as ideology: Michael Burawoy, "Toward a Marxist Theory of the Labor Process: Braverman and Beyond," *Politics and Society* 8 (1978): 247–312.

13. Foster and Ford, *Syndicalism*, p. 6; Foster, "Is Government Necessary to the Operation of Industry?" My description of Jones is from Bruns, *The Damndest Radical: The Life and World of Ben Reitman* (Urbana: University of Illinois Press, 1987), pp. 230–33, and Rosalyn Fraad Baxandall, *Words on Fire: The Life and Writing of Elizabeth Gurley Flynn* (New Brunswick, N.J.: Rutgers University Press, 1987), pp. 11–13. A "Society Notes" column by Jones in *The Syndicalist*, Apr. 15, 1913, p. 32, describes several sabotage techniques Jones learned in the painters' union.

14. Bakunin, *Catechism of a Revolutionary*, p. 93; Paul Avrich, *Anarchist Portraits* (Princeton, N.J.: Princeton University Press, 1988), p. 61.

15. Edward Bellamy, *Looking Backward* (Boston: Houghton Mifflin, 1887; repr. 1926), pp. 59–75, 85–109, 123–37; John L. Thomas, *Alternative America:*

Henry George, Edward Bellamy, Henry Demarest Lloyd and the Adversary Tradition (Cambridge, Mass.: Harvard University Press, 1983), pp. 245–47; Howard P. Segal, "Bellamy and Technology: Reconciling Centralization and Decentralization," in *Looking Backward, 1988–1888: Essays on Edward Bellamy,* ed. Daphne Patai (Amherst: University of Massachusetts Press, 1988); perhaps more germanely, Foster's conceptions in some ways echoed Daniel DeLeon's idea of "automatic" production governed by statistics: see L. Glen Seretan, *Daniel DeLeon: The Odyssey of an American Marxist* (Cambridge, Mass.: Harvard University Press, 1979), pp. 245–47. Other syndicalists also held similar ideas: see Melvyn Dubofsky, *Big Bill Haywood* (New York: St. Martin's Press, 1987), p. 146.

16. Foster and Ford, *Syndicalism,* p. 6; James Gilbert, *Designing the Industrial State: The Intellectual Pursuit of Collectivism in America, 1880–1940* (Chicago: Quadrangle Press, 1972), p. 8; Seretan, *Daniel DeLeon,* pp. 191, 194.

17. Foster and Ford, *Syndicalism,* pp. 43, 44; "SLNA Constitution," WZF, d. 86.

18. Robert Hughes, *American Genesis: A Century of Invention and Technological Enthusiasm* (New York: Penguin, 1989), pp. 250–60; BTS, p. 70.

19. Overview essays on the new unionism include David Montgomery, "The 'New Unionism' and the Transformation of Workers' Consciousness in America," *Journal of Social History* (1974): 88–116; David Montgomery, "New Tendencies in Union Struggles and Strategies in Europe and the United States, 1916–1922," and Larry Peterson, "The One Big Union in International Perspective: Revolutionary Industrial Unionism, 1900–1925," in *Work, Community and Power: The Experience of Labor in Europe and America, 1900–1925,* ed. James E. Cronin and Carmen Sirianni (Philadelphia: Temple University Press, 1983), pp. 49–87. See also Michael Kazin *Barons of Labor: The San Francisco Building Trades and Union Power in the Progressive Era* (Urbana: University of Illinois Press, 1987) and Graham Adams, Jr., *Age of Industrial Violence, 1910–1915* (New York: Columbia University Press, 1966). Foster and Ford, *Syndicalism,* p. 41.

20. Ibid., pp. 47, 17, 31.

21. Ibid., pp. 12, 32, 39–40.

22. Ibid., pp. 26, 28, 18, 9.

23. Gil Green, interview with the author, Oct. 3, 1986; Dr. Harry Epstein, interview with the author, Nov. 22, 1986; FOIA 61-330-21; Foster biographical questionnaire, Dec. 26, Comintern, op. 261, d. 15: "Three sisters living—two married to workers, one to a salesman—conservative people, Republicans and Democrats. Live on the Pacific coast. Have only the rarest contacts with them."

24. *New York Tribune,* Sept. 22, 1919, pp. 1, 3.

25. *PWL,* pp. 44, 46–50, 36, 28, 113, 51; See also Foster testimony, U.S. Senate, Committee on Labor and Education, *Investigation of Strike in the Steel Industry,* 66th Cong., 1st sess., 1919, p. 398: according to his statement, he worked as a car inspector from 1911 to 1916 on the Chicago Northwestern line, and in the stockyards for the Soo Line.

26. *PWL,* p. 119.

27. Ibid., pp. 116–17; 123, 125, 117.

28. *The Agitator*, June 15, 1912, p. 1; *The Syndicalist* (London), September 1912, p. 6.

29. *The Agitator*, Sept. 1, 1912, p. 3; Foster was listed as national secretary of the Syndicalist League of North America, ibid., Sept. 15, 1912, p. 1; Jay Fox to Joseph Labadie, Oct. 17, 1912, Labadie Collection, Special Collections, University of Michigan. Fox wrote a brief memoir of his conversion to Communism in "From Anarchism to Communism," *Communist*, February 1925, pp. 179–81.

30. *The Syndicalist*, Jan. 1, 1913; Charles P. LeWarne, *Utopias on Puget Sound, 1885–1915* (Seattle: University of Washington Press, 1975), p. 210.

31. SLNA Constitution, WZF, d. 86; Carolyn Ashbaugh, *Lucy Parsons: American Revolutionary* (Chicago: Charles H. Kerr, 1976), p. 230. William Z. Foster, *More Pages from a Workers Life*, ed. Arthur Zipser, (New York: American Institute for Marxist Studies, 1979), p. 4. Foster was apparently unsuccessful in collecting dues: *BTS*, pp. 60, 63.

32. Pettus, "Sixty-Four Years a Union Man." Ashbaugh, *Lucy Parsons*, p. 230.

33. *The Syndicalist*, Feb. 15, 1913, p. 3, March 1, 1913, p. 4.

34. See, for instance, ibid., Jan. 1, 1913, p. 4. Foster and Ford, *Syndicalism*, p. 8. On Kropotkin, see Paul Avrich, introduction to Peter Kropotkin, *The Conquest of Bread* (London: Penguin, 1972).

35. *BTS*, pp. 60, 67. At the time that Foster was attempting to establish his SLNA, Emma Goldman, Alexander Berkman, W. Sanger, Margaret Sanger, Hippolyte Havel, and E. Byrne sought to form a syndicalist league as well. Foster, in *BTS*, called this "the petty-bourgeois, bohemian, Emma Goldman anarchist group" (p. 59). The group issued a manifesto, which appeared in *Mother Earth* on Sept. 30, 1912. While Goldman's efforts apparently did not result in the formation of a syndicalist "league," her understanding of syndicalism was quite similar to Foster's. See Emma Goldman, "Syndicalism: Its Theory and Practice," *Mother Earth*, February 1913, pp. 417–22. This article contained no reference to Foster or the Syndicalist League of North America.

For a more detailed examination of the activities of the SLNA at the local level, see Charlton J. Brandt, "William Z. Foster and the Syndicalist League of North America" (M.A. thesis, Sangamon State University, 1985), and Philip S. Foner, *History of the Labor Movement in the United States*, vol. 9, *The TUEL to the End of the Gompers Era* (New York: International Publishers, 1991).

36. Solon DeLeon, ed., *American Labor Who's Who* (New York: Hanford Press, 1925), p. 147; Lucy Robins Lang, *Tommorrow Is Beautiful* (New York: Macmillan, 1948), p. 49; Joseph Manley Kolko, interview with the author, Sept. 24, 1986. Hammersmark was a long-time associate of Lucy Parsons. See Ashbaugh, *Lucy Parsons*, pp. 234, 277 n. 2. On Hammersmark and his career in the Communist party, see *Daily Worker*, Sept. 23, 1937, and obituaries, ibid., Sept. 30, 1957, and *Chicago Tribune*, Sept. 16, 1957; *Why?* February 1913, p. 16; February 1913; Elizabeth Dilling, *The Red Network* (by the author, 1934), p. 58. Solon DeLeon, *American Labor Who's Who* p. 95; on Esther, see Hutchins Hapgood, *A Victorian in the Modern World* (New York: Harcourt, Brace, 1939), p. 196; *BTS*, p. 59. Hutchins Hapgood, *An Anarchist Woman* (New York: Duf-

field, 1909), p. 193. Theodore Draper, *American Communism and Soviet Russia* (New York: Viking, 1960), p. 40.

37. *The Syndicalist*, Jan. 1, 1913, p. 3; *BTS*, p. 64; *The Toiler*, Feb. 1914, March 1914, Apr.–May 1914. Foster probably knew Dezettel through his involvement in the Spokane IWW: *Solidarity*, Aug. 3, 1911, p. 3, carries a note identifying Dezettel as secretary of the IWW Spokane local. On the Labor Forward movement, see Elizabeth and Kenneth Fones-Wolf, "Trade Union Evangelism: Religion and the AFL in the Labor Forward Movement, 1912–1916," in *Working-Class America*, ed. Michael Frisch and Daniel Walkowitz (Urbana: University of Illinois Press, 1983), pp. 153–84. On the activities of the Kansas City League, see Charlton Brandt, "William Z. Foster and the Syndicalist League of America," and Foner, *History of the Labor Movement*, 9:87–92. Earl Browder claimed to Draper to have "planned and directed" the Labor Forward Movement in the city, "the first mass organizing campaign I took part in." Browder to Draper, Feb. 29, 1956, TD, box 1, folder 17, p. 2.

38. *The Unionist* (St. Louis), Aug. 1, 1913, p. 2; *The Toiler*, November 1913, p. 1.

39. "Speech of Earl Browder at Testimonial Dinner for Wm. Z. Foster," March 23, 1945, TD, box 5, folder 30; Browder interview with Draper, Oct. 22, 1954, TD, box 1, folder 3, pp. 1–2; James G. Ryan, "The Making of a Native Marxist: The Early Career of Earl Browder," *Review of Politics* 39 (1977): 341.

Both Browder and James P. Cannon, a founder of the American Trotskyist movement, crossed paths with Foster and the Syndicalist League in Kansas City. "For a time they worked together on a Kansas City labor paper, *The Toiler*, published by Dezettel. When the paper took Foster's line against the IWW's traditional dual unionism, Cannon withdrew and became one of the IWW's travelling organizers," according to Theodore Draper, *The Roots of American Communism* (New York: Viking, 1957), p. 68. There is no mention of Cannon in any issue of *The Toiler*, as either a contributor or a "Toiler Booster," but he seems to have been involved with a "Kansas City Free Speech League" at the time, for which *The Toiler*, at least in its first issue, carried advertisements and notices of meetings. See notices in *The Toiler* Oct. 1913, and notice by Cannon, "Free Speech Fight in Kansas City," in *International Socialist Review*, February 1914, p. 510.

Browder was a relatively frequent contributor of articles to *The Toiler*. The February 1914 issue cites him as "Secretary, Kansas City Syndicalist League," a position he held for only two months. In August 1914 he appears as secretary-treasurer of the Toiler Publishing Company. Soon thereafter, by the time of Tom Mann's U.S. tour, the name of the Kansas City league had changed to the Workers' Educational League. Also, Browder Columbia University Oral History Interview, p. 47.

40. *PWL*, p. 146; David Montgomery, *Workers' Control in America* (New York: Cambridge University Press, 1979), p. 107; Montgomery, "New Tendencies in Union Struggles and Strategies in the United States," pp. 103–5; Selig Perlman and Philip Taft, *History of Labor in the United States, 1896–1932*, vol. 4, *Labor Movements* (New York: Macmillan, 1935), pp. 370–73; U.S. Senate, Commission on Industrial Relations, *Final Report and Testimony*, 64th Cong., 1st sess., 1916, vol. 19, pp. 9706–7. Fox on the timberworkers is in *The Syndicalist*, Feb. 1, 1913, p. 1.

41. This summary from J. F. Anderson, "Labor's 'Aristocracy' and the War Babies," *Labor Age*, August 1923, pp. 4–5.

42. *International Socialist Review*, May 1912, p. 782; Louis Fraina, "Syndicalism and Industrial Unionism," ibid., July 1913, pp. 25–28; *PWL*, pp. 146–48; Carl E. Person, *The Lizard's Trail: A Story of the Illinois Central and Harriman Lines Strike of 1911 to 1915 Inclusive* (Chicago: Lake, 1918), p. 457. One prominent leader of the strike, L. M. Hawver, attended the first TUEL national conference in 1921: see Andrew Overgaard autobiographical MS., Tamiment Institute Library, New York University, p. 47.

43. Ira Kipnis, *The American Socialist Movement: 1897–1912* (New York: Columbia University Press, 1952), pp. 348–57; 391–400.

44. Foster's reaction to the McNamara case is in *Vie ouvrière* (Paris), Feb. 20, 1913, pp. 239–42, Mar. 20, 1913, pp. 367–69. Later, Foster strongly urged Fox to write more in his memoirs on the McNamara case: "You know much of interest on this matter." Foster to Fox, [n.d.], Jay Fox Papers, Gonzaga University, Spokane, Washington; Carr, "Jay Fox: Anarchist of Home," p. 10.

For one prominent Socialist's reaction to the propaganda of the Syndicalist League, see John Spargo, *Syndicalism, Industrial Unionism and Socialism* (New York: Huebsch, 1913), pp. 37, 39.

45. David Montgomery, *Workers' Control*, pp. 91, 105, 102; on Mann's visit to the U.S., see Philip Foner, *History of the Labor Movement in the U.S.*, vol. 4, *The IWW 1905–1917* (New York: International Publishers, 1965), p. 430; *The Unionist* (St. Louis) Nov. 15, 1913, p. 1; Browder Columbia University Oral History, p. 47; Tom Mann, "A Plea for Solidarity," *International Socialist Review* 14 (1914): 392–94.

46. Testimony of William Z. Foster before Meatpackers Arbitration Board, RG 280, F.M.C.S. Case Files, 33/864, Box 48, National Archives and Record Service, Annex, Suitland, Md.

47. Marriage certificate of William Z. Foster and Esther "Ruff," JMK. See *Investigation of Strike in the Steel Industry*, p. 400, for Foster's testimony that he was exempted from the draft on the ground that he was married.

In the anarchist group to which Esther belonged while in Chicago, "marriage on principle was not tolerated, since it was an enslaving institution" (Hapgood, *A Victorian in the Modern World*, p. 202). See also Hapgood, *The Spirit of Labor* (New York: Duffield, 1907). Esther, according to Hapgood, was among those in the anarchist circle who sought to convert Anton Johannsen's wife, Maggie, to "varietism" (p. 383).

48. Sophonsiba Breckinridge and Edith Abbott, "Chicago's Housing Problem: Families in Furnished Rooms," *American Journal of Sociology* 16 (1910): 290.

49. *BTS*, p. 60; *PWL*, p. 46. On Carmen's wages, see Foster testimony, before the Senate, *Investigation of Strike in the Steel Industry*, p. 398; James Barrett, in *Work and Community in the Jungle* (Urbana: University of Illinois Press, 1987), p. 91, cites a 1911 study by the University of Chicago Settlement House that estimated the minimum yearly expenditures for a family of five at $800.00. At his monthly rate, Foster was earning between $780 and $960. *Railway Carmen's Journal*, May 1922, pp. 273–75.

50. *BTS*, 68. The last extant issue of *The Toiler* is January 1915. Jay Fox,

"Organizing the Timberworkers," Fox MS., Fox Papers; Joseph Manley Kolko, interview with the author, Sept. 26, 1986.

51. *PWL*, pp. 46, 47; *BTS*, p. 90.

52. William Z. Foster, *History of the Communist Party of the United States* (New York: International Publishers, 1952), p. 118; *BTS*, pp. 68–70; Foster, "Syndicalism in the United States," *Communist* 14 (1935): 1051, 1052.

53. *BTS*, p. 69.

54. Robert L. Tyler, *Rebels of the Woods: the IWW in the Pacific Northwest* (Eugene: University of Oregon Press, 1967), pp. 64–65; Charlotte Todes, *Labor and Lumber* (New York: International Publishers, 1931), pp. 155–58; LeWarne, *Utopias on Puget Sound*, p. 219; *BTS*, p. 66; Jay Fox, "Organizing Timberworkers"; Foster's certificate as an organizer for the Shingle Weavers and Sawmill Workers Union was dated Mar. 1, 1914: WZF, d. 1; Commission on Industrial Relations, *Final Report and Testimony* (Washington, D.C.: G.P.O., 1916), 5:4207–23.

55. This account of the Butte miners' revolt is from Dubofsky, *We Shall Be All* (Chicago: Quadrangle, 1969), pp. 301–7; William Z. Foster, "The Butte Miners' Split," *World Magazine*, Dec. 14, 1974; Foster, "The Miners' Revolt in Butte," *The Toiler*, August 1914, pp. 9–10.

56. Foster has given several slightly differing accounts of his employment after 1915. These include the following. "In the latter part of 1915, while working in Swift's shops in the Stockyards, I was elected Business Agent, or more properly, Organizer of the Chicago District Council of the Railway Carmen . . ." (*BTS*, p. 83). "When the United States entered the war I was working as a car inspector on the Soo Line in Chicago; for at the expiration of my year's term as Business Agent of the Railway Carmen, some time previous, I had refused . . . nomination for a second term and had gone back to work on the road" (*BTS*, p. 90). See also Foster testimony in *Investigation of Strike in Steel Industry*, p. 398.

Foster carried a card from an organization called the Kansas City Trade Union Educational League (probably associated with the Labor Forward movement) at the time, issued in November of 1914. It read "Bro. W. Z. Foster, AFL Organizer, who is an earnest militant union man. He is cooperating with us in carrying on an educational work in the unions. . . . Please give him the floor of your Union for a few minutes." WZF, d. 86. A membership card for the Brotherhood of Railway Carmen (dated August 1914) gives his address as 2503 N. Sacramento Ave. JMK.

57. *BTS*, pp. 73–74, 81; Brandt, "William Z. Foster," p. 52; I.T.U.E.L. Circular, July 3, 1917, WZF, d. 86.

58. AFL certificate, "William G. [*sic*] Foster, General Organizer," Apr. 8, 1915, signed Samuel Gompers, WZF, d. 1; *BTS*, p. 83.

59. Ibid., pp. 74, 76; Foster, *Trade Unionism: The Road to Freedom* (Chicago: ITUEL, [1916]), pp. 11, 20, 18.

60. Montgomery, *Workers' Control*, p. 13; Foster, *Trade Unionism*, pp. 11, 26, 27; Marjorie Murphy, "The Aristocracy of Women's Labor in America," *History Workshop Journal*, no. 22 (Autumn 1986): 59–61.

61. Foster's Brotherhood of Railway Carmen Certificate was issued Mar. 1, 1916, by the Garden City Lodge and was in force only to the end of the year; WZF, d. 1. See Pat Cooper, *Once a Cigar Maker: Men, Women, and Work Cul-*

ture in American Cigar Factories, 1900–1919 (Urbana: University of Illinois Press, 1987), p. 124: "Cigar makers had a reputation for embracing newcomers who made a show of antipathy toward manufacturers, frequently electing them to office without any knowledge of their backgrounds."

62. Earl Browder to Theodore Draper, Feb. 7, 1956, TD, box 1, folder 17; Hapgood, *The Spirit of Labor*, pp. 285, 290, 206, 383. On Johannsen, see Kazin, *Barons of Labor*, pp. 73–74, 207, 299.

63. Spargo, *Syndicalism, Industrial Unionism and Socialism*, p. 194; *BTS*, p. 74.

64. Gompers to Foster, July 11, 1916, WZF, d. 84.

65. *BTS*, p. 81; "Browder Testimonial Speech," TD.

66. Foster, "The Socialists and the War," draft article "refused *American Federationist*," WZF, d. 80; U.S. Senate, *Investigation of Strike in Steel Industries*, pp. 398–99. Here, Foster states that his attitude toward the war was "that it must be won at all costs." Browder Columbia Oral History Interview, pp. 64–65; Kazin, *Barons of Labor*, pp. 241–45. Chicago Federation of Labor, Minutes, Feb. 2, 1916, p. 31, Chicago Federation of Labor Papers, Chicago Historical Society.

67. *BTS*, pp. 81–85; *Chicago Labor News* in Jay Fox scrapbooks, Fox papers; Bakunin, "Letter to a Frenchman on the Present Crisis," in *Bakunin on Anarchy*, p. 196; Foster draft, "Can the Craft Unions Become Revolutionary?" WZF, d. 86; CFL Minutes, Dec. 19, 1915, May 7, 1916.

68. Richard Frost, *The Mooney Case* (Stanford: Stanford University Press, 1968), pp. 17–18; Foster, *More Pages from a Worker's Life*, p. 4; Ashbaugh, *Lucy Parsons*, p. 230; Foster, "The Molders' Convention," *International Socialist Review*, December 1912: 486–87; Draper, *Roots of American Communism*, p. 123.

69. Lang, *Tomorrow Is Beautiful*, pp. 105–6. Frost, *The Mooney Case*, p. 270; CFL Minutes, Apr. 1, 1917.

70. Richard Edwards, *Contested Terrain: The Transformation of the Workplace in the Twentieth Century* (New York: Basic Books, 1979), p. 53.

CHAPTER 4
LABOR ORGANIZING IN "THE JUNGLE"

1. Foster recounted this story in speeches given in the early 1920s before trade union groups: see FOIA, 61-330-52; *PWL*, p. 153.

2. Melvyn Dubofsky, *We Shall Be All* (Chicago: Quadrangle Books, 1969), pp. 349–75.

3. For an account of the World War I persecution of the IWW and the subsequent flight of Haywood, see Dubofsky, see ibid., pp. 405–8, 423–37, 459–60. See also Peter Carlson, *Roughneck: The Life and Times of Big Bill Haywood* (New York: Norton, 1983), pp. 316–17. According to Carlson, Haywood had secured a promise from the Communist party to back his bail bond forfeiture.

4. *BTS*, p. 90; James R. Barrett, *Work and Community in the Jungle: Chicago's Packinghouse Workers, 1894–1922* (Urbana: University of Illinois Press, 1987), pp. 189–90.

5. John H. Keiser, "John Fitzpatrick and Progressive Unionism" (Ph.D. diss., Northwestern University, 1965), p. 190.

6. On the great migration and the role of blacks in the stockyards, see James R. Barrett, "Work and Community in 'The Jungle'" (Ph.D. diss., University of Pittsburgh, 1981), chap. 2, and Barrett, *Work and Community in the Jungle*; William M. Tuttle Jr., *Race Riot: Chicago in the Red Summer of 1919* (New York: Atheneum, 1970), pp. 74–107; James R. Grossman, *Land of Hope: Chicago, Black Southerners and the Great Migration* (Chicago: University of Chicago Press, 1989); Alma Herbst, *The Negro in the Slaughtering and Meat Packing Industry in Chicago* (Boston: Houghton-Mifflin, 1932; repr. New York: Arno Press, 1969), pp. 12–27.

7. For detailed accounts of the development of business enterprise in the stockyards, see Barrett, *Work and Community*, pp. 15–35, 193; Barrett, "Unity and Fragmentation: Class, Race and Ethnicity on Chicago's South Side, 1900–1922," in *"Struggle a Hard Battle": Essays on Working-Class Immigrants*, ed. Dick Hoerder (DeKalb: Northern Illinois University Press, 1986), p. 233; Louise Carroll Wade, *Chicago's Pride: The Stockyards, Packingtown, and Environs in the Nineteenth Century* (Urbana: University of Illinois Press, 1987); and Robert A. Slayton, *Back of the Yards: The Making of a Local Democracy* (Chicago: University of Chicago Press, 1986), pp. 3–20; Herbst, *The Negro in the Slaughtering and Meat Packing Industry*, pp. 6–7; U.S. Federal Trade Commission, *Report on the Meat Packing Industry*, part 1 (Washington D.C.: U.S. Government Publishing Office, 1919), pp. 33, 40, 76, 287; Eric Halpern, "Race and Radicalism in the Chicago Stockyards," paper presented at the 1987 annual meeting of the Organization of American Historians, Philadelphia; David Brody, *The Butcher Workmen: A Study of Unionization* (Cambridge, Mass.: Harvard University Press, 1964), p. 15.

8. William Z. Foster, "How Life Has Been Brought into the Stockyards: A Story of the Reorganization of the Packing Industry," *Life and Labor*, April 1918, p. 64; Foster, *Trade Unionism: The Road to Freedom* (Chicago: ITUEL, 1916), p. 14.

9. Herbst, *The Negro in the Slaughtering and Meat Packing Industry*, p. 18; Tuttle, *Race Riot*, pp. 74–108, 112–24; Horace R. Cayton and George S. Mitchell, *Black Workers and the New Unions* (Chapel Hill: University of North Carolina Press, 1939), pp. 228–43; James R. Grossman, "The White Man's Union: The Great Migration and the Resonance of Race and Class in Chicago, 1916–1922," in *The Great Migration in Historical Perspective: New Dimensions of Race, Class and Gender*, ed. Joe William Trotter (Bloomington: Indiana University Press, 1991), pp. 85, 89–92.

10. *BTS*, p. 91; Chicago Federation of Labor, Minutes, July 15, 1917, p. 14, Chicago Federation of Labor Papers, Chicago Historical Society; McQuillen noted in ITUEL flier, July 3, 1917, WZF, d. 86.

11. *BTS*, pp. 91–92; CFL Minutes, Dec. 2, 1917, p. 7, for Fitzpatrick's conception of purpose of Stockyards Labor Council. Dennis Lane, "A Brief History of Organization in Chicago Stock Yards by the A.M.C. & B.W. of N.A.", *Butcher Workman*, November 1919, p. 2.

12. CFL Minutes, Aug. 5, 1917, p. 18; Dec. 2, 1917; Foster, "How Life Has Been Brought into the Stockyards," p. 64.

13. CFL Minutes, Aug. 19, 1917, p. 5; *BTS*, pp. 93–94; Brody, *The Butcher Workmen*, pp. 76–77; Barrett, *Work and Community*, p. 195.

14. Brody, *The Butcher Workmen*, pp. 76–77; Barrett, *Work and Community*, p. 196; CFL Minutes, Oct. 21, 1917, pp. 22–26.

15. Ibid., Sept. 2, 1917, pp. 13–14; Philip S. Foner, *Organized Labor and the Black Worker: 1619–1973* (New York: Praeger, 1974), p. 138; Tuttle, *Race Riot*, p. 126; Herbst, *The Negro in the Slaughtering and Meat Packing Industry*, p. 31; Foner, *Organized Labor and the Black Worker*, p. 101.

16. Herbst, *The Negro in the Slaughtering and Meat Packing Industry*, p. 32; CFL Minutes, July 7, 1918, pp. 33–34. Barrett, *Work and Community*, p. 194. Foner, *Organized Labor and the Black Worker*, p. 142; *BTS*, p. 92.

17. Barrett, *Work and Community*, pp. 194–96; Brody, *The Butcher Workmen*, pp. 85–86; Cayton and Mitchell, *Black Workers and the New Unions*, p. 243; Dominic A. Pacyga, *Polish Immigrants and Industrial Chicago: Workers on the South Side, 1880–1922* (Columbus: Ohio State University Press, 1991), pp. 238–47; 182–88; CFL Minutes, Nov. 18, 1917, pp. 4–5.

18. *VOL*, Sept. 15, 1922, p. 12; Minutes, preplenum meeting of Communist Party National Committee, Mar. 23, 1939, p. 39, Philip Jaffe Collection, Woodruff Library, Emory University, Series VII.

19. See, for instance, Robert Weibe, *The Search for Order* (New York: Hill and Wang, 1967), pp. 111–32, 164–95; John Milton Cooper, *The Warrior and the Priest* (Cambridge, Mass.: Harvard University Press, 1983), p. 12.

20. Foster, "How Life Has Been Brought into the Yards," p. 65; CFL Minutes, Nov. 4, 1917, pp. 21–23; *BTS*, p. 94.

21. Ibid., p. 95; Barrett, "Work and Community," p. 303; Foster, "How Life Has Been Brought into the Yards," p. 65; CFL Minutes, Dec. 2, 1917, Nov. 4, 1917, p. 18, Nov. 18, 1917.

22. CFL Minutes, Dec. 2, 1917, pp. 7–9, Jan. 6, 1918, pp. 17–18; Brody, *The Butcher Workmen*, p. 78; Foster, "How Life Has Been Brought into the Yards," p. 66; *BTS*, p. 97.

23. Ibid., pp. 97–98; *Butcher Workman*, February 1918, p. 1; Brody, *The Butcher Workmen*, pp. 79–80.

24. See, for instance, Melvyn Dubofsky and Warren Van Tine, *John L. Lewis* (Urbana: University of Illinois Press, 1986), p. 43.

25. Foster, "How Life Has Been Brought into the Yards," p. 68; Samuel Alschuler to John Fitzpatrick, Mar. 28, 1919, Fitzpatrick Papers, Chicago Historical Society, box 8, folder 58.

26. For a description of the Union Stock Yards and Transit Company, see U.S. Federal Trade Commission, *Report on the Meat Packing Industry* 3:194. *Butcher Workman*, June 1918, p. 1. For an account of the USY & T. strike and settlement, see Samuel Alschuler to William B. Wilson, Aug. 6, 1918, and attached typescript outlining Alschuler's award and composition of work force in the yards, p. 3, Federal Mediation and Conciliation Service Files, 33/864, RG 280, box 48, Na-

tional Archives and Records Administration, Suitland, Md. Foster's descriptions of the strike are in *BTS*, pp. 99–100; *PWL*, pp. 156–59.

27. *Butcher Workman*, June, 1918, pp. 1–3. Foster's accounts do not mention the Alschuler arbitration of the wage dispute.

28. Foster's testimony is in FMCS Case Files, 33/864, RG 280, box 48, National Archives, Suitland, Md.

29. *BTS*, p. 103.

30. CFL Minutes, Apr. 7, 1918, pp. 5–6.

31. Lane, "Brief History," pp. 2, 5.

32. Lane, "Brief History," p. 2.

33. Brody, *The Butcher Workmen*, p. 83; Arthur Kampfert, "History of Meatpacking Industry Unions," unpublished MS. on deposit at the State Historical Society of Wisconsin, 2:130–32.

34. William Z. Foster to Frank Walsh, July 6, 1918, Frank Walsh Papers, New York Public Library; *PWL*, p. 161.

35. Brody, *The Butcher Workmen*, p. 80; *Butcher Workman*, December 1919, p. 2; Kampfert, "Meatpacking Unions," 2:163.

36. J. W. Johnstone to John Fitzpatrick, Mar. 28, 1919, Fitzpatrick Papers, Chicago Historical Society, box 8, folder 58; Kampfert, "Meatpacking Unions," 2:163; Leslie O'Rear, "Dennis Lane and the Kiss of Death," *The Packinghouse Worker*, October 30, 1939.

37. Brody, *The Butcher Workmen*, p. 90; Frank Morrison to John Fitzpatrick, Sept. 20, 1919, Fitzpatrick Papers, box 8, folder 62; *BTS*, p. 97; William Z. Foster, *Misleaders of Labor* (Chicago: Trade Union Educational League, 1927), pp. 159–61; Foster estimated in *American Trade Unionism: Principles, Organization, Strategy, Tactics* (New York: International Publishers, 1947), p. 31, that after the new council was formed, only two thousand workers joined it, while forty thousand others, affiliated to the SLC, refused and were expelled. Lane was contemplating a new council as early as March. See J. W. Johnstone to John Fitzpatrick, March 28, 1919, Fitzpatrick Papers, box 8, folder 58; Herbst, *The Negro in the Slaughtering and Meat Packing Industries*, p. 42.

38. Tuttle, *Race Riot* p. 141; *U.S. Military Intelligence Reports: Surveillance of Radicals in the United States: 1917–1941* (Frederick, Md.: University Publications, 1984), reel 10, 10110–853, pp. 842, 812; for Jones's and Johnstone's status as delegates from Painters Local No. 147, see CFL Minutes, May 20, 1917, p. 17, Sept. 2, 1917, p. 11; *BTS*, p. 84.

39. On the role of race in the demise of the SLC, see diverse accounts by Brody, *The Butcher Workmen*, pp. 87–89, 91; Herbst, *The Negro in the Slaughtering and Meat Packing Industries*, pp. 45–52; Alan H. Spear, *Black Chicago: The Making of a Negro Ghetto, 1890–1920* (Chicago: University of Chicago Press, 1967), p. 163; Barrett, *Work and Community*, pp. 202–24; Tuttle, *Race Riot*, pp. 108–56; James Grossman, "White Man's Union," pp. 95–99; Eric Halpern, "Race, Ethnicity and Union in the Chicago Stockyards, 1917–1922," *International Review of Social History* 37 (1992): 1–15; Pacyga, *Polish Immigrants and Industrial Chicago*, pp. 238–47.

40. Chicago Commission on Race Relations, *The Negro in Chicago: A Study*

of Race Relations and a Race Riot (Chicago: University of Chicago Press, 1922), p. 429.

41. *BTS*, p. 55; on the character of racial unity in the SLC, see Herbst, *The Negro in the Slaughtering and Meat Packing Industries*, pp. 48–51; Barrett, *Work and Community*, pp. 204–6; Earl Browder, "Some Experiences in Organizing Negro Workers," *Communist*, January 1930, p. 35. This article consists of recollections of Johnstone, related to Browder, of the SLC and the 1919 race riot.

42. Nick Salvatore, *Eugene Debs* (Urbana: University of Illinois Press, 1983), p. 3.

CHAPTER 5
THE GREAT STEEL STRIKE

1. William Z. Foster and Earl Ford, *Syndicalism* (Chicago: William Z. Foster, 1912) p. 18.

2. William Z. Foster, *More Pages from a Worker's Life*, ed. Arthur Zipser (New York: American Institute for Marxist Studies, 1979), pp. 14–15; William Z. Foster, *The Great Steel Strike and Its Lessons* (New York: B. W. Huebsch, 1920), p. 84. David Brody, *Labor in Crisis: The Steel Strike of 1919* (New York: Lippincott, 1965), pp. 102–3.

3. On the 1919 strikes, see, for instance, James R. Green, *The World of the Worker: Labor in Twentieth-Century America* (New York: Hill and Wang, 1980), pp. 93–95; Melvyn Dubofsky, *Industrialism and the American Worker, 1865–1920* (Arlington Heights, Ill.: Harlan Davidson, 1985), pp. 134–38; Jeremy Brecher, *Strike!* (Boston: South End Press, 1972), pp. 101–43; David Montgomery, "Immigrants, Industrial Unions, and Social Reconstruction in the United States, 1916–1923," *Labour/Le Travail* 13(1984): 101–13; Philip Foner, *History of the Labor Movement in the United States*, vol. 8, *Post-War Struggles, 1918–1920* (New York: International Publishers, 1988).

4. Brody, *Labor in Crisis*, pp. 13–44; Brody, *Steelworkers in America: The Non-Union Era* (New York: Harper, 1960); John Fitch, *The Steel Workers* (New York: Charities Publication Committee, 1911), pp. 75–136.

5. This account of the developing business and technology of steelmaking is drawn from Brody, *Steelworkers in America*, pp. 1–49, 78, 91, 177; Brody, *Labor in Crisis*, pp. 17, 37; Katherine Stone, "The Origins of Job Structures in the Steel Industry," in *Labor Market Segmentation*, ed. Richard C. Edwards, Michael Reich, and David Gordon (Lexington, Mass.: D. C. Heath, 1975), pp. 27–84; Richard Edwards, *Contested Terrain: The Transformation of the Workplace in the Twentieth Century* (New York: Basic Books, 1979), pp. 40–41, 61–65. On the history of metalworking crafts in one community, see Celia F. Bucki, "Dilution and Craft Tradition: Bridgeport, Connecticut, Munitions Workers, 1915–1919," *Social Science History* 4 (1980): 105–24; on resistance to the introduction of machine production, see David Montgomery, *Workers' Control in America* (New York: Cambridge University Press, 1977).

6. Brody, *Labor in Crisis*, pp. 47–50; on NWLB intervention at Bethlehem, see ibid., pp. 53–56. Valerie Connor, *The National War Labor Board: Stability,*

Social Justice and the Voluntary State in World War I (Chapel Hill: University of North Carolina Press, 1983), pp. 158–86; Melvin I. Urofsky, *Big Steel and the Wilson Administration: A Study in Business-Government Relations* (Columbus: Ohio State University Press, 1969), pp. 278–91, and John S. Smith, "Organized Labor and Government in the Wilson Era, 1913–1921: Some Conclusions," *Labor History* 3(1962): 265–86.

7. Chicago Federation of Labor Minutes, May 7, 1918, pp. 5–6, Chicago Federation of Labor Papers, Chicago Historical Society; Frank Morrison to John Fitzpatrick, Apr. 8, 1919, Chicago Historical Society, Fitzpatrick Papers, box 6, folder 47; Brody, *Steelworkers in America*, p. 214.

8. Foster, *More Pages from a Worker's Life*, p. 39.

9. *BTS*, pp. 106–7; Foster to Fitzpatrick, June 12, 1918, and Foster to Fitzpatrick, June 22, 1918, both in Fitzpatrick Papers, describe Foster's efforts at the AFL convention; "Minutes of Organizations in the Steel Industries, St. Paul," Second Conference, June 18, 1918, WZF, d. 83; CFL Minutes, July 7, 1918, pp. 31–36.

10. Foster, *The Great Steel Strike*, p. 19; Foster to Fitzpatrick, June 22, 1918; National Committee for Organizing Iron and Steel Workers, Minutes, June 17–20, 1918, in DS (cited here as NC Minutes).

11. Ibid., June 17–20, Aug. 16, 1918; Foster to Mary Heaton Vorse, Mar. 10, 1938, Vorse Papers, box 64, Archives of Labor and Urban Affairs, Reuther Library, Wayne State University.

12. Foster, *The Great Steel Strike*, p. 25; NC Minutes, Aug. 1–2, 1918, Sept. 11, 1918; Foster to Frank Morrison, Aug. 27, 1918, WZF, d. 84; Brody, *Labor in Crisis*, p. 68.

13. This account of steelworkers in Gary is drawn from Raymond A. Mohl and Neil Betten, *Steel City: Urban and Ethnic Patterns in Gary, Indiana, 1906–1950* (New York: Holmes & Meier, 1986), pp. 10–25, 30–31. See also Ray Stannard Baker, *The New Industrial Unrest: Reasons and Remedies* (Garden City, N.Y.: Doubleday, 1920), pp. 27–39, 49–51.

14. Mohl and Betten, *Steel City*, pp. 28–30.

15. NC Minutes, Sept. 7, 1918, Sept. 28, 1918, Jan. 4, 1919, Feb. 15, 1919, Sept. 26, 1919; Foster to Morrison, Sept. 19, 1918, Foster to Gompers, Nov. 8, 1918, WZF, d. 84; Saposs comment in NC Minutes, p. 14. Foster's descriptions of the work in Gary are in his testimony before the Interchurch World Commission, DS, box 26, folder 13, pp. 16–17.

16. Foster, *The Great Steel Strike*, p. 29; Dreiser quotes in Richard Lingeman, *Theodore Dreiser: At the Gates of the City, 1871–1907* (New York: G. P. Putnam, 1986), pp. 129, 130; Robert Asher, "Painful Memories: The Historical Consciousness of Steelworkers and the Steel Strike of 1919," *Pennsylvania History* 45(1978): 61–86.

17. This account is drawn from Francis G. Couvares, *The Remaking of Pittsburgh: Class and Culture in an Industrializing City, 1877–1919* (Albany: State University of New York Press, 1984), esp. pp. 7, 84–89.

18. John Bodnar, *Lives of their Own: Blacks, Italians and Poles in Pittsburgh, 1900–1960* (Urbana: University of Illinois Press, 1982), p. 263; Couvares, *The Remaking of Pittsburgh*, p. 92; Michael Nash, *Conflict and Accommodation:*

Coal Miners, Steel Workers, and Socialism, 1890–1920 (Westport, Conn.: Greenwood Press, 1982), p. 116; *Liberator*, December 1919, p. 6.

19. Walsh quoted in John Keiser, "John Fitzpatrick and Progressive Unionism" (Ph.D. diss., Northwestern University, 1965), p. 45. On the breakdown of the NWLB's authority, see Connor, *The National War Labor Board* (Chapel Hill: University of North Carolina Press, 1983), pp. 180–85.

20. Foster to Gompers, Nov. 29, 1918, WZF, d. 84; Gompers to George Lysle, Dec. 4, 1918, Fitzpatrick Papers, box 7, folder 52.

21. Commission of Inquiry, the Interchurch World Movement, *Report on the Steel Strike of 1919* (New York: Harcourt, Brace and Howe, 1920), p. 36; Foster on Debs in *Vie ouvrière*, June 5, 1914, p. 656, July 5, 1914, p. 41. *BTS*, p. 135; National Committee to Eugene Debs, Jan. 25, 1919, WZF, d. 84. This letter was apparently never sent—it appears to be the original.

22. NC Minutes Nov. 25, 1918.

23. Ibid., Nov. 25, 1918, Apr. 5, July 20, 1919; Foster, *The Great Steel Strike*, p. 51; James Reddington to William Murphy (AFL Organizer), June 14, 1919, George Lysle to James Reddington, [July 8, 1919], WZF, d. 84; Brody, *Labor in Crisis*, pp. 90–91, 93; Foster, testimony before Interchurch Commission, DS, box 26, folder 13, p. 17; Foster, *The Great Steel Strike*, p. 56.

24. Brody, *Labor in Crisis*, pp. 90. 92; Foster, *The Great Steel Strike*, pp. 53, 59, 60, 63.

25. Unpublished *Pages from a Worker's Life*, typescript, "A McKeesport Meeting," JMK; Foster, *The Great Steel Strike*, pp. 54, 57; Foster, testimony before Interchurch Commission, DS, box 26, folder 13, pp. 39, 19.

26. *New Majority*, Mar. 20, July 12, 1919; Foster to Frank Walsh, Mar. 23, 1919, Frank Walsh Papers, New York Public Library.

27. William Leiserson to David Saposs, May 15, 1919, DS, box 1; NC Minutes, Apr. 5, 1919; for Foster on the conference tactic used in packing and steel campaigns, see William Z. Foster, *Strike Strategy* (Chicago: Trade Union Educational League, 1926), pp. 50–51.

28. NC Minutes, Apr. 5, 1919. Here Foster "recommended that as a tactic to help speed up the work of organization a general conference be called in Pittsburgh in about six weeks of delegates from all the unions employed in the steel industry *that are not working under union agreements*" (emphasis added). This guaranteed that the conference would be dominated by unskilled immigrant workers, recently organized, who owed their primary allegiance to the National Committee.

29. NC Minutes, May 25, 1919; ibid., May 27, 1919, July 11, 1919, for discussion of the steelworkers department and universal transfer. Foster to P. J. Morrin, July 16, 1919, copy in Fitzpatrick Papers, Foster file. See American Federation of Labor, *Report of Proceedings, 1919*, pp. 232, 301. On the earlier "federated metal trades," see David Montgomery, *The Fall of the House of Labor*, (New York: Cambridge University Press, 1987), p. 264.

30. An example of Foster on the "sabotage" by the AFL is in *BTS*, p. 114. NC Minutes, Jan. 4, 1919 for the "general dissatisfaction" of the delegates present that the heads of the various international unions "are not more active in this

campaign." On the Amalgamated's attempt at a separate settlement, see Foster, *The Great Steel Strike*, pp. 69–72. Saposs to Heber Blankenhorn, Jan. 17, 1920, DS, box 1.

31. *The Nation*, Apr. 19, 1919, pp. 600–601; *BTS*, p. 125; *Chicago Labor News*, June 13, 1919, reprinted the entire text of Fitzpatrick's letter. See also Foster, "An Open Letter to John Fitzpatrick," *Labor Herald*, January 1924, pp. 6–7.

32. Minutes of Pittsburgh Conference in Saposs, "Organizing the Steel Workers": "Anticipating the probability of the National Committee not being successful in their efforts at negotiation the conference urged it to make immediate preparations for strike action" (p. 39).

33. NC Minutes July 11, 1919.

34. Ibid., July 20, 1919, pp. 6, 8; Martin Ryan to Foster, July 15, 1919, WZF, d. 84; Brody, *Labor in Crisis*, pp. 98–100. Foster claimed in the Senate investigation of the steel strike that the decision to take the strike vote was unanimous; U.S. Senate, Committee on Labor and Education, *Investigation of Strike in the Steel Industry*, 2 vols., 66th Cong., 1st sess., 1919, p. 382.

35. Foster to Fitzpatrick, July 28, 1919, Fitzpatrick Papers; "General Report: National Committee For Organizing Iron and Steel Workers," Vorse Papers, box 120, Steel clippings and leaflets, for official accounting of the increase in the Amalgamated's membership; Foster to Fitzpatrick, July 22, 1919, Fitzpatrick Papers.

36. Curiously enough, despite his contemporary rhetoric emphasizing the willingness of the steelworkers to strike, in later years Foster offered a different assessment: "The steel industry, with its war munitions orders suddenly cut off, had dropped rapidly in production and the workers were in a defensive mood and not inclined to aggressive organizational steps" (Foster, *Unionizing Steel* [New York: Workers' Library, 1936], p. 8). NC Minutes, Aug. 20, Sept. 4, Sept. 9 and 10, Sept. 17, 1919; telegram from Youngstown Organizing District to National Committee, Sept. 17, 1919, WZF, d. 84. In *BTS*, p. 120, Foster notes that he telephoned the committee's field organizers, urging them to "express the opinions of the local steel councils."

37. Gompers quoted in Brody, *Labor in Crisis*, p. 105; NC Minutes, Sept. 17, 1919; Fitzpatrick to Gompers, Sept. 12, 1919, WZF, d. 84; Gompers in *The World* (New York) Apr. 15, 1922, p. 9, on Foster and the timing of the strike; see also Samuel Gompers, *Seventy Years of Life and Labor*, 2 vols. (New York, E. P. Dutton, 1925; repr. New York: Augustus M. Kelley, 1967), 2:517: "In these conferences, Foster had been so insistent that the strike take place upon the day set that I began to doubt his sincerity and to believe, as I am now convinced, that his whole conciliatory policy toward the American Federation of Labor and the trade union movement was for no other reason than to gain some foothold by which he could undermine and destroy the bona fide labor movement of America and to try to reconstruct it upon the Soviet revolutionary basis."

38. James W. Kline to Foster, Sept. 15, 1919; William Haddock to W. R. Rubin [Sept. 1919]; "To W. Foster, Labor Agitator," from "Employer" [n.d.], WZF, d. 84.

39. *Philadelphia Inquirer*, Sept. 20, 1919, p. 1; S. Adele Shaw, "Closed Towns," *Survey*, November 8, 1919, pp. 58–61; Brody, *Labor in Crisis*, pp. 148–49; *New York Tribune*, Sept. 22, 1919, p. 1.

40. Brody, *Labor in Crisis*, pp. 112–13.

41. Foster, *Steel Strike*, pp. 96–97.

42. Ibid., pp. 97–98; Foster and Ford, *Syndicalism*, p. 3.

43. Steel Strike Financial Report, receipts from Oct. 22, 1919 to Feb. 18, 1920, WZF, d. 85.

44. *New Majority*, Dec. 27, 1919; Foster, testimony before Interchurch World Commission, DS, box 26, folder 13, pp. 24–26; Eva Morawska, *For Bread With Butter: Life-Worlds of East Central Europeans in Johnstown, Pennsylvania, 1890–1940* (New York: Cambridge University Press, 1985), p. 180; David Montgomery, "Immigrants, Industrial Unions, and Social Reconstruction," pp. 112–13.

45. Foster, *The Great Steel Strike*, pp. 146–48, for Foster's description of Sellins's death; *New York Times*, Aug. 27, 1919, p. 2; *Call* (New York), Sept. 26, 1919, p. 1; Foster to Upton Sinclair, Sept. 23, 1922, Sinclair Papers, Lilly Library, Indiana University. On the events surrounding Sellins's death, see Carl J. Meyerhuber, *Less than Forever: The Rise and Decline of Union Solidarity in Western Pennsylvania, 1914–1948* (Selinsgrove, Pa.: Susquehanna University Press, 1987), pp. 51–56.

46. Mary Field Parton, ed., *The Autobiography of Mother Jones* (Chicago: Charles H. Kerr, 1972), p. 214; Mary Heaton Vorse, *Men and Steel* (New York: Boni and Liveright, 1920, pp. 60–61, 68, 70–71; *Public Ledger*, (Philadelphia), Sept. 25, 1919, p. 2; Art Shields, "Anniversary of the Great Steel Strike," *Daily World*, Sept. 19, 1974; *New Republic*, Dec. 3, 1919, p. 21; *New York Tribune*, Sept. 22, 1919, p. 1; *Current Opinion*, December 1919, p. 293; John Brophy, Columbia University Oral History interview, pp. 299, 406–7; Theodore Draper interview with John Brophy, TD, box 10, folder 31; on contemporary views of the facial characteristics of radicals, see Richard Gid Powers, *Secrecy and Power: The Life of J. Edgar Hoover* (New York: Free Press, 1987), p. 73.

47. Brody, *Labor in Crisis*, p. 140; *Philadelphia Inquirer* Sept. 22, 1919, p. 1; NC Minutes, July 20, 1919 (copy in Fitzpatrick Papers, pp. 1, 7), and NC Minutes, July 11, Sept. 17, Nov. 24, 1919, mention Hammersmark, Manley, and Brown; *New York Ttimes*, Jan. 9, 1920, p. 1, on Brown; *Investigation of Strike in Steel Industry*, p. 382; *New Republic*, Dec. 3, 1919, pp. 22–23, on the role of J. G. Brown. John Kikulski, an electrifying organizer for the Stockyards Labor Council, also turned up working for the steel campaign: Philadelphia conference minutes, Saposs, "Organizing the Steel Workers," pp. 29, 40.

48. Foster, *The Great Steel Strike*, pp. 89–90; Brody, *Labor in Crisis*, pp. 106–7.

49. Gompers, *Seventy Years of Life and Labor*, 2:514–15; *Investigation of Strike in Steel Industry*, p. 112.

50. David Saposs believed that while the international presidents were reluctant, Gompers "pushed them into" the steel drive: Alice M. Hoffman, "An Interview with David Saposs," 1967, DS, box 26, folder 5; Brody, *Labor in Crisis*, p. 143.

51. Foster, "An Open Letter to John Fitzpatrick," *Labor Herald*, January 1924, p. 6. In *BTS*, p. 125, Foster describes Gompers as "a keen old fox." *Investigation of Strike in Steel Industry*, p. 117.

52. *New York Tribune*, Sept. 26, 1919, p. 5; *New York Times*, Sept. 24, 1919, p. 2; *Current Opinion*, December 1919, p. 293.

53. Brody, *Labor in Crisis*, p. 138.

54. *New York Times*, Sept. 23, 1919, p. 1.

55. *New York Tribune*, Sept. 30, 1919, p. 2. *New York Times*, Sept. 25, 1919, p. 2.

56. *New York Times*, Sept. 24, 1919, p. 2, Sept. 26, 1919, p. 2.

57. *New York Tribune*, Oct. 1, 1919, p. 9, Sept. 26, 1919, p. 1.

58. William Z. Foster, *Trade Unionism, the Road to Freedom* (Chicago: ITUEL, [1916]), pp. 12, 18–19; Foster, *The Great Steel Strike*, p. 258.

59. Foster, *The Great Steel Strike*, pp. 264–65; *BTS*, p. 123.

60. Interchurch World Movement, *Report on the Steel Strike*, pp. 35, 39; Saposs Draft, "Origins and Development of the AFL," 1921, DS, box 6, folder 10, p. 11.

61. David Saposs, "How the Steel Strike Was Organized," *Survey*, Nov. 8, 1919, p. 68; *New York Times*, Sept. 25, p. 2; *New Majority*, Dec. 27, 1919. Debs quoted in *Ohio Socialist*, Oct. 29, 1919, p. 1; *New York Times*, Sept. 24, 1919, p. 3.

62. *New York Tribune*, Sept. 24 1919, p. 2; *New York Times*, Sept. 25, 1919, p. 2; *Call*, Sept. 25, 1919, p. 3.

63. Mohl and Betten, *Steel City*, p. 35; Dominic A. Pacyga, "Villages of Packinghouses and Steel Mills: The Polish Workers on Chicago's South Side, 1880–1921" (Ph.D. diss., University of Illinois, Chicago, 1981), p. 313.

64. Mohl and Betten, *Steel City*, pp. 32–33, 42; Brody, *Labor in Crisis*, pp. 135–36.

65. Foster, *Steel Strike*, p. 110; James H. Mauer to W. C. Sproul, Oct. 14, 1919, copy in Mary Heaton Vorse Papers, Archives of Labor and Urban Affairs, Wayne State University, box 120; Mauer, a socialist, expressed admiration for Foster as distinct from other Communists in his autobiography, *It Can Be Done* (New York: Rand School, 1938), p. 240; *Call*, Sept. 25, 1919.

66. Mary Heaton Vorse to [?], Oct. 28, 1919, Vorse Papers, box 120; *Wall Street Journal*, quoted in Robert K. Murray, "Communism and the Great Steel Strike of 1919," *Mississippi Valley Historical Review* 38(1951): 458; on the repression of the strike in western Pennsylvania, see Brody, *Labor in Crisis*, pp. 147–78; Foster, *Steel Strike*, pp. 110–37.

67. *New York Times*, Sept. 25, 1919, p. 2; Foster noted quite forthrightly in his testimony before the Interchurch World Commission, DS, box 26, folder 13, p. 26, that if he had distributed *Syndicalism* during the strike he would have been jailed.

68. *Investigation of Strike in Steel Industry*, pp. 388–89, 392, 393.

69. Ibid., p. 395; Gompers, *Seventy Years of Life and Labor*, 2:518.

70. *New York Times*, Oct. 4, 1919, p. 1; Foster, *The Great Steel Strike*, pp. 153–54.

71. *Investigation of Strike in Steel Industry* p. 396.

72. Brody, *Labor in Crisis*, pp. 115–27. Wilson convened a second industrial conference: see Gary Dean Best, "President Wilson's Second Industrial Conference, 1919–1920," *Labor History* 16(1975): 503.

73. Foster, *The Great Steel Strike*, pp. 209–10; Foster, testimony before the Interchurch World Commission, DS, box 26, folder 13, p. 37.

74. *Call*, Sept. 26, 1919, p. 3.

75. *New York Times*, Nov. 8, p. 1; *New Majority*, Nov. 22, 1919, p. 3.

76. Quoted in Matthew S. Magda, *Monessen: Industrial Boomtown and Steel Community, 1898–1980* (Harrisburg: Pennsylvania Historical and Museum Commission, 1985), p. 54.

77.] Brody, *Labor in Crisis*, pp. 172–76; Gary quoted in Robert R. R. Brooks, *As Steel Goes: Unionism in a Basic Industry* (New Haven, Conn.: Yale University Press, 1940), p. 40.

78. For an example of the traditional paradigm of strike conduct, see Patricia Cooper, *Once a Cigar Maker: Men, Women, and Work Culture in American Cigar Factories, 1900–1919* (Urbana: University of Illinois Press, 1987), pp. 21, 99–100. Hannon quoted in Brody, *Labor in Crisis*, p. 165.

79. "An Interview With David Saposs," by Alice M. Hoffman, 1967, p. 23, DS, box 26, folder 5.

80. "Memo by H.B[lankenhorn] Dec. 20, 1919," DS, box 1; Hoffman, "Interview with David Saposs," p. 23.

81. NC Minutes, Dec. 13, 1919; Brody, *Labor in Crisis*, pp. 168, 175; Philip Taft, *The AFL in the Time of Gompers* (New York: Harper, 1952), p. 393.

82. *New Majority*, Jan. 17, 1920, p. 14; NC Minutes, Jan. 3, 1920.

83. Foster, *The Great Steel Strike*, pp. 242, 192.

84. *U.S. Military Intelligence Reports: Surveillance of Radicals in the United States, 1917–1941* (Frederick, Md.: University Publications of America, 1984), p. 107, reel 16, (10110–1683): In the weekly report to the F.B.I., the following account of the Feb. 4 meeting: "Despite the fact that Foster is supposed to have resigned as Executive Secretary and from active participation, he is said to have dominated [the] meeting, immediately following which, he and several other radical members of the committee held a secret meeting which the general delegates were not permitted to attend. Organizers representing the Committee are now active in and about Lackawanna, N.Y. and Pittsburgh, Pa. . . . Joe Manley, son-in-law of Foster, is said to be the leading spirit in the latter district."

85. Brody, *Steelworkers in America*, p. 262; Magda, *Monessen*, p. 51; David Saposs, "In the Wake of the Big Strike: What the Workers Thought Six Months After," *Labor Age*, January 1923, pp. 6–7; Minutes, Executive Committee, American Civil Liberties Union, Nov. 3, 1919, Jan. 5, 1919, July 12, 1920, ACLU, vol. 228. At the height of the strike, Foster had requested that the ACLU investigate civil liberties in Pittsburgh (ibid., Nov. 3, 1919).

86. NC Minutes, Jan. 3, 1920; *Labor Herald*, January 1924, p. 6; Foster's characterization of the effect of the strike's defeat on the labor movement of the 1920s is from a 1922 speech: FOIA, 61-330-20, 21. See also Allen M. Wakstein, "The Origins of the Open-Shop Movement, 1919–1920," *Journal of American History* 51(1964): 465–67.

87. Robert Murray, "Communism and the Great Steel Strike of 1919," *Mississippi Valley Historical Review* 38(1951): 465; Charles Hill, "Fighting the Twelve-Hour Day in the American Steel Industry," *Labor History* 15(1974): 19–35.

88. Untitled MS., Roger Baldwin Papers, box 4, vol. 2, Seeley Mudd Library, Princeton University.

89. Philip Taft, *The AFL in the Time of Gompers* (New York: Harper, 1957), p. 386; Anon., *The Path of Foster and Browder* (New York: Workers' Library, 1941), p. 20.

90. William Preston Jr., *Aliens and Dissenters: Federal Suppression of Radicals, 1903–1933* (Cambridge, Mass.: Harvard University Press, 1963), p. 75.

91. *Survey*, Dec. 20, 1919, p. 266; Foster, *Steel Strike*, p. 265. On continuing efforts by the Wilson administration to define the terms of postwar industrial relations, see Gary Dean Best, "President Wilson's Second Industrial Conference, 1919–1920," *Labor History* 16(1975): 505–20.

CHAPTER 6
LABOR ORGANIZER AND COMMUNIST

1. *LH*, January 1924, p. 7; the infamous Lusk Committee included the Chicago Federation's official organ, *The New Majority*, on its list of publications considered "revolutionary": *Revolutionary Radicalism: Its History, Purpose and Tactics* Report of the Joint Legislative Committee Investigating Seditious Activities, filed April 24, 1920, in the Senate of the State of New York, 4 vols. (Albany: J. B. Lyon Co.), Part 1, "Revolutionary and Subversive Movements Abroad and at Home," 2:1246.

2. Saposs notes, "Free Lancers" in "What Lies Back of Foster," DS box 6, folder 16, pp. 20, 22, 23.

3. *New Republic*, Jan. 7, 1920, p. 166; "Fosterism" was typically a label applied by the IWW; see Ben Legere, *The Futility of Fosterism* (Winnipeg, Manitoba: One Big Union Bulletin, [1923]).

4. *BTS*, p. 133.

5. Arthur Zipser, interview with the author, April 23, 1986; U.S. Senate, Committee on Labor and Education, *Investigation of Strike in Steel Industry*, 66th Cong., 1st sess., 1919, pp. 416–17.

6. Foster to Roger Baldwin, Feb. 18, 1920, ACLU, vol. 120, p. 120.

7. On this strike, see Sylvia Kopald, *Rebellion in Labor Unions* (New York: Boni & Liveright, 1924). Kopald interpreted the unrest on the railroads as reflective of a general "rebellion" against union officialdom; Foster, she felt, became the primary spokesman for this challenge: pp. 3, 27, 29, 30–31, 176–77. *New York Ttimes*, April 16, 1920, p. 2; Foster, *The Great Steel Strike*, (New York: B. W. Huebsch, 1920), pp. 246–47; on the dual union "impulses" among the strikers, see Foster, *Strike Strategy* (Chicago: TUEL, 1926), p. 30. *United States Military Intelligence Reports: Surveillance of Radicals in the U.S.: 1917–1941* (Frederick, Md.: University Publications, 1984), reel 16, 10110–1683, p. 24.

8. *The Liberator*, September 1919, p. 1; J. H. M. Laslett, *Labor and the Left* (New York: Basic Books, 1970), pp. 171–72; William Z. Foster, *More Pages from*

a Worker's Life, ed. Arthur Zipser (New York: American Institute for Marxist Studies, 1979), p. 10; Legere, *The Futility of Fosterism*, p. 28; Foster later claimed that Ryan offered him the editorship of the *Railway Carmen's Journal*: Foster, *Twilight of World Capitalism* (New York: International Publishers, 1949), p. 161.

9. *La Vie ouvrière*, Oct. 20, 1912, p. 412.

10. *New York Times*, May 9, p. 1.

11. *BTS*, p. 134.

12. *NM*, July 31, 1920, p. 5; March 26, 1921, p. 11; Nov. 27, 1920, p. 5; Nov. 13 issue reprints CFL Minutes for Nov. 7 showing deficits during Foster's tenure; James Weinstein, *The Decline of Socialism in America: 1912–1925* (New Brunswick, N.J.: Rutgers University Press, 1984), p. 273. According to H. B. Sell, "The AFL and the Labor Party Movement of 1918–1920," (M.A. thesis, University of Chicago, 1922), p. 126, the number of local unions in Chicago sending delegates to the Labor party conventions in that city declined nearly 50 percent between 1919 and 1920.

13. Minutes of Directing Committee, Jan. 5, 1920, ACLU, vol. 228 (A) (unpaginated); Foster to Baldwin, July 21, 1920, ibid., vol. 119, p. 210; Foster to Baldwin, Nov. 3, 1920, ibid., p. 221; J. L. Beaghen to Baldwin, ibid., p. 231; on Beaghen see *PWL*, p. 167.

14. Philip C. Ensley, "The Interchurch World Movement and the Steel Strike of 1919," *Labor History* 13 (1972): 222; Foster to Baldwin, Feb. 18, 1920, ACLU, vol. 120, p. 120.

15. James Weinstein, *The Decline of Socialism in America*, pp. 272–75; Laslett, *Labor and the Left*, pp. 130, 173, 225; Theodore Draper, *American Communism and Soviet Russia* (New York: Viking, 1960), pp. 29–32; John Keiser, "John Fitzpatrick and Progressive Unionism" (Ph.D. diss., Northwestern University, 1965), p. 113.

16. Interchurch World Movement, *Report on the Steel Strike of 1919* (New York: Harcourt, Brace and Howe, 1920), p. 36.

17. *PWL*, p. 276; S. T. Hammersmark to John Fitzpatrick, Sept. 1, 1920, Fitzpatrick Papers, box 9, folder 65; on Johnstone, see undated document, ibid., box 9, folder 68; Hammersmark on Cook County Farmer Labor party ballot, Apr. 11, 1922, ibid., box 11, folder 81.

18. Foster to Harry Ault, Oct. 11, 1920, Ault Papers, University of Washington, AIA 5/3, box 2, folder 2–36; Harvey O'Connor, *Revolution in Seattle* (Seattle: Left Bank Books, 1964, repr. 1981), pp. 202–3; *BTS*, p. 140.

19. Foster to Ault, Oct. 11, 1920; Foster to Upton Sinclair, Nov. 28, 1920; Foster to Sinclair, Nov. 18, 1920, both Sinclair Papers, Lilly Library, University of Indiana. "Statement of Aims of the Trade Union Educational League," Vorse Papers, Archives of Labor and Urban Affairs, Wayne State University, box 120, Steel Clippings folder.

20. Ibid.

21. *Call* (New York), Nov. 1, 1920, p. 6; J. B. S. Hardman, *American Labor Dynamics* (New York: Harcourt, Brace, 1928), pp. 27, 20; Melech Epstein, *Jewish Labor in the U.S.A.: 1914–1952* (New York: Trade Union Sponsoring Committee, 1953), pp. 40–55, 87.

22. *NM*, Jan. 15, 1921, p. 2.

23. Theodore Draper, *The Roots of American Communism* (New York: Viking, 1957), pp. 267–70; Communist Labor Party, "Report of the Committee on Program and Labor," Sept. 9, 1919, p. 11; Communist Party of America, "Program," Sept. 5, 1919, p. 6, both in *U.S. Military Intelligence Reports: Surveillance of Radicals*, reel 10, 10110–853, pp. 864–72.

24. Draper, *Roots of American Communism*, p. 199; Alexander Bittelman, "History of the Communist Movement in America," p. 442, in Investigation of Communist Propaganda: Hearings Before a Special Committee to Investigate Communist Activities in the United States, part V, vol. 4, (Washington, D.C.: GPO, 1930), pp. 435–48; Fraina in *Revolutionary Age*, Feb. 15, 1919; *Ohio Socialist*, Oct. 1, 1919; *The Toiler* (Cleveland), Jan. 15, 1921, p. 14; Robert K. Murray, *Red Scare: A Study in National Hysteria* (New York: McGraw-Hill, 1955; repr. 1964), p. 453; Bittelman, "History of the Communist Movement," p. 437, 440–41 contains a succinct discussion of the syndicalist currents in the pre-war left wing, as does Draper, *Roots of American Communism*, pp. 16–17, and James P. Cannon, *The First Ten Years of American Communism* (New York: Pathfinder, 1973), p. 316.

25. Communist Labor Party, "Report of the Committee on Program and Labor," pp. 7, 10, 12; Communist Party of America, "Program," pp. 5.

26. Draper, *Roots of American Communism*, p. 198.

27. David Saposs interview with Alice M. Hoffman, 1967, p. 8, DS, box 26, folder 5; David Brody interview with Saposs, cited in Brody, *Steelworkers in America* (Cambridge: Harvard University Press, 1960), p. 246.

28. Keiser, "John Fitzpatrick," pp. 97–98; *NM*, July 17, 1920, p. 6; Gompers quoted in Keiser, "John Fitzpatrick," p. 98.

29. ITUEL circular, July 3, 1917, WZF, f. 615, d. 86; Richard Hudleson, "*Truth* in Duluth," unpublished paper in author's possession; Bittelman, "History of the Communist Movement" p. 444; Draper, *Roots of American Communism*, pp. 78–79, 179, 181; Solon DeLeon, *The American Labor Who's Who* (New York: Hanford, 1925).

30. Browder interview, TD, box 1, folder 3, p. 2; Browder to Theodore Draper, Apr. 15, 1956, TD, box 1, folder 17, p. 2; *NM*, Dec. 4, 1920, p. 3.

31. Wayne Westergard-Thorpe, "Syndicalist Internationalism and Moscow, 1919–1922: The Breach," *Canadian Journal of History* 14 (1979): 202.

32. Foster, *History of the Communist Party of the United States* (New York: International Publishers, 1952), p. 185 states that "*Left-Wing*" Communism appeared in the United States in January 1921; Draper, *Roots of American Communism*, pp. 248–49; *BTS*, 137; V. I. Lenin, "*Left-Wing*" *Communism, an Infantile Disorder* (New York: International Publishers, 1940), pp. 33, 37.

33. *BTS*, p. 137; William Z. Foster and Earl Ford, *Syndicalism* (Chicago: William Z. Foster, 1912), pp. 24–26; Ralph Chaplin, *Wobbly* (Chicago: University of Chicago Press, 1948), p. 347; Lenin, "*Left-Wing*" *Communism*, p. 32.

34. Draper, *Roots of American Communism*, pp. 252, 282–93; Arthur Zipser, *Workingclass Giant: The Life of William Z. Foster* (New York: International Publishers, 1981), p. 65; *Truth* (Duluth), July 4, 1919, p. 5.

35. James G. Ryan, "The Making of a Native Marxist: The Early Career of Earl Browder," *Review of Politics* 39 (1977): 345–46; Draper, *Roots of American Communism*, pp. 309–10; Theodore Draper interview with Browder, Oct. 22, 1954, TD, box 1, folder 3; Draper, *Roots*, p. 310; Browder to Theodore Draper, Feb. 7, 1956, ibid., box 1, folder 17; *BTS*, p. 137; Westergard-Thorpe, "Syndicalist Internationalism," p. 200.

36. Albert Resis, "The Profintern: Origins to 1923" (Ph.D. diss., Columbia University, 1964), pp. 1–6, 13, 43–47.

37. Ibid., p. 136; *BTS*, pp. 136–39; Albert Rosmer, *Moscow under Lenin* (New York: Monthly Review Press, 1971), pp. 135–40; Westergard-Thorpe, "Syndicalist Internationalism," p. 221; Tridon quoted in Charlton Brandt, "William Z. Foster and the Syndicalist League of North America" (M.A. thesis, Sungamon State University, 1985), p. 56.

38. Resis, "Profintern," p. 164; Reiner Tosstroff, "The Red International of Labor Unions" (unpublished paper, 1992), is a recent brief history of the Profintern which quotes E. H. Carr, *Socialism in One Country, 1924–1926*, 3 vols. (London: Macmillan, 1964), 3, pt. 2, p. 938; the secret protocol is quoted in "Statement of the CP of America to the ECCI" [November 1921], Comintern, Lenin Secretariat, f. 5, op. 3, d. 381, l. 88; document signed Wallace, Andrews, Ballister, Crosby, Dixon (Browder pseud.), Emmons, Baldwin, Ballaster, Haywood, Moscow July 18, 1921, CPUSA, d. 39, l. 79; "Instructions for Work in the United States," To Comrade Cook (Foster pseud.), n.d., CPUSA, d. 81, l. 2.

39. *Resolutions and Decisions of the First International Congress of Revolutionary Trade and Industrial Unions* (Chicago: American Labor Union Educational Society, 1921), pp. 30, 62; Westergard-Thorpe, "Syndicalist Internationalism," p. 221. Until 1923, the Profintern still hoped to gain the affiliation of the IWW and the United Workers' Council of New York. At the Second Profintern Congress in 1922, the TUEL gained approval for its opposition to dual-unionism, but was also criticized for its dismissal of "independent revolutionary unions" like the IWW and the UWC, and for its neglect of the unorganized majority of American labor. To the dismay of the TUEL delegates present, the Profintern called for the creation of an "Action Committee" to coordinate the rival factions, and pointedly failed to recognize the TUEL as its official American section; Resis, "The Profintern," pp. 161, 314–16.

40. Draper, *Roots of American Communism*, pp. 255–57, 279; Lenin, *"Left-Wing" Communism*, p. 38; Haywood quoted in *Truth* (Duluth), Sept. 16, 1921, p. 2; Haywood to Lenin, Aug. 12, 1921, Lenin Secretariat, f. 5, op. 3, d. 275; "Budget for American Work," ibid., f. 5, op. 3, d. 381, l. 102.

41. Rosmer, *Moscow under Lenin*, p. 139; George Williams, *The First Congress of the Red Trades International at Moscow, 1921* (Chicago: IWW, [1922]). Browder to Leon Trotsky, May 9, 1921, Moscow, CPUSA, d. 39, l. 35. Williams claimed the TUEL was a fraud, merely a "paper" propaganda organization, and that Browder [Dixon]'s credentials were thus invalid: pp. 5, 7; Earl Browder to Lenin, May 27, 1921, Lenin Secretariat, f. 5, op. 3, d. 97; Foster to Jeno Feck, May 29, 1959, WZF, d. 6 l. 32; the *Voice of Labor* ran from July 1921 to December 1923; Walter Goldwater, *Radical Periodicals in America, 1890–1950* (New

Haven, Conn.: Yale University Press, 1964). Harry Haywood, *Black Bolshevik* (Chicago: Liberator Press, 1978), p. 300, mentions that nearly a dozen veterans of the Paris Commune attended the Fifth Profintern congress in 1930.

42. *VOL*, July 8, 1921. Foster later compiled his *Voice of Labor* dispatches from Russia into a pamphlet, *The Russian Revolution* (Chicago: TUEL, 1921).

43. Philip Taft, *The AFL in the Age of Gompers* (New York: Harper and Bros., 1957), pp. 443–53; *VOL*, July 29, 1921.

44. Ibid., Aug. 5, 1921.

45. Ibid., July 29, 1921; Foster, *Russian Revolution*, pp. 58–59; Daniel Bell, "Work, Alienation and Social Control," *Dissent*, Summer 1957, p. 207.

46. Isaac Deutscher, *Soviet Trade Unions: Their Place in Soviet Labor Strategy* (New York: Oxford University Press, 1950), pp. 33–58; Steven F. Cohen, *Bukharin and the Bolshevik Revolution: A Political Biography, 1888–1938* (New York: Oxford University Press, 1973, 1980), p. 102; Leonard Schapiro, *The Communist Party of the Soviet Union* (New York: Random House, 1960, 1971), pp. 201–5; Foster, *The Russian Revolution*, pp. 31, 53–54, 57.

47. *The Worker*, Nov. 4, 1922, p. 3; Foster, *The Russian Revolution*, p. 27.

48. Ibid., p. 28.

49. *PWL*, pp. 306–10; Unpublished *Pages From a Worker's Life* MS., "Moscow, 1921," JMK.

50. *VOL*, Aug. 26, 1921, p. 11.

51. *VOL*, Sept. 16, 1921, p. 11; Foster, *The Russian Revolution*, pp. 125, 139.

52. *VOL*, Aug. 26, 1921, p. 11; Nov. 11, 1921; Foster, *Russian Revolution*, p. 7.

53. Ibid.

54. *BTS*, pp. 157–59.

55. Ibid., p. 160.

56. Ibid., p. 162.

57. Foster, *The Bankruptcy of the American Labor Movement* (Chicago: TUEL, 1922), p. 40.

58. Foster and Ford, *Syndicalism*, p. 31. This discussion draws in part from Joan Scott, *Gender and the Politics of History* (New York: Columbia University Press), esp. pp. 1–11, 28–50, 53–67.

59. Foster biographical questionnaire, Comintern Roster File, f. 495, op. 261, d. 15; Draper, *Roots of American Communism*, p. 446, n. 33; *BTS*, p. 163, and *History of the Communist Party of the United States*, p. 185; Saposs interview with Alice M. Hoffman, p. 24, DS. Despite Foster's statement in a Comintern questionnaire that he joined the party in 1921, Earl Browder insisted that Foster joined formally only in early 1923, following his arrest and trial for participating in the Bridgman underground convention of the Communist party. See Earl Browder Oral History Memoir, Columbia University, p. 208; Browder interview with William Goldsmith, June 22, 1955, p. 29, Daniel Bell papers, "closed" section, box 9, Tamiment Institute, New York University; Browder autobiography, p. 181, TD, box 1, folder 2. I have been unable to locate a record of Foster's "formal" affiliation with the party. Since he was working closely with the Com-

munists immediately following his return to Russia, the most important issue is his public acknowledgment of his membership. During the 1923 trial itself he denied that he was a member. However, soon after the end of the trial John Pepper, writing in *The Worker* (Apr. 14, 1923, p. 2) identified Foster as a Communist. Foster could not deny this, but neither did he bother to make a formal statement acknowledging his membership.

CHAPTER 7

THE "FREE LANCE" AND THE COMMUNIST PARTY

1. William Z. Foster, *The Railroader's Next Step* (Chicago: TUEL, 1921), pp. 19, 18, 26–27.

2. Ibid., pp. 9, 10, 29, endplate; *LH*, Dec. 1922, p. 5; William Z. Foster, *The Revolutionary Crisis of 1918–1921 in Germany, England, Italy and France* (Chicago: TUEL, 1921), pp. 28–31.

3. James Weinstein, *The Decline of Socialism in America* (New York: Monthly Review Press, 1967; New Brunswick, N.J.: Rutgers University Press, 1984), pp. 266–69; "Report of Jack Travis on visit to EVD," March 25, 1922, Chicago, CPUSA, d. 93, l. 31. In this report, Foster is referred to by the pseudonym "Borden."

4. *New York Times*, Apr. 9, 1923, p. 13; John R. Commons, *Myself* (New York: Macmillan, 1934), p. 149; *New York Times*, May 10, 1923, p. 1; Charles J. Maland, *Chaplin and American Culture* (Princeton, N.J.: Princeton University Press, 1989), p. 265.

5. *VOL*, July 8, 1921, p. 9; Foster, *The Bankruptcy of the American Labor Movement* (Chicago: TUEL. 1922), pp. 19–21; *International Press Correspondence*, Mar. 1, 1923; Foster to [Leder], May 31, 1923, RILU, d. 459, l. 49; Foster to Lozovsky, July 27, 1923, ibid., d. 459, l. 96.

6. Lozovsky's given name was Solomon Abramovich Dridzo. Branko Lazitch and Milorad M. Drachovitch, *Biographical Dictionary of the Comintern* (Stanford: Hoover Institution Press, 1986); Theodore Draper, *The Roots of American Communism* (New York: Viking, 1957), pp. 319–20; Isaac Deutscher, *Soviet Trade Unions: Their Place in Soviet Labor Strategy* (New York: Oxford University Press, 1950), pp. 18–22; Albert Resis, "The Profintern: Origins to 1923" (Ph.D. diss., Columbia University, 1964), p. 10; Gil Green, interview with the author, Oct. 3, 1986; Nikita Khrushchev, *Khrushchev Remembers* (Boston: Little, Brown, 1970), pp. 259–60.

7. FOIA 61-330-113. "Borden" was one of Foster's pseudonymns; another was "Dorsey." See FOIA, 61-330-1, and Draper, *American Communism and Soviet Russia* (New York: Viking, 1960), p. 134. Dixon (Browder) to Lozovsky and Andreychine, Jan. 30, 1922, RILU, f. 534, op. 7, d. 457.

8. *Labor Herald* article, March 1922, "The Principles and Program of the Trade Union Educational League," reproduced in *Investigation of Communist Propaganda*, Hearings before a Special Committee to Investigate Communist Activities in the United States, pt. III, vol. 2, "Woll Exhibits," (Washington, D.C.: Government Printing Office, 1930), pp. 175–80.

9. *LH*, March 1922, and first TUEL circulars are reproduced in *Investigation of Communist Propaganda*, 2:180, 181, 186, 183, 185; *The Toiler* (Cleveland) Dec. 31, 1921, p. 10; *VOL*, Feb. 16, 1923, p. 4.

10. National Civic Federation [author deleted] to William J. Burns, Mar. 30, 1922; Burns reply, Apr. 4, 1922, FOIA, 61-330-16.

11. Ibid., Robt. W. Lovett to G. L. Peck, vice-president, Pennsylvania Railroad, Apr. 11, 1922, National Archives, Justice Department Files, 202600–712.

12. For general overviews of this period, see Robert H. Zieger, *American Workers, American Unions, 1920–1985* (Baltimore: Johns Hopkins University Press, 1986), pp. 1–9; James R. Green, *The World of the Worker: Labor in Twentieth-Century America* (New York: Hill and Wang, 1980), pp. 100–104, 108–11.

13. David Montgomery, *The Fall of the House of Labor* (New York: Cambridge University Press, 1987), pp. 233–37; David A. Hounshell, *From the American System to Mass Production, 1800–1932* (Baltimore: Johns Hopkins University Press, 1984), pp. 217–301; Thomas P. Hughes, *American Genesis: A Century of Invention* (New York: Penguin, 1989), pp. 269–71; Daniel T. Rogers, *The Work Ethic in Industrial America, 1850–1920* (Chicago: University of Chicago Press, 1978), pp. 51–52; Foster, "The Soviet Union in 1926," *Workers Monthly*, June 1926, p. 367.

14. David Montgomery, "New Tendencies in Union Struggles and Strategies in Europe and the United States, 1916–1922," in *Work, Community and Power*, ed. James E. Cronin and Carmen Sinani (Philadelphia: Temple University Press, 1983), pp. 97–101.

15. *LH*, June 1922, pp. 16–19, July 1922, pp. 12–15; *NM* Apr. 29, 1922, p. 5; *Railway Carmen's Journal*, June 1922, pp. 346–47.

16. *LH*, June 1922, pp. 16–19; July 1922, pp. 12–15; *NM*, Apr. 29, 1922, p. 5; ibid., Mar. 25, 1922, p. 1, p. 11 for CFL Minutes for Mar. 10; ibid., Apr. 8, p. 3; Eugene Staley, *History of the Illinois State Federation of Labor* (Chicago: University of Chicago Press, 1930), p. 394–95; *VOL*, Apr. 21, 1922, p. 1; *The Worker*, Apr. 29, 1922, pp. 1, 3; *Railway Carmen's Journal*, June 1922, pp. 346–47. Samuel Gompers, *Seventy Years of Life and Labor*, 2 vols. (New York: E. P. Dutton, 1925; repr. New York: Augustus M. Kelly, 1967), p. 518; *The American Vanguard*, Sepember, 1923, p. 6.

17. Selig Perlman and Philip Taft, *History of Labor in the United States*, 4 vols. (New York: Macmillan, 1918–35), 4:516–19; *Railway Carmen's Journal*, February 1921, p. 91.

18. *The Worker*, Aug. 12, 1922, p. 1; FOIA, 61-330-15, 30, 31, 211; *BTS*, p. 169. *Journal of the Switchmen's Union of North America*, March 1938, p. 69; Foster affidavit on the "Colorado kidnapping" in *New Republic*, Aug. 30, 1922, p. 17, and Foster to Baldwin, Aug. 11, 1922, ACLU, vol. 215, p. 168; ACLU "To Our Friends in Denver," Aug. 21, 1922, ibid., p. 41.

19. Francis Russell, *The Shadow of Blooming Grove: Warren G. Harding and His Times* (New York: McGraw Hill, 1968), pp. 537–45; Foster, *Misleaders of Labor* (Chicago: TUEL, 1927), pp. 30–40, 60–62, 73–76; Perlman and Taft, *History of Labor in the United States*, p. 522; Montgomery, *Fall of the House of Labor*, pp. 423–24.

20. *Railway Carmen's Journal*, April 1923, pp. 195–96, February 1923, p. 87, March 1923, p. 169, April 1923, p. 225; *VOL*, Dec. 15, 1922, pp. 1,3; *LH*, January 1923, p. 3.

21. David M. Schneider, *The Workers' (Communist) Party and the American Trade Unions* (Baltimore: Johns Hopkins University Press, 1928), pp. 8–10, 15; Solon DeLeon, *American Labor Who's Who* (New York: Hanford Press, 1925), p. 127, on Knudsen; *LH*, September 1922, pp. 7, 18, 30–31, July 1922, p. 18; Earl Rucker Beckner, "The Trade Union Education League and the American Labor Movement" (M.A. thesis, University of Chicago, 1924), p. 50; "Amalgamation or Annihilation: A Practical Plan of Amalgamation for the Metal Trades," Daniel Bell Papers, Tamiment Institute Library, New York University, box 6, "Metal Workers' History."

22. Melvyn Dubofsky and Warren Van Tine, *John L. Lewis, A Biography* (Urbana: University of Illinois Press, 1986), pp. 35–51; 59–71; Schneider, "The Workers' (Communist) Party," pp. 38–59; Beckner, "Trade Union Educational League," pp. 74–84.

23. Dubofsky and Van Tine, *John L. Lewis*, pp. 87–88; Thomas L. Monniger, "The Fight of Alexander Howat for the Right to Strike" (M.S. thesis, Kansas State Teachers' College, 1946), pp. 1–11; Philip S. Foner, *History of the Labor Movement in the United States*, vol. 9 *The T.U.E.L. to the End of the Gompers Era* (New York: International Publishers, 1991), pp. 208–44; *LH*, June 1923, p. 12. Howat occasionally received funds from the American Communists: see Foster telegram to Profintern [1927], RILU, d. 472, l. 87.

24. Schneider, "*The Workers' (Communist) Party*," p. 46; *LH*, Mar. 1923, p. 10; Apr. 1923, pp. 24–26; "Bittelman's Speech at Moscow in Defense of William Z. Foster," typescript, p. 3, Bertram Wolfe papers, New York Public Library, box 4; "Minutes of Progressive International Conference of the United Mine Workers of America," June 2, 1923, PH box 2; Powers Hapgood to Eleanor Hapgood, Apr. 23, 1923, ibid.; *New York Times*, June 30, 1923, p. 1; On Merrick, see Montgomery, *Fall of the House of Labor*, pp. 315–26; *Labor Herald*, June 1923, "Editorial"; *New York Times*, June 22, 1923, p. 27.

25. Melech Epstein, *Jewish Labor in the U.S.A., 1914–52*, (New York: Trade Union Sponsoring Committee, 1953), pp. 130, 133; Beckner, "The Trade Union Educational League," pp. 60–74; Steven Fraser, *Labor Will Rule: The Life of Sidney Hillman* (New York: Basic Books, 1991), pp. 180, 182–83; Benjamin Gitlow, *I Confess* (New York: E. P. Dutton, 1939), pp. 176–77; *LH*, May, 1922, p. 25, January 1923, pp. 12–13, June 1923, pp. 3–4.

26. Draper, *American Communism and Soviet Russia*, p. 455, n. 49, on the extent of the amalgamation campaign; in "Draper's 'Roots of American Communism,'" *Political Affairs*, May 1957, p. 36, Foster claims the figure 3,377 as the number of railroad locals endorsing amalgamation. In *International Press Correspondence*, Feb. 8, 1923, Foster claimed that when an amalgamation plan was sent out to twelve thousand locals, four thousand "sent in endorsements of it." Foster to Lozovsky, Dec. 16, 1922, RILU, f. 534, op. 7, d. 457; Foster to Profintern Executive, May 9, 1923, ibid., d. 459, l. 30. John Haynes and Harvey Klehr, "Communication," *Labor History* (1992): 577, for confirmation of one delivery of nearly six thousand dollars to the TUEL in 1926.

27. *LH*, February, 1923, editorial, September 1922, p. 21, January 1923, pp. 11–14, March 1923, pp. 13–14; *VOL*, Feb. 16, 1923, p. 4.

28. Foster to Lozovsky, Apr. 10, 1923, RILU, d. 459, l. 3; *VOL*, Feb. 26, 1923, p. 3; *New York Times*, Apr. 15, 1923, p. 5.

29. *American Federationist*, April 1923, pp. 315–16; J. B. S. Hardman, *American Labor Dynamics* (New York: Harcourt, Brace, 1928), p. 19.

30. R. M. Whitney, *Reds in America* (New York: Beckwith Press, 1924), pp. 28, 30. See Draper, *Roots of American Communism*, pp. 364–75, 452, n. 13, on the reliability of Whitney's exposé. Other transcripts of the Bridgman proceedings appear in *Recognition of Russia*, Hearings Before a Subcommittee of the Committee on Foreign Relations, U.S. Senate, 68th Cong. 1st sess., and in FOIA, 61-443-642.29. "Questions To Be Brought before the Small Bureau of the CI by the EC Representative of the CP of America," Lenin Secretariat, f. 5, op. 3, d. 381, l. 88; *International Press Correspondence*, Jan. 6, 1922, p. 14; Lozovsky on the American party in "The Tasks of the Communists in the Labor Movement," ibid., Dec. 13, 1922, p. 919; Joseph R. Starobin, *American Communism in Crisis, 1943–1957* (Berkeley: University of California Press, 1975), p. 287.

31. Whitney, *Reds in America*, pp. 6, 30; Harvey Klehr, "The Bridgman Delegates," *Survey* 22(1976): 91, 93.

32. Whitney, *Reds in America*, p. 28; *Recognition of Russia*, p. 369; Browder interview with William Goldsmith, June 22, 1955, p. 47, Bell Papers, "Closed Section"; *VOL*, Apr. 6, 1923, p. 1, reports 10 percent of party members as belonging to the TUEL; Joseph Kucher to Lozovsky, Mar. 5, 1923, RILU, d. 461, l. 1.

33. Whitney, *Reds in America*, p. 29.

34. Draper, *Roots of American Communism*, pp. 368, 371; Jacob Spolansky, *The Communist Trail in the United States* (New York: Macmillan, 1951), pp. 25–26; *LH*, September 1922, p. 17; FOIA, 61-330-41, 42, 43, 39.

35. *LH*, May 1923, p. 4; Foster to Baldwin, Aug. 25, 1922, ACLU, vol. 215, p. 163; Baldwin to Foster, Aug. 24, 1922, ibid., vol. 219, p. 216; Eldridge F. Dowell, *A History of Criminal Syndicalism Legislation in the United States* (Baltimore: Johns Hopkins University Press, 1939), pp. 18, 67, 135; *New Republic*, Apr. 25, 1923, p. 232.

36. Baldwin to Foster, Aug. 24, 1922, ACLU, vol. 219, p. 216; William F. Kruse to Baldwin Aug. 27, 1922, ibid., p. 332; Baldwin to Kruse, Aug. 31, 1922, ibid., p. 330; "Memo on Communist Cases," Sept. 26, 1922, ibid., vol. 220, p. 102; Minutes, National Committee, Labor Defense Council, Sept. 26, 1922 ibid., vol. 219, p. 295; Draper, *Roots of American Communism*, p. 204.

37. *New Republic*, Apr. 25, 1923, pp. 231–33; *New York Times*, Mar. 30, 1923, pp. 1, 4; *Labor Herald*, May 1923, p. 26.

38. *New York Times*, Mar. 31, 1923, p. 1, Apr. 6, 1923, p. 1, Apr. 7, p. 16; Zipser, *Workingclass Giant: The Life of William Z. Foster* (New York: International Publishers, 1981), p. 81.

39. Foster to Baldwin, Aug. 16, 1922, ACLU, vol. 215, p. 165; Wm. E. Sweet to Baldwin, Aug. 22, 1922, ibid., p. 72; ACLU publicity, ibid., p. 1; Jas. H. Causey to Baldwin, Nov. 9, 1922, ibid., p. 22; Denver *Bulletin*, Jan. 6, 1923, ibid., vol. 236, p. 449; Foster to Baldwin, Jan. 2, 1923, ibid., vol. 244 (unpaginated).

40. See chapter 6, note 59, on Foster's party membership.

41. *BTS*, p. 135; *LH*, April 1923, pp. 3–4.

42. Foster to Eugene Debs, Apr. 9, 1923, WZF, d. 5; Foster to Profintern Executive, May 9, 1923, RILU, d. 459, l. 30; Foster to Lozovsky, May 31, 1923, ibid., d. 459, l. 46; William D. Haywood to the ECCI, "Bankruptcy Is Not the Term" [1923]. Haywood's manuscript is marked "Radek" and "Trotsky," and was aimed at Foster's *Bankruptcy of the American Labor Movement*.

43. Earl Browder Columbia Oral History Memoir, p. 118; Max Bedacht to Theodore Draper, Jan. 20, 1955, TD, box 10, folder 15; *NM*, Jan. 27, 1923, p. 10; *The Worker*, Nov. 4, 1922, p. 3.

44. Earl Browder interview with Daniel Bell and William Goldsmith, June 14, 1955, Bell Papers, box 8, "closed" Browder Columbia Oral History Interview, p. 344; James P. Cannon, *The First Ten Years of American Communism: Report of a Participant* (New York: Pathfinder, 1962), p. 121 on Browder's role; Gil Green, interview with the author, Oct. 3, 1986.

45. Keiser, "John Fitzpatrick" (Ph.D. diss., Northwestern University, 1965), pp. 101–2; Beckner, "The Trade Union Educational League and the American Labor Movement," p. 90; Foster to Eugene Debs, Apr. 9, 1923, WZF, d. 5; Turman Cicero Bigham, "The Chicago Federation of Labor" (M.A. thesis, University of Chicago, 1925), p. 43; *NM*, May 12, 1923, p. 9.

46. Jay Fox autobiographical MSS., "How Anarchy Would Work," and "Syndicalism: Its Growth and Decay," Jay Fox Papers, Gonzaga University, Spokane Washington; Kenneth Campbell MacKay, *The Progressive Movement of 1924* (New York: Octagon, 1966), pp. 31–33, 54–72; J. H. M. Laslett, *Labor and the Left: A Study of Socialist and Radical Influences in the American Labor Movement, 1881–1924* (New York: Basic Books, 1970); Montgomery, *Fall of the House of Labor*, pp. 434–35; Illinois State Federation of Labor, *Official Annual Gazette*, "Proceedings of the Illinois State Federation of Labor," 1923, pp. 340–41.

47. McKay, *Progressive Movement*, pp. 61–62, 69, 70; Draper, *American Communism and Soviet Russia*, pp. 36–37; H. B. Sell, "The A.F.L. and the Labor Party Movement of 1918–1920," (M.A. thesis, University of Chicago, 1922), p. 83; McKay, *Progressive Movement*, pp. 58–59; Memorandum to Theodore Draper from Earl Browder, Mar. 16, 1959, p. 3, TD, box 38, folder 1; Max Bedacht to Theodore Draper, Jan. 20, 1955, TD, box 10, folder 15; James Cannon, *The First Ten Years of American Communism* (New York: Pathfinder, 1962), p. 121.

48. Earl Browder to Theodore Draper, Feb. 20, 1956, p. 3, TD, box 1, folder 15; C. O. Taylor to John Fitzpatrick, Apr. 24, 1923, and Fitzpatrick to Edward Kosten, Apr. 17, 1923, Fitzpatrick Papers, box 12, folder 86; Harvey O'Connor, *Revolution in Seattle* (Seattle: Left Bank Books, 1964: repr. 1981), pp. 213–14.

49. Arne Swabeck to Theodore Draper, May 14, 1956, TD, box 9, folder 11; Memorandum to Theodore Draper from Earl Browder, p. 10, ibid., box 38, folder 1.

50. Foster and Pepper quoted in Draper, *Roots of American Communism*, pp. 57–60, 73–74; *The Worker*, Apr. 14, 1923, p. 1; Resis, "The Profintern," pp. 16–17.

51. Earl Browder to Theodore Draper, Feb. 20, 1956, TD, box 1, folder 15; Browder to Draper, Feb. 20, 1956, ibid., Swabeck to Draper, May 14, 1956,

ibid., box 19, folder 11; Robert Minor, "To the ECCI," Apr. 3, 1924, ibid., box 21, folder 14; *Labor Herald*, August 1923, p. 4.

52. Gifford Ernst, *William Z. Foster: Fool or Faker?* (Chicago: Privately published, 1923), pp. 11–12; *Voice of Labor*, July 6, 1923, p. 2: Brown's name had been "signed to the call for the convention"; ibid., July 6, 1923 p. 2, on Manley.

53. This general account of the July convention is drawn from Draper, *Roots of American Communism*, pp. 44–45, 48. *VOL*, July 6, 1923, p. 2; July 14, 1923, p. 1; Browder interview with William Goldsmith, July 12, 1955, Bell Papers, "Closed," box 9; Foster to Lozovsky, Nov. 7, 1923, RILU, f. 534, op. 7, d. 460, l. 102; Foster to Charles Scott, July 27, 1923, ibid., d. 459 l. 95; Ruthenberg, Pepper, Jakira to Lozovsky, Oct. 5, 1923, ibid., d. 458, l. 130; Foster to Lozovsky, Sept. 10, 1923, ibid., d. 460, l. 8.

54. *LH*, August 1923, pp. 3, 5; Foster to Lozovsky, July 9, 1923, Profintern, d. 459, l. 91; Keiser, "John Fitzpatrick," p. 135; Draper, *Roots of American Communism*, pp. 45–46.

55. Cannon, *First Ten Years*, p. 87; Max Bedacht to Theodore Draper, June 13, 1957, TD, box 10, folder 15; Browder to Draper, Feb. 20, 1956, ibid., box 1, folder 15; *International Press Correspondence*, July 26, 1923; Israel Amter, "Decision of the CEC on the FLP," Dec. 15, 1923, RILU, d. 458, l. 215; Foster to Charles Scott, July 27, 1923, ibid., d. 459, l. 95; James P. Cannon to Charles Scott [n.d.], ibid., d. 458, l. 109.

56. Cannon, *First Ten Years*, p. 120; Alexander Bittelman, *Milestones in the History of the Communist Party* (New York: Worker's Library, 1937); Alexander Bittelman Autobiographical Typescript, Bittelman Papers, Tamiment Institute Library, New York University, box 1, folder 14, pp. 432, 431; Foster to Lozovsky, Aug. 9, 1923, RILU, d. 459, l. 102.

57. Central Executive Committee, CPUSA, to Executive Council, Profintern, June 1, 1922, RILU, d. 457; Foster to Executive Bureau, ibid., Aug. 29, 1923, d. 459, l. 115; Foster to Lozovsky, Sept. 10, 1923, ibid., d. 460, l. 8; Foster to Lozovsky, ibid., Aug. 9, 1923, d. 459, l. 102. On Foster's resistance to working with the IWW and independent unions, see Resis, "Profintern," p. 315–16; Joseph Kucher to Lozovsky, Mar. 5, 1923, RILU, d. 461, l. 1; Foster to Lozovsky, Apr. 10, 1923, ibid., d. 459, l. 3; Foster to Lozovsky May 31, 1923, ibid., d. 459, l. 46.

58. *NM*, Sept. 22, 1923, p. 1; *LH*, November 1923, p. 6; Staley, *History of the Illinois Federation of Labor* p. 384; Keiser, "John Fitzpatrick," p. 145.

59. Illinois State Federation of Labor, *Official Annual Gazette*, "Proceedings of Illinois State Federation of Labor," 1923, pp. 346, 380, 365, 373.

60. Illinois Federation of Labor, "Proceedings," 1923, pp. 380–81, 398.

61. Ibid., pp. 406, 405.

62. Ibid., pp. 405, 348, 347–48, 401, 352, 399; on the practice of "traveling fraternity" in craft union culture, see Patricia A. Cooper, *Once a Cigar Maker: Men, Women, and Work Culture in American Cigar Factories, 1900–1919* (Urbana: University of Illinois Press, 1987), pp. 75–89; *New York Times*, April 9, 1923, p. 13; Karen Halttunen, *Confidence Men and Painted Women: A Study of Middle-Class Culture in America, 1830–1870* (New Haven, Conn.: Yale University Press, 1982), p. 14.

63. *NM*, Oct. 13, 1923, pp. 1–2; American Federation of Labor, *Report of Proceedings*, 1923, p. 257; Edward B. Mittelman, "Basis for American Federation of Labor Opposition to Amalgamation and Politics at Portland," *Journal of Political Economy* 32 (1924): 99; *LH*, September 1923, p. 9; Ben Legere, *The Futility of Fosterism* (Winnipeg, Manitoba: One Big Union Bulletin, [1923]), pp. 14, 20–21.

64. William Dunne to Browder [n.d.], RILU, d. 460, l. 88; Minutes, Anglo-American Secretariat, Jan. 5, 1928, Comintern, f. 495, op. 72, d. 32, l. 26.

65. Foster to Lozovsky, May 31, 1923, RILU, d. 459, l. 46; Foster to Lozovsky, Sept. 10, 1923, ibid., d. 460, l. 8; Ruthenberg, Pepper and Jakira to Lozovsky, Oct. 5, 1923, pp. 3–4, ibid., d. 458, l. 130; "Program for the TUEL [1923]," ibid., d. 459, l. 163; Beckner, "The TUEL and the American Labor Movement," p. 27; *United Mine Workers' Journal*, July 1, 1923, p. 1.

66. *Justice*, Aug. 17, 1923, pp. 7, 11; Schneider, *The (Workers') Communist Party*, pp. 92–95; Debs to Foster, Sept. 12, 1923, and Nov. 8, 1923, WZF, d. 5.

67. This account drawn from Weinstein, *Decline of American Socialism*, pp. 290ff; Draper, *Roots of American Communism*, p. 98–102; *International Press Correspondence*, Feb. 28, 1924, p. 121.

68. Draper, *Roots of American Communism*, pp. 82–84, 96–98; "Session of the American Commission," Foster speech, TD, box 19, folder 12, pp. 5, 9; Alexander Bittelman autobiographical typescript, p. 418; *Daily Worker*, Jan. 19, 1924, Sunday Supplement; ibid., Dec. 29, 1924, p. 5; Israel Amter, *International Press Correspondence*, Feb. 28, 1924.

69. This account of Comintern politics and subsequent maneuvers in late 1923 draws from Draper, *Roots of American Communism*, pp. 105–11.

70. Israel Amter, "Decision of the CEC on the Farmer-Labor Party," Dec. 15, 1923, RILU, d. 458, l. 215; *The Worker*, Feb. 17, 1923, p. 1; "Session of the American Commission," speech by Foster, May 6, 1924, TD, box 19, folder 12, pp. 1, 3, 6–7, 9, 12, 14.

71. *Daily Worker*, Dec. 9, 1924, p. 4.

72. Foster's letter to the ECCI demanding Pepper's recall is in FOIA, 61-330-178; Foster and Cannon, "Statement of Our Labor Party Policy, Submitted by Comrades Foster and Cannon," TD, box 22, folder 20, p. 15.

73. Foster to Lozovsky, July 14, 1924, RILU, d. 465, l. 46.

74. Foster, *The Bankruptcy of the American Labor Movement*, p. 60; *International Press Correspondence*, Feb. 28, 1924; *Daily Worker*, Dec. 4, 1924, p. 3; Foster to Lozovsky, July 9, 1923, RILU, d. 459, l. 91; Foster to Charles Scott, Aug. 9, 1923, ibid., d. 459, l. 100.

75. Foster to Charles Scott, Aug. 1 1924, Profintern, d. 465, l. 47; Foster to Lozovsky, July 14, 1924, ibid., d. 465 l. 46.

76. *Daily Worker*, Oct. 24, 1924, p. 6; Nov. 15, 1924, Sunday Supplement; Nov. 1, 1924, p. 2.

77. Ibid., July 31, 1924; *Socialist World*, August 1924, pp. 6–7.

78. *Daily Worker*, Oct. 13, 1924, p. 1.

79. *International Press Correspondence*, Dec. 11, 1924; *Daily Worker*, Nov. 7, 1924, p. 2, Aug. 30, 1924, Sunday Supplement.

80. Foster to Lozovsky, July 14, 1924, RILU, d. 465, l. 46; Foster to Charles Scott, Aug. 9, 1924, ibid., d. 465, l. 50; Max Eastman, *Stalin's Russia and the Crisis in Socialism* (New York: W. W. Norton, 1940), p. 97.

81. Foster to Lozovsky, Sept. 18, 1924, RILU, d. 465, l. 71; Foster to Lozovsky, Nov. 7, 1924, ibid., d. 465, l. 83; Foster to Lozovsky, Nov. 27, 1924, ibid., d. 465, l. 99. The circulation of the *Labor Herald* in July 1922 was 11,000: *Recognition of Russia*, p. 369.

82. Foster to Charles Scott, Nov. 7, 1924, RILU, d. 465, l. 82.

Chapter 8
"Phrases Learned in Europe"

1. "Memo," Charles T. Cornell to Hywell Davis, National Archives, U.S. Department of Labor Records, RG 174, box 89, Chief Clerk's files; *Los Angeles Times*, Mar. 2, 1924, p. 1.

2. Cornell to Hugh L. Kerwin, May 6, 1924, and "Exhibits A and B," Department of Labor Records, RG 174, box 89, Chief Clerk's files, and *Los Angeles Times*, Mar. 2, 1924; for suggestions that such tactics were used in other cities, see memo to E. P. Marsh, Mar. 8, 1924, Dept. of Labor Records, RG 174, box 89 Chief Clerk's files; Marsh to H. L. Kerwin, Jan. 1, 1924, ibid. The latter memo refers to a plan of cooperation between C. O. Young, a long-time AFL organizer in the Pacific Northwest, and the departments of Justice and Labor.

3. David Montgomery, *The Fall of the House of Labor* (New York: Cambridge University Press, 1987), pp. 401, 422; Foster, *Misleaders of Labor* (Chicago: TUEL, 1917), pp. 61, 71; 73–76. *Labor Age*, August 1923, p. 5; Earl Beckner, "The Trade Union Educational League and the American Labor Movement," *Journal of Political Economy* 33 (1925): p. 431.

4. Foster, *Misleaders of Labor*, p. 61; *Machinists' Monthly Journal*, April 1925, p. 214; Montgomery, *Fall of the House of Labor*, pp. 422–23.

5. Minutes, National Committee, TUEL, Nov. 6, 1924, and attached "Program for Work in the Machinists' Union," Daniel Bell Papers, Tamiment Institute Library, New York University, box 6, "Metal Workers' History," pp. 7–12; Minutes, National Committee, TUEL, Dec. 14, 1924, Bell Papers, box 6, "Metal Workers' History," pp. 10–11.

6. *Machinists' Monthly Journal*, April 1925, pp. 214–15; David M. Schneider, *The Workers' (Communist) Party and American Trade Unions* (Baltimore: Johns Hopkins University Press, 1928), p. 21; Foster, *Workers' Monthly*, February 1925, pp. 149–50. The TUEL slate in the nominating elections is in Daniel Bell notes, untitled, and "Program for Work in the Machinists' Union," in Bell Papers, "Metal Workers' History." For the results of these elections, see *Machinists' Monthly Journal*, March 1925; *Daily Worker*, Mar. 19, 1925, p. 3 identifies the candidates on the Anderson slate who supported the TUEL "minimum demands."

7. Foster, "The Situation in the Machinists' Union and the Immediate Tasks of the Left Wing," in Bell papers, "Metal Workers' History;" J. H. M. Laslett, *Labor and the Left*, (New York: Basic Books, 1970), p. 177; Schneider, *The Workers' (Communist) Party*, pp. 24–25; *Machinists' Monthly Journal* Novem-

ber 1925, p. 637; Mark Perlman, *The Machinists: A New Study in American Trade Unionism* (Cambridge, Mass.: Harvard University Press, 1962), p. 65.

8. "Minutes of Secretariat," July 24, 1925, TD, Gitlow Exhibits, Series 2.3, reel 12.

9. Foster, "The Situation in the Machinists' Union." *Workers' Monthly*, October 1925, p. 539.

10. *Labor Herald*, September 1924, pp. 199, 200; FOIA, 61-330-186, pp. 1, 4, 7; *Workers' Monthly*, April 1925, pp. 253–54, 282–83.

11. Foster to Charles Scott, Nov. 27, 1924, RILU, d. 465, l. 98; Foster to Lozovsky, Nov. 7 and 27, 1924, ibid., d. 465, l. 83, 99; "Trade Union Work," from the ECCI and the Profintern, reproduced in *Daily Worker*, Aug. 14, 1925, p. 6.

12. Quoted in Theodore Draper, *The Roots of American Communism* (New York: Viking, 1957), p. 350; *The Worker*, Apr. 22, 1922, p. 3; James Cannon, *The First Ten Years of American Communism* (New York: Pathfinder, 1962), p. 122; *Daily Worker*, May 19, 1923, p. 1.

13. Debs, "Industrial Unionism," in *Eugene Debs Speaks*, ed. Jean Y. Tussey (New York: Pathfinder, 1972).

14. TUEL National Committee Minutes, 1923–24, TD, box 22, folder 7.

15. Jay Lovestone, "To the ECCI" [1923], Philip Jaffe Papers, Woodruff Library, Emory University, box 35, folder 1, p. 3; Browder interview with Draper, TD, box 1, folder 3, p. 3. Benjamin Gitlow quoted in *American Mercury* 68 (1949): 413.

16. *International Press Correspondence*, Apr. 16, 1925, p. 418; John Pepper, "Speech at Moscow of Pepper, Mar. 4, 1925, attacking William Z. Foster," Bertram Wolfe Papers, New York Public Library, box 4.

17. Foster and James Cannon to Zinoviev, Apr. 11, 1925; Foster to Zinoviev, May 22, 1925, CPUSA, d. 423, l. 16, 18; "From the ECCI and the RILU," signed by Kuusinen and Lozovsky, dated Apr. 30, 1925, TD, Gitlow Exhibits; *Daily Worker*, Aug. 14, 1925, p. 6, Aug. 21, 1925, p. 6; Aug. 31, 1925, p. 3; Foster to Charles Scott, June 24, 1925, RILU, d. 468, l. 75.

18. Peggy Dennis, *Autobiography of an American Communist* (Westport, Conn.: Creative Arts, 1977), p. 32. This account of the Workers' Party Fourth Convention is drawn from Draper, *Roots of American Communism*, pp. 139–42, 142–52; Benjamin Gitlow, *I Confess* (New York: Dutton, 1939), pp. 257–59; Charles Ruthenberg, *From the Third to the Fourth Convention* (Chicago: Daily Worker Publishing Co., 1925), pp. 7–9; Irving Howe and Lewis Coser, *The American Communist Party: A Critical History* (New York: Beacon Press, 1957; repr. New York: Praeger, 1962) pp. 152–60.

19. Cannon, *First Ten Years*, p. 136; *Daily Worker*, Oct. 3, 1925, p. 4; Gusev's article, harshly critical of Foster, was also published in *International Press Correspondence*, Oct. 22, 1925, p. 1121. *Daily Worker*, Oct. 8, 1925, pp. 3, 4; Dec. 21, 1925, p. 4.

20. Foster to Lozovsky, Sept. 4, 12, 1925, RILU, d. 468, l. 97, 100. Writing in the 1930s, Foster safely blamed the imbroglio on then-discredited figures: Zinoviev, he claimed, had sent the telegram as a result of prodding by Pepper, while the positioning of Cannon was "one of the most unscrupulous maneuvers I have

ever seen in any organization." Still, Foster did not hide his bitterness. The cable was "drastic and totally unexpected," and "flatly against the thoroughly democratic procedure of the Comintern." As for his brief exit from the Party leadership, he noted in one account that "I have never been convinced that our course was wrong," while in another it was termed "a mistake." See Foster, "James P. Cannon: Renegade," in unpublished *Pages from a Worker's Life*, JMK; and Foster, *History of the Communist Party of the United States* (New York: International Publishers, 1952), p. 223.

21. Gitlow, *I Confess*, pp. 186, 190; *Daily Worker*, Dec. 21, 1925, p. 4; Browder, *International Press Correspondence*, Oct. 8, 1925, p. 1089; Foster and Bittelman, "To the ECCI," Jan. 18, 1926, p. 15, TD, Gitlow exhibits; on Ruthenberg's policy toward the party's industrial work, see Draper, *Roots of American Communism*, pp. 218–19; *Daily Worker*, Sept. 16, 1925, p. 4; Oct. 12, 1925, p. 4; Aug. 14, 1926, p. 4; Nov. 30, 1926, p. 6; *Workers' Monthly*, July 1926, pp. 404–5; Ruthenberg to Organization Dept., RILU, Sept. 29, 1925, Profintern, d. 467, l. 56. On the political tone of the *Workers' Monthly*, see especially September 1925–July 1926. Jay Lovestone to Nikolai Bukharin, Nov. 1, 1925, CPUSA, d. 423, l. 31.

22. "Dear Comrades," signed "A @ B," Nov. 15, 1925, CPUSA, d. 439, l. 11; Draper interview with Samuel Darcy, Apr. 30, 1957, TD, Series 2.3, reel 8; Draper, *Roots of American Communism*, pp. 219–20, 228–29; "Bukharin's Proposal," unpublished *Pages from a Worker's Life*, JMK; "Resolution on the Broadening of the TUEL and the Building of an Oppositional Bloc in Conformity with the CI Decision" [June 1926], RILU, d. 470, l. 7; Foster, "Organization of the Party Trade Union Work" [1926], Bell Papers, box 41, "Closed"; *International Press Correspondence*, Apr. 22, 1926, p. 488; Mar. 25, 1926, p. 367; *Workers' Monthly*, July 1926, p. 404.

23. Browder MS. in Jaffe Papers, Emory University, Woodruff Library, box 38, folder 1, p. 23; *Daily Worker*, Sept. 1, 1926, p. 4; Mary Carr, "Jay Fox," p. 15; Cannon, *First Ten Years*, p. 105; Foster to Earl Browder, July 17, 1926, RILU, d. 472, l. 103; Ballam to "Al," Jan. 2, 1926, ibid., d. 470, l. 69.

24. Foster to Lozovsky, July 1, 1926, RILU, d. 472, l. 101.

25. *New Republic*, Mar. 12, 1924, pp. 60–61.

26. David Saposs, *Left-Wing Unionism* (New York: International Publishers, 1926), p. 50.

27. *Advance*, Mar. 12, 1926, p. 6.

28. Joseph Manley to Lozovsky, n.d., CPUSA, d. 406, l. 35. Howe and Coser, *The American Communist Party*, pp. 239–43; Draper, *Roots of American Communism*, pp. 221, 223–26; Bert Cochran, *Labor and Communism: The Conflict That Shaped American Unions* (Princeton, N.J.: 1977), pp. 31–33; Cannon, *First Ten Years*, pp. 140–44.

29. Minutes, Trade Union committee of CEC, Aug. 5, 1926, p. 3, TD, Gitlow exhibits; Foster to Lozovsky, Aug. 6, 1926, RILU, d. 473, l. 1; Lozovsky to Foster, Feb. 3, 1927, in "Report of Jay Lovestone," Wolfe Papers, New York Public Library.

30. Draper, *Roots of American Communism*, p. 231.

31. Howe and Coser, *The American Communist Party*, p. 247; Foster to Lozovsky, Dec. 19, 1927, RILU, d. 476, l. 182; *Daily Worker*, Oct. 8, 1925, p. 3.

32. Melech Epstein, *Jewish Labor in the U.S.A.: 1914–1952* (New York: Trade Union Sponsoring Committee, 1953), pp. 119, 134, 153; Minutes, National Committee, TUEL, Dec. 5, 1923, TD, box 22, folder 7; Kenneth Kann, *Joe Rapoport: The Life of a Jewish Radical* (Philadelphia: Temple University Press, 1981), pp. 76, 123.

33. Cochran, *Labor and Communism*, pp. 38–41; Epstein, *Jewish Labor*, pp. 145–46, 153.

34. James Cannon, *First Ten Years*, pp. 218–19; Browder interview with Theodore Draper, TD, box 1, folder 8, p. 37; Browder memo to Philip Jaffe, Mar. 27, 1959, TD, box 20, folder 15, p. 5.

35. *New Republic*, Jan. 7, 1920, p. 166.

36. *Daily Worker*, Mar. 12, 1956, p. 4. An FBI informant present quoted Foster as saying "I've hated capitalism with every G—— D—— drop of my blood and I'm not stopping now." FOIA, 61-330-800.

37. *Communist*, January 1929, pp. 55–56; *Workers' Monthly*, January 1926, pp. 131–33; "American Labor Report: 1926–1927," RILU, d. 476, l. 17.

38. J. B. McNamara to Foster, Mar. 6, 1927, WZF, d. 5.

39. Foster speech, "The Conservativism of the Working Class," Nov. 10, 1926, Wolfe Papers, box 5; Foster to Lozovsky, June 13, 1926, RILU, d. 472, l. 97; "American Labor Report: 1926–1927," Feb. 17, 1927, RILU, d. 476 l. 17; *Communist*, February 1928, pp. 100–101.

40. William Z. Foster, *Russia in 1924* (Chicago: TUEL, 1924), p. 24; Foster, *Russian Workers and Workshops in 1926* (Chicago: TUEL, 1926), p. 41; Andrea Graziosi, "Foreign Workers in Soviet Russia, 1920–1940: Their Experience and Their Legacy," *International Labor and Working-Class History* 33(1988): 38–59.

41. William Z. Foster, *History of the Three Internationals* (New York: International Publishers, 1955), p. 274; Foster, *Your Questions Answered* (New York: Workers' Library, 1939), p. 101; Foster, *The Soviet Trade Unions and Allied Labor Unity* (New York: Workers' Library, 1943), pp. 31–32.

42. Jesse Lloyd O'Connor, Harvey O'Connor, and Susan M. Bowler, *Harvey and Jesse: A Couple of Radicals* (Philadelphia: Temple University Press, 1988), p. 54; "Dear Boys" [Lovestone to Ruthenberg], Feb. 12, 1926, RILU, d. 470, l. 102; Minutes, Anglo-American Secretariat, Jan. 5, 1928, Comintern, f. 495, op. 72, d. 32, l. 18.

43. Draper, *Roots of American Communism*, pp. 249–51; Alexander Bittelman, "An Answer to Bedacht's Charge That Foster Is Non-Marxian, That He Is Not a Communist" [1926], Wolfe Papers, box 4.

44. Memo, "Workers' Party Membership," Mar. 8, 1928, Profintern, d. 481, l. 69. The individuals identified in the memo were Lovestone, Bertram Wolfe, Jack Stachel, Louis Engdahl, Benjamin Gitlow, Robert Minor, Alexander Trachtenberg, and William Weinstone. Foster speech, Anglo-American Secretariat, July 17, 1928, Comintern, f. 495, op. 72, d. 36, l. 67; Benjamin Gitlow, *The Whole of Their Lives* (New York: Scribners, 1948), p. 106.

45. Draper, *Roots of American Communism*, pp. 254–59, 261–63; Cannon, *First Ten Years*, p. 197; Stephen F. Cohen, *Bukharin and the Bolshevik Revolution* (New York: Knopf, 1973; repr. New York: Oxford, 1980), p. 259; Theodore Draper interview with Sam Darcy, May 1, 1957, TD, Series 2.3, reel 8.

46. Melvyn Dubofsky and Warren Van Tine, *John L. Lewis* (Urbana: University of Illinois Press, 1986), pp. 101–8.

47. Trade Union Committee, Central Executive Committee, May 8, 1926, EB, reel 6, folder 148; Albert Glotzer, interview with the author, Sept. 12, 1984.

48. Dubofsky and Van Tine, *John L. Lewis: A Biography* (New York: Quadrangle, 1977), pp. 126–28; Carl Meyerhuber, *Less Than Forever: The Rise and Decline of Union Solidarity in Western Pennsylvania, 1914–1948* (Selinsgrove, Pa.: Susquehanna University Press, 1987), pp. 95, 102; *New York Times* July 7, 1923, p. 1; Powers Hapgood to Mother and Father, July 26, 1926, PH, box 4; "Confidential Report, Workers' Party of America," Profintern, d. 470, l. 30.

49. Foster to Lozovsky, June 13, 1926, RILU, d. 472, l. 97; Dubofsky and Van Tine, *John L. Lewis*, p. 132.

50. *Workers' Monthly*, September 1926, pp. 494–95; "The Party's Plan of Campaign for the Miners Union" [September 1926], RILU, d. 470, l. 61; Dubofsky and Van Tine, *John L. Lewis*, pp. 128–29.

51. Foster to Lozovsky, June 13, 1926, RILU, d. 472, l. 97; Feb. 26, 1927, d. 476, l. 32; Feb. 28, 1927, d. 472, l. 39; Foster, "The Immediate Tasks of the Left Wing in the Coal Mining Industry," Feb. 25, 1927, attached to Trade Union Committee Minutes, EB, reel 6, folder, 148; Trade Union Committee Minutes, Apr. 12, 1927, TD, box 22, folder 10, p. 4; William Goldsmith interview with John Brophy, notes, p. 4, Bell Papers, box 7, "Closed."

52. Lozovsky's letters (dated Feb. 3, 1927, Mar. 16, 1927), reproduced in stenogram "Report of Jay Lovestone to the American Commission," June 7, 1927, pp. 17–23, Wolfe Papers (capitals in original), box 4; Foster to Lozovsky, Feb. 14, 1927, RILU, d. 476, l. 14.

53. Meyerhuber, *Less Than Forever*, pp. 92–93, 100; Linda Nyden, "Black Miners in Western Pennsylvania, 1925–1931: The National Miners Union and the United Mine Workers of America," *Science and Society* 41 (Spring 1977): 78–87.

54. Powers Hapgood to Mary Donovan, Dec. 23, 1927, PH, box 4; on dualist sentiment among the rank and file, see Political Committee Minutes, Sept. 15, 1927, Bell Papers, box 4, "Closed"; "Notes on Polcomm," Political Committee Minutes, Feb. 22, 1928, Apr. 9, 1928, ibid., box 1, folder 1; Browder interview with Goldsmith, July 6, 1955, ibid., box 9, "Closed"; Foster to Lozovsky, Nov. 7, 1927, RILU, d. 476, l. 138.

55. Foster to Lozovsky, Dec. 19, 1927, ibid., d. 476, l. 182; Dec. 28, 1927, ibid., d. 476, l. 185.

56. Draper, *Roots of American Communism*, pp. 284–90; Foster to Lozovsky, Jan. 12, 1928, RILU, d. 481, l. 1; Foster to Lozovsky, Feb. 8, 1928, ibid., d. 481, l. 28; *Communist*, January 1928, p. 10.

57. Powers Hapgood to Mary Donovan, Dec. 23, 1927, PH, box 4; Meyerhuber, *Less Than Forever*, pp. 102–3.

58. John Brophy to Powers Hapgood, June 20, 1928; July 8, 1928, PH, box 4;

Foster to Lozovsky, Apr. 9, 14, 21, 1928, RILU, d. 481, l. 69, 72, 143; Dubofsky and Van Tine, *John L. Lewis*, p. 130; Dallas M. Young, "The Origin of the Progressive Mine Workers of America," *Journal of the Illinois State Historical Society* (1947): 313–30 Robert Zieger, *John L. Lewis: Labor Leader* (Boston: Twayne, 1988), p. 50.

59. Meyerhuber, *Less Than Forever*, pp. 101–6; Foster, "Proposals for Policy in the Mining Industry," attached, Political Committee Minutes, May 16, 1928, p. 2, Bell Papers, box 1, folder 2.

60. Foster to Lozovsky, May 3, 9, 1928, RILU, d. 481, l. 165, 197; "The American CP Breaks Discipline; Our Leaders Refuse to Obey Moscow" [n.d.], ibid., d. 481, l. 252; "Statement of Toohey, Myerscough and Kemenovich on Mining," Political Committee Minutes, June 9, 1928, Bell Papers, box 1, folder 2.

61. Theodore Draper, "The Communists and the Miners," *Dissent* (1972): 375; Meyerhuber, *Less Than Forever*, pp. 109–11; *The Coal Digger*, Oct. 1, 1928, pp. 1, 2; National Committee of the TUEL, Minutes, June 6, 1929, Bell Papers, box 2, "Closed," folder "Trade Union Fractions"; Foster to Lozovsky, Dec. 5, 1928, RILU, d. 482, l. 196; Foster to Lozovsky, Jan. 15, 1929, ibid., d. 485, l. 18.

62. Draper, *Roots of American Communism*, pp. 309–10; Cohen, *Bukharin and the Bolshevik Revolution*, pp. 229–30, 267; Isaac Deutscher, *Soviet Trade Unions: Their Place in Soviet Labor Strategy* (New York: Oxford University Press, 1950), pp. 75–81; Bertram Wolfe, *A Life in Two Centuries* (New York: Stein and Day, 1981), p. 459; Foster faction letter, "Dear Comrade," Apr. 2, 1928, CPUSA, d. 1248, l. 104, 112; Lovestone faction letter, "Dear Comrades," Aug. 6, 1928, CPUSA, d. 1248, l. 138, 146.

63. On Foster's resistance to the new line, see Foster, "Tasks and Lessons of the Miners' Struggle," *Communist*, April 1928, pp. 197–98; "Old Unions and New Unions," ibid., July 1928, pp. 404–5. Earl Browder interview with Daniel Bell, Bell Papers, box 1, folder 3, p. 2; Max Bedacht interview with Theodore Draper, June 18, 1954, TD, box 10, folder 16; Wolfe, *A Life in Two Centuries*, p. 459; Draper, *The Roots of American Communism*, pp. 309–10, 395; Foster, "The Decline of the AFL," *Communist*, (January–February 1929), pp. 55, 57; Bedacht statement, ibid., p. 44.

64. Alexander Bittelman memoirs, New York University, Tamiment Institute Library, pp. 432, 434, 513, 514.

65. Foster to Lozovsky, Dec. 19, 1927, RILU, d. 476, l. 182; ibid., Mar. 7, 1928, d. 481, l. 45.

66. Michael W. Santos, "Community and Communism: The 1928 New Bedford Textile Strike," *Labor History* 26(1985): 230–49; Cochran, *Labor and Communism*, p. 34; Foster to Lozovsky, Sept. 7, 1928, RILU, d. 482, l. 1.

67. Harvey Klehr, *The Heyday of American Communism* (New York: Basic Books, 1984), pp. 28–30; Theodore Draper, "Gastonia Revisited," *Social Research* (1971): 17–18; BTS, pp. 233–36.

68. *The Coal Digger*, June 1, 1929, p. 12; Foster, "The TUUL Convention," *Communist*, September 1929, pp. 528–33; Lozovsky quoted in *International Press Correspondence*, July 31, 1930, p. 676; According to "Resolution of the

Political Secretariat of the ECCI on the Situation and Tasks of the CPUSA" [1930], p. 4, TD, box 6, folder 1, "the best forces of the movement must be allocated to work in the revolutionary unions," while "work in the reformist unions must be revived and intensified." Foster to Lozovsky, Sept. 6, 1929, RILU, d. 486, l. 45: Foster saw the TUUL as a coordinating body for both new unions and "National Industrial Leagues" which could consist of shop committees, "isolated" locals, and left-wing organizations of any kind in the old unions, or as in the case of the Marine Workers League, workers in the process of transforming their groups into national industrial unions.

69. "Statement on Principal Points of Difference on the Trade Union Questions in the American Party" to the American Commission [April 1929], RILU, d. 489, l. 94.

70. Draper, *American Communism and Soviet Russia*, pp. 398–404; Max Eastman, *Love and Revolution: My Journey Through an Epoch* (New York: Random House, 1964), pp. 347–48.

71. Other Trotskyists moving through the Foster group in the 1920s included Ludwig Lore and Arne Swabeck. This account is assembled from Draper, *Roots of American Communism*, pp. 407–12; Gitlow, *The Whole of Their Lives*, p. 163. *Investigation of Un-American Propaganda Activities in the United States*, Hearings Before a Special Committee on Un-American Activities (Dies Committee), House of Representatives, 75–76th Cong., 11:7115, 7122–23, 7127. Harry Hapwood, *Black Bolshevik* (Chicago: Liberator Press, 1978), p. 295.

72. Leon Trotsky, *The Militant*, Apr. 26, 1930, reproduced in *The Writings of Leon Trotsky: 1930* (New York: Pathfinder, 1975), pp. 151–56; Joseph Stalin, *Stalin's Speeches on the American Communist Party* (New York: Central Committee, CPUSA, 1931).

73. According to Earl Browder, "Foster originated the idea of myself as Secretary" in 1929. Browder Columbia Oral History interview, p. 5. See also Sam Darcy memoir, in author's possession.

Chapter 9
The Reluctant Agitator

1. Following the seventh convention of the Party in June 1930, Browder became general secretary. Arthur Zipser claims that "although the record is not clear," from 1930 on Foster was national chairman: Zipser, *Workingclass Giant: The Life of William Z. Foster* (New York: International Publishers, 1981), p. 105. Yet, the *Daily Worker* (Mar. 6, 1930, p. 1) refers to him only as the general secretary of the TUUL. In March 1929, in the aftermath of Lovestone's revolt, Boris Mikhailov, a Comintern representative, came to the U.S. and helped install a secretariat composed of Robert Minor, William Weinstone, and Foster, with Max Bedacht as acting secretary. This arrangement prevailed until October 1929. Foster was a member of the new secretariat chosen at the seventh convention. Others were Weinstone (organizational secretary), and Browder (administrative secretary); see Harvey Klehr, *The Heyday of American Communism* (New York: Basic Books, 1984), pp. 18, 25.

2. See, for instance, one major bibliography, Joel Seidman, *Communism in the U.S.—A Bibliography* (Ithaca, N.Y.: Cornell University Press, 1969), which contains 249 entries for Foster as compared with 198 for Browder. This compendium does not include *Daily Worker* articles.

3. Robert S. McElvaine, *The Great Depression* (New York: Times Books, 1984), pp. 76–77.

4. Foster, "The Growing World Offensive against Capitalism," *Communist*, Mar. 1930, p. 199.

5. Klehr, *Heyday of American Communism*, pp. 32–34.

6. Al Richmond, *A Long View From the Left: Memoirs of an American Revolutionary* (Boston: Houghton Mifflin, 1973), pp. 80–82.

7. *New York Times*, Mar. 7, 1930, pp. 1, 2.

8. Klehr, *Heyday of American Communism*, p. 34; *Daily Worker*, Mar. 7, 1930, p. 2.

9. *New Republic*, Mar. 19, 1930, p. 110; *Nation*, Mar. 19, 1930, p. 311. The decision of the chief city magistrate to refuse bail to Foster and the others was formally protested by a resolution of the New York City Bar in April, and the ACLU filed a complaint (unsuccessful) to have Foster's bail set. *New York Times*, Apr. 9, 1930, p. 3, May 2, 1930, p. 25.

10. *PWL*, pp. 185–87; *Daily Worker*, Mar. 8, 1930, p. 1, Mar. 12, p. 1, Mar. 13, p. 1.

11. The transcript of Foster's appearance before the Board of Estimate is reproduced in *Investigation of Communist Propaganda*, Hearings before a Special Committee to Investigate Communist Activities in the United States (Fish Committee), 1930, pt. 3, vol. 3 (Washington, D.C.: GPO, 1930), pp. 15–17. See also, *Daily Worker*, Mar. 15, 1930, pp. 1, 5; Mar. 21, p. 1. In the transcript, Foster states that he would advise violence in a "revolutionary situation."

12. Klehr, *Heyday of American Communism*, pp. 50–51; Browder Columbia Oral History interview, p. 350; *Daily Worker*, Mar. 29, 1930, pp. 1, 5; Mar. 30, pp. 1, 3.

13. Ibid., Apr. 12, 1930, p. 1; Apr. 22, pp. 1, 3; Apr. 23, p. 1; *PWL*, p. 266; Klehr, *Heyday of American Communism*, p. 37.

14. Israel Amter autobiographical MS., New York University, Tamiment Institute Library, p. 29; Daniel Bell notes on CP organizing conference, Mar. 3–4, 1930, p. 47, Daniel Bell Papers, box 10, "Closed"; Klehr, *Heyday of American Communism*, p. 26; John Gates, *The Story of an American Communist* (New York: Nelson, 1958), p. 110; Foster, "Prisoners," *World Magazine*, May 3, 1975, p. 21; *Labor Unity*, Aug. 13, 1930, p. 8. The ACLU worked in concert with the International Labor Defense in handling the legal affairs of the imprisoned Communists. The ACLU was largely responsible for gaining dismissal of the felonious assault charges against Foster in August. See *New York Times*, Aug. 26, 1930, p. 23; various ACLU letters and documents, Mudd Library, ACLU papers, vol. 430. The only national-level meetings of the TUUL were several national committee meetings in December: *Labor Unity*, Dec. 6, 1930, p. 1; Klehr, *Heyday of American Communism*, pp. 42–43, for the Party's dissatisfaction with the TUUL.

15. *New York Times*, Mar. 4, 1930, p. 16, Mar. 6, p. 9.

16. Edmund Wilson, *The American Jitters* (New York: Scribner, 1932), p. 179. Fish Committee, pt. 1, 4:348, 359, 379, 380, 384.

17. Wilson, *American Jitters*, p. 180.

18. Foster to Lozovsky, Sept. 6, 1929, RILU, d. 486, l. 45; Aug. 22, 1929, ibid., d. 485, l. 145; Apr. 10, 1930, ibid., d. 491, l. 70; Apr. 11, 1931, ibid., d. 496, l. 78; Klehr, *Heyday of American Communism*, p. 42. On Foster's decision to set up a department for work in the AFL, see Foster to Lozovsky, Dec. 12, 1931, Profintern, d. 496, l. 206 and Dec. 29, 1931, l. 213.

On Foster's relative optimism about unions in the metal, auto, packinghouse, and marine industries, see Foster to Lozovsky, Feb. 25, 1930, Profintern, d. 491, l. 47; April 10, 1930, d. 491, l. 70; Dec. 29, 1931, d. 496, l. 213.

19. Klehr, *Heyday of American Communism*, p. 43; Jack Stachel, "Coming Struggles and Lessons in Strike Strategy," *Communist*, March 1931, p. 205.

20. Ibid., pp. 207–8, 211, 206.

21. Foster, "On the Question of Trade Union Democracy," ibid., March 1931, pp. 200–203.

22. Darcy memoir, in author's possession; Helen North Green, interview with the author, Oct. 3, 1986; Vera Buch Weisbord, *A Radical Life* (Bloomington: Indiana University Press, 1977), p. 99; Foster's self-assessment is in Minutes, Pre-Plenum Meeting of National Committee, March 23, 1939, Jaffe Papers, Emory University, Woodruff Library, Series VII.

23. Linda Nyden, "Black Miners in Western Pennsylvania, 1925–1931," *Science and Society* 41 (1977): 94; "Report of Comrade Foster on Preliminary Discussion of Trade Union Work for Plenum," RILU, d. 496, l. 224; Minutes, "Meeting of the National Board of the TUUL," Mar. 14, 1931, ibid., d. 497, l. 8; "Program of Unity and Action," NMU Conference, July 15–16, 1931, ibid., d. 498, l. 42; Foster speech, TUUL National Committee Meeting, Oct. 3, 1931, ibid., d. 497, pp. 4–5.

24. Theodore Draper, "The Communists and the Miners," *Dissent*, Spring 1972, p. 380; Foster speech, TUUL National Committee Meeting, Oct. 3, 1931, RILU, d. 497, p. 2; Meyerhuber, *Less Than Forever: The Rise and Decline of Union Solidarity in Western Pennsylvania* (Selinsgrove, Pa.: Susquehanna University Press, 1987), pp. 114, 119–20; Klehr, *Heyday of American Communism*, pp. 44–45; (Browder) to Comrade Randolph, July 7, 1931, CPUSA, d. 2355, l. 59; J. W. Johnstone to Earl Browder, July 29, 1931, Profintern, d. 498, l. 60; Darcy memoir; *PWL*, pp. 179–84.

25. Gil Green, interview with the author, Oct. 3, 1986; Earl Browder to Lozovsky, June 27, 1931, RILU, d. 496, l. 143; *BTS*, p. 230.

26. Foster, "The Coal Strike," *Communist*, July 1931, p. 595; The best account of this strike is in Meyerhuber, *Less Than Forever*, pp. 113–31; Sam Darcy interview with Theodore Draper, May 1 and 15, 1957, TD, Series 2.3, reel 8; according to Browder, Foster was "always" against the TUUL: Draper interview with Browder, TD, box 1, folder 3, p. 1.

27. Melvyn Dubofsky and Warren Van Tine, *John L. Lewis: A Biography* (New York: Quadrangle, 1977), pp. 174–78; Robert Zieger, *John L. Lewis, Labor Leader* (Boston: Twayne, 1988), pp. 60, 65; John Brophy, *A Miner's Life* (Madison: University of Wisconsin Press, 1964), pp. 235–36.

28. "Foster's Report," TUUL National Board Meeting, Apr. 21, 1932, RILU, d. 503, l. 20, pp. 11–12.

29. Robert Zieger, *American Workers, American Unions, 1920–1985* (Baltimore: Johns Hopkins University Press, 1986), pp. 16–17; Klehr, *Heyday of American Communism*, pp. 58–59; *Detroit Free Press*, May 8, 1932, p. 1; *Detroit Times*, May 8, 1932, p. 1; Zipser, *Workingclass Giant*, p. 113.

30. Zipser, *Workingclass Giant*, p. 118; *PWL*, pp. 282–83.

31. Foster to Lozovsky, Mar. 24, 1932, RILU, d. 498, l. 9; Klehr, *Heyday of American Communism*, pp. 89–90; Gus Hall, in a radio interview in 1963, (*The Worker*, Mar. 19, 1963), explained that *Toward Soviet America* "did not represent Foster's own views after more serious discussion. It never did represent the views of the Communist Party and was quickly withdrawn from circulation by Foster." According to Browder, Foster did not write the book: see Klehr, *Heyday of American Communism*, p. 429, n. 12. Browder also told Draper that Joel Shubin, "an old Menshevik," was a "consultant" on the book; Draper interview with Browder, May 11, 1970, TD, box 1, folder 11. I consider Foster to be the main author; Shubin may have done research and edited. The themes expressed in the book are common to Foster's writings during this period. Robert McElvaine, *Down and Out in the Great Depression* (Chapel Hill: University of North Carolina Press, 1983), p. 19.

32. William Z. Foster, *Toward Soviet America* (New York: Coward-McCann, 1932), p. 16; Arthur Koestler in *The God That Failed*, ed. Richard Crossman (Chicago: Regnery Gateway, 1949, 1983), p. 16.

33. Foster, *Toward Soviet America*, pp. 111, 113, 308–9.

34. Ibid., pp. 314, 318.

35. Ibid., pp. 112, 274.

36. Ibid., pp. 286, 289, 292–93.

37. Ibid, pp. 270, 290–93.

38. Klehr, *Heyday of American Communism*, pp. 88, 80; League of Professional Groups for Foster and Ford, *Culture and the Crisis: An Open Letter to Writers, Artists, Teachers, Physicians and Other Professional Workers in America* (New York: Workers' Library, 1932), pp. 3, 15–17, 23, 24; Foster, *The Words and Deeds of FDR* (New York: National Election Campaign Committee, CPUSA, 1932), pp. 2, 15; Edmund Wilson to Theodore Draper, May 3, 1957, TD, box 18, folder 15; Dreiser interview in *World Magazine*, Sept. 11, 1971. Dreiser, who helped orchestrate a successful publicity campaign during the Kentucky miners' strike, noted that Foster "invited" him to Harlan County.

39. Klehr, *Heyday of American Communism*, p. 69; Foster, *Toward Soviet America*, p. 228.

40. Ibid., pp. 227–28.

41. Matthew Josephson, *Infidel in the Temple: A Memoir of the 1930s* (New York: Knopf, 1967), pp. 124–29.

42. *PWL*, p. 283; *New York Times*, June 29, 1932, p. 3, June 30, p. 2, Aug. 9, p. 31.

43. *Daily Worker*, Sept. 15, 1932, p. 1, Jan. 19, 1934, p. 1, Jan. 22, 1934, p. 1; Darcy memoir; *PWL*, pp. 193–94, 283–84; Foster to Weinstone, June 20, 1933, Foster to Lozovsky, Oct. 19, 1933, Foster personal file, Comintern, op.

261, d. 15, l. 44. Sylvia Kolko to Weinstone, Aug. 16, 1933, and Foster biographical statement, Foster personal file, op. 261, d. 15; Zipser, *Workingclass Giant*, p. 120; see also Foster photograph, "Borvika Sanitarium," dated June 24, 1935, WZF, d. 4.

44. Foster's first public appearance after his collapse was Nov. 18, 1935, for a brief speech at the Old Star Casino in New York City; *Daily Worker*, Nov. 19, 1935, p. 2; *PWL*, p. 180.

45. Joseph North, *William Z. Foster: An Appreciation* (New York: International Publishers, 1955), p. 36; North, "Bill Foster: An American Epic," *Masses and Mainstream* 4(1951): 18; Darcy memoir; Richmond, *A Long View from the Left*, p. 49; Joseph Freeman, *An American Testament* (New York: Farrar and Rinehart, 1936), p. 295; Paul Douglas, *Six upon the World* (Boston: Little, Brown, 1954), pp. 118–19; William Hard, "Moments in the Steel Strike," *New Republic*, Dec. 3, 1919, p. 21; *Daily Worker*, Jan. 19, 1934, p. 1; Steve Nelson, James R. Barrett, and Rob Ruck, *Steve Nelson: American Radical* (Pittsburgh, University of Pittsburgh Press, 1981), p. 291.

46. See *PWL*, "Foreword," and *BTS*, pp. 8–9. By 1949, Foster was distancing himself from *From Bryan to Stalin*, which contained some themes reminiscent of "Third Period" ideology: see *The Worker*, Sept. 25, 1949, Section 3, p. 3.

47. Foster, "The Human Element in Mass Agitation," *Communist* April 1939, pp. 346–47; see ibid., May 1937, p. 383, on *From Bryan to Stalin*: "It is partly autobiographical, but in the main it is an impersonal history."

48. Elizabeth Gurley Flynn, "The Life of a Great American Working-Class Leader," ibid., May 1939, pp. 476–77.

49. Foster, "The Human Element in Mass Agitation," pp. 348, 351–52; Foster, "Some Thoughts on Elizabeth Gurley Flynn's Autobiography," *Political Affairs*, December 1955, pp. 14–15: Flynn's autobiography, he noted, "makes no elaborate statistical or theoretical presentation." See also R. F. Baxandall, *Words on Fire* (New Brunswick, N.J.: Rutgers Universiy Press, 1987), p. 53. Foster on Haywood in *History of the Communist Party of the United States* (New York: International Publishers, 1952), p. 124: "a bold, dogged fighter, although not a theoretician." See also Robert Shaffer, "Women and the CPUSA: 1930–1940," *Socialist Review* 45(1979): 90, 93; and Van Gosse, "To Organize in Every Neighborhood, in Every Home: The Gender Politics of American Communists between the Wars," *Radical History Review* 50 (1991): 109–41.

In *Pages from a Worker's Life*, we meet very few women among the various organizers, socialists, agitators, and militant unionists whom Foster celebrates.

CHAPTER 10
THE DEMOCRATIC FRONT

1. Joseph Zack, "The Meaning of the Wage-Cutting Offensive," *Communist*, December 1931, p. 993; James Weinstein, *Ambiguous Legacy: The Left in American Politics* (New York: New Viewpoints, 1984), p. 61; Klehr, *The Heyday of American Communism* (New York: Basic Books, 1986), p. 118; Roger Keeran, *The Communist Party and the Auto Workers' Union* (New York: International

Publishers, 1986), pp. 115–16, 128; Mark Naison, *Communists in Harlem during the Depression* (New York: Grove Press, 1983), p. 170.

2. See, for instance, S. Mingulin, "The Crisis in the US and the Problems of the Communist Party," *Communist*, June, 1930, pp. 512–13; A. Lozovsky, "The Struggle for the Masses," ibid., November 1931, pp. 897–902; *Party Organizer* [n.a.] December 1931, p. 16; "Resolution of the Political Secretariat of the ECCI on the Situation and Tasks of the CPUSA" [1930], TD, box 6, folder 1, p. 6.

3. Foster, "Some Elementary Phases of the Work in the Reformist Trade Unions," *Communist*, June 1932, pp. 509–18; *Labor Unity*, Mar. 7, 1932, pp. 3–6 for a "late" example of Foster's open encouragement of united fronts in the "reformist" unions.

4. Foster to Lozovsky, Jan. 3, 1931, RILU, d. 496, l. 6; Harvey Levenstein, *Communism, Anti-Communism and the CIO* (Westport, Conn.: Greenwood Press, 1981), p. 18.

5. *Daily Worker*, Mar. 16, 1935, p. 5.

6. Robert H. Zieger, *American Workers, American Unions: 1920–1985* (Baltimore: Johns Hopkins University Press, 1986), pp. 42–44; Clarence Stoecker quoted in Lizabeth Cohen, *Making a New Deal: Industrial Workers in Chicago, 1919–1939* (New York: Cambridge University Press, 1990), p. 311.

7. Zieger, *American Workers*, pp. 44–45; *Daily Worker*, Feb. 12, 1936, pp. 1, 2, May 30, 1936, p. 2; "Minutes of Trade Union Commission," Oct. 10, 1936, Comintern, f. 495, op. 14, d. 80, l. 46; Walter Galenson, *Rival Unionism in the United States* (New York: American Council on Public Affairs, 1940), p. 20. Foster criticized the Lewis bloc for not repudiating craft unionism entirely: see Foster and Nat Honig, *Industrial Unionism* (New York: Workers' Library, 1936).

8. Klehr, *Heyday of American Communism*, p. 213; Joseph R. Starobin, *American Communism in Crisis* (Berkeley: University of California Press, 1972), p. 263; Browder interview with William Goldsmith, June 23, 1955, p. 13, Bell Papers, New York University, Tamiment Institute Library, box 9, "Closed"; Pre-Plenum Meeting of National Committee, Mar. 23, 1939, Jaffe Papers, Emory University, Woodruff Library, Series VII.

9. Dorothy Healey and Maurice Isserman, *Dorothy Healey Remembers* (New York: Oxford University Press, 1990), p. 75; Dorothy Healey, interview with the author, Sept. 16, 1986; Staughton and Alice Lynd, eds., *Rank and File: Personal Histories by Working Class Organizers* (Princeton, N.J.: Princeton University Press, 1981), pp. 74–75; interview with Herbert March, 15 July 1985, and interview with Vicki Starr, 4 Aug. 1986, both from Packinghouse Workers of America Oral History Project, State Historical Society of Wisconsin.

10. See, for instance: Foster, *Organizing Methods in the Steel Industry* (New York: Workers' Library, 1936); Foster, *Unionizing Steel* (New York: Workers' Library, 1936); Foster, *A Manual of Industrial Unionism* (New York: Workers' Library, 1937).

11. Joseph P. Kamp, *Join the CIO and Help Build a Soviet America* (New Haven, Conn.: New Haven Constitutional Education League, 1937), pp. 31–46, in Henry Kraus Papers, Wayne State University, Archives of Labor and Urban Affairs, box 16; Cohen, *Making a New Deal*, pp. 319, 341.

12. Joseph Zack, "How to Apply the Open Letter," *Communist* February 1934, p. 215; Cohen, *Making a New Deal*, pp. 305, 310–11 on the influence and attitudes of Communist organizers in the CIO in Chicago; on the importance of the TUEL and the TUUL as a "proving ground" for CIO organizers, see, for instance, oral history accounts by Nat Ganley and Len DeCaux, Wayne State University, Archives of Labor and Urban Affairs; Harvey Levenstein, *Communism, Anti-Communism and the CIO* (Westport, Conn.: Greenwood Press, 1986), p. 31.

13. Foster, "Syndicalism in the United States," *Communist*, November 1935, pp. 1044–57; Foster, *Toward Soviet America* (New York: Coward McCann, 1932), p. 212; Weinstein, *Ambiguous Legacy*, p. 49; Starobin, *American Communism in Crisis*, pp. 51–52; Maurice Isserman, *Which Side Were You On?* (Middletown, Conn.: Wesleyan University Press, 1982), pp. 8–10. Stephen F. Cohen, *Bukharin and the Bolshevik Revolution* (New York: Knopf, 1973; repr. New York: Oxford University Press, 1980), p. 103.

14. Isserman, *Which Side Were You On?* (1982), pp. 14–15; Klehr, *Heyday of American Communism*, p. 24; Earl Browder Columbia Oral History memoir, p. 400.

15. *Daily Worker*, Nov. 28, 1935, p. 5, Jan. 12, 1935, p. 2, Klehr, *Heyday of American Communism*, pp. 186–88, 214; Irving Howe and Lewis Coser, *The American Communist Party: A Critical History* (Boston: Beacon Press, 1957; repr. New York: Praeger, 1962), p. 329; Kenneth Waltzer, "The Party and the Polling Place: American Communism and the American Labor Party in the 1930s," *Radical History Review* 23(1980): 106; on the growing strength of the FLP idea on the waterfront, amidst a group of workers inculcated with a "syndicalist mood," see Bruce Nelson, *Workers on the Waterfront* (Urbana: University of Illinois Press, 1988), p. 185; Foster speech, seventh Comintern congress, July 28, 1935, Comintern, f. 495, op. 72, d. 287; "Interview of Foster with Manuilsky," May 11, 1935, ibid., d. 286. According to Sam Darcy, "Browder offered no argument when Dimitroff suggested support of FDR. Neither did Foster." The Comintern decided, according to Darcy, on a policy that FDR must be reelected but left the tactics to be worked out by American Communists in the United States. Hence, no defininte electoral line was worked out in Moscow at the seventh congress. (Darcy interview with Theodore Draper, May 15, 1957, TD, reel 8). Foster on the "line" is from William Foster to Samuel Darcy, Aug. 16, 1936, Darcy Papers, New York University, Tamiment Institute Library.

16. Gil Green, interview with the author, Oct. 3, 1986; Klehr, *Heyday of American Communism*, pp. 207–8; Bittelman memoir.

17. Foster, "Political Leadership and Party Building," *Communist*, July 1937, pp. 628, 631–35, 642–43. Foster, "On the State," *New Masses*, March 1941, pp. 17–18.

18. Foster, "Political Leadership and Party Building," pp. 632, 635, 640, 642; Foster, "Panacea Mass Movements: A Problem in Building the Democratic Front," *Communist*, November 1938, pp. 984–92; "Panacea Mass Movements, Part II," *Communist*, December 1938, pp. 1086–95.

19. Foster, "The American Federation of Labor and Trade Union Progress," *Communist*, August, 1938, p. 697; Foster, "The Industrial Union Bloc in the

AFL," *Communist International*, May 1936, pp. 629, 634; Zieger, *American Workers, American Unions*, pp. 58–59;

20. Draper interview with Browder, p. 3, TD, box 1, folder 5; Klehr, *Heyday of American Communism*, pp. 245–50.

21. Ibid., pp. 5, 162, 366–67; "Material for the American Discussion" [1939], Comintern, f. 495, op. 14, d. 120. According to this document, the Party's claim of 100,000 members in 1939 was an exaggeration; in January there was an "enrolled membership" of 88,186 and an "actually registered" membership of 66,000.

22. On Foster's attitude toward "cultural work," see "Elements of a Peoples' Cultural Policy," *New Masses*, Apr. 23, 1946, pp. 6–9. Foster's conceptions in this article betrayed a flexibility that many artists were unable to discern in the Party's everyday policies. For instance, Foster understood "cultural work" from a kind of "boring-from-within" perspective; thus, compromise was necessary. Artists needed to work within capitalist cultural institutions because they "must eat, like other people." He warned against the "left" tendency to "sweep aside all bourgeois art, past and present, as useless and dangerous, to have contempt for all art that is not immediately expressive of the class struggle, to fall into a narrow cultism of various sorts, to idealize the working class. . . ." The "right" danger, he proposed, was the idea that art is free of politics, "that the artist has no democratic message for the people, that man as artist has no relation to man as citizen, and that technical content, not social content, is the essence of art." Foster to V. F. Calverton, Aug. 10, 1925, Calverton Papers, New York Public Library.

23. Howe and Coser, *The American Communist Party*, pp. 337–40; Warren Susman, *Culture as History* (New York: Pantheon, 1973; repr. 1984), pp. 80–83; Isserman, *Which Side Were You On?* p. 11.

24. Foster, *The Twilight of World Capitalism* (New York: International Publishers, 1949), p. 167.

25. Foster, "Calverton's Fascism," *Communist*, February 1931, pp. 108–9; See also Foster and Browder, *Technocracy and Marxism* (New York: Workers' Library, 1933); Foster, "Panacea Mass Movements," *Communist*, November 1938, pp. 984–85; William E. Aiken, *Technocracy and the American Dream: The Technocrat Movement, 1900–1941* (Berkeley: University of California Press, 1977), pp. 22–28, 37–40.

26. Foster was in the Soviet Union as the opposition to Stalin coalesced at the Soviet party's congress of January–February 1934: see Klehr, *Heyday of American Communism*, p. 168. Foster, *Questions and Answers on the Piatakov-Radek Trial* (New York: Workers' Library, 1937); *Daily Worker*, Oct. 6, 1943, p. 8, Oct. 9, 1943, p. 8, Oct. 19, 1943, p. 8; Foster essay, "Soviet Democracy," in unpublished *Pages from a Worker's Life*, JMK.

27. James Cannon, *First Ten Years of American Communism* (New York: Pathfinder, 1962), p. 219; on Stalin's susceptibility to flattery and the attempts of political opponents to use it to their advantage, see Warren Lerner, *Karl Radek, The Last Internationalist* (Stanford: Stanford University Press, 1970), pp. 159–60. Trotsky quoted in "Tasks of the American Opposition," *The Militant*, June 1, 1929, p. 2.

28. Harry Epstein interview, *Daily Worker*, Oct. 19, 1943, p. 8; J. Peters, "Confidential Report," January 1938, Foster personal file, Comintern, op. 261, d. 15, l. 69.

29. Browder interview with Draper, p. 3, TD, box 1, folder 3: "[Foster] served the purpose of bringing out the opposition to anything I wanted to do. Having to knock him down in advance served to keep us on our toes, to sharpen our wits. Foster was always expressing the typical view of the man-in-the-street, and it was good to have that constantly brought in."

30. Plenum meeting of National Committee, Mar. 23, 1939, Jaffe Papers, Series VII, pp. 1–5, 9, 19, 22, 32.

31. Klehr, *Heyday of American Communism*, pp. 391–94; Isserman, *Which Side Were You On?* pp. 25–54, 74–79; David Brody, *Workers in Industrial America: Essays in the Twentieth-Century Struggle* (New York: Oxford University Press, 1980), p. 112; Foster, "Seven Years of Roosevelt," *Communist*, March 1940, pp. 236–39, 244; Zieger, *American Workers, American Unions*, pp. 70–73.

32. Draper interview with Browder, p. 4, TD, box 1, folder 3; Foster, in *Communist*, March 1941, pp. 195–96; Klehr, *Heyday of American Communism*, p. 398; Isserman, *Which Side Were You On?* p. 85. Minor was a figurehead. In addition, during Browder's imprisonments, statements promulgated by the National Committee were signed "William Z. Foster, National Chairman," over Robert Minor, "Acting Secretary." See, for instance, *Communist*, July 1941, "Support the USSR in Its Fight against Nazi War." Browder, in his Columbia Oral History memoir (p. 400) recalled Foster's significantly increased influence during his absence.

33. Stenogram Minutes, TUUL National Committee Meeting, Oct. 3, 1931, RILU, d. 497; on the defense strikes: Isserman, *Which Side Were You On?* pp. 95, 87–100; Nelson Lichtenstein, *Labor's War at Home: The CIO in World War II* (Cambridge: Cambridge University Press, 1982), p. 57; Cochran, *Labor and Communism*, pp. 156–83; *Daily Worker*, June 17, 1941, p. 1.

34. Foster in *Communist*, January 1941, p. 46; Brody, *Workers in Industrial America*, p. 112.

35. *The Worker*, Nov. 16, 1941, p. 6.

36. *Daily Worker*, Feb. 23, 1942, p. 6; *Daily Worker*, May 11, 1942, p. 1.

37. Isserman, *Which Side Were You On?* pp. 162–64; Lichtenstein, *Labor's War at Home*, pp. 136–52; William Z. Foster, *History of the Communist Party of the United States* (New York: International Publishers, 1952), p. 411; Brody, *Workers in Industrial America*, pp. 99–107.

38. James Green, *The World of the Worker* (New York: Hill and Wang, 1980), p. 188; Ronald Schatz, *The Electrical Workers* (Urbana: University of Illinois Press, 1983), pp. 140–43.

39. Foster, *Your Questions Answered* (New York: Workers' Library, 1939), p. 75. Foster on the need for political action: "New Methods of Mass Organization," *Communist*, February 1939, pp. 136–46; "Labor's General Staffs Meet," ibid., October 1943, p. 898. See also *The Worker*, Nov. 16, 1941, p. 6.

CHAPTER 11
"BROWDERISM"

1. Earl Browder, *Victory and After* (New York: International Publishers, 1942), p. 251; Maurice Isserman, *Which Side Were You On? The American Communist Party during the Second World War* (Middletown, Conn.: Wesleyan University Press, 1982), pp. 174–75; Harvey Klehr, *The Heyday of American Communism* (New York: Basic Books, 1984), p. 410; Philip Jaffe, *The Rise and Fall of American Communism* (New York: Horizon, 1975), p. 32. Evidently, Foster had not been given the opportunity to review *Victory and After* prior to publication, while other members of the National Committee had. See "Earl Browder's Speech to the National Committee," *Daily Worker*, July 20, 1945, p. 1.

2. John Lewis Gaddis, *The United States and the Origins of the Cold War* (New York: Columbia University Press, 1972), p. 139; Earl Browder, *Teheran and America* (New York: Workers' Library, 1944), p. 6.

3. Ibid., pp. 6, 14, 19; Browder, "Teheran: History's Greatest Turning Point," *Communist*, January, 1944, pp. 5, 8; Joseph R. Starobin, *American Communism in Crisis* (Berkeley: University of California Press, 1972), pp. 55–56.

4. Browder, *Teheran and America*, p. 19.

5. Ibid., p. 21.

6. Browder, *Teheran and America*, p. 41.

7. Isserman, *Which Side Were You On?* pp. 190, 192, 185.

8. *New Masses*, Dec. 14, 1943, pp. 12, 13; Browder in *Daily Worker*, July 24, 1945, p. 1; Nelson Lichtenstein, *Labor's War at Home: The CIO in World War II* (New York: Cambridge University Press, 1982), pp. 153, 207–12; Henry A. Wallace, *The Century of the Common Man* (New York: Reynal and Hitchcock, 1943), pp. 67, 80–81, 86; James Gilbert, *Another Chance* (New York: Knopf, 1981), pp. 8–9; Foster's vision of a dangerous postwar world was not just invented at the last minute as a debating point—his ideas in this regard surfaced fairly often in his wartime writings: see Foster, *The Trade Unions and the War* (New York: Workers' Library, 1942), p. 44: "At the conclusion of the war, with the obsolete capitalist system badly shattered, reactionary capitalist elements will try to steer the peace settlement and the post-war world in the direction of fascism." See also Foster, "The Reactionary Offensive and the War," *Communist*, April 1943, p. 303.

9. Draper interview with Darcy, June 11–12, 1957, TD, Series III; Darcy Oral History of the American Left interview (Tamiment Institute) tape II, side 3; Starobin, *American Communism*, p. 73, on the prevalence of the idea that Foster might be expelled if he pushed his dissent much further.

10. William Z. Foster, "To the Members of the National Committee, CPUSA," p. 1, Jaffe Papers, Emory University, Woodruff Library, box 37, folder 3.

11. Minutes, Pre-Plenum Meeting of the National Committee, Mar. 23, 1939, p. 39, Jaffe Papers, Series VII.

12. Foster, "To the Members of the National Committee, CPUSA," p. 6.

13. Minutes, National Board Meeting, Feb. 8, 1944, pt. 1, pp. 1–6; pt. 3, p. 1; pt. 4, pp. 1, 3, 4, in Jaffe Papers, Series VII.

14. Philip Jaffe, *Rise and Fall of American Communism*, pp. 61–62.

15. National Board Meeting, Feb. 8, 1944, Jaffe Papers, Series VII.

16. Jaffe, *Rise and Fall of American Communism*, pp. 62–63; Minutes, Pre-Plenum Meeting of National Committee, Mar. 23, 1939, p. 3, Jaffe Papers, Series VII.

17. *Daily Worker*, Jan. 10, 1944, pp. 1, 6; Foster, "The Hoover-Dewey-McCormick Election Threat," *Communist*, July 1944, p. 617; Browder Columbia Oral History memoir, p. 347; Harrison George, *The Crisis in the CPUSA* (Privately published, 1947), p. 98.

18. *Daily Worker*, Sept. 14, 1944, p. 5; on CIO-PAC see Isserman, *Which Side Were You On?* pp. 211–12, and Bert Cochran, *Labor and Communism: The Conflict That Shaped American Unions* (Princeton, N.J.: Princeton University Press, 1977), pp. 242–43.

19. James R. Green, *The World of the Worker*, pp. 184–85; Foster, in his letter to the National Committee, (p. 5), condemned the "middle, half-middle or above the battle position" that the Party took at the UMW convention. The Party's neutral position almost gave Reuther control of the convention, he felt. See also Roger Keeran, *The Communist Party and the Auto Workers' Union* (Bloomington: Indiana University Press, 1980; repr. New York: International Publishers, 1986), pp. 246–47.

20. Lichtenstein, *Labor's War at Home*, pp. 217, 213–14; Foster in *Daily Worker*, June 2, 1945, p. 3: wartime strikes "have the effect of compromising the labor movement in the eyes of the armed forces and the general public."

21. Earl Browder, *The Road Ahead to Victory and Lasting Peace* (New York: Workers' Library, 1944), p. 8; Browder, *Wage Policy in War Production* (New York: Workers' Library, 1943), p. 8; Cochran, *Labor and Communism*, pp. 209–11.

22. In one National Board meeting, when enumerating his objections, Foster nearly neglected to mention Browder's stand on the Labor-Management Charter; it was the last of nineteen mistakes he cited that had been made by Browder: Minutes, National Board, May 22, 1945, pt. 1, p. 6, Jaffe Papers, Series VII. *Daily Worker*, May 11, 1942, p. 6; Foster, "American Imperialism in the Post-War Period," *Communist*, June 1945, p. 499; Foster, "New Features of American Economic and Political Life," draft article, in Jaffe Papers, box 37, folder 3, pp. 24, 30, 29; David Brody, *Workers in Industrial America* (New York: Oxford University Press, 1980), pp. 176–77; Lichtenstein, *Labor's War at Home*, pp. 224–27.

23. Foster, "New Features," pp. 29, 6: "After we get well into the peace period, undoubtedly many of the governmental wartime controls will be eased, or even abolished."

24. Starobin, *American Communism*, p. 76.

25. Accounts of the famous Duclos letter and its effects on the American Party are drawn from: Gabriel Kolko, *The Politics of War* (New York: Pantheon, 1968, 1990), p. 441; Starobin, *American Communism*, pp. 74–106; Jaffe, *Rise and Fall of American Communism*, pp. 71–85 (Jaffe makes a convincing argument that the

letter itself was written in the Soviet Union); and Isserman, *Which Side Were You On?* pp. 218–33.

26. Foster's letter, along with entire text of Duclos letter, in *Political Affairs*, July 1945.

27. Kolko, *The Politics of War*, pp. 439–41.

28. Starobin, *American Communism*, pp. 85–86; Jaffe, *Rise and Fall of American Communism*, pp. 78–81.

29. Ibid., p. 79. Minutes, National Committee Meeting, June 18, 1945, pp. 1–3, 12, Jaffe Papers, Series VII.

30. Draper interview with Joseph Starobin, TD, box 16; Starobin, *American Communism*, p. 264, n. 16.

31. Ibid., p. 114; 278–79; Jaffe, *Rise and Fall of American Communism*, pp. 87–88; Foster biographical report, Foster personal file, Comintern, op. 261, d. 15, l. 203; Gerhart Eisler to P. Fedotov, report no. 3103, Sept. 11, 1949, Foster personal file, l. 236.

32. Foster was chosen as chair of the national committee at the national convention in July 1945: *Daily Worker* July 30, 1945, p. 2. The "Political Association" was reconstituted as a party, and a new constitution adopted. See also Samuel Darcy to William Dunne, July 7, 1945 and August 13, 1945, Darcy Papers, New York University, Tamiment Institute Library; George, *The Crisis in the CPUSA*, pp. 22–23.

33. Foster, "The Struggle against Revisionism," *Political Affairs*, September 1945, p. 782.

34. Ibid., pp. 788, 791, 792–93.

35. Starobin, *American Communism*, pp. 112–13; Steve Nelson, James R. Barrett, and Rob Ruck, *Steve Nelson: American Radical* (Pittsburgh: University of Pittsburgh Press, 1981), pp. 274–75.

36. From a letter to the editor, *Daily Worker*, Apr. 17, 1956, p. 4.

37. Childs quoted from *Political Affairs*, July 1945, p. 655; Starobin, *American Communism*, pp. 39–40; Gaddis, *The United States and the Origins of the Cold War*, p. 258.

38. Foster, "One Year of Struggle against Browderism," *Political Affairs*, September 1946, p. 776; "A Letter from William Z. Foster," 1950, in my possession; see also Foster, "On the Theoretical Work of the Party," *Political Affairs*, April, 1948, pp. 319–26.

39. Foster, *Our Country Needs a Strong Communist Party* (New York: New Century, 1946), p. 11; Foster, "On the Theoretical Work of the Party," *Political Affairs*, April 1948, p. 325; Starobin, *American Communism*, p. 20.

40. Theodore Draper, *American Communism and Soviet Russia* (New York: Viking, 1960), pp. 198–99; Foster, "On the Theoretical Work of the Party," p. 319; Foster, *History of the Communist Party of the United States* (New York: International Publishers, 1952), p. 124; his reference to the "wishy-washy" Socialist Party is in *American Trade Unionism: Principles, Organization, Strategy, Tactics* (New York: International Publishers, 1947), p. 15. Similar themes can be found in the writings of other Communists as well. James Cannon thought Debs's central fault was that he stood for an "all inclusive" Socialist party; this was an "excellent sentiment," albeit impractical (*First Ten Years of American Commu-*

nism [New York: Pathfinder, 1962], pp. 268–69). Al Richmond, *A Long View from the Left: Memoirs of an American Radical* (Boston: Houghton Mifflin, 1973), p. 49: "One of Foster's hallmarks was a purposeful self-discipline that excluded the bravado of Haywood and the conspicuous emotion of Debs." Len DeCaux, *Labor Radical* (Boston: Beacon, 1970), p. 120: "When I heard Debs speak, he seemed a bit confused by the complications of the post–Russian revolution world he was soon to leave."

41. *Daily Worker*, Feb. 26, 1948, p. 5.

42. Foster, "The Danger of Imperialism in the Post-War Period" *Political Affairs*, June 1945, p. 493; Jaffe, *Rise and Fall of American Communism*, p. 109.

43. *Political Affairs*, July 1945, p. 655.

44. Foster, *Problems of Organized Labor Today* (New York: New Century, 1946), pp. 6–7.

CHAPTER 12
UNIONISM, POLITICS, AND THE COLD WAR

1. William Z. Foster, "Leninism and Some Practical Problems of the Post-War Period," *Political Affairs*, February 1946, pp. 105–6; Foster, "The Wage and Strike Movement," ibid., pp. 122, 124, 127.

2. Foster, "New Features in American Political and Economic Life," Jaffe Papers, Emory University, Woodruff Library, box 37, folder 3.

3. Gilbert J. Gall, "A Note on Lee Pressman and the FBI," *Labor History* 32 (1991): 551–61; Joshua Freeman, *In Transit* (New York: Oxford University Press, 1989), p. 130.

4. Joseph R. Starobin, *American Communism in Crisis* (Berkeley: University of California Press, 1972), p. 147; Harvey Levenstein, *Communism, Anti-Communism and the CIO* (Westport, Conn.: Greenwood Press, 1981), pp. 213–14; Mike Quill to Luigi Longo, Apr. 16, 1948, EB, Series I, folder 75; Philip Jaffe, *The Rise and Fall of American Communism* (New York: Horizon, 1975), p. 144; Gil Green, interview with the author, Oct. 3, 1986.

5. On the postwar strike wave, see James Green, *The World of the Worker* (New York: Hill and Wang, 1980), pp. 194–96; Mike Davis, *Prisoners of the American Dream* (London: Verso, 1986), pp. 85–87; Foster, "The Wage and Strike Movement," pp. 121–29.

6. William Foster, *Problems of Organized Labor Today* (New York: New Century, 1946), pp. 18, 22; Foster, "Leninism and Some Practical Problems," p. 102.

7. David Brody, *Workers in Industrial America* (New York: Oxford University Press, 1980), pp. 222–25; Foster, "Leninism and Some Practical Problems," p. 102; Rankin Committee testimony in FOIA, 61-330-331; *Daily Worker*, Sept. 19, 1945, pp. 2, 6.

8. Lawrence S. Wittner, *Cold War America* (New York: Praeger, 1974), pp. 25–28; John Lewis Gaddis, *The United States and the Cold War* (New York: Columbia University Press, 1972), pp. 339–40.

9. FOIA, 61-330-412, 413, 415. Starobin, *American Communism*, pp. 156–57. Starobin points out that Foster was criticized for his emphasis on the war

danger by prominent European Communists. Indeed, when he returned to the United States, he modulated his statements in this regard to some degree: "We must particularly oppose all ideas that war is inevitable." For a time, Foster's rhetoric emphasized the divisions in the American ruling class on the issue of war. He noted that "[the] largest and most decisive section of the capitalist class, though it mainly has an eventual war perspective, equivocates on the actual question of war." See Foster, "American Imperialism and the War Danger," *Political Affairs*, August 1947, pp. 681–82. However, within months, as the Cold War further intensified and Stalin's own statements became more ominous, Foster's writings again reflected a far more dire perspective. As well, his statements in Europe do not reflect any great concern to qualify his thoughts about the war danger.

10. Foster, "On Building a Peoples' Party," ibid., February 1947, pp. 115, 113, 109, 119, 121.

11. Brody, *Workers in Industrial America*, p. 226; Davis, *Prisoners of the American Dream*, pp. 87–88; Bert Cochran, *Labor and Communism: The Conflict That Shaped American Unions* (Princeton, N.J.: Princeton University Press, 1977), p. 316: "The repeal campaign was a chimera."

12. FOIA 61-330-452, 437.

13. Levenstein, *Communism, Anti-Communism and the CIO*, p. 223; Quill, in testimony at a CIO hearing, placed the order to support Wallace in October (Cochran, *Labor and Communism*, p. 301); Starobin, *American Communism*, pp. 12, 138, 175–76; Gil Green, interview with the author, Oct. 3, 1986; Isserman, *Which Side Were You On? The Communist Party during the Second World War* (Middletown, Conn.: Wesleyan University Press, 1982), pp. 23–24; Dorothy Healey, interview with the author, Sept. 16, 1986, identifies Dennis as the "main person" behind the third-party effort, but notes that "everyone felt something had to be done to make a solid break with Truman's policies." Foster typescript, [n.d.], WZF, d. 81, on Dennis's policy and his own opposition to the "Progressive Party error" of 1948. Steve Nelson, James Barrett, and Rob Ruck, *Steve Nelson: American Radical* (Pittsburgh: University of Pittsburgh Press, 1981), p. 288, on the tenuousness of Foster's leadership in the 1940s; see Harvey Klehr and John E. Haynes, "The Comintern's Open Secrets," *American Spectator*, December 1992, on Dennis's ties with the Soviet intelligence service.

14. Cochran, *Labor and Communism*, pp. 297–98; Philip Jaffe notes, p. 328, Jaffe Papers, box 10, folder 2; *Daily Worker*, Nov. 25, 1947, p. 4.

15. Jaffe notes, p. 328 Jaffe Papers, box 10, folder 2; Foster, *History of the Communist Party of the United States* (New York: International Publishers, 1952), p. 471; Starobin, *American Communism*, pp. 170–71; Cochran, *Labor and Communism*, pp. 299–300; Levenstein, *Communism, Anti-Communism and the CIO*, p. 224; Zieger, *American Workers, American Unions* (Baltimore: Johns Hopkins University Press, 1986), pp. 129–30.

16. Foster, "Organized Labor and the Marshall Plan," *Political Affairs*, February, 1948, p. 99.

17. Foster, "The Struggle for Peace," ibid., September 1948, pp. 775–76.

18. Foster medical report, FOIA 61-330-485. Evidence of this stroke is based on Foster's own description of its symptoms to a court-appointed physician in

November 1948, and the physician's statement that a neurological examination showed "valid evidence of prior vascular spasms of the cerebral vessels." The other physician determined that he suffered from both general and cerebral arteriosclerosis.

19. Joseph Manley Kolko, interview with the author, Sept. 26, 1986; Harry Epstein, interview with the author, Nov. 22, 1986; Foster, *Twilight of World Capitalism* (New York: International Publishers, 1949). Joe Kolko's mother was Beatrice Manley Kolko, daughter of Joe Manley and Sylvia. She lived in the Soviet Union for medical reasons, and Joe was subsequently adopted by Sylvia and Emmanuel.

20. Kolko interview; Harold Foster, interview with the author, Jan. 20, 1993; Arthur Zipser, *Workingclass Giant: The Life of William Z. Foster* (New York: International Publishers, 1981), p. 173; Foster autobiographical statement, Comintern, op. 261, d. 15; *Political Affairs*, October 1961, p. 7, refers to Esther as "Comrade."

21. FOIA, 61-330-483, 432; Healey interview; Kolko interview.

22. This informant gained access to Foster's personal belongings in hotel rooms on a trip to the West Coast, Sept. 14, 1947. The source photographed some French pamphlets: 61–330–432; Kolko interview.

23. FOIA, 61-330-446, 451.

24. David Caute, *The Great Fear* (New York: Simon and Schuster, 1978), pp. 187–97; FOIA, 61-330-485.

25. FOIA, 61-330-549, 552; Caute, *The Great Fear*, p. 63.

26. Foster, *In Defense of the Indicted Leaders* (New York: New Century, 1949), p. 78; *The Worker*, Sept. 25, 1949, Section 3, pp. 4, 6, for Foster's deposition; Foster, "The Party Crisis and the Way Out, Part 1," *Political Affairs*, December 1957, p. 49.

27. George Charney, *Long Journey on the Left* (Chicago: Quadrangle, 1968), p. 235; Foster had to be pressured to include reference to a "peaceful road" in his 1952 history of the Party: see Alexander Bittelman to Foster, n.d., "Ch. I, Pt. I, Intro," Bittelman Collection, New York University, Tamiment Institute Library.

28. Foster, "Peoples' Front and Peoples' Democracy," *Political Affairs*, June 1950, p. 23; Gil Green, interview with the author, Oct. 3, 1986; Maurice Isserman, *If I Had a Hammer* (New York: Basic Books, 1988), pp. 7–9; Starobin, *American Communism*, p. 207. In his postexpulsion writings, Browder continued to emphasize Foster's "anarcho-syndicalism," proven, for instance, by Foster's emphasis on the spontaneity of the revolutionary moment. "Foster's line is not that of Marx and Lenin, it is the line of Bakunin, Most and Sorel," was a typical comment. See Browder MS. comments on Foster's "In Defense of the Party and the Indicted Leaders," EB, Series III, reel 7, folder 64.

29. Davis, *Prisoners of the American Dream*, pp. 88–89; Robert Zieger, *American Workers, American Unions, 1920–1985* (Baltimore: Johns Hopkins University Press, 1986), pp. 130–32; Green, *World of the Worker*, pp. 203–7; Cochran, *Labor and Communism*, pp. 304–41.

30. Foster was able to attend the national committee meetings in March 1950 for only one hour; FOIA, 61-330-499: "subject under doctor's care for reason of

heart condition. Continues to confer with Party leaders," went a typical report of this period. A physician reported that he was suffering from "very marked arteriosclerosis" and that "angina pectoris is evoked by minor emotional tension": Louis Finger to Carl Dorfman, Apr. 28, 1950, WZF, d. 1., l. 37. See also Zipser, *Workingclass Giant*, p. 172.

31. *Daily Worker*, Aug. 19, 1946, p. 6; *The Worker*, Jan. 15, 1950, p. 7.

32. Foster, "Marxism and the American Working Class," *Political Affairs*, November 1953, pp. 1–2, 6–7, 11–12; Foster, "The General Law of Trade Union Progress," ibid., July 1955, p. 13; Foster, "Elizabeth Gurley Flynn's Autobiography," ibid., December, 1955, p. 23.

33. Foster, "Marxism and the American Working Class," pp. 3–5; *Daily Worker*, Aug. 21, 1952, p. 5, Oct. 23, 1952, p. 2; Foster, *Danger Signals for Organized Labor* (New York: New Century, 1953); Gil Green, *Cold War Fugitive* (New York: International Publishers, 1984), pp. 120–21, suggests that Foster considerably amended and expanded a proposal by Thompson and others after the election that the Party shift away from the Progressive party candidates, and concentrate on supporting anti-McCarthy candidates in the mainstream.

34. Foster, "General Law of Trade Union Progress," pp. 12–15.

35. Starobin, *American Communism*, pp. 200–203; Isserman, *If I Had a Hammer*, pp. 7–8; *Political Affairs*, June 1949, for the "white chauvinism" campaign; Foster, "Left Sectarianism in the Fight for Negro Rights and against White Chauvinism," ibid., July 1953, p. 20. Foster later backed down a bit in criticism of the white chauvinism campaign: Zipser, *Workingclass Giant*, p. 183.

36. Foster typescript, [n.d.], WZF, d. 81; Foster speech to National Committee, May 1, 1956, ibid., d. 65. Foster blamed Dennis for "leading" in this decision, claiming he was opposed, but admitted that his own "overestimation of the progress of fascistization in the United States" made him responsible for "one phase" of it. Starobin, *American Communism*, pp. 219–20, 306 nn. 8, 10, holds Foster directly responsible for the decision, but the main source is John Gates, a bitter political opponent of Foster's. It is doubtful that Foster would have misrepresented his stand in a top-level meeting, but as he acknowledged, his ideological influence and analysis were nonetheless quite important.

37. *Daily Worker*, Feb. 10, 1953, p. 3, May 7, 1953, p. 4; Foster, "The Advance of Socialism to World Leadership," *Political Affairs*, February 1956, p. 33; *The Worker*, Oct. 16, 1949, p. 3; ibid., Spet. 25, 1949, p. 6.

38. Junius Scales and Richard Nickson, *Cause at Heart: A Former Communist Remembers* (Athens: University of Georgia Press, 1987), p. 260; Green, *Cold War Fugitive*, pp. 100–102, 121; E. J. Hobsbawm, *Primitive Rebels* (New York: Praeger, 1959; repr. New York: Norton, 1965), pp. 165–66.

39. *The Worker*, Dec. 18, 1949, p. 6; *Political Affairs*, December 1949 and April 1953, for Stalin anniversary and memorial issues.

40. All of Foster's big books were published by International. Charney, *Long Journey*, pp. 261, 286.

41. Dorothy Healey interview; records of prisoner-of-war debriefings in FOIA 61-330-627. Robert Thompson, "Comrade Foster's New Book—A Great Marxist Work," *Political Affairs*, February 1951, pp. 89, 92; Herbert Aptheker, "On Foster's History of the Three Internationals," ibid., May 1955, p. 8.

CHAPTER 13
FINAL STRUGGLES

1. *Daily Worker*, Mar. 15, 1956, p. 1.

2. Caute, *The Great Fear: The Anti-Communist Purge under Truman and Eisenhower* (New York: Simon and Schuster, 1978), pp. 50–51, 207–8.

3. William Foster, "Is the U.S. in the Early Stages of Fascism?" *Political Affairs*, November 1954, pp. 5, 19; Foster, "On the Release of the National Committee Leaders," ibid., April 1955, p. 1; Foster, "Geneva: Background and Perspectives," ibid., September 1955, pp. 9, 27; Foster, "Post-Geneva: The Fight for Peaceful Coexistence," ibid., October 1955, p. 3; Foster, "The Advance of Socialism to World Leadership," ibid., February 1956, p. 33.

4. Al Richmond, *A Long View from the Left: Memoirs of an American Revolutionary* (Boston: Houghton Mifflin, 1973), p. 369; Maurice Isserman, *If I Had a Hammer: The Death of the Old Left and the Birth of the New Left* (New York: Basic Books, 1987), pp. 7–9.

5. Joseph R. Starobin, *American Communism in Crisis* (Berkeley: University of California Press, 1972), p. 305, nn. 2, 4.

6. David Shannon, *The Decline of American Communism* (New York: Harcourt Brace, 1959), pp. 272–73.

7. "Poem for William Z. Foster," by J. Brandreth, *Daily Worker*, Mar. 15, 1956, p. 7. Birthday greetings ibid., Mar. 1–18, 1956; Foster's special birthday issue of *Political Affairs* and Khrushchev's report in *Political Affairs*, March 1956.

8. Shannon, *Decline of American Communism*, pp. 274–75.

9. *Daily Worker*, Mar. 16, 1956, p. 4.

10. Ibid., Apr. 19, 1956, p. 5.

11. Eugene Dennis, *The Communists Take a New Look* (New York: New Century, 1956), pp. 19–48; Dorothy Healey, interview with the author, Sept. 16, 1986; Shannon, *Decline of American Communism*, pp. 288–89; George Charney, *Long Journey on the Left* (Chicago: Quadrangle, 1968), pp. 222–23.

12. *Daily Worker*, Apr. 13, 1956, p. 4.

13. Ibid., Mar. 22, 1956, p. 5, Mar. 23, 1956, p. 4; Isserman, *If I Had a Hammer*, pp. 16–17; Foster to Administration Committee, July 12, 1956, Peggy Dennis Papers, Wisconsin State Historical Society, Madison, box 5, folder 5.

14. Foster, "The Road to Socialism, Part 1," *Political Affairs*, April 1956, p. 8; Foster, "The Road to Socialism, Part 2," ibid., May 1956, pp. 11–13, 18; Foster, "Marxism-Leninism in a Changing World," September 1956, pp. 50, 55, 57–58.

15. George Meyers, interview with the author, April 26, 1990; Harry Epstein, interview with the author, Nov. 22, 1986; Arthur Zipser, *Workingclass Giant: The Life of William Z. Foster* (New York: International Publishers, 1981), p. 193.

16. *Draft Resolution for the Sixteenth National Convention* (New York: New Century, 1956), pp. 57–58; Shannon, *Decline of American Communism*, p. 304, Isserman, *If I Had a Hammer*, p. 27.

17. Foster, "On the Party Situation," *Political Affairs*, October 1956, pp. 15, 17, 32; John Gates, *On Guard against Browderism, Titoism, Trotskyism* (New York: New Century, 1951), pp. 14–15.

18. Foster typescript [n.d.], WZF, d. 81; Foster speech to National Committee, May 1, 1956, ibid., d. 65, pp. 10, 20; Foster, "On the Party Situation," p. 21.

19. Foster, Speech to National Committee, Aug. 23, 1956, WZF, d. 65, p. 21; Foster, "Marxism-Leninism in a Changing World," p. 57; "On the Party Situation," pp. 20–21, 33.

20. Quoted in Shannon, *Decline of American Communism*, p. 305.

21. Charney, *A Long Journey*, pp. 282–84; Isserman, *If I Had a Hammer*, pp. 24–25.

22. Ibid., pp. 26–29; Charney, *A Long Journey*, pp. 287–89; Steve Nelson, James R. Barrett, and Rob Ruck, *Steve Nelson: American Radical* (Pittsburgh: University of Pittsburgh Press, 1981), pp. 392–96.

23. Isserman, *If I Had a Hammer*, pp. 29–30; Al Richmond, *A Long View from the Left*, pp. 380–81; Peggy Dennis, *Autobiography of an American Communist* (Westport, Conn.: Creative Arts, 1977), pp. 230–32; Ruck, Barrett, and Nelson, *Steve Nelson*, pp. 389–90.

24. Foster typescript, "The Stalin Cult of the Individual" [n.d.] WZF, d. 80; Foster speech to National Committee, May 1, 1956, ibid., d. 65.

25. Foster, "Reply to a Priest's Letter," *Political Affairs*, October 1954, p. 48; [anonymous] to William Foster, Dec. 10, 1956, WZF, d. 6, l. 17.

26. *Proceedings (Abridged) of the 16th National Convention of the CPUSA* (New York: New Century, 1956), pp. 59, 65, 62; Dorothy Healey interview.

27. Foster typescript, "Remarks on the Trade Union Resolution," Dec. 22, 1956, WZF, d. 64; Foster to New York State Board, June 6, 1958, ibid., d. 65.

28. *Proceedings, 16th Convention*, p. 195. Foster finished sixth in the voting for the twenty-member committee: see ibid., pp. 327, 195.

29. Charney, *A Long Journey*, p. 223.

30. Zipser, *Workingclass Giant*, p. 193; Harry Epstein Memoir, "William Z. Foster," in author's possession.

31. Maurice Isserman, "1956 Generation: An Alternative Approach to the History of American Communism," *Radical America* 14 (1980): 95–96.

32. Foster, "The Superiority of World Socialism over World Capitalism," *Political Affairs*, May 1958, pp. 19–28; Isserman, "1956 Generation," p. 95; Foster, "On the Draft Resolution," *Political Affairs* December 1959, pp. 51–53; "Main Political Resolution," ibid., February 1960, pp. 20–22; Foster to National Committee, Dec. 2, 1958, Dennis Papers, box 5, folder 4: "The revisionists are definitely much stronger, and exert considerably more influence, both on the fringes of the Party, and even within the Party."

33. *New York Times*, Feb. 1, 1959, p. 25; Foster, "Letter to Mao Tse Tung," *Political Affairs*, March 1959, pp. 22–31; Harry Haywood, *Black Bolshevik* (Chicago: Liberator Press, 1978), pp. 616–17. In his article, "On the Draft Resolution," p. 52, Foster called on the American Party to fight for full diplomatic recognition of China.

34. Foster, *History of the Three Internationals* (New York: International Publishers, 1955), pp. 509–12; Joseph R. Starobin, "North America," in *Interna-*

tional Communism after Khrushchev, ed. Leo Labedz (Cambridge, Mass.: MIT Press, 1965), pp. 146–49. "On the Draft Resolution," *Political Affairs*, December 1959, p. 52. On the rift between Khrushchev and the Chinese over the war danger and the possibility of a "peaceful transition to socialism," and the American Party's attempts to straddle these issues, see *New York Times*, Apr. 3, 1960, p. 1, Apr. 17, p. 15, June 4, p. 7, June 29, p. 9, Sept. 19, p. 11; for Foster's emphasis on the danger of "imperialist war," see "The Cold War and the People's Welfare," *Political Affairs*, July 1959, pp. 15–16, 20.

35. Later, the Maoist Progressive Labor Party would lay claim to Foster's political heritage: see Starobin, "North America," pp. 146–49 and Fred Carlisle, "William Z. Foster," *Marxist-Leninist Quarterly* 2 (n.d.): 64–78; see also Jaffe notes, p. 425, Jaffe Papers, Emory University, Woodruff Library, box 10, folder 2.

Another interesting aspect of Foster's influence involved the Cuban Communist party. In the fall of 1945, Foster demanded that the Cuban party congress execute a complete repudiation of Browderism. His demands were granted in a resolution couched in the most extreme terms; of Latin American parties, no other went as far as did the Cuban in accepting Foster's position. See Jaffe, "Memorandum on the Change in the American CP," Aug. 18, 1947, Jaffe Papers, box 37, folder 5, p. 9. On the resemblance between Foster and Trotsky on the war danger, see Starobin, *American Communism*, p. 126. Browder was willing to use this in his attacks on Foster's leadership: see Browder, "Open Letter to Members of the CPUSA," 1946, TD, box 5, folder 29; also Jaffe comments on Starobin MS., Jaffe Papers, box 10, folder 2.

36. Foster to National Executive Committee, Dec. 12, 1958, and Feb. 6, 1959, WZF, d. 7.

37. Foster, "Work in the Two-Party System," *Political Affairs*, January 1959, pp. 28–30; Foster, "The Struggle for a Mass Labor Party in the United States," ibid., May 1959, pp. 1–16; Foster, "The Road to Socialism, Part 2," p. 18; Foster, "The Party Crisis and the Way Out, II," ibid., January 1958, p. 55: "Trade Unions are not enough; the working class must have its own mass party; in this case a Labor-Farmer party." This critique, aimed at his long-time colleague, Alexander Bittelman, was disingenuous because it did not mention his own conception of either the timing or the basis of the Labor party, which in his mind was still entirely contingent on the future of the trade union movement.

38. Zipser, *Workingclass Giant*, pp. 179–80; Shannon, *Decline of American Communism*, p. 75; U.S. Department of the Census, *Historical Statistics of the United States* (Washington, D.C.: U.S.G.P.O., 1975), p. 166; on Soviet subsidies, see Harvey Klehr and John Haynes, "Communication," *Labor History* 33 (1992): 576–78.

39. *New York Times*, July 9, 1959, p. 20, Oct. 22, 1959, p. 16, Oct. 11, 1960, p. 48, Dec. 3, 1960, p. 6, Jan. 11, 1961, p. 6, Feb. 26, 1961, p. 31; Harry Epstein memoir, "William Z. Foster," in the author's possession.

40. Foster to Gus Hall, Dec. 5, 1960, WZF, d. 7.

41. Emmanuel Kolko to Harry Epstein, Mar. 4, 1961; Foster memo, Apr. 4, 1960, both in Harry Epstein Papers (in the possession of the Epstein family); Joseph Manley Kolko, interview with the author, Sept. 24, 1986.

42. *New York Times*, Mar. 12, 1961, p. 70; Harry Epstein, interview with the author, Nov. 22, 1986; Kolko interview; Dorothy Healey interview with the author, Sept. 16, 1986. In a letter to the American Party secretariat from Moscow, Foster deplored the American Party's lack of public support for the People's Republic (Feb. 16, 1960, WZF, d. 7).

43. Kolko interview; *New York Times*, Sept. 2, 1961, p. 15, Sept. 6, 1961, p. 37, Sept. 7, 1961, p. 35, Sept. 19, 1961, p. 39; "Foster Memorial Meeting in Moscow," *Political Affairs*, October 1961, pp. 7–12. Esther died in July 1965. Half of Haywood's ashes were interred at Waldheim Cemetery.

Epilogue

1. Joseph Manley Kolko, interview with the author, Sept. 26, 1986; Foster, *The Twilight of World Capitalism* (New York: International Publishers, 1949), p. 158; Whittaker Chambers, *Witness* (New York: Random House, 1952), p. 9; Zinoviev's aphorism is quoted in Theodore Draper, *American Communism and Soviet Russia* (New York: Viking, 1960), p. 125.

2. Max Eastman, *Love and Revolution: My Journey through an Epoch* (New York: Random House, 1964), p. 347; Eastman, *Stalin's Russia and the Crisis in Socialism* (New York: Norton, 1940), p. 97.

INDEX